SRI RAMAKRISHNA THE GREAT MASTER

Vol. II

Original in Bengali

By

SWAMI SARADANANDA
(*A Direct Disciple of Sri Ramakrishna*)

TRANSLATION
BY
SWAMI JAGADANANDA

SRI RAMAKRISHNA MATH
MYLAPORE : : MADRAS-4

Published by :

Eighth Impression
VIII-3M 3C-6-95
ISBN 81-7120-386-8
ISBN 81-7120-335-3

Printed in India at
Sri Ramakrishna Math Printing Press,
Mylapore, Madras 600 004.

CONTENTS

Part Four
AS THE SPIRITUAL TEACHER (II)

Chapter		Page
	Preface ..	567
I.	Vaishnavacharan and Gauri ..	569
II.	The Mood of the Spiritual Teacher and Various Communities of Holy Men ..	600
III.	Pilgrimage of the Master as the Guru and His meeting with the Holy Men ..	637
IV.	As the Spiritual Teacher (Concluded) ..	670
V.	Sri Ramakrishna in the Company of Devotees for Nine days: The Navayatra in A.D. 1885 ..	705
VI.	Sri Ramakrishna in the Company of Devotees: The Story of Gopala's Mother — First part ..	729
VII.	Sri Ramakrishna in the Company of Devotees: The Return Chariot Journey in A.D. 1885 and the Story of Gopala's Mother — Last part ..	743
Appendix:	The Human Aspect of the Master ..	764

Part Five
THE MASTER IN THE DIVINE MOOD AND NARENDRANATH

	Preface ..	781
I.1.	The Influence of the Master on the Brahmo Samaj ..	787
2.	The Brahmo Festival in Manimohan Mallik's House ..	799
3.	The Master in Jayagopal Sen's House ..	806
II.	The Beginning of the Arrival of the Master's Devotees previously seen in Visions ..	813

III.	Narendra's Antecedents and His first Visit to Dakshineswar	821
IV.	Narendra's Second and Third Visits to the Master	841
V.	The Master's Selfless Love and Narendranath	850
VI.1.	The Extraordinary Relation between the Master and Narendranath	859
2.	The Extraordinary Relation between the Master and Narendranath	871
VII.	The Master's Method of Testing and Narendranath	883
VIII.1.	Narendranath's Schooling in the World and by the Master	911
2.	Narendranath's Schooling in the World and by the Master	918
IX.	The Circle of Devotees of the Master and Narendranath	932
X.	The Festival at Panihati	942
XI.	The Master Moved to Calcutta	954
XII.1.	The Master's Stay at Shyampukur	964
2.	The Master's Stay at Shyampukur	972
3.	The Master's Stay at Shyampukur	996
XIII.1.	The Master in the Garden House of Kasipur	1009
2.	The Vow of Service at Kasipur	1014
3.	The Master's Self-revelation and the Bestowal of Freedom from Fear	1022
	Chronology of important events	1028
Appendix I	The Book and its Author	1030
Appendix II	The Horoscope of Sri Ramakrishna	1047
	Index	1049

SRI RAMAKRISHNA THE GREAT MASTER

PART FOUR

AS THE SPIRITUAL TEACHER (II)

PREFACE

THIS is the Fourth Part of *Sri Ramakrishna The Great Master*, and forms the second half of the section "As the Spiritual Teacher". Having read so far the middle part of the life of Sri Ramakrishna, the reader may ask why we have adopted an unchronological method[1] and why the story of the perfected state of the Master's life has been told before the events of his life from his birth to the time of his Sadhana. We reply:

First, we had no previous plan of writing the life of this extraordinary personage. We were not bold enough to cherish the high hope that it was ever possible for puny creatures like ourselves to write properly the story of a life so universal and all-embracing in scope as his. It was by force of circumstances that we happened to set our hand to it and tell the readers of the *Udbodhan*,[2] a few events of the life of Sri Ramakrishna. We did not then know that we would have to proceed so far. It is, therefore, no wonder that later events came to be described before the earlier ones.

Secondly, many tried before us to record the wonderful events of the life of Sri Ramakrishna and the story of his extraordinary Sadhanas. Although those records are seen to contain a few errors in some places, almost all the events of the Master's life on the whole have been published through them. Instead of wasting our energy in recording the same facts over again as a chronicle, we thought it reasonable to treat the subject in such a way as to explain to the reader the extraordinary significance of the divine ideas and ideals embodied in his life, which has not been done by any one so far. Again, if one does not understand what is meant by his being established in 'Bhavamukha' or in the 'mood of the Guru', one cannot at all comprehend his wonderful character, uncommon actions, and unique ideas and ideals. This was why we explained them to the reader at the very beginning.

Some will perhaps raise an objection and say, "But, in setting

[1] The reference is to the arrangement of the different parts of this book in the Bengali original. This has been changed in the translation.

[2] A Bengali monthly published by the Ramakrishna Mission, from 1, Udbodhan Lane, Baghbazar, Calcutta, in which the whole of this book was serialised as articles before it came out in the form of a book.- Tr.

about to explain in different places of your book, the Master's particular ideas and actions, you must certainly have projected your own thoughts into his, and described them to the reader in the way you yourself have understood them. Consequently, your own intelligence and discrimination have been made the standard of his incomprehensible character and ideas. Have you not lowered him in the estimation of people by thus admitting indirectly that intelligence and discrimination can comprehend the incomprehensible Master? Would it not have been better if, instead of doing so, you had stopped with merely recording the facts accurately? In that case, the record would not have lowered the Master in anyone's esteem, and people could have understood the meanings of his ideas and actions in their own way"

This is a statement which is plausible but lacking any special significance; for man has been taking, and will ever be taking, the help of his senses, mind and intellect in understanding and comprehending all matters. He has no other alternative. But this does not prove that his mind, intellect, etc., are greater than the object they try to comprehend. Although man knows that time, space, universe, self, God and other unlimited entities are beyond his mind and intellect, he has always been trying to grasp and understand them through these faculties. But we do not consider this effort to understand such abstractions as illegitimate. For such endeavours will broaden one's mind and intellect, and thus be of immense benefit.

Therefore, if we study in this way the extraordinary ideas and actions of great personages, we are ourselves benefited, while they are by no means limited or thereby dwarfed. In accordance with the degree of purity and power of penetration of their minds and intellects produced by Sadhana, people can more or less understand and explain the divine ideas and actions of those great souls. A person with greater spiritual Sadhana will be able to understand the character of Sri Ramakrishna more deeply than we. There is, therefore, nothing wrong in applying our minds and intellects to the understanding of that divine character. It will be sufficient if we guard ourselves against one mistake, viz., the notion that we have fathomed the whole depth of the Master's character. All possibility of vain dogmatism will thus be guarded against, if only we can keep this fact constantly before our minds.

Sri Ramakrishna standing in ecstasy during a *Kirtan* at Keshab Chandra Sen's house in Calcutta. He is surrounded by Brahmo devotees, with Hriday, his nephew, supporting him.

Sri Sarada Devi

CHAPTER I

VAISHNAVACHARAN AND GAURI

[TOPICS: 1. Ignorance about the Master's Teacher-mood in the early part of his life. 2. 'Bees come of themselves when flowers blossom' 3. All are equally blind in respect of spiritual matters. 4. How the Master preached religion. 5. The Master's state when he met the Brahmani. 6. Others' understanding about the Master's exalted state. 7. Convention of Pandits at Brahmani's request. 8. Vaishnavacharan and Gauri of Indes invited. 9. Vaishnavacharan's fame. 10. The Brahmani curing the burning sensation of the Master. 11. The Brahmani curing his inordinate hunger. 12. Yogic hunger: our experience of it in the Master. 13. The first example. 14. Second example. 15. Third example. 16. Fourth example. 17. Spiritual emotions and changes in the Master's body. 18. Vaishnavacharan's arrival at Dakshineswar. 19. Discussion about the Master's condition. 20. Vaishnavacharan's conclusion. 21. The Master on the Kartabhaja and allied sects. 22. Religion for men full of worldly desires. 23. The origin of the Tantras. 24. The history of the "heroic mode". 25. The two strata in each Tantra, high and low. 26. Vaishnavism and new mode of worship. 27. Origin of Kartabhajas etc., from it. 28. The Sadhya and Sadhana according to Kartabhaja. 29. Vaishnavacharan testing the Master. 30. Vaishnavacharan recognising the Master as an incarnation. 31. The miraculous power of Pandit Gauri. 32. Gauri worshipped his wife as the Devi. 33. Gauri's strange process of offering oblations. 34. Convention at Dakshineswar, including Vaishnavacharan and Gauri. 35. The conviction of Gauri about the Master. 36. Gauri's renunciation. 37. The Master quoting Vaishnavacharan and Gauri. 38. Gauri on Kali and Krishna. 39. Vaishnavacharan on regarding one's object of love as a form of the Lord. 40. The Upanishads on this subject. 41. The incarnation and Sastras.]

Those men, who are full of faith and free from malice, and constantly practise this teaching of Mine, are also freed from all work (i.e., the idea of being its agent).

—Gita III.31

1. It is the general impression of the public of Calcutta that the Master transmitted spirituality or deepened it in Kesav Chandra Sen and a few other modern-minded Hindus who had university

education, and were imbued with the Western ideas and ideals. But most people of this city are ignorant of the fact that long before this class of people knew of the Master's presence at Dakshineswar, eminent holy persons, Sadhakas and Pandits well versed in the Sastras, had come to the Master from all parts of Bengal and Northern India, and having their languid spiritual life vivified by the Master's power as the spiritual teacher and by the blazing and noble spiritual ideal presented in his life, had gone away to impart that new power and ideal to many persons elsewhere.

2. The Master used to say, "As soon as flowers blossom, bees come of themselves. They have not to be invited. When love for, and devotion to, God become truly manifested in you, all who have sacrificed their lives, or have resolved to do so in quest of God, that is to say, for the attainment of Truth, cannot but come to you under the influence of an inexplicable spiritual law." So it was indeed the Master's opinion that one should first of all realize God, and have His vision and grace. Thus to possess the power of working for the real good of humanity, one should have His command before proceeding to preach religion or work for the good of the many. Otherwise, as the Master said, "Who will accept your words? Why should people in general accept or give ear to what you ask them to do?"

3. We are all, in truth, sailing in the same boat so long as we have not realised the Lord. Puffed up with pride or learning, we may consider ourselves superior to others, living all the while in this vain world with its round of birth, dotage, and death. However much we might have progressed in the knowledge of some of Nature's laws and in technology, we shall continue to be in the realm of the Divine Mother's inscrutable Maya, and our miserable condition, resulting from our subjugation to the senses, to avarice, greed and fear of death, will persist. We are living in the same dismal unbroken darkness of ignorance regarding eternal problems like: "Who am I? Why am I here? Where shall I go? What is the aim of this game of mine — a game in which I attempt to know the Truth with the help of those very five senses, mind and intellect, which themselves deceive me at every step and lead me ever astray? Will it ever be possible to find out a way to liberation out of their clutches?" Everybody in this world lacks true knowledge and is ready to receive it. But who is to give it to him? If, in this

respect, anybody has actually anything to give, let him give as much as he can. But deluded a hundred times, man does not understand this — that he must himself have realised what he professes to teach. On the other hand, urged by the desire for name and fame and by other sundry selfish motives, he hastens to give, or feigns to give, what he does not himself possess, and as in the case of the blind leading the blind, both the instructor and the instructed together come to grief!

4. The Master, therefore, moved along a path diametrically opposed to that of all others of the world. He lived his whole life in one place, calm, tranquil and free from anxiety, and practised to the fullest extent renunciation, detachment, self-control and other virtues, and thus converted himself thoroughly into a fitting instrument in the hands of the Divine Mother. Having realized the integral truth, he blazed the trail of work for the real benefit to the world. Having attained to Reality, he opened the store-house of his knowledge for distribution, and people thirsting for knowledge began to pour in uninvited, nobody knew from where. And purified by his divine look and touch, they considered themselves blessed; by spreading his new ideas wherever they went, they became a source of blessing to others without number. For, wherever we are, we naturally give expression to the mass of ideas with which we ourselves are full. The Master used to say in the simple language of a villager: "One's belchings smell of the things one has taken. Eat cucumber, your belchings will smell of cucumber; eat radish, they will smell of radish."

5. The meeting with the Bhairavi Brahmani was an important event in the Master's life. From that time onward, while on the one hand he made rapid progress in the practice of spiritual disciplines, on the other the unfoldment of the 'teacher aspect' of his personality in clear and unambiguous terms was also taking place simultaneously. But this does not mean that the 'teacher-mood' was not in him in his earlier days. In the previous chapters it was pointed out that this mood manifested in him more or less in all periods of his life, including his boyhood, and that even his teachers who initiated him in various disciplines, got themselves corrected and spiritually perfected in contact with his personality surcharged with the power of the spiritual teacher manifesting in him.

6. Before the Brahmani came, the Master's extraordinary

eagerness and love of God were regarded, to a great extent, as insanity and physical illness, and he was placed under the treatment of eminent physicians. A physician from East Bengal, himself a Sadhaka, happened to see him in the house of Gangaprasad Sen, where the Master had gone for treatment. Although he pointed out that his bodily symptoms were the extraordinary changes produced by the practice of Yoga, nobody took his statement seriously. All, including Mathur, were certain that they were the signs of insanity, though combined with the love of God. But the learned Brahmani, well versed in devotional scriptures, was the first to point out that all those symptoms were only extraordinary bodily changes corresponding to the mental states brought on by an uncommon love of God, so rare that even the gods covet in vain to possess it. She, however, did not stop with merely pronouncing her opinion. She quoted chapter and verse from the devotional scriptures to show that such physical changes were due to supra-normal mental states and that they had appeared, from time to time, in the teachers and Yogis of the past — in Sri Radha, the supreme lady of Vraja and the embodiment of love divine, and in Sri Krishna Chaitanya, the great lord. She then proved her statements by showing the similarity of the signs recorded in the scriptures with those manifesting in the Master's body. When she did so, the Master, of course, began to rejoice like a boy strengthened by the assurance of his mother, while all the people of the Kali temple, including Mathur, were not a little astonished. And their wonder knew no bounds when the Brahmani said to Mathur, "Please bring Pandits well versed in the Sastras; I am ready to convince them of the truth of my words."

7. But to be astonished is not to be convinced. Who would so readily repose his faith in the words and scholarship of an unknown woman living on alms? Therefore, the words of the Bhairavi Brahmani would have gone the way of those of the physician of eastern Bengal, failing to make any impression on Mathur and others, had the Master not made an eager request for verification, thus taking the issue to the next stage of development. The childlike Master said importunately to Mathur, "Good scholars must be brought and what the Brahmani says must be tested." The wealthy Mathur thought, "Where is the harm in doing so? So much money is being spent on doctors and medicine for the junior Bhattacharya. When the scholars come and refute

the Brahmani's words by quoting the authority of the scriptures, which they are sure to do, at least one good result is sure to follow, viz, believing the words of the scholars, the sincere soul of the junior Bhattacharya will at least be finally convinced that he has contracted a disease. Consequently, he may make an effort to control his mind. A person becomes mad when, instead of making an effort to keep his thoughts and feelings under control, he gives them free rein and allows them to run amuck, thinking, 'What I do and understand is right, and what others understand and ask me to do is wrong.' That is exactly the way how a person becomes insane. And there is no doubt that his mental derangement, as also his physical ailment, will be aggravated, if, instead of inviting scholars, the Bhattacharya is allowed to believe freely the words of the Brahmani." Cogitating thus in his mind, partly out of curiosity and partly out of love for the Master, he agreed to convene a meeting of Pandits at the Master's request.

8. Vaishnavacharan had at that time a great reputation in the community of the Pandits of Calcutta. Again, his name and fame spread amongst the people in general also, as he used to read and explain beautifully the Bhagavata to the public in various parts of the country. This was how the Master, Mathur and the Brahmani had come to hear of him. Mathur therefore decided to invite him. There was another Pandit famous for his uncommon power and rare scholarship — Gauri of Indes. Mathur resolved to invite him also. This was how Vaishnavacharan and Gauri happened to come to Dakshineswar. We heard from the Master now and again many things about them. We shall now set out before the reader what we came to know of them.

9. Vaishnavacharan was not only a scholar but was also known to the public as a devout spiritual aspirant too. His love of God and his deep understanding of philosophy and scriptures — especially those dealing with devotion — made him, it may be said, a leader of the whole Vaishnava community. That community always extended respectful invitations to him for all public functions of religious importance and honoured him with the first place among the invitees on such occasions. When a conclusion concerning any religious matter had to be arrived at, they would always consult him and accept his decisions. Again, many devout aspirants approached him for direction into the right paths of

Sadhana and followed his advice faithfully. It is not surprising, therefore, that Mathur resolved to bring Vaishnavacharan for ascertaining whether the condition of the Master was due to excessive devotion or to some physical disease.

10. In the meantime, the Brahmani gave one important proof of the truth of her opinion on the condition of the Master, which brought as much joy to herself as surprise to others. It was this: Some time before the Brahmani arrived, the Master had been suffering terribly from an intense burning sensation all over his body. Treatments of many sorts were administered but the cure was as far away as ever. We were told by the Master himself that the pain, starting with sunrise, went on increasing as the day advanced, till it became unbearable by midday, when he had to keep his body immersed in the water of the Ganga for two or three hours, with a wet towel placed on his head. He had to come out of the water even against his will, lest he should fall a prey to some other disease because of cold. Therefore, he had to take shelter in a room of the proprietor's mansion, shut all the doors and windows, and roll on the marble floor carefully wetted with a piece of damp cloth.

No sooner had the Brahmani come to know of it, than she found a surprisingly new explanation of this ailment. She said that it was not a disease but a spiritual phenomenon, resulting from his intense love for God. She went on to say that such physical counterparts of the mental changes arising from extreme eagerness for the realization of God, had very often been seen in the lives of Sri Radharani and Sri Chaitanya. The medicine for curing this so called "disease" was also extraordinary, viz., to adorn the patient with garlands of sweet-smelling flowers and to smear his body with fragrant sandal-paste.

None, not even Mathur, it is superfluous to say, could suppress laughter at the Brahmani's 'dignosis of the disease', let alone the treatment suggested. They thought within themselves, "How preposterous it is for her to say that it is not a disease, when it could not at all be alleviated even by taking so much medicine and using so many oils like Madhyamanarayana, Vishnu and the like!" But no one could have any possible objection to the simple, innocuous and easily-arranged treatment prescribed by the Brahmani. Every one was sure that the patient himself would give it up in a day or two, finding it of no use. The person of the Master was accordingly adorned with sandal-paste and garlands of flowers following the Brahmani's prescription; and, to the astonishment of all, the burning sensation of the Master's body completely disappeared in three days. But could sceptical minds accept a truth so easily? Persons of that mentality had their explanations of the cure. It must have been a mere accidental coincidence, as in the well-known analogy of the Kakataliya, "the crow and the palmfruit[1]." The last instalment of the Vishnu oil given to the Bhattacharya for use was absolutely genuine; this was clear from the physician's words. That oil was producing a good effect and the pain would have been completely cured by its use in a day or two even without the help of the Brahmani's prescription. It is a mere accidental coincidence. The use of that oil should be continued, whatever the Brahmani might say or prescribe.

11. Shortly after, the Master was affected by what people considered another "disease". This also, we were told by the Master himself, was cured in three days by following a simple prescription of the Brahmani. The Master said, "I began to feel an inordinate hunger at that time. I could not feel satisfied however much I ate. Immediately after taking my fill, I felt hungry again, as if I had not eaten anything. I felt the same hunger, whether I took food or not. Night and day that hunger continued without cessation. I thought, 'Can this be a new disease?' I spoke about it to the Brahmani. She said, 'Fear not, my child. Such states, it is written in the scriptures, come from time to time, upon the travellers on the path to the realisation of God. I will cure you of it." So saying, she asked Mathur to keep arranged in a room stacks of all kinds of food, from flattened and parched rice to Luchi, Sandesh, Rasgolla and other edibles. Then she told me, 'My child, remain in this room day and night, and eat whatever and whenever you like.' I remained in that room, walked up and down, looked on those stacks of food and handled them, now something from one stack, now from another. Three days passed in this way, when the inordinate hunger left me, and I felt relieved."

12. We have heard that before the state of mergence of the mind in God has become natural to a Sadhaka, and sometimes even after that, such abnormal hunger is experienced by some of

[1] The reference is to the story of a crow sitting on a palm tree and a palm fruit falling accidentally at the same time.

them. We were wonderstruck at seeing such states appearing in the Master in later days also, though with some difference. He did not then experience such continuous hunger as on this earlier occasion. We found him then in Bhava taking four or more times the quantity of food he would ordinarily take and digesting it without any difficulty in spite of his weak stomach. The reader will understand the matter easily if we mention here a few such episodes.

13. We have already given the reader one instance (see III.1.32). We narrated earlier in the book, in connection with the Master's gracious dealings with women devotees, how some ladies of Baghbazar went to Dakshineswar to pay a visit to the Master with a big piece of Sar (Cream) brought from the shop of the sweetmeat-maker Bhola, how failing to meet him there, they left the Sar at the Master's room and went with great difficulty to the house of Mahendranath Gupta, the teacher, where they met him, how Pranakrishna Mukhopadhyaya, whom the Master used to call the "fat Brahmana", came suddently there, and how those ladies hid themselves under the bedstead on which the Master sat and so on. We have also narrated then how the Master returned to Dakshineswar late in the evening after having taken his meal in Calcutta, and how he felt hungry once more that night and ate almost the whole of the Sar brought by the ladies. We shall now describe here a few more such instances. We say "a few" because such events happened almost daily in the Master's life. It is, therefore, impossible to record all of them.

Old people say that until Malaria made its appearance, decimating the population, many parts of Bengal like the Districts of Howrah and Burdwan, with their vast expanses of waters, orchards and green paddy fields, had a climate that was in no way inferior to that of north-western India from the point of view of health. They say that in those days people used to go to Burdwan and such other places for a change of climate. Kamarpukur, which is situated about twenty-five miles from Burdwan, could also boast in those days of a climate conducive to health. So at a certain period of his life, the Master used to go there from time to time for recouping his health. The prolonged practice of extraordinary austerities for twelve years, without paying any heed to the body, followed by continued absorption in Samadhi, had its adverse effect even on so robust a physique as his

He had become unfit for physical work, and often fell ill. That was why, when his Sadhana was complete, the Master used to go for a change to Kamarpukur and some other neighbouring places every year for the Chaturmasya.[1] His nephew and faithful attendant, Hriday, went with him on such occasions. Mathur Babu not only paid the expenses of such journeys but sent with him provisions and other necessary articles, lest he should lack anything in that small village. When a mother sends for the first time her daughter to the house of the latter's father-in-law, she sends with her even such trifling things as tooth-picks and wicks of lamps. Exactly in the same way did Mathur Babu and his devout wife, Smt. Jagadamba Dasi, very often send everything necessary for starting a new home for the Master when he went to Kamarpukur. For, it was not unknown to them that the household of the Master at that village was like that of Siva. The members of that family never had the slightest idea of providing anything for the future, even from the time of his forefathers. The practice of that family was to remain firm on the path of righteousness, living on whatever was available. They managed the household with the paddy produced annually on the half acre of the trust land of Raghuvir. This pious family had only the grocer's shop of the village as their store; for it was only when a little money was available from farewell gifts etc., that articles of daily use like salt, oil, vegetables, etc., were purchased from that store to last for that day. On other days they lived happily on rice and wild greens available in plenty on the banks of the ponds. And at all times and in all matters, they relied wholly on the living presence of Raghuvir, their family deity. As he knew well the condition of the family, Mathur Babu had a strong desire to buy a few Bighas of paddy land and make a trust of it in the name of Sri Raghuvir. And it was the same consideration that made him send all necessary household articles with the Master.

14. The Master, we have said earlier, used to go every year to Kamarpukur during the Chaturmasya. One year, when malaria had already made its appearance in those parts and was raging with fatal effect, he went to his native village and suffered a great

[1] The four rainy months from July to October when Sannyasins are expected to stop moving from place to place and stay in a fixed place for study and meditation.

deal from that fell fever. This made him resolve not to go to his native village any more from that time, and never again did he go. He made that resolve about eight or ten years before he passed away. But this is to anticipate. We are now concerned with a visit of his to Kamarpukur several years earlier. There was constantly a crowd of neighbours, men and women, who came to see him and listen to his religious talks. A current of bliss flowed incessantly there. With him in their midst, all the ladies of the house were engaged busily in serving him and those who came to see him. No one knew how days were passing in great joy one after another. Ramlal's mother, the mistress of the house, with sister Lakshmi, her daughter, and the supremely revered Holy Mother, were all there in the house.

It was about three hours after nightfall. The neighbours, men and women, had taken leave for the night and had gone home. The Master had been suffering for a few days from indigestion and had been taking nothing but sago and barleywater at night. He took milk and barley that night also and went to bed. The ladies of the house took their meal last of all and were about to retire for the night, having finished their day's duties.

The Master suddenly opened the door of his bedroom, came out staggering in Bhavasamadhi, and addressing Ramlal's mother and others, said, "I see, you are all gone to bed. Why have you done so before giving me anything to eat?" Surprised at this, Ramlal's mother exclaimed, "Ah, how is that! You took your meal only just now!" The Master replied, "When did I? I came from Dakshineswar just now. When did you feed me?"

All the ladies wondered at this and looked at one another's face. They realized that he was speaking thus in Bhavasamadhi. But what could they do? There was no food whatever in the house to feed him with at that hour. What was the way out? Ramlal's mother had therefore to say hesitatingly, "There is nothing edible except parched rice in the house now. Will you take parched rice? Why don't you take it? That will not do harm to your stomach." Saying so, she brought some on a plate and placed it before the Master. He saw it and turning about angrily like a boy, said, "I will not take mere parched rice." She tried to persuade him and said, "You are suffering from stomach troubles; nothing else will suit you. Moreover, all the shops are closed now at this hour of the night and so it is not possible to go and buy sago or barley for you. Take this small quantity tonight; I will cook for you soup and rice as soon as I rise tomorrow morning." But he would not lend his ear to it. Like a sensitive, importunate boy the Master repeated the same words, "I will not eat it.'

There being no other alternative, Ramlal was sent out to the shop. He called a shopkeeper repeatedly and roused him from sleep. He purchased two pounds of sweets and brought that home. Together with parched rice, a little more than sufficient for a normal man, they were placed on a plate. Now the Master sat joyfully to eat and consumed the whole of it. All the household then became alarmed and thought, "Ah, a person suffering from stomach trouble, who lives on sago and barley for half the days of the month — he has taken so much food so late at night! Something serious is sure to happen tomorrow." But, strange to say, the Master was seen to be quite well on the morrow. No discomfort whatever was felt by him on account of the food taken the previous night.

15. On another occasion, when the Master was living in Kamarpukur, he was taken to Jayrambati, the native village of his father-in-law. The Master took his meal and went to bed, but shortly afterwards got up and said, "I am very hungry." The ladies of the house were beside themselves with anxiety. What could they give him to eat? There was nothing in the house; for some ceremony, attended with the feeding of a large number of people , had been performed that day, and there was therefore no food left over, except some cooked rice steeped in cold water. When the Holy Mother mentioned this hesitatingly to the Master, he asked her to bring that rice. She, however, informed him that there was no curry to take with it. The Master said, "Why don't you make a careful search? Did you not cook fish with chilli and turmeric today? Why don't you see whether a little of that is left over or not?" The Holy Mother looked into the cooking pot and found a tiny Maurala fish with a little paste-like soup sticking to it. She brought it to the Master. He was delighted to see it. He sat down to eat that boiled rice steeped in water at that dead of night, and consumed a quantity weighing about five pounds with that tiny fish for sauce, and felt himself at rest.

16. The same thing happened occasionally while he was at Dakshineswar. One night, at about twelve, the Master got up,

called Ramlal and said, "I am very hungry." What was to be done? Generally there used to be some sweets and other eatables in stock; but on that occasion there was nothing in the room. Ramlal at last went to the Nahavat and informed the Holy Mother and the women devotees about it. They got up very hurriedly, made a fire by means of straw and firewood, and prepared about two pounds of Halwa (sweet pudding) and sent it to the Master's room in a big stone cup full to the brim. One of the women devotees brought it there. She just stepped into the room, dimly lighted by a lamp in a corner where Ramlal was sitting quite nearby. She was startled to notice the Master walking up and down at that dead of night, calm and silent, with an extraordinary spiritual mood overwhelming him. She saw before her the grave and sublime face of the Master brightened with spiritual emotion — that God-intoxicated figure, that steadfast inward look of his large eyes before which the whole universe merged into and emerged from Samadhi at will, that grave majestic gait, that wholly indrawn mind, and that random pacing up and down in supernal bliss. It seemed to her that the Master's body had become much bigger in both height and bulk, as if he was not a mortal of this earth, but some god from heaven come in the guise of a human being to this earthly sphere so full of misery, wailing and death. It looked as if veiling himself with the darkness of night, that being was majestically pacing up and down the room. It seemed to her that he was out of compassion, deeply absorbed in pondering in his mind over the ways and means by which he could convert this world of death and suffering, a veritable cremation ground, into a heaven fit for gods to live in. One thing seemed certain to her: he could not be the same Master whom she had known. The hairs of her body stood on end, and she felt an indescribable awe as she approached him.

Ramlal had already placed a seat for the Master to sit on. Awe-struck and hesitating, the woman devotee went near and placed the cup of Halwa in front of the seat. The Master sat down to eat and gradually ate up the whole of it under the influence of that spiritual intoxication. Did the Master understand the thoughts of the woman devotee? Who can say? But when he saw her looking at him aghast, he asked her, "Tell me who is eating? Is it I or someone else?" The woman devotee replied: "It seems to me as if someone else is there in you, and it is he who is eating". At this the Master said: "You are right." Saying so, he smiled.

17. Many such events may be mentioned. The powerful waves of spiritual emotions produced such great changes in the Master's body that on those occasions he seemed to be a different person, and his behaviour — his bodily movements, eating, drinking, etc., — all assumed a different nature, as it were. Yet, on account of that supra-normal behaviour, no disturbance was observable in his body at the end of those spiritual moods. That the mind residing within is making and unmaking our gross body and fashioning it anew, is a fact that is accepted theoretically, but it is not known how this is effected. So many are sceptical about it. But these incidents, rather too common in the Master's life, are however proofs thereof.

18. Some say that it was from Bhairavi Brahmani that Mathur Babu came to know of Vaishnavacharan. Mathur thereupon sent him an invitation to come to Dakshineswar and advise him whether there was an element of physical ailment in the Master's spiritual states. Anyway, Vaishnavacharan came to Dakshineswar shortly afterwards. We can infer that a small meeting of scholars was arranged on that occasion. For a few devout aspirants and Pandits must have come as usual with Vaishnavacharan, and the learned Brahmani and Mathur Babu's party were also there. As the subject for discussion, they had the ascertainment of the Master's spiritual condition. Hence we call it a meeting.

19. The discussion started. The Brahmani described the Master's state as she saw it with her own eyes and as she had heard about it from people around. And comparing the Master's present state with what was recorded in the scriptures as experiences of the ancient teachers of the devotional path, she gave her opinion that his was the same state as theirs. Addressing Vaishnavacharan she said to him, "If you hold a different opinion about it, please explain to me why you do so." Just as a mother stands with the pride of a heroine to protect her child, the Brahmani, as if strengthened with some divine power, came forward to support the Master's case. And what was the reaction of the Master, the cause of the assemblage of all those august personalities? We can visualize the scene. Quite unconcerned and smiling and enjoying the bliss of the Self, he must have been sitting in the midst of the people carrying on the discussion, — sometimes putting into

his mouth a few grains of aniseed or cubebs from the small bag near him and listening to their conversation as if it was about some one else, and at other times touching the person of Vaishnavacharan to draw his attention to what he had to narrate about his own condition, and saying, "Look here, it sometimes happens like this."

20. Some are of the opinion that with the help of the subtle insight born of his Sadhana, Vaishnavacharan came to know the moment he saw him that the Master was a great soul. But that apart, we were told by the Master himself that he heard and heartily approved whatever the Brahmani said about the Master's condition. Not only that, Vaishnavacharan remarked with amazement that all the signs of the nineteen kinds of spiritual moods — the co-existence of which has been called in the devotional scriptures as the "Mahabhava", the great mood, and observed only in the lives of Sri Radha, the embodiment of spiritual moods, and in Sri Chaitanya — were seen manifested in the Master. If at all the Mahabhava manifested a little in a Jiva due to unprecedented good fortune, only two or three of these nineteen moods would find expression in him. No Jiva in the past could sustain the tremendous impact of all of them, and no Jiva in the future too will be able to do so according to the scriptures. Mathur and the others present were altogether dumbfounded to hear the words of Vaishnavacharan. And the Master also said to Mathur in joy and astonishment, "Ah, what does he say! After all I am glad to be assured that it is not a disease."

21. The above-mentioned view of Vaishnavacharan about the Master was not merely verbal; for, ever afterwards, he held the Master in high regard and had genuine devotion to him. From that time on, he came very often to Dakshineswar for the purpose of enjoying the bliss of the Master's divine company and sought his opinion on his own Sadhanas of an esoteric type, which he confided to him. Sometimes, he took him by way of a trip to fellow devotees of his sect treading the same path, so that they also might be acquainted with the Master and be blessed like himself. Mixing with them and knowing their lives and secret Sadhanas, the god-like Master, the picture of immaculate purity, got the opportunity to understand that, if one practises as Sadhana, actions blameworthy and condemnable in ordinary eyes, cherishing in one's heart the sure and sincere conviction that one is doing

it for the realization of the divine Lord, one, instead of meeting with downfall on this account, becomes gradually fit for renunciation and self-control, goes forward on the path of religion, and attains devotion to God. But, when at first he heard of those practices and saw a little of them with his own eyes, there arose in his mind, we were told many a time by the Master himself, such ideas as, "These people talk tall; why do they at the same time indulge in such low practices?" And again, we were told by the Master himself that he changed his opinion at last; for he saw that those amongst them who were sincere and had faith in God made spiritual progress. In order to remove our hatred for the followers of those paths, the Master expressed to us his conviction about them thus: "Ah, why should you indulge in hatred? Know that that is also one of the paths, but a dirty one. Just as there are several doors — the main gate, the back door, and the one for the sweeper to enter the house in order to clean the dirt there — so also know that there are several approaches to the mansion of God and that this also is one, though an unclean way. Through whatever door people may enter the house, they reach the goal all right. Still, are you to act like them or mix with them? No, you should not. But you must not also entertain any hatred for them."

22. Does the human mind, so full of worldly desires, adopt the path of renunciation easily? Does it care to be absolutely pure and sincere in its quest for God? It wants generally to cling to some impurity in purity; even when it renounces lust and gold, it is pleased with whatever smells of them. The books on the method of performing worship enjoin that one should worship the Divine Mother with absolute purity of mind, but the next moment prescribe the singing of hideous, lustful songs for Her satisfaction. This is not something to be wondered at or condemned. It only shows how adamantine is the chain of lust and gold with which the human mind is bound by Mahamaya, the mistress of countless world systems. It becomes clear too that it is impossible for a Jiva to attain liberation if She does not remove this bondage by Her grace. It becomes evident that the path along which She is helping a particular person to go forward towards liberation is beyond human understanding. And when we make a minute and comparative study of the trends and tendencies of our minds on the one hand, and the unique mystery

of the Master's life on the other, it will become abundantly clear how he transcends humanity and represents a type rarely seen in this world and how he was sojourning in this sordid world of ours out of his own will in play or compassion for us — remaining always an emperor of the realm of knowledge in the eyes of knowing ones but humbler than the humblest and lowlier than the lowliest to the superficial eyes of ignorant men.

23. In the Karma Kanda, the "work" portion of the Veda, full of the descriptions of sacrifices, oblations etc., that were performed in the Vedic age, Bhoga or enjoyment of objects of the senses like sight, taste, and the rest, in and through a system of worship of Gods, came to be recognised as the aim of human life. When the human mind became freed from desires to some extent by continued observance of those Vedic rites, worship of God with pure devotion as recommended in the Upanishads was adopted by aspirants for the attainment of the goal of life. But in the Buddhistic age, a totally different outlook and way of life came to prevail. Without any consideration of competency, a system of spiritual discipline, suited for ascetics free from all worldly desires and dwelling in forests, was prescribed to all and sundry, however much they might be burning with desire for worldly enjoyment. The then political machinery of the state also helped that attempt of the Buddhist monks. The Vedic sacrificial religion permitted controlled enjoyment of the senses to men who were not fit for total renunciation, so that they might gradually be brought to that way of life with their spiritual development. When the Vedic rituals, which were the outward forms of this outlook, were destroyed by the preachings of the Buddhist monks, they reappeared in the forms of secret Tantric Sadhanas, practised at the dead of night in solitary and uncanny places like the burning grounds. Seeing the Vedic sacrifices becoming ineffective and obsolete, the great Yogi Maheswara, the Tantras say, infused life into them and revealed them in a different form as the Tantras. There is indeed a great truth hidden in this tradition; for in the Tantras, as in the portions of the Vedas dealing with sacrifices, a union of Bhoga or worldly enjoyments with Yoga or spiritual contemplation is distinctly perceptible. But while in the Vedas, the Karmas inculcated by them are never combined with the non-dual knowledge of the Upanishads, each Tantric rite or ceremony is intimately associated with that supreme know-

ledge. For example, when you sit to worship a particular Deity, first of all you are to think that you raise the Kundalini, the coiled power, to the thousand-petalled lotus in the head and think of your existence in a non-dual state with Brahman. Then you are to think that you become separate from Him and assume the nature of a Jiva again, and that the light of Brahman becomes condensed, so to say, and manifests itself in the form of the Deity to be worshipped. You then bring the Deity out from within you and begin to worship Him. Ah, what a fine method is this attempt at meditation! Becoming one with God in love and then worshipping Him! Of course, it is perhaps only one advanced worshipper among a thousand, who can properly perform this meditation. But all can at least make an attempt, which in itself is of immense benefit to them; for by continually attempting it, they are sure to advance gradually. Thus by combining the idea of non-duality with all its rituals, the Tantras remind the aspirant always of the ultimate aim of spiritual life. Herein lies the novelty of the Tantric disciplines, as distinguished from the Vedic rituals; and it is for this reason that it has such a great hold over the people of India in general.

24. Another novelty of the Tantras is the preaching of the Motherhood of Mahamaya, the Cause of the universe, as a result of which a pure, sacred mental attitude towards every feminine form is induced. Examine the Vedas and the Puranas, you will not meet with this idea so uniformly and impressively as in the Tantras. The rudiments of the worship of the female body are, however, met with in the Samhita portion of the Vedas. They especially prescribed that it should be looked upon as pure and that at the time of marriage gods should be worshipped in it by the Mantras such as "Conceive, O One (Uma) possessing the white crescent of the moon" etc., so that the bride might conceive a beautiful child, full of vitality. But let no one think on this account that the worship of the male and female bodies was prevalent in India from the Vedic times. History has proved that this worship in a gross form was at first extant among the Sumers of Babylon and cognate people. Just as, on the one hand, the Tantra of India united in each of its ceremonies the spirit of the "work" and "knowledge" portions of the Vedas, so, on the other hand, finding that the spiritual progress of a certain class of people with peculiar tendencies would be easy through the worship of the female form,

it reverted to a great extent to a gross form of such worship combining it with the high spiritual ideal of the Vedas. The Tantra thus made that worship also a part of itself. The Tantric Virachara, the hero-mode of worship, seems to have originated in this way. The Kaula teachers, who produced the Tantras, rightly understood that men, ever eager to enjoy pleasures, could not forgo the gross sights, tastes, etc., altogether, but, if they could somehow generate in those persons a genuine reverence for the objects of enjoyment, they were certain to develop, on the strength of that reverence, spiritual qualities like self-control etc., in course of time, though they might indulge for some time in the pleasures thereof — may be to some excess in rare cases. That was why they preached: the bodies of women are veritable holy places of pilgrimage; one should give up looking upon women as human beings and always regard them as the Devi Herself. Knowing that it is a special manifestation of the Mother of the universe, one should always have devotion to, and reverence for, every female figure. One should sip a little of the water in which she has dipped her toe. One should not condemn a woman or beat her even through inadvertence.

So we read such passages as these in Tantric literature: "In her (a woman's body), O great Lady, there exist all the places of pilgrimage" (Ch. 14, Purascharanollasa Tantra). "A man who looks upon woman as a human being, O Thou of the best countenance, can have no perfection, though he may repeat Mantras; he meets with the contrary result" (Ch. 2, Uttara Tantra). "A man who drinks with devotion a little of the water into which a woman has dipped her toe or eats the leavings of the food in her plate, is sure to have uninterrupted success" (Nigama-kalpadruma). "Women are the gods, they are sacred, and they are the ornaments of society. One should never hate, condemn or beat them" (Ch. 5, Mundamala Tantra).

25. But of what avail were all these? Eventually there came a time for the Tantric Sadhakas when they gave up the ideal of realizing the knowledge of God and applied their minds to the attainment of miraculous powers. It was during this period that various kinds of unnatural Sadhanas and the worship of ghosts, ghouls, etc., entered into the body of the Tantra and converted it into its present form. This is why two broad strata, the good and the bad, the high and the low, the pure and the impure are

met with in each Tantra with their distinctiveness.. Sadhanas of the lowest stratum are sometimes seen inserted into the worship of the highest. And everyone now selects from the Tantras that kind of Sadhana which suits his own nature.

26. There appeared another change in the Tantric Sadhana on the advent of Sri Chaitanya. Thinking that the spread of dualism among the masses would be beneficial, he and his immediate successors propagated among them the Tantric Mantras and outward worship only, leaving out, to a great extent, the Tantric practices leading to the attitude of non-duality. They also introduced a novel method into the above worship. They taught that the Deity, the object of worship, should be served by one as one wished oneself to be served. The Tantric deities are conceived as purifying by mere sight the fruits, roots and other food stuff offered to them by the worshippers. The general belief is that these offered articles, taken by the aspirants, increase their spiritual inclination instead of their animal propensities of lust, anger, etc. According to the process newly started by the Vaishnava teachers, on the other hand, the belief gained currency that the Deities took subtle parts of those offerings, and sometimes they took even gross parts in accordance with the devotional ardour and earnestness of the devotee. Many other changes were also introduced by the Vaishnava teachers into their mode of worship. Chief amongst them was the pre-eminence they gave to the Tantric mode of worship called "Pasvachara"[1], which favoured external cleanliness. They preached to the people in general that by remaining absolutely clean in thought, word and deed, and knowing that the name itself was Brahman, the Jivas would attain the beatific vision through the constant repetition of the name of the divine Lord, as proclaimed in the precept, "Success is achieved through Japa, Japa and Japa alone!"

27. But the efforts of these early teachers were all in vain. Very shortly after their time, the human mind, full of desires, introduced impure ideas into the pure process of worhip prescribed

[1] Pasvachara = Pasu + Achara. Pasu ordinarily means an animal, but in the Tantra it means Jiva; hence Pasvachara is not anything censurable. It simply means the rites and ceremonies of those who still consider themselves as Jivas and have not attained oneness with Siva, who is Pasupati, the Lord of Jivas. As long as a man regards himself a Jiva, he must keep an eye on cleanliness, purity of food, etc. Hence in Pasvachara, stress is laid on these things.—Tr.

by them. Man discarded the subtle ideas and took only the gross objects. Instead of cultivating the heart-felt attraction which a woman has for the paramour, and directing it towards God, he went the length of taking a mistress himself. Thus he introduced Bhoga, worldly enjoyment, into the pure process of Yoga or union with God, and brought it down to the level of his natural inclination to a certain extent. And what else can he do? For, he is unable to live such a pure life. It is only a combination of Yoga and Bhoga that he can assimilate. He wants to realize spirituality but simultaneously covets the enjoyments of sight, taste, etc. And this was why there arose in the Vaishnava community, worship and secret Sadhana according to the doctrines of the Kartabhajas, Auls, Bauls, Darvesas, Sains, and so on. Therefore, at the root of all these is seen the current of the very ancient Vedic Karmas, that combination of Yoga and Bhoga. Along with it a tendency to combine each action with the non-dual knowledge, a process introduced by the Tantric Kaula teachers, is also seen.

28. The reader will easily grasp the foregoing reflections, if we give a brief exposition of the ideas of the Kartabhaja and allied communities regarding topics like God, liberation, self-control, renunciation, and love. Speaking of these communities, the Master told us many things about them at different times. Their teachings are recorded in verses clothed in simple language. The reader will realize, when he hears them, how far those verses help the ordinary people in understanding the ideas conveyed by those terms. The people of these communities call God "Aleklata". It is superflous to say that the word "Alek" is derived from the Sanskrit word "Alakshya", the unknown and unknowable. This Alek enters into the mind of a pure man, in other words, It manifests Itself through him as Karta, the spiritual teacher. On such a teacher they bestow the title of Sahaj, the man whose natural tendencies lead Godward. The community is called Kartabhaja, or worshippers of the spiritual teacher, because it is only a human being, truly inspired by the mood of the spiritual teacher, that is regarded by them as the object of worship. About the real nature of Aleklata, and Its influence on a pure heart, they say: "It comes imperceptibly and goes imperceptibly; nobody can see the Alek." Again: "One, who has known It, is the object of worship in the three worlds."

The sign of a Sahaj man is that he always remains "intact"; in other words, he does not lose his serenity on account of lust, even if he be always in the company of women. They say about him: "He lives with women but never indulges in sexual satisfaction." If an aspirant does not live unattached in the world of lust and gold, he cannot advance spiritually. They, therefore, teach him: "Be a cook, and distribute the curry but do not touch the cooking-pot. Make the frog dance in the mouth of the snake, but let not the snake swallow it. Bathe in the sea of ambrosia but do not let your hair be wet".

Just as in the Tantra, the Sadhakas have been divided into three classes, the "animal", the "heroic" and the "divine", so there are high and low classes of Sadhakas amongst the Kartabhajas. They speak of four classes, the Auls, Bauls, Darveses and Sains, and they say that there is none higher than a Sain. The Master said, "All of them worship the formless aspect of God." He used also to sing often a few songs of this community for us. Take, for example, the song:

"Dive, O my mind, dive into the sea of Beauty.
You will realize the treasure, the gem of love, when you will make a search in the deepest world of your heart.
Search, search over and over again, and you will realize Vrindavan in your heart.
The lamp of knowledge will constantly burn, brightly illumining your heart.
Who is he, who conducts the boat so easily on land?
Kuvir says, 'Listen attentively; meditate on the holy feet of the Guru."

Thus to worship the Guru and remain engaged in congregational devotional exercises are their chief Sadhanas. Although they do not disapprove the worship of the images and forms of deities, they generally do not worship them. The worship of the Guru in India is very ancient; it seems to have been prevalent from the age of the Upanishads. For, we read in the Tattiriya Upanishad (1-11-2), "Let the Acharya be your God." It appears that the worship of deities was not at all in vogue at that time. One is astonished to see how many forms Guru worship assumed in India, in course of time.

Besides, the aspirants have to undergo various religious

exercises in order to renounce from their minds the consciousness of difference such as "the clean and the unclean", "the good and the bad." The Master said, "The aspirants receive instructions regarding those exercises coming down from Guru to disciple." He would now and again mention a few of them also.

29. The master was often heard to say, "The Vedas and the Puranas should be heard by the ear; but the disciplines prescribed by the Tantras should be actually performed and carried into practice." It is seen too almost everywhere in India, that the followers of the Smritis practise one or another of the Tantric disciplines. Big scholars of the Nyaya and the Vedanta are, it is observed, Tantrics in practice. Learned scholars of the Vaishnava communities, well versed in devotional scriptures like the Bhagavata, are also seen to follow the secret Sadhanas of the communities like the Kartabhajas. Pandit Vaishnavacharan was one of them. He was intimately connected with their secret congregation at Kachhibagan, a few miles north of Calcutta. Many men and women of the said community lived there and were engaged in Sadhana under his instruction. Vaishnavacharan took the Master there on a few occasions. Noticing that the Master was always perfectly unaffected by lust, and seeing that on account of the love of God, he entered into ecstasy, which they had never seen before, a few women of that place tried, we were told, to test him in order to know whether he had completely conquered his passions. As a result, they paid him the respect due to one who was "intact", and naturally disposed towards God. The ingenuous Master, of innocent course, had gone on a trip there with Vaishnavacharan at his request without suspecting anything. He did not know at all that they would test him that way. Be that as it may, he never went there again, afterwards.

30 Vaishnavacharan was very much impressed by the Master's strength of character as also by his purity and devotional ecstasy. Consequently his devotion and reverence for him increased so much day by day that he never hesitated at last to admit, in the presence of all, that the Master was an incarnation of God.

31. Shortly after Vaishnavacharan began visiting the Master, Pandit Gauri of Indes also came to Dakshineswar. He was an eminent Tantric Sadhaka. On his first visit to the Dakshineswar temple, an amusing event happened. We heard of it from the Master. He said that Gauri had a miraculous power acquired

through his austerities. Whenever he was invited to a scriptural controversy, he entered the house or hall fixed for it with the loud recitation of some verse like the one from a hymn to the Devi, "Helpless that I am, to whom shall I go for shelter except to Thee, O mother of Lambodara (Ganesha having a protruding abdomen)!", preceded by the startling shouts of certain syllables like "Ha! re! re!" inciting a mood of challenge and heroism. The Master said, "The hearts of all were startled with an indescribable fright when they heard from his mouth those syllables expressive of the heroic mood together with the part of that stanza from the hymn to the Devi by Acharya Sankara uttered in a voice deep and sonorous like the rumbling of a cloud. Two results were achieved by this. First, by virtue of that sound, the power in Gauri became fully awakened; and, secondly, he stole away the strength of the adversaries by startling and charming them with it. Loudly uttering that sound and slapping his left arm with the right like wrestlers, Gauri entered the meeting and sat down with his legs folded and his knees joined together in front and the feet behind, in the fashion of the courtiers of the emperors of Delhi, and engaged himself in the controversy." The Master said that it was then impossible for anyone to defeat him.

The Master had no previous knowledge of that power of Gauri. But, as soon as he entered the Dakshineswar Kali temple and uttered loudly the syllables "Ha, re,re,re!" the Master felt prompted by some power from within him to exclaim those very syllables more loudly than Gauri. Thereupon Gauri repeated the syllables again in a louder voice than the Master. Excited at that, the Master uttered "Ha, re,re,re!" far more loudly than he. The Master used to say smilingly that a terrific uproar was created, like the din made during inroads by dacoits, on account of the louder and yet louder utterance of those syllables by both the sides. With sticks, cudgels etc., the gate-keepers of the Kali temple ran hurriedly towards the place from where the noise came. All others were beside themselves with fear. The noise of this vocal contest subsided only when Gauri could not raise his voice any more. He was thus silenced. In a somewhat dejected mood, he then entered the Kali temple, laughing loudly to cover his defeat. The Master said: "The Divine Mother afterwards revealed to me that great secret of Gauri's life — the way in which he disarmed his opponent of all his powers and himself became invincible — It was also revealed that he would no longer have that power. The Mother attracted that power 'here' (into the Master) for his good." And it was seen that, day by day, Gauri was more and more charmed by the ideal of the Master and became completely obedient to him.

32. Pandit Gauri was, we have already said, a Tantric Sadhaka. At the time of the worship of Durga every year, Gauri, we were told by the Master, made all the preparations for the worship, adorned his wife with dress and ornaments, seated her on a wooden seat decorated with Alimpana and, for three days, devoutly worshipped her as the Divine Mother Herself. The Tantra teaches that all the female figures are the forms of the Mother of the universe and that there is a great manifestation in them of the Divine Mother's power of 'sustaining and delighting' the Jivas. Man should therefore worship all female forms with absolute purity of outlook. Forgetting that the Divine Mother Herself stands veiled in female figures, and looking upon female bodies with a feeling of lust, as if they were objects of enjoyment only, one insults the Mother of the universe Herself and consequently meets with endless ruin. In the Chandi (II.6.) the gods recite the hymn to the Devi:

Vidyāḥ samastāstava Devi bhedāḥ
Striyaḥ samastāḥ sakalā jagatsu
Tvayaikayā pūritamambayaitat,
Kā te stutiḥ stavya parāparoktiḥ

"O Devi, Thou art of the nature of pure Consciousness. Again Thou art manifested as all the various sciences, high and low, from which endless forms of conceptual knowledge arise. Thou existest as all the female figures of the world. Thou alone pervadest the whole universe and art present everywhere in it. Thou art incomparable and beyond words. Whoever has been able or will be able, to describe Thy numberless noble qualities by reciting hymns to Thee?"

Many of us read this hymn daily in India; but, alas! how few of us try to look upon the female figure as the Devi Herself, pay it due respect even for a few moments and thus feel pure joy in our hearts and feel blessed. How few are those who do not insult the Mother of the universe, hundreds of times every day! O India! you are in this present miserable condition only because you insult female forms with your bestial attitude and have forgotten to serve Jiva as Siva. The Mother of the universe alone knows when She will have compassion on you and remove that bestial mood of yours.

33. We have heard from the Master himself of another wonderful power of Pandit Gauri. The eminent Tantric Sadhakas generally perform Homa at the end of the daily worship of the Universal Mother. Gauri also performed it on many occasions, if not daily. But the procedure he adopted in his Homa was very strange. He did not perform it like others. Usually people make an altar on the ground by means of bricks and sand, arrange pieces of firewood on it, and then kindle fire and offer oblations. But Gauri stretched his own left arm without any suport and placed on it one Maund (about 82 lbs.) of firewood at a time, lighted it, and offered oblations into it with his right hand. It is not a short time that Homa takes. So, it appears to us to be quite impossible for one to sustain the heavy weight of one Maund of firewood on the arm stretched in the air, and devoutly offer oblations in the prescribed way for so long a time, keeping the mind calm and bearing the heat of the fire on the arm all the while. That is why many of us could not at first believe in the feat, even when we heard of it from the Master himself. The Master understood our difficulty and said, "Ah! I saw him do it with my own eyes. That was also one of his miraculous powers."

34. Mathur Babu invited a few more scholarly aspirants like Vaishnavacharan and convened a meeting a few days after Gauri arrived at Dakshineswar. The purpose of the meeting was a debate between the newly arrived Pandit Gauri and the other scholars on scriptural evidence in order to ascertain, as before, the spiritual condition of the Master. It was convened in the morning in the music hall in front of the temple of the Mother Kali. Seeing that Vaishnavacharan was late in coming from Calcutta, the Master started for the place of the meeting with Gauri. Before entering the meeting, he went into the temple of the Divine Mother Kali, saluted Her with devotion and worshipped Her feet. As soon as he came out of the temple staggering in Bhavasamadhi, he saw Vaishnavacharan fall at his feet and salute him. No sooner had the Master, inspired by spiritual emotion and love of God, seen him than he went into Samadhi, and sat on Vaishnavacharan's shoulders. The latter felt blessed and was

beside himself with joy. He recited a hymn to the Master in Sanskrit, composed extempore by himself. Seeing that gracious and bright form of the Master in Samadhi, and hearing that graceful recital of the hymn by Vaishnavacharan with his heart overflowing with joy, Mathur and the others present were standing motionless on all sides with their eyes steadfast and hearts filled with devotion. The Master's Samadhi came to an end shortly afterwards, when all went along slowly with him and sat down in the place of the meeting.

Now began the proceedings of the meeting. But, Gauri first of all said suddenly, "As he (the Master) has bestowed so much grace on the other Pandit, I will not enter into a discussion with him today. Even if I did, I am sure to be defeated; for he is armed with divine grace today. Moreover, I find he is a person holding the same view as mine. A debate is, therefore, useless in this case." The meeting came to an end after a little conversation on other scriptural topics.

35. It must be noted that Gauri refrained from a controversial debate not due to any fear of the scholarship of Vaishnavacharan. The main reason was the conversion that had already come on him. Seeing the Master's way of life and his venerable personality, he, with the help of his keen insight born of his Tapas, felt in his heart of hearts, even in that short period of his stay there, that the Master was not an ordinary man but a great soul. For, some time afterwards the Master said to him with a view to testing his mind, "Look here, Vaishnavacharan calls this (himself) an incarnation of God; can that be so? Please tell me what you think of this." Gauri replied seriously, "Does Vaishnavacharan call you an incarnation only? I should consider his estimate very low. My conviction is that you are He, from a part of whom the Incarnations come down to the world from age to age to do good to humanity, and with whose power they accomplish that work of theirs." The Master said with a smile, "Ah, you go even beyond him! Will you tell me why you think so?" Gauri said, "I say so on the evidence of the scriptures and from my own experience. If anyone takes up the opposite view and comes to controvert me, I am ready to prove my conviction." The Master thereupon said like a boy, "You say so many things. Who knows what it is all about? I for my part don't know anything at all." Gauri replied, "Quite right. The scriptures also say, 'Thou dost not

know Thyself.' So, please say how others can know you. If you have compassion on anybody and allow him to know the truth, then only he can know it."

36. The Master smiled on hearing the Pandit's words expressive of his strong faith. Gauri's attraction for the Master grew with the passing of days. In the Master's divine company, the Pandit's knowledge of the scriptures and the merits of his Sadhana were attaining fruition, and they manifested as intense detachment from the world. He was daily losing his relish for scholarship, honour, miraculous powers, etc., and his mind was withdrawing itself to the lotus feet of God. Gauri had now no more that pride of scholarship, that love for argumentation, that arrogance — they vanished altogether. He now understood that he had spent his precious time so long in vain without making the utmost efforts to realize the lotus feet of the divine Lord. Time should no more be wasted that way. He formed the firm resolve in his mind that he should renounce his all, and depending entirely on God with a heart full of devotion, should spend the remaining few days of his life in eagerly calling on Him, so that he might have His grace and vision.

Gauri thus spent day after day and month after month in the blessed company of the Master and in meditation on God. As the Pandit was for a long time away from home, the members of his family — his wife, son and others — began to write letters to him again and again to return. For, they had some inkling from people that he was mixing closely with a certain 'mad holy man' at Dakshineswar and that his mind was consequently becoming indifferent to worldly matters. Now the thought that they might come to Dakshineswar and drag him into the worldly life again, gradually grew strong in the mind of the Pandit. This was evident from the trend of the letters he received from them. After a great deal of anxious thought, Gauri discovered a way out. Knowing that an auspicious moment had arrived, he bowed down at the holy feet of the Master and asked leave of him with tears in his eyes. The Master said, "How is it, Gauri? Why do you want to leave so suddenly? Where will you go?" Gauri replied with folded hands, "Bless me, so that I may have my desire fulfilled. I'll not return before I realize God." Since then the world has never heard of Pandit Gauri, in spite of a great deal of search.

37. The Master mentioned to us, many a time, various incidents from the lives of Vaishnavacharan and Gauri. Again, sometimes in the course of discussing some topic with us, he would tell us what opinion these learned Pandits had expressed on it. One day while he was giving instruction to a devout aspirant, the Master, we remember, said to him, "When one actually sees his chosen ideal in man, one realizes the divine Lord. Vaishnavacharan used to say, 'When one has faith in the Lila of God as man one acquires perfect knowledge.'"

38. Noticing in one of the devotees the pernicious idea of discrimination between Kali and Krishna, the Master once said to him, "What a crude idea! Know that it is your chosen Ideal alone who manifests himself as Kali, Krishna, Gauri and all others. But, do I ask you, on that account, to give up your own chosen Ideal and worship Gauri? No, not at all. But give up this attitude of exclusiveness. Hold on firmly to the conviction that it is your chosen Ideal who has become Krishna, Gauri and other Divine manifestations. Don't you see that a daughter-in-law of a household goes to her father-in-law's house, serves and pays respect to every one — father-in-law, mother-in-law, the husband's sisters, his younger and elder brothers and others — according to her relationship with them; but she shares her bed and thoughts with her husband alone. She knows that it is through the husband that all others of the household are her own. So it is through your chosen Ideal alone that you are related with the other forms of His, and you should have devotion to and reverence for them all. Know this and drive away fanaticism. Gauri used to say, 'When Kali and Gauranga are known as the same, I shall know that true knowledge has come'."

39. Again, observing that the mind of a particular devotee could not become calm on account of a great attachment to some one in the family, the Master advised him to serve and love that object of his affection as a form of the divine Lord. We told the reader before (Ch. III I 27) how he advised a woman devotee, who was very much attached to a young nephew of hers, to serve and love that child as the Boy Krishna, and how, as the result of that practice, she attained Bhavasamadhi in a short time. While he was teaching that one should have reverence for, and devotion to, the object of one's love as God, the Master sometimes used to quote Vaishnavacharan on that subject and say, "Vaishna-

vacharan used to say that if any one could look upon the object of his love as his chosen Ideal, his mind would soon turn to the Divine Lord." Saying so, he would forthwith explain it: "He used to advise the women of his own community to do so. It was not blameworthy in their case; for, they had the mental attitude of a paramour. They wanted to attribute to themselves that attraction for God, which a woman feels in her mind for her paramour." The Master, however, said that it was not a thing to be taught to the general public; for he said, "It would increase adultery." But he did not disapprove of one's loving and serving one's husband, son or some other relation as a form of God. He, it is known to us, gave this advice to many devotees who took refuge at his lotus feet.

40. On a little reflection, it will be clear that this is not a novel, or unscriptural doctrine. The great Rishi of the Upanishad teaches in the conversation between Yajnavalkya and Maitreyi, "The husband becomes dear to the wife only because the Divine Lord is in the husband. The mind of the husband is attracted towards the wife only because He is in the wife" (Brh. Up. 2-5). Rishis of India, from whom the Upanishads have come down to us, have thus been teaching us for ages to look upon all those objects and persons of the world who are considered very precious, attractive and dear by us, as part of the divine Lord who is of the nature of Love and Bliss, and to love them from this angle of view. When Narada, and other teachers of Bhakti teach Jivas to turn the deadly enemies of man, the passions of lust, anger, etc., towards God, and ask them to have recourse to the devotional attitude of a friend, a mother, or a sweet-heart towards the Lord, they are but following in the footsteps of the more ancient Rishis, the authors of the Upanishads. The Master's opinion, therefore, on this matter is clearly scriptural.

41. It is well known that the great incarnations of God bring to the religious world the gospel of a new path, quite in keeping with the authority of the ancient scriptures and in no way contrary to their doctrines. This can be understood by studying the life of any one of the incarnations of God. It has all along been our endeavour in this book to explain to the reader this fact in the life of Sri Ramakrishna, the prophet of the modern age. We meet, at every turn of his life, the same reverential attitude towards the scriptures. But, if we fail to do so, let the reader

know that it is due to the defects of our limited intellect, and not to any shortcoming of the Master, whose discovery of the new great spiritual truth "As many faiths, so many paths" has charmed the world. Not only the Vedantic non-dualism but even all those doctrines like the Kartabhaja, which we call vile and at which we turn up our nose in imitation of the clever and worldly-minded westerners, who use one standard to judge the customs and institutions of other nations and cleverly cast it aside and adopt another convenient standard for their own, — all these were accorded by the Master, the god-man, a respectable position as genuine paths to the realization of the Divine Lord and prescribed for persons according to their particular inclinations and capabilities. Urged by our intolerence of what we considered debased practices, many of us asked the Master on several occasions, "Sir, how is it that such a high-class aspirant as the Brahmani used to practise Sadhana with the five M's?"; or "Is it not wrong that a devotee of such a high calibre as the learned Vaishnavacharan did not refrain from taking a paramour as auxiliary to his Sadhana?" The Master's invariable reply used to be, "Oh, no; they did not incur any blame by it! They believed whole-heartedly that it was their path to the realization of God. One should not condemn any method practised by a person who genuinely believes in his heart of hearts that that method will enable him to realize God. The spiritual attitude of no one should be interfered with. For any attitude, genuinely understood and sincerely followed as a Sadhana, will lead an aspirant to the Divine Lord, who is the centre on which all attitudes converge. But stick to your own attitude and continue calling on Him. Never condemn anybody's attitude, nor try to make another's attitude your own." Saying so, the ever-blissful Master would begin forthwith to sing now and again:

> "Remain, O mind, in yourself, do not go to anyone else's place.
> If you make a search in your heart, you will get without any effort whatever you want.
> That philosopher's stone, the supreme treasure, can give whatever you ask for!
> How many are the gems lying scattered at the backdoor of that Supreme Being!

Do not, O mind, become restless to take painful journeys
to places of pilgrimage.
Why don't you joyfully bathe and cool yourself in the
confluence of the three streams[1] at the basic centre[2]?
What do you behold, O Kamalakanta[3]? All is unreal
magic in the world.
You do not recognize the magician who dwells in this
body."

[1] Three streams: Ida, Pingala and Sushumna. [2] Basic Centre: Muladhara Chakra.
[3] The composer of the song:-

CHAPTER II

THE MOOD OF THE SPIRITUAL TEACHER AND VARIOUS COMMUNITIES OF HOLY MEN

[TOPICS: 1. How the Master met holy men. 2. Living habits of holy men. 3. A story about it. 4. Why Sadhus came to Dakshineswar. 5. Sadhus of different types came at different times. 6. Vedantic discussions of Paramahamsas. 7. A Sadhu immersed in Bliss itself. 8. A Sadhu inebriated with divine Knowledge. 9. The Ganga water and that in a drain the same to a Brahman-knower. 10. The Ramawat Sadhu. 11. The story of Ramlala. 12. Our reactions to Ramlala episode. 13. We admire modern science because it helps increase enjoyments. 14. The Kapalika preachings and the impossibility of Yoga-bhoga coexistence. 15. Worldly people's fear at the doctrine of renunciation. 16. How Ramlala remained with the Master. 17. The Master and experience of selfless love. 18. A Sadhu's faith in the name of Rama. 19. Songs of the Ramawat community. 20. The Master's supply of Sadhu's necessities and Rajkumar. 21. The Master's spiritual reaction even on unspiritual suggestions. 22. Examples of this. 23. The Sadhus helping the Master. 24. The Sadhus' arrival coincided with the Master's Sadhanas. 25. Variation of spiritual power in incarnations. 26. Comparison of spiritual power in the Master and other incarnations. 27. Why the Sadhus and Sadhakas of all denominations came to the Master. 28. They did not come for the spiritual awakening of the Master. 29. The Master's Samadhi not a disease: conversation with Sivanath. 30. The Master's behaviour like a madman: why? 31. The Master initiating Sadhakas: example of Sri Narayana Sastri. 32. Antecedents of Sri Sastri. 33. His meeting the Master. 34. Sastriji's resolve. 35. Sastriji felt detachment. 36. Sastriji and Michael Madhusudan. 37. The Master and Michael. 38. Sastriji writing his own opinion on the wall. 39. Sastriji initiated into Sannyasa. 40. The Master's visits to monks and aspirants. 41. The Nyaya philosophy in Bengal. 42. Padmalochan, the Vedantic scholar. 43. The genius of Padmalochan. 44. Siva or Vishnu — who is greater? 45. The Pandit's love of God. 46. The Pandit coming to Calcutta. 47. The Pandit meeting the Master. 48. Why the Pandit's devotion to the Master increased. 49. The Master's knowledge of the Pandit's miraculous power. 50. The Pandit's passing away in Kasi. 51. The Master on Dayananda. 52. Pandit Jaynarayan. 53. Krishna Kishore, the devotee.]

DAKSHINESWAR

Sri Ramakrishna entered Samadhi on seeing this picture of Madonna and the Child

The reconstructed cottage where Sri Ramakrishna did Advaita Sadhana

The Sword of Kali

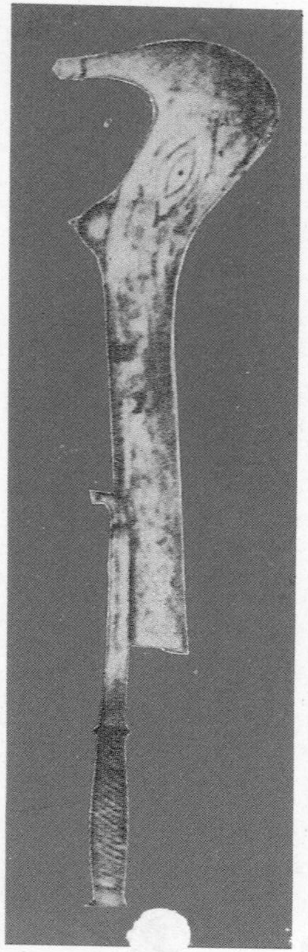

Sri Krishna's original image
— repaired by Sri Ramakrishna

The semi-circular western verandah of
Sri Ramakrishna's room, facing the Ganga.

I am the origin of all, everything evolves out of Me. Knowing thus, the wise worship Me with profound attention to the supreme Truth.

—Gita X.8

Out of compassion for them, I, abiding in a particular modification of their mind, destroy the darkness of delusion produced by ignorance, by means of the luminous lamp of knowledge.

—Gita X.11

1. Once the Master said to us, "Young Bengal'[1] like you started coming after Kesav Sen began visiting this place. But do you know how many Sadhus, world-renouncing Sannyasins and Vairagis, used to come here formerly? Since the construction of the Railways, they do not come this way so much now-a-days. But before that, all holy men used to come by the road along the side of the Ganga to bathe in the confluence of the Ganga and the sea (Ganga-sagar) and on their way to pay their obeisance to Sri Jagannath at Puri. All of them, invariably came and rested for a couple of days at Rasmani's garden. Some of them, again, stayed much longer. Do you know why? Sadhus do not stay at a place where Bhiksha[2] (food given to Sannyasins) and secluded places for answering nature's calls are not easily available. They maintain their bodies by Bhiksha only. That is why they fix their seats where Bhiksha is easily available.

2. "Again, during their journeys, when these holy men get tired, they halt for a day or two at a place in spite of the difficulty of getting Bhiksha there; but they never stay where there is scarcity of water or difficulty of getting secluded places for answering calls of nature. Good Sadhus do not perform these natural actions where all people do or where they may be seen by others; they go to secluded places far away for that purpose. Just hear a story told by Sadhus:

3. "A certain person was out in search of a holy man of true renunciation. He was told, 'Know him to be a man of true renun-

[1] The Master knew less than a dozen English words and phrases which he would use humourously now and then. "Young Bengal" was one such phrase.

[2] Sannyasins beg food from door to door as they travel. But theirs is Adainya Bhiksha i.e., begging minus the attendant humiliation. With the Lord's name on their lips Narayana Hari, they are expected to stand for a reasonable time at the door and then without the least pain or pleasure, move on.-Tr.

ciation whom you see performing the 'natural functions' at places far away from human habitation.' Remembering that, the person concerned was on the look-out for a Sadhu of that type in places considerably away from inhabited localities. One day he saw a Sadhu go farther than others for that purpose and thereafter followed him at a distance. Now, the daughter of the king of that country was told that a girl could have a good son if she could marry a true Yogi; for the scriptures say that Sadhus are born of Yogis. The daughter of the king came in search of a bridegroom after her heart to the place where Sadhus were staying. She chose that particular Sadhu, returned home, and told her father that she wanted to marry him. The king loved his daughter dearly and, as the girl persisted, he came to the holy man and tried to prevail upon him to marry his daughter, saying that half his kingdom would go with his dear daughter. But the Sadhu was firm and could not be won over. He left the place at night without anybody's knowledge. The person who was pursuing this Sadhu and watching his movements and ways of life, saw his wonderful renunciation and realized that he had come across a holy man who was indeed a knower of Brahman. He then took refuge in him, and the Sadhu took pity on him and instructed him. Through his grace he attained genuine devotion to the Lord and had the aim of his life fulfilled.

4. "It was convenient to have Bhiksha at Rasmani's Garden and there was no scarcity of water by the grace of the mother Ganga. Again, there were good secluded places to their liking in the neighbourhood. Sadhus, therefore, used to stay here in those days. Again, word travelled from mouth to mouth among the Sadhus moving about in those regions about the facilities here, and Rasmani's Garden became well known to them as a good place of rest on their way to Ganga-sagar and Puri."

5. "At particular times," said the Master, "particular kinds of Sadhus gathered here in large numbers. At one time, Sannyasins, real Paramahamsas — not the herd of vagabonds roaming about for the sake of bread — began to pour in. Large numbers of those good people were to be found in the room (his own room) day and night. And days and nights were passed in the discussion of Vedantic topics, such as the nature of Brahman and of Maya, on 'Being, Revealing, Endearing' (asti, bhati, priyam) etc.

6. When the Master used the words, "asti, bhati, priyam",

he would forthwith explain them thus, "Do you know, what they imply? It is the true nature of Brahman. It is thus explained in the Vedanta: That which is 'being', in other words, which really exists, is 'revealing', that is, manifesting Itself. Now, manifestation partakes of the nature of knowledge. The thing of which we have knowledge has manifested itself to us; and that, of which we have no knowledge, is unmanifested to us. Is it not so? That is why the Vedanta says that whenever we are conscious of the existence of anything, we become simultaneously conscious of it as revealed or manifested to us; that is, we become conscious of its nature as knowledge. And forthwith we are conscious of it as something, it is experienced as 'dear', that is, as 'bliss' residing in it and attracting us to it. Thus, whenever we have the consciousness of Existence, we have that of Knowledge and of Bliss. Therefore, what is Existence is Knowledge and Bliss and what is Bliss is Existence and Knowledge. For, the very nature of the substance Brahman, from which the universe and all things and persons in it have sprung, is Existence-Knowledge-Bliss; in other words, It exists, It manifests and It is dear. Therefore, when one acquires right knowledge, one feels, as the Uttara Gita says, that the Supreme Self exists in the place, person or thing to which your mind is attached: "Yatra yatra mano yati, tatra tatra param padam. Man's mind, it is said in the Vedas also, runs towards objects of sight, taste and other senses, because His parts are there in them.

"Hot discussions among them went on over these topics. I was then intensely suffering from dysentery and was having very frequent motions. Hridu placed an earthen pan in a corner of the room. I was suffering from such acute dysentery and at the same time listening to their discussions about the Vedantic knowledge. The Mother inspired me from within with simple solutions of those knotty problems on which they were unable to come to any conclusions. I told them of those solutions and their differences were removed forthwith.

7. "Once there came a Sadhu here. There was a beautiful glow on his face. He used to sit and smile only. He came out of his room once in the morning and once in the evening, gazed on everything around — the trees, the plants, the sky, the Ganga and so on — and, beside himself with joy, danced with both his arms raised. He sometimes rolled with laughter and said, 'Fine! How

wonderful is Maya! What an illusion has been created!' That is, what a beautiful Maya God has conjured up. That was his worship. He had the realization of Bliss.

8. "There came another Sadhu on some other occasion. He was inebriated with divine Knowledge. He looked like a ghoul. He was nude, with dust all over his body and head, having long nails and long hair. On the upper part of his body there was a wrapper of shreds, as if picked from where dead bodies are burnt. Standing before the Kali temple and looking at the image, he recited a hymn in such a way that it made the whole temple shake, as it were, and Mother looked pleased and smiling. He then went where the poor people sat and took food. But seeing that ghost-like figure of his, even they did not allow him to sit near them, and drove him away. I then saw him sharing with dogs the leavings in the leaf-plates thrown in a dirty corner. He placed one arm on the shoulder of a dog, and he and the dog were eating from the same leaf. The dog did not bark nor did it try to flee, though a stranger threw his arm around its neck. I was afraid to see him, lest I should get into that state and have to live and roam about like him.

9. "Having seen it, I came and said to Hridu, 'His is not the ordinary madness; it is the madness of supreme God-consciousness.' When Hridu was told so, he ran to see him and found that he was going out of the Garden. He followed him to a great distance and said, 'Holy sir, please give me some instruction as to how I may realize God.' At first the Sadhu did not reply. But when Hridu still followed him, he said, showing him the water in the drain by the road, 'You will realize God when the water here and that of the yonder Ganga will appear the same, as equally pure.' He said this much, and no more. Hridu tried to hear something more and said, 'Sir, please make me your disciple and take me with you.' He said nothing in reply. Having gone far, he looked back and saw Hridu still following him. Looking angry, he picked up a brickbat and threatened to throw it at him. Hridu thereupon fled away. No sooner had Hridu fled than the Sadhu threw down the brickbat, left the road, and slipped away. He could not be seen any more. Such Sadhus wander in that kind of guise lest people should annoy them. This Sadhu was in the state of a true Paramahamsa. The Sastras say, they live in the world like boys, ghouls, or mad people. Paramahamsas allow a band of boys to be around them and play with them, and learn to be like them. They try to be detached from

everything like boys who have no attachment for anything. Have you not seen how happy a boy feels when his mother dresses him with a piece of new cloth? If you say, 'Will you please give me this cloth?' he will immediately reply, 'No, I will not; mummy has given it to me.' Saying so, he will perhaps tighten his grip over it with all his force and with fearful eyes look at you, lest you should snatch it away, as if the whole of his heart then lay in that piece of cloth. But seeing immediately afterwards a toy worth half a penny in your hand, he will perhaps say, 'Give me that, I will give you the cloth.' A little later, perhaps, he will throw the toy away and run to have a flower. He is as little attached to the toy as to the cloth. That is the case with the knowers of Brahman.

10. "Some time passed that way. Visits of Paramahamsas gradually became fewer and fewer. In their place Ramayat 'Babas',[1] – men of fervent renunciation, devout and dispassionate, began to pour in, in large numbers. Ah, what devotion and what faith they had, and how steadfast was their service of the Lord! It was from one of them that Ramlala[2] came to me. That is a long story.

11. "That Baba was serving the image for a long time. He took it with him wherever he went. He cooked whatever he got by Bhiksha and offered the cooked food to it. That was not all; he actually saw that Ramlala ate, or wished to eat something, or wanted to go for a walk, or insisted on the satisfaction of a fancy, and so on. In the company of the image he was beside himself with bliss and always remained 'inebriated'. I also saw Ramlala doing all that. I sat all the twenty-four hours of the day with the Baba, and kept gazing on Ramlala.

"As days passed on, Ramlala's love for me went on increasing. As long as I remained with the Baba, Ramlala felt happy — he played and sported; but as soon as I came away from that place to my room, he also followed me immediately there. He did not remain with the Sadhu, although I forbade him to come. I at first thought it was perhaps a fancy of mine. How could it be

[1] Ramayat Sadhus are known as Babajis or 'Fathers' throughout India.

[2] The boy Sri Ramachandra. The people in the north-western part of India affectionately call boys and girls 'lalas' and 'lalis' respectively. That is why, the image of the child Ramachandra, made of an alloy of eight metals, was called Ramlala by that 'Father'. In the Bengali language also the words 'dulal and dulali' are used in the same sense. (The prefix 'du' means 'naughty').

otherwise? Could Ramlala (in the image) love me more than the Baba who had been loving and serving him tenderly all these years? Impossible!. But of what avail were these thoughts? I actually saw — just as I see you before me — that Ramlala accompanied me dancing, now preceding, now following me. Sometimes he importuned me to carry him in my arms. Again, when I took him on my lap, he would by no means remain there. He would go down to run hither and thither, collect flowers in thorny jungles, or go to the Ganga to swim and splash water there. I said over and over again, 'My child, don't do that, you will get blisters on your soles if you run in the sun. Do not remain in water so long, you will catch cold and get fever.' But he would not listen, however much I might forbid him. Unconcerned, he would go on with his pranks, as if I were speaking to someone else. He would sometimes grin and look at me with his two eyes, beautiful like the petals of a lotus, or carry on his pranks with a vengeance. He would pout both his lips and grimace and make faces at me. I would then actually be angry and scold him, 'You rascal, wait, I will give you a sound beating today.' Saying so, I would pull him away from the sun or from the water, cajoling him by giving this thing or that, and then ask him to play within the room. Again, finding it impossible to restrain his pranks, I would sometimes give him a slap or two. Thus beaten, he would pout his beautiful lips, and sob and look at me with tears in his eyes. I would feel terribly pained to see him cry. I would then take him affectionately on my lap and humour him. I actually saw and did all this.

"One day I was going to bathe, when he took an obstinate fancy to go with me. What could I do? I took him with me. Then he would not come out of the water. He turned a deaf ear to all my pleadings. At last I became angry, immersed him in the water and said, 'Be now in the water as long as you like'; and I actually saw that he panted and writhed under the water. Startled to see his suffering, I exclaimed within myself remorsefully 'What have I done!" I took him out of the water on to my lap.

"I cannot describe what agony I felt for him on another occasion, and how much I wept. That day Ramlala was obstinately demanding something to eat, and I gave him some parched rice not properly husked, in order to pacify him. I then found that his soft and delicate tongue got lacerated by the husk while he was eating. Dear me! What a great pain I felt then! I took him on my lap, wept loudly, and taking hold of his chin, sobbed out the words, 'Oh, how rash and stupid I have been! To have put this contemptible stuff into the mouth which mother Kausalya used to fill lovingly with such soft delicacies as butter, thickened milk and cream!'" As he was speaking these words, the Master's past grief burst forth anew. He became restless in our presence and wept so bitterly that we could not restrain our sympathetic tears, though we did not understand a bit of his loving relationship with Ramlala.

12. Dumbfounded to hear those words about Ramlala, we, poor jivas enchained in the prison house of Maya, looked at the image with awe, hopefully wondering if we too could see him living and moving. But ah! we saw nothing but cold metal. And how could it be otherwise? We had not got that loving attraction for Ramlala. The affection for Ramachandra had not been so intensified in our minds as to produce in us the eye of love as in the Master's case, enabling us to see the living Ramlala within oneself and outside. We see a small image only and think, "Could what the Master said have happened or can it ever happen?" It is so with us regarding everything relating to the spiritual realm, and we are resting satisfied with our load of unbelief. Do you not see, the Rishi, the knower of Brahman, says, "*Sarvam Khalvidam Brahma, neha nanasti kinchana*[1] that is, there is nothing in the world except the Reality of Brahman, Existence-Knowledge-Bliss." There is no real existence for any one of the persons or things that one sees. To this statement, we, ignorant men, are tempted to reply thus: "We also thought it might be so. But on actually examining the world, we do not find in it the slightest trace of the Reality of Brahman, the One without a second. What we see are only material substances — wood and earth, house and door, man and cow, and other things of various colours, shapes and sizes. Or at the most we see some beauty and sublimity presented by Nature — the green, but from a distance, dark-blue, snow-capped mountains arrogantly attempting to touch the azure, bespangled sky with their peaks; and the streams flowing down the slopes and valleys of these proud mountains as if to teach them by their example also what they were proclaiming by way of criticism through their murmuring sound — 'O ye mountains!

So much arrogance is not good!' Or we see the infinite expanse of the tempestuous seas riding the high breakers and rushing forth to swallow everything, but turning back, unable to go beyond the shores in spite of this continuous attack of its regiments of waves. There we come to the end of the tether of our understanding and think, "Ha, the Rishi must have spoken about seeing everything as Brahman under the influence of strong intoxicants!" To this the Rishi might reply: "No, children, practise self-control and purity and make your mind one-pointed and tranquil; then you will understand and realize what we have said — you will then actually see that the world is an intensified manifestation of your own thoughts, and that you see diversity outside because it is there in your mind." To this our reaction will be, "Revered Sir, where do we find the time for such practices — we who are restless under the tyranny of the senses and the urgency of earning our livelihood?" Or perhaps we will further say, "The list of duties you prescribe for qualifying oneself to have a direct vision of Reality you call Brahman, cannot be followed in practice in a few days or months or even years. It is doubtful whether one can do so even in a whole lifetime. Suppose we apply our minds to it in compliance with what you say, but fail to attain that Reality or Brahman and find at long last that the attainment of infinite Bliss is but a phantasmagoria! We then lose both the here and the hereafter. We are deprived of the enjoyment of worldly pleasures — transitory though they may be — as well as your infinite Bliss. What will happen to us then? No, sir, we cannot be with you. If you have got the taste of that infinite Bliss, well and good, you go on enjoying it happily for the good of generations of your disciples; only allow us to enjoy in peace the little pleasure that can immediately be had from objects of sight, taste and the other senses. Pray, don't indulge in specious arguments and causistry to spoil that little enjoyment of ours."

13. The scientist now comes forward and tells us, "I can show you with the help of instruments that one all-pervading substance, a conscious power, exists uniformly in all things and beings — in bricks and trees and plants, in men and cattle — and is manifesting itself variously. We also find that the vibration of life is indeed observable in all objects." To this we reply: "Bravo scientist! Your intellectual sweep is wide, indeed! But what is the use of having that knowledge only? The Rishis, the authors

of our scriptures also, told us more or less so, long ago.[1] You have, let us admit, demonstrated it now. But can you say that it will add to our enjoyments? Only then can we appreciate your wisdom." The scientist would probably reply to this as follows: "Wont't it? It certainly does. Just see, how convenient it is for you to get the news from various parts of the globe through the discovery of the power of electricity. How convenient it is for you to earn money, the basis of all your enjoyments, by trade and commerce carried on by means of ships, railways, mills, factories and machines, all driven by the power of steam. And how convenient it is for you to destroy your enemies, who stand in the way of your enjoyment of pleasures, by the invention of guns and cannons through an understanding of the hidden laws of explosives. This all-pervading power with which you have thus become acquainted today through science, also cannot but be of some better uses in future." Not satisfied with the reply, we would like to add: "Well, you are right in a way. But invent as soon as possible something that will yield us what we want in life — the acme of enjoyments. Can the application of your newly discovered power help us have more and more of this, the thrills of enjoyment? It is only then that your discovery will be hailed and your intelligence appreciated. Then alone we shall accept that you are not speaking under the influence of intoxicants like those authors of the Vedas and the Puranas." The scientist listens, feels the trend of our thoughts and says, "So be it."

14. The disinclination of many in the past and in the present to accept the spiritual message of the Rishis, the teachers of the Knowledge portion of the Vedas, arises from the fact that they do not say this "so be it" to the clamour of man for worldly enjoyments. They, therefore, had to live in jungles in their days, far away from the bustle of the world and remain satisfied in the company of a few people who were averse to worldly enjoyments. It is not, however, that while preaching the spiritual message, no attempt was made at any time in India to adopt the attitude of this "so be it" philosophy and subordinate spirituality to worldly values. Remember the latter part of the Buddhistic age when the Tantric Kapalikas were spreading the magical rites for killing,

[1] "Antaḥsaṃjñā bhavantyete sukhaduḥkha-samanvitāḥ" — even insentient things like trees and stones have consciousness within. The experiencing of happiness and misery is there in them also.

distracting, charming, subduing and the like. There was a great fuss about alleviating and curing bodily and mental diseases by means of various propitiatory ceremonies and exorcising of evil spirits like ghosts and ghouls. In those days no one would be recognised as a religious teacher unless he could demonstrate some miraculous superhuman powers, claimed to have been attained by austerities, and unless he could impress on his followers that he held the key to their success, enjoyments and all worldly fulfilments. Thus for a time it was preached and accepted that spiritual truth consisted in a body of esoteric doctrines that contributed to worldly enjoyments. But how could light and darkness co-exist? Consequently, the Kapalikas forgot Yoga in a short time, came down to the plane of Bhoga or enjoyment, and secretly preached in the name of religion, which is really the means for liberating man from bondage, a philosophy of enjoyments, which binds one tighter to the world of matter. The truly religious people of the country then understood once more that the two, Yoga and Bhoga, were contradictory to each other and could by no means co-exist in one and the same receptacle. When this disillusionment came, the true spiritual aspirants once again veered round to the path of knowledge preached by the seers and sought to realize that knowledge in practical life.

15. How could we concur with the views of worldly minded people and accept their philosophy of 'so be it'. For, we are narrating the story of the Great Master — one who was not of this world, and in whose mind the idea of renunciation was so deep-rooted that the touch of a metal even in deep sleep would cause the respiration to stop with the shock of a piercing pain, and would produce contraction and insensibility of the hand. He was the one on whom flashed the perception of the images of the Divine Mother Herself, the moment his eyes fell on any female figure — a perception which no amount of temptations[1] could alter. He was one who was so grievously pained and so terribly annoyed at the proposal of Mathur Babu to gift him a property worth several thousand rupees, that he grew very restless and threatened to attack his devoted Mathur with a stick. He was the one in whom was reproduced, even when recounting long afterwards, the intensity of excitement that he had felt when Laxminarain

[1] II.8.31, III.6.15, IV.1.29.-Tr.

Marwari came with a similar proposal to make a gift of a considerable amount to him, and which he described in his own graphic way by saying, "I felt as if my head was being sawn through at the proposal of Laxminarain Marwari!" And again he was the one in whose mind no objects of worldly enjoyments coming through the senses of sight, taste, touch and the rest could ever exert their attraction or cause attachments leading to any break in his perpetual experience of the super-sensuous bliss of ecstasy! O man! ever eager as you are to enjoy the pleasures of the world, we knew long ago that we would have to put up with much abuse and criticism when we chose to tell you the story of this extraordinary Master. That is not all. We knew also that you would not hesitate to slander this godly character, if any simple-hearted among your sons or grandsons, friends or relatives, would be actually attracted by our words towards that wonderful character and renounce the world and the pursuit of worldly enjoyments. But when once we have set our hand to this undertaking, we are not able to desist from it or hide the truth even partially in order to placate you. We have to narrate what we know to be the truth. There can be no peace otherwise; for some one, as it were, forces us to speak out. Let us therefore narrate, as far as we know, the story of this extraordinary God-man. Accept as much of this story as you can digest, and 'omit the head and tail.' Or if you like, you may throw the whole book away, thinking that a few cock-and-bull stories have been narrated in it by a hemp-smoker, and run every day to sip the honey from new flowers of worldly objects. Afterwards, passing through the terrible whirlpool of the world, if ever you discover through good luck — which your worldly compatriots will surely consider its opposite and call bad luck — that 'the honey of sense objects and the flower of lust' look but stale and insipid commodities, then would you turn to the life-story of this extraordinary person, have a proper appreciation of his worth, and find solace in his life and teachings.

16. In the course of his description of that wonderful behaviour of Ramlala, the Master said, "On some days the holy Baba would cook food and offer it to Ramlala but could not find him. Wounded at heart, he would then run up here (to the Master's room) and find him playing in the room. With a feeling of wounded love, he would then scold him, saying, 'I took so much trouble to cook food for you and am searching for you here and

there, but without the least consideration for all that, you are lingering here. Ah! that has ever been your way. You have no kindness or affection. You left behind your father and went to the forest; and though your poor father died weeping for you, you never returned to show yourself to him.' With these and similar words, he used to drag Ramlala to his place and feed him. Time passed in that way. The Sadhu remained here for a long time; for Ramlala did not like to leave this place (i.e., me). The Baba too could not go away, leaving behind Ramlala whom he had loved so long. Now it happened one day that, dissolved in tears, the Baba came to me and said, 'Ramlala has shown himself to me in the way I wanted to have his vision and has thus fulfilled my life's aspiration. Moreover, he said he would not go from here; for he does not like to leave you behind and go elsewhere. My mind is, however, free from sorrow and pain, as I find that Ramlala lives happily with you, playing and sporting all the livelong day. I feel beside myself with bliss to see it. I am now in such a state that I feel happy at his happiness. Therefore, I can now leave him with you and go elsewhere. Knowing that he is happy with you, I too shall feel happy.' So saying, he gave Ramlala to me, and departed. Ramlala has been here since then."

17. We have to understand from this that the holy man must have had the taste of that highest form of love which is free from the slightest tinge of selfishness by virtue of the divine company of the Master, and must have felt convinced by the power of that affection that there was no fear of separation for him from the object of his love. He must have understood that his chosen Ideal, the embodiment of pure love, would always be with him and that he could see him whenever he liked. It is doubtless that it was on some such assurance received intuitively, that the Baba left behind Ramlala, who was dearer to him than life itself.

18. The Master said, "On another occasion there came a Sadhu who had absolute faith in the name of God. He also belonged to the Ramayat denomination. He had nothing with him except a water-pot and a book. The book was very dear to him. He used to worship it daily with flowers and one day I persuaded him to lend me the book. When I opened it, I found that the only thing written in it with red ink in big letters, was 'Aum Ramah'. He said, 'What is the use of reading a large number of books? For, it is from the one Divine Lord that the Vedas and the Puranas

have come out; He and His name are non-separate. Therefore, what is contained in the four Vedas, the eighteen Puranas and all the other scriptures, is there in any one of His names. That is why His name is my only companion.' Such was the Sadhu's faith in the name of God!"

19. Thus did the Master tell us of a great many Sadhus and sing for us, from time to time, the devotional songs he had learnt from them. Take for example the songs:

"You have not, O mind, recognized my Rama. What then have you recognized? and what have you known?

One who tastes the bliss derived from taking the name of Rama, is a Sadhu. But what is he, who tastes the pleasure of worldly objects?

A true son is he, who delivers the family (from Maya's grip). But what are other sons worth?"

or

"Worship Ramachandra, the consort of Sita, the lord and king of the Raghus, the protector of Ayodhya! There is no second object of worship.

His smile and words, His gait and naughty bearing, His face and long eyes, His nose and forehead beautiful with boyish frowns and a mark of saffron and sandal-paste, giving the appearance of the morning sun,

His dazzling ear-rings, His necklace of pearls shining like stars and dangling on His broad chest, like the Ganga coming out, piercing the peak of the mountain green with flora.

This hero of the dynasty of the Raghus is there, walking with His friends on the bank of the Sarayu. Tulsidas is beside himself with joy, gazing and feasting on His beauty and craves for the dust of those lotus feet."

or

"He really lives in the world who worships Rama,
He really lives in the world who adores Him."

or

"There is no one, except Rama, who can save me."

We have forgotten the other lines of these two sweet songs.

Sometimes he recited for us the couplets he had learnt from those Sadhus. He used to say, "Sadhus always teach that one should protect oneself against the dangers of committing a theft, of being in women's company, and of telling a lie." Saying so, he would forthwith ask us to listen to what was said in Tulsidas's couplet: 'Tulsidas stands security, that God will be realized by truthfulness, obedience, and absence of covetousness. Tulsidas is a liar, if God be not realized by truthfulness, obedience, and motherly attitude towards women.' "Do you know what obedience is? It is humility. When the right kind of humility comes, egoism is destroyed and God is realized. It is also in Kabir Das's song: 'Service, worship and humility will make one easily realize the Lord of the Raghus. Be steadfast, joyfully, O brother.'"

20. On another occasion, the Master said, "At one time a desire arose in my mind that I should supply the aspirants of all communities with all the requisites of Sadhana. The idea was that getting all their requirements, they could be free from anxiety and practise Sadhana for the realization of God. I consulted Mathur about it. He said, 'Where is the difficulty, Father? I shall arrange everything just now. You may give whatever you like to anyone.' Over and above the already existing arrangement about supplying of uncooked rice, pulses, flour, etc., to each Sadhu according to his liking from the store of the temple, Mathur made provision for water-pots, Kamandalus, blankets, seats and even intoxicants such as hemp and hemp-leaves for those who would take them, and also wine etc., for the Tantric worshippers. Many Tantric aspirants used to come at that time and hold Chakras, the holy circles of community worship. I used to supply them with peeled ginger and onion as also parched rice and pulses, which were necessary for their Sadhanas, and look on, while they worshipped the Divine Mother with these and called on Her. Again, on many occasions they took me to their circle and placed me at the head of it. They requested me to take consecrated wine, but desisted from making such requests when they came to know that I felt God-intoxicated at the very mention of wine and, therefore, could not take it. As, according to their code of pious behaviour, one who sat with them had to take the consecrated wine, I used to put, in deference to their practice, a mark with it on my forehead, or smelt it, or at the most sprinkled with my finger a drop of it into my mouth, and then poured it into their drinking cups. As

soon as they drank it, some applied their minds to the Goddess, becoming absorbed in counting beads or meditation on Her, while some others, far from calling on the Divine Mother, greedily drank too much and at last became drunk. One day they behaved so improperly that I stopped giving them wine and other things any more. But I always saw Rajkumar[1] sit for Japa and abstain from all other thoughts as soon as he took the consecrated wine. But afterwards he had, it seemed, some inclination for name and fame. It was quite natural; for he had his wife and children, and on account of wants at home he had to pay a little attention to the acquisition of money. In any case, he used to take wine, only because it was helpful to his Sadhana. He, I saw, never took it greedily or behaved improperly."

21. Many thoughts are cropping up in our minds, in connection with the Master's inability to take wine. Many were the occasions on which we actually saw that on mentioning the words "hemp", "wine", etc., in the course of conversation, he became filled with divine inebriation and even entered into Samadhi. Many a time we saw the wonderful Master enter into Samadhi uttering the name of that part of the female body, at the very name of which, our rougish minds, in spite of pretension to high culture, are filled with ideas of vulgar sensuality. Or there are others who, though aware of their own weakness, yet pretend to be refined and superior, and try to hide their imperfection by calling such situation, as obscene and fly away from them. As for the Master, as soon as he got down from the plane of Samadhi and regained a little of the normal consciousness, we heard him saying in this connection, "Mother, Thou hast indeed assumed the forms of the fifty letters.[2] Those letters of Thine constitute the obscene and indecent words too. The *ka* and *kha*[3] of Thy Veda and Vedanta, and those of the obscene and indecent words, surely are not different. The obscene and indecent words as well as the Veda and the Vedanta are verily Thyself." Saying so, he entered into Samadhi once more. Oh! who will understand, far less explain, what an

[1] He used to live now and then at Kalighat, and was known by the name of Achalananda. He left behind a few disciples and grand disciples. His body was interned by his disciples with great pomp in a village near Kalighat.

[2] Fifty is the number of letters in the Sanskrit alphabet.

[3] Ka and Kha are the first two letters of the consonant series of the Sanskrit alphabet.

indescribably wonderful Light, beyond the grasp of our little minds and intellects, there was in the eyes of that extraordinary god-man, illumining all the things, good and bad, of the world! Who can have those eyes to get the vision of the realms that were open to him! Be attentive, O reader, and cherish these words of his carefully in your heart, with awe and reverence due to them, and think how deep and incomprehensible was the mental purity of that wonderful Master!

Ramprasad, on whom the grace of the univeral Mother was bestowed, sang; "I don't drink wine but nectar, crying, 'Victory to Kali' which makes my mind God-intoxicated. Wine-bibbers regard me as drunk with wine . . ." Before we saw the Master, we could not even conceive that without taking intoxicants, a man by virtue of divine bliss alone could be in such a drunken state. We remember very well how, at one period of our life, we considered the author of a book to be superstitious and foolish when he described Sri Chaitanya as losing his normal consciousness at the utterance of the Lord's name, Hari. During that period there flowed a strong current of unbelief and doubt regarding everything spiritual in the minds of all the young men of the city. It was at such a juncture that we happened to meet this extraordinary Master. Not only did we meet him, but observed him at all times, day and night, and that with the eyes of a sceptic. We saw his unrestrained dance and constant loss of normal consciousness in the bliss of Kirtan, his extreme sensitiveness to the contact of metallic objects including coins even when not aware of them, and his deep inebriation at the mention of intoxicants by their association with the inebriation of divine bliss. And what to speak of the names of God and His incarnations, when the mention of even words that rouse the basest animal passion in ordinary men by their association with sexuality could only send him into divine supersensuous ecstasy, bringing before his mind the womb of the blissful Mother of the universe, from which worlds are created every moment! Reader! Is there anything more for us to add — any quality or virtue more extraordinary or dazzling to be cited — to justify our adoring him in our heart of hearts as a divine incarnation?

22. Many a time the Master came with his devotees to the locality called Simla in Calcutta, where the house of his great devotee Ramachandra Dutta was situated, and bestowed the

benefit of his blissful company on him and other assembled devotees. One day, after one such visit, he was returning to Dakshineswar. Ram Babu's house was situated in Madhu Roy's lane. Carriages could not come to the front of the house. One had to leave one's carriage on the main road a little to the east or to the west of the house, and walk up to it. A carriage was waiting on the western main road to take the Master to Dakshineswar. The Master started in that direction and the devotees followed him. But the Master was staggering, on account of divine bliss so much, that he could not go those few steps without being helped by others. Two devotees on the two sides caught hold of his hands and helped him walk slowly. There were some people standing at the bend of the lane. How could they understand the state of the Master? They were talking among themselves, "Oh, how dead-drunk the man has become!" Though the words were spoken low, we could hear them. Smiling, we said within ourselves, "Dead-drunk indeed!"

One day in day-time, the Master went to the Kali temple to pay his obeisance to the Mother of the universe, asking our supremely revered Holy Mother to prepare a few rolls of betel as also tidy up his bedding and sweep the room during his absence. She had quickly finished almost all those works when the Master returned from the temple, as if in a completely drunken state. His eyes were red, steps hopelessly unsteady, and his words indistinct and inarticulate. He entered the room and came staggering up to the Holy Mother. The Holy Mother was then attentively doing the household work and could not at all know that the Master had come to her in that mood. The Master, like one drunk, then pushed her and said to her, "Ah, have I drunk wine?" She looked back and was astonished to see the Master in that state. She said, "No, no; why should you drink wine?" "Why do I stagger then?" said the Master, "Why can I not speak? Am I drunk?". The Holy Mother consoled him telling, "No, no; certainly not with wine. You have drunk the nectar of Mother Kali's love." Approvingly the Master replied, "You are right!"

Since the devotees of Calcutta came to the Master and had his grace, the Master would go once or twice a week to the house of one or another of the devotees. If anybody could not come to him at the fixed time and if he could not get news of his welfare from anyone else, the merciful Master would personally go to see him. Again, his mind sometimes would become restless and he would go to Calcutta to see some devotee if the latter did not come to Dakshineswar at the fixed times. It was invariably seen that such auspicious visits of his were for the good of the devotees concerned. He had not the slightest self-interest. Beni Saha had some good hackney-carriages at Baranagar. As the Master came very often to Calcutta, it was arranged with him that he should send a carriage to Dakshineswar on the Master's order. He should not raise any objection however late at night the carriage returned from Calcutta. Of course, he would get extra hire at the fixed rate for the extra time. This carriage hire was paid successively by Mathur Babu, Mani Sen of Panihati, Sambhu Mallick and Jayagopal Sen of Sinduriapati, Calcutta. But the devotee to whose house he went on a particular day, paid the carriage hire for that day, if he was in a position to do so.

One day the Master was to go to Jadu Mallick's house at Calcutta to see the latter's mother who had great devotion for him; for he had no news about the family for a long time. The Master had finished his meal and a carriage arrived, when our friend, A., came by boat from Calcutta to pay him a visit. As soon as the Master saw A., he made enquiries regarding his welfare and said, "It is very fine that you have come. I am going to Jadu Mallick's house today. I shall get down at your house on my way and see G. He could not come here for a considerable time on account of pressure of work. Come, let us go together." A., who was then newly acquainted with the Master, agreed. He had seen him only on a few occasions in a few places. He, therefore, had not known well that the extraordinary Master could get ecstasy at any place and at any time, even at the sight of things and persons considered contemptible or detestable or even unworthy to touch or look at.

Now the Master got into the carriage. The boy-devotee, Latu, now known as Adbhutananda, took with him the Master's bag, towel and other necessary articles, and followed him into the carriage. Our friend A. also got into it. The Master sat on one side of the carriage and Latu and A. on the other. The carriage started, gradually went beyond Baranagar bazar and was passing by the Mati lake. Nothing particular happened on the way. The Master saw this or that on his way and was asking Latu or A. about those sights like a boy; or he raised this topic or that, and was going on merrily as in the ordinary normal condition.

There was something like an ordinary bazar to the south of the Mati lake. And farther south there were a wine shop, a dispensary, a few stables and some tiled houses forming a warehouse for rice. The broad road to the well-known temple of Sri Sarvamangala and Chitreswari lay to the south of this place and passed by the bank of the Ganga. One had to keep to the left of that road while going to Calcutta.

Some drunkards were then sitting in one of the grog shops, drinking wine and were making merry boisterously. Some of them were singing joyfully, and some dancing with gesticulations. And the owner of the shop, having engaged his servant in selling wine to them, was standing absent-mindedly at the door of the shop. There was a big mark of vermilion on his forehead. Now, the Master's carriage was passing before the shop. The shop-keeper seemed to recognise the Master; for, when he saw him, he raised his hands and saluted him.

The noise attracted the Master's attention to the shop, and he happened to see the drunkards boisterously revelling in their drunken delight. On seeing people merry-making after drinking wine (Karana), the memory of the blissful nature of the universal Cause arose in his mind through association. It was not the memory alone, but its direct experience also followed, and he was completely filled with inebriation and his words became indistinct. That was not all. Partly stepping out of the carriage suddenly, he put one foot on the foot-board and stood up there. Like one drunk, he expressed joy at the sight, moving his hands. Making gesticulations of his body, he cried out loudly, "Very nice, fine enjoyment, bravo, bravo!"

A. said, "We had no previous indication that the Master would suddenly be in that state. He had been talking like one in the normal state. But no sooner did he see the drunkards than he got into that condition. I was benumbed with fear. In a great hurry I stretched my arms with a view to dragging his body into the carriage and making him sit, when Latu interfered and said, 'Nothing need be done; he will control himself and will not fall down.' I therefore remained quiet, but my heart went on throbbing violently for sometime. I thought, 'How very wrong it was for me to drive in the same carriage with this mad man of a Master! I will never do so again.' All these events, of course, took much less time to happen than to describe. The carriage left that shop behind and the Master sat quiet within it. Seeing the temple of Sri Sarvamangala he said, 'There is Sarvamangala. She is an awakened deity. Salute Her.' Saying so, he himself saluted the Devi when we also did so in imitation of him from that distance. Then I looked at the Master and saw him in quite a normal state, smiling gently. But the throbbing of my heart did not come to an end for a long time, thinking he might have fallen and even died.

"When afterwards the carriage came and stood at the gate of the house, he said to me, 'Is G. in? Please go and see!' I went and came back to say, 'No'. He then said, 'Well! I cannot see G.; I thought of asking him to give today's extra carriage hire. But I am now acquainted with you, will you give a rupee? Jadu Mallick, you know, is a miserly man; he will not pay more than the fixed rate of two rupees and four annas. But who knows how late at night I shall return after meeting the devotees? Again, the driver repeatedly asks us to make haste and annoys us when we are very late. Therefore, it has been arranged with Beni that the driver should not create any disturbance if three rupees and four annas are paid, and there will arise no difficulty for today's hire if you pay one rupee. That is why I say so.' Hearing all this, I handed over a rupee to Latu and saluted the Master, when he went to see Jadu Mallick."

Such 'drunken' states came daily at any time over the Master. But only a few examples of it could we record or describe.

23. Thus on many occasions the Master narrated, not only to us but to many other people, the stories of several monks and aspirants who came to the Kali temple at Dakshineswar. There are many people living even now who can bear testimony to it. We were then studying in the St. Xavier's college. It remained closed on two days a week, Thursday and Sunday. As there was a crowd of devotees with the Master on Saturdays and Sundays, we used to go to him on Thursdays also, which gave us the opportunity of hearing about various events of his life from his own lips. From the description of all these events, we could clearly understand that, besides the Bhairavi Brahmani, Swami Tota Puri, the Muslim Govinda, and the monk who came providentially to Dakshineswar (cf.III.3.10) to save the Master's body by forcibly

feeding him during his absorption in the highest Nirvikalpa plane continuously for six months, there were several other monks and spiritual aspirants who had visited the Master at Dakshineswar before we, the later English-educated disciples, went to him, and that these aspirants had received a new illumination and direction in their spiritual life from their contact with the divine personality of the Great Master. Having thus reached the fulfilment of their own spiritual life, they got the opportunity of showing the true aspirants of their denominations thirsting for spirituality, how to realize God along their own paths. Every one of them came only to learn, and having perfected his knowledge, went away to his own place. Although the Bhairavi Brahmani, Tota Puri and some others were very fortunate in coming and helping the Master in his spiritual life, they too were blessed to realize, by the power of Divine grace bestowed on them through the personality of the Master, those hidden spiritual truths which they were unable to experience in their own lives in spite of their life-long Sadhanas.

24. It does not take one long to understand another truth when one studies the order of the coming of those Sadhus and Sadhakas to the Master at Dakshineswar. And because it will be convenient to study the order in which they came, we have in this chapter tried to tell the reader these events in the Master's own words as far as possible and in their proper order and sequence, exactly as we heard them from him. We heard from the master himself that, whenever he engaged himself in the discipline and worship of particular aspects of God and realized them, the true aspirants of those communities, devoted to those aspects of the Deity, would begin to pour in, in groups, for some time, and he would be spending days and nights in their company in discussion on the particular aspects of Divinity and philosophy they represented. As soon as he attained perfection in the worship of the Mantra of Rama, the monks of the Ramayat denomination started coming to him in large numbers. No sooner had he been established in each of the devotional moods of Santa, Dasya, etc., spoken of in the Vaishnava books of Bengal, than devotees practising those moods streamed in. The then eminent Tantric aspirants of this part of the country also came to him, when he had completed the discipline prescribed in the sixty-four Tantras with the help of the Bhairavi Brahmani. Hardly had he perfected himself and

attained immediate experience of Brahman, following the non-dual doctrine, when the good Sadhakas of the Paramahamsa denomination came to him in large numbers.

25. It is obvious that there is a hidden meaning in the fact that the aspirants of different denominations came thus to have the divine company of the Master. At the auspicious advent of the incarnation of the age, it always happened thus in the world in the past and will happen so in the future. According to a mysterious law of the spiritual world, these incarnations are born in every age in order to avert the decline of religion and to brighten up the almost extinguished light of spirituality. But when we study their lives, we find that there is a difference in the manifestation of power in them, and it becomes clear that some of them came to remove the needs of a particular part of a country, or of a few particular communities, while others came to remove the lack of spirituality in the whole world. All of them are seen to promulgate their own doctrines and the knowledge discovered by them, but they keep intact the authenticity of the spiritual teachings of the preceding sages, teachers and incarnations, instead of destroying them. For, through their divine Yogic powers, they see an order of succession and a relation amongst the previous spiritual doctrines and faiths. The history of the spiritual world and the relation amongst the ancient religious doctrines always remain hidden from our vision, which is blinded by attachment to worldly objects. But these divine personages see the previous religious doctrines as strung together "like a string of pearls," and add the next required gem to it in the light of their experiences of spirituality, and quietly pass away.

26. We shall understand this clearly by the study of the history of some foreign religions. Take for example, Jesus, who came and promulgated the truths experienced by him and kept intact the religious doctrines preached by the Jewish teachers. Again, Mohammad came a few centuries later and preached his own doctrine without destroying those promulgated by Jesus. Thus the preaching of a new doctrine does not invalidate the earlier ones in vogue. Jesus does not supplant the ancient Jewish teachers, nor does Mohammad supplant Jesus. The old religions are on a par with the new ones in their efficacy in bestowing the realisation of the respective aspects of God they reveal. This is the law everywhere in the spiritual world. The same law applies to

the religious doctrines of India too. You can realize any of the particular aspects of God preached by the Vedic Rishis or the great Acharyas or the authors of the Tantras and the Puranas, if you follow with true faith and zeal the particular disciplines they have formulated for the purpose. The Master engaged himself in the disciplines according to the doctrines of all these denominations one after another, realized this grand truth, and communicated it to us.

27. "When the flower blossoms, bees come." The Master told us many a time that this was the law in the spiritual world also. It is according to this law that as soon as an incarnation of God gets illumination or realizes the truth of the spiritual world, those thirsting for religion are attracted to him in order to know and learn it. The reason why the aspirants of all denominations came to the Master, group after group, and not merely those of one denomination, is that, having traversed all denominational paths and having realized all the aspects of God realizable through them, he could give specific information about each of them. But all of these aspirants did not achieve perfection in the practice of their own doctrines nor could they recognize the Master as the "Incarnation of the Age". It was the best of them only who could do so. But each of them made progress along his own path by virtue of the divine company of the Master and was perfectly convinced that he would realize God at the right time if he went along his own path. It is superfluous to add that decline in religion arises through loss of faith in one's own path and in the possibility of realisation through it among individuals, leading gradually to the spiritual barrenness of the whole community.

28. There is wide-spread talk nowadays that the Master learnt the methods of Sadhana leading to God-realization from those monks, engaged himself in too severe austerities, and thereby went mad at one time, that his brain became deranged and there came on him the permanent physical disease of losing normal consciousness under the influence of excessive emotions. My God! We are such a herd of learned fools! The race of the Rishis of India showed in their own lives and explained to us through the Vedas and the Puranas, that the normal consciousness vanished, as one ascended to the plane of Samadhi, through the complete concentration of mind. They have left behind for us the full

explanation of it in the scriptures relating to Samadhi, a science unknown to any other people outside. And all the great souls, who have till now been regarded in the world as incarnations of God and been receiving the reverence of human hearts in all countries, experienced in their own lives this loss of external consciousness. They have also explained to us again and again that it is not really loss of consciousness but the enhancement of it to the highest pitch and that it marks the acme of spiritual progress. But, in spite of all this, if we still speak or listen to and believe those hollow words, God help us! O Reader, if you give credence to them, you may hear or accept these meaningless criticisms, but only know for certain that you are following the example of the blind men who allow themselves to be led by the blind! May you and others of similar view prosper! But kindly allow us the liberty of sitting at the feet of this wonderful God-intoxicated man. It is also better that you too try once more earnestly to understand the question before you decide one way or the other. See that your judgement is not vitiated by the outlook described by the ancient author of the Kathopanishad in the following verse: "Just as one blind man guided by another blind man, meets with disaster, so people, devoid of discrimination, who consider themselves to be intelligent and well versed in the scriptures, live in ignorance and pass through various transmigrations".

29. It is not a new thing that the Master's Bhavasamadhi is called a disease. Many persons educated in the Western way said so, even while the Master was living. But the passage of time has disproved these views, as the "insane" talks and predictions of that divinely inebriated man have received wide acceptance and revealed their significance more and more. His unique teachings are eagerly sought after and accepted by people all the world over, thus proving the utter folly of those critics who saw only a disease in his Bhavasamadhi. Their criticisms met with the same fate as a handful of dust thrown at the moon. And fully discovering that all such statements were erroneous, people came to accept the validity of the experiences and teachings of the Master with complete satisfaction. This is what is happening today also and what will happen in future too; for truth cannot be kept covered up any more than fire by a piece of cloth. It is therefore not necessary for us to expatiate further on this subject. We

would quote a word or two of the Master himself on this topic and pass on to another.

Our revered friend Sri Sivanath Sastri, who was one of the preachers of the General Brahmo Samaj, said to some of us during the life-time of the Master, that the Master's Bhavasamadhi was a disease, either hysteria or epileptic fits, produced by nervous disorder and that his unconsciousness at such times was in no way different from that of people suffering from diseases. This remark gradually reached the Master's ear. For quite a long time Sivanath had been visiting the Master frequenly, in spite of this view of his on his ecstasies. One day when Sivanath came to Dakshineswar, the Master raised this topic and said to him, "Look here, Sivanath, is it true that you call these conditions of mine a disease — tell people that I become unconscious at the time of Samadhi? Ah, fine logic! You people are all right, quite sober and wakeful, although you apply your minds night and day to insentient things like brick, wood, earth, money, etc., and I, who think night and day of Him whose consciousness makes the whole universe conscious, become unconscious! Where have you borrowed your intellect from?" Sivanath remained silent.

30. The Master used the words "Divine madness", "madness of knowledge", etc., to us every day, and frequently said to all that a powerful storm of divine love raged in his life for twelve years. He used to say, "Ah! just as, when dust is raised by a storm, all things look alike, and trees like the mango, jackfruit, etc., cannot be seen, far less distinguished from one another, even so came on me a state which did not allow me to distinguish good from bad, praise from blame, cleanliness from uncleanliness. I had one thought, one idea only, viz., how to realize Him. This was what occupied the mind every moment. People said, 'He has become mad'."

31. Some of those learned aspirants who came to the Master in those early days guided solely by their excessive devotion, were initiated by him, some into the practice of Mantras and some even into Sannyasa. Pandit Narayan Sastri was one of them. We were told by the Master himself that the Pandit lived with his teachers like the orthodox Brahmacharins of ancient days, and studied various Sastras continuously for twenty-five years. He had always a strong desire to have equal knowledge of, and mastery over, all the six Darsanas, and lived with different teachers at

Kasi and other places in the north-western part of the country and had complete mastery of five of them. But unless he studied also Nyaya, the sixth of them, under its eminent exponents at Navadwip in Bengal, he could not claim to have complete mastery over all the Darsanas. He had, therefore, come to this part of the country about eight years before he visited the Master at Dakshineswar. For seven years he lived at Navadwip to complete his studies in the Nyaya philosophy, and having done so, was ready to go home. Perhaps he entertained doubts whether he would be able to visit these parts of the country over again. So he came to see Calcutta, and among the places he visited there was Dakshineswar, where he had the privilege of meeting the Master.

32. Narayan Sastri was known as a great scholar in the country even before he came to Bengal to study Nyaya. Hearing the reputation of Sri Sastri, the Maharaja of Jaipur, we were told by the Master himself, had at one time a desire to appoint him as his court-pandit, and respectfully invited him with the promise of a high salary. But Sri Sastri's thirst for knowledge had not yet been quenched; for his eagerness for getting complete mastery over the six orthodox schools of Indian philosophy yet remained unfulfilled. So he had to reject the Maharaja's cordial invitation. Sri Sastri, we understand, belonged to some place in or near Rajputana.

33. Narayan Sastri was not like ordinary scholars. Detachment from the world was gradually growing in his heart along with the knowledge of the scriptures. He could clearly understand that no one could have real mastery of the Vedanta and other scriptures by a mere study without practice. Therefore, even before he finished his studies, there arose in his mind from time to time the idea, "I am afraid, I am not acquiring the right knowledge in this way. I should practise Sadhana for some time and try to realize what the scriptures say." But he suppressed the desire of engaging himself in Sadhana and applied his mind again to his studies, lest he should lose both, by thus giving up half-finished a subject which he had been trying to master. Now, as he had acquired a thorough knowledge of the six philosophical systems, that long-cherished desire of his was fulfilled. He now wanted to return home. He had already decided in his mind that he would do what was considered proper on his going back home. At this auspicious moment of his life he met the Master, and as

soon as he saw him, he felt drawn towards him, rather in a mysterious way.

We have already said that, at the Dakshineswar Kali temple, there were good arrangements for the boarding and lodging of guests, Fakirs, Sadhus, Sannyasins, Pandits and so on. No wonder therefore that he was respectfully received and allowed to live there as long as he liked; for, besides being a Brahmana Brahmacharin, belonging to a distant part of the land, he was a good scholar also. It was a beautiful place providing food and other necessities and affording the company of such a god-man! Sri Sastri made up his mind to spend some time here before going away. And what else could he do? The more intimately he mixed with the Master, the more did a certain feeling of love for him, combined with a desire to sound the depth of his wisdom, grow in his heart and prevail upon him. The Master too expressed his joy on getting the simple-hearted, magnanimous Sastri for a companion and spent much time with him in conversation about God.

34. Sastriji had read about the seven planes spoken of in the Vedanta. He knew from his study of the scriptures that, as soon as the mind ascended to higher and higher planes of consciousness, there came wonderful experiences and visions followed at last by the Nirvikalpa Samadhi. And it was in that state that man got merged in the immediate experience of the reality of Brahman, the indivisible Existence-Knowledge-Bliss itself, and that the delusion of the world clinging to him for ages without beginning, vanished altogether. He saw that the Master had the immediate knowledge of what Sastriji merely had read about in the books and got by heart. He found that he himself merely uttered words like Samadhi, immediate knowledge, etc., while the Master was actually experiencing these states day and night. Sastriji thought, "Ah, how wonderful! Where else shall I have such a person to teach and explain the hidden meanings of the Sastras? This opportunity must not be missed. The means of immediate knowledge of Brahman must be learnt from him at any cost. Life is uncertain indeed. Who knows when this body will come to an end? Shall I die before attaining right knowledge? That should not be. At least one sincere effort to realize God must be made. Away with the thought of home and all that for the present!"

35. As days passed on, detachment and eagerness to know the Truth grew more and more in Sastriji as a result of the divine company of the Master. The desires such as, "I shall startle all by my scholarship", "I shall become a Mahamahopadhyaya,[1] and acquire name, fame, position, etc., more than others", appeared to be contemptible aims of life to be shunned and avoided by all means; and they gradually vanished altogether from his mind. Sastriji lived with the Master like a disciple in a mood of true humility, listened attentively to his nectar-like words, and began to think within himself: "I should not apply my mind any more to anything else than God. There is no knowing when the body will meet with its end. Now, when there is time yet, efforts must be made to realize God." He reflected on the Master, "Ah, how free from anxiety he lives, knowing what one ought to know and understand in life! Even death has been conquered by him. It can no longer hold before him the horrible shadow of the 'night of destruction'. Well, the author of the Upanishads[2] says that all the wishes of such great souls become fulfilled, and that if one can truly obtain their grace, one's desire of experiencing the world again and again vanishes and one attains the knowledge of Brahman. Why then should I not pray for his grace? Why should I not take refuge in him?" Sastriji went on pondering this way and lived with the Master at Dakshineswar. But, he could not, all on a sudden, make any request to him lest he should consider him to be unfit and refuse to take him under his shelter. Time rolled on thus.

36. The following event proves that detachment from the world was becoming intense in Sastriji's mind day after day. Michael Madhusudan Datta, the great and glorious poet of Bengal, who was also a leading lawyer of those days, was at that time conducting a case on behalf of Rani Rasmani. One day he had to come to the Dakshineswar Kali temple with a relative of the Rani in order to know everything about the case precisely. After he had finished his consultations, he came to know in the course of conversation that the Master was there in the temple premises and expressed a desire to see him. When word was sent to the Master, he at first sent Sastriji to speak with Madhusudan and

[1] A title meaning "the greatest amongst the great scholars".

[2] Mundaka Upanishad III.i.10 and III.ii.1.

himself went a little after. While he was talking with him, Narayan Sastri asked Madhusudan the reason why he gave up his ancestral religion and accepted Christianity. Michael said in reply that financial pressure compelled him to do so. We cannot say whether it was reluctance to reveal his own story to a stranger that made him reply to the question in that manner. It appeared to the Master and the others present that he was actually speaking out his own mind and did not say so by way of joke or sarcasm to hide the truth about himself. Be that as it may, Sastriji became much annoyed with him to hear that answer. He said, "How is it! To give up one's own religion for the sake of a livelihood in this ephemeral world! What a mean consideration! Die as one must some day, you should rather have died than changed your religion." He thought, "And yet people call him a great man and read his books with appreciation!" A great abhorrence came upon Sastriji's mind and he desisted from speaking any more with him.

37. Madhusudan then expressed a desire to listen to some religious instruction from the Master. The Master said to us, "My mouth was pressed, as it were, by someone and I was not allowed to speak anything." Hriday and some others say that that mood of the Master left him a little afterwards, and he moved Madhusudan's mind by singing in his sweet voice a few songs of Ramprasad, Kamalakanta and other eminent Sadhakas, and taught him thereby that devotion to God was the essential thing in the world.

38. Even after Michael had bidden good-bye, Sastriji discussed and denounced Michael's playing the renegade and wrote with a piece of charcoal in big letters on the wall of the verandah to the east of the door leading to the Master's room that to give up one's own religion under the stress of one's monetary needs is a very mean act. Sastriji's opinion on this matter, written on the wall in distinct big Bengali characters, attracted our notice and produced curiosity in our mind. One day we made an enquiry and came to know everything. As Sastriji had lived in this part of the country for a long time, he had learnt Bengali very well.

39. Now comes the last known fact in Sastriji's life. One day he happened to meet the Master in a secluded place, took that opportunity to express the desire of his heart to be initiated into Sannyasa, and pressed his request tenaciously on the Master. The Master agreed on account of his eagerness and initiated him

on an auspicious day. After that Sastriji left the Kali temple. He informed the Master of his earnest desire to stay at Vasishtashrama and practise strenuous Sadhana for the realisation of Brahman till success attended on his efforts. Dissolved in tears, he asked for the Master's blessings, worshipped his feet and left Dakshineswar behind for ever. Nothing certain is known about Narayan Sastri after this, except that, as some say, he spent his days ever after at Vasishthasrama practising severe austerities, until his health broke down and death overtook him.

40. Again, the Master felt a desire to see the monks, aspirants and devotees of all communities, whenever he heard that some such person was staying in the neighbourhood. When he felt that desire, he used to go to them himself, uninvited, and spend some time with them in talks about God. No considerations of propriety or prestige such as — "Would people think ill or well of it?", "Would these unknown Sadhakas be pleased or displeased with my visit?" or "Would I myself be properly respected?" — would ever stand in the way of such self-chosen visits. He would go somehow or other to these aspirants and would not rest satisfied till he had formed a correct idea regarding their spiritual attitudes, their progress towards the goal and other relevant matters. The Master also behaved very often in the same way, whenever he heard of scholars learned in the scriptures who were also noted as spiritual aspirants. He paid such visits to Pandit Padmalochan, Dayananda Saraswati and many others, and narrated stories about their lives to us now and then. We are now going to tell the reader about Padmalochan first of all.

41. The study of the Vedanta was not wide-spread in Bengal before the advent of the Master. Although Acharya Sankara had defeated the Tantrikas of this province in theological polemics many centuries ago, he could scarcely establish his own doctrine among the people in general. Consequently, the Tantrikas accepted the highest principles of non-dualistic Vedanta and introduced a little of it into their own processes of meditation, but continued to prescribe the same forms of worship and ceremonies that were already prevalent, in spite of the afore-said influence of non-dualistic philosophy on their teachings. And the Pandits of Bengal devoted the whole energy of their fertile brain to the study of the Nyaya philosophy and created the Navya-nyaya or Neo-logic, which brought about an extraordinary revolution in logic and

epistemology. Was it due to the fact that the people of Bengal were defeated and humiliated in argumentation by Sankara, that logic, the unavoidable tool of philosophical debate, became so much prevalent amongst them? Who can say? Many a time has the world witnessed how, defeated in a certain field by a particular nation, the defeated and humiliated people have nursed a desire, and made an effort, to surpass all in that same field.

42. Although the study of the Vedanta was so scarce in Bengal, the nursery of the Tantra and the Nyaya, it was not as if no one was attracted to the study of the liberal conclusions of the Vedanta. Pandit Padmalochan was one for whom Vedanta held such attraction. After he had acquired proficiency in Nyaya, the Pandit had a desire to study the Vedanta. He went to Kasi, and studied that philosophy under competent teachers for a long time. Thereupon, he became famous as a Vedantin in a few years. On his return home, he was invited by the Maharaja of Burdwan to take up the post of a court-pandit under him. As the wonderful genius of the Pandit went on unfolding, he was gradually promoted to the post of the principal court-pandit. His fame spread throughout Bengal.

43. It will not be out of place here to allude to a remark by the Pandit indicative of his wonderful geinus. Expatiating on the theme that narrow opinions in spiritual matters were due to meanness of nature, the Master sometimes used to quote to us Pandit Padmalochan's remarks on the subject. He used to remember whatever he heard from others expressive of the liberal doctrines for which he himself stood, and to quote them in the course of conversations. But meticulously truthful as he was, he also used to mention the names of the persons from whom he first learnt them.

44. Once upon a time, the Master said, there arose a great controversy amongst the scholars of the court of the Maharaja of Burdwan as to who was greater, Siva or Vishnu. Padmalochan was not then present there. The scholars who took part grew noisy in their disputation, some supporting the one and some the other, according to the knowledge they had derived from study of the scriptures, or perhaps according to their own temperamental preference. Thus it developed into a protracted wordy quarrel between the two parties, the Saivas and the Vaishnavas. No solution of the problem could be found. Therefore, the prin-

cipal court-pandit was summoned to decide the question. Pandit Padmalochan arrived at the assembly. And when he heard the question, he said, "None of my forefathers up to the fourteenth generation saw either Siva or Vishnu. How can I, therefore, say who is superior and who is inferior? But if you want to know what the scriptures say, it has to be stated that the Saiva scriptures call Siva greater and the Vaishnava ones Vishnu. So, one's own Chosen Ideal is greater than all other deities." With this remark, the Pandit quoted as proofs verses indicating the greatness of each and concluded that both were equally great. This conclusion of the Pandit brought the quarrel to an end and everybody thanked him. We get a definite proof of his genius in this outspoken, frank and unpretentious understanding of the spirit of the scriptures, which was the cause of his great name and fame.

45. The Pandit's fame did not rest merely on his reputation for having penetrated deep into the wordy forest of the scriptures. Acquainted with the way in which his life reflected the noble qualities of liberality, non-attachment, good conduct, practice of austerities, steadfast devotion to the Chosen Ideal, etc., people came to the conclusion that he was an unusually great Sadhaka and lover of God. The co-existence of true scholarship and profound devotion to God is rare indeed in the world. So people are generally attracted towards a person in whom this combination is found. It was therefore no wonder that, when the Master heard of him, he had a desire to see that aged and noble Pandit who had been adorning the court of Burdwan for a long time.

46. Whenever there was any desire in the Master's mind, he, like a boy, became anxious to fulfil it immediately. The Master's mind evinces this trait, perhaps because he had cultivated it from his childhood. "Life is ephemeral, therefore do quickly whatever has to be done"— this is a maxim that he translated into life with the ardour of extreme sincerity. Again a little thinking will make it clear that this is a trait that will naturally dawn on a mind that is trained in the habit of steadfastness and concentration in the pursuit of its ideals. Anyway, seeing the Master eager, Mathuranath was thinking of sending him to Burdwan when the news came that, as Pandit Padmalochan had been ill for a long time, he had been brought to a garden near Ariyadaha on the banks of the Ganga for a change of climate and that, owing to the pure fresh air of the

place, he had improved a little. Hriday was sent to know whether the news was true.

He returned and confirmed the news. The Pandit too had heard of the Master and was very eager to see him. He showed great respect to Hriday, knowing that he was a relative of the Master. A day was then fixed. The Master started to see the Pandit. Hriday accompanied him.

47. Hriday said that the Master and Padmalochan were pleased to see each other when they met for the first time. The Master could find him to be a Sadhaka, of a liberal nature, amiable and well versed in the Sastras. The Pandit also had the conviction that the Master was a great soul and was in an extraordinarily advanced state of spiritual evolution. He could not refrain from shedding tears to hear the name of the Divine Mother sung by the Master in his sweet voice. The Pandit became speechless on seeing the Master lose normal consciousness in ecstasy over and over again and on hearing what experience he had in that state. The Pandit, well versed as he was in the scriptures, must have tried to compare the spiritual states of the Master with those recorded in the scriptures. But it is also certain that, in doing so, he must have felt a difficulty that day to come to any certain conclusion. For, not finding the ultimate experiences of the Master recorded in the Sastras, he could not perfectly ascertain which of the two was true — whether what was written in the Sȧstras or the experiences of the Master. Therefore, the discriminating mind of the Pandit, always accustomed to arriving at sure conclusions in all spiritual matters with the help of scriptural knowledge and his keen intellect, experienced a sort of restlessness in the midst of joy, like a spot of darkness in light.

48. On account of the love and attraction which sprang up during their first acquaintance with each other, the Master and the Pandit met together a few times more. Consequently, the conviction of the Pandit about the Master's spiritual state grew deeper and more profound. We heard from the Master himself that there was a special reason why the Pandit arrived at such a firm conviction.

Pandit Padmalochan had been practising for a long time the disciplines prescribed by the Tantras along with his study and teaching of the Vedanta philosophy. He had also some realisation as the result of his practices. The Master said that the Divine Mother revealed to him the secret of the Pandit's power, attained through certain spiritual practices. He came to know that it was only because the Devi, the Pandit's chosen Ideal, was pleased with him on account of his Sadhana and granted him a boon, that he became invincible in innumerable meetings of scholars and could keep secure his superiority. Padmalochan had always with him a towel and a water pot with a spout, filled with water. It was a favourite habit with him to take them in his hand, walk a few steps hither and thither, come back and wash his mouth and sprinkle his head with that water before he went forward to solve any problem. Nobody ever felt any curiosity to inquire into the reason for this queer habit of his, and none thought that it had any hidden purpose. The Pandit never disclosed it to anybody, not even to his wife, that he used to do so according to the commandment of his chosen Ideal and that, when he did so, intelligence, scriptural knowledge and divine grace made him invincible to others. The Devi inspired him from within to do so. From that time he followed that advice invariably and experienced its result without the knowledge of others.

49. The Master said that he could know all this by the grace of the Divine Mother. And one day, finding an opportunity, he concealed the Pandit's towel and water pot. Padmalochan could not engage himself in the solution of the problem under discussion in the absence of those things and was busy searching for them. When, afterwards, he came to know that the Master had concealed them, his astonishment knew no bounds; when, again, he understood that the Master had come to know everything about his secret earlier and had done things knowingly, the Pandit could not help reciting hymns in praise of the Master as his own chosen Ideal. The Pandit came to regard him as an incarnation of God from that time and was devoted to him accordingly. The Master said, "Though Padmalochan was so great a scholar, he had so much faith in and devotion to 'here' (me)! He said, 'When I shall come round, I'll convene a meeting of all the scholars and tell them all that you are an incarnation of God. I'll see who can refute my word.' Mathur, at one time, was for some other reason going to convene a meeting at Dakshineswar of a large number of scholars. Padmalochan who was free from avarice and who

followed the custom of an orthodox and virtuous Brahmana, would never accept a gift from a low caste man. Thinking that he would not come to the meeting, Mathur asked me to request him to be present there. At the request of Mathur, I asked the Pandit affectionately, 'Will you not come to Dakshineswar?' He said, 'I may go even to a sweeper's house with you and take my food there. Why not then to the houses of others?' ".

50. But the Pandit was not destined to come for the meeting convened by Mathur Babu. Before the meeting could be called, his physical illness increased. He bade good-bye to the Master with tears in his eyes and went to Kasi. It is said he passed away there shortly after.

When long afterwards some of the Calcutta devotees of the Master who had taken refuge at his holy feet began, in their exuberance of devotion, to describe him publicly as an incarnation, the Master on coming to know of it forbade them to do so. But they did not desist from their preaching in spite of this. Annoyed at this, he said to us, "One is a doctor and the other is the manager of a theatre. They come here now and then and call me an incarnation! They think they extol me by doing so. But what do they understand of what is meant by an incarnation? Long before they came here and called me an incarnation, many persons like Padmolochan, who spent their whole lives in the study of these things — some of them well versed in the six philosophical systems and others in three — came here and called me an incarnation. To be called an incarnation has become disgusting to me. What will they add to me by calling me so?"

Besides Padmalochan, the Master met some other famous scholars from time to time. He told us now and again, in the course of conversation, the special noble qualities he saw in them. It will not be out of place here to narrate briefly the stories of a few such distinguished men.

51. Once Swami Dayananda Saraswati, the founder of the Arya Samaj, came to Bengal on a tour and lived for some time in a gentleman's garden in the village called Sinthi in Baranagar, situated in the north of Calcutta. Although he was very well known for his scholarship, he had not then begun to preach his own doctrine, nor had he founded his organization. On hearing of him, one day the Master went there to pay him a visit. In the course of a conversation on Dayananda, the Master said to us on

one occasion, "I went to see him in the garden of Sinthi; I found that he had acquired a little power; his chest was always red. He was in the state of Vaikhari, speaking on scriptural subjects night and day; by the application of grammar, he was twisting the meanings of many words. He had in his mind the egoism, 'I'll do something, I'll preach a doctrine.'"

52. The Master said about Pandit Jayanarayan, "Although a great scholar, he was free from pride. He had fore-knowledge of the time of his death and said that he would go to Kasi and pass away there. And so he did."

53. The Master spoke many times of the great devotion Krishnakishore Bhattacharya of Ariyadaha had to Sri Ramachandra. He used to visit his house. The highly devoted wife of Krishnakishore also had much devotion for the Master. Krishnakishore's faith and devotion were of an extraordinary nature. The Master used to say that, not to speak of the Mantra 'Rama', Krishnakishore had great devotion even to its reverse form 'Mara'. For it is stated in the Puranas that the Rama-mantra was imparted in that form by Narada to Valmiki, who was then a notorious highway man. And as the result of its repeated utterance with devotion, the extraordinary divine play of Sri Ramachandra was manifested in Valmiki's mind and this made him the poet and author of the Ramayana. Krishnakishore met with much grief and misery in the world. Two of his grown-up sons died. The effect of the grief due to the death of one's son, the Master said, was so great that, even Krishnakishore, although a great devotee, could not control himself and was overwhelmed with grief.

Besides the Sadhakas mentioned above, the Master saw Maharshi Devendranath Tagore, Pandit Iswarchandra Vidyasagar and others. He spoke to us occasionally of the Maharshi's liberal devotion and Iswarchandra's zeal for the Yoga of action.

CHAPTER III

PILGRIMAGE OF THE MASTER AS THE GURU AND HIS MEETING WITH THE HOLY MEN

[TOPICS: 1. The uniqueness of the Master's life. 2. The scope of the Master's liberal doctrine. 3. The proof thereof. 4. The spread of the Master's ideas. 5. Spread of his ideas among Sadhus by his early contacts. 6. Varied experiences enhanced his capacity to teach. 7. Pilgrimage helped him understand the condition of the people. 8. Significance of the pilgrimage of divine persons. 9. "Chew the cud" after visiting temples and holy places. 10. Devotional mood and holy places. 11. The Master's advice to a devotee intent on pilgrimage to Bodhgaya. 12. "One who has it here enhanced has it there also". 13. The Master's simple faith and pilgrimages. 14. "Be a devotee but not a fool". 15. Unholiness in holy places. 16. The Master's vision of "golden Kasi". 17. Why Kasi is regarded as made of gold. 18. The Master's reaction to Holy Kasi. 19. The Master's vision at Manikarnika. 20. The Master saw Trailanga Swami. 21. His Bhavasaṃadhi in Sri Vrindavan. 22. His intense love for Vraja. 23. Gangamata of Nidhuvan. 24. The Master's service of his mother. 25. The Master's refusal to go to Gaya; why? 26. The law of effect merging in the cause. 27. Law of Karma insufficient to explain an incarnation's life: why? 28. Sankhya and incarnation doctrine. 29. Vedanta and incarnation. 30. Uniqueness of their body and mind. 31. The Master visited Navadwip. 32. The Master's views on Chaitanya's incarnationhood. 33. The Master's visit to Kalna. 34. The ascetic Bhagavan Das. 35. Religious movements during the Master's Sadhana. 36. The Master at the Harisabha in Kalutola. 37. The Bhagavata reading there. 38. The Master occupying "the seat of Sri Chaitanya". 39. Commotion over it. 40. Bhagavan Das's anger at it. 41. The Master goes to Bhagavan Das. 42. Hriday as messenger. 43. Bhagavan Das reprimanding a Sadhu. 44. Bhagavan Das's egotism of teaching people. 45. The Master criticises his egotism. 46. Bhagavan Das submits to the Master. 47. The cordial conversation between them.]

Know that all beings, that are great, prosperous and powerful, have for their origin a part of My power.

—Gita X.41.

It is not in the power of man to record everything about the divine play of the Master as the spiritual teacher established in Bhavamukha, enacted with so many people in so many places and in so many ways. We have already presented a little of it to the reader. It was also in accordance with the same mood of the teacher that he went on pilgrimages. We shall now try to narrate them to the reader.

1. As far as we saw, no action of the Master was aimless or useless. If we study even the very ordinary daily actions of his life, not to speak of the special events, they are found to be full of profound meaning. Again, in the modern age we have not seen a single life in the spiritual world so full of unusual occurrences. Ordinarily, man cannot attain the complete experience of even any one of the innumerable aspects of God in spite of lifelong Sadhanas, let alone realising Him in His various aspects as taught by different cults and religions, and attaining competency to instruct the votaries of them all in their respective paths. But the Master stands out unique, without a peer in the spiritual field. As a rule all the great spiritual teachers of the past practised only one spiritual mood, attained to the corresponding realisation, and preached it as the only path leading to God-vision. They had not the opportunity of knowing that God might be realised through various other moods also. Or, they themselves might have realized that truth, more or less, but they did not publicly declare it, thinking that such preaching might undermine the firm faith and devotion of the people to their chosen Ideals and thereby thwart or harm their realization of spirituality. But, whatever may be the motive, history bears testimony to the fact that they preached as Gurus, narrow religious doctrines only, which became in course of time a perennial source of jealousy, hatred, and even bloodshed on many occasions.

That was not all. The narrow sectarian ideals gave rise to various doctrines contrary to one another and made the path to realization of God so intricate that it appeared impossible to the human intellect to disentangle that intricacy and have the vision of God, of the Truth. Again, finding the time propitious, Westerr materialism, which regarded this worldly life and enjoyments as all in all, entered through education into India with irresistible force. It defiled the minds of boys and young men of impressionable age and flooded the country with those baneful foreign ideas and ideals of atheism and worldliness. Who can say how wide-spread

Twelve Siva Temples at Dakshineswar

The northern verandah attached to Sri Ramakrishna's room

Nahabat, where Sri Sarada Devi lived

The Bilva Tree where Sri Ramakrishna did Tantra Sadhana

that wretched condition would have been, had not religion been re-established by the advent of this extraordinary Master, a glowing example of purity, renunciation and love of God?

2. He himself practised all religions and showed that none of the different aspects of God which were realized in ancient ages by the great souls, seers, teachers and incarnations born in India and abroad — that none of these various methods of knowing Him preached by them was false. The aspirant, who has genuine faith, may become blessed by realizing God even today by proceeding along the paths chalked out by them. He demonstrated that, although there existed a mountain-like wall of partition between the Hindus and the Muslims on account of mutually contradictory social manners, customs, etc., the religious faiths of both were true; that though worshipping the same God in different ways and going forward along different paths, both of them could, in course of time, be one in love, forgetting the age-long quarrels. To the West engaged in the mad pursuit of worldly power and pleasure, he has proclaimed the warning that there can be peace only through renunciation and that this is attained only through faith in the spiritual message of the seers and incarnations of the East and the West, including Jesus Christ. The more we proceed with the study of the life of this wonderful Master, the more shall we see that he does not belong to any particular country, community, nation or religion. All the peoples of the world will have to take refuge in his liberal doctrine some day, for they cannot afford to forgo peace. Established in Bhavamukha, the Master will enter into all sects and groups in the form of those liberal ideas, and breaking asunder the limitations produced by all kinds of narrowness, cast them in his new mould, and bind them together with a cord of unity never known before.

3. That the aspirants of all the mutually contradictory and quarrelsome religious denominations of India came to the Master, saw in him the perfect ideals of their own respective spiritual moods and were convinced that he was a traveller on their own particular path, is proof of what has been said above. The spiritual ministry of the Master as the world-teacher, thus started in India for bringing about unity among the religious communities here, will not stop within the limits of India, or for that matter, even of Asia, but spread to the West too and by its serene and tranquil impact, combat the forces of irreligion and hatred prevailing there, thus

paving the way for the establishment of an era of peace all over the world never before experienced in its history. Do you not notice how quickly this work has been proceeding since the passing away of the Master? Do you not notice, again, how the ideas of the Master have entered America and Europe through the revered Swami Vivekananda, to whom his Guru was as dear as his life itself, and how they have, during this short period, produced a revolution in the thought of the world? In the irresistible march of time, this unfailing body of ideas will spread its influence over all peoples, all religions and all societies, and bring about a wonderful revolution. Who has the power to resist its progress? Who can withstand the influence of this body of ideas glowing with the benevolent power of unprecedented purity and austerity? The instruments, through which it is being spread at the present time, may perhaps be broken. Many will not perhaps be able to detach themselves and understand its source. But it is certain that all the peoples of the world will, in order to feel blessed, have to cast their lives in this mould, and to cherish carefully in their hearts this glorious mass of ideas emanating from the Master, illumining the paths of reconciliation between conflicting religions and sects.

4. Therefore, O reader, do not take as mere fables what we have narrated about the aspirants of different religious denominations of India coming to the Master and being blessed with the realization of true spirituality. First try to have a clear understanding of the spiritual height of Bhavamukha in which the Master was established and from which came all the mass of divine ideas manifesting through his mind. Then dive deep into the incidents narrated herein, and you will understand the sequence of events — how a new movement of thought with the Master as the centre was developing, first spreading its influence on the old orthodox type, next on the sections educated on modern lines, and afterwards on the world as a whole as a revolution in men's way of thinking.

5. The dissemination of the mass of ideas originating from the Master took place first amongst the aspirants of the various religious communities representing the old Indian tradition. How this took place has already been narrated partly. Whenever the Master practised any particular doctrine and realized perfection in it, the followers of that very doctrine came to him of themselves

in large numbers, saw in him their perfect ideal, and got from him before they left, the help they needed for their further spiritual development. Besides, at the request of Mathur Babu and his devout wife Jagadamba Dasi, the Master went on a pilgrimage up to Vrindavan. There is no lack of monks and devotees in places of pilgrimage like Kasi and Vrindavan and his visit to these places, therefore provided an occasion for them to contact him. Let it not be taken that this is a guess work of ours. We had heard from the Master himself, that eminent Sadhakas of those holy places met him and became blessed through the help of his power as the Guru. It is therefore necessary to record here a little of what he said.

6. The Master said, "A piece has to move through all the squares before it reaches 'home'. When one experiences all the states from that of the sweeper to that of the emperor, and is really convinced of their worthlessness, one can be in the state of a real Paramahamsa, a true knower of Brahman. This is the law for those who seek the highest knowledge for their own salvation." But regarding those who were to become real teachers of humanity, he used to say, "One can commit suicide with a nail-parer; but one requires a shield and a sword to kill another (to conquer an enemy)." If one is to become a true spiritual teacher, one has to pass through all kinds of experiences and become endowed with more power than the generality of spiritual seekers. The Master said to us again and again, "It is in the degree of power only that an incarnation of God, on the one hand, and a perfected man or Jiva, on the other, differ." Do you not see that, in the practical world of politics, geniuses like Bismarck and Gladstone have to keep an eye on the past and on the present events in the social and political life of their countries and develop foresight far more powerful than that of ordinary people? It is because of this that they see fifty years ahead of their times and estimate the possible beneficial and baneful effects that current ideas and movements can have in the future. So they set free counter-forces to combat these harmful ideas and movements that would possibly bring misery to their countries in course of time. It must be understood that the same law holds good in the spiritual world also. Incarnations, the true teachers, have to set afoot new movements after a careful study and correct assessment of the working of movements and ideas sprung from the life and teachings of the seers of the past;

what transformation the original ideas preached by those ancient seers has undergone in the course of centuries; what effects, good or bad, they have had on the lives of the people; to what extent they have degenerated; what perversions the new ideas going to be preached are likely to undergo in the course of a few centuries; whether they are likely to be more harmful to the people than the ideas and practices they are going to replace — these are the lines on which their study and assessment of the situation should proceed. For if they cannot rightly grasp these things, how can they understand the present condition of the people? And if they cannot rightly diagnose the disease, how can they prescribe the medicine? Therefore, besides acquiring the power of prescribing that medicine by practising intense austerities and the like, spiritual teachers have to pass through a great variety of conditions in the world and gain more experience than others. Do you not see, how many varied conditions of life the Master had to experience? Born in a poor cottage, he suffered intense poverty during his childhood; took up the appointment of a priest in the Kali temple; passed through the mean condition of serving another during his youth; stood the unsympathetic treatment of relatives and the ridicule and contempt of strangers for his absorption in God; and got the odium of being a mad man in the early days of his Sadhana. Side by side with this distressing situation, he also experienced the homage and reverential service worthy of a king from a man of great wealth and position like Mathur Babu as also the adoration of aspirants and devotees of various sects and denominations who accepted him as an incarnation of God. Thus through these experiences of a conflicting nature he had to stand the test of remaining perfectly unperturbed under all circumstances. Just as, on the one hand, his undivided divine love engaged him intensely in practising extraordinary austerities and opened his supersensuous and subtle Yogic vision, so, on the other, his acquiantance with all those worldly conditions enabled him to have an easy and correct grasp of the attitudes and ways of thought of various types of people in society. It endowed him with the practical skill required for dealing with them, and evoked in him sympathetic feeling with all in their weal and woe. For, it was through all these internal and external states that the Master's power as the teacher was seen to blossom and manifest itself more and more every day.

7. There is no doubt that similar results were produced in the life of the Master by his pilgrimages also. It was necessary for the Master, the spiritual teacher of the age, to be acquainted with the spiritual condition of the generality of people in the country. This need was, no doubt, met to a great extent through the pilgrimage he undertook with Mathur. That same eye of wisdom which enabled him to see through the veil of Maya, made him an expert in grasping the thoughts and attitudes of people from a few casual words, or in understanding the state of a country or society from the observation of a few events connected with them. It must, of course, be understood that this description applies only to the Master's power of understanding in the normal state of consciousness. But when he ascended the higher planes of consciousness he did not need these ordinary means of knowing like observation with the eyes and comparing the data. He was then endowed with the Yogic vision with which he could directly see into the soul of things, whether individual or social, and ascertain the means for the correction of their maladies. We saw the Master, the god-man, ascertain the truths about all things with the help of both the ordinary outward eye and the extraordinary Yogic vision. Therefore we shall be giving only a partial picture of this divine character, if we do not present the reader with both these aspects of his character — the human and the divine. That is what we are trying to do in these pages.

8. Seen from the scriptural angle of vision, there is another reason why the Master went on a pilgrimage. The scriptures say that holy sages, perfect in love and knowledge, visit pilgrim centres only to enhance the holy atmosphere and sanctity of these places. As they come and reside in those places with eager hearts to have special visions of God, they leave behind them either new manifestations of special aspects of God or enhance and illumine the previous manifestations already in existence there. So, when others come there, they experience easily a little at least of those aspects of God. When such is the elevating effect of the presence of ordinary holy personages on pilgrim centres, how much more powerful would then be the influence of the incarnations of God like the Master? The Master explained to us on many occasions in his simple language what has been said before about holy places. He said, "Know for certain, my children, that there is God's manifestation where people have practised for a long time austerities,

Japa, meditation, steady abstraction of mind, prayer and worship in order to have His vision. Their thoughts of God have become solidified there, so to speak, on account of their devotion; that is why holy thoughts and visions are so easily attained there. Numberless Sadhus, devotees and perfected souls came from age to age to these holy places in order to realize God, gave up all desires, and called on Him with all their heart. So, there is a special manifestation of God in these places, though He is uniformly present everywhere. It is like the easy availability of water in wells, pools, ponds or lakes, though it can be had in other places also, if one digs for it there."

9. Again, the Master taught us to "chew the cud" after we visit those places endowed with a special manifestation of God. He said, "Just as cows eat their fill, become free from anxiety, and then resting in one place, chew the cud, so after one has visited temples and pilgrim centres, one should sit in a secluded place, and ruminate over and get absorbed in those holy thoughts that occured to one in these sacred places. One should not apply one's mind to sights, tastes and other worldly objects, immediately after visiting them. For, in that case the godly impression gathered will not produce permanent results on the mind."

On one occasion, some of us accompanied the Master to Kalighat to pay our obeisance to the Mother of the Universe. It is superfluous to say that the special divine manifestation of the Pithasthana[1], combining with the living manifestation of the Universal Mother in the mind and body of the Master, helped to produce an extraordinary joy in the hearts of the devotees. On our way back, one of us had to go to his father-in-law's place in response to a special request and to spend that night there. On the morrow, when he came to the Master, the latter asked him where he had passed the previous night. On hearing that he had had to pass the night in the house of his father-in-law, the Master said, "Ah, what is this? You saw the Mother and came back;

[1] The story is this: The Mother, in Her incarnation as Sati, gave up Her body in Yoga, unable to bear harsh words against Her divine consort Siva, who thereupon went on travelling with the dead body dangling from His left shoulder, forgetting everything else. Vishnu, in order to relieve Siva from this precarious condition, cut from behind Him the dead body of Sati to pieces, which fell in different places of India. These spots, thus especially sanctified by one or other piece of Her body, are known and revered as Pithasthanas. —Tr.

what a great difference between 'chewing the cud' of the vision and thoughts of Her, which you ought to have done, and passing the night like worldly people in your father-in-law's house instead! One should 'chew the cud', in other words, continue to cherish the thoughts that arise in one's mind in temples and holy places of pilgrimages. How can those divine thoughts stay in the mind otherwise?"

10. Again, the Master said to us on many occasions that one could not derive much benefit from visiting places of pilgrimage and other holy places unless one devoutly cherished from beforehand holy thoughts in the mind. When he was living, many of us at different times expressed our desire to go on pilgrimage, when he said to us affectionately, "One who has it here (i.e., in the heart) has it there; one who has it not here, has it not there either.[1]" He said further, "The devotional 'moods' one is naturally endowed with or is practising, get augmented through holy associations in places of pilgrimage; but what special benefit will one derive there, if one's mind is a stranger to such 'moods'? Often it is said that so-and-so's son has fled to Kasi or some other holy place; shortly after, he writes home that he somehow secured a job there and has sent some money. Again many go to live in places of pilgrimage but start shops, business, etc., there. When I went with Mathur to the north-western parts of India, I found no difference — what is here was there also. The world seems to be the same everywhere. The same mango trees, tamarind trees, clusters of bamboos, etc., were there as here. I saw all that and said to Hridu, 'O Hridu, what have I then come to see here? Whatever was there, is here too. The only difference is that the power of digestion of the people of these parts seems to be greater than that of the people there, as could be seen from the ordure in the fields here.'"

11. The devotees, we said before, brought the Master for the treatment of his throat-disease to a hired house at first at Shyampukur in Calcutta and afterwards to a garden house at Kasipur, a little to the north of the city. Accompanied by two of his co-disciples, Swami Vivekananda went away to Buddhagaya

[1] Incarnations of God very often teach people in the same way. Once upon a time the supremely glorious Jesus said to his disciples: "To him who hath more (of faith and devotion), more shall be given and from him who hath little, that little shall be taken away."

without the knowledge of anybody a few days after the Master came to the Kasipur garden. At that time the study of the extraordinary life of Lord Buddha and conversation about his detachment from the world, his renunciation and austerity, were going on night and day amongst us. On the wall of the small room on the southern side of the ground floor of the garden house, which we always used, was written the verse from the *Lalitavistara*, indicative of the firm resolve of Buddha: "I will sit continuously on the same seat and practise meditation and steady abstraction of mind till I realise that enlightened state, which is gained only through effort lasting for ages. Let the body be destroyed in the attempt, if it is to be so." Flashing before our eyes day and night, these words always reminded us that we also would have to sacrifice our lives for the realization of God, who is of the nature of Truth. We also must follow the maxim of the *Lalitavistara:*

Ihāsane suṣyatu me śarīraṁ tvagasthimāṁsaṁ pralayañca yātu, Aprāpya bodhiṁ bahukalpadurlabhāṁ, naivāsanāt kāyamataścaliṣyati.

Thus in the midst of these endless discussions on the Buddha's detachment from the world, the Swami suddenly went away to Buddhagaya. But he did not inform anyone where he was going or when he would return. So, we thought, he would not perhaps return at all to the world any more and we would not see him again. Word came afterwards that he had put on ochre-cloth and gone to Buddhagaya. The minds of all of us were so much attracted towards the Swami that it was very painful for us to be without him even for an hour; therefore, many of us became restless and felt a constant desire to join him there. Gradually news of this reached the Master's ears also. Knowing that resolve of one of us, Swami Brahmananda told the Master about it one day. The Master thereupon said, "Why are you anxious? Where can Naren go? How long can he be away? You will see him coming back very soon." Afterwards he said smiling, "Even if you go in quest of spirituality all the world over, you will find nothing (no true spirituality) anywhere. Whatever is there, is also here (showing his own body)." The word "here", it seems, was used by the Master in two senses: first, in the sense that he was the greatest manifestation of spiritual power in his time and no one could find anything better or greater than they found in him; and secondly, in the sense that God exists within every one, and that if love for and devotion to Him could not be awakened within oneself, there is not much benefit in travelling to various places outside. Two or more meanings are thus implied in many of the Master's words. Why speak of the Master alone? It is the same case with all the incarnations of God appearing in the world from age to age; and human beings in general accept one or the other of those meanings according to their individual liking or past impressions. The person to whom the Master addressed the aforesaid words took them in the former meaning and firmly convinced that the manifestation of spirituality was nowhere to be found in the same degree as in the Master, stayed with him with his mind free from anxiety. Swami Vivekananda also came back to Kasipur in a few days.

12. At one time, a little before the passing away of the Master, a supremely devout woman devotee expressed to the Master her desire of going to Vrindavan and staying there for some time to live a life of austerity and spiritual disciplines. The Master, with a movement of his hand, said to her, "Ah! Why should you go? What can you do there? One who has it here, has it there, and one who has it not here, has it not there toc." The woman devotee could not accept those words of the Master on account of the attraction of her heart for that place and bade good-bye to him. But, she, we were told by her, could not derive much benefit from the pilgrimage on that occasion. Besides, she lost the opportunity of being with the Master in his last days, since he passed away shortly after she went away on the pilgrimage.

13. Many a time we were told by the Master, who was the embodiment of all spiritual moods, that his journeys to the holy places were undertaken with a special mental attitude. He used to say, "I thought, I would find every one in Kasi merged in Samadhi, in the meditation of Siva all the twenty-four hours; and all in Vrindavan, beside themselves with devotion and divine love in the company of Govinda! But, when I was at these places, I found everything quite the reverse." The extraordinary simple mind of the Master used to accept and believe everything like a five-year-old boy's. We have learnt to view all persons and things with a suspicious eye from our childhood. How can that kind of simple faith arise in our crooked minds! We look upon a man as a foolish, half-witted person when we see him believing anything straightaway. It was from the Master that we heard for the first time, "My children, people become simple-minded and liberal as the result of many

austerities and Sadhanas; if one is not simple-minded, one cannot realize God. It is to these men of simple faith that He manifests His real nature." Again, lest anyone should think that one must be a simpleton to have sincere faith, he would say, "You should become a devotee; but why should you be foolish on that account?" "Always, discriminate in your mind," he would continue, "between what is real and what is unreal, between what is eternal and what is transitory. And then give up what is transitory and fix your mind on the eternal."

14. Unable to harmonize these two statements, many of us got scolded by him now and again. Swami Yogananda had not then renounced the world. He required an iron pan for his house and went to Barabazar to buy one. He reminded the shopkeeper of the evil consequences of irreligiousness and said, "Look here, take the just price for the article, and give me a good thing; see that it has no cracks or holes." The shopkeeper, in his turn, said, "Rest assured, sir, I'll of course do that," and chose for him a pan and gave it to him. He believed in the words of the shopkeeper and brought it without examining it. But, when he came to Dakshineswar, he found that it was cracked! When the Master heard of this, he said, "How is that? How is it that you bought the article without examining it? The shopkeeper is there to conduct his business, not to practise religion. Why did you believe him and get deceived? You should no doubt be a devotee, but not a fool on that account! Should you be deceived by people? First examine whether the right thing has been given and then give the shopkeeper the price. See that the article does not weigh less than it should, before you receive it. Again, there are some articles for which it is customary for the sellers to give a little more than the quantity stipulated. Never neglect to take that extra quantity also." Many such examples can be given. But this is not the place for it. Suffice it to remark that in the Master extraordinary shrewdness co-existed with wonderful simplicity.

15. Mathur spent, we were told by the Master, more than a lakh of rupees on that pilgrimage. As soon as he came to Kasi,[1] he gave a feast to the Brahmana Pandits of the place. Afterwards, one day he invited them together with their families, fed them sumptuously, and gave each one of them as farewell present, a piece of

[1] This holy place is known by three names — Kasi, Varanasi and Banaras.

cloth and a rupee. Again, when he came back to Kasi after visiting Vrindavan, he played one day the part of the "wish-fulfilling tree" at the injunction of the Master, and gave to everybody whatever necessary articles he asked for — metal pots, cloth, blankets, sandals etc. When the Master saw the quarrel, tumult and even fighting amongst the Brahmanas on the very first day on which they were fed, he was extremely annoyed. He was seized with despair when he saw people very much attached to lust and gold in Varanasi as in other places. Dissolved in tears, he said to the Divine Mother, "Why have you brought me here, Mother? I was happier at Dakshineswar."

16. Although the Master was thus pained to see worldly attachment even amongst the people living in holy places, he had extraordinary visions and other experiences there, and was firmly convinced of the glory of Siva and the greatness of Kasi. From the time when he entered Varanasi by boat, the Master saw, with his spiritual eye, that the city of Siva was actually made of gold, that there was nothing made of earth and stone there. It looked as if the holy city was formed of stratum after stratum of the gold of spiritual emotions emanating from countless devotees who have been visiting the place from time immemorial. That effulgent form, the embodiment of spiritual emotions, is its eternal nature. And what is seen outside is its shadow only.

17. Even from the point of view of gross vision, it is not very difficult to understand why this city is called the 'Golden Varanasi'. Who will not admit on seeing Kasi where, from very ancient times, all the parts of India had combined to pour out incessant showers of gold to construct that wonderful city of Siva — a city with its innumerable temples and big buildings along the two miles of Ganga's banks, with its numberless bathing ghats having wide flights of steps, with its several metalled roads, decorated gateways, garden houses, monasteries, aqueducts and other reservoirs of water, and with its several charity houses providing food to large numbers of students, sadhus and the indigent poor? Who will not feel astounded to think of that heartfelt devotion of the three hundred million people of India, whose munificence has been contributing unstintedly through the ages to build up these imposing features of the Holy City? Who will not be charmed to see the irresistible force of this mighty current of spiritual feelings and be lost in an attempt to discover its origin? And who will not be wonderstruck

and say with his head bent and heart melting with devotion, "This, indeed, is an incomparable creation. It is surely not manmade. It has actually been brought into existence by the infinite compassion of the divine Lord, the refuge of the humble and the deliverer of the afflicted." Here Annapurna, the Sakti of the Lord, Herself presides, nourishing both the gross and the subtle bodies of Jivas. By the distribution of food, She supports their physical being, while She nourishes their spiritual being by imparting the knowledge of their oneness with the Lord and making salvation easy for them to attain. It is therefore no wonder that, poised in the plane of Bhavamukha, the Master could see that holy city of Siva as a golden agglomeration — a consolidation, as it were, of those spiritual sentiments that had brought it into being.

18. All luminous things, without exception, are, in the eyes of the Hindus, pure, and therefore originated from Sattva Guna. Light is one such expression of Sattva because of its luminosity. That is why the Sastras prescribe the placing of the jyoti-pradipa, the sacred lamp, near the Deities, and forbid its extinguishing. It is perhaps owing to this principle that we have been enjoined to look upon bright things like gold as pure, and forbidden to wear gold ornaments on the lower part of the body. Seeing that Varanasi was golden, the childlike Master was at first worried to think that its purity would be soiled if he were to answer nature's calls there. We heard from the Master himself that Mathur arranged for a palanquin to take the Master across the small stream, Asi, to answer calls of nature beyond it. When afterwards that mood of his came to an end, he had not to do so any more.

19. We were told by the Master of another extraordinary vision of his in Kasi. Many people take a trip on the Ganga by boat to see the five holy places like Manikarnika and others along the banks of the Ganga. Accompanied by the Master, Mathur took a similar trip. The main burning-ghat of Kasi is situated near Manikarnika. When Mathur's boat came to the Manikarnika-ghat, it was seen to be full of smoke rising from funeral pyres of dead bodies that were being burnt there. As soon as he happened to cast his eyes in that direction, the Master, the embodiment of spiritual emotions, was completely beside himself with joy and the hairs of his body stood on end. He walked quickly out of the covered portion of the boat, stood on the very verge of it and entered into Samadhi. The guides of Mathur, the boatmen, and others

of the crew, ran to catch hold of him lest he should fall down into the water and be carried away by the current. But that was not necessary, for he was seen to be standing calm and quiet, absolutely motionless; and a wonderful light and smile illumined his face, making that whole place pure and effulgent, as it were. Hriday and Mathur stood carefully beside the Master. The crew stood at a distance and viewed the strange mood of the Master with astonished eyes. When, some time after, that divine mood of the Master came to an end, all got down into Manikarnika, bathed, made gifts and performed other ceremonies that were to be performed there, before they went elsewhere by boat.

The Master then described his wonderful vision to Mathur and others. He said, "I saw a tall, white person with tawny matted hair walking with solemn steps to each pyre in the burning-ghat, raising carefully every Jiva and imparting into his ear the Mantra of Supreme Brahman. On the other side of the pyre, the all-powerful Mahakali was untying all the knots of bondage, gross, subtle and causal, of the Jivas, produced by past impressions, and sending them to the indivisible sphere by opening with Her own hands the door to liberation. Thus did Visvanatha, the divine Lord of the Universe, endow the Jiva in an instant with the infinite Bliss of experiencing Non-duality, which ordinarily results from the practice of Yoga and austerity for many cycles. Thus did He bless the Jiva with the fulfilment of the highest object of life."

The Pandits, well versed in the scriptures, who were with Mathur, heard of the aforesaid vision and said to the Master, "It is stated in general in the Kasikhanda, that if a Jiva died here, the Lord of the universe grants him Nirvana, the state of infinite Bliss; but it is not described in detail how He grants it. From your vision it is clear how it is accomplished. Your visions and experiences have therefore gone beyond even what is recorded in the scriptures."

20. While he was staying in Kasi, the Master went to pay visits to the famous holy men there. He was much pleased to see Trailanga Swami, who was one of them. He spoke many things about the Swami occasionally. He said, "I saw that the universal Lord Himself was using his body as a vehicle for His manifestation. Kasi was illumined by his stay there. He was in an exalted state of knowledge. There was no body-consciousness in him. In Kasi the sand on the river bank got so heated that no one could

set foot on it, but he lay comfortably on it. I cooked rice porridge, took it with me to him, and fed him with it. He did not speak then, as he had taken a vow to remain silent. I asked him by a sign whether God was one or has become many. In reply he hinted that, when one was in Samadhi, one knew Him as one; but as long as there was the knowledge of diversity, such as I, you, the Jiva, the universe, etc., He was the many. Pointing at him, I said to Hriday, 'This is what is called the true state of a Paramahamsa.

21. After a short stay at Kasi, the Master went to Vrindavan with Mathur Babu. He, it is said, was in a wonderful Bhavasamadhi on seeing the image of Bankuvihari—he lost himself and ran to embrace Him. When he saw cowherd boys returning from pastures and crossing the Yamuna with herds of cattle at sunset, he became filled with spiritual emotion, inasmuch as, among them, he had the vision of the cowherd Krishna, dark-blue like a newly formed cloud and bedecked with the feathers of a peacock's tail on his head. The Master visited Nidhuvan, Govardhan and a few other places of Vraja. He liked these places more than Vrindavan. Experiencing various visions of Sri Krishna and Sri Radha, the supreme lady of Vraja, he felt intense divine love in those places. Mathur, it is said, sent him by a palanquin to go and see places such as Govardhan. On one side of the palanquin he spread a piece of cloth on which he piled in stacks rupees, half-rupees, quarter-rupees, two-anna-pieces, etc., so that the Master might give them away to the poor at places of worship. But the Master became so much filled with spiritual love and affection while he was going to those places, that he could not take them in his hand to give them away. Having no alternative left, he pulled one end of the piece of cloth on which the coins were kept and scattered them amongst the poor people of those places.

22. In Vraja the Master saw many world-renouncing Sadhakas sitting within Kupas, with their backs to the doors and immersed in Japa and meditation, having withdrawn their eyes from outward things. The Master's mind was much attracted by the natural beauties of Vraja and the other sights that greeted his eyes there. Among these were its flowers and vegetation, its small hillock Govardhan, its deer and peacocks roaming everywhere fearlessly, the holymen engaged in austerity, and the simple-minded and respectful inhabitants of Vraja. Besides, at Nidhuvan, the

Master was much charmed to see Gangamata, an aged lady of great austerity and a perfected lover of God. He enjoyed her company so much that he thought he would not leave Vraja and go anywhere else, but spend the rest of his life there.

23. Gangamata was then about sixty years old. Witnessing for a long time the overwhelming fervour of her devotion to Radha and Krishna, the people of that place regarded her as Radha's principal companion Lalitha, who had assumed a body for some reason or other, and come down on earth to teach Jivas divine love. As soon as she saw him, she, we heard from the Master himself, could recognize the signs of Mahabhava, the great mood, manifested in his body as in Radhika's. She, therefore, called him Dulali, the darling friend, thinking Radhika had incarnated Herself as the Master and come down on earth. Gangamata considered herself blessed in having had that day the good fortune to meet with the Dulali by chance, and thought that her long and heartfelt adoration, service and love of the Lord had borne fruit thereby. The Master also forgot everything else when he met her, and as one long familiar with her, lived in her hermitage for some time. They were so much charmed with each other's affection that Mathur and the others, we were told, were afraid lest he should refuse to return to Dakshineswar with them. Devoted as Mathur was to the Master, we can well infer how anxious he became on account of that thought. But the filial love of the Master towards his mother became victorious after all, and conquered his inclination to remain at Vraja. The Master said to us in this connection, "I forgot everything when I went to Vraja. I thought I would no more return here. But, a few days later, I remembered my mother. I thought she would be in difficulty — who would look after her and serve her in that old age? That thought arose in the mind and made it impossible for me to live there."

24. The more we think the more do the words and actions of this extraordinary person appear wonderful owing to the unprecedented harmony in him of apparently contradictory qualities. Do you not see that, although he offered everything, body, mind, etc., at the lotus feet of the universal Mother, he could not offer truthfulness to Her? Although he gave up worldly relation with all persons, he could not forget his affection and duty to his mother. And although he never retained the slightest tinge of carnal relationship with his wife, he never forgot to maintain, in the mood of

the Guru, a loving relationship with her. Ah, how many are the examples that can be given of his extraordinary actions! Is there any spiritual teacher or incarnation of the past in whose life so many contradictions meet in such sweet harmony? Who will not admit that such a phenomenon has never been witnessed before? One may not take him as an incarnation of God, but can one find a parallel to him in the spiritual world, search as diligently as one may? His aged mother, we heard from the Master himself many a time, lived the last few years of her life at Dakshineswar under his care when he himself performed various services daily to her and considered himself blessed. Again, when his adorable mother passed away, great was the Master's grief, and he was seen to shed such profuse tears in sorrow as very few in the world are seen to do. But, although he was so much grieved at the death of his mother, the Master never for a moment forgot that he was a Sannyasin. He had the obsequies and funeral ceremonies of his mother performed by his nephew Ramlal, as he, being a Sannyasin, was precluded by the scriptural injunctions from performing them and he himself sat in a secluded place and paid off, as far as possible, his debt to his mother by weeping for her. The Master said to us about this on many occasions, "In the world, O children, the parents are worthy of supreme veneration; they should be served, according to one's power, as long as they live, and after their death their funeral ceremonies should be performed according to one's means. One who is poor, and has no resources to perform them with, should go to the forest, remember the parents and weep; it is in this way alone that the debt due to them is paid off. It is only for the sake of God that one may disobey one's parents; one does not incur any blemish thereby. Prahlada, though forbidden by his father, did not give up taking the name of Krishna. But he did not incur any blemish on that account." We felt blessed to see the wonderful manifestation of the Master's power as the spiritual teacher of people through his filial devotion to his mother in this way.

25. The Master bade good-bye to Gangamata with difficulty and returned to Kasi with Mathur. He lived there a few days when, on the occasion of the Dipavali, the new moon night of illumination, he saw the golden image of Sri Annapurna and was beside himself with love and devotion. Mathur had a desire to pay a visit to Gaya from Kasi. But the Master dissented and Mathur

gave up that desire. When the Master's father had been to Gaya, the abode of Gadadhar, he, we were told by the Master himself, had come to know in a dream that Gadadhar would be born in his family. And that was why, when the Master was born, he was named Gadadhar. He sometimes said to us that he refused to go to Gaya with Mathur lest, when he saw the lotus feet of Gadadhar there, he should become overwhelmed with love, completely forget to live in a body separate from Him, and unite with Him for all time to come. It was the firm conviction of the Master that the One who in past ages had incarnated Himself as Rama, Krishna, Gauranga and others had come down to the world in his own person. Therefore, there arose in him, we observed, an indescribable feeling at the talk of his going to Gaya, the place of the origin of his body and mind, as known from his father's dream mentioned before. He had also a similar feeling about visiting the places where other incarnations of God had brought to an end their divine play. The Master said that, if he went to those places, he would enter into such a profound absorption that his mind would not come down from there back to the sphere of mortals. The Master expressed a similar feeling, on another occasion, at the proposal of his going to Puri, otherwise called Nilachala, where the divine sport of Gauranga had ended. It was not a feeling regarding himself alone. When he knew through Yogic vision, that any one of the devotees was a part or a manifestation of a particular deity, he expressed that kind of feeling regarding him also at the proposal of his going to the particular place of the divine play of that deity, and forbade his going there. It is difficult to explain to the reader that feeling of the Master. It is not reasonable to call it "fear"; for, even those ordinary persons who experience ecstasy in their lives recognize how at death the soul merely leaves the body, and become therefore free from fear of death, knowing death to be a particular transition, like any one of the physical transitions from one stage to another, such as childhood, youth, etc. So, it is no wonder that the incarnations of God, with their capacity to enter into profound ecstasy at will, conquer death and become absolutely fearless. Neither can we call it an eagerness to live or to have the body saved, such as people in general have. For, it is for the purpose of having selfish pleasure or enjoyment that the generality of people express that eagerness. This explanation cannot be applicable to those from whose mind selfishness has for ever been washed away. How then can we explain the aforesaid feeling of the Master? Words are our instruments, that is, they are there to express the ideas that rise in our minds. But have our words got the power to express the very exalted divine ideas of great souls like the Master? We have therefore, O reader, no alternative but to give up the idea of argumentation and accept with faith the exact words in which the Master expressed his thoughts, and paint for ourselves a picture of them with the help of our imagination to the extent we have been able to grasp them.

26. The Master said — and there are many examples of it in the scriptures — that a divine manifestation arising from a place, thing or person would merge into its source on coming into intimate contact with it. The Jivas owe their origin or manifestation to Brahman; when they acquire right knowledge and approach It, they merge into It. The limited minds of you, me and all other individuals have originated from the infinite Mind, in other words, they are the manifestation of that Mind. If the little mind of any one of us grows in purity, compassion, non-attachment and other noble qualities and becomes similar and very close to that infinite Mind, then the former merges into the latter. This is the law of the gross world also. The earth has come out of the sun, into which it will immediately merge if it approaches it (the Sun), drawn by some force or other. It must, therefore, be understood, that behind that conviction of the Master, there is a particular feeling unknown to us. And, if there actually exists a Thing or Person called Sri Gadadhar (the Deity in the Gaya temple), and if the mind and body of the Master had, for some reason or other, originated or manifested itself from Him, what was there irrational in the faith that, attracted towards each other on account of love, they would be united again when the approach was close enough?

27. No inference or reasoning is necessary to explain that the lives of incarnations are not like those of ordinary men. Seeing in them the manifestation of unthinkable, unimaginable power, men's heads are bent down in reverence to them; they offer them their heart-felt worship and take refuge in them. The philosophers of India, like the great Rishi Kapila and other geniuses, made the utmost effort to pierce the mystery of the lives of those extraordinary, powerful personages. Trying to ascertain what led to such a vastly greater manifestation of power in them than in ordinary people,

they saw at the very outset that the law of Karma, common to all, was quite insufficient to solve the mystery. For, it is in search of their own selfish pleasures that ordinary people perform good and bad actions. But when the actions of those great personages are studied, such self-centred motives are seen to have been absolutely lacking in them. Therefore the desire to ameliorate the miseries of others had an irresistible pull on them. At the altar of that noble urge they completely sacrificed all their own enjoyments and pleasures. Again, it is also seen that the desire for honour, for name and fame in the world, never took root in them. They invariably gave up all such desires for honour in the world and heavenly facilities hereafter, looking upon them as mere dropping of crows. Do you not see that the two Rishis, Nara and Narayana, spent ages in practising austerity in the hermitage of Badarika in order to ascertain the means to do good to humanity? Ramachandra banished even Sita, dear to Him as His life, so that His subjects might be happy. Krishna performed each action of His with a view to establishing truth and spirituality. Buddha renounced a kingdom with all its pomp and power so that he might deliver men from the pain arising from birth, old age and death. Jesus gave up His life on the cross, so that the kingdom of Heaven might come down to this world of grief and misery, that the realm of love of the Father in Heaven, who is Love Itself, might prevail over hatred, jealousy and bloodshed. It was against irreligion that Mohammad took up the sword. Sankara applied all his powers to explain to men that true peace consisted in the realization of Non-duality. And, knowing that all the power conducive to the good of men lay in the name of Hari alone, Chaitanya renounced worldly position and enjoyments, and dedicated his life to the preaching of the name of Hari through loud singing and unrestrained dancing. What could possibly be that selfish motive or lure of pleasure that actuated them to such action, seeing that it brought on them only personal sufferings?

28. Side by side with this love of humanity, the philosophers found in these incarnations all the signs which the scriptures describe as manifesting in persons liberated in life as a result of their extraordinary spiritual sentiments and experiences. They were, therefore, forced to regard them as belonging to a new class. Kapila, the author of the Sankhya, said that they had in their minds a very generous desire to do good to humanity. Therefore,

though already liberated through the power of austerity practised in their past lives, they did not dwell in the state of Nirvana or infinite Bliss. They merged in Prakriti; in other words, they spent the period of a cycle, knowing that all the powers of Prakriti were theirs. And, therefore, the one among that class who knew himself as possessed of such powers in any particular cycle, appeared to the people in general to be Isvara during that period. For any one who knew all the powers of Prakriti as his, would be able to apply or withdraw those powers at will. Just as we can use all the powers of Prakriti that exist in our limited bodies and minds only because we know them as ours, so can they (Jivas merged in Prakriti) use all its powers at will inasmuch as they know them as belonging to themselves. Although Kapila does not admit the existence of an eternal Isvara, he has admitted the existence of all-powerful persons, each of them existsing for a cycle, and called them Prakritilina Purushas i.e. individual spirits merged in Prakriti.

29. The Vedantic thinkers however, do not, accept this rotation theory of Iswara. According to them Iswara is always the same Eternal Being who manifests himself as the Universe and the Jivas. They are therefore of the opinion that those extraordinary and powerful persons who came for the good of the world are not merely perfected individuals, but are special aspects of Isvara, the eternally pure, awakened and free Being. That is not all; each of them is born, as the world's needs demand, for a particular purpose conducive to the good of humanity. As he comes down on earth possessed of the necessary powers to accomplish his mission, he is called in the Vedanta an "Adhikarika", a person entrusted with a mission and possessed of the "Adhikara", the authority, to accomplish it. Again, seeing a higher and a lower manifestation of power in these persons and observing that the actions of some of them are performed for the permanent good of all the people of the whole world, and of others for the people of one country or a part of it only, the authors of the Vedanta have recognized the former as incarnations of God and the latter as eternally free Isvarakotis endowed with less authority. With this opinion of the authors of the Vedanta as the basis, the authors of the Puranas afterwards came forward in their effort to ascertain, with the help of imagination, how large a part of God each incarnation was, and made a little too much of their business of calculation. The author of the Bhagavata went to the extent of stating:

"All these are the manifestations of an aspect (Amsa-kala) of the all-pervading one, but Krishna is the divine Lord Himself."

We have already tried to explain to the reader (cf. III.3.22–28) how the power of the Guru is that of God Himself. Finding that the Jiva who is deluded by ignorance is unable to overcome it by his personal efforts, He Himself becomes, on account of His infinite mercy, eager to deliver him from it. This compassionate eagerness of God to enlighten and save the Jiva and the expression of His will in this respect is called Guru-bhava (Teacher-aspect) — that divine will it is that manifests as Sri Guru. The Power of the Guru has been manifesting itself now and again to us as unique personages from time immemorial, bringing enlightenment to man in ignorance. It is these persons that are being worshipped by the world as the incarnations of God. It is, therefore, clear that these persons, the incarnations of God, are the true Gurus of humanity.

30. The Adhikarikas differ very much from the ordinary Jivas in the constitution of their body and mind. Their being is made of a stuff strong enough to contain the powerful expressions of divine love and experiences of the higher plane of consciousness without any strain or elation, because these come as something very natural to them. The Jiva becomes egoistic and is overwhelmed with joy and elation when he gets a little of spiritual power and the consequent adoration of people. But the Adhikarikas do not at all get unsettled. Their discriminative faculty is not affected nor are they overcome with egoism and vanity in the least, even if they become endowed with such spiritual powers a thousand-fold. The Jiva never likes to return to the world for any reason whatever, if, being free from all kinds of bondage, he can somehow attain in Samadhi, the knowledge of the Self. But as soon as the Adhikarika persons feel this bliss, there arises in their minds the urge to share it with others. After the realization of God, the Jiva has no duty whatever left. But it is only after that realization that the duty of the Adhikarikas begins — that is, they grasp and understand the especial purpose for which they were born and begin to accomplish it. Therefore, the law regarding Adhikarika persons is that, until they execute the specific mission for which they are born, there never arises in their minds, as does in the mind of ordinary liberated persons, that passivity of outlook consisting in keeping oneself merely in readiness for the final end. But, rather, there is seen in them an eagerness to live in this sphere of the mortals

and share their weal and woe. But there is, it must be noticed, a tremendous difference between the will to live of the incarnations and that of the ordinary unenlightened Jivas. Moreover, the Adhikarika persons know when it is that their mission has been accomplished and delightfully give up their bodies in Samadhi without remaining for a second more in the world. An ordinary unenlightened Jiva cannot even know when the duties of his life would come to an end, let alone having the power of giving up his body at will in Samadhi. Rather, he feels that many desires remain unfulfilled and his longing for the continuation of his bodily life remains unabated. There are similar differences between them in many other respects also. Therefore we shall be falling into a great error if we try to judge the purpose and actions of the lives of incarnations by our own standards applicable to ordinary Jivas.

It is only against the background of these scriptural ideas that one can have a proper appreciation of such sayings of the Master as "The body will cease to live if I go to Gaya", "An eternal Samadhi will result, if I visit Puri", and so on. That is why we have discussed the subject here very briefly. The reader would have also understood from the above discussion that no mood of the Master is without scriptural authority.

The Master, we said before, refused to go to Gaya with Mathur. Therefore, no one could visit that holy place during that trip. All returned to Calcutta via Vaidyanath. It was at Vaidyanath that the Master, on his way to Kasi, was overcome with pity at the sight of the poverty of the people of a certain village and induced Mathur to feed them sumptuously and give each a piece of cloth. We have mentioned the incident in detail in another place. (cf. III 7.38).

31. Besides visiting the places of pilgrimage like Kasi, Vrindavan, etc., the master at one time went to Navadvip, the birthplace of Chaitanya, the great Lord. Mathur Babu took the Master with him there also. From what the Master told us on one occasion about Gauranga, it is clear that all truths do not always remain revealed even to the minds of incarnations of God. But, whatever truth of the spiritual world they want to know and understand, comes very easily within the range of their mind and intellect.

32. Many among us were then sceptical about Gauranga being an incarnation of God, so much so that the word "Vaishnava"

was for many of us a synonym for low class people. We also questioned the Master about it in order to remove our doubt. In reply, the Master said to us, "I also had that attitude. Formerly I thought, 'How could Chaitanya be an incarnation, as there is not the slighest mention of it in the Bhagavata and other Puranas? The shaven-headed Vaishnavas have set him up to be an incarnation'. I could never believe that. I went to Navadvip with Mathur. I thought that if he were an incarnation, something of the power of that divine manifestation must be lingering there. I shall understand it when I see this place. In order to detect whether there is any Divine presence, I took walks hither and thither — to the house of the Senior Gosain, to that of the Junior Gosain and so on; but I saw nothing particular anywhere. Everywhere I found only a wooden figure standing with its arms raised upward. I felt dejected to see it. I regretted my going there. Afterwards, I was about to step into the boat for my return trip when I saw a wonderful vision: Two beautiful boys of tender age appeared. I had never seen such beauty as witnessed in them. They had the complexion of molten gold, and round the head of both was a halo of light. Raising their hands and looking at me, they were running towards me through the sky. And I cried out immediately. 'There they come, there they come!' Scarcely had I uttered these words, than they came and entered here (his own body); I lost normal consciousness and fell down. I would have fallen into the water but for Hridu who was beside me and caught hold of me. I was shown many such things, convincing me of their really being incarnations, the manifestations of the divine Power." The Master said many such things. One day he told us of his vision of Gauranga's Sankirtan in the streets of the town. We have described it elsewhere in this book (ch. III.7.38).

33. Besides going to the holy places named above, the Master once went to Kalna with Mathur Babu. Many villages of Bengal on the Ganga have become places of pilgrimage because of the touch of the feet of Gauranga, the great Lord. Kalna is one of them. Again, every visitor, without exception, feels that glorious acts like the setting up of one hundred and eight Siva temples by the family of the prince of Burdwan, have made Kalna a place of pomp and splendour. But the Master had a different purpose in going to Kalna this time. His intention was to see Bhagavan Das, the respected Vaishnava Baba, the well-known Sadhu of that place.

34. Bhagavan Das, the respected Vaishnava "Father", was then probably more than eighty years old. It is not known to us what family he sanctified by his birth. But his glowing renunciation, dispassion and devotion to God were known to a great many of the men, women and children of Bengal. Both his legs, it is said, became paralysed in the last stage of his life on account of his sitting cross-legged day and night, in the same posture, at the same place, practising Japa, austerity, meditation, etc. But although he was more than eighty years old and had become disabled, his great zeal in taking the name of Hari and shedding incessant tears of joy out of the bliss of divine love, did not decrease; rather it increased day after day.

The life of the Vaishnava community in those regions received a new impetus due to his presence in their midst. Many a Vaishnava ascetic got the opportunity of shaping his own life after his bright example and according to his instructions. Whoever, it is said, came to pay a visit to the Baba at that time, felt in his heart of hearts the accumulated influence of his long practice of austerity, purity, devotion and renunciation, and enjoyed an extraordinary bliss before he returned. The people there took all his opinions on Sri Chaitanya's religion of love to be infallible and engaged themselves in carrying them out into practice. Therefore, the perfected Baba did not then keep himself exclusively engaged in his own Sadhana only, but spent much time in discussing and putting into practice measures for the welfare of the Vaishnava community as a whole, in guiding Vaishnava ascetics to mould their lives according to the ideal of renunciation they had adopted, and in bringing peace into the lives of worldly people by promoting their zeal in the religion of Sri Chaitanya which they professed. People used to bring to the notice of the Baba, whatever happened in any part of the Vaishnava community, such as the good or bad conduct of Sadhus in any place. He heard and reflected on them and gave instructions as to what should be done. There is always an aura of majesty and authoritativeness about those who live a life of renunciation, austerity and love; people obeyed the words of the Baba most submissively and would of themselves hasten to act accordingly. Although he had no spies, the keen eye of the perfected Baba fell on everything done anywhere in the Vaishnava community; and every person of that community felt his influence. While, on the one hand, the ardour of those of simple faith increased day by day under his protecting vision and influence, the insincere, on the other hand, felt a sort of vague fear, a sense of shrinking into themselves, to come into his notice, as a consequence of which they sought to rectify their ways.

35. Important religious movements, as we have mentioned, were taking shape in many parts of modern India, while the Master, driven by the intense urge of divine love, was engaging himself in severe austerities for twelve years for the realization of God, and while the wonderful power of the spiritual teacher was beginning to manifest in him fully. The movements of the Hari-Sabhas and the Brahmo Samaj in Calcutta and various places near it, the propagation of the "Vedic Religion", known later as the Arya Samaj, by Swami Dayananda in the Punjab and the north-western part of India, the resurgence of pure Vedanta and of the sects like those of Kartabhajas in Bengal, Radhaswamis in the North, and of Swami Narayana in Gujarat — all these religious movements were founded and propagated shortly before and after that time. It is not our intention to discuss here in detail these movements and their doctrines. We shall describe to the reader only one event about the Master in a Harisabha, situated at Kalutola in Calcutta.

36. One day the Master had an invitation from that Harisabha, and he went there accompanied by his nephew Hriday. Some say that Pandit Vaishnavacharan, whom we have mentioned before, was engaged in reading and explaining the Bhagavata there that day, and the Master went there to listen to it. But we do not remember to have heard about this circumstance from the Master himself. Be that as it may, the reading was going on, and all were absorbed in listening to it when the Master arrived there. The Master sat amongst the audience and was listening to the reading.

37. The members of that Harisabha regarded themselves as having taken absolute refuge at Sri Chaitanya's holy feet. And, in order to remember constantly this fact, they had spread a seat, and assuming the presence of the great Lord on it, were carrying on before it worship, reading and all the other devotional ceremonies. That seat was called "the Seat of Sri Chaitanya". All devoutly made salutations to him in front of that seat. They never allowed anybody to sit on it. The reading was taking place in front of that seat decorated with garlands and flowers, and it was assumed

that the great Lord was sitting on it listening, while the devotees rejoiced to think that they were sitting in his divine Presence and were blessed with drinking the nectar of Hari's words in his company. The joy and the devotional mood of the reader and the listeners became, it is superfluous to say, intensified a hundredfold on the arrival of the Master.

38. The Master lost himself listening to the nectar-like words of the Bhagavata. In the midst of it, he suddenly ran towards the seat of Sri Chaitanya, stood on it, and entered into so profound a Samadhi that not even the slightest movement of the vital force was observable in him. Seeing that extraordinary loving smile on his effulgent face and his pose with an uplifted hand and a finger pointing up as in the images of Sri Chaitanya, eminent devotees felt in their heart of hearts that the Master in Bhavamukha had become completely identified with the great Lord — that, having ascended to a higher plane of consciousness, namely that of Bhavamukha, he was not then at all conscious of the great distance of time, place and other things which, in gross eyes, separate his bodily and mental existence from those of Sri Chaitanya. The reader of the Bhagavata stopped reading and was motionless, looking at him; although unable to grasp and understand the Bhavasamadhi of the Master, the listeners also became overwhelmed with an indescribable and extraordinary awe and astonishment and remained calm and charmed. Nobody could then say anything, good or bad. Experiencing an indescribable bliss for the time being, all felt that they were carried away, so to speak, by the powerful current of the Master's spiritual mood to an indefinable realm. They did not at first know what to do, but later, impelled by that indescribable feeling, they raised a chorus of loud shouts of "Haribol" and began singing His name. While discussing the nature of Samadhi (cf.iii.7.6), we pointed out that for coming down from that exalted plane of consciousness to the ordinary state, the mind depended on the particular name of God which stimulated and brought into consciousness the infinite mass of divine ideas experienced in Samadhi. We daily observed this over and over again in the Master. When he heard the name of Hari sung, the Master became a little conscious of his own body. Filled with love and devotion, he then mixed with those who were singing in a chorus and sometimes danced charmingly in an unrestrained way and sometimes remained motionless in ecstasy

on account of the excess of spiritual emotion. The zeal of all present increased a hundredfold owing to that behaviour of the Master. They became inebriated and began singing Kirtan. Who was then to judge whether it was right or wrong for the Master to have occupied the seat of Sri Chaitanya? After singing the noble qualities of Sri Hari and of the great Lord, accompanied by vigorous dancing for a long time, all cried out "Victory to the divine Lord", and brought the proceedings of the holy function to a close for that day. The Master returned to Dakshineswar shortly afterwards.

39. Although the natural tendency of those Vaishnavas for fault-finding in others became benumbed for some time when they reached a plane of higher spiritual emotion through the divine influence of the Master's fervent singing and dancing in the holy name of Hari, it resumed its normal functioning, like the mouse of the fable of Punarmushika, after the Master came away from that place. That is indeed the defect of all the religions that neglect knowledge and teach the aspirants for God-realization to depend on devotion alone. Though the travellers on the paths of those religions reach very easily high and blissful states of spiritual moods for some time through singing the name of Sri Hari and other such devotional exercises, they come down the next moment to proportionately low states of consciousness after the high emotional surge has subsided. They are not much to blame for it; for, it is the nature of the body and mind, the evolutes of Prakriti, to lapse into lassitude after stimulation. It is the law of nature that depression follows a mood of exaltation, that lassitude overtakes the elation produced by over-stimulation. Now when depression began to set in following that high current of spiritual exaltation, the members of the Hari-sabha came under the influence of their own previous nature and impressions, and busied themselves in criticizing the Master's action. One party vindicated the Master's occupying the Seat of Sri Chaitanya in Bhavamukha and the other party engaged themselves in making strong protests. There was a quarrelsome debate between the parties. But they arrived at no decision.

This controversy spread gradually from mouth to mouth everywhere in the Vaishnava community. Bhagavan Das also heard of it. That was, however, not the only thing that mattered; but apprehensive lest cunning hypocrites desirous of name and fame should feign divine emotions and similarly occupy the seat in future, some of the members of the Harisabha went to him to ascertain how it might be prevented.

40. The high-souled Baba who had taken refuge at the feet of Sri Chaitanya was very much annoyed on hearing of the occupation of the seat of his own chosen Ideal by the unknown Ramakrishna, and blinded by anger, he did not hesitate to call him names and even to describe him as a hypocrite. The annoyance and anger of the Baba redoubled on seeing the members of the Harisabha, and he scolded them that they were culpable in allowing that improper action to be done in their presence. When, afterwards, his anger abated, the Baba issued strict instructions regarding the arrangement that should be made in order that none might behave similarly in future. But he who was the occasion of all that commotion could not know anything about these developments.

41. A few days after that event had taken place, Sri Ramakrishna, of his own accord, went to Kalna with Mathur Babu and Hriday. The boat reached the Ghat very early in the morning and Mathur kept himself busy with arrangements for board and lodging. Sri Ramakrishna, in the meantime, went out with Hriday to see the town, and ascertaining the Baba's address from people, approached his hermitage.

42. When he was to go to the presence of an unknown person, it very often happened that the child-like Master at first felt an indescribable fear and shyness. We have observed that mood of his many a time. It happened so when he went to see the Baba too. Asking Hriday to go ahead, he covered almost his whole body from head to foot with a piece of cloth and followed him to the hermitage. Gradually Hriday went up to the Baba, saluted him and said, "My maternal uncle loses himself in singing the name of God. He has been experiencing that state for a long time. He has come to pay a visit to you."

43. Hriday says that, as soon as he approached him, he could get an apprehension of the power of the Baba born of Sadhana. For, before he had spoken the aforesaid words after saluting the Baba, he heard the latter say, "Some great soul, it seems, has come to the hermitage." Saying these words, he looked around. But, as he did not see any one except Hriday coming, he applied his mind to the topic he had been discussing with those before him. A particular Vaishnava Sadhu had done something wrong. What

was to be done about him, was the topic under discussion at the time. The Baba was much annoyed at that improper action of the Sadhu and was scolding him, saying that he would snatch away his string of beads and expel him from the community. Just at that moment Sri Ramakrishna came there, saluted the Baba, and sat humbly beside the persons assembled there. His face was not clearly seen by any one as the whole of his body was covered with a piece of cloth. As soon as he came and sat down, Hriday spoke to the Baba his introductory words mentioned above. At the words of Hriday the Baba suspended the talk he was engaged in, returned the salutation of the Master and Hriday, and made enquiries about them.

44. Seeing that the Baba was counting his beads at intervals during his conversation with Hriday, the latter said, "Sir, why do you count your beads even now? You have become perfect, you have no necessity for that." We are not sure whether Hriday put that question to the Baba according to the intention of the Master or of his own accord. But it seems that he did so on his own. For, being always engaged in the Master's service and mixing with many people, high and low, in the company of the Master, Hriday had developed presence of mind to a great extent and could raise topics suitable to the time and circumstances. The Baba at first expressed humility at that question of Hriday and afterwards said, "Even though I personally do not require these things, they are very necessary for me in order to educate people. They will otherwise go astray by imitating me."

45. Always depending entirely like a boy on the universal Mother in all respects, the Master had such a natural inward reliance upon Her, that he felt a great pain to see or hear any person doing or intending to do anything under the impulse of egoism, let alone himself doing anything of that kind. Therefore, apart from using the word "I" in the sense of the servant of God on rare occasions when he was under a spiritual mood, he could never use that word in any other state of mind, or in the way we use it ordinarily in life. Anyone who saw the Master even for a short time would be charmed and astonished to see that trait of his, or to see his great annoyance at such apparently harmless but egotistic expressions used by any one else, as "I'll do such and such an action." He would be led to wonder what great offence he had committed to provoke such annoyance. Now, as soon as he came to Bhagavan

Das, the Master heard him first of all say that he would snatch away the string of beads from some one and expel him from the community. Again, a little after that, he heard him say that he had not given up counting his beads and the putting on of Tilaka, so that he might teach people better. When the Baba said again and again," "I will expel him", "I will teach people", "I have not given up putting on Tilaka", etc., the simple-hearted Master could not suppress his annoyance as we do, following the ways of the so-called cultured society. He suddenly stood up and said to the Baba, "How is it! Are you so egotistic even now? You are speaking of teaching people, of expelling them, of accepting, or rejecting things! Who are you to teach people? Only He to whom the whole world belongs, could do that. If he does not, could you accomplish it?" The covering of the Master's body had then fallen; the cloth he was wearing became loose and fell from the loins, and his face was illumined with an extraordinary divine effulgence. He was beside himself with inspiration and was, it seemed, unconscious of what, and to whom, he was speaking. Again, hardly had he said those few words when he was motionless and speechless in Samadhi on account of the excess of spiritual emotion.

46. Everybody had been showing respect for, and devotion to, the perfected Baba and no one till then had been bold enough to protest against his words or point out his defects. He was at first astonished to see that action of the Master. But unlike ordinary people who, under such circumstances, become angry and revengeful, the Baba remained calm, without any feeling of being offended. The sincerity born of his Tapas came to his help and made him understand the truth of the words of Sri Ramakrishna. He felt that there was no other doer in the world than God, that however much a man might think in his egotism that he was doing everything, he was actually a slave of circumstances and could do only what he was permitted to do and understand by the most High; and that although worldly people might think they were doing things with their own power and according to their own choice, a devotee should not fall into such error even for a moment, lest he should go astray from the path of true devotion. Thus the powerful words of the Master opened the Baba's inward vision to a great extent, showed him his faults, and made him humble and modest. Again, seeing that extraordinary manifestation of

the spiritual mood in the person of Sri Ramakrishna, the Baba became convinced that he was not an ordinary person.

47. We can very easily infer that there flowed an extraordinary current of wonderful bliss during their conversation on the divine Lord. During that talk the Master was experiencing Bhavasamadhi and enjoying unbounded bliss at short intervals; and the Baba was charmed to see that there was always manifested in the person of Sri Ramakrishna that great spiritual mood, which he had been struggling to understand through scriptural study for a very long time. Therefore his devotion and reverence for Sri Ramakrishna must have become profound. And when, afterwards, the Baba came to know that he was the Paramahamsa of Dakshineswar, who under the influence of a spiritual mood had occupied the Seat of Sri Chaitanya at the Harisabha of Kalutola, there was no limit to his sorrow and repentance. He thought, "Is it this person whom I called names for nothing!" He saluted Sri Ramakrishna with humility and asked him his pardon. Thus came to an end the play of love on the part of the Master and the Baba that day. Sri Ramakrishna came to Mathur with Hriday a little later, described to him that event from the beginning to the end and highly praised the exalted spiritual state of the Baba. Hearing all that, Mathur also went to pay a visit to the Baba and made arrangements for the service of the images of the hermitage and a special festival for one day.

CHAPTER IV

AS THE SPIRITUAL TEACHER (CONCLUDED)

[TOPICS: 1. The Vedas call a knower of Brahman all-knowing. 2. The Master's explanation of it. 3. The meaning of knowing a thing. 4. Fulfilment of the resolves of a knower of Brahman. 5. Another example from the Master's life. 6. The Master's view from two planes of consciousness. 7. Ordinary men see everything in the second way. 8. An example of the Master's two kinds of vision. 9. The Master's spiritualised view. 10. Non-attachment and the keenness of the Master's faculties. 11. Examples of the keenness of the Master's mind. 12. God altering His law. 13. The Master and lightning conductor. 14. The incident of white china-rose and red china-rose on a plant. 15. Nature as the playground of the Mother of the universe. 16. The Master's intuitive power to sense the concentration of spiritual power. 17. Sri. Chaitanya's discovery of Vrindavan. 18. The Master's intuitive powers in this respect; example of Mrinmayi. 19. The condition of the town of Vana-Vishnupur. 20. Sri Madanamohan and Mrinmayi. 21. The Master's insight into the nature of people—the first example. 22. The second example. 23. On becoming what one wishes to be. 24. The third example at Pandit Sasadhar's place. 25. The Master's mental constitution and insight. 26. An example. 27. Second example. 28. Third example. 29. The Master's spiritual experiences and verification of the Sastras. 30. The standard of non-dual knowledge 31. Vision knowable to oneself and those knowable to others also. 32. The Master satisfied only with the true nature of things. 33. The ill-will between the Saktas and Vaishnavas. 34. The Master and the removal of this. 35. Sadhus' degradation by becoming medicine men. 36. The Master's opinion on those who are Sadhus merely by dress. 37. True Sadhus breathe life into Sastras. 38. Narrow-mindedness of even true Sadhus. 39. The Master and lack of spirituality in places of pilgrimage. 40. The Master's awareness of his own liberal doctrine. 41. "As many faiths, so many Paths." 42. The Master aware of being commissioned by the Divine Mother. 43. The Master free from the ego of being a spiritual teacher. 44. The first example of it. 45. The second example. 46. The Master's realization of his own mission. 47. The Master's eagerness to meet his devotees. 48. The Master's convictions about the devotees coming to him. 49. The convictions born of his absolute dependence on the Divine Mother. 50. The meaning of the Master's words on this. 51. Divya-bhava: its meaning. 52. Sambhavi initiation and Sakti initiation. 53. No discrimination between proper and improper time in such initiations. 54. The Master is the best of teachers with the divine mood. 55. Power manifestation in incarnations. 56. The Master, Keshavchandra and devotees.]

Although unborn and changeless by nature and Lord of all beings, I am, by subjugating my Prakriti, born through Maya.
Whenever, O descendant of Bharata, religion declines and irreligion prevails, I assume a body.
I am born in every age for the protection of the good, the destruction of the wicked and the establishment of religion.

—Gita IV. 6-7-8

1. The Vedas and other Sastras say that the knowers of Brahman become all-knowing. Unlike in the case of ordinary men, no false thought ever arises in their minds. Whenever they want to know and understand anything, it becomes immediately clear to their inward vision, in other words, they can understand the truth about it. At first when we heard about this teaching, we could not understand it, and therefore opposed it and raised many specious arguments against this scriptural view without caring to know its real import. We said, "If that were true, why were the knowers of Brahman of the past ages of India so ignorant of the physical sciences? Was there any knower of Brahman in ancient India who knew that Hydrogen and Oxygen combined to produce water? Why did they not tell us that with the help of electricity, news from America, a continent which one requires six months to reach, could be received here in not more than four or five hours? Or, why could they not know that man can fly like birds in the air with the help of machines?"

2. When we came to the Master, we came to understand that, if we tried to interpret those words of the scriptures in that way, they would give us no meaning at all. The purport of the scripture is different, and unless we study the scriptural passage in the light of it, the real meaning of it cannot be understood. The Master explained that statement with the help of one or two examples from rural life. He said, "When rice is being boiled in a pot, if you take one grain from it and press it between your fingers, you at once know whether all the grains in it are boiled soft or not. Why? You have not surely pressed all the grains one by one. How do you then come to this conclusion? In the same way by examining one or two things of the world, it is understood whether the whole universe is eternal or transitory, real or unreal. A man is born, lives for some time, and then dies; a cow also does;

a tree too. Examining things in this way, you come to the conclusion that whatever has name and form follows this law. The earth, the sun, the moon, etc., have names and forms; they, therefore, are of the same nature. Thus you come to know that all things included in this universe are similar. You then know the nature of all the things of the world. Is that not so? Thus, as soon as you know that the world is truly transitory and unreal, you will cease to love it; you will give it up from your mind and will be free from desires. You will have the realization of God, the cause of the universe, the very moment you dismiss it. Is he, who realizes God this way, anything less than all-knowing?"

3. When the Master spoke these words, we felt, "This is indeed true. The man who knows this, is all-knowing in a way. To see the origin of a particular thing, its middle and its end, is indeed what we call knowledge of that thing. So, to know or understand the universe in this way must be called knowledge of it. Again, this way of understanding is applicable to all particular objects of the universe also. So one who has known the whole universe and all objects constituting it as transitory and therefore unreal, must really be called all-knowing. What the scriptures have said is, therefore, quite true."

4. From this we could also arrive at a valid meaning for a scriptural passage as, "All the resolves of a knower of Brahman come true and are fulfilled." We realize as a matter of daily experience that the knowledge of a thing is acquired by an enquiry about it with the concentrated power of thought. It is, therefore, no wonder that, whenever a knower of Brahman, who has completely mastered and controlled his mind, makes an enquiry with all the powers of his concentrated mind to know anything, he could very easily acquire the knowledge of that thing. But, there is something more to be considered on this subject — whether he who has been perfectly convinced of the transitoriness of the whole of the universe and has succeeded, through love, in having an immediate knowledge of God, the cause of the universe and the mine of all powers, will ever have the resolve or inclination to invent railway trains, construct destructive machines and various kinds of manufactured goods. If those resolves can, by no means, arise in his mind, those machines and other products cannot surely be constructed by him. From the divine company of the Master, it became clear to us that it was actually so. It is really impossible for inclinations of

this kind to arise in such minds. When the Master was laid up at Kasipur with the incurable disease of cancer in the throat, we, Swami Vivekananda and other disciples, requested him with tears in our eyes to apply the power of his mind and cure himself for our good; but he could not make such an effort or resolve. He said that, on trying to do so, he could not command a sufficiently strong urge for that resolve and added, "I could by no means make the mind turn away from Existence-Knowledge-Bliss and bring it to this cage of flesh and bones. I have always looked upon the body as a trifling and contemptible object, and have offered the mind for ever at the lotus feet of the Mother of the universe. How can I, my children, withdraw it from Her and bring it back to the body?"

5. It will be easy for the reader to understand the subject if we mention another event here. One day the Master came to Balaram Basu's house at Baghbazar. It was about ten in the morning. It had been settled beforehand that the Master should go there that day. Some young devotees, Narendranath and others, therefore, came there to have the privilege of meeting him. They were talking on various subjects, sometimes with the Master and sometimes among themselves. In the course of it, there arose a discussion about the microscope and how it enabled one to see extremely minute objects in a magnified form. Hearing that tiny things, invisible to the gross eye, could be seen through it — that a very tiny hair, seen through it, looked like a stick, that every hair on the body looked through it appears as hollow as the stem of a papaya leaf and so on — the Master expressed a boyish eagerness to see a thing or two through that instrument. The devotees, therefore, thought that they would borrow it from some one and show it to the Master that afternoon. On enquiry we came to know that Dr. Bipinbehari Ghose, a brother of Swami Premananda and an esteemed friend of ours, possessed a microscope which he had got as a prize from the Calcutta Medical College on his passing the medical examination with honours. A man was sent to him to fetch that instrument so that it might be shown to the Master. Informed of it, the Doctor came with the instrument a few hours later, at about four in the afternoon. He set it properly and asked the Master to look through it.

The Master got up, went forward, but returned without looking through the microscope. When we asked for the reason, he said, "The mind is now in such a high plane that I can by no means bring it down." We waited a long time to see if the Master's mind would come down. But on no account did it come down that day from that high spiritual plane. Therefore, he could not see through the microscope on that occasion. Having no alternative left, Bipin Babu showed those things to some of us and went away with the instrument.

6. The higher the plane of consciousness to which the Master's mind soared on giving up the body-consciousness, the more extraordinary and celestial were the visions attained in those planes. And, as he was completely separated from the body when he ascended the highest plane of non-dual consciousness, his heart-beats and the functioning of the senses stopped for some time and the body lay like a corpse. All the modifications of his mind, such as thought, imagination, etc., came to a standstill, and he dwelt in the absolute Existence-Knowledge-Bliss. Again, gradually coming down from the highest plane to lower and lower ones, the Master, like all other people, had in his mind once more the idea, "This body is mine", and only then did he see with his eyes, hear with his ears, touch with his tactile sense, and think with his mind.

7. An eminent philosopher[1] of the West had a little indication of the human mind ascending to, and descending from, the plane of ecstasy and expressed the opinion that the consciousness within the human body does not always remain in the same state. This view, it is superfluous to say, is reasonable and approved by the seers of ancient India. Man's spiritual identity really belongs to that plane of Non-dual consciousness, but he has altogether forgotten it for endless time and acquired the firm conviction that knowledge can be had only through the senses. Free from anxiety, he has, therefore, been living in the sea of the world, casting his anchor there. The Adhikarika persons like the Master, who are the teachers of the world, and known also as the incarnations of God, are born from time to time in order to destroy this delusion by behaving in their own lives in a contrary way — by living a spirit-centred life in place of a body-centred one. Such is the teaching of the Vedas and Sastras.

8. Anyway it is now clear that the Master did not see men and things of the world as we do — that is, as having their present

[1] Ralph Waldo Emerson — "Consciousness ever moves along a graded plane."

physical identity only. His view of them was what they looked like from higher and higher planes of consciousness. It was, therefore, impossible for him to have, like us, the one-sided opinion or mental attitude with respect to any object of the world. And this was why we could not understand his words and ideas, though he could understand ours. We know a man, a cow, or a mountain merely as such. He too saw that a man, a cow or a mountain was indeed a man, a cow or a mountain, but at the same time he saw that the indivisible Existence-Knowledge-Bliss, the cause of the universe, was gleaming through them. The only difference was that its manifestation was more evident in certain things and less in others owing to their thinner or thicker veilings of man, cow or mountain. We, therefore, heard the Master say as follows:

9. "I see as if all — trees, plants, men, cows, grass, water and other things — are only sheaths of different kinds. They are like pillow-cases. Have you not seen them? Some are made of coarse cotton cloth dyed red, some of chintz and others of different kinds of cloth; and in size some are quadrangular, others circular. The universe is just so. Again, just as the same thing, namely, cotton, is stuffed into all these pillow-cases, so, that one indivisible Existence-Knowledge-Bliss dwells within all the sheaths — man, cow, grass, water, mountain and the rest. My children, for me it is actually as if the Mother has covered Herself with wrappers of various kinds or hidden behind various assumed forms, and is peeping out from within them all. I was in a state in which the universe seemed like that. Noticing that state of mine, people could not understand it, and came to console and soothe me. Ramlal's mother and others began to weep. When I looked at them, I saw that it was the Mother there (showing the Kali temple) who had come and appeared so, dressed in various forms. I saw that queer guise and rolled with laughter, saying, 'Thou hast nicely dressed Thyself up!' One day I was sitting and meditating on the Mother in the Kali temple. I could by no means bring the Mother's form to my mind. What did I see then? She looked like the prostitute Ramani, who used to come to bathe in the river, and she peeped from near the jar of worship.[1] I saw it, laughed and said, 'Thou hast the desire, O Mother, of becoming Ramani today.

[1] A jar, filled with water and covered with green twigs along with leaves, flowers and a fruit, is invariably placed in front of an image. - Tr.

That is very good. Accept the worship today in this form.' Acting thus, She made it clear that a prostitute also is She, there is nothing else except Her. On another occasion I was driving along Mechhobazar road, when I saw that She, dressed beautifully and with ornaments, braided hair, and a small round mark in the middle of Her forehead, stood on the verandah — smoking tobacco from a hookah set in a socket and was enticing people in the form of a prostitute. In astonishment, I said, 'Art Thou here, O Mother, in this form?' Saying so, I saluted Her.'" We have completely forgotten to see things and persons thus from higher planes of consciousness. How can we, therefore, understand those experiences of the Master?

10. Again, when the Master remained in the normal plane of body-consciousness like ourselves, his intellect and power of observation could detect many more things and dive deeper than ours, inasmuch as even then he had not an iota of the desire for enjoyment and pleasure. The objects catering to our strong desires and providing us with pleasures and enjoyments appear in bright colours before our eyes at all times, and we pursue them through all actions of ours like eating, drinking, seeing, smelling and the rest. Our minds, therefore, neglect the things and persons that do not cater to our desires, but get attracted to those that do. We have, therefore, no opportunity of knowing the nature of the things and persons so neglected. We thus spend the whole of our lives in making or attempting to make certain things and persons our own. This is why people in general are seen to differ so greatly among themselves in the power of acquiring knowledge. Though all of us have the same senses, can we equally apply them to all objects and acquire equal knowledge? Certainly not. It is for this reason that those of us who are less selfish and have less craving for enjoyments than others, can more easily acquire the knowledge of everything.

11. It will not be out of place to give here one or two examples to show how strong the power of observation in the Master was, even when he was dwelling in the normal plane of consciousness. It is impossible to exaggerate the keenness of the power of observation noticed in the illustrations, metaphors and similies he generally used in explaining intricate problems.

a. Take for example the discussion on the intricate Sankhya philosophy that was going on one day. Speaking to us of the origination of the universe from Purusha and Prakriti, the Master said, "Purusha, it (Sankhya) says, is a non-doer; he does nothing. It is Prakriti that does everything. Purusha merely looks on all the doings of Prakriti as a witness. Prakriti also cannot do anything independently." To that audience consisting of clerks, accountants, school and college boys and a few with higher education like doctors, pleaders and magistrates — this was too abstract a doctrine to understand. Therefore, when they heard the Master's words, they stared at one another's face. Observing them, the Master continued, "Do you not remember a marriage house? Sitting and smoking tobacco from a hookah, the master has given orders, and the mistress, obedient to him, is running hither and thither with patches of the colour of turmeric in her sari, supervising everything — whether this has been completed, whether that has been started and so on. At the same time she will be welcoming all the lady guests, children and such others, and also coming up to her husband from time to time to say to him with movements of her head and hands, 'This has been done this way; that, that way; this will have to be done, and that not done.' The Master smokes and listens and gives his assent to everything, saying 'Yes, yes' to whatever she says. It is just like that." All laughed to hear the Master's words and could also understand the exposition of the Sankhya philosophy.

b. Afterwards, perhaps, came up the topic of the Vedanta, "Brahman and Its Power, Purusha and Prakriti, are identical, that is, they are not two separate entities but one and the same thing appearing now as Purusha, now as Prakriti." Seeing that we could not understand it, the Master would say, "Do you know how this is? Take for example a snake, now in motion, now at rest. When it is lying motionless, it is compared to Purusha. Prakriti is then united with Purusha and has become one with it. And when the snake is in motion, Prakriti is, as it were, separated from Purusha, and is working." All now understood the philosophical point involved, and thought, 'Ah! Why could we not understand this simple thing?' "

c. On still another occasion, perhaps, was raised the question, "Is Isvara bound by Maya like ourselves, inasmuch as Maya is His Power and exists in Him?" Hearing it, the Master said, "No, my children. Though Maya belongs to Isvara and always exists in Him, He is never bound by it. Consider this: whoever is bitten by a snake dies. The poison is always there in the mouth of the snake. Still it takes its food through its mouth, and some part of the poison must be going in with the saliva. But it is unaffected by the poison and does not die. It is just like that." All understood it was possible, indeed.

From these examples we find that when the Master dwelt in the normal state of consciousness, the real nature of anything could not escape his keen observation. Even external nature could not keep concealed from his eyes the essential qualities of its changes, let alone human nature. We are, of course, not speaking of those changes of external nature which can be detected and understood only with the help of instruments.

12. Another point to be noted in this connection is that even those exceptional changes or manifestations of external nature that do not generally attract the notice of people always came within the Master's observation, whenever he was in the normal plane of consciousness. The Divine Mother placed at all times before the Master the uncommon manifestations of nature, the exceptions to the general law, as if to impress upon his mind the idea that all kinds of manifestations in the world owed their origin to the will of God — in other words that He was the direct controller of the wheels of the destinies of all things and persons in the world. From such events as the Master came across from his childhood, we get the clear meaning of his words, "The Lord of laws can at will alter them and make new ones instead." It will not be out of place here to mention a few such events.

13. We were charmed to read in our college days a little of the discoveries of modern physics regarding the power of electricity. In our boyish liveliness, one day we raised that topic in the presence of the Master and were speaking various things to one another. Observing the repeated utterance of the word electricity, the Master expressed curiosity like a boy and asked, "Well, what are you talking about? What is the meaning of *'electictic'*?" We could not help laughing at his boyish pronunciation of that English word, which was utterly strange to him. Afterwards we told him of the general laws of electricity. We also told him of the utility of lightning-conductor, that its height should be a little greater than that of the house, inasmuch as the highest point is struck by lightning, and so on. The Master listened attentively to all our words and said, "But I saw a small shed beside a three-

storeyed house, and that wretched power of a lightning, instead of striking the latter, struck the former. What have you got to say to this? Can an all-inclusive and uniform explanation, without an exception, be given for these occurrences, my children? The law exists by the will of the universal Mother and gets reversed again by Her will." We tried to explain to the Master natural laws, but like Mathur Babu, could not find a suitable reply on that occasion. We told the Master that the lightning was attracted towards the three-storeyed house but it struck the shed because its course was suddenly deflected by some unknown cause. We continued to say that, although one or two exceptions were seen, lightning struck the highest points in thousands of other places, and so on. But the Master never accepted the statement that the events of nature took place according to inviolable laws. He said, "Let us take for granted that lightning behaves in thousands of places in the way you say, yet as there are a few exceptions, the law, it is clear, loses its uniformity."

14. There have been, the botanists have recorded, exceptions to the production of white or red flowers in the case of plants that generally produce either of them only. But they are so uncommon that it is no exaggeration to say that ordinarily we never come across such cases. But look at that event of the Master's life — at the very time of the controversy between him and Mathur Babu on the proposition that laws of Nature are not invariable but are changed by the will of God, an instance came to the notice of the Master and was shown to Mathur Babu. We refer to the incident of his showing the branch of a hibiscus plant bearing a red and a white flower on the same twig.

15. It is said the Master saw a stone as living[1]; he saw the coccyx of the human body elongate itself a little and shrink to its natural length afterwards; and he met with gods and ghosts. We heard of all these and of many more events of the Master's life. In imitation of the West we have come to the conclusion that Nature, the creatrix of the world, is insentient and absolutely destitute of the power of intelligence. We, therefore, remain satisfied with calling those exceptional events natural aberrations, and think that we have understood all the laws by which nature is

[1] Asked about it, the author said, "The Master saw a stone jump from one place to another." – Trs.

regulated. But the Master's conviction was different. He was conscious that the whole of external and internal nature was nothing but the sport of the living universal Mother, coming within our experience. He, therefore, looked upon these exceptional events as the productions of Her will in particular instances. It does not need to be stated that, on account of this conviction, the Master's mind had much more peace and bliss than ours, if not anything else. We have mentioned a few such instances of the Master's life before, and will do so later on also.

16. The Master saw all things and persons from the two standpoints mentioned before and then came to a certain conclusion about them. He did not form any opinion like us, who make observations from the ordinary plane of consciousness only. Therefore, when he undertook travels to holy places and paid visits to holy men, he estimated their spiritual values in both these ways. It was by observation from higher planes of consciousness that the Master estimated how much of high spiritual power was concentrated in any particular place of pilgrimage, in other words, how much potentiality a particular holy place had of helping man to ascend to those planes. The Master's mind, destitute of the attachment to sights, tastes, and other objects, and always pure like that of the gods, was a wonderful detector and indicator of those subtle facts. As soon as the Master went to a place of pilgrimage or a temple, his mind ascended to a higher plane of consciousness and revealed to him the divine manifestation present in that place or temple. It was from that high plane of consciousness that the Master saw Kasi golden, and could understand how a Jiva became freed from all bondage at death in Kasi. It was from the same high plane again, that he experienced a special manifestation of divine presence at Vrindavan and had the immediate knowledge of the existence of the subtle presence of Sri Gauranga at Navadwip down till today.

17. Sri Chaitanya was the first, it is said, to experience the manifestation of divine presence at Vrindavan. Before his advent, the holy places of pilgrimage at Vraja were almost forgotten. When he travelled in those places, his mind ascended to higher planes of consciousness and he experienced particular divine manifestations of Sri Krishna in particular places, where, long ago, Bhagavan Sri Krishna had actually sported. The faith that was at first generated by him in respect of these places in the minds

of his disciples like Rupa, Sanatana and others was handed down by them to successive lines of disciples until it came to be accepted by all the inhabitants of India. We could not have at all understood the aforesaid manner of Sri Chaitanya's discovery of Vrindavan and would not have entertained its possibility, had we not seen the power of the Master's mind, of rightly detecting and understanding things and persons from higher planes of consciousness. And in spite of that, how weak has been our faith in those facts? Here are, however, a few examples of this.

18. Hriday, the Master's nephew, belonged to the village of Sihar, not far from Kamarpukur. The Master, we have told the reader before, went there occasionally and spent some time before he returned to Dakshineswar. The Master was there on one occasion when there arose an altercation over some business affairs between Hriday's younger brother Rajaram and another person of the village. From words they gradually came to blows, and Rajaram, happening to find a hookah near at hand, struck him on the head with it. The injured man sued Rajaram for assault. As the event happened in the presence of the Master and as the man knew him to be honest and truthful, he cited him as a witness. The Master, therefore, had to come to Vana-Vishnupur to appear as a witness. Before he came there, he scolded Rajaram very much for being thus blinded by anger and on reaching the place said to him again, "Compound the case anyhow by giving him (the complainant) money; the case will otherwise go against you. I can by no means tell a lie. As soon as I am asked, I shall plainly say what I have seen and known." Rajaram got frightened and set about compounding the case. The Master took that opportunity to go out and see the town of Vana-Vishnupur.

19. At one time that town was very prosperous. This becomes clear from the existence there of big tanks like Lalbandh, Krishnabandh and others, of a great many old temples both ruined and surviving, and of other dilapidated buildings. It had also several features of a good residential town — good broad roads, several crowded bazaars and shops, many good living quarters and a constant flow of people coming in and going out in connection with trade and business.

20. The princes of Vishnupur, once very powerful, were great patrons of religion and learning. The town was formerly famous for the cultivation of music. The princely family became

the followers of the Vaishnava cult, shortly after the passing away of Rupa, Sanatana and the other companions of Sri Chaitanya. The image of Sri Madanamohan, installed at Baghbazar, Calcutta, belonged formerly to the princes of this place. Once upon a time, Gokul Chandra Mitra, it is said, lent a large sum of money to a prince of Vishnupur. When the time for repayment came, Mitra demanded and got in lieu of the money, the image of Madanamohan, which held very great attraction for him. Besides Sri Madanamohan, there was a very ancient image named Mrinmayi installed by the princes. The goddess Mrinmayi, it was said, was a living presence, an 'awakened' deity[1], as they called Her. Once, when the house of the prince fell on evil times, that image was broken by a mad woman. The family, therefore, installed a new image in its stead.

After visiting all other temples, the Master was going to pay his obeisance to Mrinmayi. At one place on his way, he was in ecstasy and saw Mrinmayi's face only. When he went to the temple and saw the newly installed image, he found that it was not similar to the image seen in his ecstasy. He could not at all understand the reason for the disparity. On inquiry, it was afterwards known that the new image was really dissimilar to the old one. While making the new image, the potter had actually formed the face in a different fashion in order to display his skill. The broken head of the old image was carefully kept by a Brahmana in his own house. Shortly after, that devout Brahmana had another image made to bear that head, and installed it in a beautiful spot near the pond, Lalbandh, and began to perform its daily worship and other services.

21. It is good to mention here a few examples of the Master's power of detecting the aims and attitudes of people approaching him. We have already mentioned that the Master loved the revered Swami Brahmananda, as if he were his own son. One day the Swami was standing on the northern side of the long verandah to the east of the Master's room and talking with him on various subjects. He saw a coach drawn by a pair of horses coming towards them from the direction of the gate of the garden. It was a phaeton and a few gentlemen were sitting in it. No sooner had he seen

[1] That is, she was a living deity, holding communication with human beings in various ways and helping them in their difficulties. – Tr.

it, than he could know that it belonged to a well-known rich man of Calcutta. Many people from Calcutta then used to come to see the Master. He was, therefore, not astonished that they had also come for that purpose.

But as soon as the Master's eyes fell on the phaeton, he shrank back with fear, and went in extreme hurry out of their sight into his own room and sat down there. Surprised to see that attitude of the Master, Swami Brahmananda too followed him into the room. Scarcely had the Master seen him when he said, "Go, go. If they want to come here, tell them that I cannot see them now." So charged by the Master, he came out again. In the meantime the new-comers approached him and asked, "Is not a Sadhu living here?" Swami Brahananda said, "You have been misinformed. He never gives any medicine to anyone. You might have heard of Brahmachari Durgananda. He is the person to be met for such purposes. He stays there in the hut at the Panchavati. You will meet him there."

When the new-comers had gone away, the Master said to Swami Brahmananda, "I saw such a great power of Tamas in them that I could not look at them, let alone talk to them. I fled out of fear." We found the Master thus daily understanding from an elevated plane of consciousness the high or low manifestation of power in every place, thing and person. We were compelled to accept his words, finding on repeated inquiry that such qualities, good or bad as the Master perceived, really existed in them. We propose to mention here a few more such examples and then tell the reader what he experienced from the normal plane of consciousness in those places of pilgrimage.

22. The liberal-minded Swami Vivekananda used to feel pain from his childhood at others' misery. He, therefore, always encouraged all his friends and relatives to adopt those ways and means which had benefited himself. Or, if he had been helped by some others, he would ask his benefactors to be similarly benevolent to his friends. This was the Swami's habit with regard to education, religion and all other matters. We get an indication of the above-mentioned fact from his actions. When he reached his youth, he organised meetings and associations in various places for prayer and meditation with his fellow students on fixed days. During his college life, no sooner had he become acquainted with Maharshi Devendranath and the devout Kesav, the leaders of the

Brahmo Samaj, than he took many of his friends to those personages.

Since the Swami had the sacred privilege of meeting the Master and becoming acquainted with his extraordinary detachment, renunciation and love of God, it became, as it were, a religious vow in his life to take his friends and fellow students and introduce them to him. But let no one conclude from this statement that the Swami brought any and every casual acquaintance of his to the Master. He used to take to Dakshineswar only those whom, as the result of a long acquaintance, he knew to be possessed of good character and devotion to religion.

23. The Swami thus took many such friends to the Master. But we were told from time to time, by both the Master and the Swami, that the divine insight of the Master penetrated into their inner nature and arrived at a different estimate of such persons. The Swami said, "When I found that the Master did not bestow that kind of grace on them which he had done on me by accepting me and instructing me in spiritual matters, I used to press him to bestow it also on them too. On account of boyish flippancy I was ready on many occasions to argue with him on this point. I said, 'Why, Sir? God can never be so partial as to bestow His grace on some and not on others. Why should you then not accept them as you have done me? Is it not certain that one can attain spiritual realisation by one's effort also, just as one can become a learned scholar if one puts forth sufficient effort?' The Master replied, 'What can I do, my child? Mother shows me that there is the beastly mental attitude of a bull in them. They cannot realize spirituality in this life. What can I do? And what is it you say? Can anyone become in this life what he wishes to be, by mere will and effort?' But, who lent an ear to the Master's word then? I said, 'What do you say, sir? Can't one become what one wishes to be, if one wills and makes an effort? Surely one can. I cannot believe what you say about it?' At this also the Master said the same thing, 'Whether you believe it or not, Mother shows me that.' I never accepted then what he said. But, as time passed on, more and more did I understand from experience that what the Master said was right and what I had thought was wrong."

24. The Swami said that it was by testing and appraising him thus that he could gradually believe in all the words of the Master. It will not be out of place to narrate here another event,

as told by the Swami, to show that he tested every action and behaviour of the Master. Having heard from the Swami about Pandit Sasadhar Tarkachudamani, the Master went to see him on the day of the Car Festival of 1885. In the course of the conversation he instructed the Pandit thus: "Those persons only who have got power direct from the Mother of the universe can truly become preachers of religion; the grandiloquence of other so-called preachers is in vain." He then asked for a glass of water to drink. We do not know whether the Master was thristy and wanted water, or had some other purpose. For, he told us on another occasion that it was not meritorious for a householder, if a Sadhu or a Sannyasin, a guest or a Fakir, went to his house but returned without taking anything. Therefore, when he went to any house, he asked for something to eat or drink before he returned, even if the householder did not of his own accord offer anything or forgot to do so. Anyway, as soon as the Master asked for water, a person wearing Tilaka, strings of beads and other emblems of religion on his body, respectfully brought a glass of water and gave it to the Master. But when the Master was about to drink it, he could not do so. Another man, who was beside him, saw it and threw away the water in the glass. Filling it with water again, he brought the glass to the Master. The Master drank a little of it and bade good-bye to the Pandit for that day. Everyone thought that something had fallen into the water brought at first, and hence it was that the Master did not drink it.

The Swami said that he was sitting very near the Master then. He, therefore, saw clearly that there was neither a mote nor a bit of straw nor any other kind of dirt in the water; yet the Master had refused to drink it. On pondering over the cause of it, the Swami thought the glass of water was perhaps polluted by 'contactual impurity'. For, he had heard the Master say that it was impossible for his hand to proceed to take any kind of food or drink brought by those in whom worldly-mindedness was viciously prevalent, who dishonestly earned money by cheating, robbery, or doing harm to others in any other way, and who externally assumed the guise of religion as a mere ruse for satisfying their lust and greed. He was also heard to say that he could know the nature of such persons intuitively, and his hand would invariably contract if he took such food in his hand unconsciously.

The Swami said that as soon as that thought arose in his mind, he made a firm resolve to ascertain the truth of that matter, taking advantage of the above-mentioned incident. So though requested by the Master himself to accompany him on his return journey on that occasion, the Swami helped him into the carriage, and expressed his inability to go with him, as an urgent piece of business detained him there. As the Swami was already acquainted with the younger brother of the man with the emblems of religion on his person, he called him to a secluded place when the Master had left and began to put questions to him about the character of his elder brother. Questioned thus, he hesitated at first, but afterwards said, "How can I speak of the bad character of my elder brother?" The Swami said, "I could understand the truth from that. Later on I questioned another person of that household who was acquainted with me, and came to know everything. Thus freed from doubt, I wondered how the Master could know people's minds."

25. If we want to know how, even when dwelling in the normal plane of consciousness, the Master detected the inherent and invisible qualities of all things, good as well as bad, we must first of all have an understanding of his mental constitution which provided him with an unfailing standard by which he could judge all things and arrive at correct conclusions about them. We have given the reader an indication of it in many places of this book. It will, therefore, suffice to make here only a brief mention of it. As the Master's mind was not attached to any worldly object, it could immediately get united with, or separated from, anything he wanted to accept or reject. When he rejected anything thus as undesirable, he would never again cast even a look behind at the object so renounced. Again, the Master's extraordinary steadfastness, wonderful power of discrimination and perfect attention, gave him full control over his mind and kept it steady for any length of time on any object without allowing it for a moment to think of or imagine anything else. As soon as one part of it was ready to accept or reject anything, another part of it asked instantly, "Why are you going to do so?" If it got a reasonable answer to this question, it said, "It is very good. Do it by all means." And the moment that conclusion was reached, the other part of the mind said at once; "Then stick to it firmly; you must never act contrary to it, whether you are eating or relaxing, whether you be in the waking state or be dreaming." All parts of his mind then

accepted that thing unanimously and acted accordingly. Steadfastness stood guard over and carefully scrutinized his mind's behaviour regarding it. So, even if by mistake he ever proceeded to act against the decision, the Master clearly felt as if some one from within had tied down his sense and did not allow him to act that way. We all understand the above-mentioned words when we study the Master's lifelong behaviour towards all things and persons.

26. Observe how the boy Gadhadhar had gone to school for barely a few days when he said at once, "I don't want that 'art' which teaches one 'to bundle rice and plantain'. I won't learn it." Thinking his younger brother was going astray, the Master's elder brother Ramkumar made an attempt to persuade him to acquire learning under his direct supervision in his own Chatushpathi in Calcutta. But he could not change the Master's opinion, formed during his early boyhood, that the education proposed to be imparted had mere bread-winning as its aim. The Master was not unaware that even by opening a Chatushpathi and teaching pupils according to his capacity, his brother could not maintain his family. The Master thought it was far better for his elder brother, though a Pandit of virtuous conduct, to be appointed priest in Rani Rasmani's temple, than earn money by flattering the rich, and this led to his approval of his brother's action.

27. During his Sadhana he felt that whenever he sat for meditation, his joints were getting automatically locked up with rapping sounds, as if some one from within were tightening them up in order to keep him sitting for a long time in the same cross-legged posture. And until the one within unlocked them, the Master could not, even if he tried, turn, move or otherwise use the joints of the hands, legs, neck, waist and other parts of his body at will. Or, he saw a person with a trident in hand, sitting beside him and saying, "If you think of anything except God, I will pierce your chest with this trident." Asked during the time of worship to look upon himself as identified with the Mother of the universe, his mind began to do so; but when, contrary to this identification, he was going to offer china-roses and Vilva leaves at Her lotus feet, some one, as it were, caused his hands to turn and pulled them towards his own head.

28. Again, as soon as he was initiated into Sannyasa, his

mind continued to see the one non-dual Brahman in all beings. After that when he wanted to offer oblations of water to his forefathers (Tarpana), as he was wont to do, his hand became stiff; he could not take the water to be offered in the hollow of his joined palms. That he had taken Sannyasa, renouncing all Vedic rituals, was thus brought home to him by the force working from within.

29. Many such examples can be given to prove that the detachment, discrimination, concentration and steadfastness of mind found in him were natural to him. As these experiences of the Master were exactly what are recorded in the scriptures, it is proved that what is written in the scriptures is true. The revered Swami Vivekananda said, "That is the reason why the Master came this time to play the part of an unlettered person whose only aid was his native spiritual genius. He remained illiterate, because he wanted to demonstrate that the spiritual states recorded in the Vedas and the Vedantas of the Hindus and in the religious books of other people, are all true, and that man can actually realize those states by travelling along the paths indicated therein."

30. By observing the natural bent of the Master's mind, it becomes clear that to attain the Nirvikalpa plane of consciousness and realize the non-dual Being is the ultimate experience in human life. Again, the Master said about the spiritual experience on that plane, "All jackals howl in the same way there." He meant to say that just as all jackals howl in the same way, so, each of those who attained the Nirvikalpa plane, has said the same thing about God, the cause of the universe, as viewed from that plane. About Sri Chaitanya, the incarnation of Love, the Master said, "Just as the external tusks of an elephant are for attacking his enemies and the unseen inner ones are for the purpose of chewing his food, so, in the case of the great Lord, dualism was an outward attitude, and non-dualism an inward one." It is therefore superfluous to say that non-dual knowledge, which is always of a uniform nature, was the standard by which the Master judged everything. To the degree that any ideas, actions or ceremonies helped forward individuals (or societies, which are aggregates of individuals) towards that plane, to that degree did the Master regard those ideas etc., as higher than others.

31. Again, when we study the Master's visions born of his spiritual moods, we find a distinction, namely, some are exclusively his private experiences while some were perceivable by others

also. The subjective experiences, confined within himself, were constituted of his own thoughts, solidified and embodied, so to speak, by steadfast and constant practice, and manifested to him in those forms, and these were perceivable only to him. Some others were seen by him, as he passed through higher and higher planes, until he was on the verge of the Nirvikalpa plane, or when he was abiding in Bhavamukha. The contents of such visions, although unknown to others at that time, were for him quite objectively existent, and he would foretell about their happening now or in some future time, and all actually found them coming true as facts and events. In order to realize that the former class of visions were true, one had to be endowed like him with faith, reverence, steadfastness and other virtues; or, had to ascend to that plane in which the Master had those visions. But in order to realize the latter class as true, one required no faith, no Sadhana — one had only to believe them as the results compelled one to do so.

32. From what we have said before and now about the nature of the Master's mind, one can understand that such a mind could not remain idle even in the normal state of consciousness. For, it could not feel satisfied till it had studied the nature and behaviour of those things and persons it came in contact with and arrived at reliable conclusions about them. In his boyhood he discerned that scholars studied the scriptures for the purpose of earning money, which led him to refrain from learning the art that taught him "the bundling of rice and plantain", as he derisively called it. As he advanced in age, his mind came in contact with various people in various places, and arrived at various conclusions about them. Those conclusions will be the subject of our discussion now.

33. It is superfluous to say that the ill-will between the Saktas and the Vaishnavas of Bengal, which came into existence at the time of the passing away of Sri Chaitanya, continued unabated. Although a few rare Sadhakas like Ramprasad and others realized, with the help of their Sadhana, the oneness of Kali and Krishna and preached that the ill-will was wrong and uncalled-for, it is clear from the censorious gloating, which accompanied the mutual condemnation of the deities on both sides, that the generality of the people instead of paying heed to the words of wisdom, have allowed themselves to be carried away by hatred. It is needless

to say that the Master was acquainted with that fact from his childhood. Again, applying himself to the disciplines prescribed in the scriptures of both the sects and attaining perfection in both, he realized both the paths to be equally true. He then clearly understood that the cause of the mutual hatred between the Saktas and the Vaishnavas was the vanity and egotism born of lack of spirituality.

34. The Master's father, a worshipper of Sri Ramachandra, providentially got the stone emblem called Raghuvir and installed it in his house. Although the Master was thus born in a Vaishnava family, it was evident that from childhood he had equal love towards both Siva and Vishnu. His neighbours say even now that he dressed himself as Siva at one time during his childhood, and remained in ecstasy for a few hours in that mood, and they show the particular spot where that event took place as proof of this fact. Another event may be mentioned here. At one time the Master had every one of his household initiated in the Mantras of both Vishnu and Sakti. The Master, we infer, acted in this manner only to remove that hatred from their minds.

35. It is now well known that Asoka the Great, the "man of Dharma", made up his mind to spread religion and learning for the good of humanity. He established hospitals for men and animals in various places of India for the treatment of their physical ailments and made medicinal plants, creepers, and herbs easily available to the public, by having them cultivated and collected. Moreover, through Buddhist monks, he sent medicines and medicinal herbs to foreign countries and made them available there. It is perhaps from that time that Sadhus began to collect and preserve medicines. Again, that custom became more prevalent during the Tantric age. Seeing the spiritual degradation of Sadhus on account of that custom, the authors of the Smritis in the following age raised a great objection against it. But that custom has not died even now in the conservative India. During his stay at Dakshineswar and travels to holy places, the Master saw many monks falling a prey to worldliness by developing attraction for such alien interests. Thus the Master was convinced of the lack of spirituality amongst the monks too. For, he said to us time and again, "Never believe Sadhus who prescribe and administer medicine, who practise exorcism, who receive money, and who adorn their bodies with the outward marks of religion

such as Tilakas, put on only wooden sandals, etc. Much of this is done only rather excessively to pose themselves as big Sadhus. The marks serve them as their signboard."

36. Let no one think from what has been said that, seeing the hypocritical and fallen monks, the Master, like some of the westernised people, wanted monastic communities to be abolished. For, we heard the Master say on this subject from time to time, "Even an ordinary monk in religious garb living on alms (Bhiksha) must be regarded as higher in comparision with a good householder; for though he does not practise Yoga or other religious exercises, if he possesses a good character and lives his whole life on Bhiksha, he has in this life gone much farther ahead on the path of renunciation than an ordinary householder." The aforesaid words of the Master are amongst the many instances illustrating the fact that to him renunciation of everything for the sake of God was the measure of a man's conduct and character.

37. We have already given many examples of the fact that austere and devoted Sadhus, irrespective of their community, whether they followed the path of devotion or knowledge, were much honoured by the Master. The lamp of the Sanatana Dharma, the eternal religion of India, has been kept burning by the realizations of these great souls. It is those among them who have realized God and freed themselves from the bondage of Maya, that have demonstrated and thereby maintained the authority of the Vedas and other scriptures as the repository of spiritual truths. All philosophers of this country including rationalists like the Vaiseshikas, have unanimously said that the Vedas are revealed only to the Aptas (those who have attained the truth). It was, therefore, no wonder that the Master, possessed of a profound inner vision, could know that fact and honoured them accordingly.

38. Although the Master viewed the sincere and austere Sadhus with very great favour and respect and always enjoyed their company greatly, he invariably found in them lack of one thing, which pained him much on several occasions. He saw that they could not mix alike with all communities with equal love, though it was so easy for him to do so. He noticed this narrowness even amongst the advanced aspirants, the Sannyasins treading the path of non-duality, not to speak of those travelling on the path of devotion. Even long before attaining the liberal sameness of the non-dual plane, they learn uniformly to scorn at people going

on all other paths as inferior in spiritual fitness, or, at best, to view them with condescension. The liberal-minded Master, it is needless to say, was much grieved to see that kind of mutual intolerance among people going forward to the same goal, and he clearly saw that the said illiberality or exclusiveness was produced by the lack of true spirituality.

39. When he was staying at the Kali temple at Dakshineswar, the Master got daily proof of this exclusiveness and lack of spirituality among both classes of men, householders and monks. When he travelled to holy places and temples, he found that these evils were not less, but in fact more virulent, there. The quarrel amongst the Brahmanas when they received gifts from Mathur; the Tantric Sadhakas' improper conduct at Kasi due to excessive drinking after performing the divine Mother's nominal worship, to witness which they had invited the Master; the strenuous exertion for name and fame of the Dandies (the Swamis carrying staves as their insignia); and at Vrindavan the Vaishnava Babas' lives, spent in the company of women under the pretext of practising Sadhana — all these and many more were the facts that revealed themselves in their true colours to the keen insight of the Master and helped him in understanding the actual state of the society and the country. A mere observation of these events could not, of course, have helped him very much in this respect, had he not in himself the realization of the very profound non-dual Truth. As he had already realized that Truth, the idea of the ultimate aim of individual and social life was firmly fixed in the Master's mind. It was, therefore, easy for him to sound and understand all things by testing them by that realization. And this study and experience of the daily events of individual and social life during his stay in the normal plane of consciousness helped him in ascertaining the value of all things affecting the life of man. He could with certainty ascertain thereby the goal to which true progress, civilization, morality, education, love of God, steadfast adherence to customs, Yoga, Karma and other impelling forces were taking man or would lead him, when they reached their fully developed state. Consider, how could he have understood about the progress made by a Sadhu if he had not the knowledge of what constituted true holiness? How could the very truthful Master exhort people so unequivocally to go on pilgrimages and worship the images there, if he had not known without doubt that spirituality

had been consolidated, so to say and deposited in holy places and in the images of Deities? Or, how could he understand that intolerance characteristic of all the various religions was wrong, if he had not known the direction they were taking and the goal they would ultimately lead to? Our daily experience brings us across a plethora of sects, sadhus, pilgrimages, images of deities etc., and the echoes of the tumultuous discussions of the claims of various religions and of the meanings of scriptural passages reach our ears. In the midst of these conflicting experiences we sometimes think one doctrine to be right and sometimes another, tempted by our delight in wrangles and intellectual gymnastics. Again, trying to ascertain the goal of humanity by the study and observance of the daily events of the work-a-day world, we sometimes take one thing to be the goal, sometimes another, and failing to arrive at any definite conclusion, go on oscillating and vacillating and, as it happens not unoften, turn atheists ultimately and regard worldly enjoyments as the real goal of life. What help of any consequence do we derive from this kind of experience of ours, from such ever-changing and never-abiding conclusions of ours? It is certain that without the help of great souls or world teachers, our crude minds can never understand even in a hundred lives what the Master could detect and understand straightway by virtue of the aforesaid wonderful constitution and nature of his mind. We infer from every action and behaviour of the Master what a gulf of difference there is between his mind and ours, though as minds they may appear to be similar. Devotional scriptures, therefore, have pointed out that the mind of an Incarnation of God is made of an altogether different material of pure Sattva-guna (stuff of luminosity and knowledge) untouched by Rajas and Tamas.

40. Observing thus from both the divine and the ordinary planes of consciousness, the Master came to have an intimate understanding of the present lack of spirituality in the country and the prevailing intolerance among religions from the contacts he had with people at Dakshineswar and during his visits to holy places. He dived deeper and found out that although all religious doctrines were equally true and although they help men of various natures to reach ultimately the same goal through various paths, the previous teachers were either ignorant of this truth of the unity of all religions in respect of their goal, or they intentionally re-

frained from preaching it, considering the place, time and persons to be unsuitable for such teaching. Moreover, it dawned on him that this attitude of his, free from the slightest touch of exclusiveness or hatred, was an entirely novel thing in the world. It originated with him and he was to give it to the world.

41. Many of us have now come to understand that this most liberal doctrine, namely, "All faiths are true; as many faiths, so many paths", which has charmed the world, first emanated from the Master's mouth. Some may raise an objection and say that at least a partial manifestation of that liberal principle was seen in some of the Rishis and religious teachers of the past. But when one looks a little below the surface, it becomes clear to one that those teachers culled certain portions of each of those faiths with the help of their intelligence and then made an amalgam of what they regarded essential in them. Unlike other teachers of the past, the Master excluded nothing from any faith. He practised with equal enthusiasm all of them in his own life, reached the goal as indicated by those faiths, and realized that profound truth. It is, however, not our intention here to discuss this subject in detail. The only point that we want to tell the reader here is that we get the proof of the existence in the Master's life of this liberal principle from his childhood. But, until he returned from his visits to holy places, the Master was not able to understand with certainty that it was he alone who had experienced that liberalism in the spiritual world and that, although the past seers, teachers and incarnations of God preached in society how to reach the goal through particular paths, none of them, up till then, had preached that the same goal could be reached through all the different paths. Although, at the time of his Sadhana, he made a whole-hearted offering of all his desires at the lotus feet of the Divine Mother and resolved to dwell for ever in the plane of non-dual consciousness without ever returning to the realm of Maya, the Divine Mother did not allow this to take place. Through inscrutable ways She kept up his body from destruction during the days he was oblivious of it. The Master knew that it was ordained so for the one purpose — the purpose of removing intolerence and exclusiveness from the world as far as possible. He knew moreover, that the world too was thirsting for this extremely beneficial truth. We shall make here an attempt to tell the reader how we arrived at the aforesaid conclusion.

42. That true religion consisted in practice, not in words, was the belief of the Master from his childhood. Again, he was feeling from time to time during his Sadhana, and very often after he had realized perfection, that the powers earned by long practice could be actually imparted to others or passed on to them. We have already indicated this conviction of his here and there in many places (cf.III.6,7). On many occasions in his life till then, the Master also got the proof that the Divine Mother, by Her grace, had accumulated that power abundantly in him. She had used that power as the instrument with which to bestow Her grace on particular persons like Mathur and others. Consequently till now the Master's conviction in respect of this power of his was that it was limited to the bestowal of the Mother's grace on a few blessed individuals, making his body and mind the instrument for the same. He could not understand how or when She would bestow that grace of Hers, nor did the Master's mind, unhesitatingly dependent as it was on Her like that of a child on its mother, make any effort to understand it. But never had the worldwide implication of his spiritual power — the idea of spreading the spiritual message all over the country and flooding the world with a tidal wave of spirituality — ever occured to his mind even in dream till then. Now, however, he began to feel in his heart of hearts that the Divine Mother had already started Her divine sport in this respect through his body and mind. Though he had a feeling like that, he had no idea as to the means by which it was to be achieved, what the Divine Mother would make him do, or where She would take him for its achievement. He was, however, for ever the child of the Divine Mother, and he knew only this: "The Mother is mine, I am the Mother's." No desire whatever, except the Mother's, arose in his mind. Only one desire could probably be called his own — it was the desire to know the Mother in various forms and through various paths. But the Mother Herself had made it very clear to him earlier that it was She who had raised that desire in his mind. Therefore when this new experience regarding a spiritual mission occured to his mind, the child of the Divine Mother that he was, he looked to Her alone for guidance in an attitude of absolute dependence, and the Mother continued to play with him as before.

43. From his desire to spend the rest of his life at Vrindavan in the absorption of divine love in the holy company of Gangamata,

we can clearly understand that though vague ideas of a spiritual mission were dawning on his mind, he had not the least intention even then to assume the position of a spiritual teacher like the common run of Gurus and prophets, who take up such roles under the influence of egotism. We cannot grasp or understand even a fraction of the Master's lifelong attitude: "Mother does Her own work. Who am I to work for the world and teach humanity?" But it was this very attitude that made him the wonderful instrument of the Divine Mother's work. It was this very attitude that made it possible for him to remain in Bhavamukha incessantly. It was this very attitude that led to the wonderful manifestation of the Guru-mood in his mind — or rather made him the very embodiment of that mood. So long, the Master used to lose himself when that Power welled up in him, and he could detect and understand what happened through the instrumentality of his body and mind, only after the work had been accomplished. But now his body and mind got accustomed to contain and manifest that Power without a break, in an easy and natural manner, and he was always established, in spite of himself, in the position of the true spiritual teacher. Before that time the normal state of the Master's mind was that of a humble aspirant or of a child; he then remained much longer in that mood and the manifestations of the Power as the Guru in him were few and far between. But now it was just the opposite; he remained much longer in the mood of the Guru and the manifestations of the humble attitude of an aspirant or of a child was correspondingly brief.

44. It was absolutely impossible for the mind of the Master to assume the position of the spiritual teacher under the influence of egoism. Time and again we got the proof of it in the boyish "quarrels" of the Master in Bhavamukha with the Divine Mother. Attracted by the manifestations of spirituality in the Master, big crowds gathered at Dakshineswar, like swarms of bees attracted by the perfume of a full-blown hundred-petalled lotus. In those times when we went to see the Master one day, we found him speaking with the Divine Mother from the state of Bhavamukha. He said, "What art Thou doing? Shouldst Thou bring crowds of people like that? I find no time to bathe and have my meal." That was in the very early stage of his fatal disease, and the Master was then suffering from the pain in his throat. So he said, referring to the condition of his body, "It is nothing but a broken drum.

If it is played on so much, it will get perforated any day. What wilt Thou do then?"

45. On another occasion we were sitting beside him at Dakshineswar. It was the month of October of the year 1884. The news of the illness of Pratap Hazra's mother had come, and the Master had persuaded him to go home to serve his mother. We were present on that occasion also. News came that day that Pratap had gone to Vaidyanath instead of going home. The Master felt a little annoyed at that news. After we had had a short talk on this and that, he asked us to sing a song and was in ecstasy a little afterwards. On this occasion also the Master in that ecstatic mood began to quarrel with the Mother of the Universe like a little boy. He said, "Why dost Thou bring such worthless and wayward people here? (After a little silence) I cannot do so much. Let there be at the most one-fourth or so of a seer of water to one seer of milk; but now it is not so; there are five seers of water to one seer of milk; my eyes are burning with smoke as I continue pushing the fuel into the fire. If Thou likest, deal with them personally; I cannot do so much pushing of fuel into the fire. Don't bring such people any more." Overwhelmed with awe and astonishment, we sat still, thinking as to whom the Master was referring in his talk with the Divine Mother, and how unfortunate the person was. Such quarrels arose daily between the Mother and the Master, which showed that the Master asked the Mother every day to take back from him the position of the teacher, which he regarded as totally worthless, though others yearn for it, on account of the attendant honours.

46. Thus did the universal Mother, the Divine Will, in Her inscrutable play, make the Master have extraordinary and unprecedented experiences throughout his life. She created in him such an abundance of highly liberal spiritual ideas as She had never done before in any other great teacher. Along with this fact, She showed him how much spiritual power She had accumulated in him, and how as a blessing to humanity, She had made of him a wonderful instrument for imparting that power to others. The Master was amazed to see an utter lack of spirituality in the world outside, and through the Mother's grace an accumulation of extraordinary spiritual power within himself for the removal of that want. He could not fail to understand that in this age, the Mother had once more taken to the battlefield for killing the

indomitable Raktabija, the demon of delusion produced by ignorance, so that the people in the world might again be blessed to witness that play of compassion welling up from Her, and in joy and gratitude sing hallelujah to Her, the arbiter of the destinies of innumerable universes, and the possessor of infinite auspicious qualities. Just as an excess of heat generates clouds, waning is followed by waxing, and prosperity comes on the trail of adversity, so, the long-accumulated and heart-felt want of countless people is followed by the incarnation of the Divine Mother's infinite compassion in the person of the Guru, living and moving with men. The Mother of the universe made this clear to the Master out of Her grace. She showed him again that such sport of Hers had been previously played with the Master many a time in many an age, and would be played many a time over again in future. He was to have no liberation as ordinary people have. He was, "an executive officer who would have to rush to bring order wherever there was breach of peace in the vast empire of the Divine Mother." From the words of the Master, it is clear that he realized all this at this time and not before it.

47. Ever since he understood the fact that, for the good of humanity, the divine Mother Herself had, out of Her grace, produced in his mind the liberal faith, 'as many faiths so many paths', the discerning mind of the Master applied itself to making inquiries about another matter. His mind then became anxious to know who the blessed persons were that would accept this new liberal doctrine direct from the Mother, who had chosen to dwell in him, and mould their own lives accordingly, and who, receiving power from Her, be singled out to be Her playmates in this novel sport of propagating this doctrine in this modern age so as to bring bliss to the many. In an earlier chapter on the loving relationship of the Master with Mathuranath, reference has already been made to the Master's pre-vision of these future devotees in his ecstatic states (cf.III.7.33). On account of the inscrutable play of the Universal Mother, their faces, seen before, now assumed bright living forms in the Master's mind, which hitherto was attached to nothing in the world. That extraordinary Sannyasin's mind now spent the days, as he told us many a time afterwards, in variously pondering over such matters as how many they might be, when the Mother would bring them there, which of them would perform what special work of the Mother. whether the Mother

would make them renounce the world like him or keep them as house-holders, whether at least one of the new-comers could have a complete and proper understanding of that play of the Divine Mother, or whether they would have only a partial understanding of it during their life time. For, till now there have been but few who have had even a little understanding of this extraordinary play of Hers. He said, "I then felt an indescribable yearning to see you all. The soul was being wrung like a piece of wet towel, so to say, and I felt restless with pain. I felt like weeping. But I could not do so, lest that should create a scene; I controlled myself somehow. But when the day came to an end and night approached and Aratrika music began in the Mother's and Vishnu's temples, I could no longer control myself, thinking, 'One more day has passed away and they have not come.' I then got up on the roof of the 'mansion', and cried out, calling you loudly, 'O my children! Where are you? Come.' I felt I might go mad. Then, after long waiting, you at last started coming, one by one. Only then I felt consoled. And as I had seen you all earlier, I could recognize you as you came, one after another. When Purna (literally complete) came, Mother said, 'With this the coming of those of whom you have had vision is complete. No one else of this class will come in future.' Mother showed you all to me and said, 'All these are your devotees of the inner circle.' Wonderful is the vision and wonderful its fulfilment! " Lo! who can fathom the profound depth of these words! We have quoted the Master's own words to show that these are not the inventions of any of us.

48. While he was thus gathering together the persons fit to realize and accept his own liberal doctrine, the Master had another conviction of which he personally told us now and again. He said, "All those who are living their final lives in the world will come here, and all those who have, even once, truly called on God cannot but come here." The statement evoked different lines of thought among those who heard it. It is, however, difficult to say what they were. Some came to the conclusion that it was absolutely unreasonable. Some thought it was only incoherent talk, an aberration of his faith and devotion. Some again found in it the proof of his egoism or of the derangement of his brain. Others thought that though they could not understand it, it must be true inasmuch as the Master had said so and regarded reasoning and argumentation about it as harmful to their faith. They would

not thus set their critical spirit to work. Others again thought they could understand it only if the Master ever made it clear to them; they therefore, would neither firmly believe nor disbelieve it and remained unmoved on hearing anyone speaking either for or against it. But it will not be difficult to understand the meaning of these words of the Master, if the reader has grasped what we have been at pains to clarify, namely, that the Divine Mother made the Master realize Her own liberal doctrine and established him in the position of a teacher without any artificial pose or pretension born of egoism. That is not all. If the reader looks a little below the surface, he will realize that these very words are the proof that the Master attained that high spiritual state in an easy and natural way.

49. When the Master, the child of the Divine Mother, looked at himself, it never for a moment occurred to him, completely devoted as he was to Her, that the accumulation of that extraordinary spiritual power and the ability to impart it were in any way the results of his own effort. In them he saw with astonishment nothing but the sport of the universal Mother, playing in Her own inscrutable way. Ah! what a wonderful sport has the Mother — the expert in making the impossible possible — arranged, in assuming the body-mind combination of that unlettered personality, our great Master! Ah, Her present play has surpassed a hundred, nay, a thousand times Her previous sports — making the dumb eloquent and the lame nimble enough to cross the mountain! It has charmed the world and led them to sing Her glory! By this play of the Mother, the Vedas, the Bible, the Puranas, the Koran and all other religious scriptures have been proved to be true; religion has been established, and the crying need of the world, which no one else could satisfy in the past ages, has once for all been satisfied! Bravo, Mother, Bravo! O Sportive Power of Brahman! There arose such thoughts in the Master's mind on account of that vision. The Master's mind took that vision to be absolutely true on account of his absolute faith in the Mother's words, in Her infinite grace and inscrutable power. He put questions to Her as to what the scope of that play was, who would assist in it, and in what kinds of hearts the seed of that power would be sown, and in answer to these questions he got the vision of the devotees of the inner circle and also the conviction, that those who were living their last lives and those who had called on God sincerely

even once in order to realize Him, were the persons fit to accept that extraordinary, liberal, and novel doctrine revealed through him. That conclusion, it is clear, dawned on his mind as the result of his absolute dependence on the Mother of the universe. The boy depending entirely on the Mother could not arrive at any other conclusion than that; and because of this, he ever remained absolutely untouched by egoism.

50. In the sentences, "Those who are living their final lives shall come here", and "Those who have even once called sincerely on God cannot but come here", if the word "here" is taken to mean "to the Mother's novel, liberal doctrine", it will not look unreasonable to any one and nobody will have any objection to it. But as soon as this meaning is accepted, another question is bound to crop up. Will they of themselves arrive at and accept the Divine Mother's liberal doctrine of "As many faiths, so many paths", or will it require the help of him through whose instrumentality She promulgated for the first time that doctrine in the world? The answer to this question, according to our understanding, should be determined only after observing the result of the full realization of this doctrine in the heart of the questioner or anybody else. Until that realization comes, silence is the best answer. But if the reader asks what our conclusion is, we would say that simultaneously with the right realization of that doctrine, you will also have the vision of him whom the Divine Mother has, for the first time, brought to the world as the embodiment of that doctrine, and you will of your own accord pour your heart-felt love and reverence to his Holy Presence, which is "free from pride and delusion". The Master does not demand this of you, nor does any one else. You will of your own accord offer it, out of love for the Mother. It is needless to say anything more on this subject.

51. The authors of the Tantras have said again and again that when the mood of the Guru becomes normal and natural in any person, or in other words, his personality assumes a concentrated form of it by the will of the Divine Mother, his actions, deportment, behaviour and selfless compassion for others take wonderful forms beyond the grasp of the human intelligence. Such a manifestation of it is described in the Tantras as the divine state. These scriptures also teach that the ways of instruction, initiation and other forms of spiritual ministration followed by such exalted persons are unimaginably strange, as they are not

limited by scriptural prescriptions. They can, out of compassion, awaken the power of spirituality in any one and put him instantly in ecstasy at their mere will or by touch. Or partially awakening that power in him, they can so ordain that it is completely kindled sometime later in this life itself, resulting in the realization of true spirituality. The Tantras say that in a slightly intensified state of the spiritual mood, the teacher is able to impart Sakti initiation to the disciple, and in its highly intensified state, the Sambhavi initiation. Ordinary teachers are enjoined by the Tantras to impart Māntri or Mānavi initiation. As regards Sakti and Sambhavi initiation, the *Rudrayamala*, the *Shadanwaya Maharatna*, the *Vayaviya Samhita*, and the *Sarada*, the *Viswasara* and other Tantras have all said the same thing. We quote here the verse from the *Vayaviya Samhita*:

'Saambhavi chaiva Sakti cha Maantri chaiva Sivagame
Dikshopadisyate tredha Sivena paramaatmana
Guroralokamaatrena sparsat sambhaashanadapi
Sadyah samjnya bhavejjantor diksha sa Saambhavi mata
Sakti jnanavati diksha shishyadeham pravisyati
Guruna jnanamargena kriyate jnanachakshusha
Maantri kriyavati diksha kumbhamandalapurvika'.

52. That is, Siva, the supreme Self, has taught in the Agama scripture three kinds of initiation, namely, the Sambhavi, the Sakti and Mantri. The Sambhavi initiation produces knowledge in the Jiva as soon as he sees, touches and salutes the Guru. In the Sakti initiation the Guru, with the help of this divine knowledge, makes his own power enter the disciple and awakens spirituality in his heart. The Mantri initiation consists of uttering the Mantra into the ear of the disciple after drawing a diagram, installing a jar, and performing the worship of the deity.

The *Rudrayamala* says that the Sakti and Sambhavi initiations produce immediate liberation:

Siddhai swasaktimalokya tayaa kevalayaa sisoh
Nirupayam krita diksha Saakteyi parikirtita
Abhisandhim vinaachaarya sishyayorubhayorapi
Deshikanugrahenaiva Sivata vyaktikaarini

That is, the generating of the divine knowledge in the disciple by perfected souls with the help of their spiritual power alone, without adopting any external means, is called the Sakti initiation. In the Sambhavi initiation there exists no previous desire in the mind either of the teacher or of the disciple to impart initiation or receive it. As soon as they see each other, the teacher suddenly has compassion roused in his heart and he feels a desire to bestow his grace on the disciple. And that alone produces the knowledge of the non-dual Reality in the disciple, who thereby accepts discipleship.

53. The Tantra, *Purascharanollasa*, says that, in that kind of initiation, there is no need of discrimination between the proper and improper times prescribed by the Sastras.

> Dikshayam chanchaalapaangi na kalaniyamah kvachit
> Sadgurordarsanaadeva suryaparve cha sarvada.
> Sishyamaahuya guruna kripayaa yadi diyate
> Tatra lagnaadikam kinchit na vicharyam kadaachana.

That is, O Parvati of restless eyes, there is no need to discriminate between proper and improper time for being initiated by Gurus endowed with the heroic and the divine mood. If any one has the privilege of meeting the Guru possessing the knowledge of Brahman, and the Guru mercifully invites him to be initiated, he should receive it without paying any heed to auspicious or inauspicious moments.

54. The Sastras have thus averred that such informality of procedure prevails even in the case of ordinary spiritual teachers endowed with the divine mood. How then can anyone prescribe the method of teaching others and imparting spirituality for the divine Master, who was in all respects an instrument in the hands of the universal Mother for that purpose? For, it was not that ordinary play of the divine mood spoken of in the Tantras, that the universal Mother, residing in the Master's body and mind, was then playing out of Her grace. Besides, it was not merely for the good of any individual disciple but for the good of all humanity that She was then manifesting through him this great liberal doctrine, "As many faiths, so many paths", which had not been practised or realized so far by any spiritual teacher possessed of the divine mood. Therefore we say that henceforward a new chapter opened in the Master's life.

55. The reader devoted to the Master will look askance at us perhaps on hearing these words of ours and say, "How un-

reasonable! If you regard the Master as an incarnation of God, you contradict yourself if you in any way imply by your theory elaborated above that this power of the world-teacher was absent in him at any time." In reply we say: "Brother, we say so on the very evidence of the Master's words. When they assume human bodies, even incarnations of God do not have all kinds of divine moods or powers always manifested in them. Whenever any mood or power becomes necessary, it comes. When the Master's body was reduced to a mere skeleton on account of the long struggle with the disease at Kasipur garden, the Master noticed his mental attitude and the manifestation of power in him and said to us: "What the Mother shows to me is that such a power has come into this (i.e. his body) that I need not even touch people any more. It is sufficient if she asks me to touch anyone, and that one will get awakened even by the touch.' If the Mother brings this (his body) round this time, so many people will come that you will not be able to push back the crowds from the door. It might even be so straining for you that you will have to take medicine to cure the pain in your bodies caused by the exertion." From these words, spoken by the Master himself, it is clear that he was then feeling within himself the manifestation of a power which he had never felt before. Many such examples of this may be given.

56. The Master's anxiety to meet his chosen ones could not be relieved by only calling for them in the aforesaid manner under the impulse of the divine mood. But the Divine Mother spoke to him in his heart of hearts, assuring him that almost all his devotees would know of his stay at Dakshineswar, if that news reached a certain place, namely the garden of Belgharia, and She took him there and introduced him to Sri Kesav Chandra Sen. Shortly after this event, the devotees Vivekananda, Brahmananda and others, who had been seen by the Master in ecstasy before, and who were especially fit to be blessed by his grace, began to come one after another. If the Master makes us tell the reader the story of his play with them in the divine mood, we shall do so on some other occasion. We shall now place before the reader, as an example to illustrate that phase of his life, a picture of the manner in which, under the influence of that extraordinary divine mood, he spent a few days with his devotees during the Car Festival in the year 1885, and bring to a close this part of the book.

CHAPTER V

SRI RAMAKRISHNA IN THE COMPANY OF DEVOTEES FOR NINE DAYS: THE NAVAYATRA IN A.D. 1885

[TOPICS: 1. The harmony of the divine and human natures in the Master. 2. Vijaykrishna Goswami's vision. 3. The devotees' reaction to the Master's extraordinary behaviour. 4. Swami Premananda and Samadhi. 5. Why the Master felt anxious for the devotees? 6. Narendra's query on this subject. 7. The Master honoured all worthy persons. 8. The Master's extreme steps to overcome egoism. 9. Examples of it. 10. Worldly people's contrary behaviour. 11. Religious movements. 12. Pandit Sasadhar in Calcutta. 13. The Master's desire to see Sasadhar. 14. His desires always fulfilled. 15. The Navayatra of 1885. 16. About Isan Babu. 17. Swami Yogananda's conservatism. 18. The Chariot festival at Balaram Babu's house. 19. The women devotees' devotion to the Master. 20. A woman devotee follows the Master in a state of absorption. 21. More examples of the Master's indrawnness. 22. The Master's invitation to a woman devotee to Dakshineswar. 23. "Be like a cast-off leaf before the wind." 24. The Master at Dakshineswar in Bhavasamadhi. 25. The vision of the Coiled Power and his talk in ecstasy. 26. The Master's care in feeding. 27. The Master's boyishness. 28. Pandit Sasadhar's visit. 29. The Master's description of it. 30. The Master's life helpful to have faith in the other incarnations.]

He soon becomes righteous and attains eternal peace. Proclaim, O son of Kunti, that my devotee is never destroyed.

—Gita IX 31.

If one wants to understand a little of the wonderful character of Sri Ramakrishna established in Bhavamukha, one should see him in the company of his devotees. One will get a little insight into the mystery of that divine play, if one closely observes and understands how and in what different moods he used daily to behave in his ordinary dealings of life like standing, sitting, joking, talking etc., as also in experiencing ecstasy in the company of his devotees of various nature. We shall present the reader here with the story of one such play of the Master for a few days with the devotees.

1. Even very trifling acts and efforts of this extraordinary soul were not, so far as we know, aimless or useless. It is extremely rare to find such an extraordinary harmony of divine and human natures in any one else. At least we, on our part, have not met another, during our travel in many parts of the world for the last twenty-five years. "One does not understand the value of teeth as long as they are there," runs a Bengali proverb. It has exactly been so with many of us with regard to the Master. When the devotees had brought him for the treatment of his throat-disease to Shyampukur in Calcutta for sometime, one day Sri Vijaykrishna Goswami came to see him and spoke to us to the following effect:

2. While meditating in his own room within closed doors during his stay at Dacca a few days back, Vijay had had the vision of Sri Ramakrishna, and in order to know whether it was a fancy of his brain, he tested it by continually pressing for a long time with his own hands the body and the limbs of the form that was before him. He mentioned this fact openly to the Master and to us that day. "I have travelled," said Sri Vijay, "in various parts of the country, on hills and mountains, and seen many great and holy souls, but never have I met such a one (showing the Master) anywhere else. I have seen somewhere two annas, somewhere one anna, somewhere one pie and somewhere half a pie of the power that I see fully manifested here. I have not seen even four annas anywhere." "What does he say?" said the Master to us smiling. "The other day," said Vijay to the Master, "I saw you at Dacca in such a way that I'll not believe you if you say 'no'. It is only because you are so easily available that you have created so much confusion. Dakshineswar is very near to Calcutta; we can come and pay a visit to you whenever we like. There is also no trouble in coming here — there are enough boats and carriages. We are unable to understand you only because you are thus so easily available near home. If you had been sitting on the peak of a mountain and one had to meet you after walking a long distance without food and climbing high altitudes with the roots of trees for one's support, one would probably have understood your worth. But now, because such a uniquely divine personage exists near home, we think that greater ones are there in far off remote places. That is why we run hither and thither, prepared to experience endless troubles."

3. It is truly so. The compassionate Master received as his

own almost all those who came to him and did not part company with them even if they tried to do so. He endowed them with eternal peace by erasing, now by drastic methods, now with a gentle smile, the impressions accumulated by them in their past lives and by casting them anew into new forms after the unique and attractive pattern set by him. There will remain no doubt about it, if devotees tell plainly the stories of their own lives. Overwhelmed with worldly sufferings and out of wounded feelings — because, though he had taken refuge in the divine Lord so long ago, he had not realized Him, and the Master also had not done anything for him in this respect — Narendranath once made himself ready secretly to renounce and wander away into the broad world. On coming to know of this, the Master did not allow him to do so. Knowing his intention through his divine power, he persuaded him to come to Dakshineswar to stay with him that day. Touching his person afterwards, he sang in a spiritual mood, "I am afraid to speak and also not to speak; I am afraid, lest I should lose you, O Rai." And instead of allowing him to renounce the world and go away, he kept him with him consoling him in various ways. To mention another instance, although he had the aim of his life fulfilled by the Master's accepting his "power of attorney", Girish Chandra Ghosh retained the force of his past impressions and was unable to shake off his fear and anxiety on that account. Then we see again the Master granting him freedom from fear with these words. "Is it a water-snake, O stupid one, that has caught you? You have been caught by a venomous snake — you have to die, even if you flee into your hole. Have you not noticed that, caught by water-snakes, frogs croak a thousand times before they die. Some of them are, however, able to free themselves and flee. But when caught by cobras and black-snakes, they have not to croak more than three times, the struggle being over by that time. If, however, a rare one flees by chance, it dies even after it has re-entered its hole. Know the same is the case here." But who then understood the meaning and the purpose of those words and actions of the Master? Every one thought, perhaps, that persons like him existed everywhere. Because the Master was humouring everybody's whim and was going about, unasked, from door to door with his free gift of boons and freedom from fear in his hands, so, everybody thought that there were persons in plenty of this nature to be met with everywhere. Sheltered by the compassionate Master's affectionate wing, how strong the devotees felt, how insistent they were on the satisfaction of their childish whims, and how easily they felt wounded! Almost all felt that the practice of religion was a very easy thing. They were quite certain that they could realize any mood or vision in the spiritual realm at any time they liked. There was nothing more necessary than to ask the Master persistently for it with a little eagerness — the Master would easily make them attain it immediately by his touch or words or will only!

4. Baburam, afterwards known as Swami Premananda, had the desire to have ecstasy. He went to the Master and pressed him for it, weeping, "Do help me to have ecstasy." The Master consoled him and said, "Yes, I'll ask Mother; does anything happen by my will, my child?" But he scarcely gave ear to what the Master said. Baburam repeated the same words, "Do help me to have ecstasy." A few days after he made that earnest prayer, Baburam had to go to Antpur, his native village, on some business. It was the year 1884. In the meantime, the Master was anxiously wondering how Baburam was to have his ecstasy. He said to this person and that person, "Baburam wept much and asked for ecstasy before he left. What will happen? If he does not have it, he will have no regard for the words of this place (meaning himself)." He then said to the Divine Mother, "Please ordain, Mother, that Baburam may have a little Bhava or other spiritual experience." The Mother replied, "He will not have Bhava. He will have Jnana, Knowledge." The Master was again anxious when he heard those words of the universal Mother. He went to the length of saying to some of us with deep concern, "I told Mother what Baburam asked for; but She said, 'He will have no Bhava, he will have Jnana.' Anyway, let him have at least that, so that he may have peace; that is all; I am much worried for him. He wept bitterly before he left." Ah, how anxious he felt in order that Baburam might have some kind of spiritual experience! Again, while expressing that anxiety, how the Master repeated the words, "If that does not come to pass, he will have no regard for the words of this place", as if the Master's life and all depended on Baburam's regard or disregard!

5. He said now and then with reference to the boy-devotees, "Well, can you tell me why I feel so very anxious for all these and think about what one has realised and another has not? They

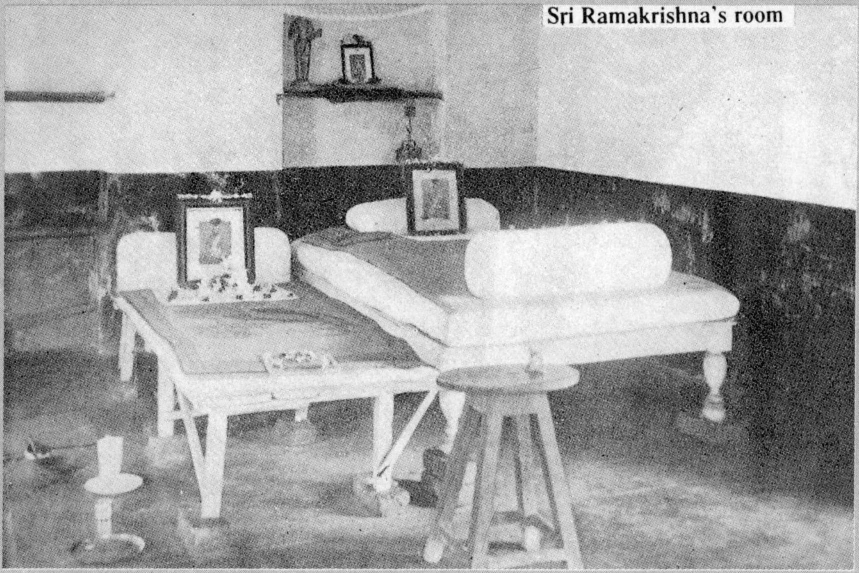

Sri Ramakrishna's room

A Guide to Dakshineswar Temple

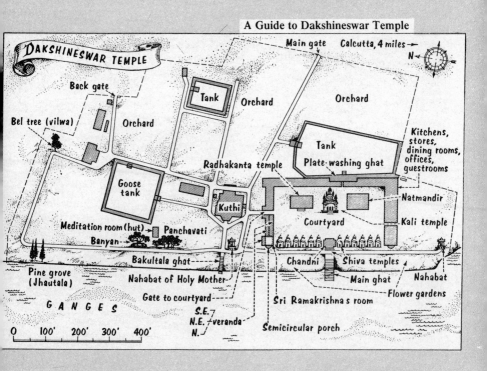

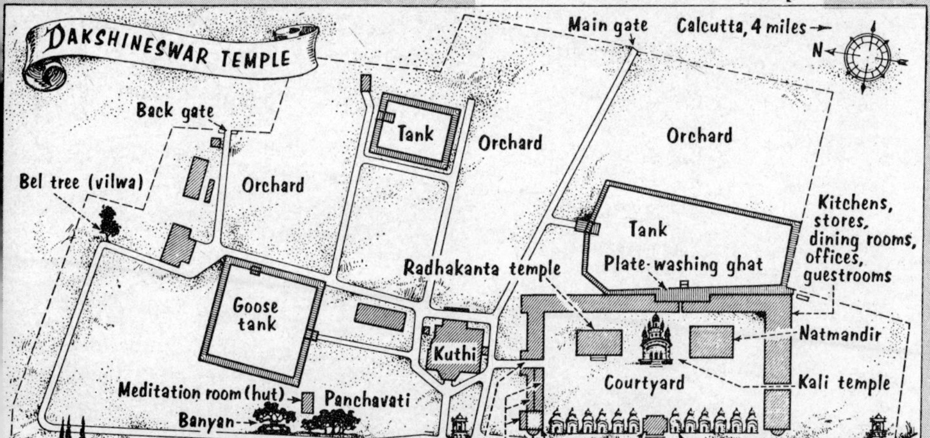
DAKSHINESWAR TEMPLE
Main gate
Calcutta, 4 miles
N
Back gate
Tank
Orchard
Orchard
Bel tree (vilwa)
Orchard
Kitchens, stores, dining rooms, offices, guestrooms
Tank
Radhakanta temple
Plate-washing ghat
Goose tank
Natmandir
Kuthi
Courtyard
Kali temple
Meditation room (hut)
Panchavati
Banyan
Bakultala ghat
Chandni
Shiva temples
Pine grove (Jhautala)
Nahabat of Holy Mother
Main ghat
Nahabat
Flower gardens
Gate to courtyard
Sri Ramakrishna s room
GANGES
S.E.
N.E. veranda
N.
Semicircular porch
0 100' 200' 300' 400'

DAKSHINESWAR

Panchavati in the early days

Ghazitala, where Sri Ramakrisha did Islam Sadhana

are mere 'school-boys'[1]; they are penniless; they have not the means of offering me a piceworth of sugar-plum. Why do I still feel so very anxious for them? If anyone does not visit this place even for two days, my heart immediately feels extremely restless to see him and have news of him. Why is it so?" The boy, so asked, perhaps answered, "I do not know, Sir, why it happens; but, it is surely for their good that you feel like that."

The Master said, "The reason is this; all these are pure in heart. Lust and gold have not yet touched them. If they apply their minds to God, they will be able to realize Him. Mine is the nature of a hemp-smoker. A hemp-smoker does not find satisfaction in smoking hemp all alone; it is necessary for him to hand over the bowl to another when he enjoys the intoxication. So is it with me. Although it is so with regard to all the boys, I don't feel so much for others as I do for Naren. If he should be late by two days, my heart would feel the pain of being wrung like a towel. Thinking what others would say, I went aside under the Tamarisk trees[2] and wept loudly. Hazra[3] said (at one time) 'How strange is your nature? You are in the state of a Paramahamsa, why then do you worry yourself thinking, why has Narendra not come? what will happen to Bhavanath? and so on, instead of remaining identified with the Lord by applying your mind to Him in Samadhi?' Then I thought Hazra was right, and that I must not do so again. When afterwards I was coming back from under the Tamarisk trees, I was shown (by Mother) a vivid picture of Calcutta, as if the city were present before me and all the people were night and day immersed in lust and gold and were suffering miserably. When I saw it, compassion welled up in my heart. I thought, 'Were I to suffer a million times greater misery for the good of these people, most gladly will I do that.' I returned and said to Hazra, 'If I choose to think of them, what is that to you, stupid fellow?' ".

6. "Naren said at one time, 'Why do you think so much of Narendar?[4] If you do so excessively, you will have to become like Narendar. King Bharata continually thought of a deer and had to be born a deer.' I have, you know, much faith in Naren's words.

[1] This he spoke in English, it being one of the few English words he knew.

[2] The Tamarisk trees in the north of Rani Rasmani's Kali Temple. It was an unfrequented spot.

[3] Pratap Chandra Hazra who stayed at Dakshineswar Temple.

[4] The Master used to pronounce the word Narendra like that.

So I was afraid to hear this. I reported it to Mother. She said, 'He is a mere boy, Why do you give ear to his words? You see Narayana in him; therefore you feel attracted towards him.' I was much relieved to hear it. I came and said to Naren, 'I don't take your words seriously. Mother has said that I feel attracted towards you because I see Narayana in you. I'll not even look at your face, rascal, the day I shall not feel His presence in you.' " So each action of the wonderful Master was strange to us but had a meaning; and he used to explain it to us lest we should think otherwise and be harmed.

7. We saw the Master always value the good qualities of all persons and pay due respect to men of honour. He said, "The divine Lord is displeased if due regard is not shown to highly respected persons. It is by His power that they have risen to rank and position; it is He who has made them such. When they are dishonoured, He is slighted." Therefore, whenever he heard of a man of special good qualities residing anywhere, we found the Master eager to see him somehow or other. If the person came to the Master, well and good; otherwise, he would himself go to him uninvited, meet, salute and converse with him. Thus satisfied, he would return. He heard of the special good qualities of Padmalochan, the court-pandit of the prince of Burdwan; of Pandit Iswarachandra Vidyasagar; of Mahesh, the famous Vina-player of Kasi; of Gangamata of Vrindavan who was inspired with the spiritual mood of a friend of God; of Kesav Sen, the eminent devotee and of several others. He sought each of them out and himself went to their doors to see them.

8. It is, of course, no wonder that the Master went unasked to anyone's door. There never arose in his mind such egotistic ideas as; "I am so great a man", or "I shall be lowering myself in the estimation of others, if I go to any and every man", or "I shall cease to be respected by them." For, he had altogether burnt up pride and egoism to ashes for ever. He carried on his head the leaf-plates, out of which the poor people had taken their food, threw them outside the temple, and washed and cleaned the place where they took their food. At one time he even partook of the leavings of those people, regarding them as Narayana Himself. Again, he washed and cleaned with his hair[1] the place where the

[1] At the time of Sadhana the Master took no care of his body; consequently, his hair grew long and got matted on account of the accumulation of dust and dirt.

temple servants answered the calls of nature and prayed earnestly to the Divine Mother, "Mother, see that I may never entertain the idea that I am superior to them." Therefore, we are not at all surprised at that extraordinary lack of egoism in him, though we cry out 'Wonderful!' even when we see a very nominal expression of it in some others. Indeed, the Master was not a person of this world, unlike all of us!

9. Throwing on his shoulder the end of the front fold of his wearing cloth, the Master was once walking in the garden of the Kali temple. A gentleman thought he was an ordinary gardener and said to him, "Hallo, just pluck those flowers for me." The Master did not utter a word but did what he was told, and slipped away from that place. Once the late Trailokya Babu, son of Mathur Babu, became annoyed with Hriday, the nephew of the Master, and ordered him to leave the temple. In his rage, he gave an indication to others that the Master also need not stay at the temple any longer. As soon as this reached the Master's ears, he placed his towel on his shoulder, smiling, and was immediately ready to leave the place. He had gone almost to the gate when, afraid that evil might befall him, Trailokya Babu came up to him and requested him to come back, saying, "I did not mean that you should leave. Why are you going away?" The Master also came back smiling as before, entered his room and sat down, as if nothing had happened.

10. Many such examples can be given. We do not feel so much astonished at such actions of the Master, though we applaud the so-called great men of the world, whose conduct even remotely resembles his. For, we have once for all unalterably settled in our minds — whether we say it in so many words or not — that, if we want to live in the world, we must look to our own interests, elbow out the weak to clear our own path, proclaim unabashedly our own glory and conceal as far as possible our own weaknesses from others. We think that one would be absolutely useless and good for nothing, if one is sincere in one's faith in, and dependence on, God and man. And it is a thousand pities that the same kind of insincerity and lack of faith in the professed ideals obtain in our politics, social etiquette, individual morals, international policies, and so on. Even those who have not eaten your 'Delhi-ka-Laddu'[1]

[1] Something having a wonderfully attractive appearance but having no substance within.

(Dead Sea fruit) repent, let alone those who have eaten it.

11. It was the year 1885. That was a time when the Master had become very well known. Attracted powerfully towards him, many new-comers daily visited Dakshineswar in those days, and had the privilege of seeing him and feeling blessed. Everybody, old and young, in Calcutta, had by then heard the name of the 'Paramahamsa of Dakshineswar' and many had seen him also. And flooding the minds of the generality of the people of Calcutta, a religious current was incessantly flowing, of course, a little below the surface. The city of Calcutta was then filled with a Harisabha here and a Brahmo Samaj there, with groups for singing of God's name here and associations for expounding the scripture there. The Master knew well the cause, though others did not. He spoke about it now and then to us as well as to other devotees of both sexes. A woman devotee tells us that one day the Master said to her in this connection, "Hallo! Know that the many Harisabhas and the other religious institutions you see are due to this (referring to his own person). Did they formerly exist? Everything had been lifeless, but since this (referring to his person again) came, all these have come to life again and a current of religion is now flowing just a little below the surface." On another occasion the Master said to us, "Did the Young Bengal that you see, care for devotion and such other things? They did not even know how to salute with their heads bent. I went on saluting them with my head bent and then they gradually learnt how to bow down their heads in salutation. I went to Kesav's house to see him. I saw him sitting in a chair. I saluted him with my head bent. At that, he just gave a nod in return. At the time of my leaving later on, I saluted him with my head completely touching the ground. He then folded his hands and once touched his head with them. The more the contacts between us increased, the more he listened to talks; and the more I saluted him with my head bent, the more did he begin to bow down his head in salutation. Did they otherwise know devotion and such other things, or had they any regard for them?"

12. During the days when the Master was associated with **the Brahma Samaj, a branch of it known as the New Dispensation** used to have big congregational gatherings. It was in those days that Pandit Sasadhar came to Calcutta for the purpose of giving expositions of the Hindu religion and of explaining the daily

religious duties of the Hindus from the standpoint of Western science. The saying, "As many sages, so many opinions" is always true in all matters. The Pandit's scientific exposition of religion was not an exception to this. But, in spite of that, there was no lack of an audience. There were great crowds of clerks and others returning from office and of students of schools and colleges. The Albert Hall, where he used to explain orthodox Hinduism, was packed with people. Every one was calm and eager to hear at least a little of the extraordinary exposition of religion by the Pandit. We remember that one day we also stood in that way for some time and heard a few words. On one occasion we too thrust in our heads with difficulty and had the privilege of seeing somehow the elderly Pandit's handsome face, adorned with a black beard, and a part of his chest bedecked with ochre coloured Rudraksha-beads. The exposition of religion by Pandit Sasadhar was the talk everywhere in Calcutta.

13. Words travel by ears, as they say. It was, therefore, not long before the news of the great soul of Dakshineswar reached the Pandit's ears, and that of the accomplishments of the Pandit reached the Master's. Some of the devotees came to the Master and said, "He is a great scholar and also speaks well. The other day he explained the couplet on Hari consisting of thirty-two letters, to mean the Devi. All heard and cried 'Bravo'." The Master heard this and said, "Is that so? I feel like hearing it once." Saying so, the Master expressed to the devotees a desire to see the Pandit.

14. When any desire arose in the pure mind of the Master, it could not but be fulfilled somehow or other. Some unseen power cleared the path to its fulfilment by removing all the obstacles to it. No doubt we had heard before that by holy living and by practising the life of absolute truth in body, mind and speech, man reaches a state wherein he cannot entertain any untruth in his mind even if he tries, that whatever desire arises in the mind of such a person becomes fulfilled in the course of time. But apart from accepting this theoretically, we could never believe that this can be an actuality in the life of any man. We, however, gradually came to accept it on seeing how the desires of the Master's mind were being fulfilled over and over again in unexpected ways. But, in spite of that fact, did we have perfect faith in his words during his lifetime? He said, "I saw within Kesav and Vijay flames of knowledge flickering like those of lamps but in Naren I saw the very sun of know-

ledge!" "Kesav" continued he, "has stirred up the world with one power; Naren has eighteen such powers in him." Those words were not the expression of knowledge gained by ordinary thought process or observation but of experiences that came to him in ecstasy. But did we even then have perfect faith in them? Sometimes we thought, "It may be true. He sees people's hearts. When he says so, there is some mystery hidden in it." Again, sometimes we wondered, "What a great difference is there between the world-renowned Kesav Chandra Sen, the eloquent devotee, and a mere school-boy like Narendra? Can the Master's opinion about them be true?" When we had such doubts about the facts of the Master's experiences, how can we say that there arose no doubt in our minds about the fulfilment of his desires, which he expressed in the same simple fashion as we do, "I have this desire"?

15. The time of Sri Jagannath's Rathayatra (Chariot Festival), arrived a few days after the Master had had a talk about Pandit Sasadhar. It is called 'Navayatra' on account of the chariot festival continuing for nine days. Many things about the Master that occured during the Navayatra of 1885 now arise in our memory. In deference to the etiquette of responding to an invitation, he went to the house of Ishan Chandra Mukhopadhyaya of Thanthania on the morning of the day of the forward trip of the chariot that year, and went from there to see Pandit Sasadhar in the afternoon. The Master participated in the chariot festival after sunset at Balaram Babu's Baghbazar house, where he spent the night. On the morrow, he came back to Dakshineswar with a few devotees in a boat. Shortly afterwards Pandit Sasadhar came to a certain place at Alambazar, otherwise called North Baranagar, to lecture on religion, and from there he came to the Kali Temple at Dakshineswar to pay a visit to the Master. Afterwards, on the morning of the day of the return trip of the chariot, the Master came again to the Baghbazar house of Balaram and stayed there in great delight with the devotees for that night and the following day and night. He returned by boat to Dakshineswar on the morning of the third day with 'Gopala's mother' and some other devotees. On the day of the return chariot trip, Pandit Sasadhar came to Balaram Babu's house to see the Master, and dissolved in tears, prayed to him with folded hands, "My heart has dried up by discussing philosophy; please endow me with a drop of devotion." The Master entered into ecstasy and touched the Pandit's heart that day. It will not

be out of place here to give in detail an account of the events of that occasion.

16. In the morning, when the chariot started, the Master as mentioned before, came to Ishan Babu's house at Thanthania in Calcutta. With him were Yogen, Hazra and a few other devotees. Rarely does one meet with a devotee like Isan — so kind, liberal and endowed with firm faith in God. His three or four sons were all educated. The third son, Satish, was a fellow pupil of Narendra. As Satish was a great expert on the Pakhoaj, the sweet voice of Narendra was very often heard from that house. Speaking of the kindness of Ishan Babu, one day Swami Vivekananda said to us, "It was by no means less than that of Pandit Vidyasagar." The Swami saw with his own eyes how Ishan Babu gave away on many occasions the whole of his own meal of rice and other preparations to beggars, and went practically without food, there being no more food available at home. The Swami also said that he saw Ishan Babu shedding tears many a time at others' sufferings, the removal of which, he found, was beyond his power. Ishan was not only kind but equally devoted to Japa. Many of us knew that he practised Japa from sunrise to sunset regularly at Dakshineswar. He was very dear to the Master, almost a favourite of his. After finishing his Japa one day, Ishan came, we remember, to offer his salutation at the feet of the Master, who in ecstasy placed his holy foot on Ishan's head. When afterwards the Master regained normal consciousness, he said emphatically to Ishan, "O Brahmana, dive, dive deep!" (that is 'be absorbed in the name of God instead of practising Japa superficially'). Ishan's Japa and morning worship at that time continued till four in the afternoon, when he took a light meal. He spent his time till sunset in talking with others or in listening to devotional songs, and then sat for his evening Japa for several hours. His sons took upon themselves the responsibility of looking after his worldly affairs. The Master blessed Ishan's house now and then with his holy presence. Ishan also during his stay in Calcutta came to see him at Dakshineswar very often, or went to the sacred temples or places of pilgrimage and spent his time in practising austerities.

On the day of the chariot festival this year, 1885, the Master came to Ishan's house and had a talk on religion with some scholars of Bhatpara. Swami Vivekananda said that Pandit Sasadhar was staying in the neighbourhood. On hearing that, the Master went to see him that day. The Swami had come to know that the Pandit was in Calcutta; for he was already acquainted with those at whose respectful invitation the Pandit had come to lecture on religion, and he frequented their College Street house. Again, as the Swami was convinced that the Pandit's symbolic exposition of religion was full of errors, he came a little more frequently to that house with a view to reason it out with the Pandit. Swami Brahmananda says that he (Swami Vivekananda) knew many things about the Pandit and told them to the Master, who, at his request, went with him to see the Pandit, and gave the Pandit much valuable instruction on that occasion. The Master told the Pandit during his very first visit to him that if one makes an attempt to preach religion without having the "badge", the power of authority from the Mother of the universe, it becomes fruitless and increases one's pride and egoism and sometimes leads one to ruin. It was, it is needless to say, as the result of these glowing and powerful words, that the Pandit gave up preaching a little later and went to Kamakhya-pitha to practise austerities.

17. The Master took leave of the Pandit that day and went with Yogen to Balaram Babu's house at Baghbazar in the evening. Yogen was then so much devoted to established rites and practices that he did not take even water in anybody's house. He, therefore, took light refreshments at home before he came with the Master, who on his part also never requested him to take food anywhere; for, Yogen's devotion to established rites and practices was not unknown to him. He knew also that Yogen used to take fruits, milk, sweets, etc., in Balaram's house, because Balaram Babu, Yogen found, had love and devotion to God and reverence for the Master. Therefore, a little after his arrival, the Master said to Balaram and the others, "He (Yogen) has not taken anything today; please give him something to eat." Balaram Babu took him lovingly to the inner apartment and gave him a light meal. We mention this here as one of the examples of how great was the Master's observation of the mental and physical conditions of the devotees, although he was often absorbed in ecstasy.

There flowed a ceaseless current of bliss in the company of the Master during the chariot festival at Balaram Babu's house. Immediately after sunset, the holy image of Jagannath was adorned with garlands, sandalpaste etc., and brought out from the shrine in the inner apartment. It was placed on the small chariot, already bedecked with cloth and flags and was worshipped again. Sri Fakir, who belonged to the house of Balaram Babu's family priest and was also devoted to the Master, performed this worship.

When studying at school, Fakir, who devoutly conformed to religious practices, lived under the care of Balaram Babu and looked after the study of the latter's only son Ramakrishna. He had great devotion to the Master from the day he first saw him. The Master loved to hear hymns recited by him. One day he taught Fakir how to recite properly the hymn to the Divine Mother by Acharya Sankara. At sunset on that occasion, the Master took him to the northern verandah of the room in which he stayed, touched him in ecstasy, and asked him to meditate. As a result, Fakir had wonderful visions and other experiences.

18. The chariot now began to be drawn forward to the accompaniment of Sankirtan, the singing of God's glory. The Master himself took hold of the rope attached to the chariot and pulled it for a short time. Afterwards, he danced beautifully to the music. Charmed with that dance and the exciting roar arising out of spiritual emotion generated by Sankirtan, all lost themselves in the love of God. Dancing, singing, and pulling the chariot, all went for a long time round and round along the verandah of the outer apartment on the first floor, overlooking the courtyard below. With salutations, the Kirtan was then brought to a close with the uttering of "Jay" (victory), separately taking the names of Jagannath, Govinda, Radharani, Chaitanya and the devotees of his inner circle and others. The holy image of Jagannath was then brought down from the chariot and installed for seven days in a different place, a small room on the second floor over the flight of steps. It was as if Jagannath had made a chariot journey to a different place and he would have a return journey to his own place again after seven days. After Jagannath had been installed in the place mentioned before, an offering of food was made to Him and Prasada was given first to the Master and then to others. The Master and Yogen passed that night at the house of Balaram Babu. Many of the other devotees went home.

19. At eight or nine on the morrow a boat was engaged for the Master to go back to Dakshineswar. When the boat came, the Master went to the inner apartment and paid his obeisance to Sri Jagannath. He received the salutations of the families of the devotees present there, and was coming towards the outer

apartment. The women devotees followed him to the end of the roof in front of the kitchen situated on the eastern side of the inner apartment, from where they went back with sad hearts; for, who would like to part from the company of that wonderful living God visible to the eyes? Taking a few steps forward from there, and then going up three or four steps, one found a door beyond which was the verandah on the first floor overlooking the courtyard below. Though all the other women devotees returned from the end of the roof, one of them forgot herself as it were, and followed him to the said verandah, as if she was not at all conscious of the presence of unknown people there.

20. After the Master had taken leave of the women devotees, he, in a spiritual mood, walked along with such an indrawn mind that he did not at all know that the ladies followed him for a certain distance and then returned, and that one of them was even then following him that way. Only those who have seen the Master walking in that manner with their own eyes, will be able to understand the extraordinary nature of it. It is difficult to explain it to others. As the result of practising mental concentration for twelve years, nay for the whole of his life, the Master's mind and intellect became so very one-pointed that they remained exactly where they were placed or exactly in whatever action they were employed; they did not in the least get distracted in any other direction. Again, his body and senses were so much under his control that they expressed to the utmost the emotion present in the mind for the time being; they could not play pranks with him. It is very difficult to explain this; for when we look at our own mind, we find that it is the battle-ground of contending thoughts, and that led by habits, our bodies and senses run after the powerful impulses in spite of our best efforts to curb them. How very different was the constitution of the Master's mind from ours!

21. Many more events can be mentioned here as examples of this. The Master one day started from his own room at Dakshineswar to pay his obeisance to Mother Kali. He came to the eastern verandah of his room, got down the steps to the courtyard of the temple and went straight towards the Kali Temple. The temple of Radha-Govinda was on the way to that temple; while going to the Kali temple, he might if he so chose, first enter the temple of Radha-Govinda, pay his obeisance to the holy image and then go to the temple of Mother Kali; but he could never do

that. He went direct to the temple of Kali and made his obeisance there. He would go to the temple of Radha-Govinda only on his way back. We thought in those days that the Master did so because he loved Mother Kali more. One day, the Master himself said, "Hallo, can you tell me why it is so? When I intend to go to the temple of Mother Kali, I have to go there absolutely direct. It becomes impossible for me to go there after taking a stroll this side or that side, or after going to the temple of Radha-Govinda and making my obeisances there. Someone, as it were, drags me by my feet and takes me direct to the temple of Mother Kali and does not allow me to bend even a little this way or that. I can go wherever I like after I see Mother Kali. Can you tell me why it is so?" We confessed our ignorance, but thought to ourselves, "Is it possible? He can first pay his obeisance to Radha-Govinda if he likes and then go to the Kali temple. But it is so perhaps because his desire to see Mother Kali is more powerful." We could not however, speak all this at once. The Master himself sometimes answered the questions thus, "Do you see? I have to do a thing just when I have a mind to do it; the slightest delay can't be brooked." Who knew then that a one-pointed mind had to be in that state and behave that way? Who knew then that the Master's mind had long become absolutely one-pointed, leaving no loop-hole anywhere, that all cross-currents of thoughts and sentiments had long stopped and there remained only one master-current there? Again, he sometimes said, "Look here, When I am in the Nirvikalpa state of consciousness, nothing remains — neither 'I' nor 'you', neither seeing nor hearing, neither speaking nor keeping mum. Even when I come down two or three steps from there, I have so much of divine intoxication that I cannot turn my attention to a multitude of persons or things. If I sit down to take my meal at that time and I am given a meal of fifty dishes, my hand would not go towards them all; it will take food to the mouth only from one spot in the plate. When such states come, the rice, pulses, vegetables, rice-porridge — all must be mixed together at one place in the plate. Then only would I be able to take it." We were astounded to hear of the state two or three steps below that of absolute sameness. He continued, "Another state comes on me when I cannot touch any one. If any one of these (pointing to the devotees) touches me, I have to cry out in pain." Who amongst us could then understand the mystery of it, that such an overwhelming amount of pure Sattva-guna was then there in the Master's mind that he could not bear the touch of the slightest impurity. He also added, "Such a state, again, sometimes comes on me during ecstasy that I can then touch him (Baburam) only. If he catches hold[1] of me then, I don't feel pain. If he feeds me I can eat."

22. Walking along with his mind absorbed, the Master came to the verandah of the outer apartment, where the chariot was drawn the previous day. He now suddenly happened to look behind and see that woman devotee following him. As soon as he saw her, he stood and saluted her again and again, saying, "Blissful Mother!" "Blissful Mother!" The devotee also placed her head on the Master's feet and saluted him in return. When she did so, the Master looked at her face and said, "Why not come, O Mother, why not come with me?" He uttered the words in such a way, and the devotee also felt such an attraction, that without considering whether it was right or wrong, she, who was then about thirty years old and had never before gone from one place to another except in a palanquin, followed the Master to Dakshineswar. Before she started, she delayed just long enough to run to the inner apartment and say to Balaram Babu's wife, "I am going with the Master to Dakshineswar." Hearing that the aforesaid devotee was thus going to Dakshineswar, another woman devotee also gave up all work and started with her. Asking the woman devotees to follow him, the Master went in that spiritual mood straight to the boat with Jogen, the Junior Naren and the other boy-devotees, and sat down there. The two women devotees also ran to the boat and sat down on the plank-flooring outside the covering of the boat. The boat started.

While going, the woman devotee said to the Master, "I feel a desire to call on Him much and to apply my whole mind to Him, but the mind by no means obeys the rein. What should I do?"

[1] As the Master had no body-consciousness during ecstasy, his limbs (the hands, head, neck, etc.) became bent and sometimes the whole body inclined on one side and was about to fall. The devotees who happened then to be beside him caught hold of those limbs and slowly set them in their proper positions and continued to hold him lest he should fall down. They uttered into his ears the names of those deities, whose contemplation had produced that state of the Master; for example, Kali, Kali; Rama Rama; Aum, Aum or Aum Tat Sat, and so on. This process being continued for some time, he would slowly regain normal consciousness. He felt great pain if any other name, except that by the contemplation of which he was inspired and absorbed, was uttered into his ears.

23. The Master (affectionately): "Why not surrender yourself to Him? One should live in the world like a leaf before the wind — a leaf plate cast off after use to be blown about by the wind whithersoever it likes. Do you know how it is? The cast-off leaf lies at a neglected corner; it flies as the wind carries it. It is just like that. One should depend on Him and live one's life — the mind should move as the wind of divine consciousness moves it. That's all."

While this talk was going on, the boat reached the temple-ghat. As soon as the Master got down from the boat, he went to the 'house' of Kali.[1] The women devotees went to the Holy Mother at the Nahavat[2] on the northern side of the temple compound. They saluted her and then started for the temple to pay their obeisance to Kali the Mother. In the meanwhile the Master came with his boy-devotees to the temple of Kali and offered salutations to Her. He then came, sat down in the music hall in ecstasy, and began to sing in his sweet voice.

> O Mother, O enchantress of Siva! Thou hast deluded the world. Thou entertainest Thyself by playing on the Vina at the great lotus in the basic centre, near the sacral plexus.
>
> O Thou Great Mantra, who movest in the three scales in the form of the three Gunas, striking the three cords, Sushumna etc., of the musical instrument, the body!
>
> O Mother! Thou art of the form of the mode Bhairava in the basic centre, Sriraga in the six-petalled lotus at the Swadhishthana centre, Mallara in the Manipura, Vasanta (in the Anahata) illumining the heart, Hindola in the Visuddha and Karnataka in the Ajna.
>
> O Thou, who art manifest as the thrice seven notes under the stress of pitch, tempo, rhythm and diatonic note!

[1] The Master called the Kali temple the house of Kali and the Radha-Govinda temple that of Vishnu.

[2] The Holy Mother went to bed in the room on the ground floor of the Nahavat and kept sundry articles there. Cooking etc., were done in the verandah in front of that room. She went to the room upstairs sometimes in the day-time and, if the number of women devotees from Calcutta was large, provided them sleeping accommodation there.

Sri Nandakumar says: 'The Supreme Truth cannot be ascertained'. For, the empirical reality, the triple Gunas, have veiled the vision of the Jiva, blinded alternately by pains and pleasures.

24. The Master sat in the northern part of the music hall in front of the Mother and was thus singing the song. The devotees, some sitting, some standing, were charmed to listen to the song. In the course of singing, the Master went into ecstasy and stood up suddenly. The singing stopped. An extraordinary smile on his lips filled the place with bliss. The devotees were looking motionless on the holy person of the Master. When he saw that the Master's body inclined a little, Junior Naren was going to hold it straight, lest he should fall down. But no sooner had he touched him than the Master screamed out in terrible pain. Finding that his touch was not then liked by the Master, he stood aloof, when Ramlal, the Master's nephew, hearing the scream from within the temple, came out quickly and caught hold of the Master's person. The Master remained in that state for some time, and after listening to the names of God, came back to normal consciousness. But he was not able to stand in the natural way, as if he was dead drunk. His legs were trembling very much.

In that condition he crawled down the steps on the northern side of the music hall to the courtyard of the temple and began to speak like a boy, "I shall not fall down, Mother, what dost Thou say?" Seeing the Master then, one actually thought that he was a child of three or four years. Gazing at the Mother as he spoke those words and keeping his eyes fixed on Hers, he was confidently getting down the steps. Shall we see elsewhere such an attitude of wonderful reliance on God even in small matters?

25. He crossed the courtyard, came to his room, went to the western verandah and sat down there. He was still in ecstasy. That mood would not leave him. Now its hold was more, now a little less. Thus the mood alternated for some time. When it increased, he lost normal consciousness. Remaining in that condition for some time, he began to say in that state of Bhava to the devotees who were with him, "Have you seen the Snake? It gives me a lot of trouble." Again, as if forgetting the devotees immediately, he addressed the snake-like Coiled Power (for it is needless to say that the Master in ecstasy saw Her just then) and

said, "Go now, I will smoke and wash my mouth; my teeth have not been cleaned." Now speaking thus with the devotees, and now with the figure seen in ecstasy, the Master came back to the normal consciousness of ordinary people.

26. When the Master remained in the normal state of consciousness, he used to be anxious for the devotees; he sent some one to the Holy Mother to know whether there were any vegetables in her store. She sent word in reply that there was nothing, and the Master became again concerned, considering who would go to the market then. How could the men and women devotees who had come from Calcutta be fed, if some vegetables were not brought from the market? After some reflection, he asked the two women devotees, "Can you go and make purchases in the market?" They said, "Yes", and went to the market and purchased and brought some greens, potatoes and two large brinjals. The Holy Mother cooked all these. From the temple also there came, as usual, a large plateful of Prasada. When the Master had finished taking his food, the devotees took Prasada. Afterwards, the reason why the Master had felt so much pain when Junior Naren held him during his ecstasy was ascertained. It was found on inquiry that on his left temple he (junior Naren) had a small tumour which was gradually becoming bigger. Doctors applied medicine to produce a sore there, lest it should prove painful. It is true, we **had heard before, that one should not touch the form of a deity,** if one has a sore in one's body. But whoever thought that the saying would thus prove true before our very eyes? He undoubtedly suffered pain, but it was beyond our power to understand the divine power within the Master which made him automatically aware of that unpleasant touch and impelled him to react with a loud scream expressive of pain even when he was absorbed in a spiritual mood and bereft of normal consciousness. It was known to us how high an opinion the Master had about Junior Naren's purity of character. In his normal state of consciousness the Master touched him as he did all others, in spite of that sore in his body, allowed him to touch his feet and moved with him in every way. So, how could Naren know that, at the time of ecstasy, the Master would not be able to bear his touch because he had a sore in his body? Afterwards, he did not touch the Master during ecstasy till the said sore was healed.

No one felt how the whole of the day slipped away in the

company of the Master in the course of various religious conversations. Afterwards, at the approach of dusk, the men devotees started home. The two women devotees also took leave of the Master and the Holy Mother, and walked back to Calcutta.

27. Two or three days after the events described above had taken place, Pandit Sasadhar was to come to see the Master at the Dakshineswar Kali temple one afternoon. The Master, who had a boyish nature, got afraid on many occasions like a boy whenever he heard that any famous person would come to see him. He felt diffident, thinking that he had no education. Besides, there was no knowing when ecstasy would come upon him, when losing consciousness of his body, his cloth, the only garment he had on, would drop off. Under such circumstances, what would the new-comer think and say? On observing his nervousness, we wondered why he was so concerned with the new-comer's impression of him. He had himself taught many people again and again, "People are nothing but worms. Nothing spiritual will be attained as long as shame, hatred and fear abide." Did he then hunger for name and fame? Not that. His attitude in this respect, was very much like that of a small boy, who shrinks through fear and shyness on seeing a stranger, but who, as soon as there grows up a little familiarity, freely indulges in various kinds of jolly pranks with him, such as riding on his back and shoulder, pulling him by the hair and so on. The Master's attitude also was similar. He could not have talked with Maharaja Yatindramohan and the famous Krishnadas Pal in the way he did, had he had the slightest desire in his mind for name and fame! [1]

Again, the Master, it was sometimes seen, was afraid because he thought that the person who came to him might be harmed. For, it was true that it would not at all matter to the Master whether the new-comer could appreciate his conduct and manners or not; but if, unable to understand them, he slandered the Master, he was sure to meet with evil. Knowing this, he felt afraid. That was why, when Girish at one time spoke various harsh words about him in his presence due to the pique and resentment of wounded love, the Master said, "Look here, let him speak of me

[1] At the very outset he said to Maharaja Yatindramohan, "But, my dear Sir, I cannot call you a Raja (king); how can I tell a lie?" Again, when, speaking of himself, the Maharaja compared himself with the great king Yudhishthira, whereupon the Master got impatient and criticised that attitude of his.

whatever he likes; I hope he has not spoken ill of my Mother."

28. There was no limit whatever to the Master's fear when he heard that Sasadhar would come to see him. He said to Yogen, Junior Naren and several others, "Please be present when the Pandit comes." What the Master meant was this. He was an illiterate man; he might not be able to speak in the proper manner with a learned Pandit like him. So we all should be present and speak with the Pandit and save the Master himself from lapses. Ah, how difficult it is to explain to others his childlike fear! But when Sasadhar actually arrived, the Master became, as it were, a different person. He was in a state resembling partial normal consciousness. On looking carefully at him, one could notice his lips slightly quivering with a smile. He then addressed the Pandit and said affectionately, "You are a Pandit; please say something."

Sasadhar: "Sir, my heart has dried up because of my study of philosophy. So, I have come to you in order to have a little of the sap of devotion. Therefore, please say something yourself and let me listen."

The Master (affectionately): "What shall I say? No one can say what Existence-Knowledge-Bliss Absolute is. That is why He at first became half-male and half-female. Why so? Because He wanted to show that both Purusha and Prakriti were He. He then came down another step from there, and became the separate Purusha and the separate Prakriti."

As he spoke thus about the hidden truths of spirituality, he became excited and stood up, and addressing Sasadhar, said: "Until the mind is joined to the Existence-Knowledge-Bliss, both prayer to God and worldly duties continue. When, afterwards, the mind merges in Him, there is no necessity for attending to one's duties. Take, for example, the line of the song 'My Nitai is a mad elephant', sung in Kirtan. When the song commences, the words are sung with correct enunciation, tone, time, measure, tempo and rhythm. It is sung, as it should be, with attention to all these things. Afterwards, as the mind merges a little in the emotion produced by the song, the words 'mad elephant', 'mad elephant' only are sung. Again, when it goes deeper still, the singer, in trying to utter the word 'elephant' (Hati) can utter only the syllable 'Ha' (that is, remains with his mouth agape)."

Speaking thus, no sooner had the Master uttered the syllable

'Ha', than he became himself completely speechless and motionless and remained in that state for about fifteen minutes, bereft of consciousness, with his face bright and serene. At the end of the ecstasy, he addressed Sasadhar again and spoke affectionately.

The Master: "O Pandit, I have seen you through and through; you are good. After finishing cooking and feeding all, a housewife places her towel on her shoulder and goes to the pond to bathe and wash her clothes and does not return to the kitchen; so, you also will finish telling others of Him and will go, never to come back."

Hearing these words of the Master, Sasadhar said, "It is all through your grace," and took the dust of his feet again and again. He heard the Master's words quite astonished, and he burst into tears, as he had thought so long that he could not realize God.

29. We shall now narrate the incident as described by the Master to a great friend of ours when the latter came to him on the day following Sasadhar's visit to Dakshineswar. The Master (affectionately): "Don't you see that there is nothing like scholarship 'here'? Only a man without any education! I was much afraid when I heard that the Pandit would come here. You see, I have no consciousness of even my cloth. I shrank into myself for fear that I might say something which might not be proper. I said to the Mother, 'I don't know the scriptures and philosophies. I know Thyself only, Mother; please protect me Thyself.' Then I said to some one, 'Be present then'; again, to some other I said, 'I shall feel somewhat confident when I see you with me.' Even when the Pandit came and sat down, fear persisted. I sat silent, and went on looking at him and listening to his words. Just then I saw the Pandit's inner nature. Mother showed me that the mere study of the scriptures was of no avail; if there were no detachment and discrimination these things were of no use. Something crept immediately afterwards towards the head, and fear vanished in no time. I became completely overwhelmed; the face turned upwards and I felt a flow of words gushing out of my mouth. The more the words came out, the more were the words pushed forward and supplied, as it were, by some one from within. It was as if a man was measuring paddy in that part of the country (Kamarpukur); one person counts the measures calling out — one, two and so on, while another sits behind him and pushes forward the paddy and supplies him with heaps of it. But I did not know at

all what I said. When a little consciousness returned, what I saw was that he (the Pandit) was weeping; he was completely changed. A state like this comes now and then; owing to fear, I would be going again and again towards the Tamarisk trees (i.e., for easing oneself). It came also on the day when Kesav sent word that he would bring with him an Englishman (the missionary Cook who was touring India) and take me in a steamer for a trip in the Ganga. When, however, they came and I got into the steamer, I was in a state like this, and there was a ceaseless flow of words. Afterwards they (showing us) said, 'You imparted much instruction.' But I knew nothing, my child."

30. How can we understand anything about these exalted states of our Master of transcending greatness! We simply become astounded and speechless without knowing how to explain them or express our feelings. Dwelling in his body and mind, a marvellous Power sported in these unprecedented ways, brought any one whom It liked to Dakshineswar with an inexplicable attraction, and gave him power to ascend to higher planes of spirituality. Even the witnessing of it could not unravel the mystery of these occurrences. But one can know from the results that these wonderful events did really happen. Beyond that none can know anything. Ah! on how many occasions did we see with our own eyes malicious men coming to the Master with inimical intentions, and the Master touching them in a state of ecstasy under the overwhelming influence of that Power and these evil men turning a new leaf in their lives with their internal nature radically changed! Jesus gave a new life to that unhappy woman Mary by a mere touch. Sri Chaitanya in ecstasy climbed on to the shoulders of some person, whereupon the latter's heretical feelings of doubt and disbelief were destroyed, and he acquired devotion to God. On reading about similar events in the lives of earlier incarnations, we used to think that they were concocted by the fanaticism of generations of disciples with the mere idea of winning more followers from among the credulous, and that by giving currency to such stories, they only acted as stumbling blocks to the progress of genuine spiritual ideas. We found it stated in the book called the *Bhakti-Chaitanya-Chandrika*, published by the New Dispensation, that Sri Chaitanya used to lose normal consciousness at the name of Hari, and we remember how we took the author to be soft-headed. Ah! how pitiably narrow we were at that time, and how pitiable our condition would

have continued to be, had we not had the good fortune to see the Master. Having had the blessing of meeting the Master, we are now in a position, as they say, "to detect wrong thatching, though we do not know how to thatch ourselves". Now we are at least saved from accepting anything and everything as religion, be it from our own wretched doubting minds within or from charlatans without. Knowing now that devotion, faith and other spiritual excellences can be directly imparted to one like anything else by a competent person, we have hope instilled into our hearts, and we are confident of attaining immortality, being blessed with a drop of the grace of the Master, who is the ocean of grace itself.

CHAPTER VI

SRI RAMAKRISHNA IN THE COMPANY OF DEVOTEES: THE STORY OF GOPALA'S MOTHER[1]—FIRST PART

[TOPICS: 1. Gopala's Mother's first meeting with the Master. 2. Govinda Chandra Datta of Pataldanga. 3. His wife, a devotee. 4. The family of her priest: Aghoramani, a child-widow of that family. 5. Her devotion and conservatism. 6. Govinda Babu's temple. 7. Spirituality in the women of the East and the West. 8. Aghoramani's second meeting with the Master. 9. The Master at Govinda Babu's garden. 10. Aghoramani's vision of Gopala. 11. Her visit to the Master in that state. 12. The Master in praise of her state. 13. His appreciation: "You have attained everything."]

I worship Sri Krishna, the milk-woman's son in the form of the cowherd, black like a newly formed cloud, having eyes like blue lotuses and blue curly hair tied up (on the head) along with the glittering feathers of the peacock. I worship the bee drinking the honey of the lotus of the milkmaid's face.

— *Hymn to Gopala*

I make firm that faith of devotees with which they seek to worship any Form whatever (of Mine).

— *Gita VII 21*

And whoso shall receive one such little child in my name receiveth Me.

— *Matthew XVIII 6*

We cannot accurately say when 'Gopala's mother' met the Master for the first time. But it is certain that when we saw her

[1] We are here going to present the reader the wonderful story of the spiritual visions and experiences of Gopala's mother, a devotee of Sri Ramakrishna, by way of an example of how the Master, established in the divine mood, was seen by us to enact his divine play with particular Sadhakas and devotees. Some may scent exaggerations in this story. To them we say, we have not added any touches whatever to it, not even to its language. We have placed it before the reader almost in the form in which we collected it from persons who, in everything they say, keep a keen eye on truth and feel repentant if they lapse from it. And they are persons who, far from being flatterers of the "Brahmani of Kamarhati", have sometimes strongly criticised some of her actions before us.

first with the Master at Dakshineswar in the month of March or April in 1885, she had been visiting him for about six months, and the extraordinary sport of the Lord as Gopala, the divine cowherd boy of Vrindavan, had also been going on with her. On that occasion 'Gopala's mother', we remember distinctly, sat facing southeast (that is, facing the Master) near the large jar containing the water of the Ganga in the north west corner of the Master's room. Though she was about sixty years old, one could not guess it; for in the face of the old lady there shone the joy and happiness of a young girl. When we were introduced to her, she said, "Are you G—'s son? You are then ours indeed! Ah, G—'s son has become a devotee! This time Gopala will not make a single exception; he will attract all, one by one. That's very good. I had previously been related to you in a worldly sense; now I am related in another, closer manner."

1. It was the month of December of 1884. The sky was so very clear. Again, there was, we remember, a little touch of cold, a bit severe, even from the beginning of the month of November that year. It was perhaps in that early winter, neither hot nor very cold, that Gopala's mother had the blessing of meeting the Master for the first time. They came by boat to see the Master from the temple garden on the bank of the Ganga at Kamarhati, belonging to Govinda Chandra Datta of Pataldanga. We say "they" because Gopala's mother did not come alone on that occasion; the widow of the said owner of the garden and a distant relation of hers, named Kamini also came with her. The name of Sri Ramakrishna was then known to many in Calcutta. So, these ladies were eager to see that extraordinary devotee ever since they had heard of him. The special service of the holy image had to be performed in the month of Kartik (November). Therefore, Govinda Babu's wife, or the 'mistress of Kamarhati' as she was called, used to live at Kamarhati during this time every year and look after the said service personally. Again, Dakshineswar was only two or three miles from Kamarhati; so, it was very convenient to come from there to Dakshineswar. The 'mistress of Kamarhati' and 'Gopala's mother' took that opportunity and came to the Kali temple of Rani Rasmani at Dakshineswar.

That day the Master respectfully made them sit in his own room and gave them many instructions about devotion, sang devotional songs for them, and bade good-bye to them, asking them to come again. While they were taking leave, the 'mistress' invited the Master to grace her temple at Kamarhati. The Master also agreed to go some day at his convenience. He highly praised the mistress and Gopala's mother that day. He said, "Ah, how beautiful is the expression of their faces and eyes! They are, as it were, floating on the current of the love of God; their eyes are full of the intense love of God. Even the Tilaka on the nose is beautiful." That is to say, the feeling of devotion within was, as it were, bubbling out naturally through their dress, facial expression, deportment and everything else about them, without any attempt at display.

2. Govinda Chandra Datta of Pataldanga was a broker at a famous European business house in Calcutta. He became very rich on account of his efficiency and perseverance. But owing to an attack of paralysis, he became unfit for service. Prior to this, his only son had died and he followed the son. Among those who survived him were his two daughters, Bhutta and Naran, and their children. But as he had considerable property, he could spend the latter part of his life in religious studies and virtuous and pious activities. Pious acts such as arrangements for discourses on the Ramayana and the Mahabharata in his house, installation of the holy images of Radha and Krishna with great pomp in the Kamarhati garden, recital of the whole of the Bhagavata and other Sastras, ceremonial gift of valuables of the weight of himself and his wife to Brahmanas, the poor and others, had all been performed by him before he passed away. Besides, there was no lack of festivals, or, as they would call it, no cessation of "thirteen festivals in twelve months", in connection with the worship of Radha-Krishna in the Kamarhati garden, and Prasada was distributed unstintedly to guests and others, the poor and the indigent.

3. After the death of Govinda Babu, his virtuous wife, the 'mistress', continued to conduct for a long time the service of the holy images with the same sort of pomp. Afterwards, the greater part of the property was lost for various reasons. Therefore, in order that there might not be any negligence in the service of the holy images, the 'mistress' herself lived there and engaged herself in supervising it. The mistress belonged to the old school of thought and life, and had to pass through much grief and suffering in her life. So her very bones, as it were, felt that there was peace in the practice of religion only. But the accursed worldly entangle-

ments were not to be so easily shaken off. She had to take into account her daughters Yajneswari and Narayani, their husbands her sons-in-law, society, position, honour and other worldly interests. But she observed with the strictest rigidity the vow of Brahmacharya from the day her husband died. She used to sleep on the floor, bathe at the three junctures of the day, take food once only in twenty-four hours, and devote her time and energies entirely to pious observances like Japa, meditation, fasts, charities, and above all to the service of the holy images.

4. The family of Govinda Babu's priests lived very near the Kamarhati temple. Nilamadhav Bandyopadhyaya, the priest, was a respectable person. 'Gopala's mother', originally known as Aghoramani Devi, was his sister. As she had become a widow in her childhood, she had been a member of her father's family all her life. Aghoramani began to spend her time in the service of the images in the temple ever since she became very intimate with Govinda Babu's wife, the mistress, as she was called. As her love for God increased, she had a strong desire to live in the temple itself on the Ganga. So she took the permission of the mistress and began to live in one of the rooms in the women's apartment. She visited her father's family once or twice a day, and spent the rest of her time in the temple premises in her round of pious duties.

Aghoramani loved to practise strict austerity and Brahmacharya like the mistress. There was, therefore, much similarity of thoughts and feelings between them. The mistress, a rich lady possessing much property, had outwardly to take into account her social position in all her actions and ways of life. But as Aghoramani had none of these, she was comparatively free. Again, as a child-widow and therefore without any issue, there were no family responsibilities to bother her. What she possessed was perhaps a sum of six or seven hundred rupees, the sale proceeds of her ornaments. That also was deposited with the mistress in government securities. Aghoramani used to live on the interest of this money and when in great want, she drew from the capital a little. Of course, the mistress also helped her and her brother in all matters.

5. Being a child-widow, Aghoramani never knew the happiness of the company of a husband. Women say, "The child-widows are extremely meticulous (about the observances of established

rites and ceremonies), so much so, that they wash even salt before using it." Aghoramani too turned to be such a one as she grew up. One day, we know, she cooked rice and was serving it from the cooking pot on the plate of Sri Ramakrishna, when somehow or other the tiny wooden spoon with which rice is stirred in the pot, was touched by him. Aghoramani did not eat the remaining rice in the pot, and threw even the stick into the Ganga. This happened when she had just begun visiting the Master. There were two or three hearths in the music room (Nahavat) at Dakshineswar. It was late on many occasions before the offering of cooked rice and other services to Kali the Mother were completed; sometimes it would be half past one. When the Master was unwell, the supremely revered Holy Mother cooked for him a little rice and soup at an early hour. Dal and Chapati were also prepared over these hearths for those devotees who spent their nights now and then with the Master. The Holy Mother cooked food over those hearths for those ladies also who came from Calcutta and other places to see the Master and spent the whole day and sometimes the night also with her at the Nahavat. On the day when Aghoramani or "the Brahmani of Kamarhati', as the Master called her in the beginning, came to visit him, the Holy Mother had to purify the hearth thrice with cowdung, Ganga water, etc., before the Brahmani would condescend to put her cooking pot over it. So great was her observance of purity and cleanliness.

6. The Brahmani of Kamarhati, again, was very sensitive from her childhood. She could not at all put up with any uncharitable remark by anybody, let alone her supplicating anybody for pecuniary help. Besides, as soon as she saw anybody doing anything wrong, she felt no hesitation in telling him of it to his very face. So, she could not get on well with any one. The room given her by the mistress to live in, was situated in the extreme south of the garden. One could have a good view of the Ganga through the three southern windows of the room which had two doors in the north and the west. The Brahmani sat in that room, observed the Ganga flow by, and performed Japa night and day. She thus spent thirty years in that room in weal and in woe before she met Sri Ramakrishna for the first time.

The Brahmani's father's family were perhaps Sakta (i.e. worshippers of God as the Mother of the Universe). We do not know what the faith of her father-in-law's family was. But she was herself a follower of the cult of Vishnu, and was initiated by her Guru in the Mantra of Gopala, God in the form of the child Krishna. Her close relation with the mistress also perhaps was responsible for it; for, the Guru family of Govinda Babu were the Goswamis of Malpara who were worshippers of Krishna, and one or two of them very often lived at Kamarhati ever since the temple was built there. But it is difficult to decide how Aghoramani had such unswerving motherly love for God and how she had the desire of worshipping Him as her son in the form of Gopala, though she, being a child-widow, had no experience whatever in this life of how a mother felt for her child. Many will say, "It was due to her previous birth and past impressions." Anyway her devotion was a fact.

7. Whenever there arises an urge for religion in the women of England or America as a result of suffering in the world or for some other reason, it gets manifested through gifts, doing good to others, or the service of the poor and the suffering humanity. It becomes their only aim to do good to people day and night. In our country it takes a different turn. Here this piety gets manifested through the observance of strict continence, the practice of austerities, the observance of established rites and ceremonies, the practice of Japa and the like. As the pratice of these disciplines dominates their lives, the spirit of renunciation dawns on them, and they become more and more inward looking in their life. The idea that the realization of God is the end and aim of human life and that therein lies real abiding peace has surcharged the atmosphere of India, and has entered into the very marrow of men and women here. Therefore, the life in solitude together with the practice of austerities on the part of the Brahmani of Kamarhati, though a matter of surprise to the people of other countries, is nothing unusual in this country.

The Brahmani of Kamarhati felt great attraction for Sri Ramakrishna ever since the day she had first met him. But why it was so, and how far-reaching it was to be, she had no idea. She felt an indescribable attraction for him but her impression of him did not go beyond what she said then, "He is a very good man, a real monk and devotee. I would like to go to him again, as soon as I get time." The mistress also felt similarly, but perhaps she never came again, lest society should speak ill of her. Besides, she had to spend much time at her Pataldanga house on account of her daughters and sons-in-law. Dakshineswar was far from there and if she were to come, she had to inform all and make the necessary arrangements. So most probably she never visited Dakshineswar again.

8. The Brahmani had no such difficulty. Therefore, a few days after her first visit, she felt one day a keen desire to come to the Master while she was performing Japa, and immediately after, she went to Dakshineswar with two or three pice worth of Sandesh of inferior quality. No sooner had the Master seen her than he cried out. saying, "Oh, you have come! Give me what you have brought for me." Gopala's mother says, "I shrank within myself to bring out that bad Sandesh, seeing that so many people brought so many good things and fed him. Besides, imagine, scarcely had I arrived when he wanted to eat that worthless stuff!" As she could not say anything out of fear and shame, she brought out that Sandesh and gave it to him. The Master also ate it with great pleasure and said while eating it "Why do you spend money and bring Sandesh? Prepare and keep cocoanut balls and bring one or two when you come. Or bring whatever you cook with your own hand, be it Chachchari of the creepers and leaves of bottle-gourd or the curry prepared with legume of drum-sticks mixed with potato, brinjals and balls of the paste of pulses. I feel a great desire to eat things cooked by you." Gopala's mother says, "There was no talk of religion and pious topics, but only of eating. I thought, 'I have come to see a strange Sadhu who talks of eating and eating only. I am a poor indigent person, how can I feed him so much? I won't come again.' But as soon as I crossed the gate of the Dakshineswar garden, he was, as it were, attracting me from behind. I could proceed no farther. I consoled my mind in various ways and dragged myself back, so to say, to Kamarhati." Just a few days after, the Brahmani walked three miles with Chachchari in her hand to see Paramahamsa Deva. As soon as she came, the Master asked for it as before, ate it and expressed joy saying, "Ah, how beautifully cooked! It is, as it were, nectar, the very nectar!" Gopala's mother's eyes were filled with tears to see that joy of the Master. She thought that, as she was a poor indigent woman, the Master was praising that ordinary stuff of hers.

In this way her visits to Dakshineswar became more and more frequent for two or three months. Thenceforward, she used to bring all the way from Kamarhati to Dakshineswar, whatever was found tasty among the dishes cooked by her. The Master also ate it all with relish. Again he asked her to bring some ordinary thing, such as a preparation of Sushni herb or Chachchari of bindweed and so on. Troubled with the request, "Bring this, bring that", and the frequent repetition of "I want to eat this. I want to eat that", Gopala's mother would think now and then, "Gopala, is this the result of my meditation on you? You have brought me to a Sadhu who wants only to eat. I'll never come any more." But that irresistible attraction again! "When and how soon shall I go there again?" this thought once again seized her soul.

9. In the meanwhile Sri Ramakrishna came once to Govinda Babu's garden at Kamarhati and expressed great joy to see the service of the holy images there. On that occasion he sang songs before the images there. He then took food and returned toDakshineswar. Seeing his wonderful ecstasy at the time of singing, the mistress and others were greatly charmed. But it is very difficult to say whether the venerable Goswamis did not feel a little jealousy and hatred lest they should lose their influence. We are told this was what actually happened.

It was a long-standing practice with the Brahmani of Kamarhati, to rise at two in the morning, finish her ablutions and sit down for Japa at three. She finished performing Japa by eight or nine, when she bathed, paid a visit to the holy images and joined in the service of the temple according to her capacity. Afterwards, when the food offering to the holy images was over, she engaged herself in cooking her own food at twelve noon. As soon as she had taken a little rest after her meal, she sat for Japa again. She witnessed the evening Arati, spent much of the night in Japa, and took a little milk before going to bed for a few hours. The 'humour of wind' was prevalent in her constitution by nature; so, she had only a little sleep. Sometimes she had palpitation of heart and a vague uneasy sensation. When the Master was told of it, he said, "That 'humour of wind' of yours is due to your meditation on Hari; if that be cured, what will be the support of your life? Please eat something whenever you feel uneasy like that."

10. It was 1884. The winter was over and the pleasant spring, abounding in flowers, arrived. Full of leaves, flowers and

songs, the earth was experiencing an awakening; a sort of madness and hilarity was there in the air. That joy and inebriation of Nature was amoral, with no distinction of good and bad as experienced by the Jiva according to his propensities derived from past impressions. Expressions of nature are the same though in common parlance we say, the virtuous are awake to the good suggestions of nature, and the vicious, to the vile. That is the difference.

During this time of the year, one morning at three, the Brahmani of Kamarhati sat for Japa. Japa finished, she began to perform Pranayama before offering the result of the Japa to her chosen Ideal, when she saw that Sri Ramakrishna was sitting near her to the left and the palm of his right hand looked half clenched. She saw him now as live and distinct as she usually saw him at Dakshineswar. She thought, "What is this? How and whence has he come here at such an hour?" Gopala's mother says, "I was looking at him with astonishment and thinking thus, while 'Gopala' (as she used to call Sri Ramakrishna) sat and smiled. Then, with a beating heart, as soon as I caught hold of Gopala's (Ramakrishna's) left hand with mine, that figure vanished into the void and a ten-month-old real Gopala, as big as this (indicating the size with her hands) and exactly like one in flesh and blood, came out of that figure. And oh, the beauty of it! Crawling, with one of his hands raised, he looked at my face and said to me, 'Mother, give me butter.' I was overwhelmed with that experience. That was a strange affair. I cried out loudly. It was a loud, unusual cry. There were no people in the house; otherwise they would have come running. I wept and said, 'My child, I am a miserable, indigent woman. What should I feed you with? Where shall I get butter and milk, my child?' But did that strange Gopala give ear to that? He only went on saying, 'Give me something to eat.' What could I do? I got up weeping, took down a dry ball of cocoanut from a hanging rope-loop, and placing it on his hand, said, 'Gopala, my child, though I give you this worthless thing to eat, don't pay me back with such fruits in return.'

11. "Then as regards Japa? How could I perform that? Gopala came, sat on my lap and snatched away the rosary. He rode on my shoulder and crawled all round the room. As soon as it was dawn, I started for Dakshineswar, running like one mad. Gopala climbed up in my arms and rested his head on my

shoulder. I held him to my breast, with one hand on his buttocks and the other on his back, and covered the whole journey on foot. The two purple feet of Gopala, I saw clearly, were dangling on my breast."

Inebriated with an intense love of God on account of the attainment of the vision of her own chosen Ideal, Aghoramani came walking from the Kamarhati garden to the Master at Dakshineswar early in the morning. Another woman devotee known to us was also present there then. We shall now tell the reader what we heard from the latter. She said:

"I was then sweeping and cleaning the Master's room. It was morning, about 7 or 7.30 A.M. when I heard someone outside crying, 'Gopala, Gopala,' and coming towards the Master's room. The voice was a familiar one and it began gradually to come nearer. I looked and found it was Gopala's mother. She was not properly dressed, and she looked like one mad, with her eye-balls drawn up, and the skirt of her wearing cloth sweeping the ground. She also seemed to be unaware of her surroundings. She entered the Master's room in that stage through the eastern door. The Master was then sitting on his small bedstead within the room.

"Seeing Gopala's mother in that condition I was completely surprised; the Master entered into ecstasy on seeing her. Gopala's mother in the meantime came and sat down near him, and like a boy, the Master went and sat on her lap. Both her eyes were shedding tears copiously. She then fed the Master with her own hand with the cream, butter and thickened milk that she had brought with her. I was flabbergasted to see it; for, I never before saw the Master in Bhava touch any woman, though I heard that the Brahmani, the Master's Guru, assumed sometimes the attitude of Yasoda and the Master in the attitude of Gopala sat on her lap. I was, however, completely astounded to see that state of Gopala's mother and the Master's mood. A little later, that mood of the Master came to an end, and he got up and sat on his bedstead. But that mental attitude of Gopala's mother would not come to an end. Beside herself with joy, she stood up and walked, dancing round the whole room like one mad, saying, 'Brahma dances, Vishnu dances and so on. The Master saw it, smiled and said to me, 'Just see, she is completely filled with Bliss; her mind has now gone to the sphere of Gopala.' Even afterwards Gopala's mother had indeed such visions while in Bhava when she became a different person, as it were. On another occasion, at the time of taking her meal, overwhelmed with spiritual emotions, and thinking that we were so many Gopalas, she fed us with rice with her own hand. As I had not married my daughter to a person of a family equal in rank with ours, she disliked me a little in her mind. With what humility she apologised to me for this on that occasion! She said, 'Did I know before, that you have so much faith and devotion in you? Gopala can touch almost none at the time of Bhava and today he sat while in Bhava on your back! Are you an ordinary person?'" The Master in fact was suddenly in Bhava to see Gopala's mother that day and at first sat on the back of this particular lady and afterwards on the lap of Gopala's mother for some time.

She arrived at Dakshineswar that day in that state and said many things to Sri Ramakrishna, shedding profuse tears in the exuberance of Bhava. She said, "There is Gopala here on my lap, there it enters into your body (Sri Ramakrishna's) . . . there it comes out again. Come, my child, come to the lap of your miserable mother." She saw the restless Gopala sometimes vanishing into the person of the Master and sometimes again coming to her in the bright form of a boy. There was no end to His childish play and pranks. She was drowned in that surge of emotion; she forgot all her austere rules and regulations; all her regard for the established rites and ceremonies was washed away. Who can control oneself when submerged in the tidal waves of Bhava?

12. From that day onwards Aghoramani became "Gopala's mother" in the real sense of the term, and the Master began to call her by that name. Sri Ramakrishna expressed great joy to see that extraordinary state of Gopala's mother. He passed his hand over her heart in order to pacify her. He then fed her with whatever good things were available in the room. Even while eating, the Brahmani, under the influence of Bhava, said, "Gopala, my child, your poor mother has spent her life in great misery; she has been earning a miserable living by selling sacred thread spun by her with a spindle. Is this why you are taking so much care of her today?"

The Master made her stay for the whole day with him. She took her bath and food there. He pacified her a little and sent her to Kamarhati a little before sunset. Gopala, seen in Bhava, was in her arms and accompained her as before on her way back to Kamarhati. When she returned home, Gopala's mother sat for Japa according to her previous habit. But could she perform it? For He, the very object seeking whom she prayed, counted, beads, and passed days and nights in meditation, was before her, playing, frolicking, importuning. At last the Brahmani got up and lay on her bedstead with Gopala beside her. The Brahmani had neither any bedding nor even a pillow to rest her head on. So for not having a soft pillow, Gopala began grumbling and would allow her no peace. Having no other course left open, the Brahmani placed Gopala's head on her left arm, and clasping him to her bosom, consoled him, saying "My child, sleep this way tonight. As soon as it is morning, I'll go to Calcutta and ask Bhuta (the eldest daughter of the mistress) to make for you a soft pillow with cotton cleared of seeds."

We have already said that Gopala's mother used to cook her own food, and feeding Gopala with it mentally, take it as Prasada, herself. The following day she went to the garden to collect dry wood to do her cooking early and feed the real Gopala in flesh and blood before her. She saw Gopala also coming with her, collecting dry twigs and piling them in the kitchen. Thus after the mother and son had collected fuel, cooking began. At the time of cooking, the naughty Gopala watched the process, sometimes sitting beside her and sometimes riding on her back. He went on prattling and making many demands on his mother, while the Brahmani sought to control him now by sweet words, now by stern threats.

Gopala's mother came to Dakshineswar once, a few days after the aforesaid event had happened. She saw the Master and went to the Nahavat, where the Holy Mother lived, and sat for Japa. Finishing the usual number of Japa and making salutation, she was going to get up when she found that the Master had come there from the Panchavati. When the Master saw Gopala's mother he said, "Why do you perform so much Japa now? You have already achieved much indeed!"

13. Gopala's mother: "Shall I not perform Japa? Have I attained everything?"

The Master: "Yes, you have attained everything."

Gopala's mother: "Everything?"

The master: "Yes, everything."

Gopala's mother: "What do you say? Have I attained everything?"

The Master: "Yes, everything. You have already finished whatever you had to do for yourself by way of performance of Japa, austerities and other spiritual practices. But you may do these things, if you like, for this body (showing himself), so that it may keep well."

Gopala's mother: "Then whatever I'll do from now on, is yours, yours, yours."

Mentioning this event, Gopala's mother used to tell us now and then, "Hearing these words of Gopala that day, I threw into the Ganga everything, the rosary, the rosary-bag etc. I then performed Japa on the fingers for the good of Gopala. Long afterwards, I began to use a rosary. I thought, 'Must I not do something? What shall I be doing all the twenty-four hours?' I, therefore, count the beads for Gopala's good."

From now on, Gopala's mother's Japa, austerities, etc., came to an end. Visits to Sri Ramakrishna at Dakshineswar became more frequent. That wave of Bhava also gradually washed away her very rigid observance of the established rules of ceremonial purity in regard to food and habits of life. Gopala occupied her mind and heart completely and there was no limit to the ways in which he taught her. And how could she now preserve intact that unswerving routine of hers? For Gopala wanted to eat at odd times, and he thrust into his mother's mouth whatever he ate. Could that be rejected? Moreover, he wept if that were rejected. Since she was incessantly floating on that extraordinary wave of Bhava, the Brahmani knew that it was the play of none else than Sri Ramakrishna, and that it was none but he who was her "Sri Krishna in the form of Gopala, black like a newly-formed cloud and having eyes like the petals of a blue lotus." She, therefore, cooked for him, fed him, and had no hesitation in eating his Prasada.

Thus did the Brahmani of Kamarhati live continuously for two months with Sri Krishna in the form of Gopala, whom she placed now on her breast, now on her back. Indeed! it falls to the lot of rare, fortunate ones only to enjoy such an unbroken surge of Bhava for so long a period and experience the vision of Pure Consciousness condensed and vivified into the divine Name (Nama), divine Abode (Dhama) and the divine Lord (Shyama). Motherly love for God is in itself rare in the world — the acquisition of such love is impossible so long as there is the slightest consciousness of the powers of God in one's mind. How much more rare, it may be easily inferred, is the vision of the divine Lord through that love condensed, as it were, with the help of unprecedented devotion! There is the saying, "Mother Kali is awake in Kaliyuga, Gopala is awake in Kaliyuga." This is perhaps why the vivid and glowing realization of these two forms of the divine Lord are sometimes met with even now.

Sri Ramakrishna said to Gopala's mother, "You have achieved much. The body cannot continue in the Kaliyuga if such a state persists for a long time." It was, it seems, the Master's wish that love for God remained for some time more in this world for the good of humanity, offering an ideal example of that form of Bhava or divine love. After the lapse of two months her Bhava and her vision of Gopala ceased to be continuous. But she got it again as before, whenever she sat quiet a little and meditated on Gopala.

CHAPTER VII

SRI RAMAKRISHNA IN THE COMPANY OF DEVOTEES. THE RETURN CHARIOT JOURNEY IN A.D. 1885 AND THE STORY OF GOPALA'S MOTHER — LAST PART

[TOPICS: 1. Car-festival at Balaram Babu's house. 2. The Master and the Sankirtan of Sri Chaitanya. 3. Balaram's devotional services. 4. Balaram's extraordinary service of the Master. 5. The Master never used "I" and "mine". 6. The Master and his suppliers. 7. The devoted family of Balaram. 8. The Car Festival at his house as an expression of devotion. 9. The wonderful relation of the Master with the women devotees. 10. The Master sending for Gopala's mother. 11. The Master's mood at the arrival of Gopala's mother. 12. The attractiveness of the Master in Bhava. 13. The Master back at Dakshineswar. 14. The Master's reaction on seeing the bundle of Gopala's mother. 15. The repentance of Gopala's mother. 16. The mental outlook of Gopala's mother. 17. Marwari devotees came to the Master. 18. The Master's outlook on presents. 19. The Master giving the presented candies to Gopala's mother. 20. No one should be told of one's vision. 21. Gopala's mother introduced to Swami Vivekananda. 22. The Master seeing a ghost at Kamarhati garden. 23. The Master feeding Gopala's mother. 24. Her vision of the universe as the form of God. 25. Gopala's mother at the Baranagar monastery. 26. Gopala's mother with western women. 27. Gopala's mother at Sister Nivedita's house. 28. The passing away of Gopala's mother. 29. The story of Gopala's mother concluded.]

To those of undivided minds who worship Me and always remain united with Me, I bring and preserve all the things they require.

— Gita IX 22

1. The Master came to Balaram Babu's house at Baghbazar in Calcutta on the occasion of the chariot festival some time after the Brahmani of Kamarhati had had the vision of the divine Lord in the form of Gopala. A crowd of devotees had assembled at Balaram's house. Beside himself with joy, Balaram Babu was receiving and welcoming them all duly. Balaram belonged to a family that was devoted to God for generations. He and his family had the Master's grace in an abundant measure.

2. At one time, we were told by the Master himself that when he had a desire to see Sri Chaitanya's Sankirtan party, he had a vision of it passing through the streets of the town. It was a wonderful sight — a boundless crowd maddened with the unrestrained love-inebriation and charm emanating from its central figure Sri Gauranga, himself lost in the fervour of devotion; a concourse over whom tidal waves of love were sweeping. That limitless sea of humanity began to move from the side of the Panchavati slowly forward in front of the Master's room. The Master said that in that procession he saw Balaram Babu's face, serenely bright with the light of devotion. It was one of the few faces that caught his attention and remained imprinted for ever in his memory. Immediately the Master saw Balaram Babu on his first visit to Dakshineswar Kali temple, he recognized him to be the person seen in that procession.

3. Balaram Babu had an estate at Kothar in Orissa. There the service of God was carried on in the image of Shyamchand (Krishna). He had also a bower in Vrindavan, where the worship of Syamasundara (the beautiful blue boy Krishna) was conducted. Besides, in his Calcutta residence service was performed to the image of Jagannath, which in later days was transferred to Kothar. "The food given by Balaram is pure," said Sri Ramakrishna, "they have been serving God, guests and Sadhus for generation after generation. His father has renounced everything and is living in the holy Vrindavan repeating the name of Hari. I can take with pleasure the food given by Balaram; as soon as it is put into the mouth, it goes down automatically as it were." Indeed of the food given by devotees, it was Balaram's, we had noticed, that he took with greatest pleasure. The Master had his midday meal invariably at Balaram's house whenever he came to Calcutta in the morning. Though he showed some discrimination in regard to the food he took, he had none if it was the Prasada of Narayana or any other deity.

4. There exists an indescribable, uncommon element in even the ordinary activities, daily or occasional, of great souls, who are indeed few and far between. Any one, who was in the company of Sri Ramakrishna, even for a day, would specially comprehend the truth of this statement. If only we analyse the simple matter of the Master's taking food given by Balaram, it

will be quite clear. At one time during his Sadhana, the Master prayed and said to the Mother, "Mother, don't make me a dry and austere monk; keep me above want." The Divine Mother also showed him that four suppliers of provisions for him had been sent to the world. The Master used to say that, of those four, Mathur, the son-in-law of Rani Rasmani, was the first, and Sambhu Mallick, the second. Surendranath Mitra, whom the Master called Surendar and sometimes Suresh, was, he said, a 'half supplier'. We had not the good fortune to see with our eyes the nature and extent of the services rendered by Mathuranath and Sambhu Babu; for we came to the Master long after they had passed away. But we have heard from the Master himself that it was a wonderful affair. We do not remember the Master to have ever mentioned Balaram to be one of the 'suppliers of his provisions'. But the privilege he got of serving the Master which we had occassion to witness, was of an extraordinary nature. His service was not inferior in any respect to that of the other 'suppliers', except that of Mathur Babu. We shall try to describe these things in some other place. Let us now say only this, namely, that Balaram Babu supplied all the food necessary for the Master — rice, candy, farina, sago, barley, vermicelli, tapioca, etc., — from the day he first went to Dakshineswar to the day when the Master passed beyond our gross vision. And Surendra or Suresh Mitra, as he was called, used to make arrangements for the food and bedding for those devotees who spent nights with the Master at Dakshineswar to serve him.

Who can say what hidden relation these persons had with the Master? And who can explain why they had that high privilege vouchsafed to them? We have understood this much that they were rare, fortunate persons, especially marked by the Mother of the universe. They would not otherwise have been born with the privilege of being helpers in the present Lila of Sri Ramakrishna. Otherwise their faces would not have been so deeply imprinted in the ever-free, pure and awakened mind of Sri Ramakrishna as to enable him to recognize them as soon as he saw them. He said, "They belong to 'here' (i.e. to him); they are born with this special privilege."

5. The Master used to say, "They belong to 'here' " instead of "They are mine". For, not the slightest I-consciousness could

find a place in Sri Ramakrishna's pure mind. It was, therefore, very difficult for him to use the words 'I' and 'Mine'.[1] Or, why say difficult, he could not at all use these two words. When it became absolutely necessary to utter them, he would say them in the sense of "I am the servant or the child of the Mother". And this also could only be said if the mind had this attitude beforehand in full. That is why, when in any case it was necessary to say "mine" in the course of conversation, the Master almost always pointed to his body and said 'of this place'. The devotees also could understand from it what he meant. For example, when he said, "such and such a person is not of 'this place'," or "it is not the attitude or idea of 'this place' ", he meant to say, "he or she was not his", or "it was not his attitude or idea".

6. Now we shall say something about the suppliers of the Master's provisions. The Master's first supplier, Mathurnath, was engaged in serving the Master for fourteen years, from the time of his first auspicious advent to the Kali temple to some time after his Sadhana was at an end. The second one, Sambhu Babu lived and served the Master from some time after Mathur Babu passed away to some time before Kesav and other devotees of Calcutta went to him. The "half supplier", Suresh Babu, lived, served and took care of him and his Sannyasin devotees from six or seven years before the Master passed away to four or five years after that event. The Baranagar monastery (which was later converted into the Belur Math) was founded in 1886 in the old, dilapidated house of the Munshi Babus at Baranagar, at the earnest request of this Suresh Babu, and he met the expenses connected with it. There are one and a half suppliers yet to be accounted for. Who are they? The American lady Mrs. Sara. C. Bull, who helped Swami Vivekananda so much in establishing the Belur Math, and Balaram Babu of whom we are speaking, — are they these one and a half? Who will now decide the question in the absence (in gross forms) of Sri Ramakrishna and Swami Vivekananda?

7. Ever since Balaram Babu went to Dakshineswar, he used to invite Sri Ramakrishna to his house at the time of the car

[1] But, in order to avoid being cumbrous, we have sometimes used I and mine in the direct form of speech of the Master, though, in the original, they were invariably the other two expressions. – Tr.

festival every year. His house, or rather the house of his brother Rai Harivallabha Basu Bahadur, who was a famous advocate of Cuttack, was situated on Ramkanta Basu's street at Baghbazar. Balaram Basu used to live in his brother's house. The number of the house was 57. It cannot be ascertained how many times the house at 57 Ramkanta Basu's street was sanctified by the presence of the Master. Who will ascertain how many people have been blessed with the privilege of seeing him there? The Master sometimes jokingly called the Dakshineswar temple, the 'fort' of Kali the Mother. It will not be an exaggeration to call this house Her second 'fort'. "All the members of Balaram's family," said the Master, "are strung to the same tune." Every one of the house, from the master and the mistress to the little children, was the Master's devotee. None of them took anything, even water, before performing the Japa of the name of the divine Lord. Every one observed the ways of pious living like the worship, holy reading, service of monks and gifts for good causes. It is seen in many families that while one or two of the members are religious, the others are of a different nature with their interest confined to worldly affairs. But in this family it was different; all were of the same nature. Rare, perhaps, are the families in the world who are selflessly religious; rarer still are those in which all the members have love for the same ideal and help one another in realizing it. That this family was, therefore, the Master's second 'fort' and that he enjoyed being there, were not matters for surprise.

8. We have already said that the service of Jagannath used to be performed in this house; so a chariot used to be drawn at the time of the chariot festival. But everything was an expression of the love of God and there was nothing of external pomp and grandeur, no decorations, music, the din and bustle of the rabble — there was nothing of all these. A small chariot used to be drawn in the quadrangular verandah in the first floor of the outer apartment facing all the four quarters and overlooking a square court below. A party of Kirtan singers came. They sang Kirtan as the chariot was drawn, and the Master and his devotees joined in the singing. But where else would one meet with such experience as that bliss, that profusion of the love of God, that God-intoxicated mood, and that sweet dance of the Master! Pleased with the pure devotion of the Sattvika family, Jagannath, the Lord of the universe,

did indeed manifest Himself in the image on the chariot and in the body of Sri Ramakrishna! The occasion was unique. Carried away by the current of pure devotion, even the hearts of godless men melted into tears, not to speak of those of devotees. After a few hours of such Kirtan, cooked food was offered to Jagannath, and after the Master had had his meal, all others took Prasad. Afterwards, late in the night, that fair of bliss came to an end, and all, except a few, went home. The writer had the privilege of participating in this blissful celebration only once in his life, that being in the Return-Car-Journey-Festival of 1885, for which Gopala's mother also had been invited at the Master's request. The Master came to Balaram Babu's house on that occasion, spent there two days and two nights, and returned by boat to Dakshineswar on the third day at eight or nine in the morning.

The Master arrived at the house in the morning. He sat for some time in the outer apartment and then he was taken to the inner one for a little refreshment. Many men devotees assembled in the outer apartment, coming in twos and threes, and in the inner apartment came all the women devotees of the Master from the neighbouring houses. Many of the latter were Balaram Babu's relatives or acquaintances. He used to send for them and have them brought to his house, whenever the Master came there. And also whenever he used to go to Dakshineswar to pay a visit to Sri Ramakrishna, he had them brought to his house and took them there with him. Many women devotees — the lady Bhavini, Asim's mother, Ganu's mother and grandmother, or again this man's mother, that person's aunt, a third's husband's sister, a fourth's neighbour and so on and so forth — all came that day.

9. We are unable to express what a sweet relation the Master, devoid of the slightest tinge of desire, had with these pure-hearted and virtuous women devotees. Many of them looked upon the Master even then as their chosen Ideal. Every one had faith in him. Again, some fortunate ones among them like Gopala's Mother knew this directly through spiritual visions. So they knew the Master as more than their own and did not feel any awe, strangeness or hesitation in his presence. When they prepared any nice food at home, in the first instance they used to set apart a portion of it for the Master before using it for the household, and either send it or themselves take it to him at Dakshineswar. It cannot be calculated how many times these ladies walked to

Dakshineswar and back home during the Master's life-time. On some occasions they returned home after sunset, on others, at 10 p.m., on still others, later than midnight after the Kirtan and festival were over at Dakshineswar. The Master, like a boy, eagerly consulted some of them regarding the medicine for his stomach troubles. If any one smiled with a touch of derisiveness at this, he would say, "What do you know? She is the wife of a great doctor; she cannot but know a few medicines." About some one among them, when he saw her intense love for the Lord, he said, "She is a Gopi perfected by God's grace." Of some other, when he had tasted the food cooked by her, he said, "She is a cook of Vaikuntha; she has a perfect hand in cooking 'Sukta'."

10. When he was taking refreshments, the Master spoke of the good fortune of Gopala's Mother to the lady devotees. "That Brahmani," said he affectionately to them, "who comes from Kamarhati and who has motherly love for God as Gopala, has had various visions. She says that Gopala stretches his hand to take food from her. The other day she came here love-intoxicated on account of experiencing many such things. When she was fed, she became a little pacified. I asked her to stay for the night, but she did not. She was equally inebriated on her way back. The cloth on her person became loose and was being dragged along the ground; she had no consciousness of it. I raised the cloth and passed my hand over her heart and head to calm her down a little. She has great devotion and she is very good. Why don't you send for her?"

As soon as this reached Balaram Babu's ear, he sent a man to bring Gopala's mother from Kamarhati; for there was plenty of time for her to arrive. The Master would be staying there for that day and the morrow.

11. The Master finished taking refreshments and came back to the outer apartment and was having talks with the devotees. Before long, the Master's midday meal was finished. The devotees also took Prasada. He took a little rest before he sat in the hall in the outer apartment and conversed with the devotees on various topics. When it was about dusk the Master was in ecstasy. All of us must have seen the metal image of the boy Gopala — it is in the posture of crawling, with this difference that its right hand is raised in the gesture of asking for some food, and its face is turned upwards as if it were looking at the face of some one, with wistful

eyes expressing delight and wanting something. The Master's body and limbs assumed exactly that posture under the influence of Bhava, except for the two eyes which remained in a half-shut, indrawn condition, not seeing anything outside. Immediately after the Master's state of Bhava began, the carriage carrying Gopala's mother arrived and stood at the gate of Balaram Babu's house; and Gopala's mother came upstairs and saw the Master in the form of her chosen Ideal. The devotees understood that it was the devotion of Gopala's mother that had brought about the sudden infusion of the Gopala-consciousness into the Master. All those present there showed her great respect and reverence, thinking how very fortunate she was. All said, "Ah, how wonderful is her devotion! The Master assumed the form of Gopala Himself on account of the urge of her devotion!" Gopala's mother said, "But I don't like such a stiff and rigid posture like a log of wood, under the influence of Bhava. My Gopala will laugh, play, walk and run. Ah! What is this? This stiff-as-wood posture! I don't want to see such a Gopala." On the day on which she first saw the Master thus lose normal consciousness in ecstasy, she really became over-whelmed with fear and said, as she pushed the Master's holy person, "Why are you in such a condition, my child?" That happened when the Master went to Kamarhati for the first time.

12. When we first went to the Master, he was nearly forty-nine years old. Perhaps it was yet five or six months to his forty-ninth year. Gopala's Mother also went to him at that time. Before we met the Master, our idea was that people would enjoy the artless dancing and gestures of a child, but that it would be nothing but ludicrous or disgusting to them when a grown-up robust youth performed such antics. Swami Vivekananda used to say, "Imagine a rhinoceros dancing like a dancing-girl!" But, coming to the Master, we had to change our opinions. Though he was advanced in age, the Master danced, sang, made various gestures — and ah, how sweet they were! "We never dreamt," said Girish Babu, "that a grown-up robust youth looked so well when dancing." But how beautiful was the posture of his body and limbs under the influence of Gopala-consciousness today at Balaram Babu's house! We did not understand then why it looked so beautiful. We only felt that it was beautiful and nothing more. We now understand that, whenever any mood came on him, it came on fully, without the admixture of any other mood with it, and with no

touch of insincerity or showing off. He was then completely inspired by, absorbed in or, as he jokingly said, 'diluted' — this was one of the few English words the Master himself employed — with that mood. The identification was so perfect that no one felt any oddity in a man past middle age acting as a boy or woman in that inspired mood. The strong waves of Bhava within burst out and completely changed his body or made it assume a different form altogether.

13. On that occasion the Master spent two joyous days and nights in the company of the devotees at the house of Balaram Babu. It was now the third day, and he was to return to Dakshineswar. At about eight or nine in the morning a boat was kept ready at the Ghat for the Master's departure. Gopala's mother and another woman devotee, it was settled, would go by that boat to Dakshineswar with the Master, besides one or two boy-devotees who had come with him for his service. Kali (Swami Abhedananda) was perhaps one of them.

Going to the inner apartment, the Master bowed down to Jagannath, received the salutations of the devotee-family, went out, and got into the boat. Gopala's mother and others also followed him to the boat. Some members of Balaram's family respectfully presented Gopala's mother with clothes etc., and knowing that she was in need of a ladle, tongs for gripping hot cooking pots, and some other articles, they made presents of them to her. A bundle containing them was also put in the boat. The boat now moved.

14. While he was going by the boat, the Master noticed the bundle and knew on inquiry that it belonged to Gopala's mother. As soon as the Master heard that it was the bundle containing the things given her by the devotee-family, his face assumed a serious attitude. Instead of addressing Gopala's mother, he began speaking on renunciation to another woman devotee named mother Golap. "One who is endowed with renunciation," said he, "realizes God. One who, after taking one's food in people's houses, comes away empty-handed, and 'sits leaning against the body of the divine Lord', can exert force on Him, because of his renunciation and dependence on Him." The Master did not speak a single word with Gopala's mother on the way that day and looked at the bundle now and again. Seeing that attitude of the Master, Gopala's mother thought, "Let me throw the bundle into the water

of the Ganga." The Master used to joke, play and make merry with the devotees like a five year old boy, but when it was necessary, he could be very strict with them. He could not put up with the slightest improper conduct on the part of any devotee. Nothing, not even the smallest thing, escaped his keen eye; as soon as anyone behaved improperly even in the slightest degree, his keen eye fell on him and the latter at once put forth his best efforts to correct himself. The Master had not to make much effort either; for, if he but looked stern and refrained from speaking with one a while, one would feel restless and repent of the fault committed. A word or two of scolding from the Master's holy mouth were enough to set right those who did not correct themselves even with this. The Master's unique way of dealing with such cases of delinquency was first to captivate the hearts of the persons concerned by working on their sentiment of affection and reverence for him, to evoke in them a sense of his selfless love for them, and then to speak to them a few words by way of correction and instruction.

15. As soon as she reached Dakshineswar, Gopala's mother anxiously went to the Holy Mother at the Nahavat and said to her, "O daughter-in-law, Gopala has been angry to see this bundle; what is the remedy now? I think I should not take the articles with me but distribute them here."

The supremely revered Holy Mother had boundless compassion. Seeing the old lady worried and pained, she consoled her and said, "Let him say so, mother. There is no one to give you these things. What will you do under the circumstances? Have you not brought these things only because you require them?"

In spite of what the Holy Mother told her, Gopala's mother gave away out of those articles one piece of cloth and one or two other things. Then with trepidations in her heart, she cooked with her own hand one or two curries and went to feed the Master. The Master, who knew all people's hearts, did not make any other remark when he saw her repentant. He then treated her as before, speaking with her smilingly. Gopala's mother also felt consoled, fed the Master, and returned to Kamarhati in the evening.

Since her first vision, Gopala's mother, as we said before, had been seeing the ideal form of Gopala for two months without a break. But this did not continue so afterwards. Let no one think on that account that, after that period, she had the vision of the form of Gopala only very rarely, at long intervals. She saw Him daily time and again whenever her heart wanted to see Him. Again, whenever anything had to be taught her, Gopala would suddenly appear before her and make her act accordingly by signs or words or by doing things Himself, thus showing her how to do them. Merging in the Master's holy person again and again, Gopala taught her that He and the Master were not different. He taught her how He should be served, by asking her for things to eat and things to lie on. Again, strolling together with some eminent devotees of Sri Ramakrishna or moving with them with especial intimacy in her presence, He (Gopala) convinced her that He and they were not different, that the devotee and the Divine were one. Therefore, the hesitation she felt in eating things touched by them gradually vanished.

16. After she became firmly convinced that Sri Ramakrishna was her chosen Ideal, Gopala's mother did not very often have the vision of the form of Gopala. Instead, she had the vision of Sri Ramakrishna very frequently and through his form, the divine Lord, who assumed the form of Gopala, taught her whatever was necessary. Deprived of the frequent visions of the form of Gopala she was very much afflicted in the beginning, and she went to Sri Ramakrishna one day and said weeping, "What have you done to me, Gopala? What fault have I committed? Why do I not have your vision (in the form of Gopala), as I used to have before?" Sri Ramakrishna replied, "If, in the Kaliyuga, one has such visions continuously, one's body does not last. It lasts twenty-one days only and then falls off like a dry leaf." Gopala's mother used always to be under the influence of divine inebriation of Bhava for two months after having the first vision of Gopala. She did everything — cooking, bathing, eating, making Japa, meditating and the like — by the force of past habits and as a matter of duty. Owing to past habits her body managed somehow or other to go through them all. But she herself always remained highly inebriated, as it were, with her spiritual mood. How long, therefore, could the body last in this way? It is a matter of surprise that it continued even for two months. The influence of that intoxication diminished a great deal at the end of two months. But, as she could not see Gopala as before, there came on her an intense eagerness to have the vision repeatedly. As a result of that, the 'humour of wind' prevailed in her constitution and she felt a great pain within her heart. She, therefore, said to Sri Ramakrishna,

"Owing to the prevalence of the humour of wind, I feel as if my heart is being sawn through." The Master consoled her and said affectionately, "It is not the humour of wind but the humour of Hari (God). What will be the support of your life if it goes? It is good that it abides. Please eat something whenever you feel too much pain." So saying the Master fed her with various good things that day.

17. Just as many of us men and women of Calcutta (Bengalis) used to go to the Master, many Marwari men and women also visited him from time to time. They came in many carriages to Dakshineswar garden, and after bathing in the Ganga, collecting flowers and performing the worship of Siva and other deities, they assembled under the Panchavati, where they dug a fire-place and cooked various preparations and offered them to the deity. They then gave at first a part of all those things to the Master and afterwards took Prasada themselves. Many of them brought for the Master candy, grapes, almonds, guavas, raisins, pistachios, dry dates, betel leaves, pomegranates, etc., offered them and bowed down to him. For, they were not like most of us; all of them knew that one should not come empty-handed to the hermitages of holy men or the places of deities, and therefore, they would without fail bring something or other with them. But Sri Ramakrishna did not himself take any of these things given by them, with the exception of one or two of the Marwaris. He said, "If they give one roll of betel, they join with it sixteen desires — 'May I win the law-suit in the court', 'May I recover from my disease', 'May I make profit in my trade' and so on."

18. The Master himself did not eat these things nor did he give them to the devotees to eat. But sometimes he would eat as Prasada a little of the cooked food they gave him after they had offered it to the deity; and he would also give it to us to eat. The only person who was thought fit to take the candy, fruits etc., given by them was Narendranath. The Master said, "He has the sword of knowledge ever unsheathed with him. He will not be harmed if he takes these things. His spiritual insight will remain unimpaired." The Master, therefore, sent these eatables to Narendranath's house through some one or other of the devotees who was available. He sent them through Ramlal, his nephew and priest of the Kali temple, on those days on which no one else was available. One day, referring to this, brother Ramlal told us that

when the Master required his service, he would call him after midday meal, and say, "Well, Ramlal, have you no business in Calcutta?" He spoke thus lest Ramlal should be annoyed to be sent too often with those things. Ramlal would reply, "I have no business there at present. But if you ask me, I shall of course go." To this the Master would say: "No, I just wanted to tell you this: you have not gone to Calcutta for a long time; you may have a liking to go there. Why don't you go just once? If you go, please take from that tin box what you want and hire a carriage on share from Baranagar; you will otherwise fall ill on account of the sun. And give Narendra these candy, almonds, etc., and bring me all news about him. He has not come here for a long time. My mind is extremely eager to hear about him." Brother Ramlal would reply, "Ah, what hesistation, lest I should get annoyed!" It is needless to say that brother Ramlal took those opportunities to come to Calcutta and add to the happiness of the devotees.

* * *

There thus came, one day, many Marwari devotees to Dakshineswar. Much candy, fruits etc., accumulated that day as usual in the Master's room, when Gopala's mother and some other women devotees came unexpectedly to pay a visit to the Master. He saw Gopala's mother and came and stood beside her. Then, while passing his hand all over her body from head to foot, he began to express his love like a child when it meets its mother. Pointing at Gopala's mother's body, he said to all, "This case is filled with Hari only; this body consists of Hari alone." Gopala's mother stood still; she was not at all shrinking, though the Master touched her feet. Afterwards the Master brought all the nice things that were there in his room and fed the old lady with them. Whenever Gopala's mother went to Dakshineswar, the Master behaved similarly and fed her. One day she asked him, "Why do you like so much to feed me, Gopala?"

Sri Ramakrishna: "Because you fed me so much in the past."

Gopala's mother: "In the past? When did I feed you?"

Sri Ramakrishna: "In a previous life."

Passing the whole day at Dakshineswar, Gopala's mother took leave of the Master before returning to Kamarhati, when the Master brought and gave her all the candy given by the Marwaris and asked her to take it with her. Gopala's mother said, "Why do you give me so much candy?" To which the Master replied (affectionately touching her chin), "You were at first molasses; you then became sugar, and now you have become candy. Now that you have become candy, eat candy and be happy."

19. All were surprised when the Master gave to Gopala's mother the candy given by the Marwaris. They felt that, by the grace of the Master, the mind of Gopala's mother could no more be affected. Having no other course left open to her, she took all the candy. What else could she do? Gopala would otherwise not cease pressing it on her. Besides, as long as the body lasted, one required everything, as Gopala's mother used sometimes to tell us. "So long as the body lasts, all things, even cummin-seeds and fenugreek-seeds, are necessary. A very strange state indeed!"

20. It was a long-standing habit with Gopala's mother to come and tell the Master everything she experienced while practising Japa and meditation. He said, "One should not tell any one else, his or her visions. In that case visions cease to appear." On being so advised, Gopala's mother one day said to him, "Why? Those are visions of you, of no one else. Should they not be told even to you?" The Master replied, "Though they are visions regarding 'this place', they should not be told even to me." Gopala's mother said, "Indeed!" Afterwards she did not, except on very rare occasions, speak of her visions to any one. A sincere and simple soul as Gopala's mother was, she had absolute faith in whatever Sri Ramakrishna said. And doubting souls like ourselves? The whole of our lives is spent in testing the truth of his words. Therefore it did not fall to our lot to translate them into practice and be happy in the enjoyment of their results.

21. One day, at this time, both Gopala's mother and Narendranath were present at Dakshineswar. Narendranath had even then a great inclination towards the Brahmo Samaj doctrine of a formless God. He had even then a great dislike for so-called idolatry, for deities, images and the like. But then he had by that time the conviction that even if people had resort to images, they might reach in time the formless Divine residing in all beings. The Master had a keen sense of humour. On the one hand, there was the very learned, intelligent Narendranath endowed with all the good qualities, fond of discussions and devoted to the divine Lord,

while on the other, there was the poor, indigent Gopala's mother of simple faith, who hoped to have the grace and vision of God bestowed on her by resorting to His name only, who never had had any literary education whatever, and never knew what discussions and argumentations were even for acquiring divine knowledge. The Master got them both together and had great fun. He asked Gopala's mother to narrate to Narendra how she first had the vision of the divine Lord in the form of the boy Krishna and how He had been having His divine play with her since then. So requested, she said, "Will that not be harmful, Gopala?". Assured by the Master that it would not be, she began to narrate, in a voice choked with emotion and with eyes brimming with tears, the whole story of the sport of the divine Lord in the form of Gopala with her for two months since her first vision of Him. She narrated how Gopala was in her arms with his head on her shoulder, how she came all the way from Kamarhati to Dakshineswar, how she distinctly saw his two purple feet dangling on her chest, how he entered the Master's body from time to time, came out again and then came to her, how he grumbled when he did not get a pillow to sleep on, how he collected wood for cooking, and how naughtily he behaved in order to get food. While narrating these events, the old lady was filled with emotions and began to visualize the divine Lord in the form of Gopala. Although Narendranath had the external covering of a rigid rationalist and spoke of acquiring divine knowledge through reason, inwardly he was always full of intense love of God. He could not refrain from shedding tears when he heard of the ecstasy, vision etc., of the old lady. Again, as she was narrating the story, she artlessly asked Narendranath all along, "My child, you are learned and intelligent; I am destitute and ignorant; I know nothing, understand nothing. Please say if these experiences of mine are mere imaginations or realities." Narendranath also assured the old lady every time and said consoling her, "Mother, what you have seen are all true." The reason why Gopala's mother questioned Narendranath about it so anxiously was perhaps because she was not then having the vision of Gopala continuously as before.

22. One day at this time the Master came to Gopala's mother at Kamarhati with Rakhal; it was about ten in the morning. For, Gopala's mother had a great desire to cook delicious dishes with her own hand and feed him once. The old lady was beside herself

with joy to have the Master with her. She gave them for refreshment whatever she could procure. When they had finished taking it, she spread a bed comfortably in the Babu's house, asked them to rest there, and girding up her loins, went to cook. She had procured various good things from others. She made various kinds of preparations and fed the Master to her full satisfaction at noon. She then affectionately made a bed for him to rest on, by spreading a sheet of cloth washed clean over her own quilt in the southern room on the first floor of the house. Rakhal also lay beside the Master. For the Master looked upon Rakhal as his own child and treated him accordingly. The Master now saw a strange thing there. We venture to state it here only because we heard it from the Master himself; otherwise we would not have narrated it. The Master used to have only a little sleep during the whole day and night. He was, therefore, lying quiet. Rakhal fell asleep by his side. The Master said, "A bad smell was felt. Then I saw two figures in a corner of the room. Their appearance was hideous. Out of their bellies, the entrails were hanging down, and their faces, hands and feet were exactly like the human skeletons arranged in the Medical College, which I had seen sometime before. They said to me humbly, 'Why are you here? Please go away from this place; we feel much pained (perhaps to remember their own condition by contrast) to see you.' On the one hand they were thus supplicating, and on the other, there was Rakhal sleeping. Seeing that they felt pained, I was going to get up and come away with my small bag and towel when Rakhal woke up and said, 'Where are you going?' Saying, 'I shall tell you later on', and catching hold of his hand, I came downstairs. Then we took leave of the old woman. She had only just finished taking her food. After seating ourselves in the boat, I said to Rakhal. 'There are two ghosts there. The Mill of Kamarhati is situated near the garden. They live in that room by smelling (for, with them smelling is eating) the bones etc., thrown away by the Europeans after they have taken their meal.' I said nothing of it to the old woman lest she should get afraid; for she has always got to live alone in that house."

23. Mati Jhil is a lake situated in front of the garden of the late Matilal Sil, a wealthy and well-known citizen of Calcutta. By the side of it is a road running in a northerly direction along the banks of the Ganga straight up to the Baranagar Bazar beyond

the bridge. The garden house of Krishnagopal Ghosh, the son-in-law of Lala Babu and his wife Rani Katyayani, is situated across this road to the east of the place, where the northern side of this lake abuts the road. It was in this graden that Sri Ramakrishna stayed as a patient for eight months, from the middle of December 1885 to the middle of August 1886, the date of his disappearance from the gross eyes of the devotees. This garden, called by the devotees as "the Kasipur garden", is a place which, alas, produces great grief, but at the same time a sublime elation too, in their hearts. Their sadness is understandable as the Master was sick there; but how could they be elated also in such a tragic situation — is a question that would naturally arise in a reader's mind. The answer is this: it was the disease in the divine person of the Master that led to the development of that wonderful bond of love that knit the devotees together into a fraternity of varying types of aspirants. It led also to the grouping of the devotees into different classes — devotees of the inner and the outer circles, would-be monks and householder devotees, Jnanis and Bhaktas. The differences between these became clearer during this period. Again it was here that the foundation of the conviction that all of them belonged to the same spiritual family, was laid. Besides, to what a large number of people did the Master's stay at Kasipur give an opportunity to contact him and become blessed by having an immediate experience of the light of spirituality. It was here that Narendranath experienced the Nirvikalpa Samadhi as the result of his Sadhana. It was again here that the twelve boy-devotees including Narendra had ochre clothes from the holy hand of the Master. And it was here again, in the afternoon (between three to four p.m.) of the first day of January 1886, in the course of his last walk in the garden path, that the Master, passing into an extraordinary ecstatic state of mind on seeing the devotees, imparted direct spiritual power to them by touching the hearts of all with his holy hand, saying, "What more shall I say to you? May you have spiritual awakening!" As in Dakshineswar, here also came every day crowds of people, men and women. Here also the Holy Mother was daily engaged in the service of the Master, preparing his food and doing other household work. Here Gopala's mother and other lady devotees also came to him and took part in the service of the Master and his devotees, some of them spending a night or two also before they returned. When, therefore, we think of the wonderful assemblage of the devotees at the Kasipur garden, it appears to us that the Mother of the universe produced the disease in the holy body of the Master only for the fulfilment of a great unknown purpose. It was here that, witnessing daily the Master's divine sports — the coming of new devotees, the Master's ever-blissful figure, the daily manifestation of his extraordinary powers, etc., — many devotees of long-standing thought that he only feigned his illness for the good of the people and that he would discard the disease at his own will and be in normal health again.

During his days at the Kasipur garden, the Master took only liquid food made of barley, vermicelli and farina. One day he expressed a desire to take thickened milk prepared by mixing with it the powder of zedoary, as was generally given to invited guests on special occasions in the houses of the Calcutta people. Nobody raised any objection to it. For, as it was possible for him to take barley, farina-porridge, etc. they thought there was little chance of thickened milk aggravating the disease. The doctors also did not raise any objection. It was, therefore, settled that Yogindra should go to Calcutta early on the morrow, purchase and bring a little of such thickened milk from the market.

Yogindra started at the appointed time. On his way he thought, "The thickened milk available in the market is adulterated with many other things along with the powder of zedoary. Will it not increase the illness if he takes it?" All the devotees looked upon the Master as the life of their lives; therefore, all had only one thought in their minds since he fell ill — and that was the thought of his recovery. It was certainly for that reason that such a thought arose in Yogin's mind. He thought again, "But I did not ask the Master about it before I left. Therefore, will he not be annoyed if I were to have it prepared by some devotee and go back with it?" Thinking in this way, Yogindra arrived at Balaram Babu's house at Baghbazar, where he had to tell the devotees the reason of his coming when he was questioned by them. All the devotees then said, "Why market-milk? We ourselves will prepare it and give it to you. But it cannot be taken there at this time of the day, for it will require time to prepare it. So, please have your meal here now. In the meantime the milk will be got ready. You can take it at three in the afternoon." Yogin agreed, and he therefore returned to Kasipur only at about four p.m. with the home-made milk.

Sri Ramakrishna had wanted to take the milk at noon and

waited a long time for it, but at last he took his usual food. Afterwards, when Yogin returned, the Master heard everything from him. He became much annoyed and said to him, "You were told to buy the milk from the market; I wished to take the market-milk. Why did you go to the devotee's house and give them trouble over it? Besides, this milk is too thick and hard to digest; can this be taken? I'll not take it." And in fact he did not touch it even. He asked the Holy Mother to feed Gopala's mother with the whole of it and said, "It is a thing given by the devotees; Gopala is there in her heart; her taking it will be the same as my doing so."

24. When the Master passed beyond the ken of gross human eyes, there was no limit to the distraction of Gopala's mother. She did not go anywhere outside Kamarhati for a long time. She lived alone in solitude. Afterwards, when she had visions of the Master as before, that mood of hers came to an end. We heard a good deal of such visions which Gopala's mother had even after the Master was out of sight. One of these was the wonderful vision she had on the occasion of her visit to see the car festival, at Mahesh on the other side of the Ganges. She saw with a heart overflowing with bliss the presence of Gopala in everything before her. She said that she then saw that the chariot, Jagannatha Deva on the chariot, those who were drawing the chariot — that vast crowd of people — all were her Gopala. But he had assumed different forms; that was all. Inebriated with affection and intense love at getting this direct indication of the universal form of the Divine, she lost normal consciousness. Once, personally describing it to a woman friend of hers, she said, "At that time I was not myself; I danced and laughed — created a second Kurukshetra (i.e. a battle scene)."

25. Whenever she felt the least restlessness in her mind, she used to come since then to the Sannyasin devotees of the Master at the Baranagar monastery, where she found her mental peace restored. On such occasions the Sannyasins at the Math used to ask her to offer cooked food to the Master and feed him. Gopala's mother also would be delighted, prepare one or two curries with her own hand, and offer them to the Master. When the monastery was removed to Alambazar, and afterwards to Nilambar Babu's house on the other side of the Ganga, Gopala's mother came to those places also, remained the whole day there and enjoyed bliss. She spent the night also there on rare occasions.

26. When Sara (Mrs. Sara C. Bull), Jaya (Miss J. Macleod) and Nivedita came to India with Swami Vivekananda on his return from the West, one day they went to Kamarhati to see Gopala's mother and were highly pleased with her talk and courtesy. Gopala's mother saw her Gopala residing in them too. She, we remember, touched their chins and kissed them affectionately. She then lovingly made them sit on her own bed and gave them parched rice, balls of coconut, etc., to eat, and asked by them, told them a little of her visions. The Western ladies ate those things with delight and were charmed to listen to her words. They asked of her for some parched rice in order to take it to America.

27. Hearing the wonderful story of the life of Gopala's mother, sister Nivedita was so much charmed that, when in 1904 Gopala's mother became very ill and incapable of doing anything and was brought to Balaram Babu's house at Baghbazar, she expressed great eagerness to take her to her (Nivedita's) Baghbazar house at 17 Bosepara Lane and keep her there. Gopala's mother too agreed without the least hesitation on seeing Sister Nivedita's eagerness. For, Gopala, we said before, had removed her idea of difference regarding everything. We remember another event as an example of it. One day at Dakshineswar, Narendranath ate a cupful of goat's meat offered to the Mother Kali and went out to wash his hand. The Master asked a woman devotee to clean that place. Gopala's mother was standing there. The moment she heard that word of the Master she removed with her own hand those leavings, and cleaned that place. When the Master saw it, he became happy and said to the above-mentioned woman devotee, "Just see how liberal she is daily becoming."

Gopala's mother lived at Sister Nivedita's residence since then. Nivedita, the Swami's spiritual daughter, served her as she would her own mother. The arrangement for her food was made in a Brahmana family near by. Gopala's mother went there at meal time every day and took a little rice. At night some one of that family personally brought to her room a few Luchis and some other preparations. She lived for about two years in this manner, and passed away in the waters of the Ganga. When she was taken according to Hindu rites, during her last days to the bank of the Ganga, Nivedita decorated her bed with her own hand, covering it beautifully with flowers, garlands, sandal-paste, etc. She had a party of Kirtan-singers brought, and dissolved in tears, she personally went with her, barefooted, to the bank of the Ganga. Nivedita spent her nights there for the two days that Gopala's mother was alive. Very early on the morning of the eighth of July 1906, when the eastern sky was assuming wonderful beauty on account of the reddish hue of the rising sun, when a few dim stars in the blue sky were still twinkling and looking down on the earth, and when the Ganga, the daughter of the "Father of mountains", was full with her high tide flooding both the banks with white waves and flowing with a sweet, gentle murmur — Gopala's mother's body was gently and reverently placed half immersed in those waves; her five vital forces united with the feet of the Divine, and she attained the eternal abode of fearlessness.

As there was no relative of hers present, a Brahamana Brahmacharin of the monastery at Belur performed her obsequies and followed the twelve-day-period of after-death observances according to the injunctions of the texts dealing with the subject.

At the end of these twelve days, Sister Nivedita, with her heart pierced with grief, invited many local ladies, known to Gopala's mother, to her own school building, and arranged for Kirtan, festival and other observances.

Before she passed away, Gopala's mother left to the care of the Belur monastery the picture of Sri Ramakrishna which she had been worshipping so long, to be kept in the temple there. She also gave a sum of two hundred rupees at that time for the service of the Master.

She considered herself to be a Sannyasini during the last ten or twelve years of her life and used to put on ochre cloth.

APPENDIX

THE HUMAN ASPECT OF THE MASTER[1]

[TOPICS: 1. People's reverence for the Master generally based on hearing of his Yogic powers. 2. Undesirability of such devotion. 3. Worshipper attains similarity with the worshipped in real devotion. 4. Light from the study of the life of an incarnation. 5. The village of Kamarpukur. 6. The wonderful behaviour of the boy Ramakrishna. 7. His search for truth. 8. The result of this search. 9. The deep meaning of the simple words of Sri Ramakrishna. 10. The Master's daily habits, his likes and dislikes. 11. Sri Ramakrishna as the awakener of spiritual consciousness. .]

1. Many people speak many things about the divine nature of Bhagavan Sri Ramakrishna. Enquiry would show that the faith and reverence of most people is based on their admiration for his super-human Yogic powers. In reply to the question "Why do you respect him?" the persons interrogated would generally say that Sri Ramakrishna could see events happening at great distances from the Dakshineswar temple; that he sometimes cured severe physical diseases by his touch; that he always had communication with gods and goddessess; and that his words were so infallible that any word coming out of his mouth, though seemingly unlikely to correspond to facts, would change and control the events of external nature. For example, the speaker might continue, it is said that even a person condenmed to death by the court was saved from sure death and was specially honoured instead, only because the Master bestowed a little of his grace and blessing on him; or that a white flower was produced on a tree which invariably produced red flowers only.

Or, others might say that Sri Ramakrishna could know men's thoughts; that his keen insight could penetrate through the external man and fathom people's mental constitution, including the inclination of their mind; that at the mere touch of his delicate hand, there appeared before the eyes of the devotees of even restless minds the forms of their chosen Ideals, inducing in them deep

[1] An article read by the author at a meeting convened at the Belur monastery on the occasion of the seventy-second birth anniversary of Sri Ramakrishna.

meditation; and that in the case of some particularly fit persons, the gate to the Nirvikalpa Samadhi opened for them at his will.

Again, some would say, "We don't know why we revere him. Ah, what a wonderfully perfect ideal of knowledge and devotion we saw in him! We do not see the like of him even among the ideal persons worshipped by the world, or among personages exalted in scriptures like the Vedas and the Puranas, not to speak of living or known human beings. To our eyes, compared with him, these seem to be of little splendour. We are unable to say whether it is a hallucination of our mind; but our eyes have become dazzled with that bright effulgence and our minds merged for ever in his love, so that they cannot turn back from him even if we try to draw them away from him. Knowledge, inference and reasoning have all been set at rest. We can say only this: "I am Thy servant, birth after birth, O Sea of Mercy; I don't know Thy destination. And mind? I don't know it either. And who wants to know it? I have by Thy command done away with everything — enjoyment, salvation, devotion, Japa, Sadhana, etc. The only thing that remains is a desire to know Thee; take me beyond that also, O Lord."[1]

It is therefore clear that, if we leave out the cases of the few last mentioned persons, all other people have devotion to, faith in, and reliance on, him only on account of his manifest external powers or his subtle mental endowments. Men of gross intellect think that, if they revere him, their diseases will be cured, or that at the time of danger or difficulty, external events will be regulated in their favour. It does not take one long to see that this current of selfishness is flowing in their minds, though they do not plainly admit it.

The people of the second class, who have a somewhat subtle intellect, revere him only because they will attain powers of clairvoyance and the like and live in places like Goloka by being counted among his followers, big or small. Or, if they are a little more advanced intellectually, they think they will attain Samadhi and become liberated from the bondage of birth, old age and death. It is easily understood that their own self-interest is at the root of this faith too.

2. Although we have had many such examples of Sri Rama-

[1] A quotation from a poem by Swami Vivekananda in Bengali.

krishna's divine powers, and although we have no doubt that devotion offered to him even with the motive of fulfilling one's own desired objects is productive of endless good, a discussion on these subjects is not our aim. Our aim is, on the contrary, an attempt to draw a picture of his human traits.

Devotion with a motive, devotion for removing any kind of want of the devotee, prevents that devotee from ascending to the highest step of the knowledge of truth. Selfishness always produces fear, which again soon makes man weak. The attainment of man's self-interest increases egoism, and sometimes idleness too in his mind, and veils his vision. Therefore, he cannot see the real truth. That was why Sri Ramakrishna used to keep a special eye on the circle of his devotees so that the said defect might not creep into them. Whenever he came to know that any new mental powers, clairvoyance and the like, had been manifested in some of his disciples as a result of their practice of meditation and other Sadhanas, he forbade them to follow those practices for some time, lest egoism should arise in their minds and make them lose sight of the aim of God-realization. We witnessed this many times. We heard him say over and over again that to possess those powers was not the aim of human life. But weak man does not proceed to do anything or revere anyone without calculating his profit and loss, and instead of learning the lessons of renunciation from the life of Sri Ramakrishna, who was a glowing example of that quality, resorts to that life for the fulfilment of his own enjoyment. He thinks that Sri Ramakrishna's extraordinary austerities, his renunciation, his unusual love for truth, his childlike simplicity, his reliance on God — all these were practised for the fulfilment of his (the devotee's) enjoyment, as it were. Human weakness is the only reason for this attitude. Therefore, a discussion of the human traits of Sri Ramakrishna will be of great benefit to us.

3. It is well known in all the religious books of all peoples that even a little of devotion, if practised rightly, makes the devotee similar to the object of his worship. The oozing of blood from the hands and feet of the devotee whose mind was absorbed in the figure of Jesus on the cross, the great burning sensation in the body of Sri Chaitanya and his occasional corpse-like states due to his identification with the pain of separation from God felt by Srimati, the motionless posture of the Buddhist devotee for a very long time before the motionless figure of the Buddha in meditation — all

these and similar examples point to this fact. We have seen with our own eyes how the love for a particular person slowly and unconsciously effects changes in one, tending towards resemblance with the object of love — how one's external gestures, deportment and currents of thought change and become similar to those of the object of one's love. If the love and devotion to Sri Ramakrishna also do not daily make our life, at least a little similar to his, it should be understood that the said love and devotion are not worth the name.

There may arise the question, "Can then every one of us become a Paramahamsa Ramakrishna? Has it ever been seen in the world that one man has become completely similar to another?" Although they cannot be exactly similar, they, we reply, can surely be like things cast in the same mould. The life of each great soul in the spiritual world is like a special mould. Cast in those moulds, the successive generations of their disciples have been preserving those different moulds till today. Man's power is small; a whole life's effort is not enough for him to become like any one of those prototypes. If, fortunately, any one is ever formed really similar to any one of the models, we call him a perfect soul and revere him as such. All the physical and mental actions — speech, thought, deportment, etc., — of a perfected man become similar to those of the great soul, the founder of the faith of which the former is a follower. The mind and body of the former become a fully developed instrument for containing, preserving and imparting to others that great power, the first manifestation of which in the founder had astonished the world earlier. Different lines of disciples have thus been preserving from time immemorial the spiritual powers transmitted by different great personalities who founded those lines.

4. Those great souls whose lives are unique expressions of Divine glory and are of immense spiritual significance leave behind new moulds formed of their lives and experiences, which become models and patterns for others to follow. Such unique personalities are worshipped as incarnations of God. Incarnations discover new religious doctrines, new paths. They impart the power of spirituality to others by a mere touch. Their energy is never directed to the glamour of lust and gold in this transitory world. It becomes clear by a study of their lives that they are born to show others the path to God-realization — and not secure their own enjoyment

or their own liberation. It is their sympathy with the sorrows of others and their love for them that urge them on to action and help them in the discovery of the path leading to the removal of the sorrows and miseries of others.

We had no idea of the hidden springs of power and holiness of the great ones known as incarnations such as Krishna, Buddha, Jesus, Sankara, Chaitanya and others, till we had the blessing of seeing the divine form of Sri Ramakrishna. We laboured under the misconception that the record of the uncommon events in their lives were later additions made by disciples with the ulterior motive of adding to their own number. And the incarnations themselves, we inferred, were queer, imaginary, mythical beings without any significance to the civilized world. Or, even when it was conceded that God could assume forms and incarnate Himself, it could not be believed that human traits like those in us would he present in these incarnations also. It could not be easily conceived that their bodies could be subject to diseases, that pain and pleasure were present in their minds, and that a fight between God and Satan could ever have gone on in them as in us, ordinary mortals. We have come to know the truth about this through the holy contact with Sri Ramakrishna. We have all read or heard of the wonderful harmony of human and divine traits in the personality of incarnations. But before we met Sri Ramakrishna, we thought there could be no harmony between childlike simplicity and austere manhood. Many say that it is only his simplicity of a five-year-old boy that attracts them. A helpless boy, ignorant of worldly ways, is an object of love on the part of all people, and they are naturally inclined to protect him. Such a feeling arose in the minds of men on seeing Sri Ramakrishna, though he was advanced in age. They were thereby charmed and attracted towards him. This is no doubt true to a certain extent; but our idea is that it was not this trait alone that attracted people in general. According to our experience, faith in, and devotion to, him arose in the minds of the visitors simultaneously with love and delight. It seems that the mighty power within, veiled by a delicate covering of childlike simplicity, was the cause of that attraction. Describing the superhuman character of Sri Ramachandra, the king of Ayodhya, the famous poet Bhavabhuti wrote: "Who can know the minds of superhuman souls, harder than adamant but softer than flowers?" The same remark applied to Sri Ramakrishna too.

The childlike nature of Sri Ramakrishna was a novel experience to superficial observers. Although a fathomless faith, unbounded simplicity, and an infinite love of truth were always manifested in his mind, worldly-minded people could, however, see in him only a simpleton lacking in worldly wisdom. He had a deep faith in the words of all people, especially of those who wear the dress and emblems of religion. The ideas current in the country and in his own village contributed a great deal to the manifestation of that wonderful trait in him.

5. A vast stretch of land extending over many square miles and covered by green paddy fields lending the appearance of a green sea or, in the absence of paddy, of an immense expanse of soil in its natural grey, presenting none-the-less the same sweep of the sea; scattered islands of human habitation consisting of small peasants' cottages of mud, neat and clean, under the shade of clusters of bamboos and trees like the banyan, date, mango and peepul; here and there the blue expansive waters of lotus-studded tanks like Haldarpukur, abounding in red lotus flowers hovered over by humming bees and surrounded by tall palm trees having leaves of still deeper blue; a few small but famous temples of stone or brick where deities like "Old Siva" are installed; the ruins of the old fort, Mandaran; the ancient crematoria on the outskirts with the bones of the village forbears lying scattered here and there; pastures covered with green grass; a dense mango grove; the noted meandering streamlet; the ever-crowded long public road from Burdwan to Puri encircling more than half of the village — this is Kamarpukur, the birth-place of Sri Ramakrishna.

6. The Vaishnava religion founded by Sri Chaitanya and his disciples is prevalent there. The peasants sing the songs composed by these poets, while working. In the evening when the day's work is done, they drown their fatigue in the bliss derived from these songs. A simple poetic faith lies at the root of this religion. For such a faith and religion as of this village, situated far away from the rough waves of the competitive struggle for existence, a boy's impressionable heart provides a very favourable field. It was all the more so in the case of the boy Ramakrishna, whose childlike behaviour was regarded as extraordinary even there. Everybody was surprised to see the sublimity of his aim and the one-pointedness of his application to them, even if they failed to understand his extraordinary actions. Hearing from the mouths of the expounders

of the Puranas that a man uttering the name of Rama becomes purified, this boy was found to reflect, "Why then does the expounder himself require even now purification by ablution and such rites?" Or, it was observed that listening but once to a drama, he could learn the whole thing by heart. and stage it in the mango-grove with his friends as the actors. Seeing and hearing their wonderful acting and music, the wayfarers on the road would stop, charmed and forgetful of their journey. The boy's cleverness manifested itself in other ways too — in making images, in painting the pictures of deities, in mimicry, in music and Sankirtan, in getting by heart the Ramayana, the Mahabharata, the Bhagavata and other scriptures by merely listening to their recitals, and in the deep apprehension of the beauty of Nature. He was, we have heard from him, in ecstasy for the first time on seeing a flight of snow-white cranes against the background of deep black rain-bearing clouds. He was then six or seven years old.

To become absorbed in the mood that came to him, was the special characterstic of this boy's mind. Pointing to the court-yard of the house of a merchant, the neighbours tell even now how the person who was to act as Siva in the "Conversation between Siva and Parvati" became suddenly ill and was unable to act his part; how everyone requested Ramakrishna to put on Siva's dress and act; and how, putting on that dress, he was so deeply absorbed in that mood that he lost all normal consciousness for a long time through identification with Siva-consciousness. The restlessness of mind proper to a boy, it is evident, did not touch him, though he was indeed a boy in age. Whenever he was attracted by anything through his eyes or ears, its picture was so firmly imprinted in his mind that it was impossible for him to be at rest without mastering it wholly and expressing it in a novel form.

7. Coming in contact with the external world, his senses developed quickly and had not to depend on books and pictures. The cardinal principle of his life was this, namely, "I shall accept anything as true only after having subjected it to close scrutiny. If it stands the test, I will reduce it to practice. And I shall not look down upon anything of the world if it is not demonstrably untrue." In his boyhood Ramakrishna, who possessed such a wonderful memory and intellect, was sent to the village school for education; but that peculiar childlike nature of his did not change. He thought, "What purpose will it all serve — this hard

study, this sitting up late at night, this rumination of the glosses and commentaries? Will this help me in attaining the truth?" Pointing to the teacher of the school, who was a finished product of that kind of education, his mind said, "You also will become like him, clever at ascribing ingenious meanings to simple words; you also will manage somehow your worldly affairs like him with some money, received as farewell presents earned by flattering the rich; and you also will read the truths recorded in the scriptures and teach them to others, but, 'like an ass carrying sandalwood', will not be able to realize them in your own life." His discriminating intellect told him, "There is no need for that bread-winning education which enables one only to 'bundle up rice and plantain'. Go rather for that supreme education which will enable you to realize the whole truth, the hidden mystery of human life." Ramakrishna gave up going to school, and applied his mind to the worship of the blissful image of the Devi. But where was peace even in that? His mind questioned, "Is it true that She is the universal Mother, the embodiment of bliss and not a mere stone image? Is it true that She accepts leaves, flowers, fruits, roots, etc., offered to Her with devotion? Is it true that a gracious glance of Hers liberates man from all kinds of bondage and endows him with divine knowledge? Or, is it a superstition of the human mind, augmented by fond imagination and tradition of ages that has produced this unreal shadowy figure? And has man thus been deceiving himself from time immemorial?" His mind became extremely eager to solve that great problem and, side by side, the sprout of intense detachment grew slowly and imperceptibly in that simple mind. His marriage now took place, but it failed to detract him from the pursuit of a solution for the above problems by offering the prospects of worldly enjoyments. His mind always remained engrossed in attempting the solution of that problem in various ways; and marriage, worldly affairs, worldly thought, earning money, enjoyment and even the extremely necessary bodily functions like eating, drinking, walking and sleeping were all reduced to a useless memory. The childlike nature of Sri Ramakrishna, which was the object of ridicule for the worldly-wise at far off Kamarpukur, became much more developed in the Dakshineswar temple, and was regarded as insanity, much more contemptible than simplicity, by the worldly wise employees of the temple. But was there any incoherence and aimlessness in it? "I'll have the immediate knowledge of the

Reality beyond the senses, I'll touch It and taste It in the fullest measure" — was not this the special characterstic of that insanity? That adamantine determination of the mind, that unconquerable perseverance, that crystal-clear sincerity and that one-pointedness of purpose which produced a novel beauty in the boy Ramakrishna at Kamarpukur, now constituted the insanity of the youth Ramakrishna at Dakshineswar! What an unprecedented event!

A violent storm went on raging unabated in his mind for twelve long years. Tossed violently by the waves of doubt and disbelief, the life's tiny boat of Sri Ramakrishna was perilously near sinking. But that heroic heart never gave way, was not frightened at the sure prospect of immediate death. It went forward along its own path with only one thing to support and sustain — the love of the Divine and faith in Him. The clamours in the world produced by lust and gold and the demands of conflicting values designated as good and bad, merit and dermit, vice and virtue, were left far below; and the mighty waves of Bhava took him up above the petty squabbles of a humdrum life. This extraordinary surge of endless emotions and the practice of severe penances shattered Sri Ramakrishna's strong body and mind, but at the same time gave them a new form and a new beauty. It was thus that the fully developed instrument for containing the Mahabhava, the supreme love of God, and for imparting great spiritual truth, was made ready.

8. Will you, O man, be able to comprehend the story of this wonderful heroism? In your gross eyes the weight and worth of a thing are determined by bulk or quantity. How can you even imagine that refinement of mind which ends in total elimination of self-centredness and egotism in a way that it becomes naturally impossible for the body and the mind of a person to indulge in any selfish effort, however small? The hands of Sri Ramakrishna used to become stiff and benumbed on consciously or unconsciously touching any metal — to grab it was then out of the question! He used to lose his way, however familiar, if he happened to come carrying from any place even trifling things like flowers and leaves without the owner's permission, until he returned to the place and abandoned the objects. If he tied a knot, his respiration remained suspended and the outgoing breath would not come out in spite of much effort till he untied it. His organ of generation would shrink instantaneously, like the limbs of a tortoise, if his

body were touched by any lewd woman. How can the ordinary human mind, entrenched in the pursuit of self-interest from the very birth, ever have the mental refinement to notice or appreciate those pure and subtle mental states of which the above-mentioned forms of behaviour are but external expressions? Can even our wildest flight of imagination enter into the sublime realm of those ideas? We have learnt from our very birth how to hide our impure ideas within and show ourselves off as purity itself. How many of us will have any scruple to conceal truth if we can become rich or famous by such deceit? Take again, courage. Many of us may not be bold enough to give ten blows for one, or to run up towards and seize a cannon vomitting fire, or to give up our life for the fulfilment of an object we cherish. Still, we appreciate that type of courage and feel proud to hear of such deed. But can we appreciate and feel a glow in our heart to witness that courage, by the promptings of which Sri Ramakrishna renounced the enjoyments of the earth and heaven and risked even his mind and body for the sake of a thing beyond the senses, unknown and unfamiliar to the world? If you can, O heroic reader, you have attained the immortality held in veneration by ourselves and others.

9. No one had the power to understand how deep were the meanings of his very trifling words and actions, unless they were explained by himself. One day he explained to us why he mentioned names of familiar persons or things or touched them as soon as his ecstasy came to a close, or why he named some article of food and said that he would eat or drink it. He said, "The minds of people in general roam in the nerve centres of the anus, of the organ of generation and of the navel only. A little purified, that mind sometimes ascends to the centre in the heart and having the vision of the light or of luminous figures, enjoys bliss. When the mind gets deeply habituated and sticks steadfastly to one ideal to the exclusion of all others, it goes up to the centre in the throat and it becomes almost impossible for it to talk of anything except that ideal on which it dwells ever more. Even when the mind has ascended there, it may go down to the lower centres and altogether forfeit that high mood. But if somehow or other, with the help of exceptional one-pointedness, it can reach the centre between the eyebrows, it goes into Samadhi and enjoys a bliss, compared with which the enjoyment of the objects of the senses in the lower centres seems to it to be contemptible; all fear of falling from there vanishes

for ever. There the light of the Supreme Self with a little veiling is manifested to it. Although there remains just a little separation from It, a clear understanding of the non-dual supreme Self is obtained as soon as the mind ascends there. The moment this centre is crossed, the knowledge of difference and non-difference vanishes altogether, and the mind is established in the perfect knowledge of Non-duality. My mind comes as far down as the centre in the throat, and that too for your education. But it has somehow to be kept down by force even there. For, as it has remained for six months in the full knowledge of Oneness, it has a natural inclination in that direction. If the mind is not tied to trifling desires like — 'I will do this, I will eat that', 'I'll see this person', 'I'll go to that place' and so on — it becomes very difficult to bring it down. And, if it does not come down, everything, talking, walking, eating, keeping the body alive and the like, becomes impossible. This is why, at the very time of going into ecstasy, I entertain a trifling desire as 'I'll smoke, I'll go to that place," etc.; but even then, the mind comes down to that object of desire only when it is mentioned again and again."

10. The author of the Panchadasi has stated at one place: "A person attaining Samadhi and its resultant powers, does not entertain any desire to change the way of life that he had been accustomed to follow before. All things or states, except the reality of Brahman, seem absolutely hollow to him." The truth of this is verified in the life of Sri Ramakrishna. Many of those conspicuous habits and ways of life observed in his day to day life at Dakshineswar after his devotional transformation, were with him even from early life. We proceed to give a few of them here.

It was his habit to keep his body, clothes, beddings, etc., very clean. He himself loved to keep things in their proper places and taught others to do so; he felt annoyed if anyone did otherwise. At the time of going to any place he enquired whether his towel, the small bag and personal requirements had all been taken without any omission. At the time of returning from there also, he would remind the disciple accompanying him, not to leave behind any of those things forgetfully. He was very anxious to be punctual in doing all things. When he had said he would do a thing, he invariably carried it out. So also if he had agreed to accept a thing from one person, he would accept it from none else but him, lest he should be guilty of falsehood. Even if insistence in such matters resulted in great inconvenience to himself, he would rather put up with it than break his word. When he saw anyone using a torn piece of cloth, umbrella or foot-wear, Sri Ramakrishna would instruct him to buy a new one if he was able to do so, or if not, himself would buy one for him sometimes. He used to say, "Fortune frowns at a man who uses such things and he loses grace." Words indicative of pride or egoism would never come out from his holy mouth. When he had to speak of his own idea or opinion, he pointed at his own body and used words like, 'The idea of this place' or 'The opinion of this place'. He used to observe minutely the configuration of all the limbs and the other features of the disciple's body, such as the eyes, the face, the hands and the feet, as well as his deportment and his ways of eating, drinking, walking and sleeping. He could by so doing accurately ascertain the course of his mental faculties, the degree of his development and the like, so that we never found him wrong in his conclusions in the course of our very intimate relationship with him.

Most of those who went to Sri Ramakrishna felt that he loved them more than he did all others. The deep sympathy that he had with the weal and woe of every one was, it seems to us, the only explanation of it. Although sympathy and love are two different things, the external characteristics of the latter are not very different from those of the former. It was, therefore, not impossible that sympathy was taken for love. It was an innate characteristic of Sri Ramakrishna's mind to become completely absorbed in a thing at the time of thinking of it. Owing to this capacity, he could exactly know the state of each disciple's mind and rightly prescribe whatever was necessary for the improvement of that state. In the course of describing Sri Ramakrishna's childlike nature we have tried to show how fully he learnt from his childhood the use of his eyes and other senses in making correct observation. He tried his best to develop this quality in his disciples too. He always impressed on them the need of applying reason before performing any action. We heard him say again and again that it was reason alone which could reveal the merits and demerits of things and make the mind go forward towards true renunciation. He had never any liking for a person of a narrow intellect or for one devoid of it. Every one heard him say, "You should be a devotee, it is true, but why should you, therefore, be a fool?" Or, "Don't be onesided and fanatical; that is not the attitude of 'this place'.

The attitude of 'this place' is, 'I shall eat the same food stuff, dressed and prepared as different dishes.'" According to him one-sidedness of intellect is a dull and drab attitude. "How monotonous!" were his words of reprimand to the disciple who could not feel delight in any but a particular aspect of the divine Lord. He used these words in such a way that the disciple had to hide his face in shame. It was undoubtedly under the impulse of this liberal and universal idea that he became engaged in practising all the modes of Sadhana of all faiths and was able to discover the grand truth, 'As many faiths, so many paths.'

16. The flower blossomed. Mad to taste the honey, the bees came flying from all quarters. Like a full-blown lotus, with its heart perfectly uncovered by the touch of the sun's rays he attracted honey bees of devotees from all directions, and he was generous to all who came and was unsparing in his effort to satisfy every one of them. Has the world ever before had the taste of that immortal honey of spirituality which Sri Ramakrishna gave it — Sri Ramakrishna, who was altogether innocent of Western education and whose life was built on the pattern of the eternal religion of India regarded by some moderns as superstition? Has the world ever before witnessed the play of that great power of spirituality which Sri Ramakrishna accumulated and imparted to his disciples, under the forceful impulse of which the people, in spite of the light of modern science, are realizing that religion is an object of immediate knowledge, something living, moving and tangible, — are perceiving that an under-current of the universal, eternal and unchangeable religion has been flowing in the hearts of all the multiplicity of religions, vivifying them all? Have the words of hope and assurance been ever before proclaimed to the world, that man, travelling from truth to truth, like the wind from flower to flower, is slowly and gradually proceeding towards an immutable non-dual Truth and will some day realize without fail that endless and boundless Truth beyond mind and speech? The "one-sided" attitude of the religious world — an attitude which the teachers of religion like Krishna, Buddha, Sankara, Ramanuja, Chaitanya and others of India and Jesus, Mohammad and others of countries abroad could not remove — was completely eradicated in his own life by that illiterate Brahmana boy who succeeded in establishing a true harmony between the apparently contradictory doctrines of various religions, and thus achieved

a grand feat impossible of achievement by others. Has any one ever seen such a picture? Is it possible to ascertain the place of this God-man in the spiritual world? We dare not try. We can say this much, that lifeless India has become much purified and awakened by the touch of his feet; that it is destined to occupy a place of glory amongst the nations of the world; that hope and blessing will emanate from it to the world around; that it has raised man above gods and has made him worthy of being worshipped by them for the privilege of his having a human body; and that the world has witnessed in Swami Vivekananda only the beginning of the display of the wonderful power which has been awakened by Sri Ramakrishna.

SRI RAMAKRISHNA THE GREAT MASTER

PART FIVE

THE MASTER IN THE DIVINE MOOD AND NARENDRANATH

PREFACE

In this Fifth Part of *Sri RAMAKRISHNA THE GREAT MASTER*, the events of the Master's life, from the time when he first became acquainted with the Brahmo devotees to the time when he came to Calcutta for treatment of his throat disease and stayed at Shyampukur,[1] have been recorded as far as possible. During this time the Master was fully established in the divine mood and all his actions and behaviour were prompted by this mood. Again, this part of his life was united for ever with Narendra's (Swami Vivekananda's) life in such sweet relationship that, when we begin to study this part of the Master's life, the story of Narendra's life presents itself simultaneously. The present part of the book has accordingly been called "The Master in the Divine Mood and Narendranath".

We could not imagine, when we began to write of the play of the divine Mother as Sri Ramakrishna, that we could ever proceed so far. Considering all things, we are convinced that it has been rendered possible by His inconceivable grace only. Bowing down, therefore, at his lotus feet again and again, we humbly place this Part before the reader.

Second day of the bright fortnight, AUTHOR
Phalgun 20, B.E. 1325 (A.D. 1919).

[1] To which has been added the last chapter dealing with the events at Kasipur, which first appeared in the Bengali monthly UDBODHAN as articles. – Tr.

A BRIEF RETROSPECT

[TOPICS: 1. The divine mood in the Master's life. 2. How the onset of the divine mood is recognised. 3. The Master and the effects of Western culture on India. 4. When does the divine mood come into play in human life. 5. The divine mood makes the divine incarnations inscrutable. 6. The seven phases of the Master's divine mood.]

1. The Master, we have said before, brought his Sadhana to a close by performing the worship of the Divine Mother as Shodasi in A.D. 1873. It will not, therefore, be improper to say that from then on he performed all the actions of his life under the impulse of the divine mood. The Master was then thirty-eight years old. So, that mood continued through his life for a little more than twelve[1] years. During this time, all his actions assumed an extraordinarily novel character by the will of the universal Mother. Under the impulse of that will, he applied his mind to impart religion and spirituality among the section of people who had a modern Western education. It is therefore clear that at the end of the full twelve years' spiritual practices, the Master spent six years in getting acquainted with his own power and the spiritual state of the people in general. Thereafter he was seen engaged with unrivalled energy in the task of re-establishing the eternal religion and arresting the decline of religion that came on India under the strong impulse of Western ideas and ideals which preached that this world was all in all. He disappeared from the scene of this world after finishing this part of his work. Now we proceed to record, according to our capacity, how he accomplished this divine task.

2. The reader might think, from what we said before, that the Master was only a spiritual aspirant till his thirty-ninth year. It was not so. We tried to explain before, in the Third Part of the book, that all those who have received the reverence and adoration of the world as Gurus, prophets or founders of religions for having led humanity to the realization of spiritual truths, were seen to have manifested the qualities of world-teachership even from their childhood. In the Master's case too we find the expression of

[1] The Master passed away in the fifty-first year of his life.

qualities in all the stages of his life, including his childhood. We have seen how under the impulse of these, he did many things during the time of his Sadhana in his youth. But since the completion of his Sadhana at the age of thirty-two, we find him doing almost everything under the impulse of this inspiration. We find this with regard to all his actions during his pilgrimage with Mathur and afterwards. So, the reason why we adopt A.D. 1875 as the date of the manifestation of his divine mood, in which he applied himself to the propagation of true spirituality, is not that it was altogether non-existent before, but that since then the divine mood expressed itself in one continuous flow and the mission of his life becomes clearly and definitely manifest; we find him from now firmly taking his stand against Western materialism and the culture and civilization based on material science. For, it had entered India and made the men and women of the country assume an outlook on life which was contrary to that of the eternal religion and was daily drifting them away from its spiritual values. So he applied himself whole-heartedly to the introduction of true spirituality among these English-educated people, so that through his guidance the lives of the people in general might be blessed with the light divine.

3. It is needless to say that there arose an especial need for doing so. The national character of India and its eternal religion, it seems, would have been completely destroyed, had it not been, through the will of God, sustained by the extraordinary spiritual power of the Master who was poised in the divine mood. A little reflection shows us that just as the Master's practice of all religions and his unique achievements through such practice, leading to the discovery of the grand truth, "As many faiths so many paths", have brought blessings on all peoples of the world, even so the twelve long years of his ideal divine life amidst people who were overwhelmed by Western ideas and ideals, served as a beacon light to them, prompting them to abandon their pursuit of pure materialistic values and return to their eternal religion. Thus was the flood-gate closed, the Sanatana-dharma re-established, and India saved from a terrible catastrophe. Here the twin purpose of his life is clearly borne out. Firstly, he brought all the extant religions of the world into line with the eternal religion of India, and demonstrated that all of them were perfectly true and that they were many and various only because the tastes and tendencies

of communities of men were many and various. And secondly, he saved the soul of India, its eternal peace and goodwill, from being caught in the whirlpool of Western materialism based on self-aggrandizement and break-neck competition. Western education was introduced into India in 1836 and the Master was born in that very year. One, therefore, is simply astonished to see the simultaneous birth by the dispensation of Providence, of the two movements, namely, the blast of the Western system of education, which was designed to sweep India from off her culture and civilization, and the counter-blast by which the evils of that system would be rendered innocuous, leaving free and clear the atmosphere in which the merits of the new system might be detached and then incorporated with India's own distinctive culture, much to her advantage.

4. The fullest realization of the divine mood, the finale of the spiritual drama, is very rarely seen in human life. When the Jiva, tightly bound by the fetters of his actions, gets liberated by the grace of God, he gets but a faint taste of this mood. For, when the control of the internal and external sense organs of a man (i.e. jiva or self in bondage) becomes as easy and natural as his breathing; when, losing its identity in the love of the Supreme Self, his little I-consciousness merges for ever in the indivisible ocean of Existence-Knowledge-Bliss Absolute; when melted in the Nirvikalpa Samadhi, his mind and intellect get rid of all kinds of dross and assume Sattvika forms; and when the series of desires in his mind, scorched to ashes by the fire of the divine knowledge, can no longer give rise to new impressions and fruits of actions — it is then and then only that the sweet play of the divine mood starts in him and his life is blessed beyond measure. It is very rarely that one has the opportunity of meeting a person blessed with the full manifestation of the divine mood and enjoying unbreakable peace and contentment. Moreover, the actions of such a man, as they do not proceed from any sense of want and therefore appear to be purposeless, remain for ever incomprehensible to ordinary minds and intellects. Therefore it is, that none but a man who is himself established in the divine mood can really understand the true nature of the said mood. It is never possible for minds and intellects like ours to comprehend the true significance of those extraordinary actions that are performed under the influence of that mood, unless and until we approach them with profound faith and reverence.

5. The full manifestation of the divine mood is seen in divine incarnations only. The religious history of the world bears witness to it. This is why the character of an incarnation seems to us to be mysterious for ever. It is possible to paint a partial picture with the help of imagination of the state of the knowledge of Brahman beyond Maya. But it is beyond our power to understand even a little of the ends and purposes of the deeds and actions of the persons who ever dwell easily and naturally in that mood, or explain why they are sometimes seen labouring as hard as limited beings like ourselves adopting definite means to definite ends, and why at other times, like gods possessed of boundless powers, they do wonderful things miraculously. The 'why' of this remains a mystery. When we foolishly try to fathom their mysterious doings, our imagination is stupefied, not to speak of our reason. It is therefore superfluous to add that it is not possible to set forth the actions of Sri Ramakrishna's life at this time in a manner satisfactory to reason as ordinarily understood. We shall, therefore, merely narrate as far as possible what he did under the influence of this mood, leaving the work of drawing any conclusion about their purpose to the future when the significance of his acts and teachings will become clear through their fruits. We generally base our estimate of a cause on that of its effects. As the effect is great, so must its cause also be great. So, when we ponder over the extraordinary nature of his acts during this period, we cannot but be convinced that the great power of the divine mood was manifesting itself through his body and mind.

6. Although all the acts of Sri Ramakrishna, who was then ever abiding in the divine mood, were performed for the sole purpose of establishing spirituality, yet they can be definitely classed into seven broad divisions: Firstly, by moulding in an extraordinary way the spiritual life of his immaculate, virtuous wife Sri Sarada Devi, he converted her into a great power-house of spirituality. Secondly, he met all the contemporary spiritual leaders of Calcutta noted for their pursuit of great ideals and their influence on society, and helped to perfect their spiritual lives by bringing his spiritual power to bear on them. Thirdly, he quenched the spiritual thirst of all people of all communities who came to Dakshineswar during this time. Fourthly, from among the devotees coming to him, he picked up those, about whom he had previous visions, as specially marked by the Divine Mother to be his associates

in the working out of his divine mission, classified them according to their capacities, and applied himself to the moulding of their spiritual life. Fifthly, he initiated some of them into the vow of Sannyasa (or the renunciation of all self-centred values for the realisation of God), and thus founded a brotherhood for propagating his own novel liberal doctrines to the world. Sixthly, he came again and again to the houses of his own devotees living in Calcutta and awakened spiritual consciousness in the members of those families and their neighbours, with the help of holy conversation and devotional services. And seventhly, he bound his own devotees with the tie of an extraordinary love and brought about such a wonderful cordial relation among them that all of them became extremely attached to one another and came to possess one soul, as it were, so that they were gradually and naturally converted into a liberal spiritual brotherhood.

We have told the reader, in the last portion of the Second Part, how the Master took up the first of the above-mentioned seven kinds of activity in 1874. We have also discussed, in the Appendix to that Part, how he took up the second kind of activity when he went to see Acharya Kesavachandra, the leader of the Brahmo Samaj of India in 1875. Again, we have given the reader a little indication of the third, fourth, and sixth classes of his activity in Chapters, V, VI and VII of the Fourth Part. We, therefore, propose to study here how and when he took up the remaining ones.

CHAPTER I: SECTION 1

THE INFLUENCE OF THE MASTER ON THE BRAHMO SAMAJ

[TOPICS: 1. Love and reverence of the Brahmos for the Master. 2. His loving relation with them. 3. The Brahmos' affinity with him. 4. The Master helped the Brahmos in Sadhana. 5. He left the Brahmos free to accept such teachings as they considered practicable. 6. The Master taught through jokes. 7. Devotion and consciousness of God as power. 8. "Don't set a limit to the Lord's nature". 9. Kesav's partial acceptance of the Master's teachings: The New Dispensation. 10. The Master's great love for Keshav. 11. The Master's influence over Vijayakrishna Goswami. 12. How far Vijay advanced in Sadhana since then. 13. Removal of misunderstanding between Keshav and Vijay. 14. Acharya Sivanath abstaining from going to Dakshineswar. 15. Acharya Pratapchandra on the influence of the Master on the Brahmo Samaj. 16. The influence of the Master on the General Brahmo Samaj. 17. The influence of the Master on the Brahmo music. 18. The Master recognised the Brahmo religion.]

1. The general public of Calcutta could know of the Master only after he met Kesavchandra, the leader of the Brahmo Samaj of India. We have said before that Kesav, who appreciated merit wherever it was found, was much attracted towards the Master from the day he first saw him. Although he was inspired with Western ideas and ideals, his heart was filled with a real love of God and it was impossible for him to enjoy the nectar of devotion all by himself. As he was getting more and more light on the path of his life's journey from the Master's illuminating words and contacts, he freely told the public about it and invited them enthusiastically to come and share with him the joy and bliss of his holy company. It is therefore seen that all the English and Bengali newspapers controlled by the Brahmo Samaj such as Sulabha Samachara, Sunday Mirror, Theistic Quarterly Review, etc., were full of discussions about the pure character, words of wisdom and the liberal religious tenets of the Master. Kesav and other Brahmo leaders were seen to repeat on many occasions the Master's words from the altar when they addressed their congregations at the end of their services and prayers. Again, whenever they had leisure, they went to Dakshineswar with a few members of their

inner circle, sometimes with the whole party, and spent some time in holy conversation with the Master.

2. Feeling delighted with the thirst for spiritual illumination and love of God of these Brahmo leaders, the Master spared no efforts to encourage them to dive deep into the sea of Sadhana and be blessed with the pearl of the immediate knowledge of God. So great was his joy in the singing of, and conversing on, God with them that he did not mind going even uninvited very often to Kesav's house for the purpose. Thus a close and intimate relationship grew up between the Master and many persons of that Society, who were real seekers of truth. He also went sometimes to the houses of the Brahmos other than Kesav and made them feel happy and blessed. For example, he often visited, especially during celebrations, the houses of Manimohan Mallick of Sinduriapati, Jayagopal Sen of Mathaghasa Lane, Venimadhav Pal of Sinthi in Baranagar, Kasiswar Mitra of Nandanbagan and others, all followers of the Brahmo faith. On some occasions it so happened that, seeing the Master suddenly enter his Brahmo prayer house while he was giving instruction from the altar, Kesav came down from it even before finishing the sermon, received the Master cordially and brought to a close the prayer of the day, in order to listen to his words and enjoy the bliss of Kirtan in his company.

3. It is with people of one's own way of thought and life that one can mix freely and feel happy without any reserve. It was not, therefore, a matter of surprise that, seeing him intermingling joyously with them in that way, the Brahmos came to the conclusion that the Master was a man of their own religious mood and persuasion. The same conclusion was entertained also by several Hindu religious communities like the Saktas and the Vishnavas, on seeing him at home in their company and forms of worship also on many occasions. For who would then have understood that the Master could behave so naturally with all sects and faiths, in fact as a faithful follower of each of them, only because he was ever dwelling in Bhavamukha? Owing to the Master's complete identification with their pattern of devotion, the Brahmo devotees had not the slightest doubt that his mind was merged in the formless but attributeful Brahman when he participated in their Kirtans and meditations; only they felt that he enjoyed a far greater bliss than they did, and truly had the direct realization of that extraordinary Light, unlike themselves who saw nothing but darkness

in their meditations. They also understood that unless they could offer their all to God and become absorbed in Him, even as he did, the taste of that kind of joy and vision would remain a far-off cry for them.

4. Seeing the love of truth, the disposition of renunciation and the thirst for spirituality and other good qualities of the members of the Brahmo Samaj of India, the Master tried to help them forward on their own chosen path of religion. He always looked upon those who loved God, irrespective of what community they belonged to, as very closely related to him, and helped them unstintedly in their spiritual quest, so that they might attain perfection by proceeding along their own paths. Again, the Master always said that all the true devotees of God were a class by themselves and never hesitated to eat and drink with them. It is therefore superfluous to say that he looked with affection upon Kesav and the members of his congregation, such as Vijaykrishna Goswami, Pratapchandra Majumdar, Chiranjivi Sarma, Sivanath Sastri, Amritalal Bose and others. Because of such intimate contact with them, it did not take him long to understand that, under the influence of Western education, they were being carried far away from the religious ideal of the nation and were regarding social reform as the acme of their practice of religion. He, therefore, tried to make them accept the realization of God as the ideal of their lives, even if their Society failed to follow them to that extent. As a result, Kesav and his party went forward very far on the path shown by him. The custom of addressing God by the sweet name of Mother and worshipping God as Mother were introduced into the Samaj; the Master's ideas and ideals entered into the music, literature, etc., of that Society and filled it with sweetness. That was not all. The leaders of that Samaj could know through the Master's life that there was much to learn from, and think about, those ideals and practices of the Hindu religion from which the Samaj had seceded under the impression that they were erroneous and superstitious.

5. The Master realized from the beginning that, imbued with Western ideas, Kesav and his companions would not rightly understand all his ideas and instructions, and that even much of what they could understand would not be to their taste. Remembering this at the time of giving them instruction, he used to tell them, "I have said whatever came into my head, you may accept

them minus their 'head and tail' ". Again, it did not take him long to know that with many members of the Brahmo Samaj, social reform and the satisfaction of the desire for worldly enjoyment came to be the aims of life. This he expressed also in jest on many occasions as follows:

6. "I went to Kesav's place and witnessed their prayer. After dilating upon the powers of the Divine for a long time, the priest said, 'Let us now meditate on Him.' I wondered how long they would meditate. But, ah, scarcely had they shut their eyes for two minutes when it was all finished! Can one realize Him by meditating thus? I looked at the faces of them all when they were meditating. Afterwards I said to Kesav, 'I have seen many of you meditate, but do you know what thought comes to my mind? Troops of monkeys would be sometimes sitting quiet, under the Tamarisk trees at Dakshineswar, as if they were perfect gentlemen, wholly innocent. But they were not that innocent; they sit and think of those roofs of houses where there were gourds, pumpkins, etc., or of those gardens where there were plantains and egg fruits. And in a short time, they would jump off into the garden with a yell, pluck those fruits and vegetables and fill up their stomachs. I saw many meditate that way.' They heard this and laughed."

The Master would thus teach us also through jokes. One day, Swami Vivekananda, we remember, was singing devotional songs before him. The Swami then used to visit often the Brahmo Samaj, practise meditation and offer prayers twice daily, once in the morning and once in the evening. He began to sing with devotion and concentration of mind, the song on Brahman viz., "Concentrate your mind on that One stainless Purusha." There is one line in that song, "Worship Him always, strive always to realize Him." In order to imprint these words in the Swami's mind the Master said suddenly; "No, no; say rather 'Worship and pray to Him twice a day.' Why should you repeat in vain what you will not do in practice?" All laughed loudly; the Swami too looked small.

7. On another occasion the Master said to Kesav and other Brahmos regarding worship, "Why do you describe His powers so much? Does the child sit before his father and think how many houses, how many horses, how many cows, how many gardens, etc., his father has? Or is he simply charmed to think how dear his father is to him, how great his love for him is? The father feeds

and clothes the child; what of that? We are, after all, His children. So, what is there to make much of, if He does all that? Instead of thinking thus, a real devotee makes Him his 'own' by love — importunes, nay, demands that his prayers be fulfilled, that He may reveal Himself to him. If one thinks so much of His powers, one cannot press one's demands on Him. The thought of His greatness creates a distance between Him and the devotee. Think of Him as your very own. It is then only that you will realize Him."

8. Besides learning the absolute necessity of striving hard to realize God and of sacrificing everything for His sake, Kesav and other Brahmos got something more from the Master. They had learnt from the Western missionaries and English books that God could never have form. It was, therefore, according to them a great sin to believe that His Presence could be felt in images having forms and to worship and offer prayers to Him there. The Master's remarks, such as, "Just as formless water gets condensed into ice having a form on account of cold, so formless Existence-Knowledge-Bliss Absolute, condensed on account of devotion, assumes forms"; "Just as a man is reminded of a real custard apple when he sees one made of cork, so, having recourse to an image having form, one attains the immediate knowledge of the real nature of God" — these made an impression on their minds, and they came to realize that there was much to say and think about what they had called "idolatry" and practices they considered irrational and contemptible. Moreover, there is little doubt that they viewed the worship of God with forms in a new light from the day the Master proved to Kesav and other Brahmos that Brahman and His power, of which the great universe is nothing but a manifestation, are non-different like fire and its burning power. They now understood that it is as erroneous to contend that God is formless but possesses attributes, as it is to maintain the reverse, namely that He is only formful but has no attributes. For form and attributes go together, and to say that anything has the one is to admit that it has the other also. As the manifested, He is the universe which is all forms; as the formless but attributeful Brahman, He is the controller of the Universe; and as the one beyond all attributes, He is the eternal substratum underlying all manifestation as names and forms, as persons and things such as God, the Jiva and the universe. Kesav and others were astonished that day to find such deep meaning in the ordinary saying of the Master, "One should

not fix a limit to the nature of God — He is with forms and without forms, with attributes and without attributes. Who can know and say what else He is besides?"

During a little more than three years since Kesav's meeting with the Master in 1875, the Brahmo Samaj of India under his able leadership was increasingly disabused of its former infatuation with Western ideas and ideals and assumed a new form. An important feature of this new development was a love for spiritual practices, which soon became pronounced enough to attract the attention of the general public. Afterwards, on March 6, 1878, Kesav gave away his daughter in marriage to the prince of Coochbihar. As the age of his daughter was a little less than what had been fixed by the Samaj as the lowest marriageable age for girls, this marriage evoked a good deal of criticism in that society; and carried away by their zeal for social reforms in imitation of the West, the leaders split into two, calling themselves the Brahmo Samaj of India and the General Brahmo Samaj. But the influence of the Master on the Brahmo Samaj did not come to an end on account of that event. His love embraced both the parties equally and the seekers after truth in both came to him as before and received spiritual help.

9. After this schism, Kesav, the leader of the Brahmo Samaj of India, made rapid progress on the path of Sadhana and his spiritual life now became very deep by the grace of the Master. Convinced that the offering of oblations, bathing in consecrated water, shaving the head clean, putting on ochre cloth and other symbolic acts help the human mind to ascend to subtler and higher strata of the spiritual realm, he more or less adopted them all. Having developed a burning faith in the eternal existence of Gauranga, Jesus and other great souls in luminous spiritual bodies as the living embodiments of different spiritual moods, serving as the perennial springs of inspiration for those moods, he applied himself from time to time to deep meditation on them, so that he might realize properly their spiritual characteristics. Kesav, it is superfluous to say, engaged himself in the practices mentioned above, because he heard that the Master, while he had been practising any particular faith, had put on the emblems peculiar to its followers. With the help of the above-mentioned practices he tried to understand the Master's newly discovered truth, "As many faiths, so many paths", which resulted, within two years

of the Coochbihar marriage, in the founding of the New Dispensation, from the pulpit of which he preached the truth, as far as he had grasped it, to the general public. We are unable to express how devoted he was to the Master and how much faith he had in him, as he knew him to be the embodiment of the said New Dispensation. Many of us saw him come to the Master at Dakshineswar and take the dust of his feet uttering again and again the words, "Victory to the new Dispensation", "Victory to the new Dispensation." Who can say how deep his spiritual life would have become, had he not passed away so soon, just about four years after he had started preaching the New Dispensation?

10. The Master looked upon Kesav as so intimately related to him that, once having heard of his illness, he promised to the Mother of the universe, the votive offering of green coconut and sugar, should Kesav recover. He went to see Kesav during his illness, and finding him very weak, could not refrain from shedding tears. He said to him, "The gardener sometimes not only prunes the branches of the plant of the Basra rose, but takes out even its roots from under the ground and exposes them to the sun and dew, so that the plant may produce big flowers. The Gardener has brought about this state of your body for that purpose." Hearing of his passing away at the end of his last illness in 1884, the Master became overwhelmed with grief, did not talk with any one and lay quiet in his bed for three days. He said afterwards, "When I heard of Kesav's death, I felt as if one of my limbs got paralysed." All the men and women of Kesav's family were greatly devoted to the Master. They sometimes took him to Kamal Kutir, the house of Kesav, and at other times came to him at Dakshineswar in order to listen to spiritual instruction from his holy mouth. To spend a day enjoying the holy conversation of the Master and in singing Kirtan with him during the Magha celebrations, came to be regarded as an indispensable item by the Brahmos of the New Dispensation, as long as Kesav lived. Moreover, Kesav used to come with his whole congregation on board a steamer to Dakshineswar now and then to pick up the Master, and then, as the steamer glided leisurely on the Ganga, there would take place on its deck Kirtan and holy conversation of the Master, in which the whole congregation would find itself lost.

11. After the separation of the two parties over the Coochbihar marriage, Vijaykrishna Goswami and Sivanath Sastri became

the Acharyas of the General Brahmo Samaj. Vijay was very dear to Kesav on account of his truthfulness and love for Sadhana. Vijaykrishna's eagerness for Sadhana, like that of Acharya Kesav, increased to a great extent after he had had the privilege of meeting the Master. As he was going forward on that path, he attained various new spiritual visions in a short time and acquired faith in the manifestation of God with forms. When Vijay first came to Calcutta for study in the Sanskrit College, he came like an orthodox Brahmana with a long tuft on his head, the sacred thread and various kinds of amulets. On becoming a Brahmo, Vijay gave up all these one day out of respect for truth as conceived by the followers of the Brahmo Samaj. He boycotted Kesav, who was to him like a Guru, out of the same respect for truth, after the Coochbihar marriage. Again, out of respect for the same truth he found it impossible to conceal his faith in God having forms and was obliged to separate himself from the Brahmo Samaj. As he lost the means of his livelihood on account of this, he had to undergo much suffering for some time for want of money. But he was not at all depressed. On many occasions Vijay clearly told us that he had received spiritual help from the Master, and that sometimes he got his visions in a mysterious way. But we do not know whether he loved and respected him as a subsidiary Guru or in some other manner; for we had heard from him that in the Akasaganga hill in Gaya, a monk mercifully made him suddenly enter into ecstasy with the help of his Yogic power and became his Guru. But there is no doubt that Vijay had a very high opinion of the Master. We have written elsewhere (cf. IV.5) in this book, what we heard about it from Vijay himself.

12. After his separation from the Brahmo Samaj, the spiritual life of Vijay became deeper and deeper as days passed. People were charmed to see his joyous, unrestrained dance and frequent ecstasy under the influence of inspiration during Kirtan. We were told thus by the Master of his spiritual condition: "Vijay has reached the room just adjacent to the innermost chamber, the acme of spiritual realization, and is knocking at its door." Vijay initiated many people in Mantras after he attained spiritual depth. He passed away at Puri, about fourteen years after the Master had given up his body.

13. It was observed that after the Coochbihar marriage, a strong ill feeling arose between the two Brahmo parties, the

Samaj of India and the General Samaj. The two parties were not even on speaking terms with each other. But we have mentioned before that persons of both the parties having a love for Sadhana used to come to Dakshineswar as usual.

One day during this period, both Kesav and Vijay came to the Master suddenly with the members of their inner circles. Of course, this happened because each party was ignorant of the other party's coming there. A sense of embarrassment was written on the faces of all as they remembered their previous quarrel. Seeing the same sense of embarrassment even in Kesav and Vijay that day, the Master said to them by way of a reconciliation: "Look here, once upon a time there arose a quarrel between Siva and Rama and a great fight took place between them. It is well known that Siva's Guru is Rama, and Rama's Guru is Siva. Therefore, it was not long before their quarrel was made up after the fight. But there could never again be a union between the ghosts, the disciples of Siva, and the monkeys, the disciples of Rama. The fight between the ghosts and the monkeys went on for ever." Then addressing Kesav and Vijay he continued, "Whatever was to happen has happened. You should no more have ill-feeling between you; let it remain among the ghosts and monkeys." After this Kesav and Vijay were at least on speaking terms with each other.

14. When Vijay left the General Brahmo Samaj because of his own direct spiritual experiences, those also who had absolute faith in him left that Samaj, which consequently was shorn much of its glory. It was Acharya Sivanath Sastri that became the leader of that party then and saved the Samaj. He had, before that time, come several times to the Master and had great love and respect for him. The Master also was very affectionate towards Sivanath. But Sivanath was in a great difficulty after Vijay had left the Samaj. He now stopped visiting the Master, thinking that Vijay's religious opinion had been changed under the influence of the Master's instruction and that was why Vijay had left the Samaj. Swami Vivekananda had joined the General Samaj a little before that time and had become a great favourite of Sivanath and other Brahmos. But although he joined the General Samaj, the Swami used from time to time to go to Kesav and the Master at Dakshineswar. The Swami said, "Questioned at that time about the reason why he had discontinued going to the Master, Acharya Sivanath said, 'If I go there frequently all the others of the Brahmo Samaj will

do so in imitation of me, and as a result, the Samaj will collapse'." The Swami said further that under that impression Sivanath advised him at that time to abstain from going to Dakshineswar saying, "The Master's ecstasy and all that are the results of his nervous weakness and his brain has got deranged on account of his undergoing too much physical hardship." We have mentioned elsewhere (cf.IV.2) what the Master said when he was told about this.

15. Be that as it may, owing to the influence of the Master, the love for Sadhana entered into the Samaj and all the seekers after truth in both the New Dispensation and the General Samaj tried to mould their lives so as to have the immediate knowledge of God. Once when Pratap Chandra Majumdar came to Dakshineswar to have the company of the Master, we asked him about the nature and the degree of the development of the spiritual ideas of the Samaj after its members came into contact with the Master. He replied, "Did we understand what religion was before we saw him? We merely played the bully. We have understood what a real religious life is, after seeing him.' Acharya Chiranjiv Sarma (Trailokya Nath Sannyal) was present there with Pratap on that occasion.

16. While the influence of the Master on the New Dispensation was evident, it was by no means negligible on the General Samaj, as long as Vijaykrishna was the Acharya there. But when Vijay and many other seekers after spirituality left it, the said influence decreased and it simultaneously lost spirituality and engaged itself in social reforms, patriotic work and similar activities. Although there was a definite decrease, the said influence was not altogether absent; the proof of it is found in the practice of Yoga, the study of the Vedanta and the pursuit of spirituality on the part of some members of the General Samaj. Some of them, we have also come to know, follow the Vedic doctrine practised by the higher stratum of the Kartabhaja community and try to cure physical diseases with the help of meditation.

17. Chiranjiv Sarma, the Acharya of the New Dispensation, has done a great deal towards the development of the Brahmo music. But, it has been found on inquiry that he composed those songs that awaken high thoughts and emotions after he became acquainted with the various kinds of the Master's visions, ecstasies and Samadhis. We quote below the first lines of a few such songs.

1. Thy formless beauty, O Mother, flashes in dense darkness.

2. The deep sea of Samadhi, endless, boundless.
3. Ah, the full moon of divine Love has risen in the firmament of Consciousness!
4. The waves of the Bliss of divine Love in the waters of the sea of Existence-Bliss.
5. Give me divine inebriation, O Mother.

It is beyond doubt that the fine poet Chiranjiv Sarma has placed all the people of Bengal and all the Sadhakas of the country under a debt of gratitude by composing these songs. Nor is there any doubt that only by seeing the ecstasy of the Master was he able to write these songs. Acharya Chiranjiv had a sweet voice. We saw the Master on many occasions go into ecstasy while he was listening to his music.

18. Thus the Brahmo Samaj became inspired by the extraordinary spiritual influence of the Master at the time. Although the Master said that the worship of the formless aspect of God preached in the Samaj was that of the unripe type (ch. III. 2), we heard from his mouth now and again, that an aspirant would succeed in realizing God if he worshipped that aspect of His with genuine faith. He never forgot to say, "I bow down to the modern knowers of Brahman", and to make salutations to the circle of Brahmos, when he bowed down to God and His devotees of all denominations at the end of Kirtans. It is clear from this that he actually believed the Brahmo religion to be one of the world faiths or paths leading to the realisation of God, preached according to His will. But he had a great desire, and took great pains, to see that the circle of Brahmos should free themselves from the Western influence, and firmly follow the true path of spirituality. He told them repeatedly about the inadequacy and danger of making social reforms and philanthropic activities the only aim of human life, however praiseworthy and indispensable they might be from the point of view of the usual conception of social life, and of regarding devotional exercises for God-realization as useless. It was the Brahmo Samaj which first publicly discussed the extraordinary spiritual life of the Master and thereby attracted the minds of the people of Calcutta in general to Dakshineswar. Every one, who sat at the feet of the Master and was blessed with the attainment of spiritual power and peace, is under an eternal debt in this respect to both the New Dispensation and the General Brahmo Samaj. The present writer, again, owes a great debt to both of them; for,

it was these two societies that placed high ideals before him and helped him in moulding his spiritual life at the beginning of his youth. Filled with reverence and gratefulness, we, therefore, bow down again and again to the Samaj, and its three Gems, namely, Brahman, the Brahmo Samaj and the circle of Brahmos, knowing them as one in their real nature. We are going to make a present to the reader of two especial pictures we had the opportunity of witnessing with our own eyes, of the Master's enjoyment of bliss in the company of the circle of Brahmos.

CHAPTER I: SECTION 2

THE BRAHMO FESTIVAL IN MANIMOHAN MALLIK'S HOUSE

[TOPICS: 1. Ascertaining the date of the event. 2. Our acquaintance with Vaikunthanath Sannyal. 3. We became acquainted with Baburam for the first time. 4. The extraordinary Sankirtan in Mani Mallick's house. 5. The extraordinary dance of the Master. 6. The Master cut jokes with Vijay Goswami. 7. The Master's love for his devotees. 8. Mani Mallik's was a family of devotees.]

1. It was, we clearly remember, the season of Hemanta (October – December). Delighted with her bath in the rains and putting on the toilet of autumn, Nature, which had been previously scorched by the summer heat, just started feeling the first touch of the cold season and drew her flowing garments a little closer to her tender, cool body. The Hemanta was almost over. We are describing the event of a day of this period. The date of the event we are going to describe here has fortunately been ascertained in the following way. Balaram Basu, an esteemed friend of ours and a great devotee of the Master, was present at the scene of the occurrence on that occasion and marked the day, as was his habit, on the margin of the almanac with a few words mentioning the fact. We have come to know from this that the event took place on Monday, November 26, 1883.

2. We were then studying in the St. Xavier's College, Calcutta, and had had the privilege of meeting the Master only twice or thrice. As the college was closed on that day, we along with Varada Sundar Pal of Comilla and Hari Prasanna Chattopadhyaya known in later life as Swami Vijnanananda settled that we should go to the Master in the evening. When we were going by boat to Dakshineswar, we remember, we were told that, like us, another passenger was going to the Master. Talking with him, we came to know that his name was Vaikunthanath Sannyal and that he also had met the Master only recently. We remember also that, when a passenger in the boat heard the name of the Master from us and used words of ridicule regarding him, Vaikunthanath's scornful retort silenced the man. It was about two or half past two in the afternoon when we reached our destination.

As soon as we entered the Master's room and bowed down at his feet, he said, "Ah, you have come today! We could not have met you, had you come a little later. I am going to Calcutta today; a carriage has been sent for. There is a festival there, a festival of the Brahmos. It is, however, good that we have met. Please sit down. What a disappointment it would have been, if you had to return without meeting me!"

3. We sat on a mat spread on the floor of the room and asked the Master afterwards, "Shall we be allowed at the Brahmo festival which you are attending?" The Master said, "Why not? You are free to go there if you like. It is at the house of Mani Mallik of Sinduriapati." Seeing a young man, not very slender, fair and wearing a red cloth, entering the room, the Master said, "Hallo! Please tell them the number of Mani Mallik's House." The young man humbly said, "81, Chitpore Road, Sinduriapati." Seeing the gentle behaviour and the calm nature of the young man, we thought he might be the son of a Brahmana officer of the temple. But when, a couple of months afterwards, we saw him coming out of the university examination hall, we talked with him and found that our impression was totally wrong. We then came to know that his name was Baburam and his home was in the village of Antpur, near Tarakeswar. He was living in a rented house at Combuliatola, Calcutta, and went and stayed with the Master now and then. It is needless to say that he is now well known as Swami Premananda of the Sri Ramakrishna Order.

The carriage arrived in a short time. Asking Baburam to take his towel, clothes, the small bag of spices, etc., and bowing down to the Mother, the Master entered the carriage. Baburam took those things and sat on the other side of the carriage. That day another person also went with the Master to Calcutta. On inquiry we found that his name was Pratapchandra Hazra.

Fortunately a passenger boat was available as soon as the Master had left. We took the boat and alighted at Barabazar in Calcutta. Thinking that the festival would take place at sunset, we waited in the house of a friend. Vaikunthanath, our new acquaintance, went somewhere else on business, assuring us that he would meet us at the proper time at the place of the festival.

We found out Mani Babu's house and it was about four when we reached there. When we inquired about the Master, a man showed us the way to the parlour upstairs. Reaching there, we found that the room was beautifully decorated with leaves and flowers for the festival and a few devotees were talking with one another. On inquiry, we were told that the midday prayer and music were over and that prayer and Kirtan would take place again in the evening. The Master had been taken into the inner apartment at the request of the lady devotees.

4. When we came to know that it would be some time before the prayer would begin, we went out. Afterwards, at dusk we came back to the place. Scarcely had we reached the road in front of the house when sweet music and the loud sounds of Mridanga greeted our ears. Knowing that the Kirtan had begun, we hastened to the parlour. But what we saw there beggars description. There were crowds of people inside and outside the hall. So many people stood before every door and on the western roof that it was absolutely impossible to push through the crowd into the room. All were craning their necks and looking into the hall with calm eyes full of devotion. They were not at all conscious as to who was or was not beside them. Knowing that it was impossible to enter the room through the front door, we went round, crossed the western roof and were near a northern door of the parlour. As the crowd here was somewhat thin, we thrust our heads somehow into the room and saw —

5. A wonderful scene! High waves of heavenly bliss were surging there in strong currents. All were lost altogether in the Kirtan, and laughed, wept and danced. Unable to control themselves, many were falling now and then violently on the ground. Swirled by emotion, they behaved like a troop of lunatics. The Master was dancing in the centre of that God-intoxicated assemblage, now going forward with rapid steps, now going backward in a similar way, to the cadence of the music. In whichever direction he was thus going forward, the people there, as if enchanted, made room for his free movement. An extraordinary tenderness, sweetness and leonine strength were visible in every limb of the Master's body. That superb dance! In it there was no artificiality or affectation, no bumping, no unnatural gestures and acrobatics; nor was there to be noticed any absence of control. On the other hand one noticed in it a succession of natural poses and movements of limbs as a gushing overflow of grace, bliss and sweetness surging from within, the like of which may be noticed in the movements of a large fish, long confined in a mud puddle,

when it is suddenly let loose in a vast sheet of water — swimming in all directions, now slowly, now rapidly, and expressing its joy in diverse ways. It appeared as if the dance was the dynamic bodily expression of the surge of Bliss, the Reality of Brahman, which the Master was experiencing within. Thus dancing, sometimes he lost his normal consciousness, sometimes his cloth would slip, which others would fasten firmly round his waist. Again, sometimes seeing someone losing normal consciousness on account of the infusion of spiritual emotions, he would touch his breast and bring him back to consciousness. Emanating from him, a bright stream of divine Bliss seemed to be spreading on all sides and enabling the devotees to see God face to face. It enabled those of lukewarm disposition to intensify their fervour, idle minds to go forward with enthusiasm to the realm of spirituality, and those extremely attached to the world to become fully free from that attachment for the time being. The surge of his divine emotion caught others and overpowered them. And, illumined by his purity, their minds ascended to an unknown high spiritual level. That Vijaykrishna Goswami, the Acharya of the General Brahmo Samaj, went now and then into a trance and lost consciousness, needs no mention; many other Brahmo devotees also were in the same condition. Besides, the sweet-voiced Chiranjiv Sarma, as he sang to the accompaniment of a one-stringed musical instrument the song, "Dance, O Children of the Blissful Mother, round and round", became absorbed in the idea, and lost himself in the Self. Then a period of more than two hours was thus spent in enjoying the bliss of Kirtan, at the end of which the following song was sung:

Nitai who has brought down the name of Hari so sweet —
has Nitai or Gour, or Advaita of Santipur brought it?
Drink the wine of the name of Hari, the essence of all beings, O my mind! and be inebriated.
Once roll on the ground and weep repeatedly uttering Hari, and saying, 'Please find a refuge for me.'
Fill the sky with the name of Hari loudly. Raise both your arms and dance uttering 'Hari' again and again, and distribute gratis the name of Hari from door to door.
Allow yourself to be pleasantly carried away day by day by the bliss of Hari's love.

Sing the name of Hari, soar to the acme of your life, and intoxicated with the bliss of God's love, destroy all mean desires!

The waves of emotion produced by that extraordinary Kirtan now gradually subsided. Then salutations were made to all the teachers of devotion and religious communities.

When all sat down at the end of the Kirtan, the Master, we remember, requested Acharya Nagendra Nath Chattopadhyaya to sing, "Drink the wine of the name of Hari, the essence of all beings, O my mind, and be inebriated", and he complied at once. Filled with fervour, he sang it sweetly, repeating it twice or thrice, which again gladdened the hearts of all.

Afterwards the Master began giving various instructions to all present in the course of the exposition of the theme that the Jiva would surely attain supreme Peace, if he could but withdraw his mind from sights, tastes and other worldly objects, and offer it to the Lord. The women devotees, who were sitting in the eastern part of the parlour behind the screen, also put various questions to him on spiritual matters and enjoyed his illuminating replies. While thus engaging himself in answering questions, the Master would now and then burst into singing a few songs in praise of the divine Mother composed by Ramprasad, Kamalakanta and other devout Sadhakas, to create a deep impression about that subject on the minds of all present. Of all the songs he sang, we distinctly remember the following five:

1. The black bee of my mind is fully engrossed in sucking the honey of the blue-lotus of Shyama's feet. 2. The kite of my mind was flying high in the sky of Shyama's feet. 3. All this is the play of the mad woman. (The Mother of the universe). 4. What is the fault of the poor mind; why do you falsely hold him guilty? 5. I grieve, O Mother, only because theft was committed in my house while I was wide awake, and Thou, Mother, wert keeping watch over me.

6. While the Master was thus singing the Mother's name, Vijay went to another room with a few devotees and engaged himself in reading out and explaining to them the Ramayana by Tulsidas. Seeing that the time for the evening prayer was nearing, he came back to the parlour to bow down to the Master before he began the prayer. As soon as he saw Vijay, the Master said jokingly, "Vijay feels great delight in Sankirtan nowadays. But I am seized

with fear when he dances; for the whole roof may crash! (All laughed) Yes, such an event actually took place in our part of the country. People build second storeys of houses there with wood and mud only. A Goswami went to the house of one of his disciples and began singing Kirtan on the first floor. As soon as the atmosphere was created and the Kirtan became quite enjoyable, dancing began. Now, the Goswami was a little fat like you (looking towards Vijay). After he had danced for some time, the roof gave way, and the Goswami descended plump to the ground floor! That is why I am afraid that your dancing might produce such an effect." (All laughed). Seeing that Vijay had put ochre cloth, the Master now said, "He has nowadays become a great lover of the ochre colour also. People dye in ochre their lower and upper garments only, but Vijay has coloured his cloth, wrapper, shirt, including even the pair of his canvas shoes. That is good. A state comes when one wishes to do so; one does not then like to put on any dress that is not ochre-coloured. Ochre is indeed the mark of renunciation; it, therefore, reminds the aspirant that he has undertaken the vow of renouncing everything for the realization of God." Vijay now bowed down to the Master, and the Master blessed him with a gracious mind, saying, "Peace, perfect peace be on you."

7. When the Master was singing the Mother's name, another event happened, which clearly proved how keen his power of observing outward things was, even though he always remained in a state of inwardness. When he was singing, he happened to look at Baburam's face and knew that he was feeling very hungry and thirsty. As he knew that he would not take anything before he himself had partaken of it, the Master had some sweets and a glass of water brought, saying that he wanted to take them. He himself took a little of the sweets and gave the greater part to Baburam and the rest to the devotees present who took it as Prasada.

Some time after, Vijay bowed down to the Master and came downstairs for the evening prayer. The Master was then taken to the inner apartment for his evening meal. By then it was past nine. In the meantime we came downstairs to join Vijay's prayer. We saw that the Brahmo devotees had assembled in the courtyard for prayer and Acharya Vijay was seated at the altar in the verandah to the north. The entire congregation, following the Acharya, was singing in chorus the Vedic passage, "Brahman is Truth,

Knowledge, Infinity" in remembrance of the glory of Brahman, preliminary to starting the prayer. The prayer now commenced and went on for some time when the Master came to the place and taking his seat along with others, joined the prayer. He sat quiet for about ten or fifteen minutes and then bowed down to the ground. Seeing that it was past ten then, he asked that a carriage should be sent for, as he would return to Dakshineswar. He then put on his shirt, stockings and a cap covering the ears for protection from cold, walked out of the place of the meeting with a slow step accompanied by Baburam and others, and got into the carriage. Acharya Vijay was addressing the circle of the Brahmos from the altar at this time and giving the usual instruction to them. We also left the meeting and started for home.

8. On that occasion, we learnt how the Master enjoyed bliss in the company of the Brahmo devotees. We do not know whether Mani Babu was a fully initiated Brahmo. But we know perfectly well that all members of his family, men as well as women, were then followers of the Brahmo religion and offered daily prayers etc., according to the prescribed order of that Samaj. There was a lady of this family who could not concentrate her mind during her prayers, knowing which the Master asked her affectionately, "Please tell me whom it is that you happen to remember at that time." Coming to know that the lady was bringing up her brother's child and that her mind always remembered him during the prayer, the Master advised her to serve that child as the very form of the boy Krishna. Putting this instruction into practice, the lady attained Bhavasamadhi in a short time. We have mentioned this elsewhere (III.1). We saw the Master on another occasion, enjoying divine bliss in the company of a few Brahmo devotees in another place. This will form the subject matter of the next Section.

CHAPTER I: SECTION 3

THE MASTER IN JAYAGOPAL SEN'S HOUSE

[TOPICS: 1. Jayagopal Sen's house. 2. The Master's method of teaching. 3. Another peculiar characteristic of it. 4. His annoyance at words not backed by realization. 5. The Master taught how to realize God in worldly life. 6. The bliss of Sankirtan.]

It was not we alone that were overjoyed and blessed with a new spiritual outlook by observing the Master's ecstasy and blissful experiences at the Kirtan at the house of Manimohan of Sinduriapati. Our friend Varada Sundar, who was a participant in it, too felt the same, and kept on making enquiries as to when and where the Master would be next attending a similar function and measuring out bliss to the assembled devotees. It was not long before his efforts were successful; for, two days later, on Wednesday morning, November 28, as soon as we met him, he blurted out, "Sri Ramakrishna will come to Kamal Kutir to see Kesav Babu this afternoon and also go to Jayagopal Sen's house at the Mathaghasa quarter later at dusk. Will you go to see him?" It was known to us that Kesav was then very ill. Therefore, thinking that the presence at Kamal Kutir of strangers like us might possibly be a cause of annoyance, we decided to go at dusk to Jayagopal's house to see the Master.

1. We took Mathaghasa to be a part of Barabazar and went there first. Then enquiring of people and pressing on and on, we reached Jayagopal's house at last when the sun had already gone down. That day, as on the previous occasion at Manimohan's house, there was a shower of rain in the afternoon. For, we remember distinctly that we made our way through mud on the road and reached our destination. Jayagopal Babu's house, like that of Manimohan, was facing west, and we remember to have entered the house turning eastward. As we passed the gate we saw a person and asked him if the Master had come. He received us cordially and asked us to proceed to the first floor by the southern flight of steps and enter the spacious parlour to the east extending from north to south. Entering that hall we saw that it was neat and clean and well furnished; there was on the floor a large mattress

covered with a white cotton sheet serving as the common seat for all, and the Master was sitting on one part of it surrounded by a few Brahmo devotees. We remember that the two Acharyas of the New Dispensation, Chiranjiv Sarma, and Amritlal Basu, were among them. Besides Jayagopal, the owner of the house, his brother, two or three friends of his living near by, and one or two devotees of the Master who came with him, were present there. We remember also to have seen there the young devotee named the junior Gopal whom the Master used to call Hutko, (literally, one who comes all on a sudden and disappears similarly). Thus seeing only about a dozen men with the Master on that occasion, we felt that that day's gathering was not meant for the public, and that to come there as we had done, was not quite right for us. We therefore decided that we steal away from that place a little before all were called to take their food.

As soon as we entered the house, we bowed down at the holy feet of the Master. "How have you come here?" asked he. We replied, "We had news that you would come here today; so we have come to see you." It seemed that he was pleased with that answer and asked us to sit down. We sat down, and thus freed from anxiety, we began to notice others and listen to his illuminating talk.

2. Although we had had the good fortune of meeting the Master for the first time only very recently, we had felt an extraordinary attraction for his ambrosial words from the very first day of our meeting. Of course, we did not then understand the reason for it; we find now how unique the method of his teaching was. There was no parade of scholarship, no logic-chopping, no festooning of fine phrases. Neither was there any studied artificiality in the use of words — any attempt to bolster commonplace ideas by clothing them in pompous words, or to obscure deep thoughts by parsimony of words as done by the Indian writers of philosophic aphorisms (i.e. Sutra literature). We cannot say whether the Master, who was the living embodiment of the ideas he expressed, paid any attention at all to the language he used. But, whoever heard him speak even once must have noticed how he held before them picture after picture drawn from the materials of daily occurrence, from the things and events the audience were familiar with, in order to imprint these ideas on their minds. The listeners also became fully freed from doubts and were perfectly satisfied with the truth of his words, as if they saw them enacted

before their very eyes. On reflecting how these pictures came immediately to his mind, we feel its cause lies in his extraordinary memory, his wonderful comprehension, his keen power of observation, and his unique presence of mind. But the Master always said that the Divine Mother's grace was the only cause of it. He used to say, "Mother sits in the heart of him who depends entirely on Her and makes him say whatever he has to say by showing it to him through unmistakable signs. Mother always keeps his mind filled with a mass of knowledge which She continues supplying from Her never-failing store of wisdom, whenever it appears to run short. Thus it is that it never gets exhausted, however much he may spend from it." Explaining this fact one day, he mentioned the following event:

There is a Government magazine to the north of the Kali temple at Dakshineswar. Some Sikh soldiers lived there for keeping watch over it. All of them were very much devoted to the Master and sometimes they would take him to their lodgings and have various doubts on religious matters cleared by him. The Master said, "One day they put the question, 'How should a man live in the world so that he may realize God?' And what I immediately saw was a picture of a husking machine before my eyes. Paddy was being husked and one person was very carefully pushing the paddy into the hole where the husking pedal was falling. As soon as I saw it, I knew that Mother was explaining to me that one should live in the world as cautiously as that. Just as the person who sits near the hole and pushes up the paddy is always careful that the pedal does not fall on his hand, so, a man engaged in worldly activities should take care always that he does not get entangled in them, by being conscious that the worldly affairs were not his. It is only then that he can escape bondage without being hurt and destroyed. As soon as I saw the picture of the husking machine, Mother produced this idea in my mind, and it was this that I told them. They also became highly pleased to hear it. Such pictures come before me when I talk to people."

3. Another peculiar characteristic that was observed in the Master's method of teaching was that he never confused the mind of his hearer by speaking unnecessary words. He discerned aright the subject and the aim of the inquirer's question and answered it in a few homely sentences. He gave the conclusion and illustrated it by vivid word-pictures in the aforesaid manner. We call this —

the statement of the conclusion — as the especial characteristic of his method of teaching. For he used to state as answer only that which he knew as true in his heart of hearts. He would not say in so many words that no other solution of that problem was possible. Neverthless that impression would be firmly created in the mind of the hearer, because of his deepseated conviction and the stress he used to lay on the expressions. If, on account of past education and impressions, any hearer brought forward contrary reasons and arguments and would not accept his conclusions, which he knew by Sadhana as true, he would wind up the topic, saying, "I have said whatever came to my mind; take as much, or as little, of it as you like (or, literally translated, accept it minus 'the head and tail')." Thus he would never harm or destroy the spiritual attitude of the hearer by interfering with his liberty. Was it that he thought that the hearer could not accept the true solution of the subject under discussion, till he had reached a higher mental state by the will of God? It seems so.

Again, he did not stop there but reinforced his talk by interspersing them with songs composed by well-known Sadhakas and sometimes quoting examples from the scriptures. That used to remove the doubts of the enquirer who, firmly convinced of the truth of the solution, would readily engage himself in moulding his life accordingly.

4. It is necessary to say one word more here. The Master told us again and again that the aspirant arrives at the non-dual knowledge by realizing his identity with the object of his worship at his journey's end, whether he treads the path of devotion or of knowledge. As proofs of this may be quoted his sayings, such as, "Pure devotion and pure knowledge are the same (thing)", or "There (in the ultimate state) all jackals howl alike (all men of knowledge speak of the same realization)". Thus although he was of the opinion that Advaita knowledge was the ultimate truth, he always taught the general public, with its hankering for worldly objects, the truth of qualified monism, and not unoften, of the love of God after the manner of a dualist. He used to be greatly annoyed at persons who, having no high spiritual experience, nor even love for God, would, nevertheless, bandy arguments in favour of non-dualism or qualified non-dualism. He did not hesitate often to condemn such actions of theirs with very harsh words. One day, the Master asked our friend, Vaikunthanath Sannyal, whether he

had read the Panchadasi and such other books. Getting a negative reply, the Master said with a sense of relief, "Good that you have not. Some boys read those books and, giving themselves airs, come here; they will not practise anything, they simply come to argue. That is a torment to me."

The reason that led us to quote the aforesaid words is that, at the house of Jayagopal, that day, a certain person put the question to the Master, "How should we live in the world to receive the grace of God?" The Master taught him the doctrine of qualified monism, punctuating the topic with a few songs on the universal Mother. We give below the substance of what he said:

5. As long as man looks upon the world as "mine" and acts accordingly, he becomes entangled in it, though he knows it to be transitory. He meets with suffering and can find no way out, even if he wants to flee from it. Saying that, the Master immediately sang, "So great is the Maya of Mahamaya that it has kept the world under a great delusion; even Brahma and Vishnu are under that delusion, let alone the Jiva not knowing it as such!" and so on. One, therefore, should associate this transitory world mentally with the divine Lord and perform every action accordingly. One must hold fast His Lotus feet with one hand and go on working with the other, always remembering that the persons and things of the world are His, not one's own. If one can do that, he will not have to suffer from worldly attachment. There will then arise the idea that whatever one does is the Lord's, and his mind will go forward towards Him. In order to imprint it firmly in the mind of the enquirer the Master sang, "O my mind, you do not know how to till (the soil of life)" and so on. The song finished, he continued, "If one lives his life in the world by having recourse to God in that manner, one will gradually feel that all the persons and things of the world are His parts. The aspirant then will serve his parents looking on them as the Parents of the universe (Brahman and His Power), see the manifestation of the boy Gopala and the Mother of the universe in his sons and daughters, and knowing all others to be the parts of Narayana, behave towards them with respect and devotion. A person who lives in the world in that spiritual mood is an ideal householder and the fear of death is rooted out from his mind. Such persons are rare indeed, but not altogether non-existent. Afterwards pointing out the means to reach that ideal, the Master said, "One should have recourse to the power

of the 'discriminating intellect' and do all actions in the light of it; one should also retire now and then from the disturbing environment of the world into the quietness of solitude and engage oneself in spiritual practices for the realisation of God." It is in this manner only that one can bring into practice the said ideal in one's life.[1] Pointing out the means, the Master sang the famous song of Ramprasad, "O mind, come let us go for a walk; you will get for the mere picking up the four fruits[2] under the wish-fulfilling tree, Kali." Again, when he used the expression 'discriminating intellect', he would explain what was meant by it. He said that with the help of that intellect the aspirant knows God as the One eternal Substance, underlying the fleeting appearances, the totality of sights, tastes, etc., which is the world, and he renounces it. But when he has known God, that very intellect teaches him that the One, who is the Absolute, has, in His play as the many, assumed myriads of forms as the individual things and persons of the universe; and the aspirant is blessed at last with the realization that God is both the Absolute and the Relative (Vijnana).

6. Then Acharya Chiranjiv began to sing with the help of his one-stringed instrument, "Make me inebriated, O Mother," and all sang in chorus after him. When the Kirtan thus began, the Master was in ecstasy and stood up. All the others also then stood round him and began to dance and sing. Finishing this song, Chiranjiv commenced singing:

Ah, the full moon of divine Love has risen in the firmament of Consciousness. Victory to the merciful One!
Behold the sea of the divine Love swollen high! Oh, the bliss of it!
Ah, the devotees like stars, glitter round Hari, the playful One and friend of the devotees!
Opening the door of heaven, the vernal breeze of the New Dispensation blows and raises waves of bliss.
The sweet smell of the nectar of divine Love spreads rapidly around and makes the Yogis inebriated with the bliss of holy contemplation.
In the shoreless sea of the world is dancing the lotus of

[1] We are indebted to 'M', the esteemed author of the Gospel of Sri Ramakrishna, for a part of the substance of this day's conversation.

[2] Namely, Dharma, Artha, Kama and Moksha i.e. moral, economical and aesthetic excellences, as well as liberation.

the Dispensation, on which sits gracefully the blissful Mother.

The bees, the devotees, overwhelmed with spiritual emotions, drink the nectar of that lotus.

Lo! There is the Mother's gracious, world-charming face so pleasing to the devotees' minds! And merged in love, holy men in companies dance and sing at Her feet.

Oh, the beauty of it! Life has become cool and refreshed on seeing all this. Holding the feet of all, Premadas beseeches every one to sing victory to the Mother.

Dancing for a long time to the accompaniment of the song, they brought to a close that day's Kirtan by bowing down to God and to His devotees. All of them took the dust of the Master's feet and sat down. He danced gracefully on this occasion also, but he did not have here that kind of deep ecstasy lasting for a long time, which we saw at Manimohan's place. The Kirtan over, the Master sat down and said to Chiranjiv, "When I heard that song of yours for the first time, I saw rising such a living, large full moon, ever so big, and would enter into ecstasy as soon as it was sung ever afterwards."

Jayagopal and Chiranjiv were then talking to each other about Kesav's illness. The Master, we remember, told some one on that occasion that Rakhal was then unwell. We do not know whether Jayagopal was a formally initiated Brahmo or not; but there is no doubt that he had great respect and reverence for Kesavchandra, the Brahmo leader, and love for the members of the Brahmo circle. Kesav sometimes went to Jayagopal's garden at Belgharia near Calcutta with his entire party and spent some time in spiritual practices. It was on one such occasion that he met the Master for the first time there, which led to the deepening of spirituality in Kesav's life, culminating in the blossoming of the flower of the New Dispensation. Jayagopal also entertained great respect for the Master ever since that day. He enjoyed great bliss in religious conversation, sometimes by coming to the Master at Dakshineswar and sometimes by inviting him to his own house. For some time, Jayagopal, we were told, paid a great part of the expenses of the Master's carriage hire for going to Calcutta. All the members of his family also had much respect for him.

Now that the night was well advanced, we took leave of the Master and started home.

CHAPTER II

THE BEGINNING OF THE ARRIVAL OF THE MASTER'S DEVOTEES PREVIOUSLY SEEN IN VISIONS

[TOPICS: 1. The Master also learnt something from the Brahmo Samaj. 2. He came to know of the influence of the Western ideas. 3. The comparative outlook of the moderns. 4. The Master unperturbed at this. 5. The Master reconciles himself to the Brahmo's partial acceptance of his teachings. 6. Calcutta people drawn to the Master through Brahmos. 7. A wonderful vision of the Master: Rakhal came. 8. The boyish nature of Rakhal. 9. Rakhal's wife. 10. How Rakhal would lose his boyishness. 11. The Master scolded Rakhal. 12. Jealousy in Rakhal's mind and the Master's misgiving. 13. Rakhal went to Vrindavan. 14. The Master's apprehension on hearing of Rakhal's illness. 15. The later life of Rakhal.]

1. We have already told the reader how the Brahmo leaders like Acharya Kesavchandra, Vijaykrishna, Pratapchandra, Sivanath, Chiranjiv, Amritalal, Gauragovinda and others were greatly benefited by coming in contact with the Master and observing in him the glorious ideals of devotion to one's faith and the total renunciation of one's all for the realization of God. Now, the question arises, "Did the Master, who had already attained the immediate knowledge of Brahman and was established in Bhavamukha, learn anything from his contact with Kesav and other Brahmos?" Many of the devotees of Sri Ramakrishna will not at all hesitate to say "No" to this in reply. But the law of "give and take" is seen always to exist everywhere in the world. Even when we go to teach a very ignorant and fickle boy, we in turn learn many things, such as the mode of teaching best suited to an intellect like his, the degree to which the past impressions of such a mind help or hinder the understanding of the subject, the process of removing the hindrances and several such lessons. It is therefore not reasonable to say that the Master learnt nothing when he came in contact with the Brahmo Samaj established on the basis of Western ideas and ideals. Our impression is quite different. We say, the Master himself learnt much when he tried to impart to the Brahmo society and church his own knowledge and spiritual

experiences obtained through his extraordinary Sadhana. It is but proper to discuss a little of the things he learnt as the result of that contact.

2. Before he came in contact with the Brahmos, the Master was living his life far from the influence of the Western ideas and ideals. With the exception of Mathuranath, all persons of note he had contacted till then were devoted followers of the ancient Indian ideals of Dharma and Moksha — some striving to do acts of piety and charity for the good of the world and themselves, and others following the eternal and glorious path of total renunciation of all possessions and desires for realising Immortality. Although he saw in Mathuranath one educated in the Western manner and possessing an outlook different from that of others, he had no opportunity to observe the lives of a sufficiently large number of people so educated and the transformation this new system of education had brought on them, making them aliens to the ancient Hindu ideals of life. For, the nature of Mathuranath had changed in a short time on account of his holy company, and so there was no occasion for the Master to study the new situation by observing him during the days of his contact with him. Coming in contact with the Brahmos, however, he saw that, although they were making efforts to realize God, they had deviated from the ancient national ideal of renunciation. His mind, therefore, engaged itself in finding out its cause. It was thus that he became acquainted for the first time with the mass of exotic ideas entering into the lives of the people of India because of Western education and training.

3. The Master, it seems, thought at first that, when Kesav and other Brahmos became acquainted with the living religious ideas realized directly by him, they would unreservedly accept them in a short time. But days followed one after another, and he found that, in spite of their coming in close contact with him, they could not get rid of the influence of Western education and place perfect faith in his direct spiritual experiences. So he came to understand that the Western ideas had struck their roots deep into the nature of young Indians, that the thinkers and scholars of the West had come to occupy the place of their Gurus and would continue to occupy it for a long time to come, and that without comparing the direct spiritual experiences of the ancient seers of India with the idea of those scholars, the Indian disciples of the latter would never accept them as true and beneficial. This was why, immediately

after giving instruction to them, the Master used to say, "I have said whatever came to my mind; you accept them selecting what suits you," or in his own phraseology, eliminating 'the head and tail'. It is needless to say that whatever ideas and experiences of the Master they accepted, they did so only because he gave them absolute freedom to pick and choose.

4. But the Master, the consolidated incarnation of the ideas and ideals of the seers of this country, was not at all disturbed by this attitude of theirs; for he had felt in his heart of hearts that the will of the universal Mother was the only cause of all kinds of events taking place in the world, and that no event could ever thwart a person who was possessed of Her command and was habituated to the guidance of it under all circumstances. Maya, the divine Power, capable of making the impossible possible, had revealed to him Her own real nature, explained it to him and endowed him for ever with inviolable, unchangeable Peace. The Master, therefore, could perfectly comprehend that it was only owing to the Divine Mother's will that Western ideas and ideals had entered India and that by Her will alone had the Brahmos and other educated communities become mere toys in their hands. So, how could he be annoyed at that weakness of theirs or withhold from them his infinite love and affection? He, therefore, remained free from anxiety, and thought, "Let them accept as much of the immediate knowledge of the seers as is possible for them; the Mother of the universe will bring forward in future such persons as will fully accept that knowledge."

5. Again, although he found that the Brahmos could not accept everything he said, he was not satisfied to give them only a partial picture of his spiritual experiences. He always told them without reserve all the hidden truths of the spiritual world, such as: "The blessed vision of God will never be had unless one renounces one's all for Him", "All the faiths are (true) paths (to the realization of God)", "At the end of each path, the worshipper becomes identified with the worshipped", "To see that one's words agree fully with one's thoughts is the most important Sadhana", "The path leading to Him is to discriminate the real from the unreal, to be free from all desires, and to perform all worldly duties with full faith in, and reliance on, God." He explained to Kesav and some others that it was never possible to be completely unattached to the body and experience higher truths of the spiritual world,

unless continence was practised with body, mind and speech. As a result of this teaching they made efforts to observe it. When, however, he found that they were unable to grasp his words fully even after repeated explanations, he came to the conclusion that, once the past impressions became deep-rooted, it was almost impossible to make one imbibe new ideas — that such effort was as futile as to teach a parrot to repeat "Radhakrishna" when once the ring of colour had appeared round its neck. He understood that those persons in whom the desire to enjoy the world had taken deep root, whether due to the influence of Western materialism or otherwise, would never be able to accept the eternal ideas of renunciation preached by this country, far less to carry them out into practice. That was why he burst into an earnest prayer, "Bring here, Mother, Thy all-renouncing devotees, with whom I am to have the joy of talking about Thee without any reserve." Therefore, it will not be unreasonable for us to say that as a result of this observation the conviction grew in him that it was only the minds of boys, unspoilt by deep-seated impressions, that would fully grasp and accept his ideas and ideals without hesitation and go boldly forward to realize the truths they represented.

6. Anyway, it did not take the general public of Calcutta long to observe how far the Brahmo leaders accepted the Master's new spiritual ideas and what changes were brought about in them. Again, when Kesav and other persons began to publish in the Brahmo periodicals some account of the extraordinary nature of his spiritual views and his ambrosial words, the people of Calcutta were much attracted towards him and began to pour into Dakshineswar to have the blessed privilege of meeting him. It was in this way that the Master's 'marked devotees' came gradually to the Kali temple there. The two householder devotees of the Master, Ramchandra Datta and Manomohan Mitra, we were told, read about him in the periodical conducted by Kesav and came to him at about the end of 1879, about four years after the Master's first meeting with Kesav. Ramchandra Datta has himself told us through some details in his book *Sri Sri Ramakrishna Paramahamsa Deber Jivan Vrittanta*, what a great revolution gradually took place in their lives on account of their good fortune in coming into contact with him. We need not repeat them here. It will be enough to say here that, although unable to accept fully the Master's ideal of the total renunciation of lust and gold for the realization of

God, they covered a pretty long distance on the path of renunciation under the influence of their devotion to and faith in him. The intensity of the devotion and faith of a householder devotee can, to a great extent, be ascertained by noticing his unstinted expenditure of hard-earned money in a good cause. Putting the Master at first in the place of his Guru and then in that of his chosen Ideal, Ramchandra invited him and his devotees again and again to his house at the Simla quarter of Calcutta and spent money so unstintedly during festivals on those occasions that one could fathom easily the depth of his faith and devotion. The Master said about him from time to time, "You now see Ram so splendidly generous. But his miserliness when he first came beggars description. I asked him to bring some cardamom, and one day he brought a pice worth of it, placed it before me, and bowed down. Guess from it what a great change has come over Ram's nature."

7. It cannot be expressed in words how blessed Ram and Manomohan felt themselves to be when the Master's grace fell on them and they were accepted and given eternal refuge at his feet and freed for ever from all fears. It was beyond their wildest dream that such a refuge could ever be found in the world! Under the circumstances it is not surprising that they now tried to take their relatives and friends to the same place of refuge. Their own families and other relatives began to visit the Master in about a year of their meeting with him. It was thus that the all-renouncing devotees, the eternal playmates of the Master in his Lila, began coming to him one by one from the last quarter of A.D. 1881. Of these, Swami Brahmananda, well known in the Order of Sri Ramakrishna, was the first to come to the Master. In his pre-monastic days, his name was Rakhalchandra. He had married Manomohan's sister, and it was from this family that he first heard the name of the Master. He came to the Master shortly after his marriage. Sri Ramakrishna said, "Before Rakhal came, I had seen in a vision the Mother of the universe suddenly bringing a boy and placing him on my lap, with the words, 'He is your son'. I startled with fear to hear it,' I said, 'How is that? How can I have a son?' She smiled and explained, 'He is not a son in the ordinary, worldly sense of the term, but your all-renouncing spiritual son.' Thus assured, I was consoled. Rakhal came immediately after I had had the vision, and I recognized him at once as the boy."

8. On another occasion, the Master said to us about Sri Rakhal, "In those days Rakhal had the nature of a child of three or four, so to say. He looked upon me exactly as his mother. He would come running at short intervals and joyfully sit on my lap without any hesitation. He would not move a step from here, let alone going home. I pressed him to go home now and then, lest his father should disallow his coming here. His father was a Zamindar, immensely rich, but equally miserly. He tried at first in various ways to prevent his son from coming. Later when he found that many rich and learned men visited this place, he did not object to his son's coming here. On some occasions he came here to meet his son. For the sake of Rakhal, I was all attention to him and he was very pleased.

9. "But no objection was ever raised against his coming here by his father-in-law's family. For, Manomohan's mother, wife and sister all used to visit this place very often. One day, shortly after Rakhal had started coming here, Manomohan's mother came with his girl wife. I was anxious lest his wife should stand in the way of his devotion to God and had her brought to me. I observed her physical features from head to foot minutely and became convinced that there was no cause for fear. Representing the auspicious aspect of the divine Sakti as she did, she would never be an obstacle on the path to her husband's realization of God. Then I was pleased and sent word to the Nahavat (i.e. to the Holy Mother), asking her to present the daughter-in-law a rupee and see her veiled face.[1]

10. "It is impossible to describe the childlike rapture that overcame Rakhal, whenever he was in my company; he simply lost himself. Every one who saw him then was wonder-struck. Inspired with spiritual fervour, I also used to feed him with thickened milk and butter, and played with him to cheer him. On many occasions I lifted him to my shoulders. Even that did not produce an iota of hesitation in his mind. But then and there I said, 'Should he grow up and live in the company of his wife, this childlike nature of his will vanish.'

11. "I also scolded him when he did something wrong. One day he was very hungry and took butter, the Prasada brought

[1] This is how a mother-in-law in Bengal sees the veiled face of her newly arrived daughter-in-law. First of all she gives some presents, generally money, then, removing the veil gently, she sees her face and kisses her.

from the Kali temple, with his own hand and ate it. I said, 'How greedy! You took the butter with your own hand and ate it, instead of controlling greed, which you ought to have learnt from here!' He shrank into himself from fear and never did so again.

12. "Rakhal then had a child's jealousy too. It was quite unbearable for him, if I loved anyone but him. He would feel wounded at heart. At that I felt greatly perturbed lest he should harm himself by being jealous of those whom Mother would bring here.

13. "Three years after he came here Rakhal fell ill and went to Vrindavan with Balaram. I had a vision a little before that, as if Mother was going to remove him from here. At this I eagerly prayed, 'Mother, he (Rakhal) is a mere boy, quite ignorant; that is why he sometimes feels piqued. If, for the sake of Thy work, Thou removest him from here for some time, keep him in a good place and in a blissful mood.' He went to Vrindavan shortly afterwards.

14. "I cannot express how very anxious I was when I was told that Rakhal was ill at Vrindavan. For, Mother had shown me before that Rakhal was in truth a 'cowherd boy'[1] of Vraja. If one goes to the place from where one came to assume a body, one very often remembers one's past life and gives up the body. That was why I was afraid that he might pass away at Vrindavan. So I eagerly prayed to Mother and She comforted me with an assurance. Mother has thus shown me many things about Rakhal. Many of those things I am forbidden to express."[2]

15. There are no limits to the things said on various occasions by the Master about this first boy-devotee of his. Whatever Mother showed the Master about him, has proved true to the letter. He became classed with the Sadhakas noted for their gravity and serenity as he advanced in age and renounced his all for the realization of God. The boy has now come to occupy the highest position in the Order of Sri Ramakrishna. Spared till now by the will of the Master, Swami Brahmananda is doing immense good to

[1] With whom the Lord, in His incarnation as Sri Krishna, had played in His childhood. The word Rakhal means a cowherd.

[2] Though the Master did not say all the things mentioned above at one and the same time, we have arranged them all here for the sake of convenience.

humanity.[1] We stop[2] saying more about him here, as he is still living in our midst.

Swami Vivekananda came to the Master three or four months after Swami Brahmananda had come to Dakshineswar for the first time. We shall now address ourselves to the narration of the incidents connected with his life.

CHAPTER III

NARENDRA'S ANTECEDENTS AND HIS FIRST VISIT TO DAKSHINESWAR

[TOPICS: 1. The Master in the divine mood. 2. The Master's first meeting with Narendranath at Surendra's house. 3. The Master inviting Narendranath to Dakshineswar. 4. His first visit to Dakshineswar. 5. What the Master thought of Narendra. 6. The Master's eagerness to see Narendra. 7. Narendra on his first meeting with the Master. 8. Narendra promised to come again. 9. Narendra's first impression of the Master. 10. Practice of religion at that time by Narendra. 11. His connection with the Brahmo Samaj. 12. The two wonderful ideas of Narendra. 13. Narendra's natural inclination for meditation. 14. Maharshi Devendranath's encouragement. 15. The many-sided genius of Narendra. 16. Narendra's inclination for study. 17. Narendra's capacity for quick reading. 18. Narendra's argumentation. 19. Narendra's love for physical exercise. 20. His courage and love for friends. 21. Securing permission to board the ship, Syrapis. 22. Trapeze incident. 23. Narendra's devotion to truth. 24. His fondness for the enjoyment of harmless pleasures. 25. Narendra's anger. 26. The equal development of Narendra's head and heart. 27. Narendra's absorption in meditation on his way to Raipur. 28. The Sannyasin grandfather of Narendra. 29. Viswanath, Narendra's father. 30. Viswanath's love of music. 31. Viwanath's Muslim manners and customs. 32. Viswanath's love for merriment. 33. Viswanath's generosity. 34. Viswanath's death. 35. Narendra's mother.]

1. The Vedas and the other scriptures say that a knower of Brahman becomes all-knowing. This saying of the scriptures is proved to be wholly true when we notice the present behaviour of the Master, who was firmly established in the knowledge of Brahman. For, not only did he now become directly acquainted with both the Absolute and its relative aspect, with Brahman and Its power Maya, but rising far above all doubts and impurities, was abiding in a state of everlasting bliss. Being established in Bhavamukha, which consists in experiencing oneness with the universal Mother, he could now understand any hidden mystery of the realm of Maya any moment he wished to know. Maya could no more conceal her nature from his mind's eye, possessed as it was of the subtle vision for penetrating her veil. And it was naturally so; for, both the Bhavamukha and the universal Mind

of Isvara, the Lord of Maya, in which the ideation of the universe remains sometimes manifested and sometimes unmanifested, are one and the same entity; all the ideas arising in the universal Mind appear clearly before one who has crossed the limit of his little I-ness and has become identified with the Universal I. The Master could know the events of all the previous births of his devotees before they had come to him, only because he had reached that state. He could know the particular Lila of the universal Mind, for the manifestation of which he had assumed his present body. He also knew that some Sadhakas of a very high order were born by the will of God to participate in that sport. He further understood who among those would help him more and who less in the manifestation of that play, and who would simply enjoy the benefit arising out of it by attaining perfection in life. Knowing that the time of their coming was near at hand, he was waiting for them with great eagerness. How could one be regarded except as an all-knowing one, who lived within the realm of Maya and knew all her secrets?

2. When one thinks of the first meeting of Swami Vivekananda with the Master, one comes to understand how eagerly the Master, established in the divine state, was waiting for his 'marked' devotees, as he saw the time of their arrival drawing near. Swami Brahmananda said that Surendranath Mitra of Simla in Calcutta came to Dakshineswar at almost the same time with him. Surendra was much attracted towards the Master at his very first visit. Drawn closer and closer to him within a short time, he took him home and celebrated a joyous festival. No good singer being available for the occasion, Surendra affectionately invited Narendra, the son of Viswanath Datta, his neighbour, to join the festival and treat the audience, especially the Master, to devotional songs. The first meeting of the Master and Vivekananda, the chief playmate in his divine sport, came to pass that way. It was probably the month of November 1881. Narendra, then eighteen years old, was preparing for the F.A. examination of the Calcutta University.

3. Swami Brahmananda said that they clearly felt that the Master was very much attracted towards Narendra as soon as he saw him that day; for, he first called Surendra and then Ramachandra to him, collected all possible particulars about the youthful singer of sweet voice, and asked them to take him once to Dakshineswar. Again, when the singing was over, he himself came to

the young man, and studying carefully his physiognomy, spoke a word or two to him and invited him to come soon to Dakshineswar some day.

4. The F.A. examination of the Calcutta University was over a few weeks after the said event. At the request of a respectable gentleman of the city, Narendra's father was arranging for his marriage with the former's daughter. As the bride was somewhat dark in complexion, her father agreed to give a dowry of ten thousand rupees. The relatives of Narendra headed by Ramachandra tried best to persuade him to consent to this marriage. But as Narendra objected strongly, the marriage could not take place. Ramchandra was a close relative of Narendranath's father. He was brought up in the latter's household, and was then practising as a physician in Calcutta. When he found that Narendra had declined to marry because of his desire to pursue the path of spiritual enlightenment, he said to him, "If you have a real desire to realize God, then come to the Master at Dakshineswar instead of visiting the Brahmo Samaj and other places." One day at this time, Surendra too invited him to accompany him to Dakshineswar in his carriage. Narendra consented, and with two or three friends, accompanied Surendra to Dakshineswar.

5. The Master told us briefly in the course of a conversation what thoughts came to his mind when he saw Narendra on that occasion. He said: "Naren entered this room on the first day through the western door (facing the Ganga). I noticed that he took no care of his body. The hair of his head and his dress were not at all trim. Unlike others, he had no desire at all for any external object. He was, as it were, unattached to anything. His eyes indicated that a major part of his mind was perforce drawn ever inward. When I saw all these, I wondered, 'Is it ever possible that such a great spiritual aspirant possessing a superabundance of Sattva, should live in Calcutta, the home of worldly people?'

"There was a mattress spread on the floor. I asked him to sit down on it. He sat down near the jar of Ganga water. A few acquaintances of his also came with him that day. I felt that their nature was just like that of ordinary worldly people and was quite opposite to his. Their attention was directed to enjoyment only.

"On inquiry, I came to know that he had learnt two or three Bengali songs only. I asked him to sing them. He began singing the Brahmo song:

"O mind, come, let us go home. Why do you travel in the foreign land of the world in a foreigner's garb?
The five elements and objects of the senses are all inimical to you; none of them are your own. Deluded with the love of others, you have forgotton the One who is your own.
O my mind, go on the path of truth. Light the lamp of love, have it always with you and go forward. Take carefully with you the secret provision of devotion.
Greed, delusion, etc., the dacoits, rob the traveller of everything.
This is why I say, 'O mind, let the two, the control of internal organs and that of the external ones, keep watch.'
When you are tired, stay in the rest-house of holy company and, when you lose your way, ask it of those who stay there.
If you find any cause of fear on your way, appeal to the King with all your might. The King wields great power there, and before him even death quails in terror.

He sang it with the whole of his mind and heart, as if in meditation. When I heard it, I could not control myself and was in ecstasy.

6. "Afterwards, when he left, there was such an eagerness in the heart, all the twenty-four hours of the day, to see him. It cannot be expressed in words. From time to time I felt excruciating pain, as if my heart was being wrung like a wet towel. Unable to control myself, I then went running to the Tamarisk trees in the north of the garden, where people do not generally go, and wept loudly, saying, "O my child! come, I cannot remain without seeing you.' It was only after weeping a little thus that I could control myself. This happened continually for six months. My mind sometimes felt uneasy for some of the other boys too who came here. But it can be said that it was nothing compared to my feelings in Naren's case."

7. We came to know afterwards from a realiable source that the Master concealed much of the extraordinary emotions that arose in his mind when he saw Narendra for the first time at Dakshineswar, and spoke to us of it with reserve. In the course of a conversation regarding that occasion, one day Narendranath

said to us: "I finished singing. Immediately afterwards the Master suddenly stood up, and taking me by the hand, led me to the northern verandah. It was winter. So to protect the room against the northern wind, the open spaces between the pillars of the verandah were covered by mat screens. Therefore, when one entered the verandah and closed the door of the room, one could not be seen by any person within or without the room. As soon as he entered the verandah, the Master closed the door of the room. I thought he might perhaps give me some instruction in private. But what he said and did was beyond imagination. He suddenly caught hold of my hand and shed profuse tears of joy. Addressing me affectionately like one already familiar, he said: 'Is it proper that you should come so late? Should you not have once thought how I was waiting for you? Hearing continually the idle talk of worldly people, my ears are about to be scorched. Not having any one to whom to communicate my innermost feelings, I am about to burst.' And so he went on raving and weeping. The next moment he stood before me with folded palms, and showing me the regard due to a god, went on saying, 'I know, my lord, you are that ancient Rishi Nara, a part of Narayana, who has incarnated himself this time, to remove the miseries and sufferings of humanity.'

8. "I was absolutely non-plussed and thought, 'Whom have I come to see? He is, I see, completely insane. Why should he otherwise speak in this strain to me, who am really the son of Viswanath Datta?' However, I kept silent and the wonderful madman went on speaking whatever he liked. The next moment he asked me to wait there and entered the room, and bringing some butter, candy and Sandesh, began to feed me with his own hand. He never gave ear to my repeated requests to give those things to me, so that I might partake of them with my companions, saying, 'They will take them later. You take these yourself.' Saying so, he fed me with all the sweets, and only after that could he rest content. He then caught hold of my hand and said, 'Promise, you will soon come to me again and all alone.' Unable to evade that earnest request of his, I had to say, 'I shall', and then I entered the room with him and sat down beside my companions.

9. "I went on observing him closely and could find no trace of madness in his deportment, conversation, or behaviour towards others. Impressed by his fine talk and ecstasy, I thought that he was truly a man of renunciation who had given up his all for God

and practised personally what he professed. 'God can be seen and spoken with, just as I am seeing you and speaking with you; but who wants to do so? People grieve and shed potfuls of tears at the death of their wives and sons, and behave in the same way for the sake of money or property. But who does so because he cannot realize God? If any one is in truth equally anxious to see Him and calls on Him with a longing heart, He certainly reveals Himself to him.' When I heard these words of his, the impression grew on me that it was not mere poetry or imagination couched in fine figures of speech that he was expressing like other preachers of religion, but that he was speaking of something of which he had an immediate knowledge — of an attainment which had come to him by really renouncing everything for the sake of God and calling on Him with all his mind.

"Trying to harmonize these words with his behaviour towards me a little while previously, I remembered the examples of the monomaniacs mentioned by Abercrombie and other English philosophers, and came to the sure conclusion that he belonged to that class. Although I came to that conclusion, I could not forget the greatness of his wonderful renunciation for God. Speechless, I thought, 'Well, he may be mad, but it is indeed a rare soul alone in the world who could practise such renunciation. Yes, mad, but how pure! And what renunciation! He is truly worthy of respect, reverence and worship by the human heart.' Thinking thus, I bowed down at his feet, took leave of him and returned to Calcutta that day."

10. As the reader will naturally have the curiosity to know the antecedents of one, the sight of whom roused such extraordinary emotions in the Master's mind, we shall now relate them briefly. At the time we are speaking of, Narendra was not a mere student of secular learning and music. He was leading a strictly continent life and was practising severe austerity under the impulsion of a spiritual urge. A strict vegetarian, he spent his nights lying on the bare ground or on a bed consisting of one blanket only. His maternal grandmother had a rented house near his ancestral home. He generally lived in a room on the first floor over the outer apartment of that house ever since he appeared for the Entrance Examination. When it was inconvenient to stay there for some reason or other, he hired a room near that house and lived separately, away from his relatives and family, engaging himself in the pursuit of his

main objective in life, namely, the realisation of God. His large-hearted father and the other members of the family thought that he was living separately only because he found it rather inconvenient to study at home on account of various kinds of distractions and disorders arising from too many persons living together there.

As a follower of the teachings of the Brahmo Samaj, Narendra believed in the formless Brahman with attributes and spent much time in meditation on Him. He could not remain satisfied, like other people, by simply becoming convinced of the existence of the formless Brahman with the help of inference and reasoning. Led by the spiritual tendencies of his past lives, his heart was incessantly telling him that if God really existed, He would never keep His own nature concealed from an eagerly seeking human heart, that He certainly must have laid down the means to realize Him, and that life would become a burden and a drudgery if it were not a quest for the realization of God. He, we distinctly remember, said as follows to us once:

11. "As soon as I went to bed, two ideas appeared before me every night ever since I had reached my youth. One vision presented me as a person of endless wealth and property, innumerable servants and dependants, high rank and dignity, great pomp and power. I thought that I was seated at the head of those who were called big men in the world. I felt I certainly had the power to achieve this end. Again, the next moment, I felt as if I had given up everything of the world and was leading a life of renunciation, putting on a loin cloth, eating whatever was available without effort, spending nights under trees and depending solely on God's will. I felt I could live the life of the Rishis and the Munis if I wanted. These two opposite pictures, according to which I could mould my life, thus arose in my mind. But the latter would grip the mind in the end. I thought that it was in this way alone that man could attain real bliss, and that I should follow this path and not the other. Brooding on the happiness of such a life, my mind would then merge in the contemplation of God and I would fall asleep. It is a matter of astonishment that this happened every night, for a long time."

12. Even at that young age Narendra found out, without the advice of any one, that meditation was the best method for the realization of God. This bespeaks the greatness of his spiritual past and the impressions derived from it. When he was about

four or five years old, he used to buy in the market small images of Sita, Rama, Siva and other gods and goddesses. Bringing them home, he would adorn them with ornaments and sit motionless in front of them with closed eyes in imitation of meditation. He would, however, open his eyes now and then to see if, in the meantime, any matted hair, hanging from his head, had entered the earth like the aerial roots of some trees. For, he had heard from the old ladies of the household that Munis and Rishis sat in meditation for such a long time that their matted hair came down and entered the earth that way. His revered mother said that one day he entered a secluded part of the house with a boy named Hari, a neighbour, without the knowledge of any one, and sat there for so long a time in imitation of meditation, that the whole household ran about in search of him, thinking that the boy had wandered away from home and lost his way. Afterwards, seeing that particular part of the house barred from within, someone broke into it and saw him sitting motionless in meditative posture. His behaviour was, no doubt, the expression of a childish imagination, but it clearly shows what wonderful spiritual tendencies he was born with. Anyway, no one of his relatives knew that he used to practise meditation every day at the time we are speaking of. For, he barred his room and sat for meditation after all the household had gone to bed. He would sometimes be so much absorbed in it that the whole night would pass away before he came back to normal consciousness.

13. Narendra's tendency to meditate was greatly enhanced on account of an event that took place about this time. One day he went with his friends to see the revered Acharya Maharshi Devendranath of the Adi Brahmo Samaj. On that occasion the Maharshi lovingly made the young men sit near him, gave much good instruction and requested them to practise meditation on God every day. Addressing Narendra he said that day, "The characteristics of a Yogi are manifest in you; if you practise meditation, you will soon experience the results recorded in the Yoga scriptures." Narendra had reverence for the Maharshi even before for his pure character. Therefore, there is no doubt, that, on his advice, he applied his mind to the practice of meditation with greater zeal than before.

The signs of a many-sided genius were perceptible in Narendra from his childhood. He got by heart all the aphorisms of the Sanskrit grammar book named Mugdhabodha. Placing him on his lap every evening, an old relative of his taught him the names of his forefathers, hymns to gods and goddesses and the aphorisms of the said grammar. At the age of six he was able to learn by heart the whole of the Ramayana done to music. If it was sung anywhere in that quarter, he was sure to be present there. One day at a certain place near by, a singer of that epic, while singing a part of the musical composition, could not recall a certain passage; Narendra immediately repeated that portion for him and got appreciation and some sweets from him. At the time of listening to the reading of the Ramayana, Narendra used to look round to see whether Hanuman, the great hero and servant of Ramachandra, was present there in fulfilment of his vow to be present wherever the glory of Rama was being sung. On account of his strong memory, he deserved to be called a 'Srutidhara', one who grasped whatever he heard even once and retained it in his memory ever afterwards. This was why his method of learning his lessons from his childhood was not like that of the other boys. When he was admitted into the school, a tutor was engaged for him to help him in learning his daily lessons. Narendra said, "When he came to our house, I brought my English and Bengali books to him, and showing him the particular books and the portions in them that were to be learnt as lessons for the day, I laid myself down or sat quietly. The teacher repeated twice or thrice the spelling, pronunciation, meaning etc., of the words of those portions of those books, as if he was himself learning the lesson and went away. That was sufficient for me to learn them." When he grew up, he would start the study of his text books only two or three months before the examination. At other times he read extra-books of his own choice. Thus, before appearing for the Entrance Examination, he had read practically all the important books in English and Bengali literature and many books on history. But, as a result of adopting this method, he had sometimes to labour hard immediately before his examinations. One day, explaining how he solved the difficulty caused by this habit of his, he said, "I found just two or three days before the Entrance Examination that the pages of Euclid had not been even turned over. I then sat up the whole night to study it. I mastered all the four books on the subject in twenty-four hours and appeared for the examination." It is needless to say that he could do so only because he had a robust body and an extraordinary memory by the grace of God.

14. When it is said that Narendra spent his time in reading books other than his text books, let no one think that he read novels and plays only and wasted his time. At certain particular times a great inclination to study books on particular subjects arose in his mind. He then mastered all the books he could collect on that subject. For example, in 1879, the year of his Entrance Examination, he felt an urge for reading the important available books on Indian History and read Marshman, Elphinstone and others. During his study for the F.A. Examination he mastered one by one all the available books on Logic in English, such as those by Whitley, Jevons and Mill; and when he was reading for the B.A. examination, he had a great desire to study the Histories of England and other European countries, both ancient and modern, as also books of Western philosophy. Similar was his passion for other branches of learning.

15. As a result of reading a vast number of books, Narendra's power of rapid reading developed to an extraordinary degree from the time of his appearing for the Entrance Examination. He said, "Since then, when I took up a book, I did not find it necessary to plod through it line by line in order to understand the author. I could grasp the point by reading the first and the last lines of a paragraph. Gradually that power became developed and it was not necessary to read the paragraphs also in the aforesaid way. Sometimes I read the first and the last lines of each page and the content was known. Again, when the author was explaining a particular point of view with arguments in any part of his book, I could understand his whole chain of reasoning by merely reading the beginning of his arguments."

16. At that time Narendra became very fond of argumentation as the result of much study and deep thinking. But he never indulged in sophistry. He always used to support only that which he knew to be true in his heart of hearts. But, if anyone expressed before him an idea or opinion against what he knew as true, he would never listen to it passively. He would bring to bear upon the topic a formidable array of arguments and silence the opponents in no time. Rare were the persons who did not bend their heads before his reasoning. It goes without saying that his defeated opponents

did not view him with a friendly eye. Hearing but a few words of the opponent, he could understand the trend of the arguments in support of the other's position and he would be ready with his reply beforehand. Asked how he could find such fine arguments ever ready to defeat his opponent, he once said. "How many new thoughts are there in the world? If those few thoughts are known together with the reasons for and against them, no necessity for further thinking ever arises, and one is always ready with the replies. For, whatever reason the opponent might adduce in favour of his position, it cannot but be one or the other of those few. Rare indeed are the persons who can give to the world new ideas and thoughts on any subject."

Born with a keen intellect, an extraordinary memory and the power of deep thinking, Narendra could master everything in a very short time, and hence had no lack of leisure for recreation and sports and games as well as for enjoying the pleasure of the company of his friends. Seeing him thus spending much time in mirth and merriment, people thought he did not attend to his studies at all. Trying to imitate him in these matters, many boys actually spoiled their career as students.

17. Narendra had as great a love for the practice of all kinds of physical exercises as for the acquisition of knowledge. When he was a child, his father bought a pony for him. As a result, he became a good horseman as he grew older. He learnt almost all forms of physical exercises — gymnastics, wrestling, boxing, stick-and-sword play, swinging club, swimming and the like. As a consequence he became physically very strong and agile, besides being highly skilled in all these physical feats. In those days general competitions were held in these arts and the successful persons were awarded prizes in the Hindu Fair established by Navagopal Mitra. Narendra was sometimes seen amongst these competitors.

18. From his childhood, Nature had equipped him with indomitable courage and love for his friends. These qualities helped him very much by making him the foremost in all the groups he entered and a leader in his student-life and afterwards. Once when he was but eight, he went with his friends to Metiaburuz to the south of Calcutta to see the Zoological gardens of Wazid Ali, the former Nawab of Lucknow. The boys raised subscriptions from among themselves and hired a boat at the Chandpal-ghat for their trips to and fro. On their way back, one of them became sick

and vomited in the boat. The Muslim boatman became very angry, and when the boat reached the Chandpal-ghat, told them that he would not allow any one of them to get down, if they did not clean the boat. The boys asked him to have it cleaned by some one and were ready to pay for the labour; but he did not agree. Then there arose an altercation and gradually there was going to be a free fight between the two parties. All the boatmen that were there came together and were ready to beat the boys. The latter did not know what they should do. Narendra was the youngest of them all. In the confusion that arose on account of the altercation with the boatman, he gave them the slip and got down from the boat. Seeing how very young he was, the boatman did not prevent him from doing so. When he stood on the bank, he saw that the affair was gradually growing to be serious. When he was considering how he could save his friends, he saw two English soldiers going for a walk. Narendra walked up to them at a brisk pace, saluted them and caught hold of their hands. Although his knowledge of English was quite rudimentary, he somehow explained the affair to them in a few words and signs, as he went on pulling them towards the place of occurrence. The two soliders, charmed with the behaviour of this young boy of pleasing looks, took kindly to him. They came with quick steps to where the boat was, understood the situation, and raising the canes in their hands, commanded the boatmen to let go the boys. Seeing that they were white soldiers of the army, all the boatmen moved away to their own boats. Narendra's friends heaved a sigh of relief. The soldiers were pleased with Narendra's free and fearless behaviour and invited him to go to the theatre with them. Narendra, however, declined the invitation with thanks and bade them good-bye.

19. There are other events also of his boyhood which prove his great courage. It will not be out of place to mention one or two here. Narendra was ten or twelve, when Edward VII, the then Prince of Wales, visited India. A gigantic man-of-war of the British navy, the Syrapis, came to Calcutta at that time and many people of Calcutta were granted permits to go on board to see the ship. Desirous of seeing it along with his friends, the boy Narendranath went to the office at Chowringhee with an application for getting a permit; but he saw that the gate-keeper did not allow any one except very respectable people to go in. So as he stood close to the entrance, revolving in his mind over the ways and means to

approach the English officer, he saw several people coming out with permits from the office. He saw that all of them went to a verandah on the second floor of that office. Narendra thought that it was perhaps the place where the English officer was receiving the applications and issuing permits. Searching some other passage leading to that place, he found that in one corner on the side of the house there was a narrow flight of iron stairs for the use of the servants of the English officer, leading to the room behind the said verandah. Knowing full well that there was a great probability of his being ill-treated if any one happened to see him, he took courage in both hands and went up to the second floor by that flight of stairs. Entering the verandah through the officer's room, he saw that applicants were crowding round him and he was incessantly signing permits with his head bent over a table. He stood behind all of them and getting the permit at the right time, saluted the officer and came out of the office by the front staircase like all others.

20. At that time, there was a club on the Cornwallis Street for the purpose of teaching physical exercise to the boys of Simla, a locality in Calcutta. It was Navagopal Mitra, the founder of the Hindu Fair, who had established it. As it was very near Narendra's house, he went there every day with his friends and practised physical exercise. As these boys were acquainted with Navagopal Babu, who was there for some time previously, he put them in charge of the management of the club. One day, the boys failed, in spite of great efforts, to erect a heavy wooden frame for a trapeze. A crowd assembled on the road to see the boys do it, but no one was ready to help them. Seeing a stout English sailor standing in the crowd, Narendra requested him to help them. He gladly agreed and joined the boys. The boys then began to pull up the head of the frame by means of a rope and the sailor was helping them in making its two legs enter slowly into the sockets. The work was going on well when the rope broke and the wooden frame fell back on the ground. And one of its legs suddenly went up and struck the sailor on the head. He fell unconscious. Seeing the sailor unconscious and his wound bleeding profusely, every one concluded that he was dead, and afraid of the police, fled away in all directions. Narendra and one or two of his close friends only stayed on there and applied their minds to inventing some means to bring the sailor back to life. Narendra tore a part of his own cloth, soaked it in

water, bandaged the wound and went on sprinkling water on the sailor's face and fanning him. When he regained consciousness, he was carried into the building of a school near by known as the Training Academy. Word was sent to Navagopal Babu to come soon with a doctor. The doctor came, examined the sailor and said, "The wound is not serious; he will require a week's nursing to come round." He recovered within that period, thanks to Narendra's nursing and the good arrangement for medicine, diet, etc. that he made. Then raising an amount by subscriptions from a few respectable gentlemen of that quarter, Narendra gave it to the sailor as provision for his onward journey and bade him good-bye. We have heard of many other events indicative of Narendra's coolness in the face of dangers and difficulties even during his boyhood.

21. Narendra was truthful even as a boy. When he reached his youth that zeal for telling the truth increased a hundredfold. He said, "I never terrified children by speaking of hobgoblins as I was afraid of uttering a falsehood, and scolded all whom I saw doing it. As the result of English education and my frequenting the Brahmo Samaj, the devotion to verbal expression of truth increased so much then."

22. Narendra was always in smiles because he was born with a robust frame, a keen intellect, a wonderful memory and a pure heart. He engaged himself in all kinds of gymnastics with abandon, learnt dancing and cultivated music, both vocal and instrumental. He also joined his friends in all sorts of mirth and merriment with gusto, but all this only so long as they did not overstep the limits of morality. Unable to understand the cause of that cheerfulness of his, superficial observers very often counted it a defect of his character. But the spirited Narendra took no notice of people's praise or blame. His proud head and heart never condescended to disprove their false calumniation.

Kindness to the poor was something inborn in him. In his childhood, whenever a beggar came to the house, he gave him whatever he wanted, even valuable clothes and utensils. The members of the family scolded him when they came to know of it and took the articles back from the beggars, paying them money. When this had happened a few times, one day his mother kept the boy confined in a room on the first floor of the house. At that time a beggar came and prayed loudly for alms, and Narendra threw down to him through a window a few pieces of his mother's precious clothes.

23. His mother used to say, "Narendra had a great foible even from his childhood. If he was angry at any time for any reason, he lost himself altogether and would shatter furniture and other things to pieces and scatter them in all directions. I prayed to Visvanatha at Kasi for a son and vowed Him offerings if one should be born, and He perhaps sent me one of His demons. Otherwise, why should he behave like a demon when angry?" She, however, discovered a wonderful remedy for that anger of the child. When she found that he could by no means be quietened, she remembered Viswanatha and poured one or two jarfuls of water over his head. And the wonder of it was that the boy's anger would at once vanish! Shortly after he had met the Master at Daskshineswar, one day Narendranath said to us, "I might not have gained anything else by this practice of religion; but it is certain that I have gained control over my terrible anger by His grace. Formerly I used to lose all control over myself in rage and be seized with repentance afterwards. But now if anyone does me a great harm or even beats me severely, I don't become so very angry."

24. People with the head and the heart equally well-developed are very rare in this world. It is those who are so endowed that make a mark in society. Again, those who manifest their own uniqueness in the spiritual world are also seen to possess a well developed power of imagination from their childhood. This becomes clear when we study Narendra's life. The reader will easily understand this, if one or two examples are given.

25. At one time Narendra's father stayed for some time at Raipur in Central India on some business. Knowing that he would have to live there for a long time, he had his family brought to that place shortly afterwards. The charge of taking them was entrusted to Narendra. He was then fourteen or fifteen only. The place was not then connected by railway. So one had to travel by bullock cart for more than a fortnight through dense forests full of beasts of prey. Although he had to suffer many physical hardships, he did not feel it at all on account of the opportunity it gave him to enjoy the wonderful beauty of the forest regions. His heart was altogether charmed when he was directly acquainted for the first time with the boundless power and endless love of Him who had adorned the earth with such incomparable robes and

decorations. He said, "What I saw and felt when going through the forest has for ever remained firmly imprinted in my memory, particularly a certain event of one day. On a particular day we had to travel by a mountain road passing through a valley of the Vindhya ranges whose peaks, rising very high in the sky, were over-looking us from both the sides. Bending under the weight of fruits and flowers, various kinds of trees and creepers covered the mountain slopes in their matchless beauty. Birds were flying from arbour to arbour or down on the ground in search of food, filling the quarters with their sweet notes. I saw all bullock carts arriving at a place where two mountain peaks, coming forward as in love, locked themselves up in an embrace over the narrow forest path. Observing carefully below their meeting point, I saw that there was a very big cleft from the crest to the foot of the mountain on one side of the path, and filling that cleft, there was hanging in it an enormous honey-comb, the result of the bees' labour for ages. Filled with wonder, as I was pondering over the beginning and the end of that kingdom of bees, my mind became so much absorbed in the thought of the infinite power of God, the controller of the three worlds, that I completely lost my consciousness of the external world for some time. I do not remember how long I was lying in the bullock cart in that condition. When I regained normal consciousness, I found that we had crossed that place and come far away. As I was alone in the cart, no one could know anything about it." It was perhaps the first time when, with the help of a strong power of imagination, he entered the closed region of deep meditation and was completely merged in it.

26. We shall give here a brief account of Narendra's forefathers and bring the present chapter to a close. The Datta family of Simla, divided into many branches, was one of the ancient families of Calcutta. This family was the foremost amongst the middle class Kayasthas in wealth, social position, and learning. Narendra's great-grandfather, Rammohan Datta, an advocate, earned enough money, maintained a large family and commanded the respect of his friends and particularly of his neighbours at Gaurmohan Mukerjee's Lane in Simla where he lived in a house which was his own self-acquired property. Durgacharan, his son, inherited enormous wealth from his father, but developed dispassion for the world at an early age and embraced the life of an itinerant monk. Durgacharan, it is said, was devoted to monks and holy

men from his boyhood. That inclination of his kept him engaged in the study of the scriptures from his youth and made him a good scholar in a short time. Though married, Durgacharan had no attachment to the world. He used to spend much time in the company of holy men in his own garden. Swami Vivekananda said that his grandfather Durgacharan left his family for ever shortly after begetting a child, as enjoined by the scriptures. Though he left his family and went away, Durgacharan twice met his wife and relatives by the will of Providence. His son Viswanath was then two or three years old. His wife and relatives came to Kasi perhaps in search of him and stayed there for some time. As railways did not exist then, people of respectable families used to come by boat to Kasi, the abode of Viswanatha (the Master of the worlds). Durgacharan's wife too accompanied a pilgrim party going to Kasi. At one place on her way, the child Viswanath fell into the waters of the Ganga. His mother saw it first and immediately jumped into the water. The unconscious mother was lifted into the boat with great effort. It was found that even in that unconscious condition, she was firmly clasping the arm of the child. It was thus that the unbounded love of the mother saved the life of the child.

In Kasi, Durgacharan's wife went daily to visit Lord Visvesvara. One day, as the road was slippery on account of a shower, she slipped and fell in front of the holy temple. A casual passer-by, a monk, saw this and went up to her quickly. He lifted her up carefully, made her sit on the step of the door of the temple, and began to examine whether she had any serious injury. But the moment the two pairs of eyes met, Durgacharan and his wife recognized each other. And the monk Durgacharan, without looking at her for a second time, disappeared from there.

It is a convention that a monk should visit his birth-place which, according to the scriptures, is superior even to heaven, twelve years after he embraces the life of an itinerant monk. Durgacharan, therefore, came once to Calcutta after twelve years and stayed in the house of a former friend of his, whom he requested earnestly to see that the news of his coming did not reach his relatives. His friend, a worldly man, disregarded the request of Durgacharan and communicated the news secretly to his relatives. They came in a party and took Durgacharan home almost by force. He went home with them, but never spoke with any one. He was kept in a closed room, where he sat in a corner with eyes shut, silent and motionless like a log of wood. It is said that he sat there like that for three days and three nights continuously without changing his seat. His relatives were afraid that he might fast unto death if he was kept confined and so kept the door of the room open. It was seen on the morrow that the monk Durgacharan had disappeared unnoticed.

27. Acquiring great learning in Persian and English, Viswanath, the son of Durgacharan, became an attorney of the Calcutta High Court. He was generous and loving to his friends. Although he earned a good deal, he could leave nothing behind. It was perhaps a quality which he inherited from his father, that he could not be economical. Viswanath's nature differed greatly indeed from that of an ordinary man of the world in many respects. For example, thoughts of the morrow never disturbed him. He helped all without any discrimination whether they were deserving or not. Though extremely affectionate to his relatives, he was none-the-less non-attached enough to feel no anxiety on their account even when he got no news of them for long periods while staying away from the family.

28. Viswanath was intelligent and possessed of great understanding. He had great love for music and other fine arts. Swami Vivekananda said that his father had a sweet voice and could sing beautifully Nidhu Babu's Tappa (light music) without learning music systematically. Contrary to the general impression of the times, he regarded music as a harmless pastime and made his eldest son Narendranath learn it with the same care and attention as he was prosecuting his studies. His wife Bhuvaneswari Devi too could perfectly master devotional songs with their tune, cadence, etc., which she had heard sung but once by wandering Vaishnava minstrels.

29. Viswanath had a great love for reading the Bible and the lyrics of the Persian poet Hafiz. A chapter or two from the Holy Bible dealing with the life of the sweet and glorious Jesus were among his daily readings. He sometimes read to his wife, sons, and others a little of these and of the love lyrics of Hafiz. He admired and adopted some Muslim manners and customs while he lived for some time in places like Lucknow, Lahore, etc., and they stuck to him for life. It is perhaps due to this that the habit of taking Pollau daily was introduced into his family.

30. Viswanath was as grave and serious as he was witty and

humorous. If any one of his sons or daughters did anything wrong, he did not scold them severely but made it known to his or her friends in such a way that he or she was ashamed and never did it again. The reader will understand this from an event we cite here as an example. One day his eldest son, Narendra, had an altercation with his mother over a certain matter and spoke to her one or two harsh words. Instead of scolding him for it, Viswanath wrote with a piece of charcoal in big letters on the door of the room in which Narendra received his companions that Naren Babu had used such and such words towards his mother. Whenever Narendra and his friends were about to enter that room, their eyes fell on those words; and Narendra looked small for a long time, reminded of his own misbehaviour.

31. Viswanath maintained a large family which included distant relatives. He was prodigal in supplying them with food and other necessaries of life. Living on his bounty, some of his distant relatives led idle lives while some others went further and relieved the tedium of their lives by having recourse to strong drinks and other intoxicants. When he grew up, Narendra very often complained that his father had been generous to a fault towards those persons. Viswanath gravely replied, "You are too young and immature to imagine how full of misery this human life is. When you come to understand it, you will view with a forgiving eye these miserable souls who use intoxicants to snatch a momentary relief from their all too bitter experiences of life."

32. Viswanath had many sons and daughters. All of them were endowed with innumerable good qualities. But most of the daughters died young. Narendranath was very dear to his parents, as he was born after the birth of three or four daughters in succession. His father died suddenly of heart-failure, when Narendra was preparing for the B.A. examination in the winter of 1883. This sudden death of the over-generous Viswanath left the family penniless.

33. We have heard much of the greatness of Narendra's mother Sri Bhuvaneswari. She combined in herself great physical beauty and devotion to deities. Her cleverness and intelligence were amply proved by her able management of the very big family of her husband, the sole responsibility of which fell on her shoulders. She managed it so easily and efficiently that she was not in want of enough time for knitting and other artistic pursuits. Her educa-

tion was extremely limited, extending not beyond the reading of the Ramayana, the Mahabharata and some other religious books. But she learnt orally many things from her husband, sons, and others so well that in conversation she was taken to be highly educated. Her memory and her power of retention were indeed great. She could repeat from memory even what she had heard only once, and she remembered very old sayings and events as if they were of the day before. Fallen on bad days after her husband's death her mettle was put to the test. She however showed wonderful patience, calmness, frugality and adaptability to the sudden change of circumstances. The lady who spent a thousand rupees monthly to manage her household affairs, had now only thirty rupees a month to maintain herself and her sons and daughters. But she was never for a day seen to be dejected. She managed all affairs of her family with that meagre income in such a way that those who saw it took her monthly expenditure to be much higher. One shudders indeed to think of the terrible condition into which Bhuvaneswari fell on the sudden death of her husband. There was no assured income with which to meet the needs of her family; and yet she had to maintain her old mother, sons and daughters brought up in opulence, and meet the expenses for the education of her children. Her relatives who had been enabled to earn a decent living by her husband's generosity and influence, in place of coming forward to help her in her bad days, found now an opportunity to do something that was to their great liking, and that was to do their best to deprive her even of her legitimate possessions. Her eldest son Narendranath, possessed of many good qualities, failed to find a job in spite of his best efforts in many directions and losing all attraction for the world, was getting ready to renounce it for ever. One naturally feels respect and reverence for Sri Bhuvaneswari when one thinks of the manner in which she performed her duties even in that terrible condition. When we discuss the close relationship of Narendranath with the Master, we shall have to revert again to the topic of the straitened circumstances of the family during this period. Therefore, instead of giving a further detailed description of it here, let us now tell the reader of Narendra's coming to Dakshineswar for the second time.

CHAPTER IV

NARENDRA'S SECOND AND THIRD VISITS TO THE MASTER

[TOPICS: 1. The delay in Narendra's second visit to the Master. 2. His wonderful experience through the Master's power. 3. Narendra's reflections. 4. His resolution to study the Master carefully. 5. The Master behaved towards Narendra like one long familiar. 6. Narendra's third visit. 7. His loss of normal consciousness at the Master's touch in ecstasy. 8. The Master questioning Narendra in that state. 9. The Master's wonderful vision about him. 10. Narendra's conviction about the Master. 11. Change in Narendra's conception of the Guru. 12. Narendra's progress in renunciation. 13. Narendra's resolve not to accept teachings without testing. 14. Narendra's conduct since then. 15. The then mental state of Narendra.]

1. It is found that men of great principles and self-reliance, when they find greatness in others, readily recognise the same and rejoice at it. Again, if they find greatness manifested in any one to an extraordinary degree, their minds constantly dwell on the thought of it, and the more they do so, the more are they ravished and dazed in admiration. They are not, however, overpowered by this admiration all of a sudden and made to give up their own path and take to a life of imitation of the person they admire. It is only through long association and the sweet bond of love developed thereby that such admiration begins to have a tangible effect on their lives. Narendra was in that state when he first met the Master at Dakshineswar. Although attracted by the Master's extraordinary renunciation and veracity, Narendra was not at first prepared to accept him as the ideal of life. Recollections of the Master's wonderful character and behaviour, no doubt, arose again and again in his mind for some time after his return from his first visit to Dakshineswar; yet, he felt no urgency in fulfilling his promise to visit him a second time. An important reason for this indefinite postponement of the visit was his impression that the Master was a monomaniac, as his study of Western psychology forced him to conclude. Besides, he had many other preoccupations engaging his attention. In addition to the practice of meditation and application to college studies, Narendra was then engaged daily in under-

going a systematic course of training in music and in physical exercises. Moreover, in imitation of the Brahmo Samaj, he was then forming associations for prayer and discussion in different parts of Calcutta for the mental and spiritual improvement of his friends. Was it, therefore, a matter of surprise that his thought of going to Dakshineswar remained suppressed for a month? Although he was thus held back by his sense of daily duties, his memory and truthfulness were inciting him to go alone to Dakshineswar in fulfilment of his promise as soon as he could find time. So, we find Narendra one day wending his way alone to Dakshineswar for the second time about a month after his first visit. We give the reader here that day's events as described to us by Narendra himself.

2. "I had no idea that the Dakshineswar Kali temple was so far from Calcutta; for I had gone there only once and that by carriage. I used to visit Dasarathi Sannyal, Satkari, Lahiri and other friends at Baranagar and thought that Rasmani's garden must be somewhere near their houses. But the journey seemed to be never ending, however far I proceeded. Anyway, enquiring of many people, I reached Dakshineswar at last and went direct to the Master's room. I saw him sitting alone, merged in himself, on the small bedstead placed near the bigger one. There was no one with him. No sooner had he seen me than he called me joyfully to him and made me sit at one end of the bedstead. I sat down but found him in a strange mood. He spoke indistinctly something to himself, looked steadfastly at me, and began slowly coming towards me. I thought another scene of lunacy was going to be enacted. Scarcely had I thought so when he came to me and placed his right foot on my body, and immediately I had a wonderful experience. I saw with my eyes open that all the things of the room together with the walls were rapidly whirling and receding into an unknown region and my I-ness together with the whole universe was, as it were, going to vanish in an all-devouring great void. I was then overwhelmed with a terrible fear. I knew that the destruction of I-ness was death, so I thought that death was before me, very near at hand. Unable to control myself, I cried out loudly, saying, 'Ah! What is it you have done to me? I have my parents, you know.' Laughing loudly at my words, he touched my chest with his hand and said, 'Let it then cease now. It need not be done all at once. It will come to pass in course of time.' I was amazed to see how

that extraordinary experience of mine vanished as quickly as it had come when he touched me in that manner and said those words. I came to the normal state and saw things inside and outside the room standing still as before.

3. "Although it has taken so much time to describe the event, it actually happened in a much shorter time. It produced a great revolution in my mind. I was puzzled and went on thinking what it was that had happened. I have seen how that unique experience came and vanished suddenly by the power of this wonderful person. I had read in books about mesmerism and hypnotism. I was led to wonder if it was anything like these. But my heart refused to admit it. For, persons of great will-power spread their influence on weak minds only and bring about such conditions. But I am by no means such; rather I have been till now feeling proud of being very intelligent and possessed of great strength of mind. It could not be that I was charmed and made a puppet in his hands, as ordinary people are when they fall under the influence of some extraordinary man. I had never allowed any such influence to gain control over me; rather I was a hostile subject in so far as I had from the start come to the certain conclusion that he was a monomaniac. Why should I then have been suddenly caught up in that state? I pondered over it but could not come to any conclusion; there it remained in my heart, an unsolved problem of great import. I remembered the words of the great poet, 'There are more things in heaven and earth than are dreamt of in your philosophy.' I thought that this might be one such. I reflected and came to the conclusion that the truth about it could not be ascertained. I was, however, determined to be on my guard so that this wonderful madman might not in future bring about such a change in my mind by spreading his influence and gaining mastery over it.

4. "But I continued thinking: How could I consider this person mad, when he could shatter to pieces the structure of a mind like mine possessing a strong and powerful will and firm convictions, when he could refashion it like a ball of clay into any pattern as it pleased him? But what about his behaviour and the words he spoke calling me aside on my first visit — how could I take it all as otherwise than the ravings of a madman? Therefore, just as I could not find out the cause of the aforesaid experience, even so, I could not come to any certain conclusion about this person, pure and simple-hearted like a child. From my boyhood

I could never accept any conclusion about any person or proposition as final, unless it had been arrived at after proper observation and investigation, reasoning and argumentation. That nature of mine received a severe shock that day, which created an anguish in my heart. As a result of this, there arose a firmer determination in my mind to understand thoroughly the nature and power of that wonderful person.

5. "My time passed that day in various thoughts and resolutions. But the Master appeared to be a different person altogether after that event and began to feed me lovingly and behave in all matters like one long familiar with me. His behaviour resembled that of people towards their dear friends or close relatives whom they meet after a long separation. He fed me, talked to me, expressed his affection for me and cut jokes with me as best as he could, and still he remained unsatisfied, as if all these fell far short of what he wanted to do. That love and behaviour of his also caused not a little anxiety in me. Seeing the shades of evening falling, I took leave of him for that day. Pained to the core of his heart, he extracted a promise from me, as on the previous occasion, that I would return to him at the earliest, and then he allowed me to go home. And I left Dakshineswar musing on what had happened and on how to solve the problem."

6. We do not know how long after his second visit Narendra went again to the Master. But seeing that, after his acquaintance with the Master's wonderful power, he was seized with a strong desire to understand its sources, it will not be wrong for us to surmise that the delay was not long. The eagerness must have brought him to the lotus feet of the Master at the earliest possible opportunity. Probably the next visit might have taken place at the end of a week, during which period he had to attend college. For by nature, when his mind was seized of any problem, Narendra paid no attention to his food, dress or leisure, and found no rest in his mind till he could solve it. It is therefore certain that his mind was in a similar condition in the effort to comprehend the Master. Again, it is also certain that on this, his third visit to the Master, he must have gone with his mind made very firm and guarded, lest it should succumb to his influence as on the previous occasion. But what happened was inconceivable. We give the reader here what we heard about it both from the Master and Narendranath.

7. On that occasion the Master asked him to accompany him

for a walk to Jadu Mallik's garden close by, probably because there was a crowd at the Kali temple at that time. May be there was some other reason also. Jadunath himself and his mother had great respect and reverence for the Master. They had given orders to the chief officer of their garden that, even if they were absent, the parlour facing the Ganga should be opened for the Master to sit in, whenever he came for a walk there. The Master walked with Narendra for some time in the garden on the bank of the Ganga that day. Talking with Narendra, he came to that parlour, sat down there and entered into ecstasy. Shortly afterward Narendra was sitting near at hand and calmly observing that state of the Master, when the latter suddenly approached and touched him as before. Although he exercised great caution because of his previous experience, Narendra became completely overwhelmed at that powerful touch. He lost consciousness completely that day, not partially as had happened on the previous occasion. When he regained consciousness after sometime, he saw that the Master was passing his hand on his chest. On seeing him come to the normal state, the Master smiled gently and sweetly.

Narendra did not tell us anything of the nature of the experience he had after he had lost his consciousness. We thought he did not express it to us, because it was a secret. But we realized later from what the Master told us one day about this event in the course of his conversation on this topic that it was natural for Narendra not to have known it. The Master said:

8. "When Narendra had lost his normal consciousness, I asked him that day many questions, such as who he was, where he came from, why he came (was born), how long he would be here (in this world) and so on. Entering into the depths of his being, he gave proper answers to all these questions. These answers of his confirmed what I thought and saw and knew about him in my visions. It is forbidden to reveal those things. But I have known from all these that on the day when he will know who he is, he will no more remain in this world; he will immediately give up his body through Yoga, with the strong power of will. Narendra is a great soul perfect in meditation."

Later, the Master told us once again a little of the visions he had had about Narendra. We narrate them here for the convenience of the reader. For, when we learned of those visions from the Master, we understood that he had those experiences before

Narendra came to Dakshineswar. The Master said:

9. "One day I saw that, through samadhi, my mind was going up by a luminous path. Going beyond the gross world studded with the sun, the moon and the stars, it entered first of all into the subtle world of ideas. The more it began to ascend to subtler and subtler strata of that realm, the more did I see beautiful ideal forms of deities existing on both sides of the path. It came gradually to the last extremity of that region. I saw a barrier of light there separating the realm of the divisible from that of the indivisible. Leaping over it, the mind entered by degrees the realm of the indivisible. I saw that there was no more any person or thing there having a form. As if afraid to enter there, even the gods and goddesses possessing heavenly bodies exercised their authority only over realms far below. But the very next moment I saw seven wise Rishis having bodies consisting of divine Light only, seated there in Samadhi. I felt that in virtue and knowledge, love and renunciation, they had excelled even the gods and goddesses, not to speak of human beings. Astonished, I was pondering over their greatness when I saw before me that a part of the homogeneous mass of Light of the "Abode of the Indivisible", devoid of the slightest tinge of difference, became solidified and converted into the form of a Divine Child. Coming down to one of those Rishis, and throwing its soft and delicate arms round his neck, the Divine Child embraced him, and afterwards calling him with its ambrosial words, sweeter than the music of the Vina, made great efforts to wake him up from his Samadhi. The Rishi woke up at the delicate and loving touch and looked on at that wonderful Child with half-shut eyes, free from winking. Seeing his bright face, full of delight at the sight of the Child, I thought that the Child was the treasure of his heart, and that their familiarity was a matter of eternity. The extraordinary Divine Child then expressed infinite joy and said to him, 'I am going, you must come with me!' The Rishi said nothing at that request, but his loving eyes expressed his hearty assent. Afterwards, looking on the Child with loving eyes, he entered again into Samadhi. Astonished, I then saw that a part of the mind and body of that Rishi, converted into the form of a bright light, came down to the earth along the reverse path. Hardly had I seen Narendra for the first time than I knew that he was the Rishi." [1]

[1] The Master described this vision to us in his extraordinary, simple language.

10. Narendra must have been astounded when that change in his mental state was produced for the second time by the influence of the Master's wonderful power. He felt in his heart of hearts how unavailing the power of his mind and intellect was, compared with that insuperable divine power. His former impression about the Master, that he was a monomaniac, was changed. But it cannot be said that he understood the meaning and purpose of what the Master said to him in seclusion on the occasion of his first visit to Dakshineswar. The Master, he felt, must be an extraordinarily great soul possessed of divine power to have turned at will the mind of a man like himself and given it a higher direction. And with that he also understood that, as the Master's will was completely identified with the Divine will, his condescension towards him that day was a rare blessing unattainable by all, and that it was therefore not a small piece of good fortune for him to have had the grace of such a sublime soul without asking for it.

11. Narendra was compelled to come to the aforesaid conclusion and to change many of his former conceptions in the wake of it. He had formerly great objection to accept another man as Guru or spiritual guide; for, as a man, that person who was accepted as a Guru must necessarily be subject to all the weaknesses and limitations under which he himself was labouring, and it was thus senseless to subject himself to another such human being and carry out his behests unquestioningly. It is needless to say that that attitude was confirmed when he joined the Brahmo Samaj. As the result of the events of these two days, his convictions in this respect were severely shaken. He understood that such souls, though rare, are actually born in the world — souls whose extraordinary love, purity, penance and renunciation far surpass the conception of God existing in the little minds and intellects of ordinary men. Therefore, if they are accepted as Gurus, ordinary men will be greatly benefited. Consequently, he was ready to accept the Master as the Guru; but he could not go so far as to accept indiscriminately whatever the Master said.

12. The idea that God could not be realized without renunciation prevailed in Narendra's mind from his boyhood. It

---

It is impossible for us to reproduce perfectly that language. Having no other course left open to us, we have kept his language as far as it lay in our power, and have expressed it briefly here. Asking him about the child of his vision one day, we came to know that the Master himself had assumed the form of that Child.

was inherent in him and must have been due to the impressions he brought with him from a previous existence. This accounts for the fact that, although he became a regular member of the Brahmo Samaj, he was never inclined to join their meetings and associations for the reform of the institution of marriage. This idea of renunciation, latent in him, now grew wonderfully, as he had the blessed privilege of meeting the all-renouncing Master and of being acquainted with his extraordinary powers.

13. But one thing became the greatest concern of Narendra's thought from now on. On coming in contact with such great and powerful souls, the human mind, he thought, generally believes in every word they say without weighing it properly or even without weighing it. At all costs he must guard himself against this, he thought. Therefore, although he was now cherishing great respect and reverence for the Master on account of the events of the two days described above, he was nevertheless determined never to accept anything regarding the Master's visions and experiences without personally having an immediate knowledge of them, or subjecting them to the most rigorous test of reason even if it led him to incur the displeasure of the Master. Consequently, just as on the one hand, he was solicitous of keeping his mind always ready to receive the unknown truths of the spiritual world, so, on the other hand, he engaged himself, since then, in putting to a severe test the Master's wonderful behaviour and visions.

14. At his first meeting with the Master, Narendranath had considered him to be a monomaniac, because of the strange words with which the former addressed him. It must, however, have been evident to the keen intellect of Narendra that these words yielded a consistent meaning, if the Master were looked upon as an incarnation. But how could his truth-seeking and rational mind accept this fact all of a sudden? So he decided that if ever God gave him the power of understanding those words and happenings, he would discuss them. Thus relegating the problem to a distant corner of his mind, he now devoted himself to learning from, and discussing with, the Master how to realize God and be blessed.

15. A powerful mind feels a strong resistance from within when, at the time of accepting a new truth, it has to change its former convictions. Narendra was in that predicament. Though acquainted with the Master's wonderful power, he could not completely

accept him, and though feeling attracted, he tried to stand aloof from him. We shall see later how matters developed as a consequence of this attitude of his.

CHAPTER V

THE MASTER'S SELFLESS LOVE AND NARENDRANATH

[TOPICS: 1. The extraordinary experiences of Narendra in his early life. 2. Narendra's direct experience of the Master's divine powers. 3. Narendra's fitness for spirituality. 4. The Master's attraction for Narendra. 5. The Master's attempt to give Narendra the Knowledge of Brahman on the very first day. 6. The difference between Narendra's wonderful experience of the first and the second day. 7. The Master's apprehension about Narendra. 8. Why the Master was attracted to Narendra. 9. This attraction was but natural and inevitable. 10. The Master's love for Narendra was unworldly. 11. Swami Premananda's testimony about that love. 12. Swami Premananda's first visit to Dakshineswar. 13. His experience of the Master's solicitude for Narendra. 14. Vaikunthanath on the Master's love for Narendra. 15. Narendra unmoved by it.]

1. Narendranath, as we have already said, was born with very rare and noble tendencies. This fact accounts for a number of unusual experiences he used to have even before he visited the Master. We narrate here a few of them as examples. Narendra said: "I used to see all my life a wonderful point of light between my eyebrows, as soon as I shut my eyes in order to go to sleep, and I used to observe attentively its various changes. So that it might be convenient to see it, I used to lie on my bed in the way people bow down touching the ground with their foreheads. The extraordinary point kept changing its colours and increasing in size, became gradually converted into the form of a ball, and bursting at last, covered my body from head to foot with white liquid light. As soon as that happened, I lost consciousness and fell asleep. I believed that all people went to sleep that way. I was long under that impression. When I grew up and began to practise meditation, that point of light used to come before me, as soon as I closed my eyes, and then I concentrated my mind on it. In those days I daily practised meditation with a few friends according to the instruction of Maharshi Devendranath. We talked among ourselves about the nature of visions and experiences that each of us had. At that time I came to know from what they said that they never had the vision of such a light and that none of them went to sleep in that way.

Again, since my childhood, it happened sometimes that when I saw a thing, place or person, I had the impression that I was very familiar with it or him; I thought I had seen it or him somewhere before. I tried to recollect, but failed. But that could never convince me that I had not seen them before. This happened very often. Perhaps I was in the company of friends in some place and there was a discussion on a certain subject; at that time someone made a remark and immediately I remembered, 'Ah! I have had talks on this subject with them in this house long before and this person made the same remark at that time also. I tried to recollect, but could not make out when and where I had talked thus with them. When I came to know of the doctrine of rebirth, I thought I might perhaps have been acquainted with those places and persons during a previous life and that a partial recollection of them sometimes came to my mind in that manner. I was afterwards convinced that such a conclusion on the subject was not reasonable. Now[1] it appears to me that before I was born I must have somehow seen, as a cinematographic film, those persons with whom I was to be familiar in this life, and a memory of these arose in my mind from time to time after I was born."

2. It was on hearing of the pure life and of the ecstasy of the Master from many people[2] that Narendranath came to see him. He then never imagined even in dream that when he saw him, he would undergo any mental change or have any wonderful ex-

[1] Narendra told us of this extraordinary experience of his soon after we became acquainted with him; But he came to this latter conclusion only during the last part of his life.

[2] When he came to Dakshineswar, Narendra, we said before, was about to appear for the F.A. examination from the General Assembly's Institution, Calcutta. The liberal-minded scholar, Mr. Hastie, was then the Principal of the college. Narendranath had great regard for this English gentleman for his many-sided genius, pure life, and his loving behaviour towards the students. One day as the professor of literature fell suddenly ill, Mr. Hastie came to teach literature to the F.A. students. In the course of a discussion on the poems of Wordsworth, he made mention of the poet's going into a trance when he (the poet) experienced the beauty of Nature. As the students did not understand what a trance was, he explained it to them properly and at last said, "That state is produced by purity of mind and its concentration on one particular object. A person fit for such a state is rarely seen. I have seen Ramakrishna Paramahamsa of Dakshineswar attain that state among contemporaries. You will understand it if you go and see once that state of his." Hearing thus of the Master for the first time from Mr. Hastie, Narendra saw the Master first at Surendra's house. Again, as he frequented the Brahmo Samaj, he might have heard of him there also.

perience. But events proved otherwise. The experiences he had had before seemed to be commonplace and trifling compared with the extraordinary ones he had on these two days of his second and third visits to the Master. His uncommon intelligence had to accept defeat when he tried to fathom the depth of the Master's personality — the knotty problem seemed to elude solution. For he could find not an iota of reason to doubt that it was through the inscrutable divine power of the Master that he had had those wonderful experiences. And the more he mused on it, the greater grew his amazement.

3. One is simply flabbergasted when one thinks of the wonderful experience Narendra had during his second visit to the Master. Such an experience, according to the scriptures, occurs in the life of an ordinary person as the result of long practice of austerities and renunciation; and when it appears somehow, the man is beside himself with joy to feel the manifestation of God in the Guru, and entirely surrenders himself to him. It is no small surprise that Narendra did not do so. It can be accounted for only by accepting his extraordinary spiritual capacities. He did not altogether lose himself, only because he ranked very high in regard to spiritual fitness. And it was because of this uncommon fitness of his that he could restrain himself so wonderfully. What was more, he engaged himself for a very long time in testing the extraordinary character and behaviour of the Master and in ascertaining their cause. But, although he could check himself and did not completely surrender to the Master, it is an undeniable fact that he was greatly attracted towards him.

4. The Master on his part felt a strong attraction for Narendra from the day they met. Possessed of the immediate knowledge of Brahman, the high-minded Guru became restless owing to an anxious eagerness to pour all the realizations of his spiritual life into the mind of the very worthy disciple, as soon as he met him. That profound eagerness cannot be measured. That unmotivated restlessness, free from the slightest tinge of selfishness, occurs in fulfilment of the divine will in the minds of the Gurus who are perfectly poised and contented in the Self alone. It is under this kind of higher impulsion that world teachers impart the saving knowledge to worthy disciples and help them shake off the shackles of desire and attain to perfection.[1]

[1] This is known in the scriptures as the Sambhavi initiation IV 4.

5. There is no doubt that the Master felt inclined to induct Narendra at once into ecstasy, thus making him a knower of Brahman on the very first day he came alone to Dakshineswar. For when, three or four years after this, Narendra surrendered completely to the Master and was again and again praying to him to grant him Nirvikalpa Samadhi, the Master would allude to this event and say jestingly to him in our presence, "Why? Did you not then say that you have parents to serve?" "Look here," said he another time, "a man died and became a ghost. He lived alone for a long time and sorely felt the need of a companion. Whenever he heard that a man had met with an accident and died he ran to the spot thinking that he could get the much-needed companion; for the belief is that people who meet with death in this way turn into ghosts. But the ghost found much to his chagrin that the dead man was saved from becoming a ghost either by the touch of the water of the Ganga or by some other purifying agency. So he had to return every time quite disconsolate and was forced to live a lonely life. The poor fellow's want of a companion was never satisfied. I am also exactly in that position. On seeing you, I thought, 'this time perhaps I shall have a companion.' But you too said that you had your parents. So I could not have a companion." Thus would the Master refer to that day's event and very often jest with Narendra.

6. Noting the terrible fear gripping Narendra's mind when he was at the point of attaining Samadhi, the Master ceased making further efforts to raise his mind to that high level for the time being. The Master's mind was, however, assailed by doubts. He doubted the truth of the visions and the experiences he had had about Narendra some time previously. This is, we guess, the reason why he overwhelmed him with his power, when Narendra came to Dakshineswar for the third time, and knew from him many secrets of his life. His anxiety was removed only when he found Narendra's answers to his questions tallying exactly with his own visions. This proves that Narendra did not have the same kind of ecstasy at Dakshineswar on both the days.

7. After the test the Master was free from anxiety in a way; but some apprehension was still lurking in his mind. For, Narendra, the Master saw, had in him in full measure, the eighteen qualities or manifestations of power, the possession of even one or two of which enables a man to acquire extraordinary fame and influence

in the world. This concentration of powers, he apprehended, would lead to an undesirable contrary result, if Narendra failed to direct them properly into the spiritual channel by realizing the ultimate truth about God, man and the world. If that should happen, Narendra would found a new sect or religion and be famous in the world like other spiritual leaders or prophets. But in that case, it would not be possible for him first to realize himself and then disseminate the grand catholic truth of the spiritual world, the realization and propagation of which were the crying needs of the modern age, and the world would thus be deprived of its greatest blessing. Therefore, there arose then an ardent desire in the Master's heart that Narendra should follow him in all respects, and like him, have the immediate knowledge of the grand spiritual truths for revealing the same to the world. The Master used to say, 'Just as water-weeds are seen to grow in pools, small ponds, etc., where there is no current of water, so sects confined within narrow circles arise whenever man remains content with partial spiritual truths, regarding them as the whole." One is surprised to think in how many ways the Master tried to make Narendra a fit recipient of the perfect truth, lest possessed of extraordinary intelligence and mental qualities as he was, he should go astray and form a sect of his own.

8. This strange and strong attraction of the Master for Narendra, which he had from their very first meeting, did not abate and assume a natural state till he was convinced that there was no more possibility of Narendra going astray in the manner mentioned above. A little reflection on this phenomenon clearly shows that some of its causes were rooted in the Master's extraordinary visions about Narendra, and others in the fear lest, coming under the influence of the modern age, he should willingly take upon himself some such bondage as the desire for a wife, wealth, or fame, and fail even partially to fulfil the ultimate aim of his great life.

9. As a result of the Master's long period of Sadhana and renunciation his limited individual consciousness disappeared and he became eternally identified in consciousness with the cause of the universe and felt the Lord's work of doing good to humanity as his own. Through the power of this knowledge, he came to know that it was the will of the benign, all-pervading Person that the very great work of removing the causes of the decline of religion in the modern age should be accomplished with his body and mind as the instruments. And it was through the power of the same know-

ledge that he knew that Narendra was not born to secure some puny little selfish end of his own, but had come down on earth, out of intense love of God, to help him in the work of doing good to humanity. Is it, therefore, surprising that he should regard the selfless, eternally free Narendra as supremely his 'own' and be strongly attracted towards him? Strange though it might appear to superficial observers, this attraction of the Master for Narendra would appear quite natural and inevitable to an observer with a penetrating eye and a knowledge of the background described above.

10. It is beyond our power to give an indication of how intensely the Master regarded Narendranath as his own and how deeply he loved him from the day he met him first. The reasons that prompt worldly people to regard others as their own and bestow their love on them were conspicuous by their absence in this case. And yet we have never seen anywhere anything comparable to the joy felt by the Master in the company of Narendra or of anxiety when separated from him. Nor had we before any idea of how a man could love another so intensely without the intervention of any selfish motives. When we saw the Master's wonderful love for Narendra, we were convinced that the world was sure to witness the day when man would realize the manifestation of God in man and feel blessed by pouring out truly selfless love on that manifestation.

11. Swami Premananda came for the first time to the Master shortly after Narendra had come to be with him. For some reason, Narendra could not come to Dakshineswar for about a week or so. Premananda was simply amazed to see the Master's agonizing pain of separation from Narendra and used to describe it to us on many occasions.

12. He said once, "Swami Brahmananda and I went to the Haltkhola Ghat to take a boat, when I saw Ramdayal Babu there. Knowing that he was also going to Dakshineswar, we got into a boat together, and it was almost dusk when we reached Rani Rasmani's Kali temple. We came to the Master's room and were told that he had gone to the temple to pay obeisance to the Mother of the Universe. Asking us to stay there, Swami Brahmananda went towards the temple to bring him. I saw him holding the Master very carefully and coming with him, saying, 'Steps, — go up here, go down there' and so on. I had already heard that the Master

used to become overwhelmed with emotions and lose normal consciousness. Therefore, I knew that he was in ecstasy when I saw him thus coming, reeling like a drunken man. Entering the room in that state, he sat on the small bedstead. Coming shortly afterwards to the normal state, he asked me a few questions about myself and my relations, and began to examine the features of my face, hands, feet, etc. He held in his hand for some time my forearm from the elbow to the fingers to feel its weight and then said, 'Nice'. He alone knew what he understood by that. Then he asked Ramdayal Babu about Narendra's health. Hearing that he was all right, the Master said, 'It is long since he came here. I should very much like to see him. Please ask him to come once.'

13. "A few hours were delightfully spent in religious talks. We took our meal at 10 p.m. and lay down in the verandah to the east of the Master's room and to the north of the courtyard. Beds were arranged for the Master and Swami Brahmananda in the room. Scarcely had an hour passed, when he came out from his room, with his cloth under his armpit, to our bedside, and addressing Ramdayal Babu, said affectionately, 'Are you sleeping?' Both of us sat up hurriedly on our beds and said, 'No, Sir.' The Master said, 'Look here, as I have not seen Narendra for a long time, I feel as if my whole soul is being forcibly wrung like a wet towel. Please ask him to come once and see me. He is a person of pure Sattva, he is Narayana Himself; I cannot have peace of mind if I don't see him now and then.' Ramdayal Babu had been frequenting Dakshineswar for some time past. The boy-like nature of the Master was not, therefore, unknown to him. Seeing that boy-like behaviour of the Master, he knew that he was in ecstasy. He tried to console him, saying that he would see Narendra as soon as it was morning and ask him to come. But that mood of the Master was not at all alleviated that night. Knowing that we were having no rest, he would retire to his room now and then for some time. But the next moment he would forget this and come to us again and begin to speak of Narendra's good qualities, expressing pathetically the terrible anguish of his mind on account of Narendra's long absence. Seeing that terrible pang of separation of his, I was astonished and thought, 'How wonderful is his love! And how hard-hearted that person must be for whom he entertains such a poignant longing that compels him to behave in so pathetic a manner! The night passed that way. In the morning we went to

the temple and paid our obeisance to the Divine Mother. Then bowing down at the feet of the Master, took leave of him and returned to Calcutta."

14. Once in the year 1883, Sri Vaikunthanath Sannyal, a friend of ours, came to Dakshineswar and saw the Master extremely anxious, because Narendranath had not come for a long time. Sannyal said, "The Master's mind was filled to the brim by Narendra, as it were; he spoke of nothing else but Narendra's good qualities. Narendra,' said he addressing me, is a man of pure Sattva; He is one of the four of the 'Abode of the Invisible' and one of the seven Rishis.[1] There is no limit to his good qualities.' Saying so, the Master became much worried and was shedding incessant tears like a mother separated from her child. Seeing him unable to control himself, we were rather puzzled about the significance of all his behaviour. Just then he went with rapid steps to the verandah to the north of his room. After weeping bitterly for some time, he sobbed out with a choked voice, 'Ah! I cannot do without seeing him!' Controlling himself a little, he now came into the room and sat down beside us, saying pathetically, 'I wept so much, but Narendra did not come. The longing to see him had produced a terrible anguish, as if my heart were being wrung; but he does not at all realize the intensity of the attraction I feel for him.' Saying so, he became worried again and went out of the room. Returning a little later, he said, 'What will they think on seeing that I, a man of such advanced age, am weeping and panting so much for him? You, however, being my own people, I don't feel ashamed in your presence. But what will others think when they see this? But by no means can I control myself.' We were speechless to see the Master's love for Narendra. We thought Narendra must be a god-like person. Why otherwise should the Master be so much attracted towards him? We then said, consoling him, 'Ah, it is indeed wrong of him, Sir. He knows you feel so much pain on account of his absence, and still he does not come.' Shortly after this event, one day he introduced me to Narendra. I saw that the Master was as delighted when united with Narendra as he was worried when separated from him. We went later to Dakshineswar on the Master's birthday. The devotees that day adorned him beautifully—dressed him up in new attire, and adorned him with

[1] Sanaka, Sanandana, Sanatana and Sanatkumara are the four, and the seven will include the three more — Sana, Sanat-sujata, and Kapila — Tr.

flower-garlands, sandal-paste, etc. Kirtan was being sung in the new verandah to the east of his room, near the garden. Surrounded by the devotees, the Master listened to the Kirtan, now entering into ecstasy, now making the Kirtan interesting by improvising extempore a line or two. But he could not enjoy the bliss fully on account of the absence of Narendra. He looked around from time to time and said to us, 'Narendra, I see, has not come.' At about noon Narendra came and bowed down at his feet in the assembly of the devotees. As soon as the Master saw him, he jumped up, sat on his shoulders and went into ecstasy. Afterwards coming to the normal state, he engaged himself in conversing with, and feeding, him. He listened to the Kirtan no more that day."

15. One is surprised to think of that intense and unearthly love, of which Narendra was the recipient from the Master. One can clearly understand how strong Narendra's love for truth was, when one finds that in spite of that unusual and ceaseless shower of selfless love, he remained firm and unmoved, and went forward to test the Master at every step, so that he might attain the wholly unalloyed truth. Surprising as this was on the one hand, the Master's magnanimity and absence of egoism were no less amazing on the other. When one finds that, instead of feeling wounded on account of that unbecoming attitude of Narendra, he submitted himself gladly to be tested in order that the disciple might have the satisfaction of realizing spiritual truths thoroughly investigated and verified by himself— one's surprise simply transcends all limits. Thus the more we study the relation of the Master with Narendra, the more are we charmed on the one hand to see the determination of the latter to accept all things only after testing them, and on the other, to witness the eagerness of the former to bring home high spiritual truths to the disciple even though it meant standing the humiliation of tests and criticism. Through such a study we can understand how a true Guru teaches a highly qualified disciple by keeping intact the latter's spiritual attitudes, and how thereby the former comes at last to occupy for ever a place of high regard and reverence in the heart of the disciple.

CHAPTER VI — SECTION I

THE EXTRAORDINARY RELATION BETWEEN THE MASTER AND NARENDRANATH

[TOPICS: 1. How long Narendra had the Master's holy company. 2. Five aspects of the behaviour of the Master towards Narendra. 3. The Master's attitude based on wonderful visions. 4. The reason why the Master tested Narendra. 5. How the Master looked upon Narendra. 6. The erroneous impression of the ordinary people about Narendra. 7. The author heard Narendra's praise from the Master. 8. The author's first erroneous impression about Narendra. 9. The author's first meeting with him at a friend's house. 10. The outward behaviour of Narendra at that time. 11. Narendra's talk on literature with the friend. 12. The author came to understand Narendra's greatness through the Master. 13. The Master recognized Narendranath from the beginning. 14. The Master praising Narendra publicly: the reason for it. 15. The Master on the inherent powers of Narendra. 16. Narendra's protest against it. 17. Narendra's power of argumentation. 18. An example; the Master came to the General Brahmo Samaj to see Narendra. 19. The result of it. 20. Lights put out to break up the crowd. 21. Narendra escorting the Master to Dakshineswar. 22. Narendra protests to the Master for loving him so much.]

1. Narendranath had the privilege of enjoying the holy company of the Master for five years. The reader might conclude from this that he spent those years continuously at the holy feet of the Master at Dakshineswar. It was not so. Like all the other devotees of Calcutta, he also used to come from home and pay visits to the Master during those years. But he, it is certain, visited Dakshineswar at short intervals, as he became an especial object of the infinite love of the Master from the very beginning. It came gradually to be regarded as an essential duty of Narendra to go there once or twice a week, and when there was leisure, to spend two, three or more days there. It is not as if there was no deviation from this rule at times. But being greatly attracted to him from the beginning, the Master did not allow him to break that rule very often. When Narendra could not come to Dakshineswar for a week for any reason, the Master would be quite restless to see him, and sending him word through some one or other, he would have him brought to him; or he himself would go to Calcutta and spend

a few hours with him. There were, as far as we know, no gaps in Narendra's regular visits to Dakshineswar for two years following his acquaintance with the Master. But he was compelled to break that rule when the whole responsibility of managing his family affairs devolved on his shoulders after the sudden death of his father, soon after his appearing for the B.A. examination at the beginning of 1884.

2. When we try to analyse the Master's dealings with Narendra during those five years, we find five main divisions: Firstly, from the beginning of Narendra's visits to him, the Master had known with the help of his inward vision that a highly qualified person like Narendra was very rare in the spiritual world and that Narendra was born to render him great assistance in the work which the Divine Mother had entrusted to him, namely, the work of renovating the Eternal Religion to serve the needs of modern times by clearing it of its age-long undesirable accretions. Secondly, he bound Narendra to himself for all eternity with the cord of infinite faith and love. Thirdly, he tested him in various ways and got confirmed the truth of his inward vision regarding Narendra's greatness and his mission in life. Fourthly, he trained Narendra in various ways and moulded him to be a fit instrument to fulfil that great mission. Fifthly, when the disciple's education was complete the Master instructed Narendra, now possessed of the immediate knowledge of Brahman, how to proceed with the work of establishing religion and at last confidently placed him in charge of this work as well as of the Order founded by himself.

3. The Master, as we have already said, had had some wonderful visions about Narendra's greatness even before he came to Dakshineswar. It was owing to the influence of those visions that he regarded Narendra, ever since their acquaintance, with an eye of infinite faith and love. That current of faith and love flowed uniformly in Narendra's heart throughout the Master's life and bound him to the Master with a cord of love that knew no rupture. It was against this background of faith and love that the Master taught Narendra and sometimes tested him too.

4. The question may be posed: "Why did the Master test Narendra, though he knew his greatness and the purpose of his advent with the help of his own Yogic visions?" The simple reason is that even God-men like the Master — not to speak of ordinary people — when they enter the realm of Maya and assume

The Kali Temple at Dakshineswar

Panchavati, the scene of Sri Ramakrishna's Sadhana

Swami Vivekananda (Narendra) at Cossipore in 1886

a body, have their vision more or less blurred, and there arises a possibility of error regarding the things seen by them. That is why such tests sometimes become necessary. Explaining this to us, the Master said, "You cannot give a lasting shape to gold without mixing it with some baser metal." Even so, the bodies and minds of even incarnations cannot be produced out of pure Sattva, which reveals knowledge, if a little of Rajas and Tamas are not mixed with it. There was, by the Divine Mother's grace, a wonderful manifestation of spiritual knowledge and visions in the Master while he was undergoing Sadhana. On many occasions he doubted the truth of those visions and could accept them fully only after testing them. Was it, therefore, surprising that he would now test the wonderful visions he had had about Narendra before accepting them as true?

5. It must be admitted that, of the five modes of the Master's behaviour towards Narendra mentioned above, three of them — namely, faith blended with love, testing, and teaching — began simultaneously. We have already given the reader a brief account of the first of the Master's modes of behaviour towards Narendra, namely his faith in, and love for, him. We shall have to say much more about it later. For, the Master's life had never before been so intimately united with that of any one of the devotees who had taken refuge in him as with that of Narendra. As soon as he met one of his great disciples, Lord Jesus said, "I will build my spiritual temple on the steady and immovable foundation of the life of this man of firm faith." Urged by Providence, such a conviction arose in the Master's mind, too, the moment he met Narendra. The Master had the vision that Narendra was his son, his friend, born to carry out his commands, and that the lives of Narendra and of himself were eternally intertwined with an unbreakable cord of love. But such love is an exalted spiritual love in which the lover gives complete freedom to the beloved, yet keeps the other as one's own from age to age. It is a love in which each of the pair feels happy to give his all to the other, wanting nothing in return. It is doubtful indeed whether the world has ever witnessed such an episode of selfless love enacted before, as in the lives of the Master and Narendra. We are quite conscious of our incapacity to explain clearly to the reader all the phases of this extraordinary love. We shall, however, give an indication of it in the interests of truth and then discuss the Master's behaviour towards Narendra in detail.

6. Just as Narendra saw the Master's purity, renunciation and single-minded devotion and became attracted to him since the first meeting, even so, the Master, it seems to us, was charmed to see his boundless self-confidence and love of truth, and made him his own from the first day they met. If we leave aside the Master's Yogic visions about Narendra's greatness and his glorious future, and try to find out the cause of their wonderful mutual attraction, what we have said before becomes evident. People in general, devoid of insight, regard Narendra's wonderful self-confidence as arrogance, his boundless vigour as insolence, and his unyielding love of truth as a feigning or as an example of undeveloped intellect. It is doubtless that they came to these conclusions from seeing his absolute indifference to people's praise, his plain-speaking nature, his free and unhesitating behaviour in all matters and, above all, his disdain to conceal anything for fear of anybody. One of his neighbours, we remember, said to us about Narendra before we had been acquainted with him: "There is a boy in that house; I have never seen a more hopelessly spoilt one than him: Having taken his B.A. degree, he has become extremely vain, as if the vast world did not count at all with him. He starts singing audaciously in the presence of his father and other superiors, keeping time on kettle drums with his palm and distended fingers. He goes along smoking a cigar in the presence of the elders of the quarter — such is his behaviour in all matters."

7. Shortly after this we got another entirely different description of Narendra and his ways, and that was from the Master. It was our second or third visit to him. Speaking with Ratan, the chief officer of the garden house of Jadunath Mallik, and pointing to us, the Master said, "These boys are good. This boy has passed one and a half examinations (I was preparing for the F.A. examination that year); he is polite and calm. But I have not seen another boy like Narendra. He is as efficient in music, vocal and instrumental, as in the acquisition of knowledge, in conversation as well as in religious matters. He loses normal consciousness in meditation during whole nights. My Narendra is a coin with no alloy whatsoever: toss it up, and you hear the truest sound. I see other boys somehow pass two or three examinations with the utmost strain. There it ends, they are spent-up forces. But Narendra is not like that. He does everything with the greatest ease, and passing an examination is but a trifle with him. He goes to the

Brahmo Samaj also and sings devotional songs there; but he is not like other Brahmos. He is a true knower of Brahman. He sees Light when he sits for meditation. Is it for nothing that I love Narendra so much?" We were charmed to hear those words, and desiring to be acquainted with Narendra, asked him, "Sir, where does Narendra live?" The Master replied, "Narendra is the son of Viswanath Datta of Simla, Calcutta." Afterwards, when we returned to Calcutta and made inquiries, we came to know that the young man, so much praised by the Master, was the very person whom our friend, his neighbour, had calumniated so vehemently. Quite astonished, we thought how improper our judgements on others' characters often turn out to be, when we base them on the casual activities of those persons!

8. It will not be out of place here to mention another incident connected with this topic. A few months before we heard the Master describing Narendra's good qualities as stated above, we had the good fortune to meet him one day at the house of a friend. That day we only saw him, but did not talk with him on account of an erroneous impression. But the words he spoke that day were so deeply imprinted on our memory that even after the lapse of many decades, it seems that we have heard them but yesterday. Before describing them, the circumstances under which we heard those words should be narrated; otherwise one will fail to understand why we carried that wrong impression about Narendranath on that occasion.

9. The friend in whose house we saw him that day had hired a two-storeyed building in front of Narendra's dwelling house at Gaur Mohan Mukherjee's Lane in the Simla quarter. We had been fellow-pupils in the same school for four or five years. Two years before our friend was to appear for the Entrance Examination, he set out for England, but could not proceed farther than Bombay. Failing in his ambition, he became the editor of a newspaper, wrote essays and poems in Bengali, and rose to be an author of a few books. He had been married a short time previously. After that event, we heard from many sources that he was living an indifferent moral life and that he did not hesitate to earn money by various dishonest means. It was only for the purpose of ascertaining the truth of this that we went without notice to his house that day.

10. Informing him of our arrival through a servant, we were sitting in a room of the outer apartment, when a young man entered

the room, and lolling against a bolster, began humming a Hindi song in an absolutely nonchalant manner, which indicated his familiarity with the owner of the house. The songs, as far as we remember, related to Sri Krishna; for the two words, "Kanai" and "flute" distinctly fell on our ears. His song about the 'black one's flute', his meticulously clean, though not ultra-fashionable, dress, his well-tended hair, and his absent-mindedness verging on coldness — all these joined together to confirm the adverse impression we had of him from his familiarity with our unprincipled friend. Seeing him behave unabashedly in that manner and smoke tobacco afterwards, ignoring our presence altogether, we concluded that he was a faithful follower of our unprincipled friend and that the latter had acquired his evil ways by mixing with such young men. Anyway, we also did not try to get introduced to him, as he assumed an attitude of great indifference and continued to be in his own mood even though he noticed us.

11. Our boyhood friend came out shortly after. Though we were meeting each other after a long interval he spoke only a word or two to us. Leaving us aside, he began to talk delightfully on various subjects with the above-mentioned young man. Though we resented that indifference he showed to us, we thought it was against etiquette to take leave suddenly. So we sat there, listening to the conversation on English and Bengali literatures, which our friend, the litterateur, held with the young man. Although, when they began the conversation, they were to a great extent agreed as to the function of high class literature, namely, that it should correctly express human sentiments, there arose a difference of opinion between them regarding the question whether a composition expressing any and every kind of human sentiment should be called literature, only because it correctly represents it. Our friend, as far as we can remember, took up the affirmative position, whereas the young man held the contrary opinion. He refuted our friend's position and tried to convince him that no composition, simply by virtue of its expressing a sentiment, good or bad correctly, could be classed as a piece of high class literature, if it did not accord with good taste and establish a high ideal. In support of his own position, the young man mentioned the books of famous English and Bengali literary men beginning with Chaucer and showed how each of them gained immortality because he adhered to this high principle. The young man said in conclusion, "Although man feels all kinds

of good and bad sentiments, he has always been straining to express some particular ideal in his mind. It is only in the realization and manifestation of that particular ideal that all the difference between man and man exists. Thinking that the enjoyment of sights, tastes, etc., is permanent and real, ordinary men make the realization of it the aim of their life. They idealize what is apparently real.[1] There is little difference between such people and beasts. High class literature can never be created by men of this type. There is another class of men who, unable to remain satisfied with the realization of the pleasure of enjoying what is seemingly real, feel higher and higher ideals within and are anxious to mould all outward things after that pattern — they want to realize the ideal.[2]
It is this class of men only who create real literature. Again, those among them who have recourse to the highest ideal and try to realize it in life, have generally to stand outside worldly life. I have seen the Paramahamsa of Dakshineswar alone to have realized that ideal in life. That is why I have reverence for him."

12. We were, of course, astonished with the scholarship of the young man and with his power of expression as evinced by his advocacy of those profound ideas. But we were disappointed to think that there was no agreement between his words and way of life; for how could he be otherwise so closely associated with a bad character like our friend? We then took leave of our friend. It was a few months after this event that we happened to hear the Master's encomiums of Narendra and the noble qualities of his head and heart, which prompted us to visit him at his home to get introduced to him. To our utter astonishment we then found that the much praised Narendranath was none other than the young man we saw the other day at our old friend's house.

13. Ordinary people, satisfied with walking along the beaten track, happened to regard Narendra very often as arrogant, insolent and ill-behaved, judging him only by his external conduct; but the Master never fell into that error. From the very start of their acquaintance, he could understand that "arrogance and insolence" arose from his great self-confidence, which in itself was the result of the extraordinary mental powers hidden in him; that his absolutely free behaviour indicated nothing but the self-control natural to him; and that his indifference to other people's opinion about

[1] This sentence was spoken in English.

[2] This sentence too was spoken in English:– Tr.

him arose from his absolute self-satisfaction with the purity of his own character. He had the conviction that in due time, the extraordinary nature of Narendra would fully blossom like a lotus of a thousand petals, and be well established in its own incomparable glory and greatness — that coming into collision with the hard realities of the world and scorched by its miseries, his arrogance and insolence would melt into infinite compassion; that his extraordinary self-confidence would reinstil hopes in the broken-hearted; and that his free behaviour, remaining within the bounds of restraint in all respects, would impress on others the lesson that in self-control alone lies the path to real freedom.

14. That is the reason why the Master praised Narendra exceedingly; but even after that he remained unsatisfied, as if he felt the inadequacy of one tongue alone to do justice to Narendra's great qualities. Though he particularly knew that a weak mind, when it always meets with praise in public, develops egoism which brings ruin, he waived aside that caution in respect of Narendranath. The reason of his doing so was that he was thoroughly convinced that Narendra's heart and head dwelt in a region too high for that weakness. The reader will comprehend it when we give here a few examples.

15. One day the noble-hearted Kesavchandra Sen, Vijayakrishna Goswami and other well-known Brahmo leaders assembled together and were seated with the Master. Young Narendra was also sitting there. The Master went into ecstasy and looked at Kesav and Vijay with a gracious eye. Afterwards, as soon as his eyes fell upon Narendra, a bright picture of his future life got immediately painted on the canvas of the Master's mind, and comparing the fully developed lives of Kesav and others with it, he looked very affectionately at Narendra. After the meeting came to an end, he said, "I saw Kesav has become world famous on account of the abundance of one power, but Narendra has in him eighteen such powers in the fullest measure. The hearts of Kesav and Vijay, I saw again, are brightened by a light of knowledge like a flame of a lamp; but looking at Narendra, I found that the very sun of knowledge had risen in his heart and removed from there even the slightest tinge of Maya and delusion." A weak-minded man devoid of inward vision would have been puffed up with pride and lost himself, had he been so praised by the Master himself. But the reaction of Narendra's mind to such praise was quite opposite.

His mind, possessed of extraordinary inward vision, dived into itself and compared impartially its own condition then with the innumerable good qualities of Kesav and Vijay. Seeing himself unworthy of such praise, Narendra protested strongly against the Master's remark, saying, "Sir, what are you saying? People will regard you as a madman when they hear this. Ah, what a great difference exists between the world-famous Kesav and the noble-hearted Vijay on the one hand, and a mediocre school boy of no consequence like myself on the other! Please never make such comparisons again." The Master was pleased to hear his protest and said affectionately, "What shall I do, my child? Do you think it was I who said so? Mother showed me all that; that is why I said so. Mother has always shown me the truth and never an untruth; that is why I spoke it out."

16. It was not always that the Master could satisfy Narendra by merely saying that Mother had made him see this or say that. Doubting the truth of all such visions of the Master, the bold, plain-speaking Narendra would very often say, "Who can say that it is the Mother that is showing you all these things? They may as well turn out to be the creations of your own brain. If I had had such experiences, I would certainly have taken them as whims of my own brain. Science and philosophy have proved beyond doubt that our eyes, ears and other organs of sense very often deceive us, especially when there is a desire in our mind to see a particular object as endowed with a particular quality. You are affectionate to me and want to see me great in every thing; this is perhaps why such visions appear to you."

17. Thus Narendra often tried to explain to the Master, with the help of apt illustrations, how the researches and investigations of modern western physiology and psychology have shown the erroneous and illusory nature of all the visions experienced by certain classes of people generally designated as mystics. When the Master's mind dwelt in higher planes of consciousness, he regarded that boyish attempt of Narendra as an indication of his truthfulness and was all the more pleased with him for that. But when the sincere, childlike mind of the Master resided in the normal plane of consciousness, Narendra's keen arguments overwhelmed him and made him anxious from time to time. He then became perplexed and thought, "Ah! Narendra, truthful in body, mind and speech, is not a person to tell a lie! It is written in the scriptures also that

only true ideas, and never false ones, would arise in minds of highly truthful persons like Narendra. Is there then the possibility of error in my visions? But I had tested my visions before in various ways and found that the Mother always showed me what was true and never what was untrue. Moreover, I had repeated assurances on their truth from Her holy mouth. Why then does Narendra, to whom truth is the very life, say that my visions are fabrications of my whims? Why does his mind not accept them as true as soon as I tell him of them?" Thus worried, he would at last place the matter before the Divine Mother and be free from anxiety on hearing from Herself the words of assurance: "Why do you give ear to his words? He will accept in a short time all these as true." The reader will understand what has been said above better, if we describe here an incident as an example:

18. The Brahmos had then become split into parties on account of the difference of opinion regarding the Cooch-Bihar marriage, and the General Brahmo Samaj had been founded a few years previously. Although Narendra used to pay visits to Kesav from time to time, he regularly attended the sitting of the said Samaj and used to sing devotional songs during its Sunday prayers. Once Narendra could not go to the Master at Dakshineswar for a week or two. For days the Master awaited his coming, when at last, disappointed, he decided to go himself to Calcutta and see Narendra. Afterwards he remembered that, the day being Sunday, Narendra might have gone out to see someone and that he might not be able to see him even if he should go to Calcutta. At last he came to the conclusion that he would surely meet him at the General Brahmo Samaj, where he was sure to go to sing devotional songs during the evening prayers. It, no doubt, occured to his mind that the sudden and unexpected visit of his might be considered a nuisance by the Brahmo devotees. "But why so?" came the thought to him the next moment, "I went thus several times to Kesav's Samaj and they were invariably happy on that account. And did not Vijay, Sivanath and other leaders of the General Brahmo Samaj too come often to Dakshineswar?" But in taking this decision, one important fact escaped the notice of the simple-hearted Master. It did not strike him even for a moment that, observing the change in the religious views of Kesav and Vijay after they came in contact with him, Sivanath and many other Brahmos of the General Samaj had gradually discontinued their

visits to him. It was quite natural for the Master not to have noticed it; for, during the whole of his life he had felt in his heart of hearts that the religious ideas of man undergo radical changes as his mind ascends to higher and higher planes of spiritual consciousness and he becomes the recepient of the Lord's grace. So, how could the Master understand that the Brahmos, who were noted as lovers of truth and as ardent fighters in its cause, would now take a different course and put a limit to spiritual experiences?

19. It was dusk. The pure hearts of hundreds of Brahmo devotees, swollen with emotions, soared high, wafted by the Mantras like "Brahman is Truth, Knowledge, Infinity" (Taittiriya Up. 2.1), and got absorbed in the contemplation of the lotus feet of the divine Lord. Prayer and meditation came gradually to an end, when the Acharya addressed the circle of Brahmos from the altar and gave them instructions for the promotion of the spirit of devotion to God in them. It was at this time that the Master entered the Brahmo temple in a state of partial consciousness and went forward towards the Acharya seated on the altar. Many of those present had seen him before. Therefore the news of his coming did not take long to circulate amongst the congregation. Of those who had not seen him before, some stood up on the floor and some on the benches to see him. Thus there was noise and disorder in the assembly and the Acharya had to bring his sermon to a close. Narendra, who was seated in the circle of the devotional singers, understood the reason of the Master's unexpected visit there and came to him. But, having decided that the Master was the cause of bringing about the aforesaid difference of opinion amongst the Brahmos such as Vijay and others, the Acharya on the altar and the other eminent members of the Samaj remained very cold and indifferent to him, and abstained from showing even the ordinary courtesy offered to a casual visitor.

20. The Master, on his part, came to the altar without looking in any direction and happened to enter into ecstasy. The eagerness of the congregation to see that state of his increased the disorder and confusion, which showed no sign of abating. When it was found that order could not be restored, all the gas lights in the hall were put out in order to break up the unruly assemblage, which, however, made the confusion worse confounded, as all rushed towards the door in the dark to come out.

21. When Narendra saw that no one of the Samaj cared to welcome the Master, he was stung to the quick. He now anxiously

busied himself in bringing the Master out from the prayer hall in that darkness. Soon after, when his ecstasy came to an end, Naren brought him out through the back door of the Samaj with great difficulty, got him into a carriage and escorted him to Dakshineswar. Narendra said, "It is impossible to describe the pain I felt to see the Master thus ill-treated on my account that day. Ah, how much did I scold him for that action of his that day! But he! He neither felt hurt at the humiliation, nor did he give ear to my words of reproach, supremely satisfied as he was that he had me by his side.

22. "Seeing that the Master failed to pay attention to himself out of his love for me, I did not hesitate on occasions to speak very harsh words to him. I said, 'King Bharata, we are told in the Puranas, thought continually of a deer and became a deer after his death. If that is true, you should beware of the consequences of your thinking much of me. So please be on your guard.' The Master, simple as he was like a boy, became much perturbed to hear those words of mine and said, 'Right you are! Ah my child! what a calamity if it should happen so! But I cannot do without seeing you. What is to be done?' Sad and frightened, the Master went to refer the matter to his Divine Mother. He returned shortly, beaming with delight, and said, 'Away, rascal! I shall never again give ear to your words. Mother said: 'You regard him as Narayana Himself; that is why you love him. The day you do not see Narayana in him, you will not even cast a glance at him.' That day the Master swept aside with one word all the objections that I had raised before against his extraordinary love for me."

CHAPTER VI: SECTION 2

THE EXTRAORDINARY RELATION BETWEEN THE MASTER AND NARENDRANATH

[TOPICS: 1. The Master's words about Narendra's greatness. 2. Food offering brought by Marwari devotees. 3. Narendra's devotion unaffected by food. 4. Narendra's progress. 5. The Master made Sri. M. argue with Narendra. 6. Kedarnath Chattopadhyaya, the devotee. 7. Kedar's power of reasoning. 8. Narendra on Kedar. 9. Narendra and Rakhal. 10. Narendra's protest against non-dualism. 11. Pratapchandra Hazra. 12. Narendra's admiration for his intellectual capacity. 13. Narendra's visit to Dakshineswar and the Master's behaviour. 14. The Master touching Narendra in a mood of spiritual inebriation. 15. Narendra's wonderful experience. 16. The author's conversation with Narendra on one occasion. 17. Narendra mentioned a wonderful incident. 18. Narendra's unique experience at the author's house.]

1. The Master's keen insight readily detected from the beginning that Narendra's pure mind and heart were always actuated by high ideals, in whatever work they were seen engaged at any time. This was why the daily behaviour of the Master with Narendra had a rare delicacy about it. The Master himself observed many rules regarding eating, drinking, sleeping and starting for a place, as also about meditation, praying and counting of beads in order to encourage his devotees to do likewise, lest their devotion should suffer. But he used to say unhesitatingly again and again in the presence of all that no harm would befall Narendra if he did not observe those rules. "Narendra is eternally perfect", he would say, "he is perfect in meditation. The fire of knowledge, ever ablaze in him, would reduce to ashes all blemishes pertaining to food[1]. His mind, therefore, will not be tarnished or distracted even if he takes whatever he likes at any place and from any person. He daily cuts to pieces Maya's bondages with the sword of knowledge; Mahamaya, therefore, fails to bring him under Her control." Ah! in how many such profuse expressions did the Master convey

[1] The Hindu believes that the articles of food that he takes not only builds up his physical being, but has also an effect on his moral and spiritual nature, by increasing or decreasing the lethargy, energy and keenness of the mind and the sense organs.

his appreciation of Narendra, making us mute with surprise!

2. The Marwari devotees came to pay their obeisance to the Master and made presents to him of various articles of food, such as candy, nuts, almonds, pistachios and the like. The Master himself took none of these; neither did he give them to any one of the devotees that were there with him. He said, "They (the Marwaris) do not at all know how to make gifts without a motive; at the time of offering even a roll of betel to a holy man, they attach to it prayers for the fulfilment of large numbers of desires. A good deal of harm is done to one's devotion when one takes food given by such persons." The question, therefore, arose what should be done with the things given by them. The Master said, "Go and give them to Narendra. He will not in any way be affected if he takes them."

3. Narendra one day took his meal in a hotel, and came and said to the Master, "Sir, today I have eaten in the hotel what all people call forbidden food." He knew that Narendra said so, not because he wanted to get credit for his act, but in order that the Master might be forewarned, if he had, on the score of that act, any objection to his touching him or using the utensils like water-pots, cups, etc., kept in his room. Promptly the Master replied, "No blemish will affect you on that account. If anyone eats pork and beef but keeps his mind fixed on the Divine Lord, it is like taking the sacred Havishya; on the other hand, if anyone eats greens and vegetables but is immersed in worldly desires, it is not in any respect better than eating pork and beef. I don't consider it wrong on your part — this taking of forbidden food. But had any one of them (pointing to all others) come and told me so, I could not have even touched him."

4. It is almost impossible to explain exactly to the reader the love, praise and liberty in all matters that the Master bestowed on Narendra ever since they met for the first time. It is doubtful whether a parallel to this behaviour, in which the teacher leads a large-minded disciple with so much reverence for his inherent capacities, can be found anywhere in the whole spiritual history of the world. The Master could not remain satisfied without speaking out all his innermost thoughts to Narendra; he wished also to consult him on all matters. To test the strength of the faith and the intellect of other devotees, he sometimes made them argue with him. He never requested him to accept anything as true without thoroughly

testing it. This behaviour of the Master, it is superfluous to say, increased a hundredfold in a very short time Narendra's devotion, reverence and self-confidence as also his capacity for personal endeavour and his love of truth. This infinite confidence and love of the Master surrounded Narendra on all sides like an impregnable wall and protected him from all kinds of temptations and mean conduct even unconsciously, thus enabling him to enjoy his natural love of unbounded freedom without any of its attendant dangers. Narendra's love for the Master grew so deep and intense that he surrendered himself to him for all eternity within a year of his first meeting him. But did he then know how far the current of the Master's selfless love carried him forward towards the goal of life? Perhaps not. Filled and contented as his heart was with a blissful and heavenly joy never felt before, Narendra was yet to know how unique and unattainable a thing it was — a thing coveted even by the gods. For, with his experience only of the extremely selfish and hard-hearted world, he had no object with which to compare this rare love. It will not be out of place here to give a few examples to make this clear to the reader.

5. Sri M., the author of The Gospel of Sri Ramakrishna, had the good fortune of meeting the Master at Dakshineswar in the month of March, 1882, a few months after Narendra had come to him. He himself has recorded in that book how he had the opportunity of coming to the Master several times at short intervals, as he was then living at Baranagar, and how a few ironical remarks of the Master removed his pride of learning and converted him for ever into a humble scholar. Narendra said, "One day at that time I spent a night with the Master at Dakshineswar. I was sitting quiet for some time under the Panchavati, when the Master suddenly came there and catching hold of my hand, said smiling, 'Your intellect and learning will be examined today. You have passed two and a half examinations only; a teacher who has passed three and a half[1] has come today. Come, let me see how you fare in conversation with him.' Willy-nilly, I had to go with the Master. When I reached his room and was introduced to M., I began to talk with him on various subjects. Having thus engaged us in a talk, the Master sat silent and went on listening to our words and

[1] Narendra was then studying for his B.A. examination while Sri M. had passed that examination and was studying law (B.L.). The Master put these facts in that way.

observing us. Afterwards, when Sri M. took leave and went away, he said, 'What matters it, even if he has passed those examinations? The teacher is womanish in character — shy. He cannot talk with emphasis.' Thus pitting me against others, the Master used to enjoy the fun of it."

6. Kedarnath Chattopadhyaya was one of the lay devotees of the Master. He, it seems, used to visit the Master for some time before Narendra came to Dakshineswar. As he was employed at Dacca in East Bengal, he could not come to the Master except during vacations, like that of the autumn worship of the Mother of the universe. Kedar was a devotee and Sadhaka, and engaged himself in the practice of the spiritual moods and attitudes described in the Vaishnava scriptures. He shed tears when he heard devotional songs. The Master, therefore, praised him before all. Seeing Kedar's faith and devotion, many people of Dacca developed great respect and reverence for him. Many, again tried to mould their spiritual lives according to his instructions. When too many people began to come to the Master, he sometimes got tired of discussing religious topics with all; and we are told, one day, when he was in ecstasy, he prayed to the Divine Mother, "Mother, I cannot talk so much; give a little power to Kedar, Ram, Girish and Vijay[2], so that people may go to them first, learn a little, and at last come here (to me) to have their spiritual awakening in a word or two." But this was long afterwards.

7. Taking leave for some time from his duties, Kedar came to Calcutta and had the opportunity of visiting the Master now and then. Having him, the Sadhaka devotee by his side, the Master was delighted and started talking with him on religious topics and introduced other devotees to him. One day Narendra came to the Master during that period and saw Kedar with him. While he was singing devotional songs at the Master's request, Narendra observed Kedar entering into ecstasy. Afterwards, the Master set Narendra to reason with Kedar. Kedar was a good debater in his own way, and used sarcastic words now and then to point out the unreasonableness of the words of the opponent. The words with which he silenced his opponent one day, were much liked by the Master. If any one raised similar questions before him (the Master), he very often said in reply that Kedar had given such and such a reply to

[2] Kedarnath Chattopadhyaya, Ramchandra Datta, Girishchandra Ghosh and Vijaykrishna Goswami.

such a question. That day the opponent raised the question, "If God is actually merciful, why has He created so much pain and misery, suppression and oppression? Why do thousands of people die of starvation during famines from time to time?" Kedar replied, "I was unfortunately not invited by the Lord to attend the meeting in which He, in spite of His being merciful, decided to keep going pain and misery, tyranny and oppression in His creation. How then, can I know the reason?" But Kedar was silenced that day in the presence of all by Narendra's keen intellect.

8. The Master asked Narendra after Kedar left, "Well, how did you find him? Have you noticed his great devotion to the Lord, —how he sheds tears at the very mention of the Lord's name? One whose eyes pour forth streams of tears at the name of Hari, is a person liberated in life. Kedar is splendid — isn't he?" The immaculate and vigorous Narendra hated from the bottom of his heart those persons who, having a male body, assumed a womanish attitude, be it for the sake of religion or for any other reason. That a man should approach God and find relief in weeping instead of strengthening his own determination and perseverance, always appeared to him to be an insult to his manliness. Although entirely dependent on God, a man, he was of opinion, should always remain a man and should surrender himself to Him like a man. Therefore, unable to approve whole-heartedly those words of the Master, he said, "But, Sir, how can I know it? You know people's nature; it is for you to say it. Otherwise, simply by seeing a man weeping and wailing, one can never know if he is good or bad. If a man gazes at a point intensely for some time, the lachrymal ducts and glands are strained and tears flow. Again, most of those who weep, singing or listening to songs describing Srimati's separation from Sri Krishna, do so, there is no doubt, by remembering their own separation from their wives or by ideally placing themselves in that condition. People like me, totally unacquainted with that condition, will not easily feel inclined like others to weep even when listening to Mathura-kirtan[1], noted for its pathos." Thus, when asked, Narendra always gave his independent opinions fearlessly to the Master on matters he knew to be true. The Master too was always pleased with this, and was never displeased. For, the Master, who knew people's hearts, certainly felt that Narendra, to whom

[1] These describe the intense pang of separation of the Gopis of Vrindavan at the departure of Sri Krishna to Mathura:- Tr.

truth was life, had not on his conscience the slightest burden of a trifling fib, or, as the Master would himself put it, "He had kept the inner chamber of his mind clear of dubious expressions."

9. Narendra had joined the Brahmo Samaj shortly before he met the Master. He had then signed the pledge of the Brahmo Samaj to the effect that he would believe in the only God who is one and formless, and worship and meditate on Him alone. But the idea of becoming a Brahmo convert by adopting the social usages and customs prevalent in the Samaj, never crossed his mind. Rakhal had been known to Narendra before, and he used to spend much time with him. It was not a matter of surprise that, charmed with the loving behaviour of Narendra, Rakhal, who possessed the soft and gentle nature of a child, reposed trust in him and was regulated in all matters by his strong will-power. Therefore, advised by Narendra, he also signed that pledge of the Brahmo Samaj then. Rakhal met the Master shortly afterwards, and instructed by him, the dormant love for the worship of God with forms was once more awakened in Rakhal's heart. Narendra began visiting the Master a few months later and was highly pleased to see Rakhal there. Rakhal, he found a few days afterwards, went with the Master to the temple and bowed down to the images of the deities. The truthful Narendra was chagrined at that, and reminding Rakhal of his former pledge, reproved him thus: "You have been guilty of false conduct inasmuch as you have signed the pledge of the Brahmo Samaj, but yet go to the temple and bow down to the deities." The gentle-natured Rakhal remained silent when his friend spoke those words and was afraid and hesitant to meet him since then. Knowing afterwards the reason why Rakhal behaved in that manner, the Master explained the matter to Narendra in sweet and convincing words, saying affectionately. "Look here, don't blame Rakhal any more. He shrinks from you. He has now faith in God with form; so what can he do? Can every one have the conception of the formless God from the very beginning?" Narendra also desisted from blaming Rakhal since then.

10. The Master understood that Narendra was a highly qualified person in the domain of spirituality and tried to infuse into him the belief in the truth of non-dualism from the very first day he met him. He used to give him books like the Ashtavakra Samhita to read as soon as he came to Dakshineswar. But books like these then appeared to be blasphemous and atheistic in the eyes

of Narendra, who was performing the dualistic mode of worship of the formless Brahman with attributes. As soon as he had read a little of Ashtavakra Samhita at the request of the Master, he blurted out, "What is the difference between this and atheism? Should the created Jiva think of himself as the Creator? What can be more sinful than this? What ideas can be more unreasonable than saying, 'I am God, you are God, all things that are born and die are God.' The brains of the Rishis and Munis, the authors of such books, must have been deranged. Otherwise, how could they have written such things?" The Master smiled to hear these words of the plain-speaking Narendra, but instead of suddenly attacking his spiritual attitude, he said, "You may not accept them now; but why do you condemn the Munis and Rishis because of that? And why do you put a limit to the nature of God? Go on calling on Him who is Truth itself and then believe that to be His true nature in which He will reveal Himself to you." But Narendra did not give ear to these words of the Master. For, whatever was not established by reason, appeared to him to be untrue, and it was his nature to stand against all kinds of untruth. He, therefore, did not hesitate to adduce reasons against the doctrine of non-dualism to many besides the Master, and even used sarcastic words against it from time to time.

11. A person named Pratapchandra Hazra used to live in the Dakshineswar garden at that time. Pratap's worldly circumstances were not then as affluent as before. Therefore, in spite of his attempts at spiritual attainments, a desire for money very often got the upper hand in his mind. But keeping it a secret to himself, he would speak of high selfless service to the Lord and try to gain praise thereby. Calculation of loss and gain at every step became so natural to him that even at the time of spiritual practice he could not forgo it. The idea of attaining some miraculous power by means of Japa, austerities and the like, with which he could satisfy his desire for money, seemed sometimes to creep into his mind. The Master knew that attitude of his mind from the very first day and advised him to call on God, giving up all ulterior motives. But the weak-minded Hazra did not only disobey his advice, but under the urge of pride, delusion and self-interest preached, whenever he had leisure, to those who came to see the Master, that he too was not a lesser Sadhu. But along with this, he seemed to have in his mind a little real desire of becoming honest. This was evident from the

fact that although the Master knew of this conduct of his and although he sometimes scolded him sharply for it, he did not drive him away from there once for all. But he warned some of us against mixing much with him, saying, "That fellow, Hazra, has a great calculating mind; don't give ear to him."

12. In addition to the good and bad qualities described above, Hazra had a sceptical temperament. Compared with other persons of similar education, he was quite intelligent. Therefore, he could understand a little of the discussions on the doctrines of the Western agnostic philosophers carried on by English educated persons like Narendra. The intelligent Narendra was, therefore, pleased with him and spent at his convenience an hour or two in conversation with Hazra whenever he came to Dakshineswar. Hazra, of course, had to bend his head before Narendra's keen intellect. He listened with great attention to Narendra's words and sometimes prepared a smoke for him. Seeing that attitude of Narendra towards Hazra, many of us said jokingly. "Mr. Hazra is Narendra's 'ferend' (friend)."

13. The Master happened very often to go into ecstasy at the very sight of Narendra. Afterwards, when he regained partial consciousness, he quite joyfully used to have long spiritual talks with him. At those times he tried through words and deeds to infuse high spiritual truths into his mind. Now and then he would feel like hearing devotional songs, but as soon as he heard the very sweet voice of Narendra, he would enter into ecstasy once more. But Narendra's songs would not stop on that account. He became absorbed and went on singing songs, one after another, for a few hours. When the Master regained partial consciousness, he sometimes requested Narendra to sing a particular song. But he would not be fully satisfied till at last he had heard from Narendra the song, "Thou art whatever there is." Afterwards some time was spent in talking about various subtle truths of the non-dual doctrines, such as the difference between Jiva and Isvara, the real nature of Jiva and Brahman and the like. Thus there was a strong surge of bliss whenever Narendra came to Dakshineswar.

14. One day the Master told Narendra many things indicating the oneness of Jiva and Brahman according to the non-dual philosophy. Narendra heard those words, undoubtedly with attention, but could not comprehend them, and went to Hazra at the end of the Master's talk. Smoking and discussing those things

again with Hazra, he said, "Can it ever be possible that the water-pot is God, the cup is God, whatever we see and all of us are God?" Hazra also joined Narendra in ridiculing the idea and both of them burst into laughter. The Master was till then in the state of partial consciousness. Hearing Narendra laugh, he came out of his room like a boy with his cloth in his armpit, and coming to them smiling, said affectionaly, "What are you both talking about?" He then touched Narendra and went into ecstasy.

15. Narendra said to us afterwards, "There was a complete revolution in the state of my mind in a moment at the wonderful touch of the Master. I was aghast to see actually that there was nothing in the whole universe except God. But I remained silent in spite of seeing it, wondering how long that state would last. But that inebriation did not at all diminish that day. I returned home; it was all the same there. It seemed to me that all I saw was He. I sat for my meal when I saw that all — food, plate, the one who was serving as well as I myself — were nothing but He. I took a mouthful or two and sat quiet. My mother's affectionate words, — 'Why do you sit quiet; why don't you eat?' — brought me to consciousness and I began eating again. Thus, I had that experience at the time of eating or drinking, sitting or lying, going to the college or taking a stroll. I was always overwhelmed with a sort of indescribable intoxication. When I walked along the streets and saw a carriage coming along before me, I did not feel inclined, as at other times, to move away lest it should collide with me. For I thought, 'I am also that and nothing but that.' My hands and feet always remained insensible at that time. While taking food, I ceased to feel that I was taking. It seemed to me as if someone else was taking the meal. Sometimes I lay down while eating and got up in a short time to continue eating. On some days I thus ate much more than the usual quantity of food. But that did not cause any disease. My mother was alarmed and said, 'I am afraid you have some severe ailment within.'

Again she said sometimes, 'He may not live more.' When the overwhelming intoxication diminished a little, the world appeared to me to be a dream. Going for a walk on the bank of the Hedua tank, I knocked my head against the iron railings round it to see whether what I saw were dream rails or actual ones. On account of the insensibility of my hands and feet, I was afraid that I might be going in for paralysis. I could not escape that terrible intoxicating mood and overwhelming condition for some time. When I came to the normal state, I thought that it was the indication of non-dual knowledge. So what is written in the scriptures about it is by no means untrue. Since then, I could never doubt the truth of non-duality."

16. On another occasion we heard of another wonderful event also from Narendra. He mentioned it to us in the winter of 1884 when we had become very familiar with him. But we infer that the event occurred at this time. Therefore we narrate it to the reader here. We remember that we went to Narendra's house at Gaur Mohan Mukherjee Street in Simla, a little before midday on that occasion and were with him till eleven at night. Swami Ramakrishnananda also was with us that day. The unearthly attraction that we felt for Narendra since we first met each other, became multiplied a thousand times that day by the dispensation of Providence. The only opinion that we entertained about the Master before was that he was a perfected man, that is, a person who had known God. But that day the words of Narendra about the Master penetrated into our hearts and shed a new light on our minds. The extraordinary events, like those recorded in the biographies of great souls, the teachers of the world such as the holy and glorious Jesus, Chaitanya and others, which we had read about and had been disbelieving so long, were, we understood that day, taking place daily in the Master's life. He granted devotion to those who had taken refuge in him by a touch, or by his will he untied the knots of their heart and effaced its past impressions. He made them enter into ecstasy and realize divine Bliss. Or he changed the course of their lives into spiritual channels in such a way that the realization of God followed very soon and they were blessed for all eternity. Narendra, we remember, took us for a walk at dusk that day to the banks of the Hedua tank while relating the divine experiences he had had in his life by the grace of the Master. Immersed in his self, he remained silent for some time, and at last burst out in a song sung in his charming voice and pouring out the wonderful bliss of his heart:

"Gora Ray distributes the wealth of love.
Nitai Chand calls 'come, come';
Come, O you, who long to have it.
Jarfuls of love are being poured out,
Yet it does not get exhausted.

Santipur is being flooded and
Nadia is swept off.
Nadia is swept off by the current of Gora's love."

17. The song came to an end. In a soliloquy, as it were, Narendra said gently, "He is actually distributing love. Gora Ray is bestowing love, devotion, divine knowledge, liberation and whatever else one may desire, on whomsoever he likes. Oh, the wonderful power! (He sat silent and motionless for a while.) I was lying on my bed at night with the door of my room bolted from within, when he suddenly attracted me and took me — the one that lives within this body — to Dakshineswar. Giving a great deal of instruction to me and talking on various subjects, he allowed me to return. He can do anything he likes; this Gora Ray of Dakshineswar can do anything."

18. The darkness of dusk had intensified into the jet-black of night We could not see each other; nor was it necessary. For, the glowing mass of Narendra's spiritual emotion had entered deep into our heart and produced such an intoxication in our mind that even its frame, the body, was actually reeling and even the world whose palpable reality was evident to us so long, receded, as it were, into the realm of dream. Moreover, the truth, that under the impulse of pure and unalloyed grace, the infinite God appears as a finite human being, setting in motion the wheel of religion and destroying the bondage of the past impressions of thousands of Jivas — this truth, which, according to the majority of the people of the world, is but a figment of the imagination — then stood revealed to us in its living, blazing form. How time slid away, we did not know. But suddenly we heard the clock strike nine. I was reluctantly thinking of taking leave of Narendra, when he said, "Come, let us go. I'll accompany you for a short distance." As we were going, similar interesting discussions were started, and we became soon absorbed in them. It occured to us when we reached home near Champatala, that it was foolish on our part to have let Narendra come so far. Therefore, inviting him to the house, we asked him to take a little refreshment, after which we accompanied him up to his house, and returned. I remember distinctly another incident of that day. As soon as he entered our house, Narendra stood motionless, saying, "I feel I have seen this house before. I find everything here is known to me; all the rooms and the ways leading to them are all fully known

to me. Oh, how strange and wonderful! The reader might remember that we described before in another place how Narendra had such experiences in his life from time to time and what he said about the cause of this phenomenon. So we do not repeat them here.

CHAPTER VII

THE MASTER'S METHOD OF TESTING AND NARENDRANATH

[Topics: 1. The Master's way of testing, 2. The ordinary method of examination. 3. The Master's ecstasies on meeting persons of particular spiritual moods. 4. The four methods of his testing people. 5. Ascertaining the mental impression from physiognomy. 6. The wonderful knowledge of the Master in this respect. 7. Ascertaining the nature of a man by the weight of his forearm. 8. Character traits revealed by other features. 9. Hanuman Singh, the gate-keeper. 10. Ascertaining the spiritual nature of women. 11. The Master on Narendra's physical characteristics. 12. More observations on the same subject. 13. The Master's impression about boys. 14. He observed every action of the devotees who came to him. 15. Examples. 16. High tide in the Ganga. 17. All activities should be oriented towards God-realisation. 18. Faith is not credulity. 19. The Master's varying teachings to persons of different temperaments. 20. The Master's instructions to Yogananda. 21. A different instruction to Niranjan. 22. Instruction to women devotees. 23. The story of Harish. 24. "This is not a case for showing kindness". 25. Instructions based on the daily trifling actions of persons. 26. The Master's ascertaining the spiritual growth of individuals through their estimate of himself. 27. Further explanation of this. 28. Differing estimates of him by different devotees. 29. The example of devotee Purnachandra. 30. The Master on Purna's spiritual fitness. 31. His loving behaviour towards Purna. 32. Purna's estimate of him. 33. The Master's instruction to him. 34. The greatness of Purna, though he lived in the world. 35. Vaikunthanath, the second example. 36. No one whose words and actions do not agree should be believed. 37. The Master's story on this topic. 38. The devotees tested the Master. 39. First example; the story of Yogananda. 40. The good impression of Yogindra and his intelligence. 41. Yogindra an Iswarakoti. 42. Yogindra's marriage and after. 43. Yogindra spent nights at Dakshineswar. 44. Yogindra suspected the Master. 45. Yogindra's suspicion removed. 46. Yogindra surrendered himself to the Guru. 47. The Master's observations on Narendra. 48. A funny incident. 49. Narendra's self-control. 50. Physical characteristics of devotion in Narendra. 51. Narendra unperturbed at the Master's indifference. 52. Narendra and supernatural powers.]

We have already stated elsewhere how, ever since his first meeting with Narendra, the Master had discovered his high spiritual qualifications and potentialities, and how his extraordinarily selfless affection for Narendra was beginning to bind him to the Master by a cord of affection. He, nevertheless, now and then tested him, even as he proceeded with educating him in spiritual matters. It is necessary, therefore, to give here a short account of his modes and ways of testing Narendranath.

1. When the Brahmo Samaj was about to be split over the difference of opinion regarding the Cooch-Bihar marriage, the Master said to Kesav, "You take anybody and everybody without examining him in order to add to the number of your society. Is it surprising, therefore, that it is dissolving? I do not accept anyone without examining him thoroughly." Astonishing, indeed, are the various ways through which the Master used to test the devotees with or without their knowledge, before he accepted them. One wonders how and whence one, who passed off as an illiterate person, acquired the mastery of those unseen and unheard-of methods. Naturally the question crops up: "Was it the self-revelation of the knowledge acquired in his previous lives? Or was it the result of his acquiring super-sensuous vision and all-knowingness by dint of his Sadhana as in the case of the seers of old? Or again, was it an expression of the power that was his by virtue of his being an incarnation, as he declared himself to be to his inner circle of devotees?" Although these queries naturally arise in our minds, we are not now going to press them for a solution. We are merely concerned with giving as far as possible an accurate description of the series of events, and leave it to the reader to come to his own conclusion regarding them.

2. The reader will have a comprehension of these extraordinary methods, if we give a few incidents illustrating them. But before trying to understand them, he must know certain things regarding those ways and means of testing adopted by the Master. As soon as some one came to him, the Master looked at that person in a peculiar way. If his mind felt attracted to him on doing so, he talked to him on religion in a general way and asked him to see him from time to time. As the person repeated his visits, the Master tried to come to a sure conclusion regarding the dormant spiritual tendencies in him by observing minutely, without his knowledge, the formation of his limbs, his mental tendencies, the intensity of his desire for worldly enjoyments, especially his attachment to lust and gold, as also how far his mind had been or was being attract-

ed towards him. He gathered these data by observing how he talked, acted and behaved. His observation was so keen and thorough that it took him but a few days to have a perfect knowledge of the character of that person. Afterwards, if it were at all necessary to know of anything deeply hidden in the person's mind, which the external observation did not clarify, the Master fathomed it with the help of his subtle Yogic insight. One day he said to us regarding this, "When I am alone during the last hours of the night, my mind is often engaged in thinking about the welfare of you all. Mother reveals everything about you: how far each one of you has progressed, what blocks the further spiritual progress of any one and so on." Let not the reader think from these words of the Master that his Yogic eyes opened during those hours only. It is clear from his words spoken at other times, that he could at will ascend to higher planes of consciousness and attain that vision at any time. Take for example his words, "Just as one looking at a glass case sees all the things within it, so, as soon as I look at a person, I see all about him — his thoughts, the impressions of his past and so on."

3. This was the method which the Master generally adopted when he tried to acquaint himself with the nature of the ordinary devotees. From this, however, he deviated to a smaller or greater extent in the case of especial devotees of the inner circle. The Divine Mother gave him a pre-vision of them in higher planes of consciousness. We have said elsewhere in this book, that the body and the mind of the Master became, by the extraordinary power of his Sadhana, a wonderful instrument wherewith he could conserve spiritual powers in himself and know of their existence in others. This was literally true. As soon as the Master saw a person with a particular spiritual mood, his own mind would be coloured by that mood under some Divine impulse. Again no sooner did he contact a person poised in a particular spiritual plane than his own mind naturally ascended to that plane and revealed to him the ideas of that person's mind. The reader will understand what we mean, if he recalls what has been narrated earlier about the Master's experiences in connection with Narendra's first visit to him.

4. This did not, however, preclude him from applying the ordinary methods, adopted to know the character of people in general, in the case of his devotees of the inner circle too. When he dwelt in the normal plane of consciousness, he observed their

talk and behaviour as well as those of other devotees, not even excepting Narendra; not until then, could he be free from anxiety. The matter being so important, the reader must be made acquainted with it fully. We can divide the ways and means adopted by the Master to examine his devotees into four main divisions. As we have already stated their broad principles, we may now explain them to the reader with the help of illustrations.

5. Firstly, the Master ascertained the strong past impressions of a newcomer by observing his physical characteristics. In the process of our thoughts being transformed into actions, they leave especial marks in particular parts of our brain and our body. Modern physiology and psychology have proved this fact to a great extent and confirmed our belief. The Vedas and other scriptures, however, have been telling us this for a long time past. The Vedas, the Smritis, the Puranas, the Darsanas and all other scriptures of the Hindus have unanimously proclaimed that the mind creates the body. With the current of a man's thoughts moving constantly in a good or bad channel, his body changes and assumes forms helpful to the fulfilment of those thoughts. Many proverbs are current amongst us regarding the ascertainment of the character of people by the observation of the formation of their bodies and limbs. It has been regarded up till now to be absolutely necessary to examine the body as a whole and all its limbs, the form of the hands, the feet etc., of the bride and the disciple at the time of marriage and initiation, respectively.

6. It was, therefore, not surprising that the Master, a believer in all the Sastras, should observe the form of the bodies and limbs of his own disciples. But occasionally, he used to say so many things in the course of conversation about it to us that we wondered whence he could have got so much information on the subject. We sometimes asked ourselves whether there was any big book on the subject coming down from ancient times, reading or hearing which he had come to know all these things. But as we had not so far seen or heard of such a book, the idea had to be given up as having no basis. So it was only with great astonishment that we listened to him, as he narrated how the formation of each limb and sense-organ of the body of men and women resembled a particular object of our daily experience, and what good and bad qualities were indicated by such resemblance. "Take, for example, the eyes of a person," he would say: "In the case of some, they are

like the petals of a lotus; in the case of others, like the eyes of a bull; and in the case of still others, like those of Yogis. A person having his eyes like the petals of a lotus has good thoughts in him; one whose eyes are like those of a bull has lust predominant in him; the Yogi's eyes have an upward look and are reddish; and the eyes like those of gods are not very large but long, reaching very near the ears. Those who are in the habit of looking through the corners of their eyes now and then at the time of conversation, are more intelligent than ordinary people." Or he would start the topic of the nature of the general formation of people's bodies and say, "A person of devotion has a soft body by nature and the joints of his arms and legs are not thick-set (that is, can be easily turned round); even if his body is thin, the bones, muscles, etc., in it are placed in such a way that the joints do not seem very angular." In order to ascertain whether a person's intelligence tends towards good or evil, the Master would hold that person's forearm (from the elbow to the fingers) in his own hand and ask him to hold it relaxed. He would then feel its weight. If it was felt lighter than that of people in general, he regarded him as a person with a pure mind. The Master, we mentioned before, thus caught hold of the forearm of Swami Premananda (alias Baburam) and felt its weight on the day of his first visit to Dakshineswar. But as he did not say why the Master did so, we also did not mention there anything about the purpose for which it was done. Our conclusion, however, was borne out by an incident on another occasion. We mention it below.

7. When the Master was staying in the garden at Kasipur, one day, the author's younger brother, Charuchandra Chakravarti, came there to see him. The Master was highly pleased to see him. He made him sit beside himself, made many kind enquiries, and gave him various spiritual instructions. When the author came there, the Master asked him, "Is the boy your brother?" When the author said, "Yes", the Master continued, "He is a nice boy, a little more intelligent than you. Let me see whether his intelligence tends to good or evil." Saying so, he immediately held in his hand the forearm of the boy's right hand, weighed it and made the remark, "beneficent intelligence". Afterwards he asked the author affectionately once more, "Shall I attract him too? (that is, shall I make his mind turn away from worldly life towards God?) What do you say?" "It will be good, Sir", replied the author,

"please do so." The Master thought a little and said, "No; let me not do it; I have taken one, and if I take another now, your parents, especially your mother, will be much pained. I have offended many Saktis[1] during my life; no more of it now." Saying so, the Master gave him more instructions and some refreshments and bade him good-bye.

8. The Master said that, like the formation of the limbs etc., sleep, calls of nature and other ordinary physical actions of persons possessed of different past impressions, differed widely. Therefore, experienced people, he used to say, found clues in these acts also for ascertaining the character of men. For example, he said, during sleep all did not breathe in the same way. A worldly man breathed in one way and an all-renouncing one did it in a different way. At the time of answering calls of nature the former would have his stream of urine deflecting to the left, while the latter would have it to the right; that the faeces of a Yogi were not touched by hogs and so on.

9. The Master described to us an event pertaining to this. A man named Hanuman Singh was appointed to guard the Dakshineswar temple during Mathur Babu's time. Although he was one of the several gate-keepers, Hanuman Singh enjoyed greater respect; for not only was he a well-known wrestler but also a wholehearted spiritual aspirant. Another wrestler came to Dakshineswar and challenged Hanuman Singh with the idea that he could defeat him and take his place. Hanuman Singh saw his sturdy body, physical strength etc., but he did not hesitate to accept the challenge. A day was fixed and persons like Mathur Babu were appointed judges to decide which of them was superior.

The new wrestler began to prepare himself for the combat by eating heaps of nutritious food and practising physical exercise for about a week before the appointed day. On the contrary, Hanuman Singh, who was a devotee of Mahavira, took his bath in the morning, repeated as usual the Mantra of his Chosen Ideal during the whole of the day and took one meal only in the evening. Everyone thought that Hanuman had got frightened and had given up hopes of success. The Master loved him, and, therefore, asked him the day before the competition, "You have not prepared your physique by practising bodily exercise and eating nutritious food;

[1] That is, women, looked upon as the embodiments of the Divine Mother's creative and preservative powers.

do you think you will succeed in the competition with the new man?" Hanuman bowed down to him with devotion and said, "I'll certainly win if your grace is bestowed on me. It is not by eating a heap of food that strength comes to the body; the food must be digested. I secretly saw the faeces of the other wrestler and found that he was eating food beyond his power of digestion." The Master said that Hanuman Singh actually defeated that man in wrestling on the day of the competition.

10. The Master said many things about the formation of the limbs of women's bodies as well as those of men. Observing these, he specified some women as Vidya Saktis, in other words, as those helping men in their Godward progress, and others as Avidya Saktis, that is, those who drag men towards worldliness. He said, "The Vidya Saktis take only a small quantity of food, require only a little sleep and have naturally little attachment to the senses. Their hearts are especially filled with joy to hear their husbands talk of God; they themselves talk of the Lord, and give their husbands a high spiritual impulse, always protecting them from mean inclinations and actions and assisting them in all matters, so that they may be blessed by realizing God at last. The nature and actions of the Avidya Saktis, on the other hand, are of quite an opposite kind. They are seen to hanker after many physical comforts and require much food and sleep. Their chief aim is to prevent their husbands from paying attention to anything except contributing to their own happiness. If their husbands speak to them about spiritual things, they become displeased and annoyed." The Master sometimes said that the external form of that particular sense-organ, with the help of which women acquire the prerogative of motherhood, indicates their inward attachment to sensual enjoyment. He also said that its forms varied. Some of its forms indicated the absence of strong animal instinct. Again, he said that those whose buttocks bulge out like the hind parts of black ants, have that instinct to an inordinate degree.

11. Thus, there is no limit to what the Master told us about ascertaining human character by physiognomical observations. He regarded it as one of the means of knowing the character of people, and he examined Narendra and all other devotees with its help. On thus examining Narendra, he was pleased, and said to him one day, "All the parts of your body have good characteristics. The only defect is, that you breathe a little heavily when asleep.

Yogis say that one breathing so heavily is short-lived."

12. The observation of the mental states as revealed in the actions of men was the second means he employed, and the assessment of their attachment to lust and gold, the third. The Master used to observe a new-comer silently for some time; then, when he had decided to take him into his circle, he would try to make him give up those defects by giving him various instructions and a gentle scolding, if necessary. Again, along with the decision of choosing the man, he would settle whether he would mould his life as of a monk or of a lay disciple, and would impart instruction accordingly from the beginning. The Master, therefore, asked every visitor if he was married, if the financial condition of the family was sufficient for providing plain living, and if there was any near relation who could take up the responsibility of maintaining his family in case he renounced the world.

13. The Master was always seen to have a great compassion for students of schools and colleges. He said, "Their minds have not yet been distracted by wife, children, fame and other worldly entanglements. (If rightly educated) they could apply their whole mind to God." He, therefore, made a great effort to impart spiritual ideas to them. He expressed that opinion with the help of various illustrations. He used to say: "The mind is like a bundle of grains of mustard seed; once they are scattered, it becomes almost impossible to collect them together"; or "Once the coloured ring appears round the neck, it is very difficult to teach the parrot to pronounce 'Radhakrishna'"; or "The footprints of cows on unburnt tiles can easily be effaced, but when the tiles are burnt, those marks cannot be obliterated," and so on. He, therefore, put questions particularly to the students of schools and colleges uncontaminated by worldly life, and gathered whether the natural tendency of their minds was towards worldly enjoyment or renunciation, and if he thought them fit, guided them on the latter path.

14. The Master did not, however, stop simply with making out the mental state of a particular person by observing all his actions minutely; he investigated closely and saw how simple and truthful he was, how far he translated into action what he expressed in words, whether he performed every action with proper discrimination, and how far he was convinced of the truth of what was taught and so on. Here are a few examples.

15. A boy had been frequenting Dakshineswar for a few

days, when one day the Master asked him suddenly, "Why don't you get married?" "Sir," replied he, "my mind has not yet come under my control; if I am married now, I shall get attached to my wife and that will destroy my power of discrimination between what is beneficial and what is not. If I can ever conquer lust, I shall get married." The Master knew from this that, although there was attachment within, the mind of the boy had been attracted towards the path of renunciation, and said smiling, "There will be no necessity for marriage when you have conquered lust."

Talking to another boy one day at Dakshineswar on various topics, he said, "Will you please tell me what it is; I can by no means keep a piece of cloth always on my loins — it does not remain there, I fail even to know when it falls off. And I, a man so advanced in age, have to go about naked. But, nevertheless, I don't feel my nakedness. Formerly, I had no consciousness at all of who saw me in that state. Knowing that those who see me feel shame, I now keep a cloth on my lap. Can you stand (naked) like me in the presence of people?" The boy replied, "Sir, I am not sure, but I can put off my cloth if you ask me to." He said, "Just let me see; go round the courtyard of the temple with your cloth tied round your head like a turban." The boy said, "I cannot do that but I can do so before you only." The Master heard it and said, "Many others also say so. They say, 'We don't feel shame in putting off the wearing-cloth in your presence but feel it before others.'"

16. We remember another event in this connection. It was a night flooded with moonlight — the second or the third night of the dark fortnight. The flood-tide came to the Ganga shortly after we went to bed. The Master left his bed and ran to the embankment, calling everyone, "Come you all, to see the tide!" He danced like a boy to see the calm white water of the river, converted into high waves crested with foam, coming like one mad with a terrible force, and surging upward and leaping upon the embankment. We were drowsy when the Master called us. We were a little late in following him; for we had to get up and take care of our dress. Therefore, scarcely had we reached the embankment, when the tide passed away. Some of us saw a little of it while others saw nothing at all. The Master was so long happy by himself. When the tide went away he looked at us and said, "Well, did you witness the tide?" Hearing that the tide went away when we were putting on our dress, he said, "Ah, fools, will the tide wait for you to put

on your dress? Why did you not leave your cloth behind like me?"

17. In answer to the Master's questions such as, "Are you going to marry? Will you take service?" Some of us would reply, "Sir, I don't wish to marry, but I shall have to take service." But the answer seemed to the Master, who was a great lover of freedom, to be extremely unreasonable. He said, "If you will not marry and perform the duties of a family man, why should you be a servant of another for life? Offer your whole heart and mind to God and worship Him. A man, born in the world, cannot do anything greater than that. If you find it quite impossible to lead a single life, marry; but know once for all that God-realization is the ultimate aim of life. Tread the path of righteousness and live a householder's life." This was his definite opinion on the matter. Therefore, he felt a great blow at heart when he heard that any one of his young devotees, whom he considered as having more than average spiritual potentialities, had married, or was wasting his energy by taking service like ordinary people without any special reason for earning money, or was engaging himself in any other worldly occupation with a view to acquiring name and fame. One day, hearing that one of his boy-devotees, Niranjan (later Swami Niranjanananda), had taken service, the Master said to him, "You have taken service for maintaining your old mother; so, I can put up with it. Otherwise, I could not have looked at your face." When another boy-devotee, Naren junior, married and came to see him at the Kasipur garden, he threw his arms around his neck, as one does when mourning the loss of a son, and shed incessant tears, saying over and over again, "May you not forget God and completely sink in the sea of the world!"

18. Under the impulse of a new-born love of God, some devotees put a wrong interpretation on the saying, "No one can progress in spiritual life without faith," and started believing anything and every person without any discrimination. As soon as the keen eye of the Master noticed this, he understood their mistake and warned them. He, no doubt, advised people to tread the path of religion with faith alone as the guide. But he, nevertheless, advised them to exercise their power of discrimination to decide what was desirable and what was not. An intimate disciple of his once purchased an iron pan from a shopkeeper after reminding him of the divine chastisement that would fall on him if he dishonestly sold a bad article to him. When he came home, he found

that the pan given by the shopkeeper had a crack in it. The Master came to know of it and scolded him saying, "Should one be a fool because one has to be a devotee of God? Has the shopkeeper set up a shop to practise religion? And should piety be the reason for you to believe him and take the pan without even once examining it? Never do so again. If you want to buy articles, you should ascertain their real price from a few neighbouring shops, examine them thoroughly at the time of buying them, and you should not come away without demanding also the extra quantity of those articles which it is usual to give the customer when the transaction is over."

19. There is a tendency among people of certain temperament to become too mild and soft in the name of spiritual living with the result that it leads them sometimes astray from the spiritual path. This happens very often with men and women of tender nature. Therefore, the Master always taught such people to be stern and those of the opposite nature to be tender. The heart of one (Swami Yogananda) was too tender. It is doubtful whether we ever saw him being angry or using harsh words even when there was good reason for it. Unable to see his mother shed tears, he all of a sudden bound himself one day with the tie of matrimony, though it was completely against his nature and intention. The protecting power and the words of assurance of the Master alone saved him on that occasion from the terrible despair and repentance to which he fell a victim on account of that action of his. The Master kept a careful eye on him so that he might learn to control his tendency to excessive tenderness and mildness, and cultivate the habit of proceeding to do any action only after due deliberation. How the Master taught him with the help of trifling things will be clear when one or two incidents are mentioned here. One day a cockroach was seen in the case in which the Master's clothes and other things were kept. The Master said to him, "Catch the cockroach, take it outside the room, and kill it." He caught it and went out, but set it free instead of killing it. As soon as he came back, the Master asked, "Well, have you killed the cockroach?" Embarassed he said, "No, Sir, I set it free." The Master scolded him and said, "Ah! I told you to kill it and you set it free! Act exactly as I tell you; otherwise, you will follow your own whim in serious matters in future and will have to repent afterwards."

20. While he was coming to Dakshineswar one day in a boat,

Yogin (the same as Swami Yogananda), when questioned by one of the passengers, said that he was going to the Master at Rani Rasmani's Kali temple. Hardly had that man heard this when he started calumniating the Master thus: "Oh! He is a mere pretender, practising deceit on the public. He eats good food, lies on cushions, and turns the heads of school boys." Yogin was touched to the quick to hear those words; he thought of giving the man a bit of his mind. But under the influence of his mild nature, the next moment he thought, "Many people, without exerting themselves in the least to understand the Master, entertain quite a wrong conception of him and speak ill of him. What can I do in the matter?" Thinking so, he did not make the slightest protest against what that man said and remained silent. When he came to the Master, he related this incident to him in the course of conversation. Yogin was under the impression that the Master, who was devoid of egoism and was therefore never moved by praise or blame, would laugh it away when he heard about the incident. But the effect produced on the Master was very different. Seeing that event in a different light, he remarked, "Ah, he spoke ill of me without any reason, and you came away, listening silently without doing anything! Do you know what the scriptures say? One should cut off the head of the man speaking ill of one's Guru or leave that place. And you did not utter a single word of protest even against all that calumny!"

21. The reader will understand how the Master's instructions varied according to the temperaments of the taught, when we mention here another such event. Niranjan (the same as Swami Niranjanananda) was, by nature, of an impetuous temperament. While coming to Dakshineswar in a boat one day, he heard the passengers speak ill of the Master in the same manner as above. He at first protested very strongly against it. But as his protest did not make them desist, he became terribly angry and was ready to retaliate by sinking the boat. Niranjan was very strong and stout, and was an expert swimmer too. All shrank in fear to see him getting purple with anger, begged his pardon, and implored him to refrain from sinking the boat. The Master came to know of it afterwards and scolded him, saying, "Anger is a most dangerous and reprehensible sin. Should one be under its spell? As a mark made on water vanishes immediately, so does the anger of a good man. Mean-minded men speak many improper things. If one is to quarrel with them over such matters, one will have to spend

one's whole life time that way. Consider such men as no better than insects and be indifferent to their words. Just think what a great wrong you were going to commit under the influence of anger. What offence did the helmsman and oarsmen give you? You were ready to cause harm even to those poor people."

22. The Master gave similar instruction to women devotees as he did to men. He, we remember, warned a lady of mild temperament in the following words: "Suppose you feel that a certain acquaintance of yours takes great trouble and helps you in all matters, but unable to control the infatuation for beauty, his weak mind begins pining for you. Should you in that case give a free rein to your kindness to him or be severe upon him, deal him a hard kick and live far away from him? So, take note that one cannot afford to be kind to anybody and everybody under all conditions. There should be a limit to one's kindness. One should take into consideration the time, place and person in bestowing one's kindness."

23. We remember another incident relevent to this topic. Harish was a strong young man. He had a beautiful wife and a young child. His financial condition was good on the whole. He had paid but a few visits to the Master at Dakshineswar, when his mind became filled with the great idea of renunciation. Seeing his straightforward nature, steadfastness and calm mood, the Master was pleased with him and became his protecting angel. From that time, Harish began to spend most of his time at Dakshineswar in the Master's service, continual meditation, Japa and other forms of spiritual practice. His people pressed him to return home, but nothing — the pressure from his parents, loving invitations from his father-in-law or the bewailing of his wife — could move him. He took almost a vow of silence and proceeded along his path instead of taking notice of any remark from anybody. With a view to drawing our attention to his calm and steadfast temperament, the Master sometimes said, "Those who are men in the true sense of the term will be like Harish — they will remain dead to all provocations and will not give expression to any reaction."

24. While Harish thus lived at Dakshineswar, giving up all his worldly concerns, and engaging himself in Sadhana and devotional practices, word was brought to him one day that all the members of his family had become very much stricken with grief, and that his wife, unable to bear his separation any longer, had become

overwhelmed with sorrow and had almost given up food and drink. Harish heard it but remained silent as before. With a view to knowing his mind, the Master took him aside and said," Your wife is so much grieved. Why don't you go home and let her see you once? In a way it may be said that there is no one[1] to look after her. So, what is the harm if you are a little kind to her?" Harish said humbly, "Sir, this is not a case for showing kindness. If I am to be kind here, it is possible that I may become overwhelmed with worldly attachment and forget the main duty of my life. Pray, don't command me so." The Master was highly pleased with what he said and used to quote his words to us from time to time and praise his detachment.

25. Many examples can be given to show how the Master observed our ordinary daily actions and thus assessed the good and bad qualities of our minds. Seeing Niranjan take too much of ghee (clarified butter), he said, "To take so much of ghee! Will you at last abduct people's daughters and daughters-in-law?" Once the Master became displeased with a person for some time, because he slept too much. When another person, led by the strong desire to study the medical science, neglected to obey him, the Master said, "Far from giving up desires one after another, you are adding to them; how then can you expect to make spiritual progress?" We have placed before the reader many examples of this nature from time to time in connection with other topics. It is therefore needless to multiply them here.

26. Knowing with the help of the aforesaid methods the natural temperament of those who had taken refuge in him, the Master not only instructed them how to modify or rectify the defects, but tried again and again to find out how far the instructions were carried out. Besides, he was seen to adopt a particular means in order to ascertain the degree of the spiritual progress made by certain persons. The means was this and that was his fourth method: The Master made it a rule to observe whether the attitude of devotion and reverence, under the impulse of which a particular person came to him for the first time, was daily increasing or not. With a view to knowing it, the Master sometimes asked how far a particular person understood his own spiritual states or conduct of his. At other times he observed whether that person had perfect faith in all his words or not: and at still other times he helped him

[1] Harish's mother was not alive. That was perhaps why the Master said so.

in various ways, such as introducing him to those of like nature, close relationship with whom was likely to deepen his spiritual mood. Ultimately he became assured of a disciple's spiritual progress only when he found him develop a natural appreciation of him (the Master) as the highest manifestation of the spiritual ideal in the modern world.

27. The reader will no doubt be surprised to hear the abovementioned words. But a little thought will make it clear that there is nothing to be surprised at the idea; on the contrary, it was but reasonable and natural for the Master to say so. He had no alternative but to behave that way, because he actually felt that in him there was a manifestation of spirituality to an extent never known before. We have tried to explain, elsewhere, dear reader, that as a result of the long practice of austerity, meditation and Samadhi, egoism had been completely destroyed, and the very possibility of any error or delusion in him, too, had vanished for ever.

Unlimited memory and infinite knowledge manifested in his mind. Consequently a conviction had dawned on his mind that through him was being revealed a spiritual ideal which humanity had never before witnessed anywhere else in the world. Therefore, he had naturally to believe that all those who properly comprehended it and tried to illumine their lives with the light of that ideal, would easily make spiritual progress in the modern age. It was, therefore, not surprising that he should scrutinise thoroughly whether those who came to him arrived at a proper understanding of what has been stated before about him, and whether they were making efforts to mould their lives after the highly liberal ideas manifested in him.

The Master expressed the above-mentioned conviction of his mind in various ways. He used to say, "A coin of the time of the Nawabs is not legal tender during the period of the Badshas"; "You will straight away reach the goal if you move on as I say"; "He who is living his last life, who has come to the end of his series of transmigrations, (i.e., who is to be liberated in this life) alone will come and accept the liberal doctrine of this place"; "Your chosen Ideal is residing here (showing himself); if you meditate on this, you will be meditating on Him" and so on. We shall give here a few examples to illustrate how the Master used to ascertain, through enquiries, the extent of the faith and understanding that the disciples had of him. The reader will then be in a better position to grasp what we have stated here.

28. Whoever has had the blessing of meeting the Master and receiving his grace knows that the Master, when alone or in the company of the select few, would suddenly put this question to a fortunate devotee, "Well, what's your idea about me? Who am I?" This question used to be put generally to persons who had for a considerable time been closely known to him. But this was not always the case. Sometimes he chose to put this question to a devotee on his first visit or very shortly after. These were the devotees, whose coming had long ago been announced to him through Yogic visions. What a variety of answers he used to get from them, cannot be described. Briefly they were: "You are a 'true Sadhu', 'a true devotee of God', 'a great soul', 'a perfected man', 'an incarnation of God', 'an equal of Krishna, Buddha, Chaitanya and other great ones'" and so on. Again asked thus, a person named Williams[1], a Christian, expressed his opinion that the Master was "Jesus himself, the Son of God, the embodiment of Eternal Consciousness." We cannot say how far all these persons understood him; but they, in making these statements, expressed their own ideas of the Master and of God at the same time. The Master, for his part, looked at those answers of theirs in the light mentioned above, and behaved towards them and instructed them according to the spiritual attitude of each. For, instead of destroying anybody's spiritual attitude, the Master, being the embodiment of all spiritual attitudes and sentiments, helped everyone to develop his own mood and attitude to the highest degree and ultimately realize the Divine Lord whose real nature is Truth and who is beyond time and space. But he was very particular to notice whether the man expressed his own idea or was prompted by another.

29. Purna[2], a disciple, was a mere boy when he came to the Master. It seemed he was just a little over thirteen then. Sri Mahendra, the great devotee of the Master, was then the headmaster of the school at Shyambazar, established by the broad-minded

[1] This person, we came to know from a reliable source, came to the conclusion that the Master was an incarnation of God after paying but a few visits to him, and renounced the world according to his instruction. He engaged himself in practising austerities at some place in the Himalayas to the north of the Punjab till he died.

[2] Purnachandra Ghosh.

Vidyasagar. He used to bring to the Master at Dakshineswar those boys who by nature were found to possess love of God. Thus he took to him, one after another, Tejchandra, Narayan, Haripada, Vinod, Junior Naren, Pramatha (Paltu), and other boys of the Baghbazar quarter who took refuge in the Master. Some of us, therefore, called him in fun "the kidnapping teacher." Hearing it, the Master would say smiling, "It is the right appellation for him." One day while teaching the boys of class three of the school, his mind was attracted by the fine nature and sweet talk of Purna and shortly afterwards he made arrangements for introducing the boy to the Master. The arrangements were of course made secretly. For Purna's guardians were men of a harsh temperament; so if they should know of it, both teacher and pupil were sure to meet with rough treatment at their hands. Purna, therefore, came to school at the usual time and went to Dakshineswar in a hired carriage and returned to the school before it was closed for the day. He went home at the usual hour.

30. The Master was highly pleased to see Purna that day, and, giving him instruction and light refreshments with great affection, said at the time of his return, "Come whenever it is convenient for you; come in a carriage; there will be arrangements here about the payment of your carriage hire." He said to us afterwards, "Purna is a part of Narayana and a spiritual aspirant possessing a high degree of Sattva. In this respect, he may be said to occupy a place immediately below Naren. The coming of Purna marks the end of the arrival of that class of devotees whom I saw in a vision as specially commissioned to come here for spiritual realisation. Therefore, no more persons of that class will come here in future."

31. Purna had an extraordinary change in his mental state that day. The memory of his past relation with the Master was awakened. It made him completely calm and indrawn. Incessant tears of bliss streamed forth from his eyes. For fear of his guardians, he had to make a great effort to control himself before he went home that day. There appeared since then a very great eagerness in the Master's mind to see Purna often and feed him. He sent him various kinds of food whenever there was an opportunity. He instructed the man who took them to Purna to hand them over to him privately. For, if that were known in his household, there was a possibility of his being ill-treated.

32. On many occasions we saw the Master shedding incessant tears because of his eagerness to see Purna. Seeing us full of surprise at this behaviour, he said one day, "You are amazed to see me thus attracted towards Purna; I don't know how you would have felt had you seen the longing that arose in my heart when I first saw Naren and how very restless I was on that occasion." Whenever he was eager to see Purna, the Master would come to Calcutta at midday, and going to Balaram Basu's house at Baghbazar or to the house of anyone else of that quarter, would send word and have him called from school. It was at one of such places that Purna had the privilege of seeing the Master for the second time and was completely merged in his self that day. The Master on that occasion fed him with his own hand like an affectionate mother and asked him, "Well, what's your idea about me? Who am I?" Overwhelmed by an extraordinary impulse of the heart and swelling with devotion, Purna replied, "You are the Divine Lord, God himself."

33. The Master found no limit to his joy and astonishment that day when he knew that the boy Purna could accept him as the highest spiritual ideal as soon as he saw him. He blessed the boy with all his heart and gave him instruction about the secret of spiritual practice and initiated him with a potent sacred Mantra. Afterwards, returning to Dakshineswar, he said to us again and again, "Well, Purna is a mere boy; his intellect has not developed, yet how has he understood it? Under the impulse of divine impressions some others also gave the same answer to that question. It is surely due to the impressions accumulated during previous lives that the picture of untarnished truth naturally appears to their pure Sattvika mind."

34. Purna had to marry by the force of circumstances and live a family life. But all those who were closely related with him unanimously bear witness to his extraordinary faith, reliance on God, love of Sadhana, freedom from egoism, and selflessness in all respects.

35. We shall give another example of the Master putting that question to the devotees who took refuge in him. There was a picture of the great lord Sri Chaitanya in Sankirtan in his room at Dakshineswar temple. The Master showed this picture to a person very well known to us, shortly after that person came to Dakshineswar, and said, "Do you see how all these are filled with divine emotions?"

That person: "Sir, they are all low-class fellows."

The Master : "How is it? Should one say so?"

That person: "Yes Sir; I belong to Nadia. I know these Vaishnavas are generally low-class fellows."

The Master : "You belong to Nadia; then I make another salutation to you. Well, Ram and others call this (showing his own person) an incarnation. Let me know what you think of it."

That person: "Sir, do they use a word of such low import?"

The Master : "How is that? They say 'incarnation of God', and you say it is of 'low import!'"

That person: "Yes sir; an incarnation is a part of God; to me it seems you are Siva Himself."

The Master : "What do you say!"

That person: "That thought comes to my mind; pray, what can I do? You have asked me to meditate on Siva; but I cannot succeed in it, though I try daily to do so. As soon as I sit down for meditation, your gracious face appears radiant before me. I can by no means bring in Siva by removing it, nor do I feel inclined to. So, I meditate only on you as Siva."

The Master: (affectionately smiling) "Oh! Don't speak like that. For I know, I am like a tiny hair of yours. (Both laughed) I had much anxiety about you; I am now freed of it today."

We do not know whether that person understood at that time why the Master spoke the last words quoted. On such occasions our hearts swelled with joy to feel that the Master had become pleased, and we yearned no more to go deep into the significance of his words. The Master, we feel, said those words to that person because he knew that the person had accepted him as the highest spiritual ideal.

36. The Master tried his best to see that the devotees who took refuge in him, did so only after they had observed him and his ways minutely and were convinced of his genuineness. For, he used to tell us very often, "Observe a holy man in the daytime, observe him at night and then have faith in him." The Master always encouraged us to observe whether a holy man practised what he taught others. He said that one should not believe a man whose thoughts, words and actions do not tally with one another. We heard the Master sometimes tell a story in this connection.

37. There was a man whose young son always suffered from indigestion. One day the father took him for treatment to a famous

physician in a remote village. The physician examined the boy and diagnosed his disease. But, instead of prescribing medicine for the patient, he asked him to come again on the morrow. When the father went to him the next day with his son, the physician said to the boy, "Give up taking molasses and the disease will be cured; there is no need to take medicine." Hearing these words, the father said, "Sir, you might have very well said this yesterday; in that case, I need not have taken so much trouble to come so far today." The physician replied, "Don't you see? I had a few jars full of molasses here yesterday. You perhaps noticed it. Had I forbidden the boy yesterday to take molasses, he would have thought that the physician was a peculiar person indeed; he takes so much of molasses himself and asks me to refrain from it! Thinking so, he would not have any faith in my words, not to speak of regard for them. That is why I did not tell you so before removing the jars of molasses."

38. Instructed by the Master himself, all of us minutely observed his behaviour and ways of life in order to see whether they tallied with his professions. Some, again, did not hesitate to test him. It was seen that he gladly put up with all this undue liberty we took with him, knowing that it was done in all sincerity and would go to strengthen our faith and devotion. The following incident is a clear example of this.

39. We have already told the reader certain things about Swami Yogananda. He was the hero of this story, and it was from him that we heard it afterwards. We shall first give a brief introductory description of Swami Yogananda before we begin to narrate the story. The premonastic name of Yogananda was Yogindranath Ray Chaudhuri. He was born in a well-known family of Savarna Chaudhuris. His father Navinchandra was a rich zamindar at one time and the family had been living for generations in the village of Dakshineswar itself. In Yogindra's home the worship of the Deity was always performed, and the place resounded ever with Kirtan and the recital of the Mahabharata, the Bhagavata and other scriptures. It was so during his childhood and even before. The Master said that he went to that house many times during the period of his sadhana with a view to listening to the discourses on Hari and was acquainted with some of the members of the house. But by the time Yogindra passed his early boyhood, the family had lost a major part of their property owing to domestic quarrels

and various other reasons, and the Chaudhuri family was fast approaching penury.

40. Yogindra was calm, mild and possessed of a sweet nature from his childhood. He was born with extraordinary good qualities. From his early boyhood, in fact ever since self-awareness dawned in him, he had always the feeling that he was not of this world — that his real home was not here but in a certain distant group of stars where all his familiar companions were still staying. We never saw him becoming angry. Swami Vivekananda said, "If there is any one amongst us who has conquered lust in all respects, it is Yogin." Although he was sometimes scolded by the Master to eradicate his tendency to naively believe all sorts of people, Yogindra was not foolish. In spite of his being quiet and always engaged in his own duties, his active mind would be observing the actions of all people, and the conclusions he arrived at about them proved to be invariably true. This developed in him some sort of pride in his own intelligence.

41. Being a resident of Dakshineswar, he had the blessing of meeting the Master when he had hardly reached his youth. The Master was highly pleased to see him when Yogindra was introduced to him for the first time. He became convinced that he was one of those who had been shown by the Divine Mother long ago as destined to come to him for spiritual enlightenment; nay, he came to know a little after, by the grace of the universal Mother, that he was one of those six persons who belonged to the class of Isvarakotis.

42. We have said elsewhere that Yogindra married suddenly against his own will on account of his mother's pathetic weeping. He said, "As soon as I married, the thought came to me that the hope of God-realisation was now a mockery. Why should I go to the Master whose very first teaching was the renunciation of lust and gold? I have spoilt my life on account of the tenderness of my heart. It cannot be undone now. The sooner I die the better for me. I used to visit the Master daily before; but, after this event, I altogether stopped going to him and passed my days in utter despair and repentance. But the Master did not forsake me. He sent word again and again, calling me to him; but when he saw that I did not go in spite of all that, he hit upon a peculiar device. A certain person of the Kali temple had given me a few rupees to buy some articles for him before my marriage. There was a balance of a few annas

left. I sent him the articles through a man and sent word also that I would soon send him the balance of money. The Master knew of this, and feigning anger, one day sent a man to tell me on his behalf, 'What sort of a man are you? You have neither returned the balance, nor even sent word when you will return it to the person who gave you money to buy his article! What you ought to have done was to submit an account of the money spent and to pay up the balance.' These words touched my pride, I was grievously wounded. I thought, 'The Master has taken me to be a cheat after such a long period of intimate relationship! Well, I'll go there somehow today and put an end to the quarrel, and afterwards I will never again turn my steps towards the Kali temple.' I was almost dead with despair, repentance, wounded pride and resentment. In the afternoon I went to the Kali temple. I saw from a distance that the Master was standing outside his room, as if in ecstasy, with his cloth in his arm-pit. As soon as he saw me, he came quickly forward, saying, 'Oh! what if you are married! Marry a lakh of times, no harm can touch you if you but have the grace of this place (meaning himself). If you want to live a family life and realize God at the same time, once bring your wife here; I'll make both her and you fit for that; and if you want to renounce wordly life and attain Him, I'll make that too quite possible for you.' These words of the Master spoken in a divine semi-absorbed mood penetrated deep into my heart, and the former darkness of despair vanished into the void. I bowed down to him with tears in my eyes. He, too, affectionately caught hold of my hand and entered his room with me. He did not give ear to what I was going to say about the settlement of the account and the return of the balance amount, for which I had come."

Yogindra was born with the mood of an all-renouncing Sannyasin. He married, but that mood of his did not at all undergo any change. He began devoting his time increasingly to the service of the Master, now his only refuge. Yogin's parents began to complain when they saw their son indifferent to worldly affairs and to the acquisition of money. He said, "One day while mother was making that complaint, she remarked, 'Why then have you married if you don't like to apply your mind to money?' I said, 'I told you again and again at the time that I do so, only because I could not bear to see you weep.' Highly incensed at these words, his mother replied, 'You don't say so! How could you marry for my sake, unless you had a desire to do so! Whoever will believe that!' Absolutely stunned at these words of hers, I thought, 'Ah, my Lord! She is the very person whose suffering I was unable to witness and for whose sake I was ready to forsake Thee! Away with it! There is no one else in the world except the Master whose thoughts and words tally. An absolute abhorrence for the world possessed my mind ever since. I started spending nights also with the Master since then."

43. Spending the whole day with the Master, one day Yogindra saw that all the devotees who were at Dakshineswar temple took leave of him just before dusk and went home. Yogindra gave up the idea of going home on that occasion, thinking that the Master might be in difficulty if he were in need of anything at night, when no one would be near him. The Master too became highly pleased to see Yogin pass the night there. Absorbed in spiritual talks they did not notice that the night was fairly advanced; it was ten. The Master then took some light refreshment. After Yogindra finished his meal, the Master asked him to sleep within the room and himself went to bed. When it was past midnight, the Master had a desire to go out and attend calls of nature; he looked at Yogin but found him fast asleep. Thinking that Yogin would be troubled if he woke him up, he proceeded alone towards the Panchavati and then went to the group of Tamarisk trees.

44. Yogindra was noted all his life for his short hours of sleep. His sleep came to an end shortly after the Master had left. Seeing that the door of the room had been left open, he sat up in his bed, and not finding the Master on his cot, wondered where he might have gone at that dead of night. He saw the Master's spouted and other water-pots in their proper places, and therefore thought the Master might be strolling outside. A terrible suspicion then gripped his mind. "Has the Master then gone to the Nahavat, where his wife lives? Does he also deny in action what he professes in words?"

45. Yogindra said, "No sooner had that thought crossed my mind than I became simultaneously overwhelmed with suspicion, fear and various other feelings. I decided that however cruel and unbecoming it might be, truth must be found out. I then stood at a place near at hand and began watching the door of the Nahavat. Scarcely had I done so for a couple of minutes when I heard the clattering sounds of slippers coming from the side of the Panchavati.

Very soon, the Master came up and stood before me and said affectionately, 'Ah you are standing here, I see.' I shrank within myself in shame and fear, thinking, 'Oh! I entertained such a mean suspicion of his character!' I stood there with my head hung down and could give no reply to him. The Master understood everything from my face, but instead of taking offence, at once reassured me and said, 'Well, it is all right. Observe a Sadhu in daytime as well as at night, and believe him then only.' Saying so, he asked me to follow him and proceeded towards his room. I could sleep no more that night, thinking what a great offence I had committed under the impulse of a suspicious nature."

46. Swami Yogananda fully atoned for the above-mentioned offence by surrendering himself to the Guru in all respects and laid down his life in the service, at first of the Master, and after his (the Master's) passing, in the service of the Holy Mother. A Yogi like Yogindra, having the experience of Samadhi, possessed of intense detachment and qualified equally for devotion and Divine Knowledge, is scarcely seen. He passed away in the year 1899 to merge in the Supreme Self.

47. We mentioned before that the Master always observed minutely every action of Narendra since he came to Dakshineswar. Consequently, he knew that courage, valour, self-control, love of religion, self-sacrifice for a good cause and other good qualities were the innate virtues of Narendra's heart. He knew that the hold of good impressions on his mind was so strong that it was impossible for him to do any mean action like ordinary people, even under the stress of adversity or temptations. And as to his devotion to truth, observing his austere devotion to it, the Master was so much impressed that he believed every word of his, and had the firm conviction that he would very soon reach such a state that truth and truth only would come out of his mouth and never an untruth even by mistake, and that even the chance ideas crossing his mind would prove to be true. He, therefore, always encouraged him in his regard for truth and said, "One who clings to truth with body, mind and speech is blessed with the vision of God who is Truth itself. A man who never deviates from truth for twelve years, attains whatever he desires."

48. We remember here a funny event regarding the Master's firm faith in Narendra's truthfulness. One day, in the course of a conversation he was explaining that the nature of a devotee is like

that of a Chataka bird. He said, "Just as a Chataka always looks to the cloud to quench its thirst and depends on it in all respects, even so, a devotee depends on God alone to quench the thirst of his heart and remove all his wants." Narendra was then sitting there. He suddenly said, "Sir, although it is generally believed that a Chataka drinks no water except rain-water, it is not true; it quenches its thirst with waters of rivers and other reservoirs of water like all other birds. I saw a Chataka bird drink such water." The Master said, "How is that? Does a Chataka drink such water like other birds? Such a long-standing conviction of mine is then proved to be false, I see. As you have seen it, I can have no doubt about it." The Master who was possessed of a boy's nature, did not rest satisfied by merely saying so. He thought that just as that conviction of his was proved to be false, so his other convictions might also prove to be so. Thinking thus, he felt much dejected. A few days after this talk, Narendra suddenly called the Master and said, "There, just see there, Sir! yonder Chataka is drinking water from the Ganga." The Master came in a hurry to see it and said. "Where is it?" Narendra showed a bird, which, the Master found, was only a small house-bat drinking water. He said smiling, "It is a house-bat. O rascal, you took a house-bat for a Chataka and caused me such great anxiety. I will no more believe in all that you say."

49. The mind of an ordinary man very often assumes in the presence of a lady an attitude of undue tenderness — of politeness, appreciation of beauty, and other noble emotions. According to the scriptures, this is not due to the impulse of a noble esteem, but due to that of subtle impressions of a sexual nature. Such impressions and their manifestations were totally absent in Narendra. The Master noticed this with great joy and was firmly convinced that Narendra would never be deflected from the path of self-control by the attraction of female beauty. One day, comparing Narendra with another devotee[1] who had received great respect from us at one time on account of his frequent trances, the Master said, "He loses himself in the care of, and affection for, ladies. But with Narendra it is quite different. I observed minutely, and found him in such situations saying, as it were, with his head turned about, 'Why are they here?' "

50. The Master said on many occasions that, although there

[1] Nityagopal. He assumed the name of Swami Jnanananda later in life.

was an unusual manifestation of Vedantic knowledge and the sterner qualities in Narendra's mind, there was no dearth of tenderness and devotion in it. He came to that conclusion by observing his mental states manifested through ordinary actions as well as his physical characteristics. Observing the loveliness of the features of Narendra's face, we remember him to have said one day, "Can persons of 'dry knowledge'[1] have such eyes? You have within you the womanly emotion of devotion as well as knowledge. Those who have within them merely the sterner qualities do not have round their nipples the black marks like those produced by a marking-nut. Arjuna, the great hero, did not have those marks."

51. The Master tested Narendra by other means known and unknown to us, besides the four kinds of general means mentioned above. Of those means we shall now tell the reader one or two important ones only. The Master, we have said before, used to busy himself about Narendra when the latter came to Dakshineswar. The moment he saw Narendra at a distance, his entire mind would run out of his body, as it were, with great speed and bind Narendra in an embrace of love. It is impossible to say on how many occasions we saw the Master go into ecstasy saying, "There's Na-, there's Na-". But a break came in this situation. At a certain phase of their relationship, it was noticed that the Master became quite cool and indifferent to Narendra. One day Narendra came as usual, bowed down to the Master, sat in front of him and waited long. But the Master remained supremely indifferent, not even inquiring about his welfare, let alone expressing his loving concern for him. Narendra thought that the Master was perhaps under the influence of spiritual emotions. Having waited long, he came out of the room and began to talk with Hazra, smoking. Hearing that the Master was talking to others, Narendra came back to him. But the Master did not speak a word to him and lay down on his bed with his face turned in the opposite direction. The whole day passed in that manner and evening approached; still Narendra found no change in the Master's attitude. So he bowed down to him and returned to Calcutta.

Hardly had a week elapsed, when Narendra came again to

[1] That kind of Vedantic knowledge which views the world to be wholly non-existing, drawing therefrom the corollary of absolute indifference to the sufferings of humanity and dumb creation and pooh-poohing the attitude of devotion to an all-pervading Personal God — Tr

Dakshineswar to find the Master in the same mood. On that occasion also he spent the whole day in various talks with Hazra and others, and started home before dusk. Narendra came for a third and a fourth time, without finding the slightest change in the attitude of the Master. But without feeling at all distressed or wounded on account of it, he continued paying visits to the Master as usual. The Master sent from time to time some one to bring him news of Narendra's welfare when Narendra was staying at home, but he continued to behave towards him with the same indifference whenever he came. At the end of more than a month, when the Master saw that Narendra did not desist from visiting Dakshineswar in spite of his indifferent attitude, he had him called to him one day and asked, "Well, I do not speak even a single word to you; still you are coming here. Why do you do so?" Narendra said, "Do I come here to hear what you speak? I love you; I wish to see you; that is why I come." Highly pleased with the reply, the Master said, "I was testing you to see whether you would cease coming if you did not get proper love and attention. It is only a spiritual aspirant of your order that can put up with so much neglect and indifference. Any one else would have left me long ago and never come here again."

52. We shall mention one more event and bring the present topic to a close. It will be well understood from this how intense was Narendra's eagerness for the direct realisation of God. One day the Master called him aside to the Panchavati and said, "As the result of practising austerities for long I have got all the eightfold supernatural powers like assuming the minute dimension of an atom and the rest. But where is the occasion for a person like me, who cannot even keep his cloth properly round his waist, to make any use of them? So, I am thinking of asking the Mother to transfer all these to you. For, She has told me that you will have to do much work for Her. If all these powers are imparted to you, you will be able to use them when necessary. What do you say?" Narendra had become acquainted with the infinite manifestation of Divine power in the Master since the day he first saw him at Dakshineswar. He had, therefore, no reason to disbelieve these words of his. But his inherent love of God would not allow him to accept those powers without careful consideration. Narendra thought seriously and asked, "Sir, will they help me in realizing God?" The Master replied, "They will be of no help to you in that respect, but they

will stand you in good stead when you engage yourself in God's work after realizing Him." Hearing these words, Narendra said, "Sir, I have no need of these things. Let me realize God first and then it can be decided whether to accept them or not. If I obtain these wonderful powers now, I may, goaded by selfishness, forget the aim of life and happen to make improper use of them. That will be wholly ruinous to me." It is beyond our power to say whether the Master was actually ready to impart such powers as assuming atomic dimension, etc., to Narendra, or spoke like that only to test his mind. But this much we know for certain that he was highly pleased to see Narendra unwilling to accept them.

CHAPTER VIII: SECTION 1

NARENDRANATH'S SCHOOLING IN THE WORLD AND BY THE MASTER

[TOPICS: 1. Narendra and the Master a point of contrast in their nature. 2. Narendra a free thinker. 3. Influence of social conditions and of his father on him. 4. Narendra dissatisfied with Western thought. 5. Narendra's vacillation between the Eastern and the Western systems of thought. 6. His resolve to attain to God remained unchanged. 7. Narendra's faith in God remained intact. 8. Narendra's Sadhana. 9. His devotion to the practice of meditation. 10. His vision of Buddha.]

1. Contrasting his own nature with that of Narendra, the Master would speak to us from time to time, "The person who is in this (himself) has the nature of a woman manifested in him, while the person who is in Naren has in him the manifestation of the nature proper to a man." It is difficult to ascertain what the Master exactly meant by these words. But we get a reasonable meaning when we study the paths along which they proceeded, the principal means which they adopted in their search for God, the ultimate Truth. For, the Master, it was observed, engaged himself in practising the various scriptural disciplines with full faith in them as soon as he was instructed by the Guru, while the behaviour of Narendra in this matter assumed an entirely different turn. Narendra, first of all, applied his intellect to ascertain whether there was any possibility of error in the words of the scriptures and of the teacher, and began practising them only when he regarded them as standing the test of reason. Although possessed of a firm faith in the existence of God owing to past impressions, Narendra all through his life entertained the idea that all men, without an exception, are liable to errors and superstitions; and that there is no reason why one should accept indiscriminately any word of any human being. It is superfluous to add that subjecting every expression of faith and devotion to the test of reason. and functioning exclusively in that attitude of mind in all matters of life, both sacred and secular, is generally regarded as a masculine trait in the modern age.

2. Environment plays a great part in influencing and mould-

ing human life at all times and in all places. It is, therefore, not at all surprising that its power and influence is seen in Narendra's life. Even before going to the Master, Narendra, by the exercise of his uncommon intellect, became well versed in English literature, in European and Indian histories, and in Western logic, and was thoroughly imbued with Western ideas, whose radical principle of research and free thinking entered into his very marrow as early as then. It was therefore natural that he should entertain doubts about the truth of the words of the scriptures in many cases and shrink from accepting any particular man as the Guru in any sense except that of an experienced teacher.

3. The ideals of life of Narendra's guardians and the condition of the contemporary Calcutta society contributed not a little to that attitude of his. His grandfather had a great faith in the Hindu scriptures all his life, and he became a monk; but Narendra's father lost that faith in consequence of his Western education, and became a free thinker. The poems of Hafiz, the Persian poet, and the words of Jesus recorded in the Bible, were regarded by him as the highest limit of spiritual ideas. This limitation of his spiritual horizon was largely the result of his incapacity to read the Gita and other Hindu Sastras on account of his ignorance of the Sanskrit language. When one day he saw Narendra perusing religious texts, he presented a copy of the Bible to him and said, "If there be anything called religion, it is contained in this." Although he thus praised the Bible and the poems of Hafiz, his life was not spiritually moulded by the ideas contained in those books too. Spirituality seems to have been alien to his nature, and the admiration he expressed even for those books was only superficial. According to him the ultimate aim of life was to earn money, live a happy life himself, and contribute to others' happiness by helping them as far as possible. One can see from this and a study of his daily life how lax was his faith in God, the individual self, and the hereafter. Western materialism, based on the idea that this world was all in all, produced in the minds of persons like Narendra's father, a terrible doubt about metaphysical entities, and in many cases gave rise to an atheistic bent of mind. They were sure that there was nothing to be learnt from the ancient Rishis and the Sastras, these being, in their eyes, the sources of all superstition and weakness. Consequently, devoid of the spiritual backbone and faith in religion, they cherished one set of ideas inwardly but

behaved in a different way outwardly, thus becoming more and more selfish and hypocritical. The Brahmo Samaj, established by that great intellectual Raja Rammohan Roy, tried for a short time to stem that country-wide tide of atheism and materialism; but under the high pressure of Western civilization, that organization too was split into two parties on account of internal quarrels, and lost its original splendour soon. It became also increasingly evident that the followers of both the parties allowed themselves to be carried along by the prevailing materialistic thought current at the time.

4. Narendra became well acquainted with Western sciences and philosophy after his F.A. examination in 1881. He had already mastered the doctrines of Mill and other Western logicians. There arose now a great yearning in his heart to master Descartes's doctrine expressed briefly as "I think, therefore I am" *(cogito ergo sum)*, the atheism of Hume and Bentham, Spinoza's pantheism, Darwin's doctrine of evolution, Comte's positivism, Spencer's agnosticism and other philosophical doctrines of Western thinkers in order to ascertain the nature of Reality. Hearing of the great fame of the German philosophers, he tried to get acquainted as far as possible with the doctrines of Kant, Fichte, Hegel, Schopenhauer and others. Again, in order to know how the nerves and the brain are formed and how they function, he went from time to time to the Calcutta Medical College with his friends and applied his mind to the study of physiology and listened to the lectures on the subject. Consequently he had much knowledge of Western philosophy even before he passed the B.A. Degree Examination in 1884. But as a result of these studies the current of unrest only flowed all the nore swiftly in his mind inasmuch as the knowledge acquired thereby proved clearly the utter inadequacy of the human mind and intellect to define their own scope and to reveal a glimpse of the truth existing beyond these limits, far less to give us any sure means for the realization of God, that Absolute Truth, and the attainment of eternal peace.

5. Narendra clearly understood with the aid of Western science and philosophy that stimuli from external sources, reaching the brain through the sense organs, evoke various reactions from the brain, which result in constant mental changes giving pleasurable and painful experiences. Man has direct knowledge only of these mental changes and their results occuring in himself, and even that

only as mediated by space and time. Beyond that, the source from which the external stimuli are supposed to come, remains unknown and unknowable to him. This limitation holds good also for the internal world and the real nature of man himself. In respect of the internal world, though man has a vague awareness of an unknown entity producing the sense of I and other ideas, he cannot grasp the nature of that in itself because of the intervention of space and time. Thus kept back by the impregnable wall of space and time, the human mind finds itself absolutely helpless in whatever direction, inward or outward, it proceeds in search of the ultimate Reality. Narendra thus came to recognise that the five senses of knowledge, the mind and the intellect, with the help of which man has been attempting to unveil the mystery of the universe, cannot succeed in revealing its ultimate cause; that the sense perceptions on the basis of which man proceeds to build his arguments and draw conclusions, are themselves full of errors and mistakes; and that for this reason all the attempts of the Western savants to ascertain the existence of a self apart from the body have been a miserable failure. The ultimate conclusions of Western philosophy regarding the spiritual truth did not, therefore, appear to be reasonable to Narendra. There arose also a serious doubt in his mind as to which of the two alternatives would be the better — whether to found philosophy in imitation of the West on the acceptance of the naturalness and truth of the sense perceptions of man, who is ever attracted to the enjoyments offered by those very senses, or to accept unquestioningly according to the practice obtaining in the East, the uncommon realisations of great souls like the Rishis, the Buddha, and Jesus, who had overcome the thraldom of the senses, in spite of the fact that their experiences ran counter to those of ordinary men depending exclusively on the senses.

6. Although a greater part of the conclusions of Western philosophy regarding spirituality appeared to Narendra to be unreasonable, he greatly extolled the Western discoveries in the field of material sciences and their scientific method of observation and experiment. In his examination of the truths of psychology and spirituality, he always took the help of their discoveries and method of analysis. He always tried since then to analyse and understand the extraordinary realizations of the Master, and only those of them which stood these tests, he accepted as true and fearlessly followed in practice. Though a terrible restlessness for the

realization of the Truth was gnawing his heart, still it was against his nature to do anything unintelligently or to respect any one out of fear. If atheism were the inevitable result of the exercise of discrimination to the utmost of his power, he was ever ready to accept that even. He would not shrink from truth or from the endeavour to solve life's mystery even at the cost of his life, not to speak of the enjoyment of pleasures in the world. Having, therefore, a steadfast eye on the pursuit of the ultimate truth, he now engaged himself in the study of Western thought, accepting, however, only its more positive and healthy features. He gave up the straight path of faith and devotion under its influence, as doubts oppressed and sometimes overwhelmed him. His extraordinary perserverance and intellectual powers, however, prevailed finally and helped him to have the ultimate aim of his life fulfilled at last. But people at large, without a proper understanding of all this, thought that Narendra accepted indiscriminately all the opinions published in Western books. His partiality at the time for the Western philosophic outlook and for Western thinkers became so well-known among his friends, that when one day, after having read the Gita, he eulogized it highly, they were taken aback and reported the matter to the Master. The Master, too, said, "I hope he did not do so because some Western scholars had expressed that opinion."

7. One thing, however, is to be carefully noted, that Narendra had met the Master and had had a few extraordinary spiritual experiences before he came into contact with Western thought which produced the great revolution in his ideas. We have already told the reader of those experiences. It is clear that they helped him very much in placing firm faith in the existence of God. Otherwise, it is difficult to ascertain whether and how far he would have been carried away by the Western ideas and doctrines which proved that God, the cause of the universe, was unknown and unknowable. Although they would not have altogether destroyed his faith in the existence of God on account of the strong spiritual impressions of his past, there was every chance of its being terribly shaken by the impact. But that was not to be. For, was not his life being moulded by Providence for the accomplishment of a special task in the world? The Guru, the knower of Brahman, in whom he found a refuge by the grace of God, said to him over and over again, "God always hears the plaintive prayer of man; He can be seen,

heard and touched palpably, being more real than the fact of our worldly experience. I stake my credit on this." On another occasion, he said to him, "If you cannot accept the form of God or the common well-known ideas about Him because they are the products of human thought, but at the same time have faith in the existence of a God as the controller of the universe, He will certainly bestow His grace on you, provided you offer such a plaintive prayer as this, 'O God, I don't know Thy nature; do Thou manifest Thyself to me as Thou really art!'" It is superfluous to say that these words of the Master reassured him immensely and made him apply his mind to Sadhana with greater zeal than ever.

8. Hamilton, the Western philosoper, has said at the end of his book on philosophy that the human intellect can give only a mere indication of the existence of God, the Controller of this world, and there its function ends. It is not in its power to reveal the nature of God. So, here philosophy ends; and "where philosophy ends there religion begins." Narendra liked these words of Hamilton very much. He quoted it to us many times in the course of his conversations. Narendra, however, did not give up the study of philosophy, though he applied his mind to Sadhana. He practically spent his time in music, meditation and study.

9. Narendra adopted a new method of practising meditation from that time on. We have already said that in our meditation on the Lord, with or without forms, we can think of Him only anthropomorphically. Before he realized this, Narendranath used to apply his mind during meditation to the thought of the formless Brahman with attributes as prescribed by the Brahmo Samaj. But coming to the conclusion that even this conception about the nature of God was anthropomorphic, he now gave up that kind of meditation also and prayed to the effect: "O God, make me fit to see your real nature." He then removed all kinds of thought from his mind, and keeping it still and motionless like the flame of a lamp in a windless place, tried to remain in that state. As the result of doing so for a short time, Narendra's mind, which had all along been restrained, used to merge in itself so deeply that even the consciousness of time and of his own body disappeared now and then. He sat for meditation in his room when all the household had gone to bed and spent whole nights that way on many occasions.

10. As the result of that, one day, Narendra had an extraordinary vision. Later, he described it thus to us in the course of

conversation: "There flowed in my mind a current of serene bliss when I kept it still, devoid of all objects. I felt for a long time even after the end of the meditation, a sort of intoxication under its impulse. So, I did not feel inclined to leave the seat and get up immediately. One day when I was sitting in that condition at the end of the meditation, I saw the extraordinary figure of a monk appear suddenly, — from where I did not know, — and stand before me at a little distance, filling the room with a divine effulgence. He was in ochre cloth with a Kamandalu in his hand. His face bore such a calm and serene expression of inwardness born of indifference to all things that I was amazed and felt much drawn towards him. He walked forward towards me with a slow step, with his eyes steadfastly fixed on me, as if he wanted to say something. But I was seized with fear and could not keep quiet. I got up from my seat, opened the door and walked out of the room with rapid steps. The next moment I thought 'Why this foolish fear?' I made bold and went back into the room to hear the monk, but he was no longer there. I waited long in vain and felt dejected, repenting that I had been stupid enough to fly away without listening to him. I have seen many monks, but never have I found such an extraordinary expression in any other face. That face has been indelibly imprinted in my heart. It may be a hallucination, but very often it comes to my mind that I had the good fortune of seeing the Lord Buddha that day."

CHAPTER VIII SECTION 2

NARENDRANATH'S SCHOOLING IN THE WORLD AND BY THE MASTER ---- (contd.)

[TOPICS: 1. Narendra as an attorney's junior. 2. His resolution to observe life-long continence. 3. His inclination to become a Sannyasin. 4. Narendra continued visiting the Master. 5. How he spent his time with him. 6. Bhavanath Narendra and friends of Baranagar. 7. The sudden death of Narendra's father. 8. A deplorable change in his worldly circumstances. 9. Narendra's description of that condition. 10. Grinding poverty. 11. Temptation by women. 12. His mother's admonition. 13. Atheism due to the wounded feeling. 14. The Master's continued faith in his character. 15. Gnawing unrest. 16. Gaining peace on account of an extraordinary vision. 17. His resolve to become a monk. 18. Delays it at the Master's behest. 19. His prayer to the Master for relief from poverty. 20. Narendra's vision of the Divine Mother. 21. Narendra's failure thrice to pray to the Divine Mother for riches. 22. Narendra got faith in the worship of God in images. 23. The Master's happiness over this. 24. The Master's keen sense of affinity with Narendra. 25. Vaikuntha came to Calcutta with Narendra.]

1. Narendra spent his time in seclusion, in studies, in the practice of austerity, and in frequenting Dakshineswar. Planning his future, Narendra's father employed him at that time to learn the profession of an attorney as a junior to Nimai Charan Basu, the well-known attorney of Calcutta. For finally settling his son in the life of the world, Viswanath now began searching for a suitable bride. But his hopes in this respect were being delayed from fulfilment, as Narendra had a great objection to marriage and as he, Viswanath, could not, on his part, find out a suitable bride.

2. The Master sometimes happened to go to Narendra's study at Ramtanu Basu's Lane and give him various instructions regarding Sadhana. At that time he always encouraged him to observe continence and warned him against foolishly binding himself down to matrimony at the plaintive persuasions of his parents. The Master said to him, "As the result of observing continuous continence for twelve years, man has his retentive nerve opened. His intellect can then penetrate into subtlest things and comprehend them; it is with the help of that intellect only that God can be

realized; it is only to such a pure intellect that He reveals Himself."

3. At that time there arose an impression in the minds of the ladies of the house that Narendra was unwilling to marry owing to his close assosiation with the Master. Narendra said, "One day when the Master came to my study and was giving me the instruction to observe life long continence, my grandmother overheard everything and informed my parents of it. They began making great efforts from that day to get me married lest I should become a monk by moving with a Sadhu. But of what avail was all that? All their efforts against the strong will of the Master failed. Even when everything was settled, the marriage negotiations broke off in a few cases on account of the difference of opinion between the two parties about trifling things."

4. Although Narendra's frequent visits to the Master at Dakshineswar were not to the liking of any one of his household, no one ventured to make any remark about it to him. For Narendra, the dearest son of his parents, paid no heed from his childhood to the restraints set by any one on his conduct and took the liberty of behaving as he liked in everything. All the household knew that, if they tried to prevent the keenly intelligent Narendra from carrying out his will in any important resolution of his in the manner people do with a boy or a weak-minded young man, the result would most likely be the contrary. Narendra, therefore, went on visiting the Master at Dakshinswar as before.

5. The sweet memory of the days Narendra spent with the Master at Dakshineswar during this period filled his mind with infinite joy throughout his life. He said, "It is difficult to explain to others how blissfully I spent my days with the Master. It is simply astonishing to think how, through play, merriment and other ordinary daily activities, he gave us the most exalted spiritual education and moulded our lives without our knowledge. A powerful wrestler instructing a boy displays only a little of his skill and power — just what is needed for the purpose of teaching. He produces self-confidence in the boy, sometimes by appearing to defeat him only with great difficulty, and sometimes by allowing himself to be defeated by him. The Master assumed such an attitude in teaching us, his disciples. He saw 'a whole sea in a drop of water', as they say. Through ecstasy he had the knowledge that the seed of spirituality hidden in our hearts would one day develop into a fully developed tree with flowers and fruits. He would praise and

encourage us in every way and at all times. And observing very carefully each of our actions, he kept us under restraint by giving us instruction lest we should get entangled in worldly attachments, desires and ambitions and fail to reach our spiritual goal. But we would not know at all that he observed us so minutely and controlled us so effectively. That was an extraordinary skill which the Master displayed in teaching us and moulding our lives. We felt that the mind, although getting a little concentrated at the time of meditation, could not dive deeper for want of a proper object. We asked him what we should do in such a situation, and in reply he used to tell us what he himself had done in similar circumstances and suggested various useful methods. When I sat for meditation during the last part of the night, the mind, I remember, became distracted and deflected from the object of meditation on account of the noise produced by the whistling sound of the jute Mills of Alambazar. When I referred the matter to the Master, he advised me to concentrate my mind upon the sound of the whistle itself, and I derived much benefit from doing so. On another occasion, I apprised him of my difficulty in forgetting the body and concentrating the mind on the goal and sought his advice. The Master, recounting Sri Tota Puri's instruction to him when he was practising under him, said, "He pierced my forehead between the eyebrows with the sharp tip of his nail, saying, 'Concentrate your mind upon that pain.' And actually I found that the pain produced by that nail impression could be kept uniformly in the mind as long as I liked, and I completely forgot even the existence of all the other parts of the body, let alone the distractions of the mind by them. " The secluded Panchavati, the place of the Master's Sadhana, was very well suited for our meditation and other spiritual exercises. Why speak of spiritual exercises alone? We spent much time there in play and merriment also. At those times the Master often joined us and added to our happiness. There we ran about, climbed trees, and sitting in the swing formed by the cable-strong Madhavi creepers, swung freely and merrily; and sometimes we picnicked, cooking our meals ourselves. Seeing on one such day that I cooked the food with my own hand at the picnic, the Master himself took that cooked rice and other preparations. I knew that he did not take cooked rice out of the hands of people other than Brahmanas. I was therefore going to arrange for him the offered food of the temple. But he prevented me from doing so and said, 'Nothing will happen to me if I take food cooked by a person of pure Sattva like you!' I raised repeated objections, but he did take the rice cooked by me that day without paying attention to my remonstrances."

6. A devout person of pleasant looks named Bhavanath Chattopadhyaya, who had been visiting the Master for some time, became acquainted with Narendra and contracted friendship with him. Bhavanath was dear to the Master on account of his faith, devotion, humility and simplicity. Seeing his tender nature, which resembled that of a woman, and his uncommon love for Narendra, the Master sometimes said jokingly, "You were perhaps the life-companion of Narendra in a previous birth." Bhavanath lived at Baranagar, and whenever there was an opportunity, took Narendra to his house and fed him. Satkari Lahiri, Bhavanath's neighbour, was very well acquainted with Narendra; and Dasarathi Sannyal was Narendra's class-mate and friend. Whenever Narendra was available, they spent days and nights with him. So, now and then, on the occasions of his visit to Dakshineswar or sometimes when specially invited by them, Narendra used to spend a few hours or a day or two with these Baranagar friends of his.

7. The even flow of the course of Narendra's life got a violent jolt, early in the year 1884, sometime before the result of the B.A. Examination was out. His father, Viswanath had had a nervous breakdown sometime previously on account of over-work. One night at about 10 p.m., he suddenly died of heart-failure. Invited by his Baranagar friends, Narendra had gone to them in the afternoon of that day and occupied himself in singing devotional songs till about eleven at night. He then lay in the same room after taking his meal with them, and was engaged in conversation with his friends till late in the night. At about 2 a.m. his friend Hemali arrived with the startling news of his father's sudden demise. Narendra started home immediately.

8. Narendra returned home and performed the obsequies of his father. On making inquiries afterwards, he came to know that the worldly circumstances of the family were extremely deplorable. Instead of leaving some property behind, his father had left only a debt, having spent more than what he had earned. Their relatives had improved their worldly circumstances with the help of Narendra's father, but in place of being grateful to the family, found in its present helpless condition a splendid opportunity for self-aggrandisement. They turned inimical and even plotted

to eject the family from their home. It might well be said that there was in fact no income for the family and yet five or six persons had somehow to be maintained. Brought up in a high style of living till now, Narendra now felt helpless. He knew not what he should do to maintain the family. He went about from place to place in search of a job, only to meet with frustration everywhere. It is said that when an unfavourable period occurs in one's life, even a hundred efforts on the part of one prove utterly futile. Three or four months elapsed, one after another, after the death of Narendra's father, but still the sky of Narendra's life continued to be as overcast as ever with clouds of poverty and uncertainty, devoid of any sign of the sunshine of relief to break its gloom. It is doubtful if he ever waded through such darkness again in his life. Talking of this period, he said sometimes to us:

9. "I went about hither and thither in search of a job even before the period of mourning was over. Suffering from lack of food and walking barefooted, I went from office to office with an application for a job in my hand in the blazing midday sun. Sympathizing with me in my sorrow, some of my very intimate friends would be with me some days, but on other days they could not be. But I was disappointed everywhere. From that very first experience of the hard realities of the world, I felt keenly that selfless sympathy was very rare anywhere, and that there was no place here for the weak and the poor. Those who deemed it a piece of good fortune to be able to help me only a day or two previously, now thought it fit to do the contrary. They made a wry face at me, and although able to help, showed reluctance to do so. When I had such experiences, the world very often seemed to me to have been created by a demon. One day, at that time, when I was going from place to place in the sun, my sole, I remember, got blistered. Extremely fatigued, I had to sit down in the shade of the Ochterloney Monument in the Maidan. A friend or two were with me that day or met me there by chance. One of them, I remember distinctly, sang by way of consoling me: 'Here blows the wind, the breath of Brahman, His grace palpable. . .' When I heard the song, I felt as if he was inflicting severe blows on my head. Remembering the sheer helpless condition of my mother and brothers, I burst out in resentment, despair and disappointment: 'Shut up. Those who are in the lap of luxury and do not know what the pinch of hunger means, and those whose nearest and dearest ones are not starving

and going naked — to such people, in the midst of the fullest enjoyment of life, such flights of imagination appear sweet and pleasing. I also had such days and felt similarly, but now, confronted with stern reality, all these sentiments seem to be a terrible mockery.'

10. "Maybe, the friend was highly offended to hear those words of mine. But how could he understand what a severe grinding poverty it was that had drawn those words out of my mouth? On leaving my bed in the morning and making secret enquiries, I found on some days that there was no food sufficient for all the household, and as there was no money in my pocket, I went out telling mother, 'I have an invitation to lunch with a friend of mine.' During those occasions, on some days I took very little food, and on others went without any food at all, so that the others of the family might have sufficient to eat. I was too proud to speak out these things to any one in the family or outside. Rich friends took me to their houses or gardens now as before and requested me to add to their pleasure with music. Unable to avoid them, I sometimes went with them and entertained them. But I did not feel inclined to express to them the feeling in my mind. They, too, never made enquiries of their own accord. A rare few of them, however, did ask me affectionately now and then, 'Why do you look so dejected and weak today? Please tell us the reason.' One of them, coming to know of my condition from another without my knowledge, began sending money to mother with anonymous letters from time to time, and thus put me under an eternal debt.

11. "Knowing of my poverty, some of those boyhood friends of mine, who had lost their character in youth and were earning some money by dishonest means, found now an opportunity and tried to drag me into their company. Some among them, who had met with a sudden change of circumstances like myself and adopted detestable means of earning their livelihood, I found did actually feel pained for my sake. Mahamaya, too, did not lag behind. She also found it a good opportunity to tempt me. A wealthy woman had had an evil design on me for a long time. Thinking that it was an opportune moment, she sent word proposing that I might accept her property with herself and put an end to my poverty. I rejected her suit with bitter contempt and sterness. Soon after, another woman came to allure me in that way, but I said to her, 'Ah, my child, how innumerable are the evil deeds you perpetrated so long for the satisfaction of this worthless body of

yours! Death is very near at hand. Have you made any provision for that day? Give up low-mindedness and call on the divine Lord.'

12. "In spite of all my trials, my faith in the existence of God did not vanish so long, nor did I doubt that 'God is good'. I used to wake up from sleep in the morning, remember the Lord, and leave my bed taking His name. Then with firm determination and hope I used to go from place to place in search of some means of earning money. One day, I was leaving my bed as usual, calling on the Lord, when my mother heard my words from the adjacent room and suddenly said, 'Stop, lad! you have been constantly repeating the name of the divine Lord ever since your childhood, — and now see how your divine Lord has left nothing undone!' These words hurt me terribly. Cut to the quick, I pondered, 'Does God actually exist? If so, does He hear the plaintive prayer of man? Why is there then no response to so much of prayer which I proffer to Him? Whence has so much of evil come in the creation of a benign Creator? Why is there so much of calamity in the kingdom of one who is all bliss?' Vidyasagar, pained at the suffering of others, asked himself at one time, why, if God were all goodness and all bliss, lakhs of people fell into the terrible jaws of famine and died for want of a morsel of rice. That query resounded in my ears as the reverberation of the bitterest mockery at all easy and easy-going optimism. My heart was pierced through by a feeling of wounded love, and doubt in the existence of God assailed my mind.

13. "It was against my nature to do something and conceal it from others. Nor could I, from my childhood, conceal, out of fear or from any other motive, even the least shade of thought, let alone my actions. Was it, therefore, surprising that I should, in the mood that seized me then, go aggressively forward to prove to the people that God did not exist, and that even if He did, there was no need to call on Him; for it was futile to do so? Consequently, a rumour soon spread that I had become an atheist and was mixing with people of bad character, and did not shrink from drinking and even from frequenting houses of ill-fame. Consequently, my heart, which had never been too docile from childhood, became steeled all the more on account of such false calumny. Even unasked, I was publicly telling one and all that not only had I no objection to anybody's drinking wine or going to a brothel with a view to forgetting his hard lot in this world of pain and misery, if he could feel happy thereby, but that I would myself do likewise

the very day I was perfectly convinced of becoming happy for a moment like them by doing so, and that I would not retract my steps for fear of anybody.

14. "News travels from ear to ear. It did not take long for these words of mine to get variously distorted and reach the Master's ears at Dakshineswar and those of his devotees in Calcutta. Some came to see me with a view to ascertaining the real state I was in, and they let me know by hints and suggestions that they were ready to believe something at least, if not all, of what they had heard. On knowing that they could stoop to believe me to be so degraded, I became terribly wounded at heart, and my injured feelings forced me to react by an anti-God campaign. I tried to prove that it was a great weakness to believe in God for fear of being punished. And quoting Hume, Mill, Bain, Comte and other Western philosphers, I started a fierce argumentation with them to prove that there was no evidence for the existence of God. Consequently, as I came to know afterwards, they went away far more convinced of my fall than ever before. I was happy to know that, and I thought that the Master would hear of it from them and would perhaps believe it too. The moment this thought crossed my mind, my heart was filled with a tragic sense born of wounded feeling. I came to the conclusion that there was no harm if he did so, inasmuch as people's opinions, good and bad, were worth so little. Later, however, I was surprised to hear that the Master had heard of it all from them, but had not expressed himself either way at first; but when afterwards Bhavanath wept and said to him, 'Sir, it was beyond even our dream that such would be Narendra's lot', he excitedly said, 'Silence! you fellows! The Mother has told me that he can never be degraded like that. If you mention it again to me, I'll not be able to put up with your presence.'

15. "But of what avail was it to indulge in atheism on account of pride and egoism? The extraordinary experiences that I had had from my childhood, more especially those that came subsequent to my meeting the Master, arose in bright colours in my mind, the next moment, and I thought, 'God certainly exists and the means to realize Him also certainly exist; otherwise what is life for; what is its worth? That path has to be searched out, however great the pain and misery the search might entail.' Time glided by and the mind wavered and doubted, and peace receded further than ever. My worldly wants too, showed no signs of abating.

16. "The rainy season followed the summer. The same search for a job continued as before. One day, drenched in rain and having had no food for the whole day, I was returning home at night with tired legs and a mind more weary than the body. The exhaustion was so great that, unable to proceed a single step further, I lay like a log of wood on the open verandah of a nearby house. I cannot say whether I lost consciousness altogether for some time; but I remember that thoughts and pictures of various colours, one after another, arose and vanished of themselves in my mind. I had no power to drive them away or to concentrate on one particular thought. I suddenly felt as if within my mind many screens were raised one after another by some providential power, and I saw in the innermost recesses of my heart the solutions of the problems which so long had baffled my intellect and distracted my mind — problems such as 'Why are there malignant forces in the creation of a benign God?' and where is the harmony between the stern justice and the infinite mercy of God?' I was beside myself with joy. Afterwards, when I resumed my walk home, I found that there was not an iota of fatigue in my body and that my mind was filled with infinite strength and peace. The day was then about to break.

17. "I became absolutely indifferent to the praise or blame of the world. And, firmly convinced that I was not born to earn money, serve the family and spend time in worldly enjoyment like people in general, I was secretly getting ready to renounce the world like my grandfather. When the day for starting on my itinerary was fixed, I heard the news that the Master would come to a devotee's house at Calcutta that day. I thought this a very good opportunity; I would see my Guru before I renounced home for ever. As soon as I met the Master, he said to me in a very earnest and compelling manner, 'You must come to Dakshineswar with me today.' I offered various excuses, but he was inexorable. I had to drive with him in his carriage. There was not much talk on the way. After reaching Dakshineswar, I sat with others in his room for some time, when the Master entered into ecstasy. In a moment he came suddenly to me, and taking my hand in his, began singing as tears flowed:

'I am afraid to speak,
And am equally afraid not to speak.
The doubt rises in my mind

Lest I should lose you, Ah my Rai,[1]
Lest I should lose you.

18. "For long I kept back the surge of the strong emotions of my mind, but could no more check their force. My breast too was flooded with tears like that of the Master. I was quite sure that the Master knew everything. All the others were astonished to see that behaviour of ours. Some asked the Master the reason for this after he came back to the normal state, when he smiled and answered, 'It is something between ourselves.' Afterwards, sending away all others, he called me to him at night and said, 'Know that you have come to the world for the Mother's work; you can never live a worldly life. But remain in your family for my sake as long as I live.' Saying so, the Master immediately began shedding tears again with his voice choked with emotion!

19. "I took leave of the Master and returned home the next day. And immediately, a hundred thoughts about the family occupied my mind. I now began going from place to place as before and made various efforts to secure a living for the family. I worked in the office of an attorney, and also translated a few books. By this means I earned a little money, and the household was managed somehow with it. But these were all temporary jobs; and in the absence of any permanent work no smooth arrangement for the maintenance of mother and brothers could be made. I remembered a little later that God would grant the Master's prayers. I must make him pray for me so that the suffering of my mother and brothers for want of food and clothing might be remedied; he would never refuse to do so for my sake. I hurried to Dakshineswar and asked persistently that he must pray to the Mother that the pecuniary difficulty of my mother and brothers might be removed. The Master said to me affectionately, 'My child, I cannot say such words, you know. Why don't you yourself pray? You don't accept the Mother; that is why you suffer so much.' I replied, 'I have no knowledge of the Mother; please pray to the Mother yourself for my sake. Pray you must; I will not leave you unless you do so.' The Master said with affection, 'I prayed to the Mother many times indeed to remove your sufferings. But as you do not accept the Mother, She does not grant the prayer. Well, today

[1] There is a pun on the two words "Ah Rai"; When separate, they mean "Ah Rai" (Radha); and when not, they mean, "Lest I should lose" —Tr.

is Tuesday, a day especially sacred to the Mother. The Mother will, I say, grant you whatever you ask for. Go to the temple to-night, and bowing down to Her, pray for a boon. My affectionate Mother is the Power of Brahman; She is Pure Consciousness embodied. She has given birth to the universe by Her will. What is it that She cannot do, if She wills?'

20. "A firm faith arose in my mind that all the sufferings would certainly come to an end as soon as I prayed to the Mother, inasmuch as the Master had said so. I waited for the night in great expectancy. The night arrived at last. Three hours of the night had elapsed when the Master asked me to go to the holy temple. As I was going, a sort of profound inebriation possessed me; I was reeling. A firm conviction gripped me that I would actually see the Mother and hear Her words. I forgot all other things, and became completely merged in that thought alone. Coming into the temple, I saw the Mother was actually Pure Consciousness, was actually living, and was really the fountain-head of infinite love and beauty. My heart swelled with loving devotion; and, beside myself with bliss, I made repeated salutations to Her, praying, 'Mother, grant me discrimination, grant me detachment, grant me divine knowledge and devotion; ordain that I may always have an unobstructed vision of Thee.' My heart was flooded with peace. The whole universe completely disappeared, and the Mother alone remained filling my heart.

21. "No sooner had I returned to the Master than he asked, 'Did you pray to the Mother for the removal of your worldly wants?' Startled at his question, I said, 'No, Sir; I forgot to do so. So, what should I do now?' He said, 'Go quickly again and pray to Her.' I started for the temple once more, and coming to Mother's presence, became inebriated again. I forgot everything, bowed down to Her repeatedly, and prayed for the realization of divine knowledge and devotion before I came back. The Master smiled and said, 'Well, did you ask Her this time for removing your worldly wants?' I was startled again and said, 'No, Sir; hardly had I seen the Mother when I forgot everything on account of the influence of an indescribable Divine Power and prayed for knowledge and devotion only. What's to be done now?' The Master said, 'Silly boy, could you not control yourself a little and make that prayer? Go once more if you can, and speak out to Her your wants. Be quick!' I started a third time; but as soon as I entered the temple,

a formidable sense of shame overpowered my heart. I thought, 'What a trifling thing have I come to ask of the Mother! It is, as the Master often says, just like the folly of asking a king, after having received his grace, for gourds and pumpkins. Ah, how low is my intellect!' Overpowered with shame and aversion, I bowed down to Her over and over again, saying, 'I don't want anything else, Mother; do grant me divine knowledge and devotion only!' When I came out from the temple, it occured to me that it was certainly the play of the Master, otherwise how could I fail to make the prayer to Her, though I came with that purpose as many as three times? Then I insisted that he must ensure for my mother and brothers freedom from lack of food and clothing, saying, 'It is certainly you who made me intoxicated that way and prevented me from praying.' He said affectionately to me, 'My child, I can never offer such a prayer for anyone; it does not indeed come out of my mouth. You would, I told you, get from Mother whatever you wanted. But you could not ask Her for it; you are not meant for worldly happiness. What am I to do?' I said, thereupon, 'That won't do, Sir. You must utter the prayer for my sake; it is my firm conviction that they will be free from all sufferings if you only say so.' As I kept on persisting, he said, 'Well, they will never be in want of plain food and clothing.' "

22. What has been described above was, it is superfluous to say, a turning point in the life of Narendranath. The hidden meaning of the Motherhood of God and of Her worship in symbols and images had not been comprehended by him so long. Before this, he had looked upon the images of the deities installed in the temples with contempt, never with love and respect. The whole mystery of such worship now became clear to his mind and made his spiritual life fuller and richer. The Master felt an unspeakable joy on account of that. The reader will understand this when we mention what a friend of ours (Sri Vaikunthanath Sannyal) saw and heard at Dakshineswar when he came on the morrow. He said:

23. "I became acquainted with one Tarapada Ghosh, as he and I served in the same office. Narendranath was a great friend of Tarapada. Therefore, I saw Narendra sometimes in that office. Besides, one day Tarapada told me in the course of conversation that Paramahamsa Deva loved Narendra dearly. Still I did not try to get acquainted with Narendra. One day at

noon I came to Dakshineswar and saw the Master sitting alone in his room and Narendra sleeping on one side, outside the room. The Master's face was beaming with delight. No sooner had I approached and bowed down to him than he pointed to Narendra and said, 'Look here; that boy is very good. His name is Narendra. He never accepted the Divine Mother before; it was only last night that he did so. He was in straitened circumstances. I, therefore, advised him to ask Mother for money. He however could not ask Her for it; he said he felt ashamed to do so. Coming back from the temple, he asked me to teach him a song addressed to Mother. I taught him the song:

> 'Thou art the saviour, O Mother!
> Beyond the cause of all things, Thou art the substratum of all the three Gunas.
> I know Thee, O Mother, O bestower of mercy on the poor
> As the destroyer of irremovable misery in great distress.
> Thou art in water, Thou art in land, Thou alone art the primeval Cause, O Mother!
> With forms and without form,
> Thou existest in all hearts and in all eyes.
> Thou art Sandhya, Thou art Gayatri,
> Thou art the support of the universe, O Mother,
> Thou takest us, helpest us across the shoreless sea of the world,
> Thou the delighter of the heart of the eternally existing Siva!

'He sang that song the whole night. So, he is sleeping now. (Smiling with joy) Narendra has accepted Kali; it is very good; is that not so?' Seeing that he was happy like a child on account of that, I said, 'Yes, Sir; it is very good.' A little afterwards he smiled and said again, 'Narendra has accepted the Mother; it is very good; what do you say?' He thus expressed his joy, saying it over and over again.

24. "On waking up, Narendra came and sat beside the Master in the room at about four in the afternoon. It seemed that Narendra would now take leave of him and return to Calcutta. But the Master entered into ecstasy as soon as he saw him, and touching Narendra's body with his, sat almost on his lap, saying, 'What I see is that this (his own person) I am, and this too (Narendra's person), I am.

Truly I say, I see no difference. Just as the water of the Ganga seems to be divided into two parts when a stick is placed on it, but actually there are no divisions but only one whole mass of water existing, — such is the case here too. Do you understand it? What exists but Mother? What do you say?' Speaking thus he suddenly said, 'I'll smoke.' I hurried to prepare a smoke for him and gave him the Hookah. Smoking a puff or two, he returned the Hookah, and saying, 'I will smoke with the bowl', took it in his hands and began smoking. Smoking three or four puffs, he held it near Narendra's mouth and said, 'Just have a puff, a puff through my hands.' Narendra shrank, at which the Master said, 'What ignorance! Are you and I different? This am I, that also am I.' Saying so, he held both his hands again in front of Narendra's mouth with a view to making him smoke. Thus compelled, Narendra smoked two or three puffs with his mouth through the Master's hands and then stopped. Seeing him stop smoking, the Master himself was again going to smoke.

At that Narendra said hurriedly, 'Sir, wash your hands and then smoke.' But the Master paid no heed to the words. He said, 'You, rascal, you are awfully conscious of differences', and smoked with his own hands that had been touched by Narendra's lips while smoking, and spoke many things in that ecstatic mood. The Master considered all food stuff, of which a portion had already been given to another, or which had come into contact with the mouth, as polluted, and he could not himself take such stuff. Seeing him act in violation of this rule towards Narendra that day, I was surprised, and thought how near to his heart Narendra must be.

25. "Our talks went on till it was 8 p.m., when we saw that the Master's ecstasy came to an end. Then we took leave of him and walked back to Calcutta." Afterwards on many occasions we heard Narendra say, "Ever since our first meeting, it was the Master alone, and no one else, not even my own mother and brothers, who always had uniform faith in me. That faith and that love of his have bound me to him for ever. It was the Master alone who knew how to love. He did love, while others only feign to love for the sake of their self-interest."

CHAPTER IX

THE CIRCLE OF DEVOTEES OF THE MASTER AND NARENDRANATH

[TOPICS: 1. The marked devotees of the Master came by 1884. 2. The Master's behaviour with this class of devotees. 3. The Master rouses their spiritual consciousness in his divine mood. 4. What the Master's divine touch proved. 5. Each devotee felt the Master to be a person of his own mood. 6. Balaram Basu an example. 7. Balaram's early behaviour on meeting the Master. 8. Balaram's doubt about the virtue of non-injury. 9. His doubt removed by an example. 10. The two groups of devotees. 11. His method of teaching men in general. 12. Narendra's pre-eminence amongst the devotees. 13. Narendra's deep understanding of the Master's words. 14. Serving Jiva as Siva.]

1. All those devotees of the Master mentioned before, whose coming to Dakshineswar he had seen in his Yogic visions, arrived there before the close of 1884. For, Purna came to him in the beginning of 1885. After bestowing his grace on him, he said, "With Purna's arrival, the coming of that class of devotees whom I saw in visions, is completed. No one else of this class will come hereafter."

2. Many of the above-mentioned class of devotees had come to the Master during the period between the middle of 1883 and that of 1884. Narendra was then struggling against dire poverty to maintain his family; and Rakhal had gone to Vrindavan for some time. With a kind of fore-knowledge of events, the Master would sometimes announce the coming of devotees of this class thus: "One belonging to this place is coming today from this direction (pointing to a particular direction)." Or as soon as one came, he would receive him lovingly and say, "You are a person belonging to this place." In the case of a few fortunate ones, he felt special attraction and became eager to see and feed them and have a talk with them on spiritual matters. He would observe their nature, which was derived from their past impressions, and introduce them to devotees of a similar nature who were already in the habit of visiting him, so that they might have the opportunity of spending their leisure in religious discourse with people who thought on the same lines as themselves. Again, he would visit

the houses of some such devotees unasked and would please their guardians with charming conversation, clearing their way to come to him.

3. Shortly after the arrival of such a devotee, he would call him aside, ask him to meditate, and then touch under the influence of divine inspiration certain parts of his body like the chest or the tongue. By that potent touch, the devotee's mind would become indrawn into a trance in which his accumulated impressions of the past got activated and produced spiritual realisation in him. Consequently, on account of that touch, one would have the vision of a divine Light or of the luminious figure of a God or Goddess; another would be in deep meditation or feel a bliss never experienced before; a third would have the knots of his heart suddenly loosened and removed and experience an intense eagerness for God-realization; a fourth would be inspired with spiritual emotions and enter into Savikalpa Samadhi; and a rare one would get a foretaste of Nirvikalpa Samadhi. There was no limit to the number of persons who came to him and thus had the vision of luminous forms. We heard from the Master himself that Tarak, one day, thus experienced a great upsurge of aspiration accompained by a tremendous fit of wailing, as a result of which all the knots of his heart were loosened. Owing to that potent touch, Junior Naren entered into ecstasy during his meditation on the formless aspect of God. But the experience of a foretaste of the Nirvikalpa Samadhi on account of that touch was seen in the life of Narendranath alone. Besides touching the devotees in that way, the Master initiated some of them in Mantras. At the time of initiation, he did not examine the horoscopes of the disciples nor did he perform worship like ordinary preceptors. But observing the accumulated impressions of their past with his Yogic vision, he pointed out their Mantras saying, "This is your Mantra." We have heard from him that he bestowed his grace in that way on Niranjan, Tejchandra, Vaikuntha and some others. He did not initiate any one in a Sakta or a Vaishnava Mantra merely because that person was born in a Sakta or a Vaishnava family. After a careful scrutiny of the inner tendencies, he would sometimes initiate a Sakti worshipper with a Vishnu Mantra and a Vishnu worshipper with a Sakti Mantra. It is therefore evident that he observed every one's tendency and prescribed everything accordingly.

4. It is recorded in the scriptures that great souls can, by their

will or touch, impart spiritual power to others and turn the course of their minds to higher channels. Even the lives of prostitutes, lecherous persons and other perpetrators of sinful actions have thus been changed by the influence of great souls, not to speak of those of the disciples of their inner circles. The manifestation of that power is seen in varying measure in the life of each of the great souls such as Krishna, Buddha, Jesus, and Chaitanya, who have all along been worshipped as incarnations in the world. But of what avail is it that it is so written in the scriptures? Having no direct knowledge of the extraordinary actions of the personages of that class for a very long time, the world totally lost its faith in them. Even faith in God is very often regarded nowadays as a sign of mental weakness born of superstition, and even more so faith in His incarnations. It was very necessary in the modern age for an extraordinary person like the Master to be born in this world in order to remove that lack of faith from the minds of men in general and make them spiritual. Seeing the manifestation of that power in him, we are now coming to have faith in the similar powers of the great souls of the past. Even if one may not accept the Master as an incarnation of God, one cannot, when one sees that power in him, deny that he was an extraordinary person belonging to the same class as Krishna, Buddha, Jesus, Chaitanya and other great souls.

5. Among those devotees, whom the Master had known before they actually came there, were people of various ages, classes and spiritual moods, such as the young and the old, householders and monks, worshippers of God with form and of God without form. In spite of all these differences, there was one common point observable in them all. Each one of them had an unshakable faith in, and single-minded devotion to, his own path of Sadhana and the chosen Ideal, and was ever ready to undergo any amount of sacrifice for the realization of God. The Master tied one and all to himself with the cord of his love and guarded everybody's particular spiritual mood and behaved towards him in a way that made him think that he, although an expert in all religious doctrines, had greater love for the path along which the devotee himself was proceeding. There was no limit to the disciples' love and devotion to the Master on account of that impression of theirs. Again, as soon as they transcended the narrow circles of sectarianism one by one, and came to posses liberal views by virtue of his company

and under the influence of his instructions and teachings, they were astonished and charmed on becoming aware of the perfection of his comprehensive vision. We mention here, by way of an example, an ordinary event.

6. Balaram Basu of Baghbazar was born in a Vaishnava family and was himself a great follower of that faith. Though living in the world, he was untouched by it, and though possessing great wealth he was never proud on that account. He used to spend four or five hours in worship and religious study every morning and was so careful in observing the virtue of non-injury that he never hurt even insects, for any reason whatever. As soon as the Master saw him for the first time, he received him lovingly, as if he was already familiar with him. The Master said, "He is a devotee of the inner circle of the great Lord Sri Chaitanya. He belongs to this place (meaning himself). I witnessed in ecstasy how the great Lord Chaitanya together with the revered souls, Advaita and Nityananda, brought about a flood of Hari's name in the country and inebriated a number of men, women and children by means of Sankirtan sung by a wonderful party. In that party I saw him (Balaram)."

7. Keeping the Master's company, Balaram underwent wonderful transformation and progressed rapidly in the spiritual realm. Going beyond the limit of external worship and other kinds of ritualistic devotion enjoined by the scriptures, he could, in a short time, live in the world completely reliant on God, discriminating the real from the unreal. Offering, as the Vaishnava ideal of spiritual discipline requires, his all — his own life, wife, son, wealth, etc. — at the lotus feet of the Lord, he lived like a servant of His in His world, ever ready to carry out His commands. Balaram came to have only one aim in life, namely, to live in the holy company of the Master as much as possible. He could not remain satisfied with himself enjoying the peace born of the grace of the Master, but busied himself with making suitable arrangements for his friends and relatives also to come in contact with the Master and to enjoy the bliss derived therefrom. Many people thus felt blessed to have the Master as their refuge on account of Balaram's devotional attitude of being a servant of the Lord.

8. As in the matter of external worship, Balaram's opinion about the observance of the virtue of non-injury also got changed in a short time. Before he came into contact with the Master,

he never used to hurt even mosquitoes, though they distracted his mind at the time of worship. It would, he thought, destroy his piety altogether. Now, one day the thought suddenly crossed his mind that the practice of religion consisted in making the distracted mind concentrated on God, and not in always engaging oneself in saving the lives of mosquitoes, insects, birds and other creatures. Therefore, if the mind could be helped to concentrate on Hari for a short time by killing a few mosquitoes, that act should, far from being considered irreligious, be regarded as highly beneficial from the point of view of the ultimate end of life. Balaram said, "The long-standing eagerness of the mind to observe the virtue of non-injury got a rude shock at that thought; but the mind, assailed by doubts, found itself swayed by the new thought. I, therefore, started for Dakshineswar to consult the Master about it. On my way I went on thinking the matter over, 'Did I ever see him kill mosquitoes like others?' I could not remember such an act. As far as I could see, he was more devoted to the observance of the vow of non-injury than I. I recollected that, when one day he saw a man treading a field, green with newly grown grass, he felt as if the man was stamping on his breast and became restless with pain. So keen was his sensibility to that one Power of consciousness that gave life and vitality to all things, including the grass in the field, and that pervaded them through and through! So the decision forced itself upon me that it was quite unnecessary to ask him the question as my doubt on the question must only be a deceptive device of my mind. Let me, however, go and see him. The mind will then become purified, I thought.

9. "I reached Dakshineswar and came to the door of the Master's room. But, before I entered it, I was astounded to see from a distance what he was then doing. I saw him bringing out bugs from his own bed and killing them! As soon as I approached, and bowed down to him, he said, 'There are many bugs breeding in the pillow. They bite me day and night, produce distraction of the mind and disturb sleep. I am, therefore, killing them.' There was now no need to put a question on the topic. My mind became free from doubt on hearing his words and seeing his action. But, astonished, I thought, 'I have been coming to him at all hours and without notice for the last two or three years; I came in the day-time and returned at night. If I came at dusk, I took leave only when the night had advanced more than three hours. I came and

went thus three or four times every week. But never did I happen to see him do such an act. How could it be? The solution is this: I was not prepared for the lesson at first. My spiritual mood would have suffered had I seen him do so before; I would have lost faith in him as a consequence. The supremely compassionate Master, therefore, never acted thus in my presence before."

10. Besides the devotees whom the Master had seen in visions before, many other men and women came to Dakshineswar during this time to see him and have peace. He received these also affectionately and blessed them, some by instruction and others by a touch in a state of Divine inspiration. As time thus passed on, the circle of devotees, having the Master as the centre of attraction, became wider and wider. He took special care to mould the spiritual lives of the boys and unmarried young men who were among them. He pointed out the reason for this on many occasions thus: "The perfect realization of God can never be attained if one does not apply one's whole mind to it. The boys have with them their whole minds which have not become distracted by wife, sons, wealth, honour, fame and other worldly objects. If they try now, they can offer their whole minds to God and be blessed with His vision. That is why I have a greater zeal in guiding them on the path of spiritual realization." Whenever the Master found an opportunity, he took each of them to a secluded place and instructed him in the higher methods of spiritual realization, such as Yoga, meditation, etc., and advised him to practise perfect continence by not entering into matrimony. Further taking a person's fitness into consideration, he selected the Chosen Ideal suited for his worship and meditation, as also the special spiritual mood from among the Santa, Dasya and the rest that he should cultivate towards the selected aspect of the Deity for his rapid progress in spiritual life.

11. Let no man think that Sri Ramakrishna had less grace on, and compassion for, householder devotees when he hears of his greater zeal in teaching the boys. He did not ask them to practise and study the higher spiritual truths, only because he knew that many of them had no time or capacity to do so. But he guided them constantly, so that they might gradually overcome the attractions of wealth and sex, and have the ideal of their lives achieved in due course by realizing God through the path of devotion. He taught them first of all to live 'in God's world' and not 'in their own', and while doing their duties, to give up all attachment, all sense

of "my and mine" and be like a servant working in the houses of a respected Master. The Master also encouraged them to observe continence according to their capacity. "Husband and wife," he observed, "should offer their minds to God and live in the world like brother and sister after one or two children are born." Besides, he directed them always to tread the path of truth and move with all in a simple, artless way; to give up luxury and remain contented with plain food and clothing only, fixing their gaze steadfastly on God; and to remember and think of God daily at the two junctions of the day and night and perform worship and Japa and sing Kirtan. He advised those householders who were unable to practise even that, to sit in a secluded place at dusk and take the name of Hari while clapping their hands. He advised them also to congregate with their relatives and friends and sing the name of God. At the time of giving instruction to men and women in general, he was heard to say, "Devotion according to Narada, is the only path in the Kaliyuga; people will be saved if they but sing loudly the name of God. People of the Kaliyuga depend on food for their life; they are short-lived and of meagre powers; that is why such an easy path for the realization of God has been prescribed for them." Again, sometimes he would say, lest they should lose heart by hearing of Yoga, meditation and other difficult paths of Sadhana, "A man who has turned a monk must, of course, call on the Divine Lord. For, it is for this very purpose that he has renounced all the duties of the world. What credit or uniqueness is there in his doing so? But God becomes highly pleased with one who remembers Him even once, while he carries the very heavy load of duties towards one's father, mother, wife, son and others in the world. God thinks, 'It is no small credit on the part of this man that he can turn to Me even for a short while, in spite of so heavy a burden lying on his shoulders. This man is indeed a hero among devotees.'"

12. Words fail us to express how high a place the Master gave to Narendra even among the especial devotees seen by him in visions, let alone the ordinary class of devotees who came without any such earlier intimation through visions. Pointing out a few amongst the devotees previously seen in visions, he said, "They are Isvarakotis, in other words, they have been born in this world to accomplish a particular work of the divine Lord." Comparing Narendra with those few men, he said to us one day, "Naren is a

Purna Chandra Ghosh

Durga Charan Nag
(Nag Mahashay)

Vijay Krishna Goswami

Surendra Nath Mitra

Shambu Charan Mallik

Ramchandra Datta

Balaram Bose

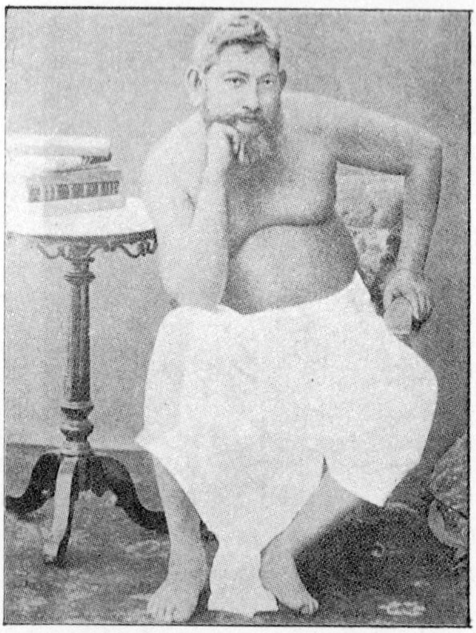

Girish Chandra Ghosh

lotus of a thousand petals, while the others of this class are also lotuses no doubt, but of ten, fifteen or at the most twenty petals only." He said on another occasion, "So many men have come here; but no one else like Naren has come." It was also seen that no one could so correctly understand and express, as Narendra did, the import of the Master's wise words and extraordinary actions. Hearing Narendra's exposition of the Master's sayings, we were astonished at times and led to think, "Ah! We also heard these words from the Master, but we could not understand that they have such deep meaning." We mention here one such case as an example.

13. Sometime in 1884, a friend of ours came to Dakshineswar and found the Master sitting in his room surrounded by devotees. Narendra also was present there. Various spiritual talks, interspersed with merriment, were going on. There arose the topic of the Vaishnava religion in the course of the conversation, and explaining briefly the essence of that doctrine to all, the Master said, "That doctrine teaches that one should always be careful to observe three things, namely, a taste for God's name, kindness to all beings and the service of the Vaishnavas. God is what His name is. Knowing the non-difference between the name and the possessor of the name, one should always take His name with love and devotion. Knowing the identity of the devotee and the Divine, of the Vaishnava and Krishna, one should always respect, worship and salute holy men, the devotees. And one should have the conviction in one's heart that the whole universe belongs to Krishna; and therefore, one should have compassion for all beings." No sooner had he uttered the words, "compassion for all beings", than he suddenly went into ecstasy. Regaining partial normal consciousness in a short time, he continued, "Talk of compassion for beings! Insignificant creatures that you are, how can you show compassion to beings? Who are you to show compassion? You wretch, who are you to bestow it? No, no; it is not compassion to Jivas but service to them as Siva."

14. All went on listening to those words of the Master spoken in that ecstatic mood; but none could detect and understand their hidden import at that time. It was Narendranath alone who, coming out of the room at the end of Master's ecstasy, said, "Ah what a wonderful light have I got today from the Master's words! What a new and attractive Gospel have we received today through

those words of his, wherein a synthesis has been effected of sweet devotion to the Lord with Vedantic knowledge, which is generally regarded as dry, austere and lacking in sympathy with the sufferings of others. In order to attain the non-dual knowledge, we have been told so long that one should have to renounce the world and the company of men altogether, and retire to the forest, and mercilessly uproot and throw away love, devotion and other soft and tender emotions from the heart. Formerly, when the aspirant tried to attain that knowledge as prescribed in ancient works, he regarded the whole universe and each person in it as obstacles in the path of his spiritual progress — an attitude which produced in men a sort of antipathy towards society and often led them away from the true spiritual path. But from what the Master in ecstasy said today, it is gathered that the Vedanta of the forest can be brought to human habitation, and that it can be applied in practice to the work-a-day world. Let man do everything he is doing; there is no harm in that; it is sufficient for him, first, to be fully convinced that it is God who is manifested before him as the universe and all the beings in it. Those with whom he comes in contact every moment of his life, whom he loves, respects and honours, and to whom his sympathy and kindness flow, are all His parts, are all He Himself. If he can thus look upon all the persons of the world as Siva, how can there be an occasion for him to regard himself as superior to them or cherish anger and hatred for them or an arrogant attitude towards them, or even to be kind to them? Thus serving the Jivas as Siva, he will have his heart purified and be convinced in a short time that he himself is also a part of God, the Bliss Absolute, the eternally pure, wakeful and free Being.

"We get a great light on the path of devotion too from these words of the Master. Until he sees God in all beings, the aspirant has not the remotest chance of realizing true devotion and having the aim of his life fulfilled in a short time. Those aspirants who adopt the path of action or that of concentration for the realization of God, will also get much light from these words. For, as embodied beings can never rest for a moment without doing work, it goes without saying that only work of the nature of service of Jiva as Siva should be performed, and action done in that spirit will enable them to reach the goal sooner than otherwise. If the divine Lord ever grants me an opportunity, I'll proclaim everywhere in the world this wonderful truth I have heard today. I will preach this truth to the learned and the ignorant, to the rich and the poor, to the Brahmana and the Chandala."

The extraordinary Master always entered the realm of ecstasy in this way and constantly brought wonderful light regarding knowledge, love, Yoga and Karma to illumine the path of human life. But unfortunate as we were, we could not then comprehend the implication of his words. It was the supremely intelligent Narendranath who understood those divine words as far as it was humanly possible, and expressed from time to time their sublime significance to our amazement.

CHAPTER X

THE FESTIVAL AT PANIHATI:

[TOPICS: 1. Narendra became a school headmaster. 2. The enmity of his kinsmen. 3. The Master's illness. 4. Worsening of the illness due to talking and Bhavasamadhi. 5. The festival at Panihati. 6. The Master's desire to attend it. 7. Starting for Panihati. 8. Why the Holy Mother did not accompany the party. 9. The scene at the festival. 10. Mani Sen's house. 11. His temple. 12. The Master danced in Bhavasamadhi. 13. Bhavasamadhi on the way to Raghava Pandit's house. 14. The wonderful beauty of the Master in Bhavasamadhi. 15. The zeal and joy of the Kirtan party on seeing the Master. 16. All were attracted towards him. 17. A plateful of Prasada. 18. Bestowal of grace on Navachaitanya. 19. Arrival at Dakshineswar. 20. The Master on the Holy Mother's sagacity. 21. The Holy Mother's words on the subject. 22. Annoying experiences of Snanayatra day.]

1. We have said before, how Narendranath took refuge in the Master and how the Master blessed the family to be ever above want of plain food and clothing. Narendra's worldly circumstances changed gradually thenceforward; and although they were not affluent, the family never again had to experience the sort of dire poverty that they had to pass through before. A branch of the Metropolitan School was opened at Champatala in Calcutta shortly after the event; and Narendra was appointed the Headmaster there through the kindness of Pandit Isvara Chandra Vidyasagar. He worked as a teacher there for about three or four months, probably from the month of May of the year 1885.

2. Although the worldly circumstances of Narendra improved a little, he was harassed a great deal now by the enmity of his kinsmen. When they found an opportunity they occupied the best houses and the best places of his ancestral property by hook or by crook. He had therefore to leave his house for some time and live in his grandmother's at Ramtanu Basu's Lane. And, in order to come by his just right he instituted a case in the High Court and got everything settled. Nimai Charan Basu, an attorney and his father's friend, helped him much in this case. Now that he had to spend much time in looking after the case and preparing for the impending B.L. Examination, he had to resign his post of

teachership after three or four months only. There was also a graver reason for it. The Master was now attacked by an inflammatory affection of the throat, and as it increased gradually, Narendra felt the necessity of himself being present with him and making arrangements for his nursing and treatment.

3. Seeing the Master suffer from the excessive heat of the year 1885, the devotees requested him to use ice. Observing that he felt relieved by taking ice, many of them, when coming to Dakshineswar, now began to bring it. He too liked to take it with sugared drinks, and made merry like a boy. But there started a pain in his throat after he had used it for a month or two. It was probably the month of April when he felt the pain for the first time.

4. More than a month elapsed, and the pain did not abate; and scarcely had the month of May come when the disease developed new symptoms. It increased when he spoke much or went into ecstasy. It was at first diagnosed as the inflammation of the pharynx due to cold and an ordinary plaster was prescribed. But finding it ineffective after a few days' use, a devotee called in Dr. Rakhal of Bowbazar who was known to be an expert in such diseases. The doctor diagnosed the disease and prescribed an unguent and medicine for applying outside and inside the throat. He asked us to see as far as possible that the Master did not talk much for some days and did not often go into ecstasy.

5. The thirteenth day of the bright fortnight of the month of Jyaishtha (May-June) was now drawing near. An annual fair of the Vaishnava community is held on this day in the village of Panihati on the Ganga, a few miles north of Calcutta. The story of the burning renunciation and detachment of Raghunath Das Goswami, one of the companions of the great Lord Chaitanya, is well known throughout Bengal. Leaving behind a very beautiful wife and immense riches, Raghunath, the only son of his father, came to Santipur to take refuge at the feet of Sri Chaitanya, who sent him back to await at home the ripening of his too insipient dispassion for worldly life. In implicit obedience to this command of the great lord, Raghunath returned home, and keeping hidden in his heart the strong desire for renouncing the world, he began helping his father and uncle in worldly matters like the management of the family. Although he thus continued to live at home, he could not do without seeing the companions of Sri Chaitanya now and

then. He used to visit them with the permission of his father, pass a few days in their holy company and return home. Days thus passed, and Raghunath lived on at home, biding his time for renouncing it. In course of time Sri Gauranga was initiated into Sannyasa and went to live at Puri. Placed in charge of the preaching of the Vaishnava religion, Nityananda, one of the leaders of Sri Gauranga's movement, made the village of Khardaha, situated on the Ganga, the chief centre of his work, and travelled far and wide to many places of Bengal singing and preaching the name of God and initiating many people into that faith.

Once when Nityananda with his friends and disciples of the inner circle was staying and preaching at the village of Panihati, Raghunath came to see him, and was asked by him to feed him and the circle of devotees with flattened rice, curd, milk, sugar, plantain, etc., mixed into a paste and offered to the Deity. Raghunath gladly consented and gave a sumptuous feast to the hundreds of people who had come to see the revered Nityananda on the bank of the Ganga on that occasion. When Raghunath went to bow down to Nityananda and take leave of him at the end of the festival, the latter embraced him in a partial trance and said, "The time is now ripe; if you now renounce the world and go to the great lord at Puri, he will accept you and will place you under Sanatana Goswami for your training with a view to perfecting your spiritual life." Raghunath leaped in joy at that command of Nityananda; he paid a short visit to his house and renounced the world for ever and went to Puri. Raghunath left the place, but in commemoration of this event the Vaishnava devotees hold an annual fair in the village of Panihati on the Ganga, in the name of Gauranga and Nityananda with a view to having similar grace of the divine Lord. This afterwards came to be known to the devotees as the 'Festival of the flattened rice at Panihati'.

6. The Master had, we have mentioned elsewhere, joined that festival many times before. But, owing to various reasons, he had not done so for a few years since his devotees, educated in the Western ways, came to him. He expressed the desire of going and witnessing the festival this year together with his devotees, and said to us, "A fair of bliss — a veritable mart of the name of Hari — assembles there on that day; you 'Young Bengal'[1] have

[1] The two words were spoken in English.

never seen such a thing. Let us go and witness it." Although a party of devotees like Ramchandra and others became very happy at the proposal, some of them thought of the pain in the Master's throat and tried to dissuade him. In order to satisfy them he said, 'I'll take here a little food early and return after staying there an hour or two; that will not do much harm. The pain in the throat might increase if I have much of ecstasy, but I shall be careful to keep it in check." All objections were thrown to the winds at those words of his, and the devotees began to arrange for his trip to Panihati.

7. It was the thirteenth day of the bright fortnight, the day of the Panihati festival. About twenty-five devotees in two boats came to Dakshineswar at 9 a.m. Some came there on foot. A separate boat hired for the Master was seen tied at the Ghat. A few women devotees had come very early morning. They joined the Holy Mother in arranging a meal for the Master and the devotees. All took their food and were ready to start by 10 a.m.

8. When the Master had taken his meal, the Holy Mother sent word to him through a woman devotee, asking him if she too might go. The Master said to the devotee, "You all are coming, I see; let her come if she likes." When these words were thus reported to her, the Holy Mother said, "Many people are going with him and there will also be a very big crowd; it will be very difficult for me to get down from the boat and witness the festival. It is better that I do not go." The Holy Mother gave up the idea of going. She fed the two or three women devotees who were to accompany the Master, and asked them to go in the same boat with him.

9. A large number of people were already assembled round the old pipal tree on the bank of the Ganga when the party reached Panihati at about 12 noon. The Vaishnava devotees were enjoying the bliss of Sankirtan in many places. But, although they did so, many of them did not seem to have actually lost themselves in singing the name of the divine Lord. It was everywhere a sort of lifeless affair. Both before and after arriving at Panihati, Narendranath, Balaram, Girishchandra, Ramchandra, Mahendranath and other principal devotees earnestly and repeatedly requested the Master not to mix with any Kirtan party and get inebriated. For, if he did so, ecstasy would be inevitable and the pain in his throat would increase thereby.

10. The Master got down from the boat and went direct to the house of Mani Sen. Happy at his coming, all the household of Mani Babu bowed to him and took him to the parlour and seated him there. It was a room well-furnished in the English fashion with tables, chairs, sofas, and other facilities. After a short rest of ten or fifteen minutes there, he got up with all others to pay obeisance to the Lord, Sri Radhakanta, in the temple of that family.

11. The temple was situated very near the parlour. We came direct through the side door to the music hall adjoining the temple and were blessed to see the images of Radha and Krishna. The images were beautiful. Gazing on the images for a while, the Master made salutations to them in a divine semi-conscious mood. Coming five or six steps down from the music-hall, one reaches the quadrangular temple courtyard with suites of rooms on all the four sides. The gate is so situated that one sees the images as soon as one enters the courtyard of the temple. When the Master was making salutations, a Kirtan party entered the courtyard through that gate and commenced singing. It appeared that the practice was for each party that came to the fair to start singing Kirtan in the temple courtyard first and then proceed to the bank of the Ganga and chant the Lord's name. A tall, fat, middle-aged man of fair complexion, with sacred thread and tuft of hair on his head and his body adorned with sandal-paste and marks of the sacred wheel and other holy emblems, came to the courtyard counting beads in a small bag. With an upper garment hanging from his shoulder, a white clean washed "Rally's 49" cloth without coloured border worn in a very tidy manner, and a bunch of coins in a fold of that cloth at the waist, he seemed at the very first sight to be a tramp of a Goswami who had come out fully dressed to the fair to make a little money by playing on the faith of others. In order to excite the Kirtan party and probably to show himself off to the new-comers as a great devotee, he came and immediately joined the party and began to roar, dance and gesticulate as if he were in trance.

12. The master stood on one side of the temple after making salutations. Smiling to see the Goswami feigning ecstasy and the orderly disposition of his dress and ornaments, he said to Narendra and other devotees beside him in a low voice, "Mark the hypocrisy." There was seen a gentle smile on the lips of everyone at that merry remark of his. And all were free from anxiety to think that he

had kept himself under control without experiencing any spiritual emotion. But the next moment, before the devotees had any idea of the 'how' and 'when' of the matter, the Master, in the twinkling of an eye, came down in one bound to the middle of the Kirtan party and passed into ecstasy, losing all consciousness. The devotees then hurried down from the music hall and stood around him. He sometimes gained partial normal consciousness and danced with the stride of a lion, and sometimes lost outward awareness and stood still. Dancing under the influence of the spiritual emotions, he was now proceeding, now receding with a rapid step to the timing of the music. He seemed like a fish swimming about in great delight in a sea of bliss. Each movement of his limbs clearly indicated it. But it is impossible to give expression to the wonderful manifestation of that fully natural and unrestrained power of bliss where beauty and tenderness had blended together in a sweet harmony. We have witnessed many beautiful dances full of gesture by both male and female dancers, but never did we have a glimpse of that happy synthesis of power and beauty as we did in the unrestrained and yet perfectly balanced dance of the Master, when he lost himself in the divine moods of spiritual emotions. When his body, overflowing with the intense joy of divine feeling, swayed to and fro with quick steps, one seriously wondered whether it was made of any solid, physical substance at all. One felt as if waves, mountain high, rose in a sea of bliss, and were going forward carrying everything before them and merging that very moment in that sea, liquid in liquid, only to vanish out of sight. No one had to explain how great a difference there existed between the genuine and the counterfeit. The Kirtan party did not turn their eyes to the Goswami any more but surrounded the Master and sang with zeal and happiness multiplied a hundredfold.

13. About half an hour elaspsed this way, when seeing the Master in a somewhat normal consciousness, the devotees tried to take him away from the midst of the Kirtan party. All should, it was decided, return to the boats after paying their obeisance to the pair of images and the Salagrama, (the round stone-symbol of the Supreme), which Pandit Raghava, a companion of the great lord Sri Chaitanya, had daily worshipped in his house situated a little more than a mile from that place. The Master consented and started with the devotees from Mani Sen's temple. But the Kirtan party did not desist from following him. They followed

him, singing the name of God with great fervour. The Master went forward a few steps only, when he stood motionless in ecstasy. When he regained partial consciousness, the devotees requested him to walk on. He took three or four steps and was in ecstasy once more. As this happened over and over again, the devotees were compelled to proceed very slowly.

14. We do not remember to have ever seen the divine effulgence and beauty, which we saw that day in the person of the Master in ecstasy. It is not in human power to describe that wonderful beauty of his divine person. We never imagined before that such a change could come on a man's body in the twinkling of an eye under the influence of spiritual emotions. His fairly tall figure, as seen by us daily, looked much taller and appeared to be as light as a body seen in a dream. Getting brighter, the slightly dark colour of his body turned into a fair complexion. Brightened by the Divine mood and lit up by an incomparable smile playing on his slightly parted lips, his face beamed with glory, peace, bliss and compassion, and spread a wonderful light which illumined all sides. Bewitched, as it were, by the sight, the vast congregation forgot all other things and followed him almost unknowingly. The bright ochre colour of the silk he put on, became one with the lustre of his body, and he was mistaken for a person surrounded by flames of fire.

15. As soon as the Master came out of Mani Babu's temple and reached the public road, the Kirtan party saw his divinely bright beauty and charming dance as also his repeated and deep ecstasy. His sight worked up their zeal to a high pitch, and they began singing:

"Who takes the name of Hari on the bank of the Ganga the
river Divine?
It seems Nitai, the bestower of the divine love,
has come.
Who takes the name of Hari,
And sings victory to Radha?
It seems Nitai, the bestower of the divine love,
has come,
Our Nitai, the giver of love, has come!
How can our hearts be soothed without him?
Here comes our Nitai, the bestower of love!"

16. When they were singing the last line, they pointed their

fingers at the Master and danced with great delight, repeating it over and over again; "Here is our bestower of love." That zeal of theirs attracted the attention of all who came to the festival and they began to pour in there. Those who came and saw the Master were at once charmed, and joined the Kirtan in great enthusiasm, or amazed at the rise of indescribable divine emotion in their hearts, remained rooted to the ground for some time and then followed the Master silently looking on him with unwinking eyes. The zeal of the party gradually seized all present around, and also attracted a few other Kirtan parties that now arrived, to join it. Thus a vast congregation of people surrounded the Master in ecstasy and proceeded with slow steps towards the cottage of Pandit Raghava.

17. The women devotees had a few platefuls of sweets offered to Sri Gauranga and Nityananda under the Pipal tree on the Ganga, and were bringing them for the Master. A little before they arrived at the house of Pandit Raghava, an ugly, ill-formed Vaishnava in the garb of a religious mendicant came — nobody knew whence — snatched a plateful of Prasada from the hands of a woman devotee, and as if swelling with love and spiritual emotions, put a little of it into the mouth of the Master with his own hand. The Master was then standing still under the influence of the ecstatic mood. As soon as the man touched him, the whole of his body winced and this disturbed his ecstasy. He spat out the food and washed his mouth. It did not take anybody long to know that that Vaishnava was a hypocrite. Seeing that all were casting glances of annoyance and ridicule, the fellow slipped off. The Master then took Prasada from one of the devotees, ate a particle of it himself, and gave the rest to them.

18. It took a long time, about three hours, to walk a distance of one mile and reach Pandit Raghava's house. The Master took half an hour to go to the temple and touch the Salagrama and pay his obeisance to the images and take rest. The vast crowd of people that came with him, dispersed in various directions. The devotees brought him to the boat when they saw the crowd had thinned. But here also, there came to pass a wonderful event. Knowing that the Master had come to the festival, Navachaitanya Mitra of Konnagar became eager to see him and was searching everywhere for him.

Now seeing the Master in the boat, about to start, he came towards him running like one mad. He fell at his feet and wept on, moved by the intensity of the emotions surging in his heart, and prayed, "Deign to bestow grace on me!" The Master responded to the eager and fervent prayer of the devotee by touching him in an exalted mood. We do not know what extraordinary vision he had as a result of that touch, but found his uncontrolable mood of weeping suddenly changing into one of intense delight in the twinkling of an eye. He danced in an unrestrained manner in the boat, as if he had lost the consciousness of the world outside. He sang the Master's glory in various hymns and bowed down to him over and over again. When some time had elapsed this way the Master passed his hand over Navachaitanya's back and soothed him by giving him various instructions. Although Navachaitanya had seen the Master many times before, he could not receive his grace earlier. He was blessed to receive it that day. He then placed his son in charge of his worldly affairs, lived in a cottage in his own village on the Ganga like a Vanaprastha, and spent the rest of his life in spiritual practices and in singing hymns glorifying the name of the Master. The aged Navachaitanya used to have ecstasy during Sankirtan from now on, and many loved and respected him on seeing his devotion-soaked and blissful figure. He was thus able by the grace of the Master to awaken the love of God in the hearts of many people during the last part of his life.

19. When Navachaitanya bade good-bye, the Master said that the boat might start. Scarcely had we gone a little distance when it was dusk, and we reached the Kali temple at Dakshineswar at about 8.30 p.m. The Master sat in his room, and the devotees bowed down to him and took their leave of him to return to Calcutta. All were getting into the boat when one of them, a young man, remembered that he had forgotten to put on his shoes and ran to the Master's room to bring them. The Master asked him the reason of his coming back and said jokingly, "It is fortunate that you remembered this before the starting of the boat; otherwise it would have acted as a jolt on the joyous experiences of this day." The young man smiled at these words, bowed down to him and was ready to leave when the Master asked him, "How did you enjoy the day? It was a veritable fair of Hari's name. Wasn't it?" When the young man assented to the description, the Master asked him again, "How did you enjoy the day? A fair of Hari's name! Isn't it?" When the young man again assented, the Master mentioned the names of those of his devotees who had trances at the place

of the festival. He eulogized Junior Naren, saying, "That dark-complexioned boy has been visiting this place only for a short time, and already he is having trances. The other day, his trance would not come to an end — he was devoid of normal consciousness for more than an hour. He says, 'My mind merges in the formless aspect of God now-a-days.' Junior Naren is a good boy; isn't it so? Please go to his house some day and have a talk with him. Will you?" The young man assented to all his words and said, "But, Sir, I like no one as much as I do Senior Naren; I therefore, do not feel inclined to go to Junior Naren's house." The Master scolded him for saying so, and said, "You, brat, how are you so one-sided! The Divine Lord has a flower-basket containing various kinds of flowers. He has got various kinds of devotees. It is a sign of a low mind not to be able to mix with all and enjoy bliss. You must one day go to Junior Naren. What do you say? Will you?" Having no alternative left, he bowed his assent and bade good-bye. This young man, it was afterwards known, went within a few days to see Junior Naren according to the Master's advice, and felt blessed in getting thereby a solution for what he said was a very complicated problem of his life. The boat reached Calcutta that night at about 10 p.m.

20. The women devotees stayed with the Holy Mother that night. Knowing that there would be a great celebration at the Kali temple on the Snanayatra day, which happened also to be the anniversary of the installation of the Devi, they decided to return to Calcutta only after witnessing that festival. While taking his meal at night, the Master said to one of them in the course of a talk about the Panihati festival, "The crowd was indeed very great; besides, all were observing me on account of my ecstasy. She (the Holy Mother) did well in not accompanying us. Had people seen her with me, they would certainly have said, 'The Hamsi and the Hamsa[1] have come.' She is very intelligent." In order to give another example of the extraordinary intellegence of the Holy

[1] The syllable *'hamsa'* in the word *Paramahamsa* means a 'swan' and '*Parama*' means 'supreme'. So the literal meaning of Paramahamsa is 'Swan Supreme'. It is applied to the monks of the Orders of Sankaracharya, as they reject the world and worldly enjoyments as being unreal, and accept Brahman as the Real, even as the swan is supposed to reject water and accept milk only from a mixture of the two. And Sri Ramakrishna was a monk of the same Order. The Master expressed it rather serio-comically.

Mother, he added, "When the Marwari devotee Lakshminarayan wanted to make a gift of ten thousand rupees to me, I felt as if my head was sawn through; I said to the Mother, 'Hast Thou come to tempt me again even as late as now, Mother?' In order to test her (Sri Sarada Devi's) mind I had her called to me at that time and said to her, 'Look here, he wants to give that sum. Since I cannot accept it, he wants to transfer it to your name. You may accept it. What do you say?' As soon as she heard this, she said, 'How can I accept it? The money can never be accepted; if I accept it, it will be the same thing as your accepting it. For, if I keep it with me, I cannot but spend it on your service and other necessities. So it comes to the same as your acceptance. People love and respect you for your renunciation; the money, therefore, can by no means be accepted.' I heaved a sigh of relief."

21. When the Master had taken his meal, the women devotees went to the Holy Mother at the Nahavat and told her what the Master had said about her. She said, "I could understand from the very way in which he sent me word in the morning regarding my going to Panihati, that he did not heartily approve of it. He would otherwise have said, 'Yes, certainly she may go.' When he placed on me the responsibility of making the decision on the matter, and said, 'Let her come, if she likes' I decided it was advisable to give up the idea of going."

22. The Master had no sleep that night on account of the burning sensation in his body. It happened perhaps because people of various kinds of character had touched his divine person during the festival. For, when impure men of polluted minds touched his person and took the dust of his feet for the purpose of becoming free from diseases or with some other motive, he, it was observed, very often suffered from that kind of burning sensation. The festival of Snanayatra took place on the day following the Panihati festival. We could not be present at Dakshineswar on that occasion. Many men and women, we were told by the women devotees, came to see the Master that day. One of them, called A's mother, pressed him to help settle her property and thereby damped his bliss. Seeing her sitting beside him at the time of his midday meal, the Master was annoyed, and did not speak afterwards; he could not also take his meal as usual. Afterwards, when another woman devotee, an acquaintance of ours, went to pour water into his hand for a wash after his disturbed meal, he said to her privately,

"People come here with a view to having divine love and knowledge. This woman wants the settlement of her property to be made here! Now look at that! She has brought mangoes and sweets with this selfish motive in her mind; I could not put even a bit of them into my mouth. Today is the day of Snanayatra. Ah, how much of ecstasy I used to have on this day in other years! The inebriation produced by that ecstasy used to continue for two or three days. I could have nothing at all today. High moods could not come on account of the atmosphere here and the contact with people of various states of mind." As A's mother stayed that night at Dakshineswar, the Master's annoyance did not abate even at night. He said to a woman devotee at the time of his taking the night meal, "Too much crowding of women here is not good. Trailokya, the son of Mathur Babu, is here. What will he think of it? It is one thing if one or two women come here now and then, and stay here a day or so; but it is quite a different thing if a crowd is here. I cannot put up with such a rush of women." Thinking that they were the cause of the Master's annoyance, the woman devotee became much dejected on that occasion and returned to Calcutta as soon as it was morning. There was great pomp on the occasion of Snanayatra in the Kali temple on account of worship, Yatra and other items of celebration, but the devotees could not feel any joy that day for the above reason. From these incidents the reader will understand to a certain extent how keenly mindful the Master was of daily occurrences, and how he controlled and guided the devotees for their good, in spite of the fact that he constantly lived in high planes of spiritual consciousness.

CHAPTER XI

THE MASTER MOVED TO CALCUTTA

[TOPICS: 1. Panihati experience aggravates the Master's throat pain. 2. The Master ignoring it. 3. The causes of the disease. 4. The Master quarrelling with the Divine Mother in Bhavasamadhi. 5. Great influx of devotees at Dakshineswar. 6. The Master's predictions about the time of his passing away. 7. His service of Jivas as Siva. 8. His power of detecting the past impressions in the minds of people. 9. An example. 10. Aggravation of the disease and bleeding from the throat. 11. At Balaram's house for treatment. 12. The disease diagnosed as cancer. 13. Spiritual ministry at Balaram's house. 14. An event in Balaram's house.]

1. The pain in the throat of the Master increased after his taking part in the Panihati festival. There had been intermittent showers of rain that day. The doctors expostulated with the devotees that the disease had increased because he had spent a long time with his body and feet exposed to the rains. They said that the consequences would be serious if such irregularity happened again. Consequently, the devotees were determined to be careful thereafter. Boyish in temperament as he was, the Master put the whole blame for his breach of medical prohibitions that day on the shoulders of Ramachandra Datta and a few other elderly devotees and said, "Would I have gone to Panihati if they had forbidden me a little more emphatically?" Although he was not a professional doctor, Ram Babu had studied in the Campbell Medical School and taken a diploma in medicine. As he was a lover of the Vaishnava faith, he had rather encouraged the Master to go to Panihati. He was, therefore, regarded as deserving the greater part of the blame on that account. One day a friend of ours came to Dakshineswar at that time and found the Master sitting quietly on his small bedstead with an unguent on his throat. He said, "I saw in the Master's face the very picture of that gloomy expression which a boy bears, when he is prevented by way of punishment from doing something and is kept confined in one place. I saluted him and asked what the matter was. He showed me the plaster on his throat and said, 'Just see; the pain has increased and the doctor has forbidden me to speak much!' 'Ah Sir!' said I, 'you, I am told, went to Panihati the other day. That is perhaps why the pain has

increased.' To this he replied like a boy with a wounded feeling of love, 'Just see; there was water above, water below. In the sky there were dripping rain clouds, and on the roads, mud and mire. And still Ram took me there, and made me dance the whole day! He has passed an examination and is a doctor. Would I have gone there, if he had forbidden my going strongly?' I said, 'Yes, Sir, Ram is quite wrong. Anyway, what's done is done. Now please be careful for a few days and it will be cured.' He was pleased to be told so and said, 'Can one, however, do without speaking at all? Just see, what a great distance you have come from! Should I not speak a word with you? Is it possible to do otherwise?' I replied, 'I am fully satisfied even by seeing you. Why should you then speak? I don't mind your silence under the circumstances. When you are cured, we shall certainly be hearing many great things from you again.' But he did not lend an ear to these words of mine. He forgot the doctor's prohibition, his own suffering and all other things, and began talking with me as before."

2. The month of Ashad (June-July) passed. For more than a month the Master had been undergoing treatment and the pain did not show any sign of abatement. Though he felt it less at other times, the pain increased during the full moon and new moon days and the eleventh days of both the fortnights of the lunar month. It was absolutely impossible for him at that time to swallow any kind of solid food or vegetable. The Master, therefore, took on those days milk with a little rice or coarse flour of wheat boiled in milk only. Doctors examined him and diagnosed that he had contracted the ailment known as 'clergyman's throat'; that is, his organ of speech had been too much exercised in giving religious instructions to people day and night, and his throat was about to develop that particular disease. Doctors prescribed medicine, diet, etc., after diagnosing the disease. Although the Master completely followed most of the prescriptions, it was violated in respect of two points. Unable to control himself on account of his deep love of God and infinite compassion for the people parched by the heat of worldly misery, he could not avoid entering into ecstasy, nor could he cease talking to them. As soon as there arose any talk about God, he continued to enter into ecstasy as before; and when people, blinded by the darkness of ignorance or overwhelmed with grief and sorrow, came to him in quest of illumination, consolation and peace, he would, losing himself in compassion

for them, throw all medical prohibitions to the winds, and proceed to instruct those enquirers and bless the afflicted.

3. Many men with spiritual longing were coming to the Master then. Besides the earlier devotees, new persons numbering five or six, were daily seen to knock at his door, thirsting for spirituality. It had become a daily occurrence ever since Kesav had come to Dakshineswar in the year A.D. 1875 and begun to proclaim his glory. Therefore for the past eleven years, the Master was often led away by his zeal for the relief of the spiritually hungry and thirsty, and was not able to keep regular hours for daily bath, meals and rest. Besides he had very little sleep owing to the impulsion of the Mahabhava. At the time when we were staying with him at Dakshineswar, we saw on very many occasions that he got up shortly after he went to bed at 11 p.m. and strolled in an ecstatic mood. He now opened the western door, now the northern, and went out; again, though sometimes lying quietly on his bed, he was fully awake. He left his bed three or four times during the night, and yet he rose daily as soon as it was 4 a.m., waited for the light of the dawn, remembering, thinking on, and singing the glories of the divine Lord and would then wake us. Is it therefore surprising that his body should have got worn out on account of his sleeplessness at night and his excessive labour in giving spiritual instruction to many people during the day?

4. Although the Master did not tell any one that his body was getting too tired and exhausted, we had an inkling of it in his loving quarrels with the universal Mother, but could not completely understand it. One of us went to Dakshineswar one day shortly before the Master fell ill and saw that, seated on his small bedstead in an ecstatic mood, he was addressing someone saying, "Thou bringest all worthless people here. One seer of milk adulterated with five seers of water! My eyes are red and swollen and my bones reduced to powder with pushing wet fuel into the fire and by constant blowing through my mouth. I cannot work so much. If it is Thy pleasure, do it Thyself. Bring good people here — those who will attain spiritual awakening even by a word or two." On another occasion he said to the devotees who were with him, "I was saying to Mother today, 'Give a little power to these — Vijay, Girish, Kedar, Ram, and the Master (M., the author of the Gospel), so that the new people may come here after they have got their angularities somewhat rounded by them.'" Regarding the question

of remoulding the spiritual attitudes and lives of people, he said to a woman devotee at one time, "Pour water yourself, and let me prepare the mud." While staying still at Dakshineswar, finding that the crowds at his door thirsting for spiritual ministration was on the increase, the Master once said in ecstasy to the Divine Mother just a few days after he first felt the pain in his throat, "Shouldst Thou bring so many people? Thou hast produced a veritable crowd; I don't find time to bathe and take my meal. It is only a drum, and that too one with holes in it (meaning his own body). How long can it last if it is played on day and night?"

5. By the end of the year A.D. 1884, the presence of the Master at Dakshineswar came to be widely known all over Calcutta. His unique personality, his frequent experience of ecstasy, his ambrosial words conveying the highest teachings of religion in very simple form, his unique power of rousing the spiritual potentialities of aspirants, his unselfish love for every one without distinction of caste or creed — all these were the general talk among the people of Calcutta, and large numbers of them began to pour into Dakshineswar to see him, and many of them, having seen him once, to repeat their visits. But their number cannot be estimated; for, there was never an opportunity for all of them to come together at one place on the same day. And this was good in a way. For had it not been so, the inner circle of the Master's devotees, who were feeling elated over their own swelling numbers and by the awareness of their object of love and worship becoming the object of love and worship of an ever-increasing circle of people, would have recognised an evil foreboding in these developments and their joy would have been overcast with a shadow of fear and dejection; for, had they not heard the Master repeat time and again, "When many people will regard this (me) as God and love and respect this (me), it (the body) will immediately disappear?" Had they been meeting frequently, they would surely have discussed this matter and made themselves unhappy thereby.

6. The Master gave us from time to time many hints about the time of his passing away. But, blinded by his love, we did not then pay heed to his words, though we heard them uttered somewhat explicitly. Nor could we comprehend their import though we understood them literally. All then had but one idea in their minds, viz., how all their friends and relatives could enjoy through the Master's grace the peace which they themselves were enjoying.

Therefore, the fear that he might pass away never crossed their minds. The Master had said to the Holy Mother as follows, four or five years before he had the throat disease: "When I shall take food out of anybody's and everybody's hand, pass nights in Calcutta, and give a portion of my food to others first and then take the rest myself, know that the time of my passing away is fast approaching." The course of events was actually turning out to be as predicted, even some time before he contracted the disease in his throat. Invited to the houses of people in various places in Calcutta, the Master was now taking all kinds of food, except cooked rice, out of the hand of anybody and everybody. He accidentally spent nights also at Balaram Babu's house now and then. As Narendra was ill with dyspepsia and did not come to the Master at Dakshineswar for many days, thinking that there could be no arrangement about his diet there, the Master had him brought in the morning to Dakshineswar one day, fed him early with a part of the rice and soup cooked for him, and took the rest himself. The Holy Mother objected to this and expressed a desire that she should cook for the Master again, when he said, "My mind did not shrink from giving a portion of the food first to Naren. So there will be no harm in that. You need not cook again." The Holy Mother said later, "Although the Master said so, I felt uneasy on remembering his words spoken long ago."

7. Although his body became exhausted on account of excessive strain in teaching people, the zeal of his mind in this respect was never seen to wane. As soon as a fit person arrived, he could know his fitness in his heart of hearts, and losing himself in the influx of a divine power, would either instruct him or touch him and thus open for him the path to spiritual progress. It used to happen like this. The newcomer's spiritual mood would evoke a response from the Master's mind, throwing into the background all other moods of his for some time. He would then see with his divine vision how far that person had gone towards perfection and why he could go no farther. Next he would remove all obstacles on that person's path and make him ascend to higher planes of consciousness. Thus he always served the Jivas as Siva till the last moment of his life, and thus slaked the spiritual thirst of numerous people of all stations of life. It was, indeed, as a result of their strivings and the good deeds of several past lives, that this spiritual thirst was generated in them, and now they became,

at the Master's hand, the recipients of the highest of all gifts — the supreme Light of Knowledge and the Abode of Fearlessness.

8. We always saw clearly a power in the Master of detecting the hidden ideas and the past impressions in the minds of people. This can be said to be a good proof of the fact that physical health or illness never touched his mind. But although he knew completely the mystery of other people's minds, he never divulged it to any one with a view to showing off his extraordinary power. He let any one know only that fragment of his power which would do good to him and point out a higher path to him, or, in the case of a fortunate few, make their faith in the Master himself firm and unshakable. We give here an ordinary example of it for the benefit of the reader.

9. Hearing that the pain in the Master's throat had increased, one of our acquaintances, a lady, was about to go to see him in the month of August in the year 1885. Another lady of the locality came to know of it and said to her, "There is nothing else in the house today to send to the Master through you. Will you please take with you a potful of milk?" The former refused and said, "There is no lack of good milk at Dakshineswar, and there is, I know, an arrangement to provide him with milk. Moreover, it will be very inconvenient to carry it. Milk, therefore, need not be taken."

On reaching Dakshineswar, she saw that it was not possible for the Master to take any diet except milk mixed with rice on account of the pain in his throat, and that the Holy Mother was very anxious, as the milk-woman could not, for some reason, give the daily quota of milk. The lady devotee now repented of her not bringing the milk from Calcutta. She began inquiring whether milk was sold anywhere in the village, and came to know that not far from the temple, there was an upper-Indian, known as Mrs. Pande, who had a cow and was selling milk. She went to her house but was told that all her milk had been sold except about three ounces of it, which she had already boiled. Being told by the lady devotee that she needed it very badly, the milk woman sold it to her. With the milk thus procured, a thin pudding of rice-milk was made and the Master fed with it. He then got up to wash his mouth and the lady devotee helped him by pouring water into his hand. Afterwards the Master called her aside and said to her with affection, "I feel much pain in my throat, will you please utter the

Mantra you know to cure diseases and pass your hand once over the throat?" Hearing these words, the lady was amazed for some time. She then passed her hand over the Master's throat as desired by him, and then, coming to the Holy Mother, she said, "How could he know about my having this Mantra? Long ago I learnt it from a woman of the Ghoshpara community, knowing that one can accomplish certain desired ends with it. Afterwards I abandoned it when I came to understand that one should call on God without any motive. I had told everything of my life to the Master except my initiation in the Mantra of the Kartabhaja sect, lest he should dislike me for it. How could he then know about it?" Informed thus, the Holy Mother smiled and said affectionately, "He can know all the thoughts and actions of others. But that does not affect his good will towards others. He never dislikes any one for doing anything, if one is sincere and one's motives are good. You need not be afraid. I also had been initiated in that Mantra before I came here. I told him about it, and he replied, 'It does not matter that you were initiated in the Mantra; now offer it at the lotus feet of your chosen Ideal.'"

10. Some time passed, but the pain in the Master's throat was only on the increase in spite of all treatment. The devotees thought again and again over the situation, but could come to no decision about the future course of action. Just then an event took place, which made them take an immediate decision. A lady of Baghbazar had invited the devotees that day to supper at her house. She had a great desire to bring the Master too, but knowing that he was ill, gave up that hope almost completely. Nevertheless, thinking that it might be possible for him, without any difficulty or adverse effect, just to take a drive and grace the occasion by a brief visit to her place, she requested a devotee to go to him at Dakshineswar. As that person did not return even by 9 p.m., she had the guests seated for their meal without further delay. Just then, the person sent to Dakshineswar returned and informed that the pharynx of the Master bled that day and so he could not come. Those present — Narendra, Ram, Girish, Devendra, Mahendra and others — became very anxious on hearing it, and after holding some deliberations amongst themselves on the matter, came to the conclusion that a house in Calcutta should be hired and the Master brought there immediately for treatment. Seeing Narendra dejected at the time of taking food, a young man asked him the reason for it,

to which he replied, "He, who is the source of all our joy, is perhaps going to leave us this time. I have come to know from medical books and talks with doctor friends that this kind of throat disease gradually develops into cancer. Hearing of the bleeding today I suspect the disease to be that one for which the medical science has not discovered any cure yet."

11. When, next morning a few elderly devotees went to Dakshineswar and requested the Master to move to Calcutta for treatment there, he agreed. All knew the Master's love of the Ganga, and so when the devotees found that the river was visible from the roof of a small house at Durgacharan Mukherjee's street in Baghbazar, they hired it and brought him to stay there shortly afterwards. But when the Master, who was habituated to living in the open atmosphere of the spacious garden of the Kali temple, entered that small house, he found it impossible to live there, and walked immediately to Balaram Basu's house on Ramkanta Basu street. Balaram received him lovingly and requested him to stay there until a suitable house was available. He agreed to it.

12. The search for a suitable house went on. Thinking that it was not proper to waste time, the devotees meanwhile called the well-known physicians of Calcutta and secured their opinions about the Master's disease. Gangaprasad, Gopimohan, Dwarakanath, Navagopal and some others were called in. They examined the Master and diagnosed that he had contracted the incurable disease *Rohini*, the inflammatory affection of the throat. Gangaprasad, questioned privately by a devotee, said, "Rohini is what the Western doctors call cancer. Although there is a treatment of the disease prescribed in the books, it is considered incurable." Seeing that no hope was held out by the physicians and knowing that too much drugging never agreed with the Master's constitution, the devotees thought it desirable to have him treated according to homoeopathy. In about a week, the house of Gokulchandra Bhattacharya, situated on the Shyampukur street, was hired for the Master to live in and he was placed for some time under the treatment of Dr. Mahendralal Sarkar, the famous doctor of Calcutta.

13. The news of the Master's coming to Calcutta spread from mouth to mouth all over the city. Coming in batches to see the Master, many known and unknown people made the house of Balaram ring with joy as on a festive occasion. Although he

remained silent from time to time to conform to the doctor's advice, the plaintive prayers of the devotees always made him talk to them on spiritual matters with such a zeal and energy that it seemed that he had come to Calcutta for that purpose only, — that he had come for sometime to the doors of those who could not go up to Dakshineswar to gain the light of spirituality from him. Every day of that week's stay at Balaram's, from early morning to the time of his midday meal, and again, after a rest of about two hours, to the time of his night meal and retirement to bed, he solved the complicated problems of the spiritual lives of many people, and attracted many persons to the path of spirituality through discussions on various topics regarding God and spiritual life. Entering into the deep realm of ecstasy while listening to devotional songs, he filled to overflowing the hearts of many individuals thirsting after religion, with a flood of peace and bliss. None of us had the good fortune to be present there at all times on all days. The owner of the house also had many a time to be busy elsewhere, making various arrangements about the Master and the devotees. It is therefore almost impossible to have a detailed description of that week. So we shall content ourselves with mentioning one event only, to explain to the reader how the Master passed those days in the house of Balaram.

14. We were studying at college then. So, we had leisure enough to see the Master only once or twice a week. We came to Balaram's house one afternoon and found the hall on the first floor packed to capacity with people, when Girish and Kalipada commenced singing with great zeal:

> "O Nitai, hold me!
> Today my heart feels an unknown sensation, as it were."

Entering the room with great difficulty, we saw the Master, who was in ecstasy, seated in the western extremity of the room facing the east. We saw his lips adorned with a wonderful smile of bliss and graciousness and his right leg raised and stretched. A person who sat before him was holding that leg very lovingly and carefully on his breast. That man had his eyes shut and cheeks and chest flooded with tears. All sat motionless in that room, filled as it was with a divine presence emanating from the Master. The song went on:

> Today my heart feels an unknown sensation, as it were.
> Hold me, O Nitai!

I am now being carried away by the waves
That rose in the river of love,
As Nitai distributes the name of Hari.
To Nitai, I have written the bond with my own hand,
To which the 'eight friends'[1] are witnesses.
How can I pay off my debt to the creditor of love?
For, all my accumulated wealth has run out,
And still the debt remains unpaid.
Now I am going to be auctioned on account of that debt of love.

The song now came to an end. The Master had partial consciousness some time after and said to the person before him, "Say, Sri Krishna Chaitanya! Say, Sri Krishna Chaitanya! Say, Sri Krishna Chaitanya!" Thus making him utter that name thrice consecutively, the Master regained his normal consciousness shortly afterwards and began talking to others. On inquiry, we came to know that the name of that person was Nityagopal Goswami, that he was a professor of a college at Dacca, and that hearing the news of the Master's illness, he had come to see him. The Goswami had an impressiveness of form, which was enhanced by his devotional zeal.

[1] The eight main female friends of Radha, the divine consort of Krishna. — Tr.

CHAPTER XII: SECTION 1

THE MASTER'S STAY AT SHYAMPUKUR

[TOPICS: 1. A description of the Shyampukur house. 2. Dr. Mahendralal Sarkar engaged to treat the Master. 3. His diet and nursing at night. 4. Bashfulness of the Holy Mother. 5. The proposal of bringing her to Shyampukur. 6. The Holy Mother's capacity for adjustment. 7. The route from Kamarpukur to Dakshineswar. 8. The Holy Mother's travel up to Tarakeswar. 9. In the dreary tract of Telo-Bhelo. 10. The Bagdi couple. 11. Their solicitude for the Holy Mother. 12. The Holy Mother bidding goodbye to the couple. 13. The Holy Mother at Shyampukur house. 14. The boy devotees serve the Master.]

1. The house now hired for the Master extended lengthwise from east to west and was situated on the north side of the Shyampukur street. As soon as one entered the house, one saw on one's left and right, a pavement and a narrow open verandah to sit in. Going a few steps forward, one found to one's right a flight of steps leading to the first floor, and in front a courtyard with two or three small rooms on its eastern side. Going upstairs by the staircase, one saw to one's right a long room extending north to south, meant for visitors to sit in, and on the left, the corridor leading to the rooms extending east to west. This corridor led first of all to the door of the hall called the parlour. This was the room which the Master occupied. To its north and south there were two verandahs, the northern one being broader. To its west, were two small rooms in one of which some of the devotees slept at night, while the other was given to the Holy Mother to live in at night. Besides, there was a narrow verandah to the west of the room intended for all to sit in. The steps leading to the roof were situated to the east of the corridor to the Master's room and there was a covered terrace about six feet by six feet near the door leading to the roof. The Holy Mother spent the whole day on that terrace and cooked there the necessary diet for the Master. The Master came from Balaram's to this house some time in the second half of Bhadra or the beginning of the month of September, 1885, and spent a little more than three months there. From there he moved to the garden house at Kasipur a day or two before the month of Agrahayan (Nov.-Dec.) came to an end.

2. In accordance with their previous decision, the devotees called in Dr. Mahendralal Sarkar for the treatment of the Master, a few days after he had come to the Shyampukur house. During the life-time of Mathur Bàbu, the doctor had come a few times to Dakshineswar for the treatment of Mathur's family and was not altogether unknown to the Master. But that was long ago. It was, therefore, quite natural for the famous doctor to have forgotten everything connected with those visits, and so the devotees called him without telling him the name of the patient whom he was going to treat. But he recognized the Master as soon as he saw him, and examining him and diagnosing the disease with great care, prescribed medicine and diet. Afterwards he spent a little time in conversation on spiritual matters and about the Kali temple at Dakshineswar, before he bade good-bye to him that day. On that occasion, the doctor, so far as we remember, asked the devotees to inform him every morning about the Master's physical condition. He accepted his usual fee at the time of his leaving when the devotees offered it to him. But coming on the morrow to visit the Master, he came to know in the course of conversation that the devotees had brought him to Calcutta and were meeting all the expenses. He was pleased to see their devotion to their Guru and declined to accept fees any more. He said, "I'll treat him without taking any fee and help you in your noble endeavours according to my capacity."

3. The devotees could not be free from anxiety in spite of having the assistance of a highly experienced physician. They were convinced in a few days that persons should be appointed to serve the Master day and night whenever necessary, and to prepare his diet carefully. Knowing that neither of those two wants could be removed merely by spending money, the devotees decided to bring the Holy Mother from Dakshineswar to remove the second want and take the help of the boy-devotees to remove the first. But great obstacles lay ahead. For, they were at a loss to understand how the Holy Mother could live there alone, as there was no inner apartment for ladies in the house. Again the guardians of the boy-devotees would be highly displeased if they were to come there daily and pass nights without sleep.

4. Many of the devotees were in great doubt about the Holy Mother's coming there. They were rather justified in their doubt, for did they not know of her exceptional shyness and modesty?

Although she was staying in the Nahabat in the north of the garden at Dakshineswar and had engaged herself daily in the service of the Master all these years, no one else, except two or three boy-devotees whom the Master himself introduced to her, ever saw her holy feet or heard her voice during that long period. Although she lived the whole day in that small room and prepared varieties of food twice daily for the Master and the devotees, no one could know that anyone was engaged in doing those duties there. She left her bed every day a little after three in the morning, long before anyone else rose from sleep, and having performed the personal duties of the morning, including ablutions in the Ganga, she entered that room and never came out during the whole day. Calmly and silently she finished all her work with wonderful quickness and engaged herself in worship, Japa and meditation. On one occasion during a dark night, while she was going down the steps of the Ghat under the Bakul tree in front of the Nahabat, she almost trod on a crocodile which was lying on a step. Fortunately at the sound of her footsteps, it jumped into the water. She never again went to the Ghat without taking a light with her.

5. Not one of the devotees could imagine how the Holy Mother, who had been living in that small Nahabat room for so long a time, unseen by anyone, could give up all her bashfulness and live the whole day in the midst of menfolk in that house. Finding no alternative, they were compelled to talk to the Master on that matter. The Master reminded them of her nature as described above and said, "Will she be able to stay here? However, ask her and see whether, knowing all the circumstances, she likes to come here. If she does, let her come." A messenger was sent to the Holy Mother at Dakshineswar.

6. No one, the Master said, could attain peace or reach his desired goal, if he could not adjust himself to changed circumstances, to the change of time, place and person when required; or who failed to act up to the principle, as the Master himself put it, "As the man so the treatment; as the time so the movement; as the place so the action." Although she always kept herself surrounded by the impregnable screen of bashfulness and modesty, the supremely revered Holy Mother had that instruction from the Master and learnt to regulate her life accordingly. The reader will be able to understand clearly, from the description of her first visit to Dakshineswar (cf. II. 20) and from the event mentioned below,

how easily and naturally she could, whenever necessity arose, free herself from all habits and past impressions and behave correctly without the least fear or hesitancy.

7. In those days the Holy Mother, for want of money and cheap conveyance, had many a time to come on foot from Jayaramvati and Kamarpukur to Dakshineswar. The wayfarers who undertook journeys that way had to proceed to Jahanabad (Arambag) and by crossing the ten-mile-long field of Telo-Bhelo come to Tarakeswar, and thence, traversing similarly the field of Kaikhola reach Vaidyavati, where they crossed the Ganga. At that time there were ambuscades by dacoits in those two vast fields. It is said even now how many wayfarers lost their lives at their hands even in the morning hours, at midday, and at dusk. Even today one meets with a very terrible image of Kali, having a mouth with large projecting teeth in the middle of the field about two miles from the two small contiguous villages of Telo and Bhelo. She is known amongst the local people as the "Kali of the dacoits" of Telo-Bhelo. The decoits, it is said, worshipped Her before proceeding to kill human beings and commit other cruel deeds. Travellers did not venture in those days to cross the two fields except in groups in order to protect themselves from the hands of the dacoits.

8. Once the Holy Mother was coming on foot from Kamarpukur to Dakshineswar with the daughter and the younger son of Rameswar, the Master's elder brother, as also some other men and women. They reached Arambag, and thinking that there was yet sufficient time to cross the field of Telo-Bhelo before dusk, most of the members of the party were for continuing their journey instead of halting for the night at Arambag. Although very tired on account of the journey, the Holy Mother did not tell anybody of her difficulty but proceeded with the party. But scarcely had they walked four miles before she felt unable to keep pace with her companions and began to lag behind. They waited a little for her and on her joining them, asked her to walk faster and moved on again. When they came to the middle of the field, they found that she was lagging far behind the others. They waited there once more for her and said when she came up, "At this pace it will be very late at night before we cross this dangerous field, and there is the chance of all of us falling into the hands of dacoits." Feeling that she had become the cause of inconvenience and apprehension to so many

people, the Holy Mother forbade them to wait for her on the way, saying, "Go direct, all of you, to the next stage at Tarakeswar and rest there; I shall try to be with you as soon as possible." Seeing that it was nearing sunset, her companions found it convenient to take her words literally. They walked away fast and were soon out of sight.

9. The Holy Mother then began to walk on as fast as she could. But on account of extreme physical exhaustion, her pace slackened, and hardly had she reached the middle of the dreary tract when darkness enveloped the earth. Extremely anxious, she was thinking of what she should do, when she saw a tall, jet-black man with a staff on his shoulder coming forward with a rapid step towards her. It appeared that another person, seemingly a companion of his, was also coming a little behind him. Seeing that fleeing or crying was in vain, the Holy Mother stood still and awaited their coming with an apprehensive heart.

10. The man came up to her in a few moments and asked her in a harsh tone, "Who are you standing here at such a time?" With a view to pleasing him, the Holy Mother called him 'father' and submissively said, "Father, my companions have left me behind and it seems I have lost my way too. Will you kindly accompany me to the place where they are? Your 'son-in-law' lives at Rani Rasmani's Kali temple at Dakshineswar. I am on my way there. He will be very pleased if you will kindly take me up to that place." Scarcely had those words been spoken when the other person also came up. The Holy Mother saw that it was not a man but a woman, the wife of the man. She became highly reassured to see that woman, and catching hold of her hand and addressing her as 'mother', said, "Mother, I am your daughter Sarada. Left behind by my companions, I was in great danger. You and father have fortunately happened to come! I don't know what I would have done otherwise."

11. The hearts of the Bagdi[1] robber and his wife melted on account of the absolute reliance, the sweet words, and the unhesitating and simple-hearted behaviour of the Holy Mother. They forgot the social barriers of caste and other such considerations under the upsurge of parental affection for her, and looking

[1] A rather low caste people but generally noted for their physical strength and valour. Formerly, they made very good soldiers. Later, when the British stopped recruitment in Bengal, many of them turned dacoits. — Tr.

on her as their own daughter, solaced and comforted her. Afterwards, considering her physical fatigue, they took her to a small shop in the neighbourhood and arranged for her stay there for the night, instead of allowing her to proceed on her way to the next village of Telo-Bhelo. The woman spread her own cloth and prepared a bed for the Holy Mother while the man brought puffed rice and sweetened parched rice for her to eat. Thus with parental care and love, they asked her to sleep, themselves guarding her for the whole night. They woke her in the morning and reached Tarakeswar with her in about an hour after sunrise. They took her to a shop there and asked her to rest. The woman then addressed her husband and said, "My daughter had nothing to eat last night. So go and offer worship to Father Tarakeswar Siva, and then bring fish and vegetables from the market. She must be fed well today."

12. While the man had gone to procure things from the market, the companions of the Holy Mother came there in search of her and felt joy to find that she had reached the place safely. The Holy Mother then introduced to them her 'father' and 'mother' who had given her shelter at night, saying, "I cannot say what I would have done last night if they had not come and saved me." Afterwards, finishing worship and cooking and taking food, they rested a little at that place. When they were all ready to start for Vaidyavati, the Holy Mother expressed her infinite gratefulness to the man and the woman, and begged their permission to take leave. In later days the Holy Mother used to say, "We became so much attached to one another within that one night that I felt highly moved and shed incessant tears at the time of taking leave of them. At last I requested them to come to see me at Dakshineswar at their convenience, and only when they promised to do so, could I come away from them with great difficulty. When we left, they came with us a great distance, and the woman wept bitterly, plucked some peas from the neighbouring field, and tied them at the end of my cloth, saying plaintively 'Sarada, my child, please take these with the parched rice you will be eating at night.' They kept the promise they made to me. They came to Dakshineswar a few times with some sweets. He (the Master) also heard everything from me and pleased them by receiving them lovingly and behaving towards them like a 'son-in-law' on those occasions. Although gentle and well-behaved now, it seems to me that my 'dacoit father'

must have committed dacoity several times before."

13. Now on hearing that the Master's ailment might aggravate if his diet were not prepared strictly according to the medical injunctions, the Holy Mother came gladly to the Shyampukur house to take up that work, without in the least minding her own inconvenience in staying there. One is surprised to think how she stood every kind of inconvenience and did her duty for three months, staying in a house of one apartment only, among unknown men. Although there was only one place for all to take bath, no one knew when she finished her ablutions in the morning and went up to the terrace near the steps leading to the roof of the second floor before 3 a.m. She spent the whole day there, prepared diet for the Master at proper times, and then sent word downstairs through Swami Adbhutananda (Latu) or old Swami Advaitananda (Gopal-da). At that time people were asked to move away, and she brought the diet downstairs and fed the Master herself or we, the disciples, did the feeding, according to convenience. At midday she took her food and rested there. At 11 p.m., when all were asleep, she came down from that place and slept till two in the morning in the room on the first floor allotted to her. Fortifying her heart with the hope of seeing the Master cured, she spent day after day in that way. She stayed there so silently and unnoticed that even many of those who visited the house daily could not know that she lived there and took upon herself the hardest and the most important work in the service of the Master.

14. When the problem of preparing the diet was thus solved, the devotees applied their minds to the removal of the other want, namely, that of rendering personal service to the Master at night. Narendra himself took charge of it and began staying there. Encouraged by his example, Gopal (junior), Kali, Sasi and a few other smart young men came forward to join him in that work. All of them were firmly determined to live the life for the highest ideal, namely, the realization of God. Inspired by the blazing renunciation of the Master, by his holy words and company, and by their love and regard for him, they resolved to dedicate themselves to his service. Their guardians did not object to their coming to the Shyampukur house and serving the Master till they understood their ultimate purpose. But, as the Master's illness increased, they altogether stopped going to colleges for study or even to their own houses to take food. The guardians then became suspicious.

Their suspicion gradually yielding place to alarm, they started adopting various means, proper and improper, to dissuade the young men from their devoted service. The boy-devotees, it is superfluous to say, could not have remained firm and unmoved but for Narendranath's example, inspiration and encouragement. Although only four or five persons at that time dedicated their lives and commenced the vow of service at the Shyampukur house, the number of those who undertook the vow multiplied almost four times by the time of its completion in the Kasipur garden.

CHAPTER XII: SECTION 2

THE MASTER'S STAY AT SHYAMPUKUR

[TOPICS: 1. The part of householder devotees in serving the Master. 2. Sacrifice by the householder devotees. 3. The disease knits the devotees together into an Order. 4. The devotees' three conceptions about the Master. 5. The devotees' love for one another. 6. Devotees' experience of special spiritual manifestation in the Master. 7. Dr. Sarkar's attraction for the Master. 8. The doctor's love of truth. 9. Para Vidya and Apara Vidya. 10. The Lord is limitless. 11. The intellect gives up but the heart hankers after more. 12. The pulse of boy-devotee in Bhavasamadhi was examined. 13. The "heat" (pride) generated by learning. 14. The humility of the doctor. 15. "There is substance in him". 16. The Master leads the doctor along the path of spirituality. 17. Failure of medicine causes anxiety to the doctor. 18. Much harm due to a slight irregularity. 19. The doctor's reverence for the Master increases. 20. The doctor's opinion about incarnations of God. 21. The disease aggravated. 22. The wonderful Bhavasamadhi of the Master at the annual worship of Kali. 23. The preparation for the worship. 24. The Master sat silent. 25. Girishchandra worships the Master in Bhavasamadhi. 26. The devotees too worship him. 27. The devotees' direct spiritual experiences about the Master. 28. Balaram's association with the Master resented by his relatives. 29. They obstruct Balaram. 30. The early life of Balaram. 31. Balaram meeting the Master. 32. Balaram's cousin Harivallabh's coming to Calcutta. 33. The Master's desire to see Harivallabh. 34. Girish bringing Harivallabh to the Master. 35. The Master's touch and its result. 36. Increasing number of devotees. 37. The Master's attractive sweetness. 38. An example; Upendra, a sub-judge. 39. Upendra's experience of the Master. 40. God is both with form and without form. 41. Atul's annoyance at brother Ram's words.]

1. The devotees, however, did not feel free from anxiety even after making the above-mentioned arrangements for the Master's treatment, diet, and twenty-four hour nursing attention. For, they had understood from the pronouncement of some of the best physicians of Calcutta that his throat-disease, though not altogether incurable, was none-the-less very difficult to treat, and that it would take a very long time for him to get relief. It was, therefore, a matter of concern for them now as to how the expenses could be met for continuing the service till he finally recovered. This was natural. For, Balaram, Surendra, Ramachandra,

Girishchandra, Mahendranath and others who brought the Master to Calcutta for treatment — all of them were not very affluent. None of them had the means for taking the sole responsibility of meeting the Master's expenses together with those of his attendants, after meeting the demands of their own family budgets. Urged by the current of heavenly hope, light, bliss and peace that flowed in their hearts because of the Master's presence in their midst, they took up that work without any consideration whatever of the future. But it was quite unreasonable to expect that this holy current would always be in flood-tide and would know no ebb when the thought of the future came to disturb their peace and bliss. And as a matter of fact the current did not flow uniformly. But it is wonderful that as soon as such moments came, they experienced marvellous spiritual manifestations of the Master which made that anxiety vanish altogether, and their hearts were again filled with zeal and strength.

An experience of unrestrained bliss carried them to a plane far beyond the reach of the intellect, and they saw in a flash of divine illumination that he whom they accepted as the supreme goal of all living beings — the very God as man, the veritable Narayana himself — and his birth, austerities, and even ordinary acts, not to speak of the present sufferings due to physical illness, were all for the good of humanity. Otherwise how could there be bodily illness in the Supreme Person, all of whose resolves came true and who was beyond the miseries of birth and death, of disease and dotage? They were convinced that he was feigning illness and staying there in order that those who had not the leisure and opportunity to go up to Dakshineswar to see him might come and get the light of the Spirit kindled in their hearts, that the disciples might get the privilege of serving him and thereby have the ideal of their lives fulfilled.

They perceived in the Master's change to Calcutta a hidden purpose that it would give to many a man turned materialistic in outlook — an outlook due to the influence of Western education and the supposed wisdom of ill-understood natural sciences — an opportunity to observe his life based on the direct experience of the Divine, and thereby become converted to the ideal of renunciation, recognising the utter futility of a life of sense enjoyments. Why then, the disciples thought, should there be any apprehension about the scarcity of funds? He who had given them the privilege of serving him would also give them the power to see it through.

2. Let not the reader think that the above remarks are but an outburst of emotionalism on our part. We have recorded them only because we actually saw the devotees discussing these matters, as they gathered day in and day out around the Master. Many a time have we witnessed how, perturbed by the apprehension of possible deficiencies in the Master's service for want of money, they would gather together for mutual consultation, but would invariably disperse with a reassurance generated by their above-described mood. One of them said, "The Master will make his own arrangements. And what even if he does not? What anxiety is there as long as there is one brick upon another there (showing his own house)? I'll mortgage my house and defray the expenses of his service." Another said, "I'll be able to manage the service, just as I manage to meet the expenses at the time of the marriage or illness of my sons and daughters. There is no cause for apprehension as long as there are a few ornaments on the person of my wife." A third, again, instead of giving expression to such a feeling, curtailed the expenditure of his household and met unstintedly the expenses of the Master's service. It was under the influence of such a mood alone that Surendra personally bore the entire house-rent and Balaram, Ram, Mahendra and Girish together supplied whatever else was necessary for the Master and his attendants at that time.

3. The divine bliss that the devotees thus felt in their hearts had its support in the Master and helped very much now in drawing them together and binding them with the cord of love. Although the order of the devotees of Sri Ramakrishna is said to have started at Dakshineswar, it took form at Shyampukur and the Kasipur gardens, and grew so fast there that many of the devotees were of the opinion that one of the purposes served by the Master's disease was to bring about that development.

4. As time passed on, the loose talks and imaginations of the devotees about the purpose of the Master's disease and the time of his recovery, took definite shape and divided them into several well-defined groups. The discussions on these points were strongly reinforced by the account of the extraordinary events of the Master's early life and the wonderful conclusions of these devotees on them. One party thought and expressed openly to all that the physical disease of the Master, an incarnation of God,

was simply a feigning and not a reality. He had assumed it knowingly in order to accomplish some particular purpose and when that purpose was fulfilled he would again show himself as before. Girish, with his very great power of imagination, was the leader of that party. Another party was of the opinion that the Mother of the universe, in complete compliance with whose infinite will the Master was accustomed to live and do all kinds of acts, kept him ill for some time, in order to fulfil a particular hidden purpose of Her own, which would bring about the good of humanity. May be even the Master himself was not able to unravel that mystery. As soon as that purpose of Hers should be fulfilled, he would come round. Still another party expressed the view that birth, death, old age, and disease were natural to the body; all these would occur as long as the body lasted; that was the explanation of the Master's bodily disease. What, then, was the necessity for so much talk and speculation on it and for bringing in a supernatural, hidden cause to explain the situation? They were not ready to accept any conclusion about the Master without analysing it by means of reasoning and inference and arriving at a valid conclusion. They were the rational and practical group, eschewing sentimentalism. In place of speculating, they would like to serve the Master and work for his cure even endangering their own lives; they would try their best to follow the high spiritual ideals he stood for and cast their lives in the mould he had prepared; and they would, while serving him patiently, engage themselves in the spiritual practices he had instructed them in. It is superfluous to say that Narendranath, as the representative of the young disciples of the Master, expressed the last-mentioned view.

5. Although the Master's disciples, having different temperaments, thus held different opinions on such matters, on one point they were all in perfect agreement. All of them had the fullest faith in the fact that they would come to the supreme goal if they lived their lives according to his highly liberal teachings and attained his grace by engaging themselves in his service with all their heart. That was why there was amongst them no lack of love for one another, though one party believed him to be an incarnation of God, another the Guru or world teacher, a third a super-man, and still another a man-god.

6. We will now mention a few events that we witnessed ourselves and that are corroborative of the various kinds of spiritual

manifestations of the Master to the disciples. Those events were seen also by persons who could not be classed as disciples but who simply came to see him at that time.

7. Dr. Mahendralal Sarkar, who had taken charge of the Master's treatment, was trying his best to cure him. For many days he came to see the Master three times — morning, noon and evening. Every day after examination, prescription and other duties connected with his patient, he would spend some time in conversation with him on spiritual matters. As he repeated his visits, he gradually began to feel the attraction of the liberal spiritual ideas of the Master, and whenever he had leisure, he would spend two or three hours in his company. One day when the Master was about to express his gratefulness to the doctor for spending such a great portion of his valuable time there, the doctor hurriedly stopped him and said in his blunt way, "Well, do you think I spend so much time for your sake only? I have also a personal interest in it. I derive great joy in talking with you. Although I met you before, I did not find time to mix with and know you so intimately, busy as I was with many things. I like you so much, you know, because of your love of truth. You cannot deviate a hair's breadth in your speech and actions from what you know as true. Elsewhere I find that they say one thing and do another. I cannot at all put up with that. Don't think I am flattering you. I am not a fellow of that sort. I am a graceless son of my father, as they say; I would speak out plainly even to him, if he should do anything wrong. That is why I have gained notoriety for a sharp tongue!" Smiling, the Master rejoined, "Yes, I have heard of it: but so far I have got no proof of it, though you have been coming here so long."

8. The doctor replied smiling, "That is a piece of good luck for both of us. Otherwise, had anything appeared to be wrong, you would have found that Mahendra Sarkar is not the sort of a person to tolerate it. However, don't think I have no love for truth. I have been running hither and thither all my life only to establish what I know to be true; that is why I have taken to Homoeopathy; that is why 'The Association for the Cultivation of Science' has been founded; so also with all other works of mine."

Some of us, as far as we remember, hinted at that time that although the doctor had love for truth, he had love for the discovery of only relative truths (Apara Vidya), not leading direct to the realization of Brahman, but the Master's pursuit all his life has been after supreme Knowledge (Para Vidya) leading to the immediate Knowledge of Brahman, or the ultimate Truth.

9. A little excited, the doctor said, "That is the very bee in your bonnet. What are Para and Apara with regard to knowledge? What is higher or lower in connection with the revelation of truth? Again, even if you make an imaginary distinction, it must be admitted that one will have to attain Para Vidya through the Apara. We can comprehend God, the primeval cause of the universe, more clearly through the truths we know directly from the study of the natural sciences. I don't take into consideration those fellows, the atheistic scientists. I cannot even understand what they say; they are blind, though they have their eyes intact. But if anybody says that he has understood the whole of the endless and the beginningless God, he is a liar and a cheat; a lunatic asylum is his fit residence."

10. The Master smiled and said with a look of pleasure at the doctor, "Right you are; those who ascribe a limit to God are low-minded; I cannot bear their words."

11. Saying so, the Master asked one of us to sing the song of Ramprasad, the foremost of devotees, beginning with: Who knows, O my mind, how Kali is? The six philosophies cannot see Her. Some one then sang:

"Who knows, O my mind, how Kali is?
The Six Philosophies cannot see her.
Kali as the Hamsi co-habits with the Hamsa in the cluster lotuses.
The Yogi always meditates on Her in the lotuses, from the basic one to the thousand-petalled in the brain.
There are lakhs of proofs that Kali is the Self of one who is contented in the Self.
She, the saviour, resides according to Her sweet will in the hearts of all beings as the divine will.
Do you know how big is the Mother's womb in which is contained the macrocosm, Brahman's universe?
The great Gatherer (i.e. the Destroyer) alone has known the truth about Kali:
Who else knows it so?
Prasad sings: people might smile, but I must swim across the sea.

The heart has understood, but the intellect will not; a dwarf (that I am) attempts at catching the moon."

While listening to the song, the Master explained at intervals its import to the doctor in a low voice. When the singer sang, 'My heart rests satisfied but not the intellect,' the Master stopped him, saying, "Oh! It is all topsy-turvy there; it should be, 'My intellect rests satisfied but not my heart.' In trying to know God, the intellect easily understands that it is not for it to comprehend the endless and the beginningless God; but the heart is reluctant to feel it; it continues in its attempt to realize Him."

The doctor was charmed to hear the interpretation and said, "That's it. That fellow, the intellect, is extremely mean; meeting with a slight difficulty it asserts, 'It cannot be'. But the heart does not approve of it; and that is how all these discoveries have been made, and many more will be."

12. Seeing that one or two young men were in a trance and lost normal consciousness while listening to the song, the doctor came to them and examined their pulse, and said to the Master, "It seems they have no consciousness of external objects as in a fainting fit." Observing them to regain their previous normal consciousness when the Master passed his hand over their chest and uttered the name of God in their ears in a low tone, he said to the Master once more, "It seems to be all your play." He smiled and said, "It is not my play, but His will. Their minds have not yet become distracted by wife, son, money, name, fame, etc., and that is the reason why they become merged in God as they listen to the glory of His name."

13. The previous topic was raised again and the doctor was told by some devotees that although he (the doctor) accepted God and did not ascribe a limit to Him, there are several scientists who had done away with God; and there are others, who, while accepting His existence, proclaimed at the top of their voice that He was what they conceived Him to be, and that He had no power except what they credited Him with. The doctor replied, "Yes, that is very true; but do you think it is due to knowledge? No, it is the 'heat' generated by learning; it is due to an intellectual indigestion of knowledge. They think that they have solved the whole mystery of the universe because they have been able to know a trifling few things of His creation. These are the people with much learning

but little of experience. But those who have both these qualifications are free from this perverted outlook. As for myself, I can never entertain such an idea."

"You are right," said the Master. "With the acquisition of knowledge there comes egoism: 'I am a scholar, what I have understood is the only truth; others' opinions are wrong.' Man labours under many bondages. The pride of learning is one of them. You are so learned but fortunately you have escaped this kind of pride. That is due to His grace."

14. "What I have known and understood," said the doctor, a little warmed up, "seems to be very little, — almost nothing. There is no reason to get proud of it. So vast and varied are the things I am yet to learn about, that I think, or actually see, that every man knows many things which I don't know. I, therefore, don't feel humiliated to learn anything from anybody. It appears to me that I may have many things to learn even from them (pointing to us). I am ready to take the dust of the feet of all out of this consideration."

15. The Master heard it and said (showing us), "I also say to them. 'O Friend, as long as I live, so long do I learn'." Then pointing to the doctor, the Master continued, "Do you see, how free from pride he is? He has certainly substance in him and hence such an attitude." The doctor then bade good-bye.

16. As the doctor's faith in, and love for, him increased, the Master took greater care to lead him on the spiritual path. Besides, knowing that cultured people like talking with the cultured, the Master sent now and then selected disciples like Mahendranath, Grishchandra and Narendranath from among his disciples to have talks with the learned doctor. When he had become acquainted with Girish, the doctor witnessed the Buddhacharita staged on one occasion and extolled the play to the skies. He also saw some other plays of his. Similarly, he was charmed by a talk with Narendra, and invited him to lunch one day. Again, when he came to know of Narendra's proficiency in the art of music, he requested him to sing some devotional songs for him some day. A few days afterwards, when one afternoon the doctor came to see the Master, Narendra sang for him for over a period of two or three hours and thus kept his promise. The doctor was so pleased with the singing on the occasion that, before bidding good-bye, he blessed Narendra, embraced him, and kissed him, saying to the Master,

"I am very happy to see a boy like him come to follow the path to God-realization." Thereupon the Master looked at Narendra with evident pleasure and said, "Gauranga, it is said, came down to Nadia at the loud calls of Advaita; this time everything indeed is for him alone!" Whenever thenceforward the doctor came to see the Master and Narendra happened to be present there, he would invariably listen to a few devotional songs sung by him.

17. It was autumn, the time for the worship of Sri Durga in Bengal. At that time the illness of the Master varied from day to day, increasing on some days and decreasing on others. The treatment was making very little impact. One day the doctor came, and noticing that the disease had aggravated, ventured a remark, "There must have been some irregularity in diet. Please tell me what you ate today." The Master told him what food he had taken that day. He had had his usual rice-gruel, soup and milk in the morning, and milk and liquid food like barley-water in the evening. On hearing it the doctor said, "No, I can't take it; there must have been some departure from the prescription. Well, tell me please what vegetables were used for the soup." The Master replied, "There were potatoes, green plantains, egg-plants and also a piece or two of cauliflower." "Ah!" exclaimed the doctor with a start, "You have taken cauliflower! Here, you see, is a grave irregularity! Cauliflower is very hot and difficult to digest. How many pieces have you eaten?" "I did not eat a single piece," was the mild protest of the Master, "but then, I saw they were in the soup." The doctor replied, "It is immaterial whether you have actually eaten them or not; but there was certainly the juice of cauliflower in the soup. Your digestion has, therefore, been impaired, and the disease has increased today." The Master protested telling, "How is that? I have not taken cauliflower nor have I had disorder of the bowels; it is difficult to accept that the disease has worsened because of a little juice of it in the soup."

18. The doctor continued, "None of you have any idea as to how much harm can be done by some such slight alteration. Let me tell you an event of my life; you will understand the matter when you hear it. My power of digestion has always been bad; I have suffered from dyspepsia from time to time. Therefore, I am very careful about my food and strictly observe dietetic rules. I take nothing brought from the market. I have ghee and oil made at home. Still, at one time I caught a bad cold and contracted

bronchitis of a stubborn nature, which refused to be cured. It then crossed my mind that there was certainly something wrong regarding my food. But even detailed investigation could reveal no defect in the food I was taking daily. But sometime after, it suddenly came to my notice one day that the servant was feeding our cow with kidney-beans. I was being given the milk of that cow. On inquiry I came to know that a few maunds of that kidney-beans had been procured from a certain place. As no one liked to eat it lest one should catch cold thereby, it was being used to feed the cow. The two events, namely my feeding the cow with kidney-beans and my catching cold coincided perfectly as cause and effect. To verify it, I stopped feeding the cow with kidney-beans, and true to my guess, the cold subsided. It took me a long time on that occasion to be completely cured. I had to spend about four or five thousand rupees to go for a change of climate and other measures to effect complete recovery." The Master smiled to hear it and said, "Oh, dear! It is, I see, like the case of the man who passed by a tamarind tree and caught cold." All laughed. Though that inference of the doctor seemed a little too far-fetched, nobody raised any question about it, as they saw his firm faith in it. His prohibition was accepted and cauliflower was at once discarded from ingredients of the Master's soup.

19. The Master's love for him, together with his simple and sincere behaviour and his deep spirituality, attracted the doctor towards him, and a sort of reverence for him was slowly filling the doctor's heart. His words and actions on occasions clearly conveyed it. He was now regarding not only the Master but also his devotees with a loving eye and became convinced that they were not making of the Master a false idol. But it is not easy to say how he looked upon their profound faith in, and great devotion to, him. It seems that it appeared to him to be a little excessive. Yet he could clearly understand that they did not adopt their attitude for show or for any selfish motive. He, therefore, seems to have regarded it as something eluding his comprehension. Although he mixed intimately with the devotees and his keen intellect was engaged in solving the problem, it remained still an enigma to him. For, in spite of his being a believer in God, he was so deeply influenced by Western education that he was unable to understand how one could worship or revere a mere man as Guru or as incarnation of God, even when one actually saw in him an extraordinary

manifestation of divine power. He was against this attitude only because he could not understand it. The cause of this general antagonism of the modern educated people to it is not far to seek. Generations of disciples of those who are being worshipped in the world as incarnations of God, exaggerated certain things connected with their lives in such a way that they have made it impossible for others to believe these. The disciples, no doubt, did so in their zeal to propagate the glory of their Masters. But this false zeal has evoked antagonism. One day the doctor plainly communicated his difficulty in this connection before the Master. He said: "I can understand love, worship, and other forms of devotion to God, but a world of confusion arises as soon as that infinite God is said to have come down as man. It is difficult to understand that He incarnated Himself as the son of Yosoda[1], the son of Mary[2], the son of Sachi[3] and so on. That host of 'sons' has ruined the country." The Master smiled at these words and said to us, "What does he say? It is, however, true that low-minded fanatics many a time wanted to make them appear so great and act in such a way that these reactions are naturally produced in people's minds."

20 Girishchandra and Narendranath had from time to time many controversies with the doctor on the aforesaid opinion of his about God's incarnations, as a result of which he became a little wary of giving expression to such an opinion without due consideration. For, it was proved that many reasonable arguments could be given against his view. But what could not be accomplished by reason was done by the extraordinary love and sweetness of the Master and by the wonderful spiritual manifestations in him which the doctor saw with his own eyes. And that changed his opinion gradually to a great extent. The sudden appearance in the Master of the extraordinary manifestation of power that we witnessed (cf. II.8) during the annual worship of Durga at the juncture of the eighth and the ninth days of the bright fortnight of the lunar month of Aswin (September – October) that year, gave the doctor also an opportunity to witness and examine it. He was present there that day with another doctor friend of his and examined the heart beats etc., of the Master with instruments. His doctor friend did not refrain even from poking his finger into the open eyes of

[1] Sri Krishna. [2] Jesus Christ. [3] Sri Chaitanya.

the Master to see if they would wink. As a result of their examination, they were amazed, and they had to admit that science could not throw any light so far on the state of Samadhi in which one appeared to be dead externally to all intents and purposes, as was the case with the Master; that in the light of this the Western psychologists' characterization of this state as mere unconsciousness and their refusal to accept any dimension other than the sensuous was only a demonstration of their ignorance and unreasonable stubbornness; that in God's creation there are many things the mystery of which had not at all been explained by Western science and philosophy so far; and that there was very little likelihood of this mystery ever being solved in future. As the point has already been discussed elsewhere, it is needless to repeat here how factually true were the mental experiences of the Master on occasions when he appeared externally like one dead.

21. The month of Aswin (September – October) and that of Kartik (October – November) were over, and the day of the worship of Kali was approaching; but no improvement in the physical condition of the Master was seen. The good effect that the treatment produced at first was fast disappearing and there was apprehension lest the disease should assume a more serious turn. But the bliss and the cheerfulness of the Master's mind appeared to the devotees to increase rather than decrease. Although Dr. Sarkar visited him frequently now as before and changed medicines repeatedly, he did not get the expected result and considered the change of the season to be the cause; and that condition, he thought, would pass as soon as the cold of winter advanced a little.

22. The devotees witnessed an extraordinary spiritual manifestation of Divinity in the Master at the time of the annual worship of Kali also, as they did at the worship of Durga. At one time Devendranath had a desire to bring an image and worship Kali in it. Thinking that it would be a matter of great joy if he could carry that resolve into practice in the presence of the Master and his devotees, he made a proposal to perform that worship at the Shyampukur house. But the devotees thought that the Master's body would get more exhausted on account of the zeal, excitement and noise at the time of the worship and tried to dissuade him. These words of the devotees appeared to be reasonable to Devendra, who consequently gave up that idea. But on the day before the worship, the Master said all of a sudden to a few devotees, "Collect

all the ingredients for a brief worship; Mother Kali must be worshipped tomorrow." Happy to hear him say so, they began consulting others. But as they had no other instructions from the Master regarding the preparations for the worship except the aforesaid words, all kinds of suggestions were offered. Unable to come to a decision regarding such details as whether the worship was to be performed with sixteen ingredients or five, whether cooked rice was to be offered or not, who was to officiate as priest, etc., they decided at last to keep ready sandal-paste, flowers, incense, light, fruits, roots and sweets only and wait for further instructions from the Master, which they could carry out afterwards. But the Master gave them no further instructions even till the morning of the day of worship.

23. It was 7 p.m., the time of sunset. Seeing that the Master did not suggest to them anything more regarding the worship and was sitting quiet on his bed, the disciples washed clean a portion of the floor to the east of his bed, brought the collected articles and placed them there. While he was at Dakshineswar, the Master sometimes worshipped himself with sandal paste, flowers and other ingredients. Some of the devotees had witnessed it. At last they came to the conclusion that on that occasion also he would worship the universal consciousness and its power in the symbol of his own mind and body, or in other words perform the scriptural worship of oneself as identical with the Mother of the universe, as sanctioned by the scriptures. It was therefore no wonder that they should place the ingredients of worship near the Master's bed in the aforesaid manner. The Master did not in any way dissuade them from doing so.

24. All the articles were gradually brought. Incense was burnt and lamps were lighted and the room became illumined and filled with fragrance. Seeing that the Master was still sitting quietly, the devotees sat beside him. Some among them awaited his command and looked at him with a concentrated mind while some others meditated on the Divine Mother of the universe. The room was thus completely silent; and although there were thirty or more persons in it, the room seemed to be vacant altogether. Some time passed that way; but the Master even then sat quietly without himself beginning to perform the worship or asking anyone of us to do it.

25. The elderly devotees, Mahendranath, Ramchandra

Devandranath, Girishchandra and others, as well as the young devotees, were present. Many of them were surprised to notice the Master's silence about the worship. But Girishchandra, whom the Master often described as having a super-abundance[1] of faith, had a different sentiment surging in his heart. It struck him that the Master had no need to worship Kali for his own sake. If it was suggested that he had a desire to perform the worship under the impulse of pure devotion, why was he sitting thus quietly without doing so? There must be some other reason. Might it not be then that these preparations were meant for the devotees, so that they might be blessed by worshipping the Mother of the universe in the living image of the Master's person? It was certainly that. Thinking so, he was beside himself with joy, and suddenly taking the flowers and sandal-paste that were lying there before all, he offered handfuls of them at the lotus feet of the Master, uttering. "Victory to Mother!" At this, all the hairs of the Master's body stood on end, and he entered into profound ecstasy, his face radiating effulgence, his lips adorned with a divine smile and both his hands assuming the attitude of granting boons and freedom from fear. All this indicated the manifestation of the Divine Mother in him. These events occurred in such a short time that even many of the devotees who were near thought that Girish saw the Master in ecstasy first and then offered flowers at his holy feet, while to those who were a little farther away, it seemed that the luminous image of the Devi suddenly appeared before them in the body of the Master.

26. It is superfluous to say that there was no limit to the joy of the devotees. Each of them managed to take flowers and sandal-paste from the tray, and uttering a Mantra according to his liking, worshipped the lotus feet of the Master and filled the room with the repeated sounds of 'Jai' (victory). Some time passed this way when the ecstasy of the Master came to an end and he was in a state of partial consciousness. The fruits, roots, and other things collected for the worship were then brought to him and were given to him to eat. He, on his part, took a little of all those things and blessed the devotees so that their knowledge and devotion might increase. Afterwards they took his Prasada and sang the

[1] "Four or five annas more than the sixteen annas which go to make a rupee," as the Master used to put it.

glory of the Devi and the greatness of Her name till a late hour in the night.

The devotees experienced a joy that they had never felt before at this especial worship of the Divine Mother that year, the memory of which remained fresh in their minds ever after. And whenever sorrows and miseries came and they became dejected, that serene face of the Master, brightened with a divine smile and his hands promising boons and freedom from fear, appeared before them and reminded them that they were all under the protection of the Divine.

27. During his stay at Shyampukur, it was not only on such especial days of worship as the above that the devotees experienced the divine power and the divine nature of the Master, but they were witnessing its manifestation off and on without any differentiation of day or time. Needless to say, it strengthened their faith in him as a God-man. But it may be noted that such revelations did not take place before all and sundry. It was given only to a few devotees to witness them. They in their turn, communicated them to other devotees with similar results. This will be clear to the reader if we mention here a few events as examples.

28. We mentioned elsewhere certain matters connected with Balaram. Some of his relatives became ill disposed towards him because he and his family had developed love and reverence for the Master. They had sufficient reason to be so. Firstly, they held religious doctrines that were too narrow, and they were given too much to the observance of external rites and ceremonies, according to the training and education prevalent in the Vaishnava families in which they were born. They could not, therefore, comprehend the liberal doctrine of the Master; for he had the firm conviction that all religions and the different devotional traditions are true as means for realizing God. Besides he was not putting on any kind of external emblem of religion. All these were beyond the comprehension of these tradition-bound Vaishnava relatives of Balaram. They, therefore, regarded Balaram's liberal tendencies, acquired through the Master's grace and company, as lack of, and deviation from, religiosity. Secondly, wealth, honour, noble birth and other kinds of worldly superiority very often develop in man a peculiar kind of pride and egoism. These relatives of Balaram were also victims of this weakness. It was a matter of pride and glory to them to have been of the family of the late Krishnaram Basu of holy memory. So they felt wounded at heart

when they heard that Balaram forgot the great prestige and reputation of the family and went at any time, like an ordinary man, to the Master at Dakshineswar to be instructed by him in spiritual matters, and that, worst of all, he did not hesitate to take there his wife, daughters and other ladies. They were, therefore, determined to dissuade him now from such behaviour.

29. Proud people, when they find honest means unavailing to attain their desired end, do not hesitate to use foul ones. Some of the relatives of Balaram were now in that state of mind. They tried their best to dissuade him from going to the Master, first by reminding him that there were in the Vaishnava tradition itself well-recognised and orthodox saints like Bhagavan Das of Kalna to whom he could resort if he wanted holy company, and next by appealing to him that he should not bring discredit to the aristocratic traditions of their family by his conduct. When such appeals proved ineffective, they assumed an attitude of hatred towards the Master and did not even hesitate to calumniate him sometimes. It must of course be said that they received their reports about the Master at second hand. On the basis of it, they began to denounce him as devoid of single-minded devotion to his chosen Ideal, heterodox in matters of food, drink, customs, and usages, and antagonistic to the use of the emblems of the Vaishnava religion like marks on the forehead. Seeing that this did not produce any effect, they at last brought various distorted accounts of the Master and Balaram to the ears of his cousins Nimai Charan Basu and Harivallabh Basu.

30. The noble quality of kindness and the spirit of renunciation and dispassion which were dominant in Balaram convinced him that estates and other properties could not be managed properly without occasional recourse to cruel means. So he left his estates and other properties in the charge of Nimai Basu. Although what he got from him as the income of his property was hardly sufficient to meet all his requirements, he somehow managed his worldly affairs with it. He was also not physically fit to manage his affairs himself. In his early youth, he became so badly dyspeptic that he had to give up taking rice for twelve years at a stretch and live on barley water and milk. He spent a great part of that period at Puri for regaining his health. He then passed his time in Japa, worship, holy company, paying daily obeisance to the image of Jagannath and so on. He had thus opportunities for being well acquainted with whatever good or bad there was in the Vaishnava

community. His meeting with the Master took place on his return to Calcutta on some business after a long period of absence from that city.

31. Balaram had to come to Calcutta for a few weeks at the time of the marriage of his eldest daughter. His peace of mind during his full eleven years' life at Puri was not otherwise disturbed. His cousin Harivallabh Basu purchased the house at 57, Ramakrishna Basu Street, shortly after Balaram's return to Calcutta. His father and cousins secretly conferred together and asked him to live in the newly bought house, lest he should renounce the world on account of his intimate relation with the holy men at Puri. Deprived of the sacred company of holy men and the daily visits to the temple of Sri Jagannath, Balaram felt dejected and came to live in Calcutta with a heavy heart. He seems to have intended at first to go back to Puri somehow or other after a short stay; but he completely gave up that resolve when he met the Master, and decided to live permanently in Calcutta. Now he began to feel much worried from time to time, lest Harivallabh Basu should ask him to vacate the house, or Nimai Basu should call him to Kothar to look after the estates and other properties, thus depriving him of the holy company of the Master.

32. Anxious thoughts sometimes foretell future events. This held good in Balaram's case now. His apprehension came true. At the secret instigation of his relatives, both his cousins sent him letters hinting that they were displeased with him. And the news that Harivallabh Basu would soon come to Calcutta and stay with him for a few days with a view to settling some important matters in consultation with him, also reached him duly. Although the soul of Balaram was not distressed on that account since he felt that he had done nothing wrong, he was, however dejected lest the force of circumstances should take him away from the Master. After a great deal of anxious thought he at last came to the conclusion that he would not leave the Master behind during the Master's illness and go elsewhere, even if his cousins were to decide against him. Harivallabh Basu came to Calcutta in the meantime. Balaram made every arrangement to ensure that his cousin had no trouble or inconvenience during his stay with him. He then remained firm in his own resolve, and without fear or anxiety, continued visiting the Master openly every day.

33. The face is the best mirror of the mind. The Master understood that there was a struggle going on in Balaram's mind as soon as he saw his face when he came to him on the day Harivallabh Basu arrived at Calcutta. The Master looked upon Balaram very much as his own. Sympathizing with him in his trouble, the Master called him aside, and putting a number of questions to him, came to know everything about the situation and said at last, "What sort of man is he? Can you bring him here some day?" Balaram replied, "As a man he is very good, Sir, learned, intelligent, magnanimous and charitable; he gives away a lot, and is a devoted soul too. His only defect is the one that the rich generally suffer from, namely, he is a little too credulous. He has come to entertain some misunderstandings about me on the basis of the report of others. He is displeased with me, solely because I come here. So I doubt if he would come here at my request." The Master then said, "You need not then ask him. Please call Girish here."

Girish came and gladly agreed to bring Harivallabh. He said, "Harivallabh and I were class-mates in our younger days. So, I usually go to see him immediately I come to know he has come to Calcutta. Therefore it is not at all out of the way for me to meet him. I'll go to see him this very day."

34. Girish came to Dakshineswar the next day with Harivallabh Basu at about 5 p.m. and introduced him to the Master, saying, "He is Harivallabh Basu, my boyhood friend. He is the Government pleader at Cuttuck. He has come to see you." The Master welcomed him lovingly, and seating him close to himself, said, "I heard of you from many people and had a desire to see you. I had a fear that you might have a calculating disposition. (To Girish) But I now see it is not so. (Pointing at Harivallabh) He has the simplicity of a boy. (To Girish) Do you notice his eyes? One can never have such eyes if one's heart is not full of devotion. (Touching Harivallabh suddenly) O yes! you seem to be very much my own. With you I don't feel like keeping any distance." Harivallabh bowed down to the Master, took the dust of his feet, and said, "That is your grace."

Girish said, "It is natural that he should have devotion for the Lord; for, he is born in a family of noted devotees. People think so highly of the devotion of the late Krishnaram Basu. He is considered worthy of being remembered every morning when they take the name of pious souls. The fame of his piety has brought glory to this part of the country itself. Who would have devotion if not they who are born in his family?"

There then arose a discussion on the topic of devotion to the divine Lord. The Master began to speak to those present on various aspects of the subject and maintained that the supreme achievement of human life was to attain unfailing faith in God, devotion to Him, and absolute dependence on Him. While talking, he entered into ecstasy. When a little later he regained partial consciousness, he asked one of us to sing a devotional song. He began explaining in a low voice the import of the song to Harivallabh, when he entered into deep ecstasy once more. When the song came to an end, it was seen that two or three young devotees also were in a trance. And, completely charmed with the Master's words that touched everyone's heart, Harivallabh shed tears of love. He took leave of the Master sometime after it was dusk.

35. While we were at Dakshineswar, we very often saw the Master deftly touch a new-comer in the course of a conversation when the latter began arguing against his doctrine, or when any one came in a mood of antagonism against him for some reason or other. This had the effect of making the person amenable to his advice. Of course, he behaved that way only with those he felt pleased to see. One day he told us the reason of it, of his own accord. He said, "Under the influence of egoism and the feeling that they are in no way inferior to anyone, people do not like to accept others' words. As soon as they touch the Being who resides within this (his body), that tendency loses its force, that egoism cannot raise its head again on account of His divine power, even as a snake, touched with a particular herb at the time of raising its hood, bends its head low. That is why I touch their persons during talks with them."

The above-mentioned words of the Master came to our mind on seeing Harivallabh Basu take leave of him with reverence in his heart and in an attitude completely contrary to what he had before. It is needless to say that the thought that Balaram was doing something wrong in visiting the Master, never again crossed the minds of his cousins.

36. The physical condition of the Master grew worse during his stay at Shyampukur; and, keeping pace with it, as it were, the number of people coming to see him and attain his grace also

increased daily. Householder devotees like Harish Chandra Mustafi and Manidranath Gupta, and young devotees like Sarada Prasanna Mitra (who became afterwards well known in the monastic Order of Sri Ramakrishna as Swami Trigunatitananda) as also several others saw the Master here for the first time. Again, although many like Swami Abhedananda had paid a visit or two at Dakshineswar, it was here that they got the opportunity of coming into intimate contact with him. The Master observed their nature and past impressions and guided them accordingly along the path of Sadhana either of pure devotion, or of devotion fortified by the discipline of knowledge. He never missed an opportunity to give them individual instruction privately and urge them to go forward along the spiritual path. The Master, it is known to us, was one day teaching a young man the different ways of sitting and other bodily postures fit for the meditation on God with form and on God without form. Sitting in the posture of Padmasana, placing the back of the right hand on the palm of the left hand and then raising both the joined hands to the level of the chest, he said with his eyes closed, "This is the best posture fit for all kinds of meditation on God with forms." Next, remaining seated in that posture of Padmasana, placing his right and left hands on his right and left knee respectively, bringing together the tips of the thumb and the forefinger of each hand while the other finger remained straightened, and steadying his eyes between the eyebrows, he said, "This is the most common posture for the meditation on God without forms." Scarcely had the Master said those words when he entered into ecstasy, and bringing the mind forcibly down shortly afterwards to the plane of normal consciousness, he said, "No more can be shown. As soon as I sit in that posture, the mind becomes absorbed and merges in ecstasy. The vital airs within the body go upwards and the sore in the throat gets hurt thereby. The doctor, therefore, has especially enjoined that ecstasies should be avoided." The young man became very sorry and said, "Why did you demonstrate all those things? I did not ask for it." He replied, "That is true, but can I do without demonstrating or expounding a little to you?" The young man was surprised to think of his infinite grace and the great inclination of his mind to ecstasy.

37. There was such a unique sweetness in all the actions of the Master that many new-comers were simply overwhelmed by

it. We mention below an event as an example. We heard of it from Atulachandra Ghosh, the great Girishchandra's younger brother, who had exceptional love for his friends. We shall try to record it in his own language as far as possible:

38. "Upendra[1] was an intimate friend of mine; he was a sub-judge living away from home. After my acquaintance with the Master, I wrote to him, 'When you come here next, I shall show you a wonderful object.' He came during the Christmas holidays and reminded me of it. I said, 'I thought of introducing you to Sri Ramakrishna Paramahamsa. But he is now ill and is staying at Shyampukur. Doctors have forbidden him to talk. You are a new-comer; so, how can I take you there now?' That day passed. Another day, Upendra came to see my brother (Girishchandra) when there arose a talk about the Master. My brother said to him, 'Why don't you go with Atul some day and see the Master?' Upendra said, 'He has been telling me for the last six months that he would take me there; but when I came here and reminded him of it, he said, it would not be possible now.' I heard these words and said to my brother, 'Even we are not always allowed to go in now. How can I then take a new-comer?' My brother said, 'Anyway take him once; that done, the Master will show himself to him and love him if he is lucky enough.'

39. "Later, one afternoon I took Upendra there. The Master's room was packed with an audience sitting on two long mats spread on the floor, reaching up to his bed, and talks on various commonplace subjects were going on — talks on painting (for, the painter Ananda Bagchi was there on that day), on melting gold[2] in the goldsmith's shop and so on. We sat for a long time, but there was not a single word except words of that nature. I thought, 'I have brought this newcomer here today, and it is this very day that all kinds of useless talks are going on! What an

[1] Upendranath Ghosh. He was related to Bhupendra Nath Basu of Shyambazar.

[2] The Master sometimes told us an amusing story of the dexterity of goldsmiths in stealing gold and silver. Atul Babu refers to that here. The story is this: A man came to a goldsmith's shop with a few friends in order to sell an ornament and saw an old goldsmith who had his whole body decked with marks of sacred coloured earth and sandal-paste, his head with a tuft of hair, and his neck with strings of beads. He was sitting outside his house and taking the name of Hari in a very profound mood. His three or four assistants had put on similar marks and beads, and were engaged themselves in making various kinds of jewels inside the house.

idea about the Master would he (Upendra) carry with him?' I felt extremely restless in mind. I was looking at him at intervals with apprehension. But, whenever I looked at him, I saw in his face an evident expression of pleasure, as if he was enjoying those talks quite well. I then asked him by a sign to leave, but he signed back to me to wait a little more. I gave him similar hints twice or thrice, and then he rose up and came to me. I then asked him, 'What were you listening to so long? What is there to listen to in these talks? Do we call you 'simple' without a reason?' We

---

Seeing the marks and dress of piety of the old goldsmith and his assistants, that customer and his friends thought that these goldsmiths were pious people and would not cheat them. They then placed the jewellery they had come to sell before the old goldsmith and requested him to ascertain its exact price. The old man seated them lovingly and asked an assistant to prepare a smoke of tobacco for them. He then tested the ornament on the touchstone, told them the price of that quality of gold, and with their permission, handed it over to an assistant inside the house to melt. The assistant began immediately to melt it and suddenly remembering God, cried out "Kesava! Kesava!" On account of the association of divine ideas in his mind, the old man also simultaneously uttered in a loud voice "Gopala! Gopala!" An assistant inside the house repeated immediately afterwards "Hari! Hari! Hari!" The one who brought tobacco handed over the bowl to the newcomer in the meantime, and said aloud while entering the house, "Hara! Hara! Hara!" As soon as he said so, the first-mentioned assistant threw dexterously some melted gold into a pot filled with water standing before him, to be appropriated by them.

The newcomers did not understand that for the goldsmith and his assistants the aforesaid names of the divine Lord had unusual meanings. Instead of saying Kesava, the name of God, they were enquiring "Kesava", which in Bengali means "Who are they?" In other words, they wanted to know whether the newcomers were intelligent or foolish. As answer to this question, the old man said "Gopala" not in the sense of the boy Krishna, but in the sense of "Go-Pala", a herd of cattle, implying thereby that they were as foolish as a herd of cattle. And by the two words Hari and Hara (the names of Vishnu and Siva respectively), they meant "Let me then steal" (hari) and "Do steal" (hara). Pleased with their devotion and steadfastness in religion the newcomers smoked tobacco without suspecting any foul trick. They had the melted gold weighed, took its price, and returned home cheerfully.

Bankim Chandra, the famous novelist of Bengal, took up a sceptical attitude and put to the Master various complicated questions on religion when the Master met him at the house of Adhar Chandra Sen, his very loving devotee. After giving proper replies to those questions, the Master said to Bankim Chandra, by way of a joke: "You are Bankim (crooked) by name and also by action." Pleased with the Master's answers to his questions Bankim Babu said, "Sir, you must come to our Kanthalpara house some day; there are arrangements for the service of the divine Lord and all of us take the name of Hari." The Master replied in fun, "How do you take the name of Hari? Is it as the goldsmiths took it?" Saying so, the Master narrated the aforesaid story, which evoked a peal of laughter from the audience.

used to call him so because he had a tattooed mark on his forehead. He replied, 'Oh! no; it was nice to listen to. I only heard of universal love before; but never saw it manifested in anyone. I have experienced it today in him (the Master) when I saw him making merry on trifling topics like that with all around. But I must come once again; I have three questions to ask.'

"I took Upendra with me the next morning. There was practically none with the Master then. Only one or two attendants and Sri Mallick, my brother-in-law, were there. I said to Upendra over again before we started, 'Ask him personally what you have to ask. You will then get answers to your satisfaction. Don't ask these questions through anybody else.' But he was of a bashful nature, and he happened to do exactly what I told him not to do. He put the question through Sri Mallick. The Master gave answers which, I understood from the expression of Upendra's face, were not to his satisfaction. I then said to him in whispers, 'It is bound to be so. Did I not tell you again and again to ask him personally what you had to ask? Why don't you put questions personally? Why have you engaged a pleader to hold a brief for you?'

40. "He took courage and put personally one question to the Master, 'Sir, has God forms or has He not? And if both, how can two such contradictory natures be in Him at the same time?' The Master answered immediately, 'He is both with form and without form, like water and ice.' Upendra had taken the science course at college; so, that example given by the Master was to his entire satisfaction. He was pleased to get that answer, which he understood with the help of his knowledge of science. He asked that one question and refrained from asking the two others, bowed down to the Master and took leave of him. When we came out, I asked him, 'Upendra, you said you had three questions; why did you put only one and come away'? He replied, 'Don't you understand? All the three questions of mine have been solved at once by that one answer.'

41. "Brother Ram (Ramchandra Datta), perhaps you remember, used to take an early meal at home at that time and come very often to the Master with a small bundle containing his office dress. He spent an hour or two there before he changed his dress and went to office. When the Master was answering Upendra's question, he came suddenly to that room, putting on his office dress, and heard those words of the Master. As soon as we came

out, brother Ram ventured to say, 'Brother Atul, bring him (Upendra) here. The Master's answer to his question will be too difficult for him to understand. He will have to read my book Tattvaprakasika in order to understand the Master's words.' I was annoyed at this and did not hesitate to say, 'Is it not a fact, brother Ram, that you have been coming to the Master for the last seven years, long before we all saw him? Ah! And you say he will not understand the truth from what the Master has said but will understand it through the persual of your book! What the Master could not make clear, your book will! What a queer idea! But if you want to give Upendra your book to read, you may do so; that is a different matter.' Brother Ram became a little embarrassed, and handed over the book to Upendra."

CHAPTER XII: SECTION 3

THE MASTER'S STAY AT SHYAMPUKUR

[TOPICS: 1. The Master's seeing sores in his body. 2. Restrictions regarding new-comers. 3. An actress seeing the Master. 4. Sentimentalism amongst the devotees. 5. Ramachandra outdoing Girish in this. 6. Vijayakrishna Goswami fanned the flame. 7. Narendra's efforts to check sentimentalism. 8. Sentimentalism produces no permanent change in life. 9. Artificiality in tears, horripilation and other bodily changes are bad. 10. Narendra's words carrying conviction. 11. Narendra ridiculed sentimentalism. 12. His efforts to establish true renunciation and love for God in place of sentimentalism. 13. One's life will be similar to that of the Master if one loves him. 14. Narendra's endeavour to make the devotees critical in accepting new ideas. 15. Mahim Chakravarthi's hankering for name and fame. 16. The tiger skin of Mahima. 17. Mahimacharan's Guru. 18. The religious Sadhana of Mahimacharan. 19. Mahimacharan at Shyampukur. 20. A debate between Mahima and Narendra. 21. Narendra taught equal regard for all true Sadhakas. 22. Prabhudayal Misra, the Christian missionary. 23. Furthur deterioration of the Master's illness.]

1. While he was staying at Shyampukur, one day the Master had a wonderful vision. He saw that his subtle body came out of his gross body as he was strolling up and down in the room, and he observed that its back was covered with sores, especially in the region of the throat. He wondered at the cause of such sores, when the Divine Mother of the universe explained to him that people who had committed various evil deeds had become pure by touching him; the burden of their sins was thereby transferred to him and consequently he had those sores in his subtle body. We had heard the Master say sometimes at Dakshineswar that he was willing to be born lakhs of times to do good to living beings. It was, therefore, no wonder that he should joyfully speak of it to us without being at all affected by it. We were charmed to remember and discuss his infinite grace. But the devotees, especially the younger ones, however, took particular care to see that no newcomers should bow down to him and touch his feet till he regained his former health. Some of the devotees, too, thought of their unrestrained early lives, and decided that they would not any more touch the holy person of the Master, as it meant suffering

for him. But some rare persons like Narendra, on being apprised of this experience of the Master, engaged themselves in an inquiry and research into the truth of this doctrine of vicarious suffering (or the theory of one taking upon oneself voluntarily the sufferings consequent on another's sinful actions) — a doctrine which is fundamental to the Christian, Vaishnava and some other faiths.

2. Girishchandra observed the attempt at preventing newcomers from visiting the Master and said, "There's no harm in trying to do so, but it will be impossible. For, that is the very purpose of the Master's advent." As days passed, the surmise of Girish proved true. For while perfect strangers could be prevented, the newcomers known to the devotees could not be. So the earlier decision was changed, and it was settled that no one unknown to any devotee should be allowed to approach the Master. And even those who were known should be told beforehand not to bow down to him and touch his feet. But even this rule had to be violated occasionally when perfect strangers with unusual devotional fervour came to see the Master.

3. There took place a funny incident in connection with the working of this rule. While the Master was at Dakshineswar, he had, on one occasion, gone to witness a certain religious drama staged in the theatre managed by Girishchandra, and on that occasion he had praised the actress who took the leading part. The actress had the good fortune to worship the feet of the Master while he was in an ecstatic mood at the end of the play. Since then, she looked upon him as God Himself and was adoring him accordingly. She was also seeking for an opportunity to meet him again. She now became very eager to see the Master once more when she heard of his serious illness. As she was acquainted with Kalipada Ghosh, she entreated him persistently to help her in this matter and placed her entire reliance on him for the fulfilment of her longing. Now Kalipada was a follower of Girish in all matters and did not believe that the Master's illness would increase if an evil-doer became repentant and touched his holy feet; for he was convinced that the Master was the Incarnation of the age and nothing could affect or injure him. He, therefore, had no fear or hesitation in taking that actress to the holy Master. He took counsel secretly and one day dressing her like a European gentleman, as "young Bengal" used to do then, came with her at dusk to the Shyampukur house where the Master was staying. He in-

troduced her to us as a friend of his, took her to the Master, and told him who she really was. None of us was in the Master's room at that time and Kalipada had, therefore, no obstacle to overcome. Knowing that the actress had come in that dress to throw dust in our eyes, the Master, fond as he was of merriment, had a hearty laugh. Pleased with her faith and devotion, he praised her courage, strategy, and reverence. He gave her a little spiritual instruction that she might have faith in and reliance on, God, and bade good-bye to her soon afterwards. She shed tears of joy and repentance, touched adoringly his holy feet with her head and went away with Kalipada. We came to know of this afterwards from the Master, and seeing that he was joking, smiling and expressing joy on account of the trick played on us; we could not be cross with Kalipada.

4. Although the faith and devotion in the hearts of the devotees increased by leaps and bounds owing to the Master's company and the services they rendered to him, there arose now a possibility of their minds running along a path which was not only full of dangers but led in a direction opposed to true spirituality. The temporary surgings of emotions now became dearer to them than austere renunciation and difficult self-control. The devotees could not understand that such sentimentalism, sweet though it be, could not impart to them the power of winning victories over lust, anger, and the hosts of other enemies of man, if it was not based on renunciation and self-control. There were several causes that produced this sentimentalism. The first of the causes was the ordinary man's partiality for easy paths and quick returns. Most people who are considered religious want a path that will offer them both the world and God, enjoyment and renunciation. Rare are the fortunate few who regard them as contrary in nature, like light and darkness, and do not fall into the above-mentioned error. They understand that these two cannot be harmonized without the risk of compromising the ideal of renouncing one's all for God-realization. Those who want to achieve the impossible feat of keeping close to both the shores take out their life's boat just a little away from this shore of the world, resolutely discard all thought of farther journey, and lie there safe at anchor for ever. The Master, therefore, tested variously everybody as soon as he came to him and ascertained whether he "lay safe at anchor" or not. If he knew that he was doing so, he would reveal to him only

that much of the ideal of renunciation as he could understand and accept. This was the reason why his teachings differed with different persons according to their fitness. He gave different kinds of instructions to his householder devotees and to his unmarried disciplies. That was the reason why, while giving instruction to people in general, he said that devotion as expounded by Narada and the singing of the name of Hari were the most efficacious means in the Kaliyuga. The study of religion and the scriptures became so obsolete amongst the public at that time that it was doubtful whether one in a hundred understood the meaning of the phrase "devotion as expounded by Narada". People did not know that the renunciation of one's all out of love for God had also been taught by Narada. It was therefore no wonder that, prompted by their weak nature, the ignorant devotees of the Master sometimes fell into the error of clinging to both the lives, the worldly and the spiritual, and of regarding the increase of sentimentalism as the acme of religious experience.

Again, another cause leading the devotees to that error probably lay in that they did not see the very firm basis on which the extraordinary emotionalism of the Master was established; for the great austerities and ascetic practices that the Master had undergone during the Sadhana period of his life were far off occurrences which they had never witnessed and were therefore little aware of. But this development of sentimentalism received its most powerful impetus from the time Girishchandra gave his spiritual "power of attorney" to the Master, and being fully convinced that the Master was the incarnation of the age, began preaching it at the top of his voice to one and all with great joy and enthusiasm. Although many had had that idea regarding the Master, all of them obeyed his ban on revealing it. For the Master had been warning them that when large numbers of people came to regard him as an incarnation and began to flock to him, that would mark the time of his demise and disappearance from the world. But Girishchandra had his own way of thinking. He could never in his life conceal any thought or action of his, good or bad. He, therefore, could not obey that interdict of the Master. He forgot the fact that his keen intelligence, his life full of various experiences and his heart surcharged with infinite zeal and faith, enabled him to understand the true greatness of the Master and helped him to surrender himself to him completely. So he invited one and all quite indiscriminately to do what he himself had done. Neglecting, therefore, the necessity of personal effort, devotional exercises, renunciation, and austerity, and uttering the cheap shibboleths like — "We have given him the power of attorney", "We have surrendered ourselves to him", and so on — people came to regard the realization of God as a matter of easy attainment. Girishchandra's infinite love for the Master could have prevented his preaching it that way, had he not been misled by his extreme intelligence. He had fully accepted that the Master had assumed a body to arrest the decline of religion and to give a new spiritual awakening to mankind, and that he was voluntarily undergoing the miseries of birth, old age and sickness, so that suffering Jivas could take refuge in him and be freed from the "threefold miseries[1]". His intelligence dictated to him that, the facts being so, the Master would never pass away without completing his mission. He was, therefore, not to be blamed if he invited people to take refuge in the Master and to have peace and divine bliss like himself.

5. The intelligence of many elderly devotees like Ramachandra was then overpowered by the keen intelligence and argumentation of Girishchandra. Ramachandra, we have said before, was born in a Vaishnava family. It was therefore no wonder that he should truly take the Master to be Sri Krishna and Sri Gauranga. But he had observed a certain amount of restraint in proclaiming his theories before Girish began preaching his ideas about the Master. The advent of Girish, however, served like adding fuel to the fire of his zeal. He did not, however, stop with merely preaching that the Master was an incarnation of God, but indulged in speculations to establish the identities of particular devotees of the Master with particular devotees of his in his previous incarnations as Gauranga and Krishna. And, it is needless to add, that those who experienced bodily changes and sometimes lost normal consciousness on account of temporary surges of sentimentalism, occupied a high spiritual rank in his judgement.

6. While the devotees allowed themselves to be carried off by the current of sentimentalism, thanks to their firm conviction that the Master was the incarnation of the age, Vijaykrishna

[1] These are the miseries, due to the soul's association with the body, due to other creatures like tigers, snakes, etc., and due to natural agencies, such as lightning, flood, etc.

Goswami came from Dacca to see the Master and declared before all without any reserve how, at the time of meditation in his room at Dacca, the Master had appeared there physically before him and how Vijay touched his body and limbs (cf. IV.5). This acted like a high wind fanning a wild fire. Five or six of the devotees then used to undergo bodily changes and to lose partial consciousness as soon as they listened to devotional music. They gave up the royal road of spiritual practice supported by reason and discrimination, and began to habituate themselves to the morbid attitude of waiting for miracles to happen. They were of the belief that anything might be brought about at any time by virtue of the divine power of the Master and they were standing on the tiptoe of such expectations.

7. When this unhealthy sentimentalism was being regarded by the devotees in general as the acme of religious life, it was only the keen intelligence of Narendranath, the greatest of the Master's devotees, that could foresee the baneful effects of such developments. He felt that this type of sentimental mentality was no substitute for the real spiritual excellences like renunciation, self-control, singleminded devotion and the rest, — nay, it was, on the other hand, a positive danger if it were given free rein. Narendra tried to explain this to them and save the situation. The question may arise, why the Master was indifferent, even though he saw the possibility of the devotees going astray? It may be said in reply that he was not so; but knowing that genuine emotion freed of all artificiality was one of the paths leading to the realization of God, he was seeking a favourable occasion to guide them on that path by observing who among those devotees were actually fit for it. For, we heard him say time and again, "Nothing comes about but at the proper time, however much we may wish for it"; "Success has its own time"; "Everything awaits the right time" and so on. Again, who knows that he was not observing Narendra in his crusade against that error of the devotees and was waiting for the result of his efforts? Or, it may be that it was his intention to make Narendranath the instrument in the matter and have the corrective administered through him.

8. Thinking that the circle of young devotees, possessed of firm bodies and determined minds, could easily understand his words, Narendra adduced reasons and arguments against this growing tide of sentimentalism. He said, "The sentimentalism

that does not produce a permanent change in human life but makes man eager to realize God at one moment, but at the very next has little power to make him desist from lust and greed, has no depth, and is therefore of little value in life. Though under its influence some might shed tears and experience horripilation and other bodily changes, or even a temporary withdrawal of normal consciousness, it is, I am perfectly convinced, produced by nervous weakness. A man should surely eat nutritious food and take the help of a physician, if he cannot suppress it through the exercise of his will power."

9. Narendra added, "There is much of artificiality in those bodily changes and absence of normal consciousness. As our control over ourselves grows firmer, our real genuine sentiments go deeper. It is only in the lives of very rare persons that spiritual sentiments become so powerful as to assume the form of tidal waves, overflowing even the firm dam of control, and manifest themselves as bodily changes and temporary cessation of normal consciousness. Foolish men cannot understand this and reverse the process. The depth of spiritual sentiments, they think, is attained as the result of those bodily changes and the loss of normal consciousness. They, therefore, make conscious efforts to induce those effects in themselves. That will and effort of theirs develop gradually into a habit and weaken their nerves increasingly as days pass on, so that in course of time those changes come on them at the slightest appearance of a sentiment. Consequently, they become insane or afflicted with a chronic malady by indulging freely in them. In trying to practise religion, eighty per cent of people turn cheats and about fifteen per cent mad; the remaining five only attain the immediate knowledge of the infinite Truth and are blessed. Hence beware."

10. We could not at first take those words of Narendranath to be true. But we had to do so when shortly afterwards it was discovered, by chance, that one devotee, sitting in seclusion and singing certain verses conveying certain sentiments, was deliberately practising to induce the desired bodily changes appropriate to that sentiment; that the charming dance of another one was only a demonstration of a kind of dance which he had previously practised by observing a different devotee perform it in a state of semi-trance; and that a third one's dance was an instant fit of imitation on seeing the beautiful dance of another devotee. Again,

observing that a devotee had trances more and more frequently, Narendra convinced him in private of his folly in thinking that this was a desirable achievement and advised him to practise the control of sentiments and eat comparatively nutritious food if he wanted to save himself from these morbid developments. As a result of following his advice for a fortnight, the devotee acquired health and self-control to a great extent. When many saw these facts demonstrated before their very eyes, they had to believe in Narendra's words, and they ceased to regard themselves unfortunate because they did not have bodily changes and cessation of normal consciousness like the other devotees.

11. Narendra did not stop at preaching this with the help of reason and arguments only, but when he scented the slightest artificiality in anybody's sentimentalism, he ridiculed and made merry over it in the presence of all, and the devotee felt embarrassed and humiliated. Again, he would raise the topic of man's imitating the gestures of woman, as was prevalent in the practice of Sadhana of a class of Vaishnavas, and the extremely ridiculous form which it sometimes assumed. He thus roused a peal of laughter amongst the devotees and held to ridicule those of us who were inclined to that kind of sentimentalism, saying that they belonged to the class of "women friends" of the Lord. In fact, Narendranath, a lion among men, could not at all put up with the idea that, because a man had come forward to practise religion, he should give up his virility, self-exertion and his indomitable search after truth, and should, instead, practise weeping and confine himself to imitating the gestures of women in response to the singing of Vaishnava lyrics. He, therefore, serio-comically called as 'Siva's demons' those devotees who took to virile forms of Sadhana and had devotion tempered by the discrimination between the real and the unreal, while he nick-named those of the opposite nature as 'women friends' of the Lord.

12. Narendranath could not rest satisfied simply with effecting a breach in the circle of sentimentalists with his reason and sarcasm. He was fully convinced of the fact that mere preaching did not produce its effect till a new mental attitude could be substituted in its place, and he made great efforts towards that. He gathered the young devotees during his leisure, sang together with them devotional songs that awakened in their hearts the idea of the transitoriness of the world, and of renunciation and devotion

to God, and thus tried to keep burning in their hearts the flames of those sterling spiritual qualities. Coming to see the Master, many returned shedding tears, because strong detachment and love of God were roused in their hearts as the result of listening to these songs and hymns sung by Narendra in his sweet voice. He used to sing:

> "O Thou, the sea of nectar who art a concentrate of Bliss and Consciousness! Life overflows with joy when we sing Thy name."

* * * *

> "I am neither the mind nor the intellect, neither the ego nor the mind-stuff;
> I am neither the ears nor the tongue, neither the nose nor the eyes;
> I am neither the ether nor the earth, neither fire nor air;
> I am Siva, Bliss and Consciousness Absolute!"

Again, he would narrate stories from the life of the Master dealing with the Sadhanas that he spontaneously performed as a result of his profound love of God, or explain the unique greatness of the Master in a manner that amazed the disciples. Or, at other times, he would quote passages from the Imitation of Christ and say, "The life of anybody who truly loves the Lord will be perfectly moulded in His pattern. Therefore, whether we truly love the Master or not will be best proved by this test.' Moreover he reminded us of the Master's saying, "First tie the non-dual knowledge in the corner of your cloth and then do whatever you like." He then explained to us that all the Master's emotionalism arose with that knowledge as its basis. The devotees had, therefore, to make efforts to attain that non-dual knowledge first.

14. Narendra encouraged us very often to cultivate the habit of testing any new idea before accepting it. Hearing that physical ailments could be cured with the help of the concentration of the mind, he once gathered us together in a room, and engaged us in that practice for curing the Master's ailment. Again, he always tried to see that the devotees kept themselves aloof from irrational observances. The event mentioned below may be cited as an example.

15. Mahimacharan Chakravarti's house was situated op-

Monastic Disciples of Sri Ramakrishna

Swami Vivekananda

Swami Brahmananda

Swami Premananda

Swami Akhandananda

Swami Saradananda

Swami Shivananda

Swami Trigunatitananda

Swami Yogananda

Swami Abhedananda

Swami Vijnanananda

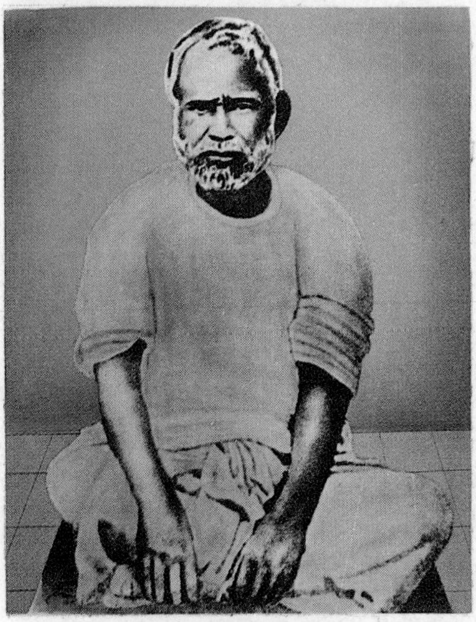

Swami Adbhutananda

Swami Ramakrishnananda

Swami Turiyananda

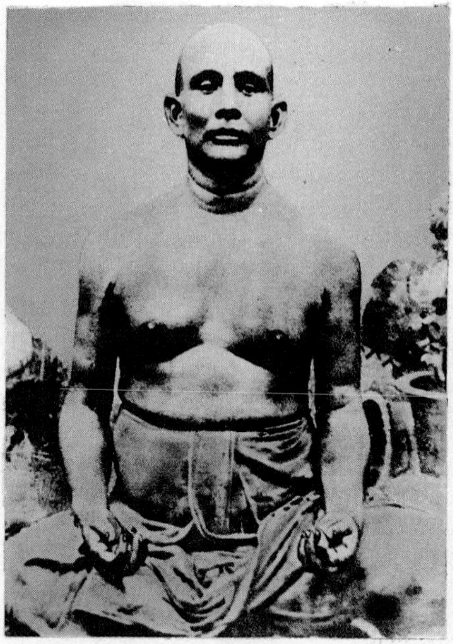

Swami Subodhananda

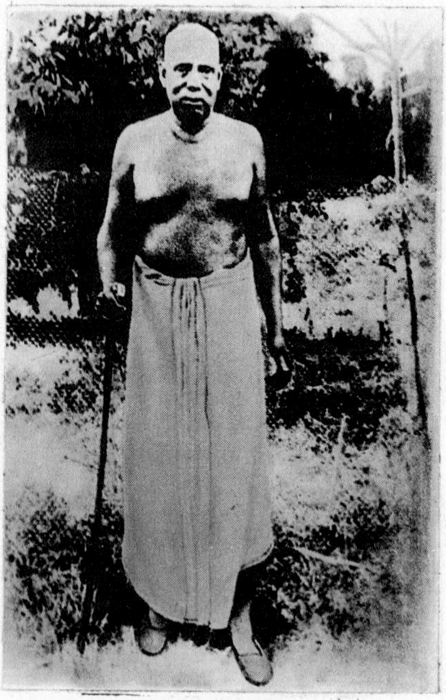

Swami Advaitananda

Swami Niranjanananda

posite the place where the southern part of the Mati pond met the Kasipur Road. He was blessed with many good qualities, but he was always eager to show himself off as greater than he actually was. He did not, it seems, even hesitate to have recourse to falsehood if that would fetch him honour. This anxiety that people should regard him as wealthy, learned, intelligent, religious, generous and possessed of all other praiseworthy qualities regulated each and every action of his life, even to the extent of making him a laughing stock sometimes. Once Mahimacharan started a free school and called it, "The Educational Section of the Institute of the Oriental Aryans" (Prachya-aryasiksha-kanda-parishat). He called his only son by the name of "The holy face of one having the moon on his head" (Mriganka-mauli-puta-tundi); he had a deer which he called Kapinjala after the name of that anchorite. For, did it become a scholar like him to call things or persons by short, simple names? He had a collection of various English and Sanskrit books. When we became acquainted with him, one day we went to his house with Narendranath and asked, "Have you, sir, read all these books?" With elaborate humility he replied that he had. But Narendra brought out some of those books the next moment, and finding that their leaves had not even been cut, asked the reason for it. Mahima replied, "Do you see, brother, people took the books after I had read them, but they failed to return them. So I bought these books again to replace the lost ones. I don't allow anyone to take out books from here anymore". But Narendra discovered in a short time that none of these books had their leaves cut. Narendra was, therefore, certain that he kept those shelves of books only with a view to pass off as a great scholar as also to provide an additional decoration for his drawing room.

16. At the time we became acquainted with him, Mahimacharan introduced himself to us in the course of conversation as a spiritual aspirant on the path of knowledge. He used to visit Dakshineswar many years before the devotees of Calcutta went to the Master. At the time of certain festivals he would go to Dakshineswar wearing on ochre-dyed cloth and Rudraksha beads, and holding a one-stringed instrument in his hand, would seat himself for Sadhana in a pompous manner on a tiger skin spread under the Panchavati. He hung the tiger-skin on a wall in a corner of the Master's room when he returned home. This was enough for the Master to understand the man. For, one day on being asked

about the ownership of the tiger skin, the Master said, "It has been kept here by Mahima Chakravarti. Do you know why? People will see it and ask me to whom it belongs; and when I mention his name, they will consider him to be a very big Sadhaka."

17. Once when there was some talk on initiation, Mahimacharan is reported to have said, "The name of my Guru is Agamacharya Damaruvallabha." Again, he said at other times that he had also been initiated, like the Master, by Tota-puri, the itinerant Paramahamsa. "I met him," he said, "at a certain place when I went on a pilgrimage in the western part of the country and got initiated. He had asked the Master to live his life as a devotee, while he instructed me to live in the world as a Sadhaka on the path of knowledge." It is superfluous to add that the truth of his words was known only to himself and to Him who knows all hearts.

18. The only Sadhana one saw him practise was the uttering of the Pranava with his voice in unison with the note of his one-stringed instrument, together with 'shouting' a verse or two from books like the Uttara Gita at intervals. He said that this practice of his was the discipline inculcated by the eternal path of knowledge; no other discipline was necessary if one practised it. This itself would awaken the coiled power and one would see God. The holy image of Sri Annapurna was installed in Mahima Babu's house, and it seems the annual worship of Sri Jagaddhatri used to be performed there. It is inferred from these facts that he must have been born in a Sakta family. He seemed to have followed the method of the Sakta Sadhana in the latter part of his life. For, while he drove in a small buggy, he was heard to cry out at intervals, "Tara, That Thou art; Thou art That." He had a small estate, the income from which was sufficient to satisfy his worldly needs.

19. Mahima Babu came to visit the Master on two or three occasions during the Master's stay at Shyampukur. On those occasions, after enquiring about the welfare of the Master, he came and sat down in the room that was intended for all people, and hummed a Mantra in unison with his one-stringed instrument, and while doing so, talked at intervals on religious subjects to others. Charmed with his personal beauty enhanced by the ochre cloth he put on, and impressed by his gigantic corporeal frame and the glamour of his words, many used to put spiritual questions to him. The Master also sometimes used to tell him, "You are a scholar. Please go and give them (all present) some instructions." For, it

was not unknown to the Master that Mahima had a great desire in his heart to have a few disciples and to spread his own name.

20. One day Mahima Babu came to Shyampukur and spoke on many things and tried to establish that the method of discipline adopted by him was the easiest and the best, all the other methods being low and tortuous. Narendra could not bear it when he saw the young devotees of the Master listening to this without a protest. He brought forward contrary arguments and proved Mahima's position to be untenable, saying, "What is the proof that one will see God by uttering Mantras in unison with the music of the one-stringed instrument, as you are doing?" Mahima Babu replied, "Sound itself is Brahman. God cannot help revealing Himself in response to Mantras uttered in unison with musical notes. Nothing more need be done." Narendra retorted, "Has God made such an agreement with you in writing? Or will He appear before you with stealthy tread like a snake charmed by Mantras and herbs, when you raise the pitch of your voice and utter mystical syllables like 'Hum' 'Hum'?" It is needless to say that Mahima Babu's preaching did not prove the more interesting for Narendra's arguments and he bade good-bye earlier that day.

21. Narendranath also kept a watch over the devotees of the Master to see that they paid due respect to the true Sadhakas of all religious communities. "Paying reverence to the Sadhakas of one's own community only and condemning all others, as people in general do," he said, "is as good as showing disrespect to the Master's doctrine, 'As many faiths, so many paths,' and therefore, to the Master himself." We remember an event of this sort which happened during our stay at Shyampukur.

22. One day a Christian missionary by name Prabhudayal Misra came to see the Master. We did not at first take him to be a Christian owing to his ochre cloth. When in the course of conversation we came to know from him what he was, he was asked why he, a Christian, had put on ochre cloth. He replied, "I was born in a Brahmin family. Should I give up the customs and practices that have come down to me from my forefathers only because I have the good fortune to have faith in sweet Jesus and accept him as my chosen Ideal? I believe in the Yoga scriptures, and with Jesus as my chosen Ideal I practise Yoga exercises daily. I have, of course, no faith in the distinctions recognised by the caste system, but I do believe that it is prejudical to the practice

of Yoga to take food out of the hand of anybody and everybody. So, I take self-cooked food every day. Consequently, though a Christian, I have been realising, one after another, the results of Yogic practices such as seeing light and the rest. The Yogis of India devoted to the Supreme Being, have been wearing ochre cloth from time immemorial. So I prefer this dress to any other." Narendranath put him question after question and brought out all his dearest and innermost ideas one by one. Thus knowing him to be a Yogi and a holy man, he paid great respect to him and asked us also to do likewise. So, many of us touched his feet and bowed down to him. We sat together in one place and took the Prasada of the Master consisting of sweets. He expressed his view about the Master, that he regarded him as Jesus himself.

23. Narendranath thus guided the devotees of the Master on the right path during those days when the Master's disease was daily worsening. Dr. Sarkar became anxious on seeing that the very medicines that had produced more or less good results before, were found no longer efficacious. Coming to the conclusion that this was due to the polluted atmosphere of Calcutta city, he advised that the Master should be removed to some garden house outside the city. The first half of the month of Agrahayan (Nov.–Dec.) was not now over. Knowing that the Master would be unwilling to change house in the next month of Paush (Dec.–Jan.), the devotees did their utmost to find out a suitable house. In a short time they hired for a monthly rent of eighty rupees the garden house of the late Gopal Chandra Ghosh, the son-in-law of Rani Katyayani, situated on the eastern side of the main road leading to the Baranagar Bazar, where the northern path of the Mati pond of Kasipur touched that road. Surendra Nath Mitra of Simulia, Calcutta, one of the closest of the devotees of the Master, promised to pay the whole rent.

When the final settlement regarding the house had been made, an auspicious day was fixed consulting the almanac to shift the furniture and the utensils from Shyampukur to the new house. After making all the necessary arrangements, the devotees brought the Master from Shyampukur to the garden house of Kasipur in the afternoon of the penultimate day of the month of Agrahayan (Nov.–Dec.,). They felt great joy in their minds when they saw the Master joyous over the seclusion and the open air of that place, adorned with trees full of fruits and flowers.

CHAPTER XIII: SECTION 1

THE MASTER IN THE GARDEN HOUSE OF KASIPUR[1]

[TOPICS: 1. Kasipur. 2. The garden house of Kasipur. 3. The Master came and started training his boy devotees. 4. The garden house carrying these memories should be acquired by the Ramakrishna Mission.]

The Kasipur garden house is situated on the broad road that runs through the north of Calcutta and connects the Baghbazar quarter with Baranagar, three miles from the city.

1. On both sides of that road from the north of Baghbazar bridge to the cross-roads, a little to the south of that garden, are seen the cottages of poor labourers and small shops full of articles necessary for their daily use. There are, however, seen here and there some brick-built edifices like a few jute mills, the iron factory of the Dost Company, the firm of Ralli Brothers Ltd., one or two gardens or dwelling houses, the police station and the fire brigade station situated to the south-west of the Kasipur cross-roads. Not far to the west stands the famous temple of Sri Sarvamangala Devi, as if to bear witness to the terrible differences in the living conditions of the poor and the rich. Again, as the Sealdah railway station was improved and extended, many tin-roofed godowns have now been built on the said road, marring even the little beauty it had a few years ago. Although this ancient road is thus not pleasing to the eye of a poet or an artist, it has some value in the eye of the historian. For, Nawab Siraj[2], it is said, advanced along this road and occupied the British fort of Govindapur, and besides, a palace of the notorious traitor Nawab Mirzaffar once stood on this part of the road, a little more than half a mile from Baghbazar. This portion of the road from Baghbazar to the cross-roads of Kasipur is not beautiful; but the part of it extending from there to the Baranagar bazaar cannot be called unattractive. Going a little further north from the said cross-roads, one meets with the

[1] Written by the author and published in the monthly Bengali magazine Udhodhan, but not included in the first edition of the book published during his lifetime.

[2] Siraj-ud-daula, the last independent Nawab of Bengal, Bihar and Orissa. — Tr.

southern part of the Mati pond, and opposite to it, on the eastern side of the road, stands the beautiful residential home of our well-known friend, the late Mahimacharan Chakravati referred to in the previous chapter. The Railway Company has now purchased the greater part of the garden surrounding this house and extended a branch of the railway to the bank of the Ganga through it, which has robbed the house of all its former beauty. Going a little further north from there, one sees on one's left the northern side of the Mati pond, and opposite to it, on the eastern side of the road, the high wall and the iron gate of the Kasipur garden. To the west of the western portion of Mati Jil (pond) there were a number of beautiful garden houses along the road, some of them being on the banks of the Ganga. Of these again, the best and the most beautiful was Mati Lal Sil's garden, which, after its acquisition by the Calcutta Electric Company, has been shorn of all its serene beauty of earlier days and is now filled with sprawling buildings and the din and bustle of industry. A dilapidated residential house of the Basaks was situated on the Ganga to the north of this garden. As rows of Tamarisk trees stood on both sides of the path leading from the road to this house, a wonderful beauty of form and sound always soothed the eyes and the ears of visitors. While we were staying with the Master at the garden house of Kasipur, we very often went to the Sil's garden for a bath in the Ganga, and as the Master liked Gulchi flowers, we plucked them from the big trees growing by the side of the Ghat and presented them to the Master. Very often, again, we went through the path adorned with those beautiful rows of Tamarisk trees, and reaching the Basak's uninhabited garden house, sat down on the bank of the Ganga. A little to the north of this garden lay the spacious bathing Ghat belonging to the late Prananath Chaudhuri, and to the north of it again stood the beautiful temple of Sri Gopala, belonging to Rani Katyayani, wife of the famous Lala Babu. We sometimes went to that place too for taking bath in the Ganga and for paying our obeisance to Sri Gopala. The late Gopal Chandra Ghosh, son-in-law of Rani Katyayani, was the owner of the garden house of Kasipur. The devotees hired it from him at the monthly rent of eighty rupees, at first for six months, and then on bond for another three months. Surendranath Mitra of Simla, Calcutta, a great devotee of the Master, signed the bond and paid the whole rent.

2. The Kasipur garden was a very beautiful place, though

Cossipore Garden House, where Sri Ramakrishna entered Mahasamadhi on 16 August 1886

Balaram Bose's house in Calcutta

COSSIPORE GARDEN-HOUSE

Śri Ramakrishna's room and the bed he used

Sri Sarada Devi's room

not big. It had an area of about fourteen bighas ($4\,^2/_3$ acres). This quadrangular piece of land was a little longer from east to west than from north to south and was surrounded by high walls. A row of three or four rooms almost touching the middle of the northern compound wall were meant for the kitchen and the stores. Facing those rooms and on the other side of the garden, there was a two-storeyed residential house. It had two rooms upstairs and four downstairs. Of the rooms on the ground floor, the one in the middle was a spacious hall. To the north of it there were two small rooms side by side. From the western one of these rooms a flight of wooden steps led to the first floor. The room on the eastern side was occupied by the Holy Mother during her stay there. The above-mentioned hall extending from east to west and the room to the south of it, which had also a verandah on the east, were used by the devotees for sitting and sleeping. Above the hall on the ground floor, there was a square hall of equal dimensions forming the first floor. It was this that served as the Master's sick room. To the south of it there was a small terrace surrounded by parapet walls, but open above. Here the Master sometimes strolled or sat. And to the north of it there were the roofs of the room through which the steps led upstairs and a small square room equal in size to, and situated above, the room fixed for the Holy Mother. Here the Master used to take his bath. It was also used at night by one or two attendants.

On the eastern and the western side of the residential part of the house were two flights of steps leading to the hall on the ground floor, which was surrounded by a brick-built circular garden path. In the south-west corner of the garden and joined to its western wall there was a small room for the gate-keeper, and to the north of it was the iron gate. A semi-circular garden path, broad enough for carriages, went north-east and joined the circular road round the residential house. There was a small pool to the west of the residential quarters. Opposite to the western stairs leading to the hall and on the other side of the garden-path, there was a flight of steps leading down to the said pool. In the north-east corner of the garden there was a pond four or five times bigger than the said pool, having two or three one-storeyed rooms to the north-west of it. Besides, there was a stablé in the north-west corner of the garden, to the west of the above mentioned pool, and situated side by side, there were two dilapidated, brick-built rooms for the gardeners near the middle of the southern wall of the garden. In the rest of the space in the garden there were mango, jack, lichee and other fruit-bearing trees. The garden paths were adorned with flower plants on both the sides. Much of the land near the pool and the pond was used for growing greens and vegetables for the kitchen. Again, spread at intervals among the trees, there were lawns covered with green grass, adding much to the beauty of the garden.

3. The Master came to this garden house on the 11th of December, A.D. 1885. The disease had gradually worsened during these eight months, and his tall, strong body was reduced to a mere skeleton. But none-the-less his mind, perfect in self-control, went on increasingly disregarding the fury of the disease and the pain arising from it. He appeared to all observing eyes to have girded up his loins to complete the work already begun, of teaching and training up the Order of his devotees by imparting to them the necessary instructions without a break or pause, both individually and collectively. Moreover, we were constantly witnessing the fulfilment of his prophecy about himself, so often mentioned to the devotees at Dakshineswar. He had said on various occasions: "Before I pass away, I'll cast the whole secret to the winds (that is, I'll divulge my nature as a God-man)"; "when many come to know (my divine glory) and whisper about it, this case (my body) will cease to be; it will go to pieces according to my Mother's dispensation"; "It will be ascertained at that time (during my illness) which amongst the devotees belong to the inner circle and which to the outer", and so on. It was here that we could understand the truth of his predictions about Narendranath and other devotees, such as, "Mother has perforce brought you (Narendra) down to the world to do Her work; you cannot but follow me; where else will you go?"; "They all (the boy-devotees) are like the young ones of the Homa bird that rises very high up in the air where it lays eggs, which start falling towards the earth with great accelerated speed. One is afraid that they will all be shattered to pieces when they reach the ground; but that does not happen. Out of the falling eggs are hatched young ones, which fledge immediately before touching the ground. The fledglings spread their wings and fly up again into the air to reach their parents, who wait above for them to come up. Similarly, they (the boy-devotees) also will renounce the world and go forward towards God before they are

chained to the world." Besides, it was here that he moulded the life of Narendranath and placed the circle of devotees, particularly the boy-devotees, in his charge, and gave him detailed instructions about guiding them. It needs no mention, therefore, that the work the Master accomplished at Kasipur was fraught with the weightiest significance.

4. A very strong desire rises naturally in the minds of all, that the said place where the Master accomplished those grave and profound actions of his life, may be associated with the Ramakrishna Mission[1] to serve as a permanent memorial to those blessed deeds of the Master, so that generations of human beings might feel inspired by the serenity and spiritual stimulations which those surroundings associated with the last days of the Master could give. But alas, a very great obstacle to its fulfilment has arisen. The Railway Company, we understand, is trying to acquire it. It is, therefore, superfluous to say that this place of the Master's divine sport will soon assume a different form and be converted perhaps into jute godowns or railway yards or into some such ugly constructions. But if that be the will of Providence, what can we, weak mortals, do? Let us, therefore, helpessly console ourselves with the thought: "What exists in the mind of Providence, will unavoidably come true."[1]

[1] This earnest desire of the venerable author has since been fulfilled. The Railway Company's intention to acquire the site did not fructify, and it has now come into the possession of the Ramakrishna Math recently (1946). The preservation of the holy atmosphere of the place has therefore become possible. At present a Monastery of the Ramakrishna Order is situated there. The old buildings have been repaired without interfering with their original shape, and the sacred spots associated with the Master's last days are all marked. Also a great religious festival, attracting mammoth crowds is held there on the 1st of January every year to celebrate the anniversary of the Kalpataru day.

CHAPTER XIII: SECTION 2

THE VOW OF SERVICE AT KASIPUR

[TOPICS: 1. The Master's joy to be at the garden house. 2. Men and money needed for the Master's service. 3. Narendra's resolve to stay at the garden house to serve the Master. 4. The Master depended on the universal Mother alone. 5. The Master directing arrangements. 6. Formation of the circle of would-be monk devotees. 7. Slight improvement in the Master's health. 8. Cooking done by the Holy Mother aided by sister Lakshmi. 9. The lay disciples and financial matters. 10. Narendra inspired the boy devotees to God-realisation. 11. The boy devotees burnt desires in the Dhuni-fire.]

1. The Master, we have said before, came from Shyampukur to the Kasipur garden on the penultimate day of Agrahayan (Nov.–Dec.), inasmuch as custom forbade making a journey to a new place in the month of Paush (Dec.–Jan.). The residential house in this garden was more spacious and more secluded than the Shayampukur house, which was situated on a road filled throughout **the waking hours with the din caused by the people of the city.** In whatever direction one might cast one's look in this Kasipur house, one's eyes were soothed with the green leaves of trees, the bright colours of flowers, and the blue and dark-blue hues of the tender and mature grass on the lawns. Although the beauty of this garden cannot stand comparison with the wonderful natural beauty of the Kali temple at Dakshineswar, it is worth mentioning that it appeared to the Master to be very pleasant after continuous stay of about four months at Calcutta. As soon as he entered the spacious room on the first floor set apart for him, he was drawn out by the beauty of the surrounding area. He came out by the southern side of the room, and taking his stand on the terrace of the first storey, enjoyed the beauty of the garden for sometime. The Holy Mother, too, was very pleased, seeing that she would not have to live here cribbed and cabined as in the Shyampukur house and also would have the opportunity of serving the Master under better surroundings. It is therefore superfluous to say that the joy of the attendants knew no bounds when they found both of them so very pleased with the garden house.

2. A few days passed in attending to the deficiencies of the place

that came to the notice of the attendants. Narendranath thought over them and easily came to the conclusion that more men and money would be required now than before, if those who had taken upon themselves voluntarily the charge of the Master's service were also to live at that garden house situated far away from their homes as also of the doctor treating the Master. It was evident that unless all matters were thrashed out duly and steps taken from the beginning, difficulties would naturally crop up in the way of the service of the Master. Balaram, Surendra, Ram, Girish, Mahendra and others, who had all along been thinking of the financial side of the matter, found out after due deliberation the ways and means of meeting the expenditure. But as regards the question of men, Narendranath himself would have to think it out as before. He would, therefore, have to spend the greater part of his time at the Kasipur garden. If he did not show the way, many of the young devotees could not do so, lest they should incur the displeasure of their guardians or their studies should suffer. For, during the Master's stay at Shyampukur, they used to go home to take their food and come back to engage themselves in his service, which would now be impossible for them to do on account of the long distance between Kasipur and Calcutta.

3. Narendra was preparing for his Law examination (B.L) that year. Although it was absolutely necessary for him to stay in Calcutta for his studies and for looking after the suit pending before the High Court regarding the partition of his ancestral property necessitated by the enmity of his kinsmen, he dismissed that idea completely from his mind in order to serve the Guru, and he decided that he should bring his law books to the Kasipur garden and read them at leisure, if possible at all. Thus we see that till then Narendranath's plan was to prepare himself for the Law examination, and also side by side serve the Master. For, having no alternative before him, he had decided that he should pass the Law examination and by a few years' hard labour earn money sufficient for the bare maintenance of his mother and brothers, and that having made arrangements for them, he should retire from the world and devote himself entirely to spiritual practices. But alas! many of us do make such good resolves, but how many succeed? Many of us calculate that we might allow ourselves to be carried away to some extent by the currents of worldliness, and then show our inner strength by veering round and swimming

against those currents on to the safe haven of spirituality, and start working accordingly. But how many of us can save ourselves from being caught in the whirpool and succeed in reaching the shore? Narendranath was the foremost among the first class spiritual aspirants, and he had received the infinite grace of the Master. What about the above mentioned resolve of his? Is he likely to stand by that resolve even when faced by the unforeseeable complications of his domestic milieu? Or is he also going to be a victim at the altar of compromise? Be patient, O reader, we shall soon see how and by what path Narendranath was helped to reach his goal by the infallible power of the Master's will.

4. We have been so far speaking of what the devotees were doing for the service of the Master. The question may now be asked conveniently, "Did the Master now depend on the devotees for everything without thinking about himself at all? Can we expect such indifference on the part of the Master who, as we saw him at Dakshineswar, kept, on the one hand, a keen eye even on the small affairs of the daily life of all concerned and on the worldly and spiritual conditions of each devotee, and was, on the other, having simultaneously the immediate experiences of the truths beyond the Vedas and the Vedantas? Should we not expect some positive effort and guidance on his part?" It has to be said in reply that he depended wholly even now, as before, on the Divine Mother alone — his eyes being directed to Her alone for all he needed and not to any human agency. Whatever service, personal and financial, that he accepted from each devotee, — he had known it beforehand to be so ordained by the Divine Mother Herself for their own good. The more we proceed to tell the story of the Master's life, the more will this important fact become clear.

5. Again, he used to undo the arrangements made by the devotees when they were not to his liking, sometimes with their knowledge and sometimes without it, whenever he felt they would feel pained thereby. He, for example, had called Balaram to his side at the time of his coming to Calcutta for treatment and said: "Look here, it is quite against my liking that people should arrange my daily meals by subscription; for I have never lived so. You may ask whether I was not doing so at the Kali temple of Dakshineswar? For, the temple authorities were jointly managing the affairs of the temple, though they lived separately. Under these circumstances you may say that I was jointly maintained by them,

that is, with their subscription, so long as I lived in the temple. But the fact is otherwise. There was no occasion for me to live by subscription even then. It had been arranged ever since the time of Rasmani that the monthly pay of seven rupees that I used to be given when I performed the worship, should be paid to me together with the Prasada of the deities as long as I lived there. It may, therefore, be said in a way that I lived on a pension.[1] So please pay personally the expenses for my food as long as I am outside Dakshineswar for treatment." Again, when the garden house at Kasipur was hired for him, he came to know that the monthly rent of that house at Kasipur was a big amount (namely, eighty rupees), and he was wondering how his devotees who had to maintain their big families — many of them with considerable difficulty — could possibly bear the expense. He at last called to his side the devotee Surendranath, who was by profession a superintendent of the Dost Company, and said, "Look here, Surendra, they are all petty clerks earning small incomes and find it difficult even to maintain their families. Can they raise so much money by subscription? Therefore, please pay the whole amount of the rent yourself." With folded hands Surendra gladly agreed, saying, "As you command." One day the Master was telling us that, owing to his weakness, it would soon be difficult for him to go out for answering calls of nature. The young devotee Latu[2] felt pained to hear those words of the Master on that occasion. He made the Master as well as all of us smile even in that state of sorrow when, with folded hands, he chimed in sweet broken Bengali, "Sir, here I am, your sweeper." Thus did the Master make things convenient for the devotees by introducing appropriate rearrangements of his service.

6. Proper arrangements about everything were being gradually made, and all the young devotees, more than the number strictly required for the service, came one after another. Narendra kept them engaged in meditation, devotional exercises, studies, holy conversations, and discussions on scriptural topics in such a way that they did not feel how the days slipped by; so absorbed

[1] The Master pronounced the word as 'pencil'.

[2] He is now well known in the circle of the devotees by the name of Swami Adbhutananda. He was a native of the district of Chhapra. Although he could understand Bengali, there were various peculiarities when he spoke that language, which were very sweet to hear, like the lisping of a child.

were they in the great joy of all these. The pure, selfless love of the Master on the one hand, and the wonderful spirit of friendship of Narendra and his noble company on the other, united together to bind them in such a sweet and tender, yet hard and unbreakable, bond that they actually began to consider one another to be much more intimately related than the people of the same family, so much so that if any one had unluckily to go home on some very urgent business on a certain day, he would invariably come back the same evening or the next morning. Although not more than twelve[1] in number, all of them remained there to the end of the Master's mortal life and completed their vow of service by renouncing the world. They loved their Guru as dearly as their lives and were wonderfully dexterous in all manner of work.

7. A few days after his coming to Kasipur, the Master came downstairs one day and strolled for a short time along the garden path round the house. The devotees were happy to see it and hoped that he would soon be strong and regain his health if only he could take walks like that everyday. But he felt weak the following day, either on account of his catching a cold due to the contact with the cold air outside or for some other reason, and could not take a stroll for some time to come. The cold of course was cured in two or three days, but his weakness continued. The doctors, therefore, prescribed for him some special soup, by taking which he got over that weakness to a great extent in a few days, and he felt healthier than before. This improvement continued for about a fortnight, and Dr. Mahendralal too felt very glad to notice this, when he came to see him on one of these days.

The young attendants had to go to Calcutta every day to tell the doctor about the Master's health and bring the requisites for his diet. Both of these duties were left at first in charge of one man. That gave rise to great inconvenience; so it was decided that thence-

[1] In order to satisfy the curiosity of the reader, the names of those twelve are given below: Narendra, Rakhal, Baburam, Niranjan, Yogindra, Latu, Tarak, brother Gopal, (who was the only old man amongst the young devotees), Kali, Sasi, Sarat, and Hutko ('abruptly appearing') Gopal. Sarada could stay for a day or two only from time to time owing to hard pressure from his father. Harish came for a few days and went back home and his brain got deranged there. Hari, Tulasi, and Gangadhar practised Tapasya at home and came there at intervals. Besides these twelve, two others joined Mahimacharan Chakravarti shortly afterwards and lived in his house.

forth two persons should go to Calcutta for those two urgent items of work. If it was found necessary to go to Calcutta for any other reason, a third person would be deputed. Moreover, the young devotees began to do all the duties by turns, such as keeping clean the house, going daily to Baranagar to make purchase from the market, rendering personal service to the Master day and night, and whatever else they were called upon to do. Narendranath engaged himself in superintending every action of theirs and in doing whatever work came up suddenly by chance.

8. The Holy Mother, however, was in charge of preparing the Master's diet as before. When any special food was prescribed for the Master, the details of the method of preparing it were learnt from the doctor. And one or two devotees like brother Gopai, with whom she did not observe *purdah* and spoke freely, would go and explain to her the method of cooking it. Besides preparing the diet, the Holy Mother personally used to carry the food to the Master twice daily, once a little before midday and the second time shortly after sunset. She would be waiting on in the room till the Master finished his meal, when she would take back the cups and plates. Lakshmi Devi, the niece of the Master, was brought to Kasipur to help the Holy Mother in cooking and other works and to keep her company. Over and above that, some of those women devotees who visited the Master often at Dakshineswar came here at intervals and stayed with the Holy Mother for a few hours and sometimes for a day or two. Thus in a week everything was running smoothly.

9. The householder devotees also were not free from anxiety at that time. They gathered either in Ram's or Girish's house to decide upon the maximum service, personal or pecuniary, that they could render to their beloved Master. They knew that they could not spare the same time or amount of money every month; hence they had to meet once or twice a month to take decisions beforehand.

10. Most of the young devotees did not go home even for a short time till everything began to move in an orderly manner. Those who had unavoidably to go, returned in a few hours and sent word home somehow, that they would not be able to go home regularly and live there as usual till the Master had regained his health. It needs no mention that no guardian, when he came to know this, approved of this readily. But what could the guardians

do? The brains of the boys had been spoilt, as they put it. They thought that more harm than good might befall them, if they tried to interfere directly. So they allowed the boys to go their own ways, trying all the time to win them over slowly through indirect pressure and persuasion. When both the classes of devotees, the householders and the Brahmacharins, joined heartily and with determination in the great vow of service to the Master, and everything was going on smoothly like a machine, Narendranath was free from anxiety. Having now the time to think about his own affairs, he made up his mind to go home soon for a day or two. He made it known to us all at night and went to bed; but he had no sleep. He got up in a short time. Seeing Gopal and one or two others of us awake, he said, "Come, let us go and stroll in the garden and have a smoke." He said, while walking, "The Master is suffering from a fell disease. Who can say if he has not made up his mind to give up his body? While there is time yet, let us make as much of spiritual progress as we can by service, meditation and devotional exercises. Otherwise, when he passes away, there will be no limit to our repentance. To postpone calling on the Lord till desires are fulfilled! This is exactly how our days are passing, and we are getting more and more entangled in the net of desires. It is these desires only that lead to destruction and death. So let us give up desires; yes, let's give them all up."

11. The winter night of the month of Paush (Dec.–Jan.) was drowsing away in utter silence. The infinite blue above was looking steadfastly at the earth with a hundred thousand starry eyes. Below, the ground under the garden trees was now dry on account of the powerful rays of the sun, and was well cleansed and fit to sit on. Narendra's mind, inclined to dispassion and detachment and accustomed to meditation, felt, as it were, within, that external silence merging in itself. Instead of walking any more, he sat down under a tree. Shortly afterwards he saw a dry heap of grass and broken branches of trees and said, "Set fire to it. Holy men light Dhunis under trees at this time. Let us also light a Dhuni and burn up our desires within." A fire was lighted. We pulled along similar heaps of dry fuel lying on all sides and offered them as oblations to that fire, thinking, all the while, that we were offering the desires of our minds as oblations and felt a wonderful bliss. We felt as if our worldly desires were burnt up and our minds grew pure and serene, and we were approaching

God. We thought, "Ah, why did we not do this before? It has given us so much bliss!" We then resolved to light such Dhunis whenever opportunities should occur. When two or three hours elapsed in that way and no more fuel could be found, we extinguished the fire, returned to our places and went to bed again. It was then past four in the morning. Those who could not join us in lighting the Dhuni felt sorry when they woke up at day-break and heard of it. They were grieved at not being called. Narendranath said by way of consolation to them, "The whole thing was not pre-planned. And who could know beforehand that it would be so blissful an experience? We shall gather together from now on and light a Dhuni whenever we find time. We need not worry on that account."

Narendra went away to Calcutta in the morning as settled before, and returned to Kasipur in a day with a few law books in his hand.

CHAPTER XIII: SECTION 3

THE MASTER'S SELF-REVELATION AND THE BESTOWAL OF FREEDOM FROM FEAR

[TOPICS: 1. The Master felt a little better under Dr. Rajendra's treatment. 2. The Master's self-revelation and blessings to the disciples. 3. Did the Master act as the wishfulfilling tree? 4. Who were present during this self-revelation? 5. Vaikunthanath pestered the Master for having spiritual experiences. 6. How he felt at the touch of the Master. 7. Without due preparation high spiritual experiences cannot be retained.]

1. We have already told the reader how one day the Master came out of his room and walked in the garden for a short time. Feeling weak on account of it, he did not venture to do so again for about a fortnight. Although there was no change of treatment during that period, there was a change in the person of the doctor treating. Rajendranath Datta, born in the family of the rich and famous Akrur Datta of Bowbazar, Calcutta, laboured hard and spent much money over a prolonged and deep study of Homoeopathy and its propagation in the city. Through association with him the well-known physician, Dr. Mahendralal Sarkar, became convinced of the efficacy and efficiency of Homoeopathy and adopted that method in his profession. Rajendra Babu had heard from people of the illness of the Master. He knew that if he could cure him, the reputation of Homoeopathy would be established among many; so he selected a medicine after much study and thought. He was acquainted with Atul, the younger brother of Girish. He, as far as we remember, met Atul somewhere at this time and asked him about the Master's illness. He then expressed his intention of treating the Master and said, "Please tell Mahendra that I have selected a medicine after much thinking. I hope to get good results with it. I would like to try it once if he is agreeable." Atul reported this to the devotees and to Dr. Mahendralal Sarkar, and as no one had any objection to it, Rajendra Babu came to visit the Master in a few days. After listening to the description of the disease from the beginning he administered Lycopodium (200). The Master derived much benefit from it for more than a fortnight. The devotees thought he would perhaps soon become strong and healthy as before.

2. Half of the month of Paush (Dec.–Jan.) passed away and it was the first day of January 1886. As the Master felt rather well that day, he expressed a desire to come out of his room and have a walk in the garden for some time. It was a holiday and the householder devotees came one by one and in groups, shortly after midday. Thus when the Master came downstairs at three in the afternoon, more than thirty people were engaged in conversation in the garden under the trees, or inside the house. As soon as they saw him, all got up out of reverence and bowed down to him. He came down to the garden path through the western door of the hall on the ground floor and was slowly proceeding southward to the gate when all followed him at a little distance. When he came to the middle of the path leading to the gate, he saw Girish, Ram, Atul and a few others, sitting under the trees to the west of the path. They also saw him and saluted him from there and came joyfully to him. The Master addressed Girish, all of a sudden before anybody had spoken a word, and said, "Girish, I find, you say to one and all everywhere so many things about 'this' (that I am an incarnation of God); what have you seen and understood (about me) to make you do so?" Girish remained completely unmoved, and kneeling down on the ground near the Master's feet, said in a choked voice with his hands folded and face turned upwards, "What more can I say of Him, whose greatness Vyasa and Valmiki could not find words to express?" The Master was charmed at the fervent utterance of Girish, and blessing all the devotees assembled there through their representative Girish, said "What more shall I say to you? May you all be blessed with the spiritual awakening." Beside himself with love and compassion for the devotees, hardly had he said those few words when he entered into Bhavasamadhi. Those words of profound blessing, untouched by the slightest tinge of the ego-sense, directly entered the devotees' hearts, where they raised high billows of bliss. They forgot time and space, forgot the disease of the Master, forgot their previous determination not to touch him till he recovered, and were aware only that an extraordinary divine Being, out of sympathy for them in their plight, feeling excruciating pain at their misery and overflowing with compassion for them, had come down from heaven and called them affectiontely to Him for giving protection, like a mother sheltering her children against all ills by covering them lovingly with the upper part of her sari. They

became eager to bow down to him and take the dust of his feet; and filling the quarters with cries of "Victory to Ramakrishna", began saluting him one after another. As they were thus bowing down to him, the sea of the Master's compassion transcended all bounds and brought about a wonderful phenomenon. We had almost daily seen the Master at Dakshineswar losing himself in grace and compassion for certain devotees and blessing them by his extraordinarily potent touch in the state of divine semi-consciousness. He now began touching each of the devotees assembled on that day in that divine mood. The joy of the devotees, it is superfluous to say, knew no bounds at that act of the Master. They felt that he would not henceforward keep concealed the fact of his divinity either from themselves or from anybody else in the world; and nevertheless, knowing, as they did, their own defects, their spiritual destitution, their incapacity, they had not the slightest doubt that all alike, the sinner as well as the afflicted, would find a refuge at his feet, a touch of which dispelled all fear for ever. Unable to utter a single word owing to that wonderful occurrence, some were only looking steadfastly at him as if they were under the spell of a Mantra, some others called aloud to all within the house to come and be blessed by receiving the Master's grace, and still others collected flowers and worshipped him with them, uttering Mantras. Soon the ecstasy of the Master came to an end and the devotees too were again in the normal state of their consciousness. Bringing thus to an end his walk in the garden that day, he went into the house and sat down in his room.

3. Some devotees like Ramchandra have described the happening of that day as the transformation by the Master of himself into the wish-fulfilling tree (Kalpataru). But, it is more reasonable, it seems to us, to call it "the self-revelation of the Master" or "the bestowal of freedom from fear on all devotees by revealing himself". The Kalpataru, it is said, gives to all whatever good or bad they ask for. But the Master did much more; he made clear through that event the fact of his being a God-man and of his bestowal of protection against, and freedom from, fear on all, without the slightest discrimination. Be that as it may, of all the people that felt blessed by having his grace on that day, Haranchandra Das is worthy of being particularly mentioned. For, as soon as he bowed down to him, the Master in ecstasy placed his lotus foot on Haran's head. It is only on a few occasions that

we saw him bestow his grace in this way.[1] Ramlal Chattopadhyaya was present there on that occasion and also received the Master's grace. Asked about it, he said, "I could formerly see a part only of the holy Person of my chosen Ideal with my mind's eye at the time of meditation — when I saw the lotus feet, I could not see the face; again perhaps I saw the Person from the face to the waist, but could not see the holy feet; and whatever I saw never seemed to be alive. But no sooner had the Master touched me that day than the form of my chosen Ideal appeared suddenly from head to foot in the lotus of my heart and moved and looked benign and effulgent."

4. We remember the names of nine or ten only of the persons who were present on the spot during this day's occurrence. They were Girish, Atul, Ram, Navagopal, Haramohan, Vaikuntha, Kishori (Ray), Haran, Ramlal and Akshay. Mahendranath (the writer of the Gospel of Sri Ramakrishna) was also perhaps present. But it is a matter for wonder that none of the future Sannyasin devotees of the Master was present there at that time. Narendranath and many others of that group had been engaged in Sadhana, besides the Master's service, during the previous night for long hours, and feeling tired, they were sleeping inside the house. Although Latu and Sarat were awake and saw what was taking place from the roof of the first floor to the south of the Master's room, they refrained voluntarily from going there. For, as soon as the Master went downstairs to have a walk in the garden, they put his clothes and bedding in the sun and were cleaning the room. Thinking that it might cause inconvenience to the Master if they left their duty half-finished, they did not feel inclined to go there.

5. We asked a few others including Vaikunthanath about their experience on that day. We shall bring this subject to a close by recording what Vaikuntha told us. Vaikuntha met the Master at about the same time as we did. We have already mentioned something of how the Master gave him instructions and moulded his life since then. The Master rendered his life full of bliss by initiating him in a Mantra. Vaikuntha engaged himself in Sadhana since that time and was striving his best that he might have the

[1] Haranchandra of Beliaghata had a job in the office of Messrs. Finlay Mayor Company. During the last few years of his life he used to celebrate an annual festival in memory of the grace the Master bestowed on him on this occasion.

vision of his chosen Ideal. Knowing that he could not succeed in his attempt without the Master's grace, he was from time to time plaintively praying to him for it, especially when the Master became physically ill and came to Calcutta and then to Kasipur for treatment. During this period also, twice or thrice, Vaikuntha got the opportunity of humbly beseeching him for the fulfilment of his heart's desire. The Master smiled graciously, comforted him, and said, "Why don't you wait? Let the disease of the body be cured a little, and I shall do everything for you."

6. Vaikuntha was present on the spot at the time of this day's occurrence. As soon as the Master had blessed two or three of the devotees by his potent touch, Vaikunta came before him, bowed down to him with devotion and said, "Sir, please bestow your grace on me!" The Master said, "But you have been given everything." "When you say," said Vaikuntha, "everything has been given, it is certainly so; but kindly do so, that I too can understand it." Saying, "So be it", the Master touched his chest only for a moment in the ordinary way. "But," said Vaikuntha, "as the result of it, a great revolution took place in my mind. I saw the figure of the Master lit up with a gracious smile in the sky, in the houses, trees, plants, men and in whatever else I looked at. I did not know how to contain my delight within myself, and seeing both of you, Sarat and Latu, on the roof, I called aloud saying 'O you all! Wherever you be, come without delay!' That mental attitude and vision of mine continued for some days throughout my waking state. I became amazed and charmed with the holy vision of the Master in all things. It continued to be so wherever I went, to the office or elsewhere on any business.

7. "I could not attend to the work on hand and it suffered. On finding that my work was suffering, I tried to forget that vision for sometime, but failed in my attempt to do so. I then understood a little why Arjuna felt afraid to see the universal form of the divine Lord and prayed to Him to withdraw it. I remembered the statement of the scriptures that liberated souls always remain in the same elevated state. Only after this experience I could understand the extent of desirelessness the mind has to develop to have the capacity to remain in that high state. For hardly had a few days passed when I felt it difficult to live in the same mental attitude and with the same vision. Sometimes it occured to me, 'Am I going mad?' I then prayed to the Master again with fear, 'O lord, I am not able

to contain this mental state; please ordain that it may come to an end.' I now think, 'Woe be to human weakness and stupidity! Why did I pray so? Why did I not keep my faith firm in him? And why did I not wait patiently to see its ultimate developments? I might at most have become mad or the body might have dropped off.' For as soon as I prayed in that manner, the said vision and mental state came to an end one day. My firm conviction is that they were removed by the same extraordinary Being from whom I had got them. But he preserved compassionately a partial capacity of the mind to recapture it, perhaps because there arose no prayer in my mind for its complete removal. I felt blessed and amazed at the sudden appearance of this vision a few times daily — the vision of the gracious figure of the Master made effulgent by the divine mood."

CHRONOLOGY OF IMPORTANT EVENTS

Year	Events
1775	Birth of Kshudiram.
1791	Birth of Chandra Devi.
1799	Kshudiram's marriage with Chandra Devi.
1805	Birth of Ramkumar.
1810	Birth of Katyayani.
1815	Kshudiram's migration to Kamarpukur.
1821	Marriages of Ramkumar and of Katyayani.
1824	Kshudiram's pilgrimage to Rameswaram.
1826	Birth of Rameswar.
1835	Kshudiram's pilgrimage to Banares and Gaya.
1836	Birth of the Great Master, Thursday, 18th February, before 5 A.M. (Wednesday according to Indian calculation)
1840	Birth of Sarvamangala.
1843	Death of Kshudiram.
1848	Marriages of Rameswar and of Sarvamangala.
1849	Birth of Akshay.
1850	Ramkumar's opening of a Sanskrit school in Calcutta.
1852	The Master's coming to Calcutta.
1853	Birth of the Holy Mother.
1855	The consecration of the Dakshineswar temple. The Master's appointment as the priest of Kali. The coming of Hridaya Ram.
1856	Death of Ramkumar and the Master's appointment as the priest of Kali. His first divine inebriation and great vision.
1857	Correction of Rani Rasamani.
1858	Appointment of Haladhari as the priest of Kali.
1859	The Master's marriage.
1860	The Master's second visit. Mathur's vision of the Master as Siva and Kali.
1861	Death of Rani. Arrival of Bhairavi Brahmani.
1862	The Master's Tantra Sadhana.
1863	Completion of Tantra Sadhana and the arrival of the

Master's mother at Dakshineswar.

1864 Mathur's gift of a "mountain of food."

1865 Arrival of Tota Puri and the Master's Sannyasa.

1866 The Master's stay of six months in the non-dual state.

1867 The Master at Kamarpukur with the Brahmani and Hriday. The Holy Mother's arrival at Kamarpukur.

1868 The Master's pilgrimage.

1870 The Master's visit to Kalna and Navadwip and meeting with Bhagavandas.

1871 Death of Mathur.

1872 The Holy Mother's first arrival at Dakshineswar.

1873 The Master's Shodasi Puja (1872?) The Holy Mother's return to Kamarpukur and Rameswar's death.

1874 The Holy Mother at Dakshineswar for the second time.

1875 The Master's meeting with Kesav Chandra Sen.

1876 The Holy Mother's illness. Death of Chandra Devi.

1877 The Holy Mother's third visit to Dakshineswar.

1879 The Master's marked devotees started coming: Ram and Manomohan.

1881 The Master's first meeting with Narendranath. Dismissal of Hriday.

1882 The Master's visit to Pandit Vidyasagar.

1883 The author's meeting with the Master.

1884 Death of Kesav. Gopala's mother's first meeting with the Master, and the end of the coming of the marked devotees.

1885 The Master's last visit to the Panihati festival. His removal to Shyampukur and later to Kasipur.

1886 The Master's self-revelation (Kalpataru day, 1st Jan.) and Mahasamadhi, 16th August.

APPENDIX 1

THE BOOK AND ITS AUTHOR

This is the first complete English version of *Sri Ramakrishna Lila-prasanga*, a faithful record and exposition in Bengali of the various aspects of the life of Sri Ramakrishna (1836-86), whom the late reputed French savant Romain Rolland introduced to the Western world as "the Messiah of Bengal". Indeed, Sri Ramakrishna's life was a significant spiritual event of the last century. His chief disciple, Swami Vivekananda, declared, "His (Ramakrishna's) life was a thousandfold more than his teaching, a living commentary on the texts of the Upanishads, nay, he was the spirit of the Upanishads living in human form. Nowhere else in this world exists that unique perfection, that wonderful kindness for all that does not stop to justify itself, that intense sympathy for man in bondage. He lived to root out all distinction between man and woman, the rich and the poor, the literate and the illiterate, the Brahmanas and the Chandalas. . . . He came to bring about the synthesis of the Eastern and Western civilizations. Indeed, not for many a century has India produced so great, so wonderful a teacher of religious synthesis. . . . The new dispensation of the age is the source of great good to the whole world, specially to India; and the inspirer of this dispensation, Sri Bhagavan Ramakrishna, is the reformed and remodelled manifestation of all the past great epoch-makers in religion." Such a life may be presented and interpreted only by a thoroughly rational mind endowed with a high order of intuitive insight and almost an encyclopaedic knowledge of the spiritual realm.

Sri Ramakrishna Lila-prasanga, the original Bengali biography of Sri Ramakrishna, based as it is on first-hand observation, assiduous collection of materials from different sources, patient sifting of evidence by way of an earnest effort for precision, and backed up by lucid interpretation of all relevant intricate problems connected with religious theories and practices, may easily be ranked as one of the best specimens of hagiographic literature.

The book was published serially in five volumes in Bengali.

The first two volumes (Parts III & IV) contain learned discourses by way of explaining and illustrating the aspect of Sri Ramakrishna as a Guru (spiritual guide). His early days and his vigorous spiritual practices in youth are delineated in the following two volumes (Parts I & II) respectively. The last (Part V) depicts the manifestation of Divinity in and through the life of Sri Ramakrishna.

But, unfortunately, the book was incomplete. It did not cover the last few months of Sri Ramakrishna's life. However, Romain Rolland was perfectly justified in stating, "Incomplete though the work remains, it is excellent for the subject."

Regarding the author, the French savant cogently remarks that he "is an authority both as a philosopher and as a historian. His books are rich in metaphysical sketches, which place the spiritual appearance of Ramakrishna exactly in its place in the rich procession of Hindu thought." Really, the masterly treatment of the subject gives a glimpse of the marvellous capacity of the author. His wide experience, vast erudition, spirit of rational enquiry and, above all, his far-reaching spiritual achievements may be discerned even by a casual reader of the book.

An acquaintance with some details of the author's life may prove interesting and helpful to the readers of the present English publication of the work. It will enable them to appreciate its worth as an authentic and comprehensive record of an epoch-making spiritual phenomenon, the hallowed life of Sri Ramakrishna. Hence the following outline:

The author was Swami Saradananda, one of the outstanding monastic disciples of Sri Ramakrishna. Before he took Orders his name was Sarat Chandra Chakravarty. He was born in December 1865, of a fairly well-to-do Brahmin family residing in central Calcutta.

His early life showed unmistakable signs of a saint in the making. Sedate and polite by nature, he had a robust physique, a sharp intellect and a highly sympathetic heart. Easily the best boy of his class, Sarat Chandra made his mark also in the debating society of his school, though it was not possible for him to hurt anybody's feelings by a harsh word or a caustic taunt. His loving heart invariably prompted him to serve any ailing acquaintance, be he a relative, a friend, a neighbour or a menial, — and this even if the disease was an infectious one. To crown all, a remarkable feature of Sarat Chandra's mental make-up was its precocious bias for religion. Even as a little boy he evinced an instinctive craving for religious rites. Mimic worship was the child's favourite play. As he grew up, this play gradually turned into the most serious pursuit of his life.

Born of an orthodox Brahmin family, he inherited a profound reverence for the traditional Hindu religion. Towards the end of his school-days his faith was fairly secured on rational grounds as he came in touch with a sophisticated form of Hinduism through the New Dispensation Movement of the Brahmo Samaj. His ardour for spiritual growth got a fresh stimulus when in St. Xavier's College he contacted the Holy Bible and became inspired by the life and teachings of Jesus. Lastly, it was during his college-days that he lighted upon an exalted spiritual guide who resolved all his possible doubts regarding the truth behind all religions, and by whose surging spiritual power the course of Sarat Chandra's life was entirely changed.

The spiritual guide was Sri Ramakrishna, then known as the Saint of Dakshineswar, a northern suburb of Calcutta. The news of a towering spiritual personality residing in a Kali temple in that suburb had been spreading for some years among the Calcutta public through several Calcutta journals, particularly under the auspices of the Brahmo Samaj. This was drawing a stream of pious visitors, young and old, from Calcutta to meet the saint. Sarat Chandra and his cousin Sasi (later Swami Ramakrishnananda) were caught in the current. Both of them were then college students and were in their teens, when one day in October 1883, they went over to pay their respects to the saint.

Sri Ramakrishna appeared to be waiting for such pious young souls. As soon as he met them, he hailed them with delight and made them his own by his endearing and edifying talks. By his sweet and simple words he burnt deep into their minds the supreme need of renouncing sense-enjoyments for realizing God. They felt instinctively that in Sri Ramakrishna they had found a worthy guide on the spiritual path.

After this first visit Sarat Chandra made it a point to come alone to meet the saint every Thursday, which was a holiday in his college. The enchantment of Sri Ramakrishna's incomparably pure and selfless love was upon him, and as days went on, he began to feel an irresistible attraction towards the holy man. Through repeated contact with him, Sarat Chandra's ideas about practical religion became clearer and clearer, and he advanced step by step on the spiritual path as directed by Sri Ramakrishna.

Even in his early youth, Sarat Chandra's spiritual aspirations were pitched very high. He was not after washy sentiments, nor even after visions. God in any particular form was not his quest. He wanted to see Him manifested in all creatures. Though told by Sri Ramakrishna that this was the finale of spiritual attainment and could not be easily achieved, Sarat Chandra said that nothing else could satisfy him, and that he was determined to get to that blessed state, whatever difficulties might stand in the way. Evidently Sri Ramakrishna was pleased to find such a prodigious mental calibre in the young aspirant, and suggested that the latter should make friends with Narendranath (later Swami Vivekananda), a potential spiritual giant.

Within a year of his first visit to the saint, Sarat Chandra came to be attached to Narendranath by a bond of intimate friendship. One day in October 1884, hearing from Narendranath about his marvellous mystic experiences connected with Sri Ramakrishna, Sarat Chandra's perspective of the Saint of Dakshineswar became radically changed. He perceived that Sri Ramakrishna was not merely a saint but a spiritual personage ranking with the Prophets and Incarnations he had heard about.

Naturally, after the above incident, Sarat Chandra's love and esteem for Sri Ramakrishna soared to spontaneous adoration of Divinity in the garb of the holy man. With unquestioned faith he resigned himself to the loving care and guidance of the saint as his Guru, and devoted himself heart and soul to spiritual practice, as far as the limits of his home environment and academic career would allow. Sri Ramakrishna, on his part, recognizing in Sarat an aspiring soul of a very high order with a brilliant past, poured out his unstinted grace upon the young disciple and vitalized his budding spiritual genius.

Things went on smoothly till the middle of the year 1885, when Sri Ramakrishna was laid up with a serious attack of throat trouble (cancer) and was brought to a rented house in the northern quarter of Calcutta for treatment. The alarming news came to Sarat Chandra like a bolt from the blue. The terrible shock he received, however, served eventually as a fillip to his spiritual progress. The moorings of worldly life seemed immediately to give way. With anxious concern for the health of his beloved

Guru, he rushed to his bed-side, playing truant from his home and bidding adieu to the Calcutta Medical College, which he had recently joined. Shortly, he began to live day and night with Sri Ramakrishna, and followed him when after about four months he was removed to a garden house in Kasipur, a northern suburb of Calcutta. With his phenomenal zeal for nursing, Sarat Chandra kept on tending the Master till the last moment of the latter's earthly life.

Sri Ramakrishna's illness lasting for about a year proved to be a signal, as it were, for his picked, young disciples to tear themselves away from their home life and be eventually banded together into an incipient holy brotherhood under their pre-eminent leader Narendranath. They came obviously to nurse their beloved Guru, but stayed on to be drilled into monastic life. It was in the Kasipur garden house that one day Sarat Chandra with most of his comrades received from Sri Ramakrishna the ochre cloth, the distinct garb of a Hindu monk. It was here that, under the Master's instructions and encouragement, they learnt to beg their food like Sannyasins in order to practise complete resignation to Providence as well as to purge their minds of deep-rooted egotistic tendencies. Thus inspired by their Guru with the highest spiritual ideals, and ushered symbolically into monasticism, they forgot all other concerns except the service of their beloved Master and an intense devotion to spiritual practice.

In this way the lofty aim of realizing God was rooted deeply in their minds. The world and its humdrum affairs had no attraction for them. And this state of their minds became more intense after the Master passed away in August 1886. Soon after that, a monastery was started for them in a rented house at Baranagar, not far from the Kasipur garden house. Though for a time Sarat Chandra returned home reluctantly, yet as soon as the monastery was started, he began to visit it off and on and spend long hours in the company of his comrades, absorbed in spiritual practice or in talks about the life and teachings of the Master. Apprehending that his eldest son Sarat was tending to be a recluse, and failing to turn his mind towards worldly life by arguments, Sarat's father, Girish Chandra, took the extreme step of cutting off all contacts of his son with his fellow disciples by locking him up in a room. Unruffled, Sarat Chandra accepted the unenviable solitary confinement in his own house, and fully utilized his loneliness in focussing his mind on his spiritual objective. However, one day when one of his sympathetic younger brothers furtively unlocked the room, Sarat Chandra silently walked out of the house and went straight to the Baranagar monastery. Shortly after this, he and some of his brother disciples assembled in the village home of Baburam (later Swami Premananda), and there, inspired by their leader Narendranath's exhortation during a night-long vigil round a sacred fire, they took the solemn vow of Sannyasa, that is, monasticism for life.

Thus, step by step and without any fuss, Sarat Chandra forged ahead on the path chalked out for Hindu monks. A period of austere monastic life in the Baranagar monastery followed. Without paying any heed to the meagre allowance of food and dress that the slender resources of the monastery provided for these educated middle-class youths, they braced themselves up for the arduous task of realizing the Divine. No other concern could stand in the way of their one-pointed spiritual endeavour. Meditation, hymns, prayers, scriptural study and discussion on religious topics were all that absorbed most of their time and energy.

Thus the young spiritual aspirants kept themselves busy and were not in a mood to rest before they reached their goal. On one auspicious day in the Baranagar monastery, they performed the prescribed sacred rite known as Viraja Homa and thus ceremonially joined the traditional Hindu monastic Order. Though their monastic life was virtually started by Sri Ramakrishna during his last days in the Kasipur garden house, and was reinforced by their solemn vows in the village home of Baburam under the inspiration of Narendranath, it was from this day that they commenced a new life as sanctioned by Hindu religious texts. Wiping out all previous impressions about their castes and social positions related to the families of their birth, they discarded even their previous names and titles. From this day Sarat Chandra came to be known as Swami Saradananda.

Soon, however, Saradananda, like most of the inmates of the Baranagar monastery, was seized by a passion for leading the lonely life of a wandering monk (Parivrajaka). Even the company of his brothers as well as the comparatively secure life within the monastery sat on his nerves as an unbearable bondage. He felt an indomitable urge for moving about from place to place as an unfettered soul in pursuit of his spiritual aim, depending absolutely on God for food and shelter. Sacred cities, river banks and Himalayan retreats, rich with spiritual associations piled up by saints and sages through scores of centuries, made their irresistible appeal to his pure mind.

His first sojourn outside the Baranagar monastery was at Puri, the sea-side holy city of Jagannath. After a time he came back, and went out again to spend a considerable time in various sacred places in Northern India. Through Banaras and Ayodhya he proceeded to Hrishikesh, where, absorbed in spiritual practice, he stayed on for some months leading the traditional life of Hindu monks. In the summer of 1890, he climbed up the Himalayas to visit Kedarnath, Tunganath and Badrinarayan, and in July came down to Almora, where within a month he met Swami Vivekananda. With the latter he went again to Hrishikesh through the Garhwal State. Then, after spending some time in Meerut and Delhi with Swami Vivekananda, he went down to Banaras, visiting on the way holy places like Mathura, Vrindavan and Prayag (Allahabad). After another period of intense spiritual practice in the holy city of Banaras, he had an attack of blood dysentery, which eventually brought him back to the Baranagar monastery in September 1891. On recovery, he went to Jayramvati to pay his respects to the spiritual consort of Sri Ramakrishna, known to the devotees as the Holy Mother.

The itinerary of a wandering monk like Swami Saradananda may be followed in detail, but the path traversed by his mind speeding through spiritual experiences cannot be mapped. How, when and by what stages his spiritual genius unfolded itself completely, cannot be traced. Thus the most interesting and substantial contents of his life remained like a sealed book in the bosom of the sage.

In 1892 the monastery was shifted from Baranagar to Alambazar, a place nearer to the Dakshineswar temple. For a fairly long time before and after that, the brotherhood had no knowledge of the whereabouts of their leader Narendranath, till they were thrilled to learn that their itinerant brother had crossed the seas and burst upon the American society in the wake of the Chicago Parliament of Religions as Swami Vivekananda, the Cyclonic Monk of India. From March 1894, the latter kept himself in touch with the brotherhood of the Alambazar monastery through regular correspondence, and went on inspiring it to step out of the traditional monastic seclusion and to inaugurate a new Order of Hindu monks accepting as its motto individual salvation together with the service of deified humanity. Two years later he called Swami Saradananda to assist him in his Vedanta movement in the West. Accordingly, on the first of April 1896, Swami Saradananda reached London, where about a month later Swami Vivekananda arrived for the second time from America.

After delivering a few discourses in London, Swami Saradananda had to go over to the United States and join the Vedanta Society that had already been established by Swami Vivekananda in New York. There he set about doing some solid work through his interesting lectures on the Vedanta and the ideas and ideals of the Hindus as well as through his edifying classes on the Yoga System. He made precious contributions to the Greenacre Conference of Comparative Religions, the Brooklyn Ethical Association and to the interested *elite* of Boston and New York by way of introducing the Hindu view of life to the American public. His talks coming out of the fullness of the heart had a marked effect on the audience. Besides, his calm, dignified and courteous bearing, his catholic outlook and universal love won for him many friends and admirers over there. Under his vigilant care the Vedanta Society in New York was being placed on a sound footing, when a call from the leader made him cut short his work in the West and sail for India *via* Europe on the 12th of January, 1898.

Swami Vivekananda, the leader, had come back to India in January 1897, and in the midst of a hectic period of broadcasting his message practically all over India, from Colombo to Almora, he had started working breathlessly at the foundation of the Ramakrishna Order of monks and the Ramakrishna Mission. On the first of May of the same year, he inaugurated the Ramakrishna Mission, an Association of lay and monastic members for carrying on spiritual and humanitarian work. Within a year after his arrival, the monastery at Alambazar was shifted temporarily to Nilambar Mukherjee's garden house at Belur, where close by, on the western bank of the Ganga, a suitable site was purchased for building up a permanent monastery for the brotherhood. At this stage Swami Saradananda's service was requisitioned for piloting the Ramakrishna Mission as its Secretary as well as for organizing the management of the monastery.

Swami Saradananda reached the monastery in the above garden house early in February 1898 and took up the responsible duties allotted to him. At the beginning of the next year the monastery was shifted to its permanent site, now known as the Belur Math, and within a couple of years after that Swami Vivekananda placed the monastc organization on a stable legal basis by executing a Trust-Deed and incorporating in that organization the ideas, ideals and activities for which the Ramakrishna Mission Association had been started. In this new set-up also Swami Saradananda was chosen by the leader to function as its Secretary. It may be mentioned that later on, when for certain practical considerations the Ramakrishna Math and Mission were split up into two parallel organizations, the Swami continued to direct the affairs of both of them as their Secretary. With the allegiance of a faithful follower, Swami Saradananda stuck to this post right up to the end of his life, considering it to be a sacred task entrusted to him by Swami Vivekananda.

However, Swami Saradananda, equipped with his fresh experience of the Western methods of organization, quickly brought the internal affairs of the monastery into perfect order. Under his care and guidance, a routine life divided between spiritual practice, scriptural study and household jobs went on like clock-work within the monastery. Moreover, with his knowledge of the needs and temperaments of the Western people, he applied himself in right earnest to training up preachers for the West from among the deserving young monks.

On top of these, he had to attend to quite a number of occasional duties at the instance of the leader. Within a few months of his arrival from America, he had to take an active part in conducting the Ramakrishna Mission plague relief work in Calcutta; several months later he had to act as a guide for some Western disciples of Swami Vivekananda in their tour through a number of historical sites in Northern India. Early next year, shortly after the monastery had been shifted to its permanent site, he had to engage himself in collecting funds for the Belur Math in the course of a lecturing tour through some of the important States in Rajasthan and Sourashtra in North-western India. Coming back to the Math shortly before Swami Vivekananda left for his second visit to the West, he devoted himself with his usual zeal to his normal duties within the monastery. Towards the end of the year he visited some important towns in Eastern Bengal, and roused the spiritual fervour of the interested people in those parts by his inspiring talks and instructions.

Swami Vivekananda returned from his second tour in the West towards the end of 1900; he executed the Belur Math Trust-Deed in January 1901; and in July 1902 he passed away, leaving the Ramakrishna Math and Mission to the care of the Trustees, of whom Swami Brahmananda and Swami Saradananda held the pivotal positions of the President and the Secretary respectively. In spite of the severe shock of separation from their beloved and esteemed leader, Swami Saradananda proceeded to shoulder the onerous responsibility of the day-to-day administration of the Math and Mission under the inspired guidance of the President Swami Brahmananda, the spiritual child of Sri Ramakrishna.

Shortly, Swami Saradananda took upon himself the additional task of running and editing the Bengali monthly magazine, *Udbodhan*, that had been started about three years back under the direction of Swami Vivekananda and was being ably conducted by one of his brilliant colleagues, Swami Trigunatitananda. As the latter had to leave India for joining one of the preaching centres of the Mission in the United States, the magazine was about to stop for want of a capable organizer, when Swami Saradananda stepped in. Under his efficient and persevering care the *Udbodhan* went on gaining in popularity, as had been desired by the departed leader, and its financial condition gradually looked up. After several years of keen struggle and hard work it became possible for the Swami to move the *Udbodhan* Office to a permanent house of its own.

It was to find a permanent Calcutta residence for the Holy Mother that the Swami felt the urge of getting up the building as quickly as possible, even by incurring a loan on his own responsibility. The upper storey of the house was reserved for her residence when she would come to stay in Calcutta in order to bless the monks and novitiates of the Ramakrishna Order as well as hundreds of devotees from far and near. She graced this house by her first visit on May 23, 1909. Of course, the additional purpose of the house was to accommodate the office of the *Udbodhan*, which was fast developing into a publication concern mainly of Bengali books comprising mostly of what is known as Ramakrishna-Vivekananda literature. The ground-floor was set apart for this. This is why even to this day the house is known to the devotees as the Mother's House, and to the general public as the *Udbodhan* Office.

However, it was to pay off this loan that Swami Saradananda hit upon the idea of writing and publishing an authentic biography of Sri Ramakrishna. With supreme enthusiasm he bent himself to see the work through, sharing all the time the ever-increasing burden of directing the affairs of the Ramakrishna Math and Mission. He vigorously applied himself to collecting all available data and sifting them with scrupulous care in order to bring out a correct account of the Master's life, as far as that was possible, relying on nothing but indubitable evidences. Day in, day out, year after year, the Swami would remain absorbed in this work before a tiny writing desk in a small room, though distracted now and then by visitors or by pressing duties in connection with the Math and Mission. This was the genesis of the brilliant Bengali production, *Sri Sri Ramakrishna Lila-prasanga*, that came out first serially as articles in the *Udbodhan* since 1909 and then in five volumes between the years 1911 and 1918.

In 1909 the Ramakrishna Mission was organized as a separate body for carrying on philanthropic and educational activities among all sections of people, irrespective of caste, creed or colour. Branch centres of the Ramakrishna Mission as well as those of the Ramakrishna Math were opened one after another in different parts of India and in certain foreign lands, and these went on multiplying as years rolled on. Besides, occasional relief works during wide-spread calamities due to floods, famines, earthquakes or epidemics in this country had to be organized and conducted from time to time. Naturally, the task of piloting all these as the Secretary of both the Math and the Mission became more and more arduous as years went by. Yet Swami Saradananda was always found equal to the occasion. With his usual calmness he would silently and unostentatiously direct the affairs, meeting embarrassing situations sometimes and solving many a complicated problem arising out of them. It was through his bold and sagacious handling that a number of political suspects aspiring for spiritual life could join the Ramakrishna Order and put in valuable work unmolested by the Government. When the political authorities looked askance at even social service organizations, it was through his efforts that the Ramakrishna Mission could carry on its activities unhampered by any governmental measure.

Beneath the intense and multifarious activities of Swami Saradananda, one may perceive the supernormal lineaments of his inner life. It is through a seer's responses to the world outside that one may possibly get a clue to the source of his inspiration and energy. The following incidents of Swami Saradananda's life obviously give such a clue.

Towards the end of 1898, while he was travelling in a tonga from Rawalpindi to Srinagar in Kashmir in order to meet Swami Vivekananda and his party, he gave a convincing proof of his marvellous equanimity in the face of a perilous situation. It so happened that all of a sudden the horse took fright and crazily rushed downhill with the vehicle at a breakneck speed. Luckily, its mad career was arrested some way down by a big tree standing on the sloping hill-side, when Swami Saradananda quietly came out of the carriage. At that very moment a heavy boulder crashed down from above and, sparing his person by a few inches, fell upon the horse and killed it on the spot. Absolutely calm all through the incident that might very well have cost his life, the Swami remained a disinterested witness of the entire scene like a true Sthitaprajna, one whose consciousness is anchored in the higher Self.

The extraordinary quietude of a liberated soul before a precarious situation was also demonstrated through some other thrilling incidents of his life. On his voyage to London in 1896, when his ship was overtaken by a cyclone in the Mediterranean, the Swami sat unmoved, witnessing dispassionately the panicky stampede and desperate cries all about him. On another occasion, later in life, while crossing the Ganga in a country boat that was about to be capsized by a violent storm, the Swami sat unperturbed, as if there was nothing serious about him to take notice of. His absolutely unconcerned attitude went so far as to impel his panicky companion to make a rude gesture. Such behaviour of the dismayed companion drew only a genial smile from the Swami.

Another incident of a different nature has a peculiar significance, reminding one of Sri Ramakrishna's vision of Swami Saradananda's previous life as a companion (apostle) of Jesus. On his way to London from India, when he visited St. Peter's Cathedral in Rome, his mind was abruptly whisked off to a superconscious plane, and he fell into a deep mystic trance (Samadhi). What he actually saw and felt at that time remained a closely guarded secret of his life. One may reasonably guess, however, that the holy Cathedral associated with the sacred memory of the apostles of Jesus stirred up a vivid recollection of his previous life as had been visualized by the Master, and drowned for the time being his consciousness of his immediate surroundings.

Swami Saradananda's spiritual eminence indicated through these significant incidents of his life was verified by a few hints given by him on some rare occasions. On the pages of his personal diary one finds repeated mention of his direct communion with the Divine Mother. Then his following explicit admission while dedicating his illuminating Bengali book *Bharater Shakti-Puja* (Worship of the Divine Mother in India) may be cited as another instance to the point: "The book is dedicated with great devotion to those by whose grace the author has been blessed with the realization of the Divine Mother in every woman on earth." This shows to what a peak of spiritual experience his mind had been lifted. Indeed, such a realization is the very goal of Mother Worship (Tantrika Sadhana). Incidentally it may be mentioned that Swami Saradananda went through a course of this kind of spiritual practice within about a couple of years after his return from the West. Later in life, in answer to the repeated and earnest queries of a monastic attendant regarding Swami Saradananda's spiritual attainment, a significant hint escaped unawares from the Swami's usually tight lips: "Nothing beyond my spiritual experience has been recorded in the book, *Sri Sri Ramakrishna Lila-prasanga*." And this book is replete with spiritual realizations of various kinds, including the highest one of transcendental oneness in Nirvikalpa Samadhi. This hint sums up the core of his inner life as that of a liberated soul — a seer of the ultimate verities of life and existence.

However, over and above all other activities of Swami Saradananda connected with the Math and the Mission as well as with the composition and publication of his Master's biography, his primary concern appeared to be looking after the ease, convenience and health of the Holy Mother. He regarded her as the Divine Mother incarnate and placed himself completely at her service. Whether she stayed in her rural home at Jayramvati or in the city, the Swami was all attention to her. The Calcutta house was erected, as we have seen, mainly for facilitating her comfortable sojourn in the city. And for doing this as quickly as possible, he did not mind running into debt; nor did he mind undergoing strenuous labour for about nine years at a stretch in the production and publication of *Sri Sri Ramakrishna Lilaprasanga* in order to clear off that debt. Indeed, his devotion to the Holy Mother cannot be fathomed. Seated in a small room downstairs in the Calcutta house, he would be found regulating the stream of her visitors exactly like her door keeper. Sometimes he would sportively introduce himself to strangers as the Mother's janitor. One could learn from his bearing that it was a glory and privilege to be allowed to serve the Holy Mother even in this way. Throughout her last stay in the Calcutta house during her fatal illness in 1920, with what anxious care the Swami would go into minute details regarding her medical treatment and nursing, sparing no pains, though in vain, for bringing her round!

Three years later in April 1923, the Swami had the satisfaction of perpetuating the sacred memory of the Holy Mother by getting a temple erected and dedicated to her in her native village Jayramvati. During the dedication ceremony, the benignant mood of the Holy Mother seemed to possess the Swami's mind as he went on like her, gracing with spiritual initiation all sorts of people who approached him on that occasion. One could feel the spiritual fervour radiated by the Swami on the festive days connected with the ceremony.

The dedication of the Holy Mother's temple was perhaps the final oblation offered by Swami Saradananda by way of completing his life-work, which was one long-continued sacrificial rite. After the successive exits of some of the stalwarts of the brotherhood, the passing away of the Holy Mother in July 1920, followed within two years by that of Swami Brahmananda, the first Abbot and inspired guide of the Order, shook even the unmoved Swami. These bereavements appeared to squeeze out the Swami's zest for work. That was why after seeing through the construction and dedication of the Holy Mother's temple, the Swami practically detached himself from active work and went on spending long hours in meditation. He gave up writing and was never in a mood even to finish his *magnum opus*, *Sri Sri Ramakrishna Lila-prasanga*.

The only thing that concerned him at the moment was to instil into the junior members of the Order unflinching faith in the ideas and ideals left by its founder, Swami Vivekananda, and also to train up a batch of young monks for sharing the burden of piloting the organization that he had been carrying on his own shoulders.

For this purpose, in 1926, he called a Convention of representatives from all Math and Mission centres; he surveyed before them, through his inaugural address, the origin and growth of the Ramakrishna movement that was careering at the time at top speed, cautioned them against the possible pitfalls on the path ahead and exhorted them emphatically to stand firmly by the ideals, so that they might march onward clearing all hurdles in the way. In the wake of this Convention, the Swami set up a Working Committee for advising the Secretary of the Math and the Mission on practically all administrative problems. As the remaining elders were about to disappear from the stage, it was in the fitness of things that a fresh batch of junior monks should be trained for stepping into their shoes. This device of the Working Committee inaugurated by Swami Saradananda served not only the purpose for the time being but also has proved to be a permanent and useful administrative link of the Math and Mission.

Thus enthusing the young members of the Order by holding aloft the ideas and ideals they were to strive after, and devising ways and means for realizing them in practice through successive generations, he laid down with complete satisfaction the charge entrusted to him some three decades back by his beloved leader Swami Vivekananda, and placidly entered Mahasamadhi on August 19, 1927.

An illumined soul, freed completely from all kinds of bondage, is not restricted by any prescribed code of life. Even the idea of duty ceases to have any meaning to him who has seen through the universe and realized the all-pervading Oneness as its essence.

Yet such a liberated soul, when commissioned by the Divine Will to work for the uplift of humanity, does display distinctive traits of character befitting the role he is made to play. Swami Saradananda's role was to demonstrate through his life the pattern of an ideal Karma-yogi. With perfect non-attachment and self-possession he would go on scrupulously discharging the duties before him, paying equal attention to the minor as to the major ones. Neither frown nor favour, nor any number of difficulties could swerve him from the straight and strict path.

Indeed, he held up the model of an ideal worker as desired by Swami Vivekananda. His rational mind, compassionate heart, pure and perfectly poised mind, indomitable energy and rare organizing ability combined to set up such a model. "Infinite patience, infinite purity, and infinite perseverance," as Swami Vivekananda wanted to see, were in his blood. The latter once remarked, "Sarat's blood is as cold as that of a fish, nothing can inflame it." His heart was "deep as the ocean, broad as the infinite sky," as Swami Vivekananda would have it. Swami Saradananda saw potential divinity even in the worst sinner, and tried to the last to work it up with extreme love and sympathy. Truculent and refractory persons thrown over by his colleagues found refuge under his benign care, and they naturally gathered round him. Indeed, he was a living illustration of the truth of Swami Vivekananda's assertion, "The man of renunciation sees all with an equal eye, and devotes himself to the service of all." Without any air of superiority, he treated all people alike with love and tenderness. He never cared for his personal ease and comfort. He would hardly accept any corporeal service even from his own disciples. But he was ever ready to face any amount of hardship or even to hazard his life for helping others out of danger. While crossing a ravine on the Himalayas on his way to the Badrinarayan temple, he handed over his stick to one of the fellow pilgrims, an unknown old woman, without thinking for a moment what a risky adventure it would be for him to get over the steep hill-side without a staff in his hand for support. He would be found by the bed-side of patients suffering from contagious fatal diseases, whom their own kith and kin would not dare contact. His solacing words would give relief to many a person aching with mental agonies.

A distinctive mark of personality was stamped on his general demeanour. It was an object-lesson on decorum. Even those who were punctilious about etiquette would be captivated by his winning manners. The patience he would usually exhibit while listening to and answering even silly questions from youngsters was surely marvellous. His sweet and soothing voice would often take the edge off any harsh word that he might have to utter by way of rebuking an offender. It would sound like a mother's appeal to her erring child. Yet this motherly voice was balanced by an awe-inspiring solemnity, and these combined effectively to produce the desired effect on the conscience of the guilty.

Swami Saradananda was an exemplar of methodical work. Slow, steady and regular in his movements, he would regard even a trifle with as much serious attention as it deserved. Any undertaking, big or small, was equally sacred to his thorough-going mind as an act of worship. Always cool in judgment, he was hardly found to rush to any decision on insufficient or unreliable data before him. He was perfectly rational, considerate and psychological in his methods while dealing with men and their affairs.

Lastly, love for orderliness was an innate virtue with him. Though quite simple in his requirements, he would scrupulously see that everything about him was kept neat and tidy. Possibly, this trait was reinforced by the example of his Master, Sri Ramakrishna, who had been a past master in simplicity with orderliness.

From the above sketch one may get an idea of the part that the author of *Sri Sri Ramakrishna Lila-prasanga*, Swami Saradananda, had to play as one of the prime organizers of the Ramakrishna Math and Mission. It will ever remain a perfect model to be emulated by all who will seek personal salvation along with the well-being of the world as their aim of life.

SWAMI NIRVEDANANDA

APPENDIX 2

THE HOROSCOPE OF SRI RAMAKRISHNA

By Narayanachandra Jyotirbhushana

शुभमस्तु। शकनरपतेरतीताब्दादयः १७५७। १०। ५। ५९। २८। २९। सन १२४२ साल। एतच्छकीय-सौर-फाल्गुनस्य षष्ठदिवसे, बुधवासरे, शुक्ल-पक्षद्वितीयायां तिथौ, पूर्वभाद्रपदनक्षत्रस्य प्रथमचरणे, सिद्धयोगे, वालवकरणे, एवं पञ्चाङ्गसंशुद्धौ रात्रि-चतुर्दशविपलाधिकैकत्रिंशद्दण्डसमये अयनांशोद्भव-शुभकुम्भलग्ने, (लग्न स्फुटराश्यादिः १०। ३। १९'। ५३''। २०''') शनैश्चरस्य क्षेत्रे सूर्यस्य होरायां सूर्यसुतस्य द्रेक्काण शुक्रस्य नवांशे बृहस्पतेर्द्वादशांशे कुजस्य त्रिंशांशे एवं षड्वर्गप-रिशोधिते पूर्वभाद्रपद-नक्षत्राश्रितकुम्भराशिस्थिते चन्द्रे बुधस्य यामार्द्धे जीवस्य दण्डे कोणस्थे गुरौ केन्द्रस्थे बुधे चन्द्रे च लग्नस्थे चन्द्रे त्रिग्रहयोगे धर्मकर्माधिपयोः शुक्रभौययोः तुङ्गस्थितयोः वर्गोत्तमस्थे लग्नाधिपे शनौ च तुङ्गे पराशरमतेन तु राहुकेत्वोस्तुङ्गस्थयोः (यतः उक्तं "राहोस्तु वृषभं केतोर्वृश्चिकं तुङ्गसंगितम्" इत्यादिप्रमाणात्) अत एव उच्चस्थे ग्रहपञ्चके असाधारणपुण्यभाग्ययोगे शुक्लपक्षे निशि जन्महेतोः विंशोत्तरी-दशाधिकारे जन्म एतेन बृहस्पतेर्दशायां तथा देशभेदेन दशाधिकारनियमाच्च अष्टोत्तरीयराहोर्दशायां अशेषगुणालङ्कृत-स्वधर्मनिष्ठ-क्षुदिरामचट्टोपाध्याय-महोदयस्य (सहधर्मिणी-दयावती-चन्द्रमणिदेवी-महोदयायाः गर्भे) शुभः तृतीयपुत्रः समजनि।

तस्य राश्याश्रितं नाम शम्भुरामदेवशर्मा। प्रसिद्धनाम गदाधरचट्टोपाध्यायः। साधनासिद्धिप्राप्त-जगद्विख्यातनाम श्रीरामकृष्णपरमहंसदेवमहोदयः ॥

जन्मकुण्डली —

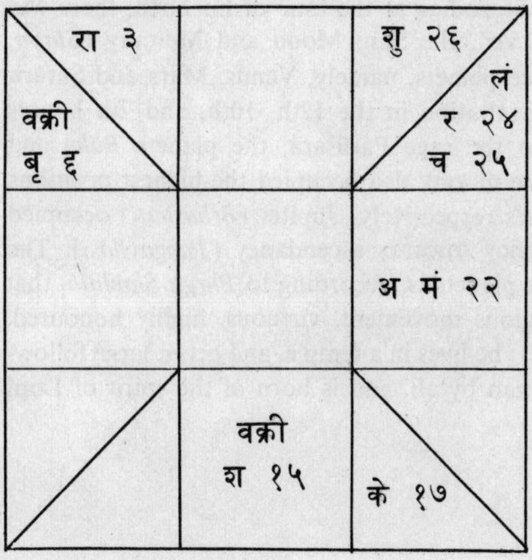

३। १९ 'होरा लं ०। ४६'

वक्री अ बु २४

दिवा — २८ । २८ । १५			दिवा — २८ । ३१		
४	२४	२०	५	२५	२१
१	५१	४६	२	५१	४१
४६	२६	५६	४५	४१	४८
४४	किं	६	१६	२	७

जाताहः   पराहः

चान्द्रफालानुस्य शुकपक्षीयद्वितीया जन्मतिथिः ।

पूर्वभाद्रपदनक्षत्रमानं ६० । २५ । ०

तस्य भोगदण्डादिः ५२ । १२ । ३१

भुक्तदण्डादिः ८ । २ । २६

जन्मकोष्ठीफलम्—

धर्मस्थानाधिपे तुङ्गे धर्मस्थे तुङ्गखेचरे। गुरुणा दृष्टिसंयोगे लग्नेशे धर्मसंस्थिते ।।
केन्द्रस्थानगते सौम्ये गुरौ चैव तु कोणभे। स्थिरलग्ने यदा जन्म सम्प्रदायप्रभुर्हि सः ।।
धर्मविन्माननीयस्तु पुण्यकर्मरतः सदा। देवमन्दिरवासी च बहुशिष्यसमन्वितः ।।
महापुरुषसंज्ञोऽयं नारायणांशसम्भवः। सर्वत्र जनपूज्यश्च भविष्यति न संशयः ।।

इति भृगुसंहितायां सम्प्रदायप्रभुयोगः तत्फलं च ।।

Śrī Rāmakṛṣṇa was born in the year A.D. 1836 on the 2nd day of the bright fortnight of the month when the sun was in the zodiac of Aquarius (*Kumbha*—February 18), early in the morning at about 5 a.m. His birth took place when it was *Siddhi Yoga* owing to the auspicious union of *Śukla Dwitīya* with *Pūrvabhādrapada Nakṣatra*. His natal star was *Pūrvabhādrapada* (Pegasi), the twenty-fifth lunar mansion. In his *Janmalagna*, *i.e.*, in the zodiac at the time of his birth, there was the conjunction of the three planets, viz., the Sun, Moon and Mercury (*Sūrya*, *Candra* and *Budha*) and the other three planets, namely, Venus, Mars and Saturn (*Śukra*, *Maṅgala* and *Śani*) were in exaltation in the 12th, 10th, and 7th houses respectively. And again, according to the sage Parāśara, the planets *Rāhu* and *Ketu* (two other ascending nodes of the moon) also occupied the highest positions as they were in the 2nd and 8th houses respectively; Jupiter (*Bṛhaspati*) occupied the 3rd house and so it had a tendency towards ascendancy (*Tungavilāsi*). The result of this natal arrangement of the planets is, according to *Bhṛgu Saṁhitā*, that the man becomes the head of a religious movement, virtuous, highly honoured, always engaged in doing virtuous deeds; he lives in a temple, and gets a large following of disciples; he is called a great man by all, and is born of the spirit of Lord Nārāyaṇa; he is worshipped by all.

INDEX

A

Abercrombie, 826
Abhedānanda, Swāmī, 448, 751, 991; at the Kasipur garden house, 91, 92; his vision of Vaikuntha, 428; devotes himself to the service of the Master 970
Abhimāna (Bhakti), 265
Acālānanda, 615
Ācārya, Śankara, 87; Advaita, 482, 589; Kesavacandra, 786; Vijayąkrishna Goswami, 793; Ciranjīv Sarma, 796; Nāgendranāth Cattopadhyāya, 803; Amritlal Bāsu, 807; Pratāpcandra, 813; Gaura Govinda, 813; Maharshi Devenranath, 828
Acintya-bhedābheda, 443
Adainya Bhikshā, 601
Adbhutānanda, Swami, in attendance on the Master in Kasipur, 382, 618, 619, 970, 1017, 1018, 1025
Adharcandra Sen, 993
Adhikara 658
Ādhikārika Purusha, birth and development of the idea of, 6, 8; Sri Ramakrishna as, 295, 297, 341; definition of the term, 404; two divisions of, 658, 659, 660, 674.
Ạdhirūḍha, 262
Adhyāsa, 112
Adhyātma Rāmāyaṇa, 90, 175, 187, 190, 283
ĀdiBrāhmo Samaj, 828
Ādi Gangā, 211
Advaitācārya Goswāmī, 195, in the Master's vision of Sri Caitanya's sankīrtan, 360, 802, 935, 980
Advaita, non-dual knowledge, 444, the Master on, 809; Advaitānanda Swāmī, 394, 970
Āgama, 702
Āgamācārya Damaruvallabha, 1006
Āgāmi Karma, destruction of, 464
Aghoramaṇi, see Gopala's Mother.
Agradwīp, a place of pilgrimage visited by Rāṇi Rāsmani, 132
Āhirītolā, 422
Aitihya, 368,
Ājñā cakra, 416, 721
Ākāśagangā Hill 794
Akrur Datta, 1022
Akṣay, birth of 34; after the death of his mother, 70, 71; the Master's fondness for him 80; appointed worshipper of the Mother in the Kali Temple, Daksineswar, 283; his appearance, 320; his love of Sadhana, 321; marriage of, 322; illness and death of, 322; the Master's agony at his death, 389, 130, 353
Akṣay, Master, 1025
Alakṣya, 588
Ālambāzār, Jute mills of, 353, 920; Monastery,761,361,395,714
Alankāra Sāstra, 264
Albert Hall, exposition of Religion by Pandit Sasadhar in, 713
Ālek, 588
Āleklatā, 588
Ālimpana, 335, 592
Allah, 299, 304
Ālipur Suit, 211
Āmalaki, in the Pañcavati, 157, 184
America, spread of the ideas of the Master in 542, 640, 671, 734, 762
Āmodar River, 24
Amrtlāl Bāsu, 789, 807, 813
Anāhata cakra, 416, 721
Anāhata Dhwani, 232
Aṅganyāsa, 153
Anjali, 354
Annadā Bagci, 992
Annameru, 236, 346
Annapūrṇa, 132, 138, 313, 650, 654 installation in Cānak of, 350, installation of image in Mahimācaran's house, 1006
Āntpur, 708, 800
Anupa Goswami, 21
Anur, village two miles N. W. of Kāmārpukur, 32, 36, 62, 115
Anurāga 275
Apāna, 288
Aparājitā, 184
Aparāvidyā, 977

Apatya-Bhāva, 255, 268
Āpta, 6, 7, 691
Ārāmbāg, 22, 967
Ārati, or Ārātrika, the Master's manner of performing, 161, 319, 494, 504, 512, 513, 547, 699
Arghya, 167
Āriādaha, 535, 632, 636
Arjuna, his devotion to Kṛṣṇa 379, 454, 456, 908, 1026
Artha, 811
Arthavada, 368
Āryans, cause of downfall, 368, 369, 1005
Ārya Samāj, and Swami Dayānanda, 635, 663
Aśauca, 354
Aṣṭāvakra Saṁhitā, 90, 544, 876
Asi, 650
Aśoka, how he spread religion and learning, 690.
Aśoka, sapling of tree planted in the Pancavatil, 184
Atake, the Master's habit of taking, 340
Ātman, 9; ignorance of the knowledge of, 15
Atulcandra Ghose, reminiscences of 992, 994, 995, 1022, 1023, 1025
Āul, 588, 589
Aum, 291, 322, 612
Aum Tat Sat, 720
Avadhūta, in the Bhagavata, 534
Avidyā, how it arises, 442
Avidyā Śakti, characteristics of, 889
Āyan Ghosh, 263
Ayodhyā, 36, 196, 613, 768
Āyurvedic, 175, 354

B

Bābājī, 605
Bābu, 496, 497, 515, 758
Bābūrām, see Premānanda Swāmī
Babylon, Sumers of, 585
Badarika, hermitage of, 657
Bādṣāhs, 380, 897
Bagdi, robber and his wife take care of the Holy Mother, 968
Bāghbāzār, 312, 394, 422, 576, 682, 800, 899, 935, 960, 1009
Balarām Bāsu's house at, 673, 714, 716, 743, 747, 760, 762, 961, 900
Bain, 925
Baiṭhak-khānā-Bāzār, 154
Balarām, of Puri, 340
Balarām Bāsu 394, 434, 799, 819, 945, 972, 974, 990, 1015; the Master in the house, of, 422, 673, 749, 750, 751; in the company of the Master in Dakshineswar, 465; chariot festival in the house of, 714, 716, 717, 747, 748, 958; the Master commends the devotion of, 743, 744, 935; and of his family, 746; Gopala's mother brought to the house of, 762; his spiritual progress after he met the Master, 936; his opinion about the virtue of non-injury, 936, 937; the Master comes to Calcutta for treatment and stays in the house of, 961, 962; attempts made by resentful relatives to prevent him from going to the Master, 986, 987, 988, early life of and first meeting with the Master, 989, 990; undertakes the expenses of the Master's treatment during his last illness, 1016
Bāṅka, 384
Baṅkim, 993
Baṅkimcandra Cattopadhyaya, 993
Bakul tree, 44
Barābāzār, 648, 800, 806
Barānagar, 395, 618, 746; temple of the ten mahavidyas at, 192; two youths of, 495, Bhavanāth and Narendra's friends at 921
Baranagar monastery, 746, 761
Bārāsāt, 172
Bārrackpur, 350
Basrā rose, 793
Bāul, 73, 588, 589
Beliaghaṭa, 131, 1025
Belgharia, 355, 704, 812
Belte, 360
Belur, 351, 542, 550
Belur Math, 746, 763, 764
Bengal, 56, 125, 329, 359, 488, 536, 558, 570, 572, 576, 689, 797, 943, 968, 980, 993, 1009; Villages of, 21, 22, 463, 661, 944; Tota Purī comes to, 284, 285; Young Bengal, 601, 712, 944, 997; Nyāya Philosophy in, 630, 631; Dayānanda in, 635; Bengāli, 227, 567, 605, 629, 706, 787, 993, 1009; Book of Psalms of the New Dispensation, 796, 823; on the literature of, 829, 863, 864

Bengāli Era, 781
Beni Sāhā, 618, 620
Bentham, 913
Bhagavān, Sri Caitanya, 10, Sri Kṛṣṇa, 20; Sri Ramakṛṣṇa, 369, 371, 764; identified with the Bhāgavata and the Bhakta, 277
Bhagavān Dās, the Master's visit to, 661; renunciation and devotion of, 662; at the meeting with the Master, 665, 667, 987
Bhagavata, 39, 73, 137, 175, 187, 253, 282, 321, 490, 573, 590, 658, 661, 663, 664, 770, 902; on the number of incarnations, 216, 217, 219; the Master vision while listening to the reading of, 277; story of the Avadhūta in, 534
Bhāgavat Bandhyopādhyāya, 30
Bhagavad Gita, 90
Bhāgīrathi, 133, 287, 388, 560
Bhairava, 164, 231, 427, 536, 721; Totapuri sees one in the Pañcavati, 550
Bhairavi, Brāhmaṇī, see Brāhmaṇī 225
Bhakta, 277
Bhakti divisions of, 275, 415
Bhakti, Kāmātmikā, 275
Bhakti, Rāgātmikā; 275; the Master attains, 170
Bhakti, sambandhātmikā, 275
Bhakti Caitanya Candrikā, 727
Bhakti Granthāvalī, 262
Bhakti Sūtras, of Nārada, 377
Bharata, of the Purāṇa, 709, 870
Bharata, founder of Candra dynasty 671
Bhārata, land of, 369, 371
Bhartābhārī, gardener of the Kali temple, Dakṣineswar, 184, 425
Bhāti, the Master's explanation of the term, 602
Bhātpārā, 762
Bhattācārya, (Ramkṛṣṇa), 168, 169, 173, 479, 480, 495, 572, 573, 575
Bhāva, fantastic conception about 401; definition of, 431; effect of, 434, 575, 772; the Master's vision of the coiled power in the state of, 722; Gopala's mother in, 738, 739, 741, 753; the Master under the influence of, 750, 751
Bhavabhūti, 768
Bhāvamukha, 246, 365, 366, 482, 528, 531, 567, 638; the Master in the state of, 182, 303, 341, 426, 435, 696; the Divine Mother's mandate to the Master to remain in, 190, 294, 295, 296, 373, 412, 441; the Master's ability to understand all moods in the state of, 398, 427; explanation of the state of, 401, 413, 438, 442, 443; how one feels in the state of, 446; the Master established in, 639, 640, 650, 705, 788, 813; conclusions on the state of, 689; mental state of the Master in, 821
Bhavanāth Chattopādhyāya, 709, 921, 925
Bhāva-samādhi, the Master's first experiences of, 54,.55, 56; the Master in, 189, 216, 217, 226, 301, 326, 333, 342 464, 494, 496, 499, 509, 578, 593, 664, 669, 681, 722, 943; description of the state of, 267; Hriday's vision in, 316; a woman devotee attains, 392, 596, 805; who is qualified to attain, 520; explanation of the state of, 624; beauty of the Master in, 948; physiological reactions in the state of, 978, 982; of the Master in Syāmpukūr and Kāśipūr, 985, 1023
Bhāvinī, 748
Bhek, 270
Bhikṣā, 215, 462, 547, 601, 605, 691
Bhikṣā Mātā, 306, 462
Bhoga, worldly enjoyment, 160, 584, 588; impossible to co-exist with yoga, 610
Bholā, confectioner, 395, 576
Bhṛṅgī, and Nandi, 316
Bhūkailās, 164
Bhūr, 286, 289
Bhūrsubo, Māṇik Rājā of, 23, 54, 55; the girl from, 35
Bhutirkhal, 23, 60, 202,
Bhuvaneśwarī, 838, 839, 840
Bible, 160, 180; the Master learns of the Life of Jesus from, 338, 339, 380, 406; an event in the life of Jesus from, 460, 700, 838, 912
Bismarck, 641
Bodhodaya, 486
Bosepara lane, 762
Bowbazar, 943, 1022
Brahmā, 193, 276, 442, 738, 810, spiritual teacher is, 451
Brahmacārin, 763, Nārāyaṇ, Sastry,

625, 627
Brahmạcarya, in married lite, 471, 472, 732
Brahmamuhūrta, 287
Brahmānanda, Swāmī, 90, 394, 542, 646, 682, 683, 704, 716, 817, 818, 819, the Master's love for, 425 682, 759, 806; vision of the Master before the arrival of, boyish nature of, goes to Vrindavan and falls ill, later life of, 820; disagreement with Narendra and the Master's intervention, 876
Brāhmaṇī of Kāmārhaṭi, see Gopāla's mother, Aghoramaṇī
Brāhmaṇī or Yogeswari or Bhairavi, 172, 178, 190, 195, 237, 271, 274, 326, 346, 534, 535, 542, 554, 563, 620, 621; arrival at Daksineśvar of, 214; first conversation with the Master 215, her extradinary vision under the Pancavati 216; is convinced that the Master is an incarnation of God, 217, 219; asks the Master to undertake Tāntrik Sādhana, 220, 221; the Master undertakes Tāntrik Sādhana under the guidance of, 222 to 227; she was part of Yoga-Māyā, 234, 235; helps the Master at the time of Vatsalya Bhāva Sādhana, 248 268; in Kāmār-pukur with the Master, 303, 308, 309, 310; information about her, 313; asks the Master not to discuss the Vedanta, 404, how she assisted the Master in Sadhanas; scholarship of the Vaisnava scriptures; antecedents of, 536; yogic vision of, 537; limitations of the realizations of, 543, 544, 545, 546; discussion with Pandits on the condition of the Master, 571, 581, 582; prescribes for the master's maladies 574, 575.
Brahman, 189, 225, 228, 264, 287, 294, 295, 331, 334, 374, 379, 485, 550, 585, 587, 608, 688, 774, 785, 788, 797, 798, 802, 804, 810, 827, 921, 951, 976; realization of, 8, 9, 98, 254, 260, 297, 341, 622, 821; Sadhana for the realization of, 193, 251, 277, 289, 291, 300, 630 power of, 289, 357, 700, 703, 928 bliss of, 45, 306; knowledge of, knowers of, 97, 101, 180, 284, 297, 307, 287, 424, 464, 470, 548, 602, 605, 607, 627, 671, 675; Sankara's Conception of 112; nature of, 421, 429, 603, 790, 791; Saguna and Nirguna, 443-448; and Jivas, 656; and Maya are one, 677, the Master's attempt to impart to Narendra Knowledge of, 852, 860, 869, 877, 878; Narendra's meditation on, 915
Brahma Sakti, 554
Brahma Vārī, 142, 340
Brahma Yoni, 231
Brāhmin, in the Smrtis, 369; story of a, 382, 383; sanctifying ceremonies for a, 466
Brāhmo Samaj, 89, 351, 664, 684, 807, mode of worship, 89, 103; and Kesav, 356, 357, 358; and the New Dispensation, 712; Narendra's association with, 756, 827, 835, 841, 847, 848, 851, 863, 915; influence of the Master on, 789-798; Vijay leaves, 795; Pratapcandra on the influence of the Master on, 797; music of, 797, 798, 834; the Master's estimate of, 798; festival of, 798; what the Master learnt from his contact with, 813, 814, 815, 816; Rakhal's association with, 876
Brāhmo Samāj, general, 358, 430, 625, 792; split in, 795-798, 802; the Master's unexpected visit to, 868
Brāhmo Samāj of India, 358, 786, 787, 792, 795
Buddha, 20, 39, 40, 87, 114, 156, 251, 365, 451, 766, 471, 657, 768, 776, 898, 914, 934; magnanimity of; 245; austerities of, 257; the Master's veneration for, 340; stops animal sacrifice, 475; on the detachment of, 583; Narendra's vision of, 917
Buddhacarita, 340, 979
Buddha-Gaya, 645
Buddhism, 40
Buddhist, 23, 254, 257, 260, 261, 584, 609, 690, 766
Burdwan, 21, 24, 70, 145, 576, 631, 632, 661, 710, 769

C

Campbell Medical School, 954

Catherine, Saint, 253
Catholic, 255
Central India, 284; Narendra recounts experience of travel in, 835
Cachadi, 735, 736
Caitanya Bhāgavata, 195, 216, 217
Caitanya Caritāmṛta, 40, 216, 217
Caitanya, Sri Kṛṣṇa, 10, 20, 40, 87, 115, 171, 195, 215, 365, 378, 380, 451, 459, 471, 482, 489, 490, 582, 587, 616, 657, 680, 681, 682, 688, 717, 727, 766, 767, 768, 776, 898, 900, 934, 935, 943; the Brāhmaṇī compares the conduct and behaviour of the Master with those of, 218, 219, 572, 574; lack of records of the spiritual practices of, 257; and the practice of Madhura Bhāva, 258-263; in the Hari Sabha of Kolutola, the Master occupied the seat of, 323, 324, 663, 664, 665, 666, 669; birthday of, 329; the Master witnesses in a vision the peripatetic Sankirtan of, 360, 744; devotion of, 453; opinion of the Master about 660, 661, 688, 689; discourses in Vrindavan, 680; songs on, 880, 948, 962, 963
Caitanya Maṅgala, 261
Cakras, the piercing of, 416
Cāmara, 238, 243, 503, 512, 513.
Cāmpātala, 881, 942
Caṇḍa, 202
Caṇḍāla, 245, 367, 941
Caṇḍi, 154, 236, 240
Hymns quoted from, 557, 592
Candīdās, 265
Caṇḍikā, 226
Cāndopāl ghāṭ, 832
Candra, disciple of Bhairavi, story of, 537, 538, 540, 542
Candramaṇī, nature of, 25, 29, 30, 32, 42, 56; vision of Lakshmi, 34, 35; strange visions and experiences of, 41-47, 49; after Kṣudirām's death, 59, 62, 65; calls in an exorcist to cure the Master, 201, 202, prāyopaveśana before Siva, 208; last years of 353; death of, 354
Capāti, 555, 733
Cārucandra Cakravarti, the Master tests the nature of, 887,
Cātaka, 522, 907
Caṭṭopādhyāya, 510; Mānikrām, 24
Cāturmāsya, the Master visits Kāmārpukur during, 577
Caturmukha, 207
Catuṣpāthi, at Jhāmāpukur, 134, 141, 687
Chaucer, 864
Chātu Bābu, 131
Ciranjīv Sarma, 789, 811-813; Contribution to Brāhmo music 802, 807, 811, 812
Citreśvari, 619
Cowringhee, 832
Christ, 87, 253, 255, 982; the Master's vision of, 339; an incident in the life of, 459
Christian Mysticism, 253, 255, the Master's practice of the religion, 339; scriptures on vicarious atonement, 379, 622, 997, opinion about the Master of a 898; missionary Prabhu Dayāl, 1007
Christianity, 18, 40
Cūrni canal, 323
Coccyx, elongation of during Sādhana of Dāsya bhakti, 183
Combuliātolā, 808
Company, East India, 225, 550
Comte, 913, 925
Coochbehār marriage and its repercussions, 357, 358, 793, 794, 868, 884
Cook, missionary, 727
Cornwallis Street, physical training club of, 833
Cuttack, 747, 989

D

Dacca, Vijaykṛṣṇa Goswāmi's vision of the Master in, 706, 874, 963, 1001
Dakṣinā Kālī, Rām Prasād's song on, 381
Dāna, an essential of Madhura Bhava, 265
Danḍi, 692
Darśana, 355, 420, 886; Panḍit Nārāyaṇ Sāstri's mastery of 626
Darveś, 299, 588, 589
Daśaratha, 247
Dāśarathi, song of, 388

Dāśarathi Sannyāl, 842, 921
Dāsya-bhakti, the Master's Sādhana of, 183; a division of Rāgātmikā Bhakti; 275; and Savikalpa Samādhi, 404, 405, 415
Dāsya-bhāva, the Master's Sādhana of, 182, 228, 251, 255, 268; Hanumān, a bright example of, 444, 621, 937
Datta family, 836
Dayānanda Saraswatī, Swāmī, 630; the Master on, 635; propagation of the Vedic Religion; 663
Deoghar, the Master visits Sri Vaidyanāth at, 312
Dere Ramanand Roy of, 24, Māṇikrām Caṭṭopādhyāya of, 24; Kṣudirām's migration from, 25, 30, 36
Deśrā, 22, 70, 137
Deva, 224, 287, 338
Devaki, 489
Devamanḍal ghāt, Bhairavi Brāhmaṇī in, 535
Devendranāth Babu, 429
Devendranāth Mazumdār, 960, 983, 985
Devendranāth Tāgore, 359, 636, 683, advice to Narendra 828, 850
Devi, Hriday celebrates the autumn worship of 319, ?26, the Master's worship of Sodasi, 335, 336, 338 Annapūrṇā, 350, 351; Siṁhavāhinī, 352, Pandit Gauri Worships his wife as, 592; in the Tantras, 586; in the Caṇḍī, 592; Sarvamaṅgalā, 620; Her boon to Panḍit Padmalocan, 633, 634, 713
Dhāma, 741
Dhani Kāmāriṇī, 42, 43, 45, 46, gives alms to the Master at the time of his upanayana, 63, 64, 124, 306, 462
Dharma, worship of, 23, 65, 66, 485, 690, 811
Dharmacakra, Buddha's establishing of, 257
Dharmadās Lāhā, arranges for the first rice-eating ceremony of the Master, 49, 62, 63; Prasanna, sister of, 117, 306
Dharmapātra, Ramkumār has recourse to the practice of, 140, 141
Dhauti, 391
Dhruva, 67,
Dhuni, 61; sacredness of, 547, 549, 550, 556, 561; Narendra and other boy devotees burn desires in the fires of, 1020, 1021,
Digambar Mitra, 126, 136,
Dināјpore, 138, 210
Dīnānāth, officiates as priest of Rādhā Govinda Temple, Dakṣineśvar, 322, 335,
Darwin, 913
Dīpāvalī, 654
Dolyātra, 329, 511
Droṇācārya, Ekalavya's devotion for, 455
Duckpond, 184
Dulālī, 605; Gaṅgā Mātā calls the Master, 653
Durgā, Worship in Rāmacandra Bandyopādhyāya's house, 56, 57, 123; Hriday celebrates the autumn worship of, 318, 319, 429, 503; Mathur celebrates the worship of, 507; the Master fans the image of, 513; juncture worship of, 524, 525; Panḍit Gauri worships his wife as, 592, 980; Surendranāth Mitra celebrates the worship of, 196, 198
Durgā Caraṇ Datta, brief account of the life of, 836, 837
Durgācaraṇ Mukherji Street, 961
Durgādās Pyne, the Master corrects the pride of, 75, 76
Durgānanda Brahmacāri, 683
Durgā Prasād Sen, 208
Durvā, 28, 37; in the garden of the Kali temple, 301
Dvaita, a step in the spiritual progress of the Sādhaka, 444
Dwārakeśwar River, 22
Dwārakā, 87
Dwārikānāth Biswas, 325, 326
Dwārikānāth, 961

E

East Bengal, 874
Eastern India. Tota Puri comes to, 284
Eden Garden, 500
Edward, Prince of Wales, 832
Ekalavya, devotion to his Guru, 455
Elphinstone, Indian History of, 830
England, 542, 734, 830, 863,
English, 787, 830, 832, 833, 838, 851, 878, 1005; the Master's smattering of, 709, 751, 944; on the literature of, 864, 865

Euclid, 829
Europe, 640
European, 758, 830, 912, 997

F

Fakīr, a priest of Balarām's family, 717
Fakīr Datta, 23
Fakīr, 125, 348, 627
Fichte, 913
Francis, Saint, 253

G

Gadādhar, 37, 43, 655, 656; birth of, 47; childhood of, 48-57, 116-118; boyhood of, 59-68, 119, 120, 460-462, 687; attainments of 71, 72; influence over the people of Kāmārpukur, 73-83; accomplishments of; departure to Calcutta, 83; mental constitution of, 121, 122; activities at the Jhāmāpukur Tol of, 123, 124; return to Kāmārpukur and marriage of, 201-206; at Dakṣineśwar, 492
Gājan, 22, 120
Galilee, 460
Ganeś, story of the final attitude of, and Kartik, 227, 228, 229
Gaṅgā, 33, 131, 138-142, 153, 166, 172, 213-218, 225, 301, 316, 318, 324, 351, 357, 389, 394, 446, 481, 504, 539, 600, 602, 613, 649, 734, 740, 749, 761, 762, 764, 823, 931, 948, 949, 950, 962, 965, 1010; venerated by the people of India, 19, 322, 329, 350, 354, 853; the Master's devotion to, 141, 340, 907; the Master throws clods of earth and coins into the, 159, 193, 240; the Master's vision of the emergence of the Divine Mother from the, 232; Chandrā Devi's decision to live on the banks of, 281, 303, high tide in, 425, 891; story of Airāvata and, 491, Totā Purī tries to give up his body in, 560 the Master's boat trip on, 650; the Master's steamer trips on, 727, 793; Viśwanāth Datta saved from the waters of, 837; 'Cātaka bird drinking water from', 907
Gaṅgādhar, 1018
Gangāmātā, the Master meets, 313, 653, 654, 695, 710
Gangānārāyan, 318
Gangāprasād Sen, Medical treatment of the Master by, 175, 207, 499, 572, 961
Gangāsāgar, pilgrimage to, 132, 184, 601
Garuḍa, Rāma appears in the form of Viṣṇu before, 455
Gaurāṅga, 596, 680, 792, 944, 949, 980; the Master regarded as an embodiment of, 76, 195, 310, 346, 655, 1000; an example of the transcendental love of Śrīmatī, 273, 274 the Master witnesses in a vision the peripatetic sankirtan of, 360, 744; opinion of the Master about 660, 661; songs on, 802, 880, 881. (See also Caitanya, Śrī Kṛṣṇa)
Gauragovinda Ācārya, 813
Gaurīkānta Tarkabhūṣaṇ, Paṇḍit, 346, miraculous power of, 591, 592, 593; worships his wife as the Devī, 592; conviction about the Master, 594, 595; detachment and renunciation, 596;
Gaurhāti, 68, 80
Gaur Mohan Mukherjee lane, 863, 880
Gautami, 245
Gaya, Kṣudirām's pilgrimage to, 36; Kṣudirām's divine dream at, 37, 38; Mathur gives up the idea of going to, 314; the Master's refusal to go to, 654-656, 660
Gayā Viṣṇu Lāhā, 63, 65, 79, 306
Gāyatrī, 14, 16, 930; invocation to, 54
General Assembly, institution of, 851
Ghāt, of the Hadārpukur tank, 52, of Gangā, 131, 139, 151, 213, 217, 285, 301, 666, 751, 945, 966, 1010; Maṇikarṇikā, 312, 313; on the garden Celgharia), 355
Ghāṭāl, 22, 116, 330
Ghee, 980; excessive consumption of, 896
Ghośpāra community, 960
Girija, 537, 542; power of performing miracles, 537, 538, 539
Giriṣ Chandra Ghose 302, 342, 398, 429, 431, 724, 750, 945, 956, 960, 962, 973, 974, 982, 985, 1019, 1022, 1023; author of *Buddhacarita*, 340; gives power of attorney to the Master, 375, 378, 707; mental state of, 376, 377; regarded as a Bhairava by the Master, 427 commends the wonderful

faith of, 448, 449; conception about the Master of, 975, 1023; Dr. Sarkar's acquaintance with, 985 offers flowers at the feet of the Master in Śyāmpukur, 985 introduces Harivallabh Bāsu to the Master, 989; his infinite love for the Master, 997-1000
Gītā, 19, 187, 279, 366, 379, 915; Saṅkarā's commentary on the, 111; the Lord's promise to His devotees through, 170, verses and references thereto from, 373, 401, 436, 456, 458, 474, 477, 487, 507, 601, 637, 671, 705, 729, 743
Gladstone, 641
Gokulcandra Bhaṭṭacārya, 961
Gokulcandra Mitra, 682
Golāp Mā, 752
Goloka, 94, 765
Gopāla, 810; the Master regarded as a manifestation of, 73, 218, 237, 248, 268, 535; Aghoramaṇī regards the Master as, 729 to 743; the attitude to God as, 392
Gopāl, Rameśwar, after his death talks to, 350
Gopāl, old, 1018, 1019, 1020 (see Advaitānanda, Swāmī)
Gopāla, Aghormaṇī, regards the Master as, 734-736, 748-754
Gopālcandra Ghoṣ, garden house in Kāsipur of, 447, 1008, 1010;
Gopāl, Junior, 448, 807, 970, 1018
Gopāla's Mother, 400, 527, 714; story of, 729 to 742, 748 to 763
Gopeśwar, 21
Gopis of Brindāvan, Madhurabhāva of, 253, 259, 262, 266, 268, 272, 276, 749, 875
Gopīlāl, Goswāmī, 21
Gopīmohan, Kavirāj, 961
Gospel of Sri Ramakṛṣṇa, 344, 811, 956, 1025
Goswāmi, Utsavānanda, 346, 734, 804, 946
Govardhan hill, 313, 475, 652
Govinda, 647, 717; broken leg of the image of, 151, 152, 173, 504, 505
Govindachandra Datta of Patāldanga, 730, 731, 732; the Master visits the garden of, 736
Govind, Guru, 341
Govinda Ray, the Master is taught Islam by, 178, 298, 299, 534, 620
Gulci flower, 1010
Gunas, the three, 188, 285, 373, 381, 474, 721, 930
Guru, 134, 135, 139, 222, 247, 322, 357, 375, 738, 794, 795, 814, 858, 911, 915, 965, 981; worship of the, 7, 16, 590; mind itself becomes, 179, 180, 454; one's own experiences must tally with the words of, 179, 221
Jaṭādhāri as, 247; Totā Purī as, 287, 288; of the sikhs, 341; the Master annoyed when addressed as, 351; on the mood of the, 452-454, 701 to 703; description of a, 521; the Master as the, 638, 640, 659, 696, 698, 816; Narendra's conception and non-acceptance of the doctrine of, 847, 852, 911, 912; Yogindra's surrender to the, 906; the devotees' conception of their, 975; how the future monastic disciples served their, 1015, 1018
Gurubhāva, definition of, 452, 659
Guru Gītā, 521
Guru Śakti, 452
Guṭika, siddhi, 537
Guzarat, religious movement of Narayana Swami in, 663

H

Hafiz, 838, 912
Haladhāri, 31; comes to Daksineswar, 176; effect of his curse on the Master, 184; how his views regarding the Master changed again and again, 185 to 190 gives up worshipping in the Kālī Trmple, 282, 283
Hāldār, becomes jealous of the Master, 500; violent behaviour of, 502
Haldārpukur, 23, 52, 74, 510, 769
Hātisahar, 132
Halwa, 580
Hamilton, 916
Hamsa, 951
Hanumān, on his devotion to Rama, 444; as an exemplar of steadfast devotion, 455, 829
Hanumān Singh, 888
Hara, 152, 228, 993
Hara Gaurī, 561
Haramohan Mitra, 373, 1025
Hārancandra Dās, 1025

Hari, 66, 291, 754, 755, 902; name of, 10, 22, 120, 121, 213, 304, 329, 355, 391, 392, 454, 555, 616, 657, 662, 665, 723, 744, 875, 935, 938; Vrindāvan, playground of, 259; sabhā, 323, 664; a young devotee of, 521; Pandit Saśadhar explains a concept on, 713 songs on, 802, 803, 948, 963; festival at Pāṇihaṭi, a veritable mart of the name of, 944, 950; a story of how some goldsmiths took the name of 992, 993; the only efficacious way in Kaliyuga is, 999
Hari, neighbour of Narendra, 828
Haripada, 899
Hariprasana Caṭṭopādhyāya, 799
Harisabhā, of Kolutola, 323, 663, 666, 669, 712
Harīś, story of, 895-896, 1018
Harīścandra Mustāfi, 991
Haritakī, 391
Harivallabh Bāsu, Raj Bahādur, 747; visits the Master at Śyāmpukur, 988-990
Hātī, 725
Hātisayar, tank in Bhūrsubo, 23
Hatkhola ghāt, 855
Haviṣyanna, 872
Hazra, Pratāp Candra, 434, 709, 715, 800; sceptical temperament of, 877, 878, 879
Hedua Tank, 879, 880
Hemali, Hegel, 913
brings to Narendra news of his father's death, 921
Hemānginī, 30, 36, 57, 135, 145
Himālayas, 7, 508
Hindi, 247, 864
Hindola, 721
Hindu (-s), 338, 534; Mythology 10; society, 17; home, 32; scriptures of the, 98, 101, 886, 912; and Muslims, 299, 300; and Buddha, 340; religion 369, and Christian Religion, 460, 461; marriage, 466, national degradation of the, 469; modern minded, 569; funeral rites, 762; and Brahmo Samaj, 788, 789; belief about food, 870;
Hindu Fair, established by Nava Gopāl Mitra, 831, 833
Hinduism, 40, 713
Holy Bible, see Bible
Holy Mother, Sāradāmaṇi, 117, 346, 351, 353, 394, 397, 546, 578, 579, 580 733, 906, 959, 960; Marriage of, 205, 206; when she saw the Master for the first time, 327; mental attitude of, 328; resolves to go to Dakṣineśwar, 328; arrives in Dakṣineśwar, 328; arrives in Dakṣineśwar, 329; how the Master behaved with the, 329-336; the Master worships, 336, 337; returns to Kāmārpukur, 336; is told by the Master when he would pass away, 342; comes to Dakṣineśwar for the second time, 351; Śambhu Bābu and Captain Viswanath build a room for, 352, 539; goes to Kāmārpukur for the marriage of Rāmlāl, 465; her respectful attitude to the Bhairavi Brāhmaṇī, 308, 535; Śambhu Bābu's wife worships, 352, 539; sees the Master in a mood of divine inebriation, 617; consoles Gopāla's mother, 752; serves the Master in the Kāsipur Garden house, 759, 761, 1011, 1014, 1019; and Rakhal's wife, 818; why she gave up the idea of going with the Master to Pāṇihaṭi, 945, 951, 952; bashfulness of the 964, 965; encounter with the Bagdi footpad and his wife, 966-970; life in the Syāmpukur house, 970
Homa, performed by the Master at the time of initiation into Sanyas, 287, 288; of Tāntrik Sādhakas 593
Homa bird, the boy devotees likened to the young ones of the, 1012
Hooghly, a district of, 21
Hookah, 931
Howrah, 329
Hṛdayrām Mukhopādhyāya, 164, 191, 232, 234, 248, 281, 301, 303, 321, 322, 323, 324, 326, 327, 349, 352, 517, 645; sundry details about events related in the Master's Biography obtained from, 3, 21, 26, 36, 56, 137, 140, 151, 152, 153, 172, 174, 195, 203, 207, 213, 217, 218, 236, 271, 308, 356, 633; comes to Dakṣineśwar and devotes himself to the service of the Master, 145; his love for the Master 146, 147; appointed to assist the Master and Rāmkumar, 148; appointed to worship Rādhā-Govinda, 154; his anxiety about the Master and attempts to

bring him round, 157-158; on the Master's worship and meditation, 167-168; takes over the worship of Kālī, 176; plants a new Panchavati at the express desire of the Master 184; and Haladhāri, 186, 189; the Master's vision on the way to the house of, 195; is asked by the Master to fetch the Bhairavi Brāhmaṇī on her arrival in Dakṣneśwar, 214, 215; engages himself in nursing the Master day and night 259; on the Master's practising Islam, 298, 300; goes to Kāmārpukuṛ with the Master and Bhairavi Brāhmaṇī, 303 327; quarrels with the Bhairavi Brāhmaṇī, 309; accompanies the Master on his pilgrimage with Mathur, 311-319; death of the wife of and consequent dispassion of, 314, 315; Bhāvasamādhi and wonderful vision of 316; again becomes dull and drab; 317; attempts sādhanā and is foiled, 317, 318; celebrates Durga puja, 318, 319; serves Candra Devi, 352, 353; goes with the Master to Naṭabar Goswāmī's house 360; dismissal of, 361, 362; 711; with the Master in Kāmārpukur, 510, 511; meets a paramahamsa, 604, 651; accompanies the Master to Navadwīp, 661; in the Harisabhā at Kalutola with the Master, 663; accompanies the Master to Kālna with Mathur, 666, 667

Hutko, see Gopal Junior

Hume, 913, 925

I

Ida, 599

Idesh, 346, 573

India, 97, 371, 605, 640, 671, 674, 1008; on the religion of, 5; in the Paurāṇic age, 7, 10; in the modern age, 10, 11, 18, 19, 359, 359, 468, impact of the West on, 14-17, 639; foundations of national life in ancient, 17, history of the religions 255; the significance of the Master's practice of Islam for, 300, 338; cause of the spiritual degradation of, 343, 592; Brāhmo Samāj of, 355, 358; the vast meeting ground of various ideals, 497; origin of the Tantras in, 585; worship of the Guru in, 589; the teaching of the Ṛṣis of, 597, 623; Pīṭhasthānas in, 644; Vārāṇasī, the sacred city of, 649; religious movements in, 663; origin of the custom of Sādhus prescribing and administering medicines in, 690, 691; spirituality of the people of, 734; the spiritual awakening of, 777, 783, 814, 815

Indian, foundations of ancient national life, 17; philosophers on Prakṛti līnas, 656, 814, 830, 912

Indra, story of the Brāhmin, and, 383, 475

Iśān Candra Mallick, 361

Iśān Candra Mukhopādhyāya, the Master in the house of, 715

Iśān Caudhury, 361

Islām, 20. 255, 338, 426; Sufi Govinda Ray teaches the Master, 178, 298; behaviour of the Master while practising, 299; significance of the Master's practice of, 300

Īśwara, 285, 294, 369, 822; Kalpaniyāmaka 7, 8, 9, 10; māyā stands between Jīva and, 557, Vedantic conception of, 658; not bound by māyā, 677; difference between Jiva and, 878

Īśwara Koti, 405; according to Sāṅkhya teachers, 7; definition of the term, 404; the Master on, 459, 549 according to the authors of Vedānta, 658; the Master regarded Yogindra as, 903; and Narendra, 938;

Īśwara Candra Vidyāsāgar, 710, 715, 942

Itihāsa, 368

Iti iti, path of, 101

J

Jada samādhi, 186

Jādunath Mallick, 618, 620, 845, 862; picture of child Jesus in the house of, 338

Jadunāth Sarkar, teacher in the school of the Lahas, 51

Jagadambā Dāsī, Mathur marries, 132; involved in litigation, 211; falls seriously ill, 292; recovers by the grace of the Master, 293; regard and devotion for the Master, 303, 503, 512,

577, 641; death of, 325, 361; children of, 326; temple of Annapūrṇā Devī built on behalf of, 350
Jahānābād, 22, 967
Jaina religion, the Master's faith in, 341
Jaipur, Mahārāja of, invites Narāyan Śāstri as his Court Pandit, 626
Jānbāzār, Rāṇī Rāsmaṇī's residence in, 131, 137; the Master in the house at, 271, 500, 502, 507
Janaka, Śukā taught by, 180; Sikh Gurus believed to be incarnations of, 341
Jānakī, 196, 456
Janmāṣṭamī, 524
Japa, 54, 91, 139, 203, 381, 519, 542, 615, 652, 662, 732, 747, 765, 895, 987; the Master's performing of, 207, 224, 225, 226; Narendra in Kāśipur devotes the nights to, 448; Rāṇī Rāśmaṇī punished by the Master while performing, 554; Vaiṣṇava teachers on, 587; power of, 644, 877; Iśān Bābu's zeal in the performance of, 715; Gopāla's mother performs intensive, 736, 737, 740, 741, 756; an easy path to realization of God, 938
Japan, 14, 16
Jatādhāri, the Master initiated in the Mantra of Rāma, by, 178, 247, 248; arrival of, 242; the Master and 242, 243, 281
Jatīndramohan Thākur, Mahārāja, the Master's talk with, 724
Jātismaratwa, the Master attains 295, 296, 297
Jayā, see Macleod, Miss, J
Jayagopāl Sen, 355, 788; the Master in the house of, 806, 807, 810, 812
Jayanārāyaṇ, Paṇḍit, the Master's estimate of, 636
Jayanārāyan, Bandyopādhyaya, asks the Master about the broken image of the Govinda temple, 152
Jayrāmvāti, 203, 394, 967; Ramacandra Mukhopādhyāya of, 205, 463; the Master's marriage celebrated at, 205; the Master's visits to, 304, 469, 510, 511, 579; the Holy Mother's life in, 329; the Holy Mother falls seriously ill in, 352
Jehova, 461, 482
Jerusalem, 460, 461, 482
Jesus, 20, 39, 40, 87, 115, 171, 451, 471, 475, 622, 639, 657, 727, 898, 912, 914, 934, 982; lack of records of the spiritual practices of, 257; the Master practises the religion of, 339; the Master's vision of, 340; takes upon himself the sufferings of others, 378, 379; at the age of twelve explains the scriptures in the temple of Jehova, 460, 461; seized with divine anger drives the shopkeepers from the temple of Jehova, 482; parable of the Talents, 645
Jevons, 830
Jew, 340, 460
Jewish teachers, doctrines preached by, 622
Jhāmāpukur, Rāmkumār starts a Sanskrit school in, 71, 130; the Master's activities at, 126; 138
Jilāpī, Kāmārpukur famous for, 22
Jīva(s) or Jīvakoti, 273, 342, 585, 587, 597, 607, 652, 722, 784, 791, 1000 and divine incarnations, 9, 113, 641; the Master's Sādhana to realize that Siva is in
Jīva(s) or Jīvakoti, 273, 342, 585, 587, 597, 607, 652, 722, 784, 791, 1000 and divine incarnations, 9, 113, 641; the Master's Sādhana to realize that Siva is in all, 159, 247; distinction between Iswarakotis and, 403-404; on the attainment of Nirvikalpa Samadhi, 549; Represented by Laksmana, 557; effect of Mahābhāva on, 582; Tantrik Sādhana for, 587, 592, 593; liberated by death in Kāsi, 650, 651, 680; manifestation of, 656; and Adhikārikas, 658-660; effect of Sambhavi initiation on, 702; on the attainment of supreme peace by, 803, 810; and Non-dualism, 877, 878, 881; Seeing Siva in all, 939, 940, 958
Jīva Goswami, 275
Jīvanmukta, 405
Jnānānanda, see Nityagopal
John, the Baptist, 257
Joseph, 39, 461
Jugiṣ, Temple of, 42
Jyotis, 59
Jyot-pradīpa, 650

K

Ka, Kha, letters of the alphabet, 615
Kabīrdās, Song of, 614
Kachhibāgān, Vaiśṇavacaran, takes the Master to a private meeting at, 590
Kaikeyī, 31, 489
Kaikola, field of, 967
Kailās, Dr., mistakes the Master for a gardener, 711
Kaivarta, 132, 147, 495; Rāmkumār's scruples against accepting office from a, 136, 137
Kākatālaīya, analogy of, 575
Kalaighāt, 323
Kālī, 213, 218, 517, nil, 718, 719, 726, 747, 762; Rāṇī Rāsmaṇīs devotion to the Goddess, 132, 484; Rāmkumār accepts the service of the Mother, 151; the Master takes over the worship of, 155; the Master's mode of worship of, 167, 168, 478, 494; Haladhāri ceases to worship, 176; the Master teaches Haladhāri the truth about, 187, 188; Mathur sees the Master as Siva and, 209; songs on, 152, 355, 721, 811, 930, 977; the Master demands and receives prasāda on the occasion of the worship of Phalahāriṇī, 524, 525; on the knowledge of non-difference between Kṛṣna and, 596, 689; the Master inebriated with the love of, 617; is awake in Kaliyuga, 742; in Śyāmpukur the devotees conduct the Annual worship of, 983-985.
Kālīdās, son of Kanairām caṭṭopādhyāya, 31
Kālīghāṭ, 132, 192, 615; Rāṇī Rāsmanī and Mathur brought in their last moments to, 211, 323; Haldar, Mathur's priest at 724
Kālīnāth Datta, 323
Kālīpāda Ghosh, 962; helps an actress to see the Master in Syāmpukur, 997
Kālī's Mother, servant of Candrā Devi, 353, 354
Kālī Temple, 177, 207, 242, 391, 394, 441, 476, 495, 536, 617, 630, 642, 675, 692, 714, 718, 719, 746, 845, 894, 903, 965, 968, 1016; Rāṇī Rāsmaṇī builds the, 134; Rāmkumār accepts office of priest in the, 136, 140; installation of the Goddess in the 137, what the Master said about the founding of the, 138; the Master's reluctance to take charge as priest of, 147; the Master accepts the office of priest of 150; Hriday appointed to the service of, 155; visited by sādhus, sādhakas and perfected souls, 184, 242, 243, 298, 604, 620; Rāṇī Rāsmaṇī makes endowment of property on the, 210, 211; Bhairavī Brāhmaṇī comes to, 236; performance of Annameru ceremony by Mathur in, 238; the Master's mother comes to 281; Totā Purī comes to, 283, 284, 543; while practising Islām the Master would not enter the, 300; dismissal of Hriday from service of, 362, the Master punishes Raṇī Rāsmaṇī in, 481; to observe the actions of the Master minutely Mathur comes secretly to, 492; Prasāda of the, 524, 525, 818; the Master escorted by Girija returns to 539; Totā Purī leaves, 554, 562; the Master's vocal contest with Paṇḍit Gaurī in the, 591; meeting of scholarly aspirants convened in the, 593; the Master sees a sādhu inebriated with Divine knowledge standing before, 604; Ramlāl, priest of, 754; the Master's devotees come gradually to 816; in order to pray to be relieved from poverty Narendra goes thrice to, 927, 928; Snānayātrā day at, 951, 953
Kali yuga, 188; the Master on man's capacity for spiritual sādhana in, 184, 185, 742, 753, 938; mental sin is no sin in, 390; singing name of Hari efficacious, in, 999
Kalki, 188
Kālnā, the Master goes to, 323, 661, 666
Kalpa, a branch of study, 179
Kalpa-niyāmaka, 6
Kalpataru, the Master acts as, 1024
Kalutolā, 323; the Master occupies the seat of Sri Caitanya at the Hari-sabhā of, 663, 669
Kāmā, in the sense of aesthetic excellence, 811
Kāmākhyā, 461, 716
Kamalākānta, the Master sings songs of, 156, 481, 599, 629, 803

Kamal Kuṭīr, the residence of Keśav Candra Sen, 356, 793, 806
Kamaṇḍalu, 531, 641, 917
Kāmārhaṭi, the garden and temple of, 730, 731, 737, 738; the Brāhmanī of, 735, 736, 741, 749, 752, 755, 757; the Master visits, 758; Mrs. S.C. Bull, Miss MacLeod and Sister Nivedita visit, 761
Kāmārpukur, 54, 164, 192, 281, 321, 322, 360, 462, 469, 772; the village of, 20-24, 769; Kśudirām comes to, 26, 27; Kśudirām's life in, 31-32; Kśudirām returns from Gayā to, 38; news of Kśudirām's death at Selāmpur reaches, 58; the Master's early life in, 62, 66, 67, 74, 76, 148, 239; the Master leaves, 80; early ecstasies of the Master in, 115-122; The vision of the Master on the way to Sihor from, 195; the Master back home in, 201, 202, 203, 205, 206; Candrā Devī's prāyopaveśana before Siva of, 208; the Master goes with Hriday to 303-307, 510, 511, 576, 577, 578; the Master returns to Dakṣhineśwar from, 310; the Holy Mother in, 327, 331, 336, Rameśwar's death in, 348; discussion on the scriptures by Paṇḍits in, 460; Rāmlāl's marriage in, 465; Bhairavi Brāhmaṇī in, 535; the route to Dakṣineśwar from, 967
Kāmātmikā bhakti, 275
Kaṃbuliatola, 395, 800
Kamsa, 489
Kanailal Ghośal, an advanced sādhaka of Sakti, 172
Kanāirām Caṭṭopādhyaya, 25, 30, 31
Kant, 913
Kānthalpārā, house of Baṅkim Candra, 993
Kanyakubja, 138
Kāpālika, 609, 610; attempt to kill Sankarācārya, 489
Kapila, and Sāṅkhya philosophy 6, 656, 658
Kapila, one of the seven Ṛṣis, 857
Kapiñjalā, 1005
Kāraṇa, the two meanings of, 227, 544; Wine, 544
Karanyāsa, 153
Karma, 240, 692, 941
Karmakāṇḍa, 584
Karmayoga, the path of, 344
Karṇāṭaka, 721
Kartā, the spiritual teacher, 588
Kartābhājā, 178, 598, 663, 796, 960; the doctrine of, 588, 589, 590
Karuṇāmayī, daughter of Rāṇī Rāsmaṇī, 132, 211, 292
Kāsī, 626, 631, 635, 636, 641, 645, 660, 692, 835; Rāṇī Rāsmaṇi prepares to go to, 133 Bhairavai Brāhmaṇī leaves for, 310, 535; the Master's stay in, 311, 312, 532, 651, 654, what the Master thought about, 647, 648, 649, 650, 680, Māheś, the vīnā player of, 313, 710; Durgācaran Datta's wife in 837
Kāśikhāṇḍa, 651
Kāśipur, 617, 887, 892, 1005, 1009, garden house of, 1010; topography of, 1009, 1010; an instance of the destruction of spiritual attitude on Sivarātri day in, 89-93; the Master commends the devotion and enthusiam of Narendra in, 223; the Master's remark about his own photograph in, 345; Paṇḍit Saśādhar visits the Master in, 423; story of a young devotee brought to, 520; Narendra goes to Buddha Gayā soon after the Master came to, 645, 646; the Master's refusal to cure himself by the power of his mind while staying in, 673; the manifestation of power in the Master in, 704; the Master feeds Gopāla's mother with thickened milk in, 759, 760; the Master moves to, 964, 1008; the devotees commence their vow of service in, 971, 1014-1019; the purpose of knitting the devotees together into an order is accomplished in, 974; Rāmakṛṣna Mission has acquired the garden house of, 1013; Vaikuntha Nāth Sannyāl receives the grace of the Master in, 1026
Kāsiśwar Mitra, of Nandanbagān, 788
Kāthā, 67, 277
Kathāmālā, 486
Kātyāyanī, daughter of Kṣudirām Caṭṭopādhyāya, 25, 27, 32, 36, 37
Kātyāyanī, Rāṇī, 447, 430, 1008, 1010
Kātyāyanī, the gopis of Vraja pray to, 272
Kaupīn, 62, 125, 289

Kauslyā, 607
Kauṣītakin, 498
Kavi, 73
Kāyastha, 23, 432, 836
Kāzī, brought to his senses by Srī Caitanya, 482
Kedārghāt, in Kāśī; the Master and Mathur's party stayed in, 312
Kedārnāth, Siva, 312
Kedārnāth Caṭṭopādhyāya, a lay devotee of the Master, 874; the Master commends the devotion and reasoning power of, 875
Kenārām Bandyopādhyāya, 32
Kenārām Bhaṭṭācārya, initiates the Master in Sakti Mantra, 154, 178, 191
Keśavcandra Sen, 430, 569, 601, 683, 710, 727, 746, 786, 806, 812, 813, 814, 815, 816, 884, 956, the Master's first meeting with, 355, 704, 711, intimate relations between the Master and, 356, 357, 358, 787-795; the Cooc-Behār marriage and its repercussion on the career of, 357, founds a new faith, the New Dispensation, 358; death of, 360; the Master compares Narendra with, 713, 866-868
Ketu, in the horoscope of the Master, 46
Khārdāha, the chief centre of Nityānanda's work, 944
Khol, 361
Kīrtan, 725, 762, 788, 797, 806, 902; the Master during, 616; in Balarām Bāsu's house, 717, 747, in Dakṣhineśwar, 748, 793, 794, 858; in Maṇi Mallick's house, 801-804; in Jaya Gopāl Sen's house, 811, 812; in Maṇi Mohan Sen's house, 946-949; the Master on the importance of, 938
Kiśori, Ray, 1025
Konnāgar, 949
Korān, 180, 255, 299, 380, 700
Koṭhār, 744, 988
Kṛṣṇa, 11, 18, 39, 40, 48, 80, 87, 88, 114, 117, 150, 238, 253, 329, 357, 451, 456, 477, 524, 596, 657, 731, 741, 805, 819, 864, 875, 939, 946, 963, 982; the Master believed to be born as a part of, 73, 76; Śaṅkara on the birth of, 111; the Master identified with, 144, 196, 297, 367, 425, 465, 517, 655, 898, 1000; unperturbed at the time of death, 245; the Bhairavi Brāhmaṇī treats the Master as child, 248; lack of records of the spiritual practices of, 256; Rādhā and Vṛindāvan līlā of, 256, 257, 258, 259, 261, 262, 265 273, 274, 510, 652, 680 the Master's practice of Madhurabhāva and his attitude to, 270, 272, the Master's vision of, 275-277; the Master's practice of Sakhī Bhāva and attitude to, 385, 393; Vaisnava teachers of Bengal and, 442; Arjuna's devotion to, 454; utterances in the Gītā, 474, 477, 478, 729; Uddhava and the Gopis on the love of, 517, 518; the Master chants the name of, 555; Bhāgavata extols, 659; oneness of Kālī and, 689; in the form of Gopāla, 734, 741, 757
Kṛṣṇabāndh, in the town of Vana Viṣṇupur, 681
Kṛṣṇa Caitanya, see Caitanya, Sri Kṛṣṇa; see also Gaurāṅga
Kṛṣṇacandra Mukhopādhyāya, father of Hriday, 30
Kṛṣṇadās Pāl, 724
Kṛṣṇaganj, 361
Kṛṣṇa Kiśore Bhaṭṭācārya, the Master commends the great devotion of 636
Kṛṣṇalāl Goswāmī, 21
Kṛṣṇarām Basu, of holy memory, 986, 989
Kśatriya, 20, 298,
Kśetranāth Caṭṭopādhyāya, priest in the temple of Rādhā-Govinda, 136, 151
Kśudirām Caṭṭopādyhāya, life in Dere, 25, 26; settles in Kāmārpukur, 27-32; goes to Gayā on pilgrimage, 33-36; life after his return from Gayā, 37-38; and child Gadādhar, 50, 51; goes to Selāmpur, falls ill and dies, 56, 57; effect on Gadādhar's mind of the death of, 58
Kucākol, 321
Kula teachers, 586
Kumāri, daughter of Rāṇī Rāsmaṇi, 132, 211
Kuṇḍala, 35
Kuṇḍalinī, 585; the Master saw the awakening of, 231; the repository of past impressions, 414; its states of working and sleeping, 415, 416
Kūpas, the Master sees sādhakas in

Vraja sitting within, 652
Kūrma, Srī Dharma looked upon as, 23
Kurukeśtra, 551; a battle scene, 761
Kuśa, 423
Kuṭīghāṭ, 151
Kuvīr, song of, 589

L

Lagna, of Sri Rāmakṛishṇa's birth, 47
Lāhā, 21, 35, 46, school of the Lāhās, 51; pilgrim's rest-house, 61; Dharmadās, 64, bridal ornaments borrowed from, 206; affection for Sri Rāmakṛṣṇa, 306; discussion on the scriptures by Paṇḍits in the house of, 460
Lāhore, 838
Lakṣmaṇa, 245; in the Master's vision of Rāma, 283; 455; travelling in the forest with Rāma and Sītā, 557
Lakṣhmī, Candrādevi's vision of, 35
Lakṣhmī (Sri Ramakṛṣṇa's niece), 397, 578, 1019
Lakṣmījalā, 29, 70
Lakṣmīnārāyaṇ, the Master's reaction to the proposal of, 610 the Holy Mother's reaction to the gift of, 952
Lālā Bābu, 759, 1010
Lālbāndh, in the town of Vana Visnupur, 681, 682
Lalitā, (Radha's principal companion), Gangāmātā of Nidhuvan-regarded as, 653
Lalitavistara, verse indicative of the firm resolved of Buddha, 646
Lankā, 453, 455
Lātu, see Abhutananda
Lava, 423
Līlā, as a special manifestation of the divine power, 8, 10, 26, 245; of Bṛndāvan, 258; the Mother as the source of, 299; 438; as an aspect of God, 445, 451, 473, 745, 817, 822
Luci, 147, 575, 762
Lucknow, 838
Ludhiana, Totāpurī's association with, 551

M

M, author of the Gospel of Srī Rāmakṛṣṇa, see Mahendranāṭh Gupta
MacLeod, Miss J., 762
Mādhana, definition of the state of, 262
Madanmohan, of Vana Viṣṇupur, 67, 682
Mādhāi, the saving of, 379
Madhujugi, of Kāmārpukur, 42, 67
Madhumatī,132
Madhura bhāva, 251, 253, 255, 268, 346, 405, 415, 427; the Master's sādhana of, 172, 248, 266-277; the Master's state of mind before he undertook sādhana of, 238; the Master on the ultimate truth of, 253; the greatest contribution of Vaiṣṇava teacher, 255; Caitanya and, 260-266; Vedāntins and the sādhana of, 266; aim of practising, 268; Vaiṣṇava literature on, 522
Madhu Roy's lane, 617
Madhusūdan Datta, Michael, and Nārāyan Sāstri, 628; conversation between the Master and, 629
Madhyam Nārāyaṇ oil, 207, 574
Māgha celebrations, 793
Mahabhārata, 17, 50, 67, 125, 180, 239, 731, 840, 902; story of Ekalavya in, 455; the Master as a boy gets by heart, 770
Mahābhāva, 258; 772, 956; the Bhairavi Brāhmaṇī recognizes the Master's state as, 215; Rādhā the embodiment of, 259, 262; physical signs manifested during, 274; the Master in the ultimate stage of, 275; Paṇḍit Vaiṣṇavacāran sees manifested in the Master all the signs of, 346, 582; Gaṅgā Mātā recognises in the Master the signs of, 653
Mahādeva, 40, 281,
Mahākāli, opens the door to liberation, 651
Mahāmāyā, 871; inscrutable ways of, 110, 380, 583, in the Tantras, 585; power of, 810; Narendra tempted by, 923, 924
Mahāprasād, Atke, sanctity of, 340
Mahārāja of Burdwan, 236; 631
Mahārāja of Jaipur, 626
Mahāvākya, 178
Mahāvāyu, 415
Mahāvidyās, temple of the ten 151, 192 Ṣoḍaśī, one of the ten, (233) 469
Mahāvīra, 888; the Master; practises

Dāsyabhāva according to 182, 238
Mahāvirā, the Tirthankara, 341
Mahendranāth Pāl, the physician of Ālambazār, 361
Mahendralāl Sarkār, 447, 499, 525; attends on the Master during his last illness, 196, 961, 965, 1008, 1018, 1022; examines the Master in Nirvikalpa samādhi, 385; becomes attracted to the Master, 976
Mahendranāth Gupta, 'M', 395, 576, 945, 956, 960, 973, 1025; appointed headmaster of Vidyāsāgar's school in Shyāmbāzār, 898; meets the Master for the first time, 873, with other house holder devotees attends to the Master's requirements during his last illness, 974, 979, 984, 1015
Māheś, chariot festival at, 761
Māheś Candra Caṭṭopādhyāya, of Sihār, an officer of Raṇī Rāsmaṇī's household, 70, 135-136
Maheścandra Sarkār, an expert vinā player of Kāśi, visited by the Master, 314 710
Maheśwar, 451, 584
Mahimācaran Cakravarti, pomposity of, 1004, 1005; gurus of, 1006; the only sādhana of, 1006; debate with Narendra in Syāmpukur, 1007
Mahimna-stotra, the Master's recital of, 494
Māhut-god, story of, 374
Maitreyī, conversation between Yājnavālkya and, 597
Mallick, brother-in-law of Upendra Nāth Ghoś, 994
Mālpāra, Goswāmīs of, 734
Māna, kīrtan, 265
Mānā, bhakti, 275
Manasā, 22, 66, 116; the Bhairavi Brāhmaṇī compares herself to, 309
Mānasā Maṅgala, 116
Mānavī, mode of initiation, 702
Mandākinī, 491
Māndaran, fort of, 24, 769
Maṇikarṇikā, ghāt, the Master sees Trailanga Swami in, 312; the Master's vision at, 650-651
Māṇikcandra Bandyopādhyāya, Mānikrājā of Bhūrsubo, 23; fascinated by Boy Gadādhār, 54, 55
Māṇikrām Caṭṭopādhyāya, 24
Maṇimohan Mallick, 805, 806; grief over the death of his son, 386-390; the Master consoles, 390-391; the Master visits the house of, 788, 800
Manimohan Sen, of Pānihati, 192, 350, the Master in the house of, 946, 948
Manīndranāth Gupta, 991; Maṇipūra, 416, 721; Mantra, (-s), 33, 98, 136, 153, 165, 202, 226, 287, 291, 318, 322, 378, 470, 534, 586, 625, 651, 721, 869, 985, 1007, 1024; of Gāyatri, 29; of Sakti, the Master gets initiated in, 154; of Rāma, the Master's initiation, in, 178, 242, 247, 281, 621; of the Virajā Homa, 287; uttered by the Master during the worship of the Holy Mother, 336; difference between the human teacher and divine teacher imparting, 378, 456; of Guṭikā siddhi, 537, 538; of Rāma imparted by Nārada to Vālmīki, 636; of Sakti, the members of the Master's household initiated in, 690; three kinds of initiation, 702; of Gopāla, 734; Vijay Kṛṣṇa Goswāmī initiates many people in, 794; Wrestler Hanumān Singh's faith in the, 888; the Master imparts to Pūrṇa a, 900; the Master's mode initiating disciples in, 933; of the Kartābhajā sect, 960; the Master initiates Vaikuṇṭhanāth Sannyāl in a, 1025
Māntri, initiation, 702
Manu, 368,
Mārā, Buddhistic Satan, 257
Mārā, 636
Marshman, 830
Mārwāri devotees, come to the Master in Dakśineśwar, 754, 755, 756, the Master on the food brought by, 872
Mary, 39, 255, 460, 982
Maṭh, at Ludhiana of which Totā Purī was the Mohanta, 551
Māthaghasa lane, 788, 806
Mathurā, 266, 518, 875
Mathur Kirtan, 266, 875
Mathurā Mohan Biswās, 132, 142, 191, 238, 303, 327, 345, 550, 558, 572, 610, 634, 635, 695, 745, 814; marries Jagadāmbā Dāsī, 131; requests Rāmkumār to officiate as priest in the Kālī temple, 137; his first impressions of the Master, 142; tries to secure

the services of the Master for the temple and succeeds, 145, 149-151, 154; begins to revere the Master, 162; watches the Master at worship, 168; concerned about the condition of the Master, 172, 173; mistaken notion about the Master's condition, 199; sees the Master as Siva and Kālī, 208, 496; improvement in the worldly affairs of, 208; his conception about the Master, 209; contention with the Bhairavi Brāhmaṇī on the subject of incarnations, 213; on receiving the Master's grace, 236; undertakes the vow of gift of annameru, 237; serves holy men as directed by the Master, 241, 610; helps the Master in his practice of Madhura Bhāva, 270, 271; become a great favourite with the Master's Mother, 281; begs the Master to save Jagadambā Dasi's life, 292, 293; arranges for the Master's food during his practice of Islām, 300; takes the Master with him on pilgrimage, 311, 313, 641-648, 660, 661, 666, 669; compares himself and Hriday to Nandi and Bhrṅgi, 316; takes the Master to Ranāghāt and to his own house in Sonābere, 322, 323; selfless devotion of, 323, 324; the profound love between the Master and, 324, 325; death of, 325, 326; convinced by the Master that anything can happen by the will of God, 425, 679; relation of the Master with, 487, 488, 489, 490-495, 527-532, 573, 574; his increasing devotion to the Master, 497-506; celebrates Durgā Pūjā in his Jānbazār house in the company of the Master, 507, 508, 513; experiences ecstasy, 519, the Master's attitude to, 522, 523, 524; altercation with Bhāirāvī Brāhmaṇī, 536; convenes meeting of Pandits to discuss the Master's condition, 550, 551, 581, 582

Mati Jhil, 618, 758, 1010

Matilāl Seal, 758, 1010

Matthew, 729

Maurāla, fish, 579

Max Muller, 461

Māyā, 9, 284, 291, 368, 390, 485, 607, 613, 694, 785; incarnations always free from the meshes of, 9, but they assume a veil of, 95, 111; is beginningless and beyond time, 101, Suka Deva untouched by, 179, 273, 393; Tōtā Purī's idea about 285; power of, 289, 451, 604, 810, 860; leading Godward, 445; leading away from God, 446; Uddhava considers the love of the Gopis as within, 518; how Totā Purī came to realize the identity of Brahman and, 556, 557, 558, 560; stands between man and God-realization, 557; the Master could always penetrate all the veils of, 643, 815, 821; realization of God frees one from, 691; the Master declares Narendra free from even the slightest tinge of, 866, 871

Māyā Avidyā, 446, 554

Māyā Vidyā, 399, 446

Māyā Dēvi, 39

Mechhūābāzār, the Master sees the Mother even in the harlots of, 199, 676

Medical College, 673, 758

Medinipur, 21, 56; Kṣudirām's frequent visits to, 31, 32

Meghanād, 455

Mentaions, what they are and on what they depend for their existence, 439

Meru cakra, 416

Metiāburuz, 831

Metropolitan school, Campatala, Narendra appointed Headmaster of, 942

Mill, J.S., 830, 913, 925

Mill of Kāmārhati, 758

Mīrābāi, 384

Mīr Zāfar, Nāẃāb, 1009

Mithilā, 180

Modana, characteristic of Mahābhāva, 262

Mogalmāri, battlefield of, 24

Mohammad, 20, 622, 657, 776, regarded as a religious hero and selfless teacher, 475

Mokṣa, 811

Mokṣada, Bhairavi Brāhmaṇī's companion at Kāsī, 313

Manomohan Mitra, takes refuge in the Master, 817, 818

Mount Sumeru, 547

Mṛdaṅga, 801
Mṛgāṅkamauli Pūtatuṇḍi, 1005
Mṛṇmāyī, Goddess, image of, 682
Mugdhabodha, Narendra gets by heart all the aphorisms in, 829
Mutki, 90
Mukundapur, 23; assurance given to Candradevi by Siva, of 208, 281
Mulādhāra, 231, 414, 416, 599
Muṇḍamāla Tantra, 586
Munsi Babus of Barānagar, later becomes the Barānagar monastery, 746
Muslim, or Mohammedan, 139, 299, 300, attitude to Sufis, 255; manners and customs affected by Viśwanāth Datta, 838

N

Nabāt, Kāmārpukur famous for, 22
Nāgā, fakīrs, 125, 547, 556
Nāgakesara flower, 274
Nāgendranath Caṭṭopādhyāya, 803
Nahāvat, 213, 524, 562; Holy Mother in 331, 333, 336, 394, 580, 721, 733, 740, 752, 818, 905; Candrā Devi in, 349, 351, 354
Nāma, 741
Namāz, the Master performs, 299
Nānak, the master's reverence for, 341
Nanda 536; festival of, 151
Nandakumār, song of, 722
Nandanbāgān, 788
Nandi, and Bhṛṅgi, 316
Nara, 657; the Master identifies Narendra with, 825
Nārada, conversation between Visnu and, 94; bhakti sutras of, 377; imparts mantra to Vālmīki, 636; devotion as expounded by, 404, 597, 938, 999
Nārada Pāncarātra, 344
Nārāyana, 47, 189, 322, 557, 810, 973; the Master regards his devotees as, 427, 710, 825, 856, 870, 899
Nārāyaṇ, 899
Nārāyaṇ, Hathayogi, 391
Nārāyaṇ Sāstri, antecedents of, 625; study and attainments of, 626; lives in Daksineśwar, 544; and Michael Madhusūdan, 627, 629; later life of, 630
Nārāyan Swāmī, founder of a religious movement in Guzerāt, 663
Nārāyanī, invocation to Devī, 336
Nārāyaṇī, daughter of Govinda Bābu of Patāldanga, 732
Narendranath, 199, 413, 427, 448, 673, 707, 709, 714, 759, 762, 942, 945, 946, 958, 960, 970, 971, 997, 1012; love and enthusiasm for sādhanas of, 224; the Master's admiration for the sharp intellect of, 431; reason for the Master's great attachment to, 709-710; The Master compares Keśab and, 713-714; the Master on the spiritual insight of, 754; Gopāla's Mother and, 757; first meeting with the Master, 822-826; ideas and ideals of, 828, 911-917; qualities of head and heart of, 830-835, 907; ancestry of 836; parents of, 837-840; subsequent visits to Dakśineśwar of, 841-849; the Master's wonderful vision about, 846; extraordinary experiences in early life of, 850, 851; the Master's great love for, 852-858; relations with the Master, 859-870, 908; the Master's estimate of, 871, 872; protests against the doctrine of non-dualism, 877; and Hazra, 878, 879; at the touch of the Master, 879; the Master on the physical characteristics and natural tendencies of, 889, 890, 907, 908; in adversity after the death of his father, 921-931; with the devotees of the Master, 937, 938, 939; in attendance on the Master during his last illness, 970, 971, 979, 1015-1019; controversy with Dr. Sarkar, 982; efforts to check the growth of sentimentalism among the devotees, 1001-1003; Mahimacaran and, 1005-1007; inspires the boy devotees in Kāsipur to devote themselves to God realization, 1019-1021
Naren, Junior, 720, 722, 723, 725, 899, 933; the Master scolds, 893; the Master eulogizes, 951.
Narmadā, 284
Naṭabar Goswāmī, 361
Navacaitanya Mitra, of Konnāgar, the Master bestows his grace on, 949, 950
Navadwīp or Nādiā, 132, 138, 360, 680, 901, 980; Mathur takes the Master to, 323, 660; Nārāyan Śāstri studies

Nyāya philosophy, 626
Navagaṅgā, 132
Navagopāl, Kavirāj, 961
Navagopāl Mitra, founder of the Hindu Fair, establishes a physical training club in Cornwallis street, 831, 833, 834.
Navarasika, A Vaiṣṇava sect, 178
Navayātrā, places visited by the Master in the year 1885 during, 714.
Navīncandra Niyogi, 217
Navīncaṇdra Raychaudhuri, father of Swāmi Yogānanda, 902
Navya-nyāya, 630
Nawābs, cōīns of the time not legal tender in the time of Badshas, 380, 897
Nāyikās, of the Divine Mother, Rāṇī Rāsmaṇi one of the eight, 484
Nazareth, 460
Nepal Government, 351
Neti, 391
Neti Neti, path of sādhana, 101
New Dispensation, 358, 712, 796, 807; foundation and propagation of the, 793; influence of the Master on, 797; song of the, 811
Nidhirām, Caṭṭopādhyāya, 25, 30, 31
Nidhuvan, the Master visits, 313, 652
Nagama-Kalpadruma, 586
Nīlacāla, see Pūri
Nīlāmbar Bābu, 761
Nīlmādhav Bandyopādhyāya, 732
Nīm tree, 36
Nimaicaran Basu, Narendra as a junior to, 918, 942, 987
Nirañjanānanda, or Nitya Nirañjan, 93, 933, 1018; the Master's opinion on service expressed to, 149, 892; the Master's instructions to, 894, 896
Nirātmā, Goddess, 260
Nirvikalpa samādhi, 96, 284, 404, 521, 543, 555, 627, 688, 689, 765, 784, 853; how to attain, 103, 104; the Master attains, 178, 190, 224, 250, 290, 291, 294, 295, 406, 439, 458; the Master established in, 297, 300, 336, 385, 407, 411, 412, 426, 440, 446; definition of, 404, 439; the Divine Mother an obstacle on the Master's path to, 411; destruction of past impressions by the attainment of, 414; the Master's experiences during, 417, 418, 443, 719; Totā Purī attained, 546, 558; Narendra attained, 759
Nirguṇa, see **Brahman**
Nirukta, 180
Nirvāṇa, 260, 283, 651, 658
Nitya, aspect of God, 445
Nityagopāl, and Narendra, a contrast pointed by the Master, 907
Nityagopāl Goswāmī, in Balarām Basu's house in the company of the Master, 963
Nityānanda, Brahman, 454
Nityānanda, or Nitāi, 195, 218, 725, 802, 880, 935, 948, 962; initiates Uddharan Datta, 120; in the Saṅkīrtan of Śrī Caitanya, 360; and Raghunāth Dās Goswāmī, 944
Niveditā, sister, 762; serves Gopala's mother, 763
Nyāsa, 321, 335
Nyāyacāñcu, 477

O

Ochterloney Monument, 476, 922
Orissa, 138, 744, 1009

P

Padmalochan, Paṇḍit, 237, 276, 346, 347, 710; attainments of, 630, 631; his love of God; 631 comes to Calcutta and sees the Master for the first time, 633; the secret of the miraculous power of, 634; death in Kāsī, 635
Padmamaṇi, eldest daughter of Raṇi Rāsmaṇí, 132, 211
Padmāsana, for meditation on God without form, 991
Pakhoāj, 715
Pāl pārvaṇa, 22
Pañcabhāvas, Bhairavī Brāhmaṇī was an expert in the disciplines of, 237, 248
Pañcadasī, 296, 422, 774, 810
Pañcamuṇḍī, seat constructed under the Pancavati for the Master's Tantrik sādhana, 224,
Pañcavati, 148, 153, 157, 218, 292, 299, 317, 321, 360, 419, 425, 495, 496, 547, 559, 561, 683, 740, 744, 873, 905, 920, 1005; the Master cooks his food under

the, 142, 147; the Master spends his time in meditation in the, 168, Hriday tries to frighten the Master when he is meditating under the, 157; the Master had a vision of Pāpa Puruṣa while sitting under the, 172; the Master with his own hands plants the, 183, 184; description of a, 184; the Master seen sitting on the branch of a Banyan tree of the, 188, the Bhairavi Brāhmaṇī has an extraordinary vision under the, 216; preparations made for the Master's Tāṇtrik sādhana under the, 225; the Master offers to transfer the eight miraculous powers to Narendra in the, 232, 909; Tōtā Purī and the Master in the Sādhanakuṭīr at the, 286, 291; the Master on his return from pilgrimage celebrates a festival at the, 314; Hriday's wonderful vision of the Master as he was going towards the, 316, 317; the Master attains the vision of Jesus Christ under the, 339; a strange experience of the Master in the, 390; Yogen fascinated by Haṭhayogi Nārāyaṇ living under the, 391, 392; anecdote of a pseudo-vedantin camped under the, 421, 422; Tōtā-Purī sees a Bhairava in the, 550; Mārwāri devotees assemble after worship under the, 754

Pāṇḍe, the Holy Mother buys milk from, 959

Paṇḍit, (-s), 56, 138, 276, 355, 443, 498, 570, 572, 627; Rānī Rāsmaṇi procures sāstrik opinions from, 134, 135, 151, 504; the Lāhas convene a meeting of, 460; the Bhairavi Brāhmani requests Mathur to convene a meeting of, 573, 581; the Master's vision at Maṇikarṇikā pronounced true by, 651

Pāṇihātī, 397, 499, 954; the Master's visit in 1858 to the great festival at, 192; Manimohan Sen of, 350; story of the festival at, 943; the Master at the festival of, 944-950, 952

Paramahaṁsa (-s), 233, 295, 622, 951; Suka deva, 179, 273; Tōtā Purī, 276, 283, 1006, Trailaṅga Swāmī, 312, 652; state of a, 466, 552, 604, 641, 709; and knowledge of alchemy, 562; of Dakṣiṇeswar, 669, 712, 767, 851, 865

Parāśara, 46

Parāvidyā, on the attainment of, 977

Parinirvāṇa, 245

Pārvātī Devī, 703, 770; filial attitude of Ganeś and Kārtik to, 228, 229

Paśupatī, 587

Paśwācāra, explanation of the term, 587

Paṭol, vegetable, 468

Paṭaldāngā, 731, 734

Patañjali, Yoga aphorisms of, 296, 393, 512

Paurāṇic age, doctrine of God incarnate in, 6, 7, 8; and this sceptical modern age, 105

Persian, 298, 912

Phalahāriṇī Kālika Devī, the Master performs worship of Ṣoḍaśi on the day of worship of the, 334; the Master once demands and receives the Prasada on the occasion of worship of the, 524, 525

Phalgu, 255

Phului-Syāmbāzār, the Master's visit to 361

Piṇḍa, 37, 286

Piṅgalā, 599

Pīṭhasthānās, the story of, 644

Prabhudayāl Miśra, comes to see the Master in Śyāmpukur, 1007

Prācya-Arya-Sikṣakāṇda Pariṣat, 1005

Prahlāda, 67, 654

Prakṛti, 658, 671; or Māyā is beginningless and beyond time, 101; Puruṣa and, 261, 381, 443, 725; body and mind are the evolutes of, 665; and Puruṣa in Sānkhya Philosophy, 677

Prakṛti-lina-puruṣa, 5, incarnations belong to the class of, 658

Pramatha, or Paltu, 899

Prānakṛṣṇa Mukhopādhyāya, 396, 576

Praṇava, 356, 1006

Praṇaya, 275

Prāṇāyāma, the Master practised, 184

Prārabdha, a man of absolute knowledge is not under the control of, 464, 465

Prasāda, 138, 147, 159, 176, 192, 215, 216, 309, 717, 723, 731, 740, 749, 754, 804, 949, 985, 1008, 1017; of the Kālī temple, initial objections of Brāhmins to take, 134; in the course of Tantrik Sādhana the Master par-

takes of offal as, 231; on the occasion of worship of Phalahāriṇi, the Master demands and obtains, 524-526; of Nārāyana or any other image of God always acceptable to the Master, 744, 748; Rākhāl scolded by the Master for greedily eating, 818; an ugly ill-formed Vaiśṇava tries to feed the Master with a plateful of, 949
Prasād, Doctor, 352
Prasād, see Ramprasad
Prasanna, or Prasannamayī, sister of Dharmadās Lāha, 42, 46, 62, 73; held in high esteem by the Master, 117; her devotion to the Master, 117, 118
Pratāpcandra Majumdār, 789, 813; on the influence of the Master on the Brāhmo Samāj, 796
Pratāpcandra Hazrā, 697, 908; reproached by the Master for forgetfulness, 434; asks the Master not to worry unduly about the devotees, 709; character of, 877, 878; and Narendra join in ridiculing the truth of Non-dualism, 878, 879
Prayāg, the Master's behaviour at, 313
Prāyopaveśana, by Candra Devi for the recovery of her son, by the Holy Mother in Simhavāhini's temple, 352
Premānanda, Swami, see Baburām
Premdās, see Cirañjīv Sarma
Priya, 602
Punarmūṣika, 189, 665, fable of,
Punjab, 551, 663, 898
Purāṇa, (-s), 180, 184, 258, 276, 369, 379, 483, 585, 590, 609, 612, 623, 636, 700, 770, 886; on incarnations, 8, 9, 39, 40, 658, 659; the Master even from his early years was greatly interested in the, 40, 61, 73, 90, 124, 420, 770; the Master tells a story from the 227, 228; story of Vyāsa and Śuka from, 393; story of Airāvata and Gaṅgā in; story of King Bharatā told in the, 870
Purāścaraṇa, 544
Puraścaraṇollāsa Tantra, 586, 703
Pūri, 22, 61, 125, 132, 184, 284, 461, 601, 602, 769, 944, 987, 988; the Master believed the incarnation of Buddha to be manifest in the image at, 340; the Master does not approve of the proposal of his going to, 655, 660; Vijay Kṛṣṇa Goswāmi passes away at, 794; Raghunāth Das Goswāmi directed by Nityānandā to go to, 944
Pūrī, sect, 551-554
Pūrṇā and Sūnya are one and the same reality, 250
Purnābhiśeka, 226
Pūrnacandra Ghosh, 699, 932, introduced to the Master by Sri Mahendra, 899; the Master speaks highly of the spiritual fitness of, 899; the Master's loving behaviour towards, 899, 900; greatness of, 900
Pūrṇahuti, 337
Puruṣa, and Prakṛti, 262, 381, 443, 725; and Prakṛti in Sāṅkhya philosophy, 677
Pūrvabhādrapada, 46
Pūrvarāga, 265
Pyāri Chaudhuri, 132
Pyne, a prosperous family of Kāmārpukur, 119, 120, 306

R

Rādhā, or Rādhikā, 73, 117, 151, 185, 196, 215, 572, 574, 582, 652, 717, 731, 946, 948, 963; transcendental love of, 257-265, 271-276, 456; Gangā Mātā regards the Master as, 652
Rādhā Govinda, temple of, 136, 151, 154, 176, 186, 271, 282, 321, 322, 335, 504, 524, 718, 719, 721
Rādhākāṇta, 946
Rādhākuṇdā, the Master visits, 313, 314
Rādhāsyāmi, sect, 663
Rāga, 275
Rāgātmikā Bhakti, the Master attains, 170-175, 175, 178; divisions of, 275
Rāghav, brother of Hriday, 30, 318
Rāghav, Pandit, the Master visits the cottage of, 949
Raghuvīr, 32, 49, 50 54, 59, 68, 79, 182, 215, 216, 309, 577; devotion of Kṣudirām for, 25, 29, 57, 58; how Kṣudirām came upon the Sālagrāma of, 28, 29, 690; Candrā Devī's attitude to, 41-45, 71, 119, 208; the Master's worship of, 64, 72, 79; Rāmkumār's faith in, 129; Aksay's devotion to, 320; Rāmeśwar's devotion to, 350

Raghunāth Dās, Goswāmī, story of the renunciation and detachment of, 943, 944
Rāicaran Dās, of Krsnaganj, 361
Raipur, Narendra in meditation on his way to, 835
Rājādhirāja, the Dharma of Kāmārpukur, 23
Rājāram Mukhopadhyāya, 30, 176, 681
Rajas, 171, 288, 373, 861
Rājasika, devotion of Mathur, 508
Rājcandra Dās, 131, 132
Rājendralāl Datta, offers homoeopathic treatment to the Master, 447, 1022
Rājendralāl Bandyopādhyāya, 312
Rājendranāth Sarkār, teacher in the school of the Lāha, 51
Rājkumār, see Acalānanda
Rājnārāyan, 236
Rājarājeswari, the Master's vision of, 233
Rājayoga, 184
Rākhal, see Brahmananda, Swami
Rākhal, Doctor, diagnoses the Master's disease, 943
Rākṣasās, in Vibhīṣana's assembly, 453
Rāksaśagaṇa, evil portent, 321
Raktabīja, 698
Rāma, or Rāmacandra, 20, 24, 28, 31, 80, 124, 182, 183, 213, 238, 278, 301, 463, 489, 557, 562, 657, 720, 768, 770; the Master identified with, 144, 196, 297, 367, 425, 465, 517, 655; the Master initiated into the Mantra of, 178, 281; Jaṭādhārī's extraordinary love and attachment to, 242, 605, 606; the Master's love and devotion to, 243; the Master's visions of, 247, 283; Akṣay's devotion to, 320, 322; Rāmeśwar's devotion to, 349; Hanumān's attitude to, 344, 455; Vibhīṣanā's devotion to, 453; faith of a sadhu in the name of, 612; devotional songs on, 613; Kṛṣṇa Kiśore's devotion to, 636; story of the fight between Śiva and 795
Rāmakṛṣṇa, ancestry of, 20, 22; birth of, 46; early ecstasies, 118, 119, 121; comes to live in Dakṣineśwar, 145; blessed with a vision and mandate from the Divine Mother, 188; undertakes Tanṭrik Sādhanās, 222; confers his grace on Mathur, 235, illustration of the uncommon mental make-up of, 240; practises Vātsalya mood of sadhana, 242-251; and Madhura Bhāva, 253, 254; on the ultimate truth of Madhura Bhavā, 257; on the attainment of Advaitic consciousness, 298; practice of Islām, 299; with the people of his birth place, 306; pilgrimages with Mathur, 310-314; receives power of attorney from Girīṣ, 375-380; the unique constitution of the mind of, 407; leads the devotees forward on the path of spirituality, 427, 428; his extraordinary power over the human mind, 435; the play of the Divine power as spiritual teacher seen in, 438; an example of his power of awakening spirituality, 447-450; on devotion to the spiritual teacher, 452; first manifestation of the spiritual teacher's mood in the life of, 460, 462; his immaculate love for his wife, 470; as an incarnation of the modern age, 485, 488, 489, 490; relation with the revered Totā Puri, 446, 447; how he preached religion, 571; his reverential attitude to all religions, 597; with Bhagavān Dās of Kālna, 666-669; Vijay Kṛṣṇa Goswāmī's vision of, 706; at the Chariot Festival in Balarām Bābu's house, 717; and Gopālā's mother, 729, 737-742, 753-756, 758-763; the Master's four suppliers of necessities, 744-746; human traits of, 766-774; daily habits, likes and dislikes of, 774, 775; in Jaya Gōpāl Sen's house, 806; contact with Brahmo leaders, 813; the devotees' conception about, 974, 975; instructs increasing number of devotees at Syāmpukūr, 991, 992; self revelation and blessings to his disciples at the Cossipore Garden house, 1023
Rāmakṛṣṇa Mission, 1013
Rāmakṛṣṇa Order of Monks, 800, 819, 860
Rāmakṛṣṇa Paramahamsā Deber Jivan Vrttānta, 816
Ramakṛṣṇāyana, 67
Ramānanda Rāi, landlord of Dere, 24; deprives Kśudirām of his paternal property, 26

Rāmānanda Saṅkhāri, 23
Rāmānuja, 776
Rāmāwat, sect, 178, 190, 605; the Master's initiation in the mantra of Rāma by a holy man of, 242, 621; devotional songs of the, 612, 613
Rāmāyana, 17, 39, 50, 125, 137, 731, 840; the Master reads, 67, 239, 770; genesis of, 636; of Tulasidas, 803; Narendra learns by heart the whole of, 829
Rāmcand, see Rāmcandra Bandyopādhyāya
Rāmcandra Bandyopādhyāya, regard for his maternal uncles, 31, 34; gift of a milch cow to Kṣudirām by, 48; Kṣudirām's illness and death in the house of, 56, 57
Rāmcandra Caṭṭopādhyāya, 322
Rāmcandra Dās, 132
Rāmcandra Datta, and Girīś with the Master in Dakṣiṇeśwar, 449; the Master at the house of, 616; takes refuge in the Master, 816; and other devotees take the Master to the Festival at Pāṇihaṭi, 945; vanity of, 994; attends to the financial needs of the Master during his last illness, 823, 874, 956, 960, 972, 974, 984, 1000, 1015, 1019, 1023, 1024
Rāmcandra Mukhopādhyāya, of the village of Jayramvati, 205, 463; takes his daughter to Calcutta, 329, 330, death of, 352
Rāmdayāl Babu, 855
Rāmdhan Ghoś, of Desra, 70, invites Rāmkumār to the Kāli Temple, Daksineśwar, 137
Rāmeśwar, 68, 80, 201, 203, 205, 350; birth of, 25, 32; early life of, 59; marriage of, 68; his difficulties after the death of Rām Kumār's wife, 71; arranges Akṣay's marriage, 321; appointed priest in Radha Govinda Temple, 322; charitable nature of, 348, last wish of, 349; death of, 349; talks to his friend Gopāl after death, 350
Rāmeśwar Siva, 64
Rāmeśwar, Vānalinga Kṣudirām brings home from Setubandha, 32, 41
Rāmjay Bandyopādhyāya, 54
Rāmjivanpur, 361
Rāmakānai, see Kanairām Cattopādhyāya
Rāmkānta Basu Street, No., residence of Balaram Bāsu, 747, 961, 988
Rāmkumār, 27, 33, 45, 71, 201, 205, 283; birth of, 25; marriage of, 32; undertakes responsibilities of the family, 32; supernatural power of, 34; present at the death of his father in Sēlāmpur, 57, 58; after the death of Kṣudirām, 59; performs upanayana of the Master, 63, 64; arranges the marriage of Rāmeṣwar, 68; change in the financial condition of, 68; starts a Sanskrit school in Jhanāpukur, Calcutta, 70, 130; takes the Master to Calcutta, 81; admonishes the Master, 125, 126, 127, 128, 686; worldly conditions of, 128, 129; gives an opinion in Rāni Rāsmanī's favour, 134; requested by Rāni Rāsmanī to accept the office of priest in Dakṣineswar, 135, 136; life in Dakṣineswar, 137, 138, 139, 140, 141, 142, 145, 146, 150; teaches the Master worship and recital of scriptures etc., 154; death of, 155
Rāmlālā, image of, 178; Jatādhāri's love and attachement to, 242, 243; Jatādhāri makes a gift to the Master of, 247, 281, 611, 612; story of, 606, 607
Rāmlāl Caṭṭopādhyāya, 395, 397, 434, 525, 579, 722; appointed priest in Dakṣiṇeśwar, 350; performs funeral rites of Candrā Devī, 354, 654; marriage of, 465; the Master's great considerateness for, 755; receives the Master's Grace, 1025
Rāmlāl's Mother, 577, 578, 675
Rāmmohan Datta, 836
Rāmmohan Roy, Rājā, 359, 913
Rām Prasād, 156, 492, 689; the Master sings the songs of, 156, 160, 161, 355, 481, 629, 803, 811; a saying of, 283; songs of, 381, 616, 811, 977
Rāmratan Mukhopādhyāya, 30, 346
Rāmsaday Bandyopādhyāya, 68
Rāmsīla, birth of, 25; marriage of, 30; children of, 31; possessed by Goddess Sītālā, 54
Rāmtānu Bāsu's Lane, Narendra's study at, 918, 942

Rāmtārak Cattopādhyāya, see Haladhāri
Rānāghāt, the Master goes with Mathur to, 323, 532
Rāṇi Rāsmāṇi, 152, 154, 162, 167, 177, 184, 199, 212, 213, 292, 478, 487, 488, 497, 524, 527, 529, 550, 1017; the family of, 131, 132; her devotion to Kālī, 132; builds the temple at Dakṣinéswar, 133; overcomes all obstacles in the way of consecration of the temple, 134-136; praises the images of Siva made by the Master, 148; has firm faith in the advice of the Master, 151, 504; punished by the Master for indulging in worldly thought at the time of worship, 172, 173, 174, 476, 480, 481, 483, 486; executes a Devottara deed of Dinājpur properties, 210; death of, 211; "story of the life of", 236, 346; holds the Master in high esteem; 479, 480
Rasagollā, 468, 575
Rāsa platform, 23
Rāśi, 47
Rasiklāl Pyne, 120
Ratan, chief officer of the garden house of Jadunath Mallick, 862
Ratha, 511
Ratha-yātrā, 23, 714
Rāti's mother, 190
Ṛṣi (-s), 30, 402, 414, 485, 519, 597, 609, 623, 694, 827. 877, 912; of the Vedic period, 6, 7, 8, 343, 367, 369; Janaka, 341; on a Satya Saṅkalpa, 424; Nārada and Vālmiki, Kapilā, 656; Nara, 825; Narendra as one of the seven, 846
Ṛṣis, four, 857
Ṛṣis, seven, 857
Rohiṇi, the doctors diagnose the Master's ailment as, 961
Rūdha, stage of Mahābhāva, 262
Rudra, 8
Rudrākṣa, 65, 269, 713, 1005
Rudrayāmalā, 702
Rukmiṇī, daughter of Sītānāth Pyne, 76
Rūpa, Goswāmī, 265, 681, 882

S

Sacī Devī, mother of Srī Caitanya, 40, 982
Sādhaka, (s), 142, 185, 203, 217, 225, 250, 274, 287, 298, 307, 456, 461, 476, 554, 570, 572, 632, 729, 797, 803, 809, 819, 822, 1006; definition of, 101, Rāmkumār, 130, 136; of Sakti Kenārām Bhattacāryā, 154; Kanailāl Ghoṣāl, 172; will not suffer from want if he renounces everything for God, 170; physical and mental equipment for a successful, 171; Halādhāri, 175; a neophyte is to be guided by the experience of past, 179, 180, 221; of Hathayoga should be wary, 184; of God only could form any idea of the high spiritual state of the Master, 192, 213; the Master a unique Tantrik, 229; the nature of confirmed, 244, 246, hard inward struggles of, 249, of Madhura Bhāva, 259; the prescribed costume for a, 289; life of others compared with the Master's. 341; Paṇḍits see in the Master divine power and manifestation 345; belonging to the Jīvakoṭi class, 404; 405; experiences in samādhi of, a 417; Rāmprasād, 492, 689; pass through abnormal states as a result of practice of yoga, 575; among the Kartābhajās, 589; of all denominations come to the Master at the proper time, 621, 622, 641; the Master himself visits several, 630; Padmalocan, 632; sitting in Kūpas in Vrāja, 652; Kedārnāth Caṭṭopādhyaya, 874; Narendra has equal regard for all true; 1007
Sādhana, 90, 95, 105, 139, 146, 199, 209, 256, 257, 341, 346, 404, 430, 444, 455, 471, 476, 491, 543, 554, 574, 582, 621, 626, 648, 689, 694, 745, 765, 776, 788, 795, 809, 815, 861, 884, 885, 934, 1025; individual effort and perseverance necessary for, 94; erroneous conception of ordinary people about, 97; ultimate result of, 98; the two paths of, 101, for the welfare of other incarnations undertake, 108; an objection against some of the Master's methods of, physical changes that came over the Master during, 171, 172, 710; three main divisions of the period of the Master's, 178, 179; reason why the Master

practised, 180; of the Dāsya Bhāva as practised by the Master, 182, 183; of Parakīya love, 185; the Master practises other kinds of, 193; the Master's vision of a young sannyāsin seen during, 194; Tantrik, see Tantrik sādhana; of the vatsalya Bhāva, see Vātsalya Bhāva; prevalence of, in different ages, 256; of Madhura Bhāva, see Madhura Bhāva; of the Vedānta, see Vedānta; of Islam, see Islam; Hriday in a fit of temporary dispassion practises, 315; Akṣay's love of, 320; the Master at the age of thirty-two completes his, 334, 337; the Master realizes the ultimate result of each kind of, 343 Keśav plunges in, 357, 792; the Master on the necessity to stick to, 385; the mood of the Master at the time of, 476, 495; the Bhairavi Brahmanī assists the Master in, 535, 536, 537, of the Kartābhajā sect, 588, 589, 590, 598; an erroneous notion about the Master's, 623, 642; of Paṇdit Padmalochan, 634; religious movements in India during the period of the Master's, 662; Bhagavān Das of Kālna possessed a power born of, 666; strange experience of the Master while sitting for meditation during his, 687; the Master's purveyors during the period of, 746; the Master advances Brahmo aspirants along the path of, Vijay Kṛṣna Goswāmi under the influence of the Master advances in, 794; Hari engaged in 895; Purna's love of, 900; of Narendra, 916, 917, 918; devotion an easy path of, 938; the Master points out to devotees suitable paths of, 991; Narendra advocates a virile form of, 1003; of Mahimā caran, 1005

Sādhana Kutīr, 184, 286, 314

Sādhārani, 263

Sādhu, (-s), 21, 190, 241, 350, 546; 601, 605, 612- 614, 627, 644, 661, 662, 683, 692, 693, 736, 898; the Master suffering from the curse of Haladhāri is reassured by a, 186, should not take betelnut, 202; the Master prays to the Mother not to make him an austere, 532; story of a, 601; high state of a certain, 602; inebriated with divine knowledge seen by the Master, 603, 604; with absolute faith in the name of Rāma, 612; of all denominations come to Dakśineswar, 621, the Master's ideas and ideals first promulgated among the, Bhagavāndās scolds a Vaiṣṇava, 666; origin of the custom of prescribing and administering medicine by, 690; 691; the Master's opinion on some, 691; Hazrā pretends to be a, 877; should be observed day and night before one believes him, 906; Narendra's household afraid to allow him to move with, 919

Saguna, Brahman, 9; harmony between the doctrine of Nirguna and, 442-445

Sahacarī, a well known songstress, 236

Sahaj, 588; the sign of a, 589

Sahasrāra Cakra, 153, 231, 420

Sāhitya, 32

Saileśwar, 24

Sāin, regarded as highest of the Vaiṣṇava sects, 588, 589

Saivas, quarrel with the Vaisnavas, 631

Sajinā, with the basil held equally holy by the Master, 233

Sakhībhāva, the Master at the time of practising, 385, 535

Sakhya bhāva, 251, 255, 257, 404, 405, 415, 426; the Master practises the disciplines of, 178, 237; aspects of, 275

Śākta, (-s), 524, 733, 788, 933; the Master sees the ill will between the Vaiṣṇavās and, 690

Sakti, Adyā, 33, 139, 172, 176, 443, 524; the Master initiated in the mantra of, 154; the universe consists of Siva and, 228; Mathur's vision of Siva and, Nil; Totā Pūrī convinced of the reality of, 561; in the form of Annapūrṇa, 650; the Master got his own household initiated in the Mantra of, 690

Sākti, modes of initiation, 702, 703

Sāl, 351

Sālagrām, of Raghuvīr, 32, 947; how Kśudirām of Kāmārpukur came upon, 28, 29

Sālbāri Paragaṇā, 138

Samādhi, 8, 112, 215, 250, 257, 289, 413, 425, 444, 445, 470, 520, 623,

624, 652, 664, 765, 774, 796, 853, 897, 906, knowledge of unqualified Brahmaṇ through, 8, 96; Nirvikalpa, 96, 103, 765, 784, 853; definition of, 404; the Master attains 290, 291, 406, 407; Totā Pūri attained, 284, 558; Narendra experiences, 759; the Master in, 199, 225, 226, 227, 333, 335, 336, 355, 399, 449, 544, 594, 650, 664, 668; is not a disease of the brain, 401, 625; spirituality and eternal peace is gained only through, the piercing of the six centres and, 416; the Master's attempts to describe his experiences during, 417; the five different kinds of movement of the Kuṇḍālini on the path to, 418, 419; by a mere touch the Master could impart, 438; I consciousness in different states of, 439; Totā Purī often in, 546, 547, 558, 559, 561; even at the utterance of obscene words or songs the Master would enter into, 615, Ādhikārikas and, 659, 660; the Master's wonderful vision about Narendra seen in, 846; doctors baffled on examining the Master in, 983

Sāmādhi Savikalpa, 64, 104, 267, 404, 439, 933

Samāna, 288

Sāmānjasya, 263

Samartha, 263

Sambandhātmikā bhakti, divisions of, 275

Sāmbhavī, initiation, what it is, 702, 703, 852

Sambhucandra Mallick, 338, 409, 410; supplies the Master's necessities, 350, 351, 352, 538, 539, 618, 745, 746; death of, 352

Saṁita, 585,

Saṁskāra, 264, 369

Sanātana Dharma, 691

Sanātan Goswāmī, 265, 681, 682, 944

Sāncita 464

Sandeś, 467, 735, 825

Sandhi Pūjā, 199

Sandhyā, 25, 64, 176, 930

Saṅkara, 20, 39, 87, 115, 257, 374, 444, 451, 471, 489, 552, 591, 657, 717, 768, 776; on the assumption of human body by Kṛṣna, 111, 112; on the indivisible non-dual reality, 251; about the characteristics of the mind merged in God, 484; commentary on the Vedānta Aphorisms, 498; on the liberated person, 523; could not establish his doctrine in Bengal, 630

Sāṅkhya, the genesis of the idea of incarnations and Īśwara found in the philosophy of, 7, 657; the Master's exposition of the philosophy of, 676, 677

Saṅkīrtan, 521, 522, 770, 900, 950; of Srī Caitanya witnessed by the Master in Bhāvasamādhi, 360, 661, 744, 935, the Master during, 361, in Balaram Basu's house, 717; in Mani Mallick's house, 801, 803; in Jaya Gopāl Sen's house, 811, in Pānihati, 945

Sannyāsa, 245, 307, 308, 338, 552, 625, 687, 944; of the Master, 269; the Master performs the rites preliminary to initiation in, 286, 287, 289, 498, 543; the Master attained Nirvikalpa Samādhi on the third day of receiving, 406; the Master initiates Nārāyan Sāstri in, 629

Sannyāsin, 348, 354, 550, 552, 601, 602, 685, 691, 698, 746; the Master's vision of a, 194; liberates seven generations of his family, 473; the Master served his mother although he was a, 654; Narendra's grandfather had become a, 836

Sannyāsinī the Bhairavi Brāhmaṇī, 214, 218, 222, 536

Sannyāsirājā, 23

Sanskrit, 594, 1005; language, 17, 912; grammar, 32, 828; school, 32, 34, 71, 79, 126; college, 794

Sānta, bhakti or bhāva, 251, 252, 255, 264, 275, 404, 405, 415, 426, 554

Sāntipur, 802, 881, 943

Saptaṛṣi, see Rsis, seven,

Sar, 395, 397, 576

Sāradāmani, see Holy Mother

Sāradāprasanna, later Trigunātitānandā, 991, 1018

Sārā C Bull, 746, 762

Saratcandra Cakravarti, later Śāradānanda, 1018, 1026

Sāratimāyāpur, 25

Sarayū, 613

Sārī, 677; the Master in, 75, 270, 509

Sarvamaṅgalā, younger sister of the

Master, 50, 59, 80; marriage of, 68
Sarvamaṅgalā Devi, 619, 620, 1009
Saśadhar Tarkacudāmani, asks the Master in Kāsīpūr to cure his own disease, 423; the Master's desire to see, 685, 714; comes to Calcutta to expound Hindu religion in the Albert Hall, 713, meetings with the Master, 715, 716, 724, 725, 726
Sasibhūsan Cakravarti, later Ramakrsnananda, 880, 970, 1018
Sāstra, (-s), 25, 28, 138, 179, 189, 193, 219, 221, 345, 369, 570, 572, 604, 625, 627, 671, 674, 703; what they say about incarnations, 9; the two paths of Sādhana indicated in the 101; discussion under the Pañcavati on the 216; what they are, 269, 367; the Master performs Soḍasī Pūjā according to the injunctions of the, 335, 336; lack of faith in 343, 344, 913; incarnations of God always abide by the authority of, 597; on why divine persons go on pilgrimages, 643; the Master's spiritual experiences demonstrated the truth contained in Vedas and, 688; lives of true sadhakas breathe life into the, 691
Satan, 768; Buddhistic, 257
Sātbere, 24
Satī, 644
Satīś, son of Īśāncandra Mukhopādhyāya, 715
Sātkari Lāhirī, a friend of Narendra, 842, 921
Sattva guṇa, pure, 262, 264, 344, 373, 440, 484, 524, 650, 784, 861; incarnations possess bodies and minds consisting of, 171, 693, 720; Kālī is, 188; the mind of the divine teacher assumes the nature of, 456; Narendra a person of, 856, 857, 921; Pūrṇa possessed of, 899
Satya saṅkalpa, 424
Satyāyaṇī recension, 498
Sāvarna chaudhurī, 526, 902
Savikalpa, 435, 443,
Sāyuja, 283
Schopenhauer, 913
Setubandha Rameśwar, 32
Ṣadanwaya Mahāratna, 702
Ṣoḍaśi, the beauty of, 233; the Master performs worship of, 334, 335, 336, 337, 469, 782
Syāmā, 741, 803
Syāmbāzār, the Master in the company of Vaisnavas of, 360
Syāmbāzār, Calcutta, M headmaster of the school at, 898
Syāmcānd, in Balaram Basu's estate at Kother, Orissa, 744
Syāmkuṇḍa, the Master visits, 313, 314
Syāmnagar Mulajōr, Rāmkumār's death in, 155
Syāmpukur, the house at, 395, 525, 974, 983; the Master's visions in, 196, 197, 379, 990; the Master in Samādhi examined by doctors in, 385; Vijay Kṛṣṇa Goswāmi in, 706, 997; description of the house at, 965; proposal to bring the Holy Mother to, 966; how the Holy Mother lived in, 970; boy devotees serve the Master in, 971; annual worship of Kālī in, 983, 984; Upendranāth Ghoṣh with the Master in, 992, 993; Mahimācaran in, 1007; the Master moves to the garden house of Kāsīpur from, 1008
Syāmsundara, in Balarām Bāsu's bower in Vrndavan, 744
Siddhārtha, 489, see Buddha
Siddhiyoga, 46
Sienna, St. Catherine of, 253
Sihar, 22, 30, 70, 135; the vision of the Master on the way to, 195, 218; the Master with Hriday goes to, 360, 510, 681
Sikh, 341, 808
Sikṣā, 179
Silimpur, 30, Kṣudirām's death at, 57
Siṁhavāhinī, the Holy Mother's Prāyopaveśana in the temple of, 352
Simlā, or Simuliā, 422, 836, 863, 1008, 1010, Sures Mitra celebrates Durgā Pūjā in his residence at, 198; the Master in Ramacandra Datta's house in, 616, 817; the Master met Narendra for the first time in Sureś Mitra's house in, 822; Nava Gopal Mitra's gymnasium in, 833; Narendra's residence in, 880
Sindur 350, 386, 392, 618, 806; Master's visit to Mani Mohan Mallick of, 788, 800
Sinthi, 636, 788
Sirājuddaula, Nawāb, 1009

Sītā, 245, 367, 613, 828; the Master's vision of, 183, 238, 283; Maya represented by, 557
Sitālā, 29, 31, 41, 64, 208, 309; Ramśilā possessed by the spirit of the goddess, 54
Sītānāth Pyne, 65, 67; the Master's intimacy with the family of, 74, 75, 76, 77
Siva, 22, 31, 65, 120, 123, 159, 303, 320, 321, 381, 404, 647, 828, 901; Saileśwar, 24; temple in Dere, 24; Candrā Devī's vision and experience in front of the temple of, 42, 44, 48; the Master during his boy-hood was once asked to act as Śiva, 121, 122, 769; of Kāmārpukur, 119, 120, 280; of Mukundapur, 281; the Master makes a lovely image of, 148; Candrā Devī's prāyopaveśana before, 208; Mathur sees the Master as Kālī and, 209, Sakti and, 228, 561, 562; Kāsī the city of, 312, 649, 650; and Viṣṇu, 426; Mahimna stotra, 494, 495; serve Jīva as, 593, 939, 940, 958; controversy on who is greater of the two — Viṣṇu or, 631, 632; Sati and her divine consort, 644; Kālna with its hundred and eight temples of, 661; has taught three kinds of initiation in the Āgama scriptures, 702; story of the fight between Rāma and, 795
Śivaliṅgā, named Gopeśvara, 21
Sivanāth Sāstrī, 789, 793, 813, 868; conversation between the Master and, 625; abstains from going to Dakṣineswar, 795
Sivarām Cattopādhyāya, 33
Sivarātri, observed by the Master, 65; in the Kāśipur garden house, 91; the Master required to act as Siva on, 120, 121
Skanda Purāṇa, 184
Slokās, Aṅtahsamjñā Bhāvayante, 609; Āpāta Vairāgyavato, Asita girisamaṁ syāt, 494; Digambaro vāpi cha sambaro vā, 484; Dīkṣyām cāncālāpāngī, 702; Sāmbhavī caiva Śākticā, 703; Sarvaṁ khalvidam Brahma, 607; Tyāgenaike amṛtatvam, 520; Vidyāh samasi āstāva Devī bhedāh, 592; yatra yatra mano yāti, 603
Śmrti, (-s), 32, 59, 185, 367, 505, 590, 886; on the emergence of incarnations, 9, 369; Rāmkumār well versed in 33, 126
Snānayātrā day, on May, 31, 1885, installation of the goddess in the Dakṣineśwar temple, 133, 137, 138, 951, 953
Sneha, 275
Solomon, 255
Sonābere, 323
South India, Kṣudirām's pilgrimage in, 32
Spencer, 913
Spinoza, 913
Srāddha, 58, 64, 349, 354, 460; the Master before initiation in sannyās performs, 286
Srī, or Lakṣmī, 456
Srīdāma, 237
Srīmatī, 766, 875; transcendental love of, 273; the Master in the course of Madhura Bhāva sādhana realizes himself as, 274
Srīnāth Mallick, 361
Srīnivās Sānkharī, 78, 306, 309
Srīpur, 21, 23
Srīrāga, 721
Srutidhara, the Master from his childhood was a, 239; Narendra had the memory of a, 829
Subhadrā, 340
Sudāma, 238
Suddhodhan, 489
Sūdra, 135, 443
Sūfi, 255; Govinda Ray, 298
Sujan, 384
Sukadeva, 273, goes to Mithila and is taught by Janaka, 179; ever free from Māyā, 393
Sukhasāyar, tank of, 23
Sukhlāl Goswāmī, 21, 44; makes a permanent gift of land to Kśudirām, 26, 29; death of, 32
Sulabha samācāra, 787
Sumers, of Babylon, 585
Sumeru, Mount, 547
Sunday Mirror, 787
Sūnya, 250
Surendranāth Mitra, or Sureś Mitra, the Master's vision at the time of Durgā Pūjā in the house of, 198, 199; one of the four 'suppliers' of the Master, 745, 746; the Master and

Narendra met for the first time in the house of, 822; with the other householder devotees offers to bear the expenses of the Master in Syāmpukūr and Kāsīpur, 972, 974, 1008, 1010, 1015, 1017
Suvarna-vanik, 119, 120
Suvarṇa-rekhā, 132
Susumnā, 153, 186, 233; 599, 721; Kuṇḍalinī's rising along, 231, 416, 419
Susṇi, 736; the Master in his boylike nature exposes Mathur's wife's 'theft' of the, 529
Subāhu, the Master copied the musical compositions of, 67
Swādhiṣṭhāna, 416, 721
Swagatabheda, 442, 444
Swāhā, 288
Syrapis, Narendra cleverly secures permit to go on board the ship, 832

T

Tālāmārgo, home of Mathur's Guru, 323
Tamas, 171; the Master teaches Haladhāri that Kālī does not consist of, 188; reference in the Gītā, 373, 683; incarnation of God is untouched by, 693, 861
Tāmasika, 264
Tāṇpurā, 349
Tantra, (-s), 139, 178; discipline of, 221; the Master undertakes the disciplines of, 223, 535, description of the disciplines, 225, 226, 227, 229, 230; misuse of, 261; external emblems favourable to the practice of, 269, 338, 406, 426, 543; the three modes of worship according to, 544; history of the origin of, 584, 585; heroic mode of worship and, 586, 587, 588; the two strata of, 589; miraculous powers acquired by followers of, 590, 591, 621, 623, 630, 633; Divine state according to, 701; kinds of initiation prescribed by, 702, 703
Tantradhārka, 318
Tantra, Sārada and Viśwasāra, 702
Tantra Yoginī, 224
Tantrik Mantras, 586
Tantrik Sādhakā, 586, 592, 593, 596, 609, 614, 621, 630, 692
Tāntrik Sādhana, (-s), 212, 221, 345, 690; the Master undertakes, 223, 225; realizations of, 226; uniqueness of the Master's, 229; purpose of, 230; visions and experiences of the Master on practising, 231, 232, 233, 234; history of the heroic mode of, 585, 586
Tapas, 269, 594, 668, 1018.
Tappā, 838
Tārā, 1006
Tārāhāt, 22
Tārakéswar, 67, 329, 800; the Holy Mother goes on foot to, 968; Sivā, 969
Tārak Ghoṣal, later Swāmī Sivānanda, 932, 1018
Tārāpada Ghos, a friend of Narendra, 929
Tarkālankār, 477
Tarkākāvāgīsa, 477
Tarpaṇa, 226; the Master unable to perform, 354, 688
Tattva Prakāśikā, magnum opus of Rāmcandra Datta, 995
Tejacandra, 899, 933
Telo-bhelo, the Holy Mother Stranded in, 967, 969
Thākurgāon, 138
Thanthaniā, 715
Theistic Quarterly Review, 787
Tilak, 668, 685, 691
Tīrthankara, 341
Tol, Rāmkumār starts a, 130
Totā Purī 178, 190, 276, 308, 320, 406, 498, 534, 543, 620, 920, 1006; arrival at Dakṣiṇeśwar, 284; meeting with the Master, 285; his conception of the Mother of the Universe, 286; initiates the Master into Sannyās, 286-289; imparts instructions to the Master, 289, 307; is astonished at the Master's attainment of Nirvikalpa Samādhi, 291; story of, 546-556; how he learnt that Brahman and Sakti are the same, 558-563
Trailokyanāth Biswās, 325, 326, 711, 953; dismisses Hriday from the service of the Kālī temple, 362
Trailanga Swāmī, the Master pays a a few visits to, 312, 651
Trailokyanāth Sannyāl, see Ciranjīv Sarma

Tripura, 381
Tripurāsundarī, 335
Trisuparna-mantra, purport of, 288
Trivenī, 132
Tulsīdās, 278, 614, 803
Turīya state, 280

U

Udāna, 288
Ucchalan, the big tank of, 24
Uddhāran, Datta, Nityānanda initiated, 120
Uddhava, and the Gopis, 518, 519
Umā, 585
Upanayana, of the Master, 63
Upaniṣhad, 8, 98, 246, 251, 584; on the true knower of Brahman, 424, 425; Aitareya, 416; Bṛhadāraṇyaka, 101, 290, 597, 607; Chhāndogya, 296, 607; Jābāla, 473; Kaṭha, 416, 502, 624; Māṇḍūkya, Muṇḍaka, 160, 269, 502, 628; Kaivalya, 520; Nārāyaṇa, 520; Svetāśvatara, 8, 160; Taittirīya, 402, 589, 869
Upendra Nāth Ghoś, his experience in the Master's company in Syāmpukur, 992-995
Utsavānanda Goswāmī, father of Pandit Vaiṣṇavacaraṇ, 192, 346
Uttara Gītā, 603, 1006
Uttara Tantra, 586
Uttar Pradesh, 499

V

Vadanganj, 22
Vaidyanāth, the Master's visit to, 312, 660
Vaidyāvatī, 350, 967, 969
Vaikharī, Dayānanda in the state of, 636
Vaikuntha, 353 Kālī (Swāmī Abhedānanda) has the vision of, 428
Vaikuṇṭhanāth Sannyāl, 799, 800, 809, 929, 1025; the Master administers a mild rebuke to, 454; on the Master's love for Narendra, 857; pesters the Master for spiritual experiences, 1025
Vairāgī, 125, 601
Vairāgya, 102
Vaiśeśika,
Vaiṣṇava, (-s), 73, 74, 255, 314, 338, 345, 346, 361, 426, 457, 520, 524, 553, 573, 631, 665, 682, 692, 788, 838, 901, 933, 935, 939, 949, 986, 987, 997, 1000, 1003; of Kāmārpukur, 120; books and scriptures, 178, 219, 248, 273, 379, 415, 499, 535, 621, 769, 874; denominations, 178, 185, 587, 588, 590; sādhanās undertaken by the Master, 237, 238, 270, 271, 274, 275; teachers and Madhura Bhāva, 258, 259, 263-266, 442, 505, 662, 665-667; ill will between Sāktas and, 690; festival at Pāṇihāṭi, 943-945
Vaiṣṇavacaran Goswāmī, 178, 219, 274, 593, 663; frequent visits to Dakṣineśwar, 345, 346; the fame of, 573; participates in a discussion about the Master's condition, 581, 582; believed the Master to be incarnation of God, 590; the Master in Bhāvasamādhi rides on the shoulders of, 593; and Paṇḍit Gauri, 593, 594; on regarding the object of one's love as a form of God, 596, 598
Vajrayāna, 260
Vakulghāt, 214, 966
Vālmīki, 449, 1023; initiated by Ṛṣi Nārada, 636
Vāmācārā, 261
Vānalinga, 32
Vānaprasṭhin, 28, 950
Vānaviṣṇupur, 67; the Master's visit to, 681, 682
Vankevihāri, the Master in Bhāvasamādhi before the image of, 652
Varadāsundar Pāl,
Vārāṇasi, 36, 139; the Master in, 649, 650; shawl, the fate of a, 501; see also Kāsī
Vasantā rāga, 721
Vaśisthāśrama, 630
Vāsudeva, 489
Vātsalya Bhāva, 251, 255, 257, 275, 281; the Master undertakes the sādhana of, 238, 243; the Master initiated by Jatādhāri in the sādhana of, 247; the Bhairavi Brāhmaṇī also helps the Master in his sādhana of, 248; of the Bhairavi Brāhmaṇī towards the Master, 535
Vāyāvīya Samhitā, 702
Veda, (-s) 179, 180, 195, 244, 420, 485, 533, 590, 603, 609, 612, 765, 886;

doctrine of incarnation founded on the knowledge gained from, 7, 8; on the one non-dual Brahman, 98; what is Sādhana according to the, 101; the Master's experiences corroborated by, 276, 345, 406, 1016; content of, 367, 368, 369; tantras and the Karma Kāṇḍa portion of the, 584, 585, 586, 588; on the knower of Brahman, 671, 674, 821; revealed to the Āptas only, 691
Vedāṅgas, the six branches of study, 180
Vedānta, 251, 275, 345, 382, 407, 426, 477, 533, 551, 559, 590, 615, 663, 796; Swāmī Vivekānanda comes to believe the doctrine of non-duality spoken of in, 89, 90, 91; the Master's sādhana of, 270, 280, 291, 295; Totā Puri teaches the Master, 289; content of, 368, 369; the Bhairavi Brāhmaṇī tries to dissuade the Master from discussing, 406; the seven planes described in, 419, 420, 626; the Master sums up, 421; the Bhairavi Brāhmaṇī's ignorance of, 543, 544; on the true nature of Brahman, 603; not popular with the Paṇḍits of Bengal, 630; Paṇḍit Padmalocan, a scholar of, 630, 631; on the two divisions of Ādhikārikas, 658; Brahman and Māyā in, 677; in practice, 940
Vedānta Sāstra, 559
Vedānta Sūtras, 498
Vedāntic, 439; knowledge, 555, 908, 940; Haladhāri proud of, 189; Uddhava was a person of, 518; alone can develop brotherly feeling among the Hindus and Muslims, 300; discipline, 555; the Master practises, 282, 285; truth discussions on, 295, 422, 602, 603, 633; scriptures, on the knowledge of Brahman, 548
Vedāntin, 264, 265, 386, 498; the Master rebukes a pseudo-Vedāntin, 421, 422
Vedic, 178, 254, 338, 340, 355, 492, 688, 796, 804; religion, propagation by Swami Dayananda, 663
Veṇīmādhav Pāl, 788
Vibhīsaṇa, devotion to his guru, 453
Vidyāpati, 265
Vidyāsāgar, see Iswara Candra Vidyāsāgar
Vidyāśakti, the Master on how to ascertain whether or not a woman is, 889
Vidyāvāgīś, 477
Vikāra, Sāttvika, 262, 264
Vijayā, Daśamī, 514
Vijay Kṛṣṇa Goswāmī, 358, 789, 796, 802, 813, 868, 869, 874; vision in Dacca of, 706, 1000, 1001; the Master compares Narendra with, 713, 866, 867; leaves the Brāhmo Samāj, 793; how he advanced in sādhana thereafter, 794; the Master tries to make peace between Keśav and, 795; with the Master in Maṇi Mohan's house, 803, 804
Vilva, 31, 140, 166, 184, 203, 445, 687; tree in the temple garden, the Master performs the Tantrik rituals under the, 225; Swāmī Vivekānanda's vision of the Brahmayoni under the, 232
Vīṇā, 710, 721, 846
Vindhyāvāsini, 461
Vindhyā mountains, 836
Vinod, Junior, 899
Vipin Vihāri Ghoś, 674
Vīrācāra, 586
Virajā Homa, the Master, before initiation in Sannyāsa, performs, 288, 289
Visālākṣī, temple of the Goddess at Ānur, 62; the Master's ecstasy while he was going to the temple of, 116, 118
Viṣahārī, another name of the Goddess Mānasā, 116
Viṣṇu, 23, 39, 139, 153, 154, 175, 188, 277, 426, 644, 690, 810, 933, 993; Kṣudirām in Gayā, the holy abode of, 36, 37, 38; devotees of Sīva and, 66, 120 a conversation between Nārada and, 94, 95; the spiritual teacher is, 451; Hanumān prefers the form of Rāmā to that of, 455; dispute as to who is greater, Siva or, 631
Viśuddha, 416, 721
Viśwanātha, 37, 138, 312, 313, 835
Viśwanāth Cakravarti, 262
Viśwanāth Datta, 822, 825, 863, 918; character and attainments of, 838, 839; death of, 840, 921
Viśwanāth Upādhyāya, 351, 355; about the Master's samādhi, 412
Vivekānanda, Swāmī, 359, 366, 402,

430, 467, 471, 522, 542, 683, 704, 747, 750, 762, 765, 790, 820; reminiscences of, 90, 91; the Master's offer to transfer his miraculous powers to, 231; doubts the historicity of the Vṛndāvan Līlā, 259; on the purpose of the Master's incarnation, 269, 373, 688; on Hindu Religion and Srī Rāmakrsna, 367-371; the Master praises the renunciation of, 403; importunes the Master to cure himself, 424; on "blind faith", 431; on the Master's extraordinary power over the human mind, 435; always favoured devotion with discrimination, 522; gains through meditation the power of clairvoyance and clairaudience, 538; spread of the ideas of the Master through, 640; goes to Buddha Gayā, but returns in a few days, 645, 647; on Isan Bābu's kindness, 715; and Paṇḍit Saśadhar, 716; association with Brāhmo Samāj, 795; tribute to Yogin, 903

Vivekacūdāmani, 484, 520, 552

Vraja, 238, 680; devotional mood of the Gopis of, 105, 253, 268, 270, 272, 276; Rādhā, the supreme lady of, 572; the Master's intense love for, 652, 653, Rākhāl, a "cowherd boy" of,

Vṛndāvan, 36, 87, 196, 263, 266, 510, 647, 680, 692, 744, 932; refutation of the objections against the historicity of the līlā at, 258, 259; the Master visits, 313, 314, 531, 652, 695, 710; to console the Gopis, Uddhava was sent to, 518; Srī Caitanya discovered the places of the sports of Srī Kṛṣṇa at, 680, 681; the Master's apprehension on hearing of Rākhāl's illness in, 819

Vyākaraṇa, 32

Vyāna, 288

Vyāsa, 449, 1023; sends his son Suka to Mithilā, 179, 180; and Suka, 393

W

Wājid Ālī, Nawāb, Zoological Gardens of, 831

Whitley, book on logic, 830

Williams, declares that the Master was Jesus himself, 898

Wordsworth, Principal Hastie explains the trances of, 851

Y

Yadu, 245

Yājnāvalkya, conversation of, 597

Yamunā, 652

Yaśoda, 88, 982; attitude to Gopala, 218, 237, 268, 536, 738

Yātrā, dramatic performance, 31, 52, 137, 239, 953; the Master's interest in, 73, 79, 121, 530

Yātrāsiddhi Rājā, 23

Yoga, 7, 367, 420, 651, 691, 692, 796, 937, 938, 941, 1008; how the mind is to be fixed in, 159; and Bhoga can never co-exist, 160, 610; the Master's practice of prānāyam and, 184, 185, 186, 203; picture of the Master in a very high state of, 345; harmony between the paths of Bhakti and, 415; piercing of the six centers by, 415, 416, 417; bodily symptoms produced by the practice of, 572, 575; and Tantras, 585, 585, 588; of action, 636

Yogādyā, 67

Yogamāyā, the Bhairavi Brāhmanī part of, 234

Yogānanda, or Yogen, Yogīndra, Yogīn, 361, 434, 715, 720, 725, 761, 1018; fascinated by Haṭhayogi Nārāyan, 391; the Master's advice to, 392; wonders at the Master's demanding and receiving prasada on one occasion, 525-528; told by the Master that a devotee need not be a fool, 648, 893; his devotion to established rites and practices, 716, 717; chidden by the Master for want of spirit, 894; believed by the Master to be an Īśwara Koṭi devotee, 902; marriage and repentance, 903; treated by the Master affectionately, 904; suspects the Master only to realize his error, 905, 906; surrenders himself to the Master, 906

Yoga scripture, 827; of Patañjali, 512

Yoga Sūtra, 296, 393

Yogeśwarī, see Brāhmaṇī Bhairavi

Yogic powers, 296, 367, 622, 794, 845; of the Bhairavi Brāhmaṇī, 537; an

obstacle to God realization, 540, 541, 542; vision and power of the Master, 178, 203, 332, 341, 342, 343, 344, 345, 347, 642, 643, 764, 860, 862, 885, 898, 899, 932, 933
Yogin or Yogī, 414, 416, 558, 572, 886, 887; Jesus Christ, 339; story of a 602; Maharşi Debendranāth recognizes in Narendra the characteristices of a, 828
Yoginis, sixty-four, a place in Kāśī, 313
Yoginī Tantra, 224
Yudhiṣṭhira, Mahārāja Jatīndra Mohan compares himself to, 724